YALE ORIENTAL SERIES

BABYLONIAN TEXTS

VOLUME XII

YALE ORIENTAL SERIES • BABYLONIAN TEXTS VOL. XII

LEGAL AND ADMINISTRATIVE TEXTS OF THE REIGN OF SAMSU-ILUNA

BY

SAMUEL I. FEIGIN, Ph.D.

INTRODUCTION AND INDICES BY

A. LEO OPPENHEIM

with the assistance of
Mark E. Cohen

NEW HAVEN AND LONDON, YALE UNIVERSITY PRESS, 1979

Published with assistance from the
Yale Babylonian Collection.

Designed by John O. C. McCrillis
and set in Monotype Scotch type
by Heritage Printers, Inc., Charlotte, N.C.
Printed in the United States of America by
The Murray Printing Co., Westford, Mass.

Published in Great Britain, Europe, Africa, and Asia (except Japan) by Yale University Press, Ltd., London. Distributed in Australia and New Zealand by Book & Film Services, Artarmon, N.S.W., Australia; and in Japan by Harper & Row, Publishers, Tokyo Office.

Library of Congress Cataloging in Publication Data

Feigin, Samuel Isaac, 1893–1950.
Legal and administrative texts of the reign of Samsu-iluna.

(Yale oriental series : Babylonian texts ; v. 12)
Based on the author's thesis, Yale, 1923.
1. Assyro-Babylonian language—Texts.
2. Law—Iraq—Babylonia—Sources. 3. Babylonia—Politics and government—Sources. I. Title.
II. Series.
PJ3711.Y3 vol. 12 [PJ3873] 492'.ls
ISBN 0-300-01963-7 [492'.1] 78-4032

CONTENTS

Preface vii
Introduction ix
Catalogue 1
Indices
    Personal Names 23
    Deities 62
    Titles and Occupations 65
    Geographical Names 69
        Towns 69
        Countries 71
        Canals and Rivers 71
Seal Inscriptions 72
Texts with Seal Inscription(s) 78
Concordance of Museum Numbers 80
Autographed Texts Plates I–C

PREFACE

More than half a century has elapsed in the preparation of this volume. Its early history is detailed in the Introduction, reproduced below as it was submitted in 1952. At that time, the manuscript was entrusted to Ferris J Stephens, who devoted himself to it during the rest of his life, both before and after his retirement in 1962. He tirelessly collated each text, and made numerous improvements both in the copies and in the indices.

Upon Stephens's death late in 1969, I assumed responsibility for the volume, greatly aided by Professor Oppenheim's continuing cooperation, and by a grant from the National Endowment for the Humanities, which provided for the services of Dr. Mark E. Cohen. As research associate in 1972–73 and again in 1974–75, he updated the indices, added the list of professional names and seal inscriptions, and generally prepared the manuscript for the printer. In the list of personal names, the customary transliterations from the Akkadian were converted into connected transcriptions wherever possible. It is hoped that this departure from previous practice will augment the utility of the elaborate indices traditionally offered in this series, and justify the effort and expense entailed in their preparation and printing. Professor Oppenheim reviewed and approved all these steps, and had the satisfaction, before his sudden death on July 21, 1974, of seeing the final draft. That draft also had the benefit of a critical reading by Dr. Marten Stol, Leiden University, and, at the Yale University Press, by Jane Isay.

The help of all the individuals and institutions who contributed to this volume is gratefully acknowledged.

William W. Hallo

NEW HAVEN, CONNECTICUT
1975

Another three years have elapsed since the above was written. The further delays were necessitated by other demands on those involved with the production of the volume. They have, however, permitted further checks on the front matter and collations of the copies by those previously mentioned, especially Dr. Stol. In addition, the manuscript had the benefit of a careful review by Ulla Kasten, Museum Editor for the Babylonian Collection.

WWH

INTRODUCTION

The texts contained in this volume formed the basis of the thesis of the late Dr. Samuel I. Feigin, presented to the Faculty of the Graduate School of Yale University in 1923. It consisted of copies of the tablets and of transliterations and translations of certain documents preceded by an introduction. The title was *Early Babylonian Legal Transactions Dated in the Reign of Samsu-iluna.* Since then, the main Assyriological interest of Dr. Feigin was concentrated upon this group of documents which was planned to appear in the *Yale Oriental Series. Babylonian Texts.* He recopied all tablets and dedicated many years to the preparation of their transliteration and translation, as well as to the writing of an elaborate commentary. Up to the illness which led to his death, Dr. Feigin was working on his magnum opus, checking and rechecking his indices, collating his copies.

After the untimely death of Dr. Feigin on January 2, 1950, a manuscript of appalling size, in fact, several manuscripts in various stages of completion were entrusted to me, together with numerous file cards written in English as well as in modern Hebrew. I was thus faced with the difficult problem either of submerging myself into all the work pertaining to an elaborate edition of these interesting and difficult texts or abandoning the project entirely, pressed as I was by my obligations to the Assyrian Dictionary project, my teaching, and my personal research work. Out of esteem for Dr. Feigin, whom I greatly respected as a scholar and a man, and in view of the importance and number of the texts involved, I decided on the following course of action: the practically finished copies of the 561 texts were taken as a basis (without further collation) for the compilation of the indices offered in the present volume. The lists prepared by Dr. Feigin have been utilized as much as possible, but the sole responsibility is, of course, mine.

The name indices contain personal names, names of deities, and geographical names. The personal names are strictly alphabetically arranged, but allowances had to be made for variant writings and the inevitable inconsistencies inherent in such lists. The index of the names of the deities mentioned in the tablets attempts to offer more information than is the rule in lists of this type. The references for the occurrences of individual divine names have been broken up in order to show the contexts in which they occur. The following classification has been adopted: deities as witnesses, deities as contractants in legal transactions, deities invoked in oath formulas or mentioned in seal inscriptions, and, finally, priests and offices of the pertinent deity, sanctuaries, and sacred objects. Divine names from theophoric personal names and from date formulas have not been included.

INTRODUCTION

The Catalogue shows likewise a deviation from the normal form of such lists. In the column headed Contents, it has been my intention to identify the nature of the transaction recorded as exactly as the space limitations permit. To achieve this goal and to offer, at the same time, a maximum of information, a series of "keywords" have been used to designate the typological form and the exact content of the tablets listed.

These keywords call for an explanation. Business transactions involving loans are described as "loan" only when they contain the Sumerian phrase ŠU.BA.AN.TI.(MEŠ). In all other cases, the characteristic phrases or formulas are indicated in brackets (e.g., loan [ŠU.TI.A]) or such descriptions as *usâtum*-loan, ŠU.LÁ-loan, are used. In the cases in which the scribes have cast credit operations or similar financial transactions into the form of a ŠU.BA.AN.TI-loan, reference to the actual nature of the business transacted was made wherever it was feasible in an abbreviated form (e.g., "silver against barley") and as far as the content of the text was understandable. The term "promissory note" refers exclusively to texts of the UGU PN_1 PN_2 IN.TUK type. The receipts are differentiated according to the use of ŠU.TI.A and *namḫartu*, respectively, as well as of *imḫur(u)*. The legal texts of the normal run, such as "rent," "sale," "hire," and "adoption," are provided with short references to rare or extraordinary phrases, in order to point them out to the student interested in "Keilschriftrecht." As to the administrative texts proper, the term "account tablet" indicates that the text is drawn up in columns with headings; "itemized list" is reserved for lists of items which are added up at the end of the text, while the designation "record" refers to itemized entries which are neither added up nor provided with any indication as to the purpose of the recording. All this is necessarily subjective and, at times, rather arbitrary; still it has been introduced not only to facilitate the task of the reader but also to draw attention to the problem of establishing a typology of administrative documents as a first step toward understanding the bureaucratic techniques of Mesopotamian administration.

My thanks are due to many persons whose cooperation has helped to bring this book into being. I have to thank, first of all, Mrs. S. I. Feigin, who placed the copies of the texts and all other manuscript material at my disposal, and Professor Ferris J Stephens of the Yale Babylonian Collection, who kindly granted me permission to prepare Dr. Feigin's copies for publication and to add the indices, as well as for accepting this book for publication in the series. I have enjoyed, in my work, the assistance of Professor F. W. Geers for the tedious job of checking references; to Professors I. J. Gelb and B. Landsberger I am under obligation for advice and discussion with regard to the index of personal names.

A. Leo Oppenheim

ORIENTAL INSTITUTE
UNIVERSITY OF CHICAGO
JUNE, 1952

Text	*Year*	*Month*	*Day*	*YBC Number*	*Contents*
1	1			4260	ŠU.TI.A-loan (barley and *saḫlû*) from Shamash and a person
2	1			4907	Obligation to pay rent (Á.BI *bi-tim*) styled as a ŠU.TI.A-loan
3	1	1	30	8398	ŠU.TI.A-receipt for onions etc. for which the barley value is indicated (sealed with an alien seal; lines 10–11)
4	1	2	5	6360	Same type (Ì.SAG-oil)
5	1	4	13(?)	8227	*Namḫartu*-receipt for barley
6	1	4	14	6547	ŠU.TI.A-receipt for bitumen (ESIR.È.A)
7	1	4	17	5944	Small cattle entrusted (*paqādum*) to a shepherd and his *kaparrum* (*pîḫātum, riābum*). Note lines 18–22. The month name is written ŠU.NIGIN.NA
8	1	4	16	4957	Transportation of barley styled as barley given *ana puḫḫim* in one locality to be delivered in another
9	1	4	22	7865	ŠU.TI.A-receipt for Ì.SAG-oil priced in terms of silver
10	1	4	28	4239	Same type. (Case on pl. XCVIII)
11	1	5		8068	Rent of a house. Note that the month name is written GAR.NE.GAR instead of NE.NE.GAR
12	1	5	10	8372	*Usâtum*-loan (due: *bulṭa ikaššad*). Note seal inscription
13	1	5	10	4334	Obligation to deliver barley in another city within 20 days. Interest to be paid for delayed delivery
14	1	5	15	8524	ŠU.TI.A-receipt for silver (fragment)
15	1	5	20	8569	Promissory note (silver), creditor: Shamash (*bulṭa ikaššadma . . . šamšam ana kišādišu išakkan*)
16	1	5	20(?)	3345	ŠU.TI.A-receipt for silver (settlement of accounts). Seal on pl. XCIX
17	1	6	1	7930	Obligation to deliver wool at shearing time (*ina buqūmim*) styled as a promissory note. Tablet on pl. XCVIII
18	1	6	20	5775	ŠU.TI.A-receipt for copper and KUŠ.LU.ÚB-bags

Text	*Year*	*Month*	*Day*	*YBC Number*	*Contents*
19	1	6	20	9098	Same type for barley (ŠE.ŠEŠ and ŠE.GUD)
20	1	6	21	6449	Hire of a person styled as obligation to perform a specified work (*ana* lú.ḫun.gá *erēbum, warḫam še'am īpušuma ittallak*)
21	1	6	26	8556	Sanctions against a zabar.dab-official to appear in the capital (*ekallam ippal*)
22	1	7	4	6701	Sale of an é.dù.a-house
23	1	7	3	7928	Similar transaction between same persons as in no. 17 but styled as a loan (the wool is characterized as IGI.SAG.GÁ on the tablet, as ŠID.GÁ on the case). Tablet on pl. XCVIII
24	1	7	12	8166	Record of wool
25	1	7	28	6337	šu.ti.a-receipt for hides
26	1	7	15	7219	*Namḫartu*-receipt for barley (taxes of the Lagash canal district) with itemized account (sag.níg.ga šà.bi.ta in line 1)
27	1	7	29	9093	šu.ti.a-receipt for silver
28	1	8	4	7794	One of two brothers takes over a slave who was their joint property before (*ina zittim leqûm, tappilātum, aḫum aḫam ušerdīma*)
29	1	9	1	7978	šu.ti.a-receipt for barley (being the equivalent, šám, of *iniātim* and numun)
30	1	9	25	3380	Promissory note (silver), creditor: Shamash mu . . . a íb.ta.su.su)
31	1	10	1	4358	Promissory note (silver, the equivalent of barley). Case and tablet
32	1	10		4459	Rent of a field to grow barley (nam.giš.uru$_4$.lá še) (*imittu-šumēlu*-clause, *makāsum*)
33	1	(?)	11	6359	Same type as no. 24
34	1	10(?)	20	9097	šu.ti.a-receipt for sickles
35	1	10	25	6333	Receipt (*maḫārum*) of zabar.dab-money from cities along the Lagash canal being taxes collected by the PA.PA-official
36	1	11	10	8525	šu.ti.a-receipt of silver with itemized account
37	1	11	28	6436	Record of silver given to the ugula-íd.da
38	1	12	12	8340	šu.ba.an.ti-receipt for wool
39	1	12	1	6183	Loan (gold), creditor: Sin (*ûm ebūrim*)
40	1	12	10	6387	šu.ti.a-receipt for ì.sag-oil
41	1	12	20	8332	Record of barley amounts characterized as: *ina pî* PN (*la*) *burru*
42	1	(?)	1	6239	Sale of a house: é.dù.a . . . . x iz.zi dal.ba.na
43	2			5095	Accounting of barley (NÍG.ḪAR.ra and zíd.da). Note lines 4–5. Unusual type

Text	*Year*	*Month*	*Day*	*YBC Number*	*Contents*
44	2			6972	Rent of a field (*ana errēšūtim*) belonging to a LUKUR of Shamash (5 EZEN, *paqādum*, *liqtātum*, NINDA.LAGABxU.RA *qajatum*). Tablet on pl. XCVIII
45	2	1	20	6227	Loan (silver), creditor: Shamash
46	2	5	(?)	5564	Agreement terminating a litigation concerning a slave girl
47	2	6	1	5524	Rent of a house
48	2	6	20	5338	Settlement of accounts from a contract of transportation (*ana babālim nadānum*, route: KASKAL *ša* dIM). Expenses: *gimrum*, Á.ANŠE, AB.A.AB.DU, and BA.ZI) [Cf.AS 16:224]
49	2	7	9	7970	*Šukunnû*-transaction (cf. no. 445)
50	2	11		5440	Loan (silver against barley)
51	2	9	20	5882	Receipt (*maḫārum*) for dates
52	2	9	20	6088	ŠU.TI.A-receipt for sesame (*šibšum*)
53	2	10		8178	Same type (barley)
54	2	10	30	8401	Rent of doors (monthly payments) by a carpenter. Cf. no. 107
55	2	11	13	6150	*Namḫartum*-receipt for dates. ERÉN.MEŠ LÚ *Tu-ru-kum* mentioned
56	2	10	30	7252	Large account tablet (dealing with barley, silver, sesame, and covering two years)
57	2	10	10	9095	Loan (SAG-barley). Tablet on pl. XCVIII
58	2	12	30	8515	ŠU.TI.A-receipt for beer and SAG-barley
59	2	12	13	6556	Record of *gurnu* and SIG_5 dates being the KASKAL of 3 persons. Note line 14
60	3	1	10	5876	Obligation of the *rabiānum* to produce (*kullumum* plus *nadānum*) a person within 5 days or else to do *ḫarrānam alākum* for him
61	3	1	23	4206	Two brothers receive wool from the banker Šēp-Sîn for which they have to pay the palace. Styled as a loan. SILIM.GI.NA-clause
62	3	1	23	4272	Similar transaction to that of no. 61. Same principals and witnesses. Styled as a promissory note. SILIM.GI.NA-clause
63	3	2	1	8257	Fragment of a contract
64	3	2	30	4890	ŠU.TI.A-receipt for various materials (*annîtum esiḫtum*) for the construction of chariots
65	3	3		5957	Itemized list of small silver amounts (ŠU.TI.A in line 12)
66	3	3	10	6420	Tax-arrears deducted (*ḫarṣu*) from payments made in silver and barley
67	3	3	20	6230	*Namḫartu*-receipt for silver from tax-arrears collected by the PA.PA-official (cf. no. 35)

Text	*Year*	*Month*	*Day*	*YBC Number*	*Contents*
68	3	5		5551	ŠU.TI.A-receipt for barley (*labirtu*-tax)
69	3	5	25	5350	A person promises to pay the GUDU$_4$-priest two overdue GÚ.È-garments
70	3	6	13	4232	Obligation to pay dates for certain *kanīk šarrim* (dating from two preceding years). In case of delay, silver according to the exchange determined by the palace (KAR É.GAL-*lim*) is to be paid
71	3	6	2	8708	Promissory note (crediting the purchase price of two bulls)
72	3	6^2	20	6319	Rent of a sesame field which is to be made into a garden (*ana kirîm šubšîm u pirṣim ṣabātim*) in 3 years. In the meantime, the tenant may harvest barley and sesame (*esēpum-tabālum*-clause)
73	3	6^2	14	7081	Lawsuit concerning full payment for a house. Oath taken in Larsa by the NA$_4$.ŠEN.TAB.BA and the ḪAR.MUŠEN.NA of Shamash. Case and tablet
74	3	7	15	6744	Sale of a slave girl characterized as ÙR.RA.TU.UD.DA "born in the loft." Case and tablet
75	3	7	15	4319	Division of property
76	3	7	15	4472	Sale of a Subarean slave girl. The list of witnesses, headed by Shamash, precedes the text
77	3	7	25	6327	*Namḫartu*-receipt for *kanīkum*-documents (cf. no. 70) drawn up by several cities for ZABAR.DAB-money (*qabâm šakānum* in line 18)
78	3	8		7204	List of expenditures (ZI.GA) of barley
79	3	8		5969	Obligation to deliver bricks, styled as a loan
80	3	8	4	4948	Itemized list of barley given to certain persons and for various purposes (line 8: ŠÀ ŠE.RI.RI.GA)
81	3	8	20	6448	Same type (sesame)
82	3	8	20	6410	Same type (silver)
83	3	9	1	6442	Rent of a *šukūsu*-field (*ana errēšūtim*, tenant and owner divide 2:1). (Note variant spelling of month name: GAN.GAN.NE)
84	3	9	30	4882	ŠU.TI.A-receipt for barley (periods stated)
85	3	10	2	6443	Record of tax-arrears (dates)
86	3	10	2	6431	Same type as no. 66 (*šutaḫruṣu* instead of *ḫarṣu*)
87	3	10	1	6444	Same type
88	3	10	1	7823	Same type as no. 82
89	3	10	1	6446	Same type as no. 66
90	3	10	10	6712	Itemized list of ŠE.ḪAR.RA

Text	Year	Month	Day	YBC Number	Contents
91	3	10	20	8521	ŠU.TI.A-receipt for silver (being the rent for a house). Tablet on pl. XCVIII
92	3	11	1	6709	Account tablet (headings: ŠE.BA.É and MU.BI). Expenditures (BA.ZI.DIDLI)
93	3	11	1	7890	Loan (barley)
94	3	12	4(?)	4963	ŠU.TI.A-loan (oil against silver)
95	3	12	8	5943	Small cattle which have been entrusted (*paqādum*) are being returned to their owner
96	3	12	21	4959	Record of flour expended at the shearing (ŠU.TI.A) and for the rent of a boat (*našûm*)
97	3	(?)	(?)	5545	Loan (barley and oil)
98	4	1	5	5337	Itemized list of wool (EŠ.DÉ.A in line 11) (fragment)
99	4	2		6450	Expenditures (ZI.GA) of silver
100	4	2	24(?)	6353	Record of tax-arrears (dates)
101	4	2	15	7075	Account tablet (headings: MU.DU of the current year, silver, LÁL, MU.LÚ
102	4	3	30	6248	Sale of an É.DÙ.A-house. Note lines 19–21
103	4	3		9099	Cattle inspected (*ša innamaru*) and entrusted (*paqādum*) to a shepherd
104	4	4	1	5973	Receipt (*maḫārum*) for rent of a field
105	4	4	14	6710	Rent of a field from a NIN.DINGIR to grow barley and sesame (IGI-4-GÁL) (fragment)
106	4	4	20	6656	ŠU.TI.A-receipt for barley to be charged to the account of the giver (*ana nikkassi* PN *šakānum*)
107	4	4	20	6383	Rent of a door (same lessor as in no. 54) (annual payment)
108	4	5	1	8679	Sale of a Subarean slave (fragment)
109	4	5	4	6328	Record of *gurnu* and SIG_5 dates
110	4	5	15(?)	6390	Dates deducted from tax-arrears (*ina ribbatim labirtim ḫarṣu*). An earlier *kanīkum* declared void
111	4	6	20	7793	Rent of a ship (10 KÙR) (*ṭebûm*-clause)
112	4	5	16	7066	Itemized list of tax-arrears given to a person who is to pay the collector
113	4	7	14	6746	Payment (MU.DU) of silver characterized as KUG.BABBAR.NAM-5 by the UGULA.NAM-5
114	4	7	15	8528	Barley (being the rent for a house) credited in form of a ŠU.TI.A-loan (lines 7–8: KAR *ibaššû* KÚ *iḫarraṣ*)
115	4	7	5	8295	Rent or sale of ship (fragment)
116	4	7	24	6381	Dated order to deliver bundles of straw
117	4	8	14	9096	Rent of a *šukūsu*-field (*ana errēšūtim*; *šakākum*, *erēšum*, *imittu-šumēlu*-clause, [*širḫam*] *šakānum*)

Text	Year	Month	Day	YBC Number	Contents
118	4	10	10	7605	Itemized list of silver (named persons and ERÉN *ša li-ib-bi ma-tim*, line 21)
119	4	10(?)	10	7759	Rent of a ship (20 KÙR) (*ṭebûm*-clause)
120	4	10	14	8532	Rent of a millstone (NA_4.ḪAR *ši-mu-ru-um*) for one year
121	4	11	10	8230	Loan (barley)
122	4	11	10	6315	Itemized ŠU.TI.A-receipts (silver equivalents of dates for taxes)
123	4	12	23	7972	ŠU.TI.A-receipt for bitumen (ESIR)
124	4	11	24	8482	Same type (barley)
125	4	12	7	6318	Itemized *namḫartu*-receipts for dates
126	5	1	5	6024	Rent of a date-grove (cf. no. 434) (*ana* ŠU.GAR, *rukkubum, šukunnê šakānum, ana ḫīṭi ušuzzu, kîma ālim*)
127	5	1	29	4463	Wool bought on credit styled as a loan of unusual type
128	5	2	4	4421	Same type as no. 66
129	5	2	6(?)	4428	Record of dates delivered
130	5	2	10	4444	Expenditures (ZI.GA) of sesame
131	5	2	15	4443	Record of tax-arrears of a LÚ.ŠU.I. Same type as no. 66
132	5	2	23	4441	Same type as no. 66
133	5	2	25	4427	Same
134	5	2	25	6043	Same
135	5	4	20	6047	Rent of a field (*eqlam mala ḫašḫu libbû eqil* PN) to grow onions (rent: barley)
136	5	4	24	6531	ŠU.TI.A-receipt for bitumen (ESIR.È.A)
137	5	5	2	6373	Loan (barley)
138	5	5	14	4331	Hire of a person *ana ḫarrān šarrim* from his brother (*imittu-šumēlu*-clause, *leqûm*). Cf. nos. 140, 146, 253
139	5	5	15	6026	ŠU.BA.AN.TI-receipt for silver (*ša ina kanīkišu šaknu*)
140	5	5	25	7767	Hire of a person *ana* GI.DUB.ÍL *ekallim* from his brother (*imittu-šumēlu*-clause). Note line 6; cf. lines 7–8 with 146:8–9. Same employer as in nos. 138 and 146
141	5	6	2	5358	List of females characterized either by *ša* ^{d}DN or as NIN.DINGIR
142	5	6	3	7739	Receipt for barley
143	5	6	20	5891	Record of dates which a person has to pay to the king (*šarram ippal*)
144	5	6	30	5491	Rent of a house
145	5	7	3	8520	ŠU.TI.A-receipt for barley and oil being the hire of a person (*āgirānum*)

Text	*Year*	*Month*	*Day*	*YBC Number*	*Contents*
146	5	7	3	8510	Hire of a person (*itti ramānišu*) to do *tupšikkum*-service for a month (*imittu-šumēlu*-clause). Note lines 11–12: *ipaṭṭarma ekallam ippal*. Same employer as in nos. 138, 140, 253
147	5	7	10	4961	Loan (barley) for a business venture ([*adi*] *paṭār ḫarrāni*)
148	5	7	8	8298	Loan (wool against barley)
149	5	8	10(?)	4426	Same type as no. 66
150	5	8	10	4423	Record of dates delivered to the palace
151	5	8	10	4429	Itemized list of sesame
152	5	8	15	6313	Accounting of barley (lines 1–12 SAG.NÍG.GA ŠÀ.BI.TA, lines 13–16 ZI.GA)
153	5	8	23	6232	Sale of an É.DÙ.A-house. Case and tablet
154	5	8	23	4430	Same type as no. 66
155	5	8	20(?)	9094	Rent of a building(?) (É.TAR.RA). Cf. *BIN* II, 83
156	5	9(?)	(?)	7760	Sale of an infant by his parents (DUMU.GABA *ša* MU-1-KAM NAM *šu-nu-qi-i*[*m*](?) . . . *wi-li-id* É)
157	5	9		7599	Inventory of property (slave girl, jewelry, furniture, etc.) said to have been given to a person
158	5	9	20	8720	Warranty to produce a person (ŠU.DÙ.A . . . ŠU.BA.AN.TI) (fragment). Note seal inscription
159	5	10	10	4425	Delivery (MU.DU) of tax-arrears (dates)
160	5	12	20	8318	Loan (barley)
161	5	(?)	(?)	6242	Sale of a KISLAḪ-territory
162	5	12	30	4304	Hire of a person (KI.NÍ.TA.NI). Note line 9: INIM.TA PN DAM.A.NI)
163	6			6310	Itemized ŠU.TI.A-receipts for barley, beer, and *piḫû*-containers (Ú.SA.KA.DÙ). (*šikaru ša pân šattim*)
164	6			6329	Tablet containing receipts (DUB.ŠU.TI.A) for various commodities during two years
165	6	1		4953	Itemized record of barley and flour
166	6	1	26	4897	Fragment of administrative document
167	6	2	8	5397	Rent of the *šukūsu*-field of two persons (*ana errēšūtim, šakākum, šebērum, širḫam šakānum*, ratio 2:1)
168	6	2	15	3315	Receipt for barley
169	6	3	1	4931	Warranty to produce a person at the palace within 5 days (ŠU.DÙ.A . . . ŠU.BA.AN.TI) (*šuzuzzum, qabâm šakānum*)
170	6	3	10	5531	Same type as no. 66
171	6	3	10	5536	Same

Text	*Year*	*Month*	*Day*	*YBC Number*	*Contents*
172	6	3	10	5993	Same
173	6	3	10	6100	Itemized list of small amounts of silver (taxes not yet collected)
174	6	3	15	3332	Rent of a field to grow sesame (IGI-4-GÁL). Note seal inscription
175	6	4		4359	Loan (barley) of unusual type. Note seal inscription
176	6	4	1	5208	*Šukunnû*-transaction. Same type as 183 (fragment)
177	6	4	25	6149	Rent of a *šukūsu*-field to plant tamarisks and date palms (*zaqāpum, maiarī maḫāṣum*, GIŠ.MAR of silver [cf. no. 258]). Case on pl. XCVIII
178	6	5	13	5537	Itemized barley deliveries which entered (*erēbum*) the É.KIŠIB.BA
179	6	5	22	8326	ŠU.TI.A-receipts for various agricultural implements (*unûtum*), copied from a sealed tablet
180	6	6	1	7740	Accounting of barley (MU.DU-SAG.NÍG.GA ŠÀ.BI.TA-ZI.GA)
181	6	6	15	6424	Receipt for barley (*ezib ṭuppim maḫrîm*)
182	6	7	15	4231	Expenditures (ZI.GA) of dates, onions, and *saḫlû* (collected as *nemetti kirî*-tax)
183	6	(?)	23	4495	*Šukunnû*-transaction (NAM.GAR.GAR.RA IN.DIB). Cf. no. 176
184	6	8		7055	Fragment of legal document. Case
185	6	7	10	7654	Division of property among 4 brothers (mentioning a cow named EŠ$_4$.DAR-*ri-im-ti-ì-lí*, an object: GIŠ.PA.KU, an *amtum walittum*). Case and tablet
186	6	8		4209	Lawsuit concerning failure to destroy a tablet (partnership)
187	6	8	7	8330	ŠU.TI.A-loan (barley)
188	6	8	30	3396	Record of bricks, hired men, provisions, materials (with an obscure phrase in lines 8–9)
189	6	9	21	6523	Small cattle given (*nadānum*) for pasturing
190	6	9	7	4356	Division of property among 4 brothers (only oil and furniture)
191	6	10	10	6184	ŠU.TI.A-receipt for oil
192	6	10	12	6821	Fragment of a lawsuit
193	6	10	15	4419	Itemized record of sesame
194	6	10	20	8581	Sale of a KI.ŠUB.BA *ni-di-tum* territory which is unclaimed (*ša bēlam la išû*) by the town and the *rabiānum* (fragment)
195	6	10	20	6767	Obligation to deliver a ŠEN-kettle by a smith within a month (fragment)
196	6	11	14	5553	Loan (silver against barley)

Text	Year	Month	Day	YBC Number	Contents
197	6	11	20	8058	Receipt (*maḫārum*) for silver (being the rent of a house). Note seal inscription
198	6	11	20	8344	Loan (barley and oil)
199	6	11	25	4952	Itemized record of barley with dated entries
200	6	12	(?)	3358	Small cattle given (*nadānum*) to a shepherd (wages of the shepherd, *riābum*-clause)
201	6	12	2	5507	ŠU.TI.A-loan of copper to be paid (*šuqqulum*) before the harvest (*ebūram ibbalakatma . . . tašnî utâr*)
202	6	12	6	5546	Receipt (*maḫārum*) of barley (*puquddû*)
203	6	12	11	7079	Accounting of large amounts of barley (SAG. NÍG.GA ŠÀ.BI.TA-expenditures, lines 6–34). Note lines 36–38 where the arrears (LÁ.NI) are said to be composed of "deductions" (NÍG.TUR.TUR) and "(actual) balance" (ÍB. TAG_4)
204	6	12	19	5103	ŠU.TI.A-receipt for barley
205	6	12	24	8037	Expenditures (ZI.GA) of dates from the É. KIŠIB.BA
206	6	12	26	8767	Adoption (NAM.DUMU.NI.ŠÈ BA.DA.[RI] and NAM.IBILA.NI.ŠÈ IB.TA.AN.SAR). Note lines 18–19
207	6	12	30	4464	Rent of a slave
208	6	5	(?)	8082	ŠU.TI.A-receipt for barley (being the hire for a rented-out son)
209	6	12	30	8378	Loan of silver (unusual style)
210	6	12	30	6045	ŠU.TI.A-loan of dates (from the palace)
211	6	(?)	(?)	5994	Promissory note (wool to be delivered *ina buqūmim*). Note line 8
212	7	1	9	5367	Deposition (*burrum*) made in the KISAL of the sanctuary in money matters (HAR.RA, *nadānam qabûm, qêpum*)
213	7	1	10	7966	Receipt (*maḫārum*) for work done by harvesters during 13⅔ days
214	7	2	10	7603	Sale of a KI.ŠUB.BA-territory
215	7	2	10	6069	Rent of a field to grow barley and sesame (IGI-3-GÁL.LA)
216	7	2	10	6787	Rent of a field (*ana teptîtim*, MÁŠ.A.ŠÀ) (3 years)
217	7	3		4257	Rent of a *ḫubtum*-field (consisting of two A.ŠÀ *ne-pé-eš* PN, for shares of respectively one third and one fourth; *ana errēšūtim*) (1 year)
218	7	3(?)		7220	Settlement of a dispute concerning measurements of a territory (fragment)
219	7	3	1	6003	Fragment of a contract

Text	*Year*	*Month*	*Day*	*YBC Number*	*Contents*
220	7	3	25	6039	Sub-rent of a field (IGI-3-GÁL) to grow sesame and barley
221	7	7	22	8698	Promissory note concerning two *iniātum*
222	7	4	24	8644	Sale of a slave girl (fragment)
223	7	5		8064	Promissory note (sesame)
224	7	5		4313	A promissory note (*ṭuppu seḫtum*) concerning the making of bricks and harvesting is declared void
225	7	5	18	4246	Sale of a slave
226	7	6		5525	Loan (barley)
227	7	6	7	4197	Sale of a KISLAḪ-territory
228	7	6	8	5410	Same (fragment)
229	7	6	5	6388	ŠU.TI.A-receipt for sesame and ŠE.LÚ.SAR (Style: second pers. sing., addressing a woman)
230	7	6	11	5542	Loan (barley)
231	7	6	17	4341	Fragment of a contract (sale of a slave?)
232	7	7		8164	ŠU.TI.A-receipt for barley
233	7	7		5982	Loan (barley)
234	7	7	2	8487	Loan (silver)
235	7	7	3	5865	Same
236	7	7	19	5910	Settlement of a dispute concerning the payment of silver to the UGULA-NAM-5 (*kīma ṣimdātim, annam šūpulum*)
237	7	10	10	8681	Dates given *ana puṣṣî* (styled as a loan) (fragment)
238	7	7	14	8672	ŠU.TI.A-receipt for dates (given for the digging of a canal)
239	7	7	20	4967	ŠU.TI.A-loan (wool against barley)
240	7	8		8233	Loan (barley)
241	7	8	5	3316	Promissory note (barley against bitumen [ESIR])
242	7	8	10	5966	Loan (barley) without interest
243	7	8	22	5366	Loan (silver)
244	7	8	30	8390	Hire of a person from his father
245	7	9		5979	Loan (sheep against barley)
246	7	9		7645	Loan (oil against barley)
247	7	9	17	6734	Rent of a field (AB.SÍN and KANKAL for respectively *errēšūtum* and four years)
248	7	9	20	5342	Loan (barley). Payment: *ana šuršumišu . . . isaddarma ippal*
249	7	9	26	6376	Settlement of accounts (NÍG.ŠID *napisma*) concerning the *tēniqum* paid to a wetnurse (barley, oil, garment, wool received [*maḫārum* plus *leqûm*])

Text	*Year*	*Month*	*Day*	*YBC Number*	*Contents*
250	7	9	30	4226	Warranty to bring two slaves to Babylon within a month (ŠU.DÙ.A ŠU.BA.AN.TI)
251	7	10		4377	Loan (barley)
252	7	10	1	5433	Receipt for barley (MU.DU NÍ.TA.NI *namḫarti* PN)
253	7	10	10	8773	Hire of a person from his parents (*ana* KASKAL *ilkim alākum*). Same employer as in nos. 138, 140, and 146
254	7	10	11(?)	8296	Loan (oil against barley) (purpose: *burru* of oil)
255	7	10	17	6016	Loan (sesame NAM *zi-ra-ni*)
256	7	10	20	8045	Loan (dates)
257	7	10	20	7991	Same type as no. 237
258	7	10	21	6236	Rent of a *šukūsu*-field. GIŠ.MAR of copper as no. 177. Note lines 13–15, 16–19
259	7	10	20	8673	Two promissory notes over GÚ.GAL and *zirānu* in favor of the same creditor
260	7	10	27	4379	Loan (barley)
261	7	10	28	4352	Same
262	7	11	1	5196	Loan (barley) without interest (fragment)
263	7	11	3	6445	Same type as no. 260
264	7	11	5	3368	Record concerning copper fetters (*maškanum*) for slaves
265	7	11	8	8167	Loan (sesame) (fragment)
266	7	11	12	5975	Loan (barley) with interest
267	7	11	15	7927	Loan (barley)
268	7	11	20	8676	Loan (sesame against barley)
269	7	11	26	8694	Same
270	7	11	27	8506	Same
271	7	12		6683	Statement of two debtors called upon (*erēšum*) to pay a debt of dates
272	7	12	2	3330	ŠU.TI.A-loan (silver)
273	7	12	14	6068	Receipt for dates
274	7	12	6	4221	Sale of KI.ŠUB.BA-territory
275	7	12	7	7790	Sale of a slave girl (with infant: TUR.RA GABA *ù ša i-na* ZA.AH *wilid bitim*)
276	7	12	10	4361	Loan (barley)
277	7	12	14	9092	Sale of a Ú.SAL-field
278	7	12	21	6317	Division of property (É.DÙ.A) among 3 brothers
279	8			4380	Partnership styled as loan (silver and goods) given by the *ummeānum* to two brothers (payable after a month: ITI.SILIM.MA UD-30-KAM)
280	8	1	1	4254	Guarding a date grove (*ana maṣṣartim nadānum*). Lines 12–14 ŠÀ.KIRI$_6$ *ša inaṣṣaru unappalma ikkal*

Text	Year	Month	Day	YBC Number	Contents
281	8	1	1	4199	Rent of a date grove (*ana maṣṣartim nadānum*, NAM.KÀD.KÀD, *erâm naṣārum*, the building of a *pisé*-wall) for 4 years
282	8	1	1	5371	Rent of a prebend (MAR.ZA) (*a-na tu-ur-šu-mi-*[*im*]) (fragment). Cf. no. 329
283	8	1	25	5548	Receipt (*maḫārum*) for harvesters (from the ⟨UGULA⟩-NAM-5). Note seal inscription
284	8	2	10	8238	Loan (silver), creditor: Shamash (*ûm kaspam immaru* [*išaqqal*]). Design[1]
285	8	2	15	7160	Hire of a person from his father (cf. Á in line 7 with *kiṣru* in line 10, and also no. 155)
286	8	2	20	4269	Rent of a KANKAL-territory to grow barley and sesame (3 years). Annual rent
287	8	2	30	5657	ŠU.TI.A-receipt for silver
288	8	2	30	5362	Partnership (NAM.TAB.BA ŠU.BA.E.TE). Note lines 7–12
289	8	3	1	6174	Rent of a house
290	8	3	14	8777	Lawsuit of a woman against her father-in-law who robbed her (*mašûm*). Note lines 12–21, a list of household utensils, etc. (fragment)
291	8	3	22	4868	Rent of a date grove (GÚ.UN) (3 years). Rent in barley
292	8	(?)	(?)	7819	Loan (oil against barley). Note line 5
293	8	3	27	5347	Receipt for barley (MU.DU NÍ.TA.NI) given out as ŠE.BA of female weavers
294	8	4		8733	Rent of a KANKAL-field (GÁL.TAG$_4$.TAG$_4$.ŠE) (4 years). Line 9: MU-4-KAM *ikkalma itelli*
295	8	4	1	6412	Loan (silver) *ana* ŠE *šâmim*
296	8	4	7	6008	Loan (silver), creditor: Sin; two debtors (SILIM.GI.NA-clause). Design
297	9	4	18	5349	Sale of a GUDU$_4$-prebend
298	8	4	(?)	5945	Rent of a field (IGI-4-GÁL) to grow sesame
299	9	5	29	6099	Record of a hired person starting his service (*erēbum*) for one month
300	8	6	(?)	6083	Rent of two types of fields (fragment) to plant barley and sesame (1 year)
301	8	6	5	6076	Rent of a field (GÚ.UN). Note lines 11–14
302	8	6	10	5830	Sale of a slave girl (*i-li-id bi-tim ma-ar-ti-*⟨⟨x⟩⟩-*ša*! TU.RA)
303	8	6	15	6185	*Šukunnû*-transaction (*ekallam ippal*)
304	8	6	10	8043	Hire of a person from his father for one month
305	8	6	15	8540	Promissory note (oil). Note line 1
306	8	6	24	5502	Receipt (*maḫārum*) for silver (*qabâm šakānum aššum* PN)

1 Refers to a schematic drawing of the standard of Šamaš (or Sin) scratched into the clay. (WWH)

Text	*Year*	*Month*	*Day*	*YBC Number*	*Contents*
307	8	6	25	4357	Receipt (*leqûm*) for silver and agreement concerning a house given by the king Rîm-Sin
308	8	6	30	6194	Same type as no. 303
309	8	7	10	9101	Loan (barley)
310	8	7	20	8232	ŠU.TI.A-loan (barley) (fragment)
311	8	8	30	8347	Unusual (and obscure) administrative document
312	8	(?)	(?)	6725	Sale of a slave girl
313	8	12	1	5523	Loan (barley)
314	10	1	1	6757	Hire of a slave (?)
315	10	2	8	4345	Hire of a slave girl
316	10	4	(?)	6432	ŠU.TI.A-receipt for silver (given *ana nuššurim* for 3 years). Cf. no. 358
317	10	7	21	4303	Sale of a slave
318	10	9	3	4410	Expenditure (ZI.GA) of barley, feed for donkeys
319	10	10	5(?)	7639	Loan (barley)
320	10	9	(?)	7791	Lawsuit (and "Klageverzicht") concerning full payment for a slave girl (*kaspam gummurum, ezibtum*) (fragment)
321	10	11	1	4479	Lawsuit (before the *rabiānum* and the *šībūt ālim*) concerning a house (*šutamgurum*) (fragment). Case and tablet
322	10	11	10	4245	Sale of a slave (*wi-li-id bi-tim*) identified as the son of a slave
323	10	11	1	4214	Loan (silver) (fragment)
324	10	11	30	5435	Contract for pasturing small cattle (unusual style). (SIPA and NA.GADA, annual wages)
325	10	11	30	5577	Lawsuit (before the GAL-UKKIN.NA) concerning barley, oil, and tablets taken from Eshnunna. Note oath formula in lines 9–11
326	10	12	12	8459	Promissory note over balance of silver from a partnership (lines 6–7: MU-3-KAM *inaššarma ippalsu*)
327	10	12	16	5209	ŠU.LÁ-loan (wool) (fragment)
328	10	12	30	4263	Rent of a field (A.ŠÀ Ú.SAL KIRI$_6$) to grow barley and sesame (*imittu-šumēlu*-clause) (time: MU.BAL). Note line 2
329	10	12	30	5388	ŠU.TI.A-receipt for rent of a prebend (*turšummu* in lines 7 and 15) (fragment). Cf. no. 282
330	10	12	30	8430	Partnership (styled as a loan)
331	11	(?)	(?)	4330	Adoption (*ina mêšu ana mârūtim leqûm*), parents giving their son away, the mother receives a *tēniqum* for 3 years

Text	*Year*	*Month*	*Day*	*YBC Number*	*Contents*
332	11	1	1	4296	Rent of a *šukūsu*-field (*ana errēšūtim*, ratio 2:1, *šakākum, šebērum, širḫam šakānum, makāsum*)
333	11	1	1	5429	Hire of a slave(?) (daily wages in barley). Note line 7
334	11	1	9	6322	Bulls (one GUD.ÙR.RA) entrusted (*paqādum*) to a plowman (*ana šamaššammī epēšim*). Note lines 7–8
335	11	2	4(?)	5177	Loan (silver against barley) for 4 days
336	11	2	12	4373	Rent of a field (same type as no. 332). Note lines 10–12: *kakkussu zibbat ḫaṭṭim u šapal biltim ul ibaššîma . . .*
337	11	2	15	6377	ŠU.TI.A-receipt for barley
338	11	3	1	6323	Itemized record of ŠE.GUD and ŠE.ŠEŠ
339	11	3	6	6321	Itemized expenditures (SAG.NÍG.GA ŠÀ.BI.TA) of barley
340	11	4		8038	Obligation to deliver oil pressed out from sesame received. Note line 7
341	11	4	1	6375	Same type as no. 339 (read: SAG.NÍG.GA.RA(!) ŠÀ.BI.TA)
342	11	5	1	8029	Rent of tools for pressing sesame (fragment): DUK.UTUN, GIŠ.KUM, NA_4.HAR.ZI.BI! GIŠ.GAN.NA
343	11	5	1	5510	Loan (silver against sesame)
344	11	5	17	6654	Same (silver against barley)
345	11	5	25	6112	Itemized expenditures of ZÍD.KUM and $UTUL_2$.BA.BA.ZA SIG_5. Note lines 9–10 *a-na ṣí-ir-pi-tim ša e-rib A-bi*
346	11	5	30	6628	Same type as no. 24
347	11	6		6312	Itemized record of dates
348	11	6	10	8664	Loan (silver against 4 KÙR of x-*in-nu*)
349	11	6	10	6324	Accounting of dates (SAG.NÍG.GA ŠÀ.BI.TA, *leqûm*)
350	11	8	10	5937	Receipt for dates
351	11	8	10	6758	Same
352	11	8	(?)	6478	Same content as no. 326 (*tappûtum, šapākum*)
353	11	10	10	8642	A prebend bought previously from a person not authorized is "redeemed" (*paṭārum*) by the buyer from its lawful owner
354	11	12	11	5376	"Rent" of KASKAL-[d]IM (cf. no. 48) LAMA-[d]NIN.A.ZU. Lessor and lessee to divide equally the yield of barley (and *mimma ibaššû*)
355	11	12	20	7673	Sale of a house
356	11	12	30	5359	Division of profits among 4 brothers (*ša* x-*pu-ri-im u li-bi ma-tim*) from capital belonging to the temple. Note line 14

Text	Year	Month	Day	YBC Number	Contents
357	11	12	20	7725	A fugitive slave (profession: AD.GUB$_x$) resold. The owner is to *apālum* the first buyer from whom the slave fled
358	12	2	(?)	8413	ŠU.TI.A-receipt for silver given *ana nuššurim* for 3 years (cf. no. 316)
359	12	5		7912	ŠU.TI.A-receipts for small amounts of barley
360	12	5	26	4242	Two holders of a *ṣibtu*-field come to an agreement (*dabābum, mitgurum, eqlam šutagmulum*)
361	12	(?)	4(?)	6186	Expenditures (ZI.GA) of dates
362	12	5	(?)	8447	*Usâtum*-loan (*bulṭa ikaššadma*)
363	12	6	10	7621	Adoption KI.NÍ.TA.AN.NI (NAM.DUMU.NI ŠU.BA.AN.TI, NAM.IBILA.NI IN.GAR)
364	12	6	15	8062	Rent of a house
365	12	6	11	7816	*Šukunnû*-transaction. Cf. no. 547
366	12	7	20	7830	Itemized list of barley (expenditures)
367	12	8	10	5933	Receipt (*maḫārum*) for *gurnu* and SIG$_5$ dates (GÚ.UN). Case
368	12	11	1	6672	Receipt for dates (lines 3–4 ÍB.TAG$_4$ *našpakim ša uštannû*)
369	12	12	3	6193	Record of settling of accounts (NÍG.ŠID *napiṣma*)
370	13	4	(?)	7686	Rent of a field (IGI-4-GÁL) to grow barley (*maiarī maḫāṣum, šakākum, erēšum*)
371	13	10	20	6714	Marriage contract (unusual type) (*šûrubum ana bîti* PN, *ḫašûm, ana mê nadûm*)
372	14	4	18	6173	Itemized record of barley (fragment) (GIŠ.BÁN É *ši-iq-qa-tim*)
373	14	5	21	6040	Two persons renounce all claims against a third (fragment)
374	14	11	1	6000	Receipt for silver (GÚ.UN)
375	14	10	6	6061	Rent of a field (*e-ma qa-as-sú ú-um-ma-du*) from the son of its owner (GÚ.UN) (2 years). Note lines 10–12
376	14	12	21	6235	A person assumes the obligation to pay within 6 days for silver rings to the father of the wife in order to *qātam nasāḫum* the claim of her husband
377	15	4	1	8457	Fragment of contract
378	15	5	16	6023	Receipt for dates
379	15	8	20	8377	Receipt (*maḫārum*) for silver (GÚ.UN A.ŠÀ-^{d}AMAR.UD)
380	15	3	4	6041	Rent of a field (described: *tawirtum* and *dimātim kurritim*) for one year (GÚ.UN *ina maškanim imaḫḫar u tisīt* A.ŠÀ *ippal*)

Text	Year	Month	Day	YBC Number	Contents
381	11	6	2	9100	A person assumes the obligation to hold large cattle (GUD.EGIR.RA and ÁB.GUD) available which were sold *ina Hurraiē*, seized and entrusted to him
382	11(?)	9	20	6072	Fragment of a lawsuit (claims against the owner of a field)
383	16	7	8	5870	Receipt (*namḫartu*) for barley (*naḫlum*). Note lines 10ff.: *natbak* PN_1, *namḫarti* PN_2, MÁ.Ì.DUB PN_3, NU.BANDÀ PN_4, GÌR PN_5, KASKAL PN_6
384	16	10	1	5967	Receipt for dates. Note seal inscription
385	16	12	10	5928	Rent of a field to grow barley and sesame (IGI-3-GÁL, *inītum*)
386	17	2	20	7646	Partnership, styled as a loan
387	17	3	1	8305	Receipt (*namḫartu*) for barley (GÚ.A.ŠÀ)
388	17	7	10	8726	Expenditure of silver (lines 4–6: PN DUMU.SAL LUGAL [*i-nu-ú-ma a-na* KÁ].DINGIR.RA^{ki} [*il*]-*li-ku*)
389	17	12	5	7647	Receipt for dates (GÚ.UN)
390	19	1	10	8585	Sale of an É-KISLAḪ
391	19	5	27	6001	ŠU.TI.A-receipt for wages paid to the LÚ *kāsimum*
392	19	9	12	3393	Receipt for silver
393	19	10	15	5947	Fragment of a contract
394	19	12	30	6025	Loan (silver)
395	20	1	1	8336	Rent of a date grove (*rapāqum*, *rubbûm*, *naṣārum*, *šukunnê šakānum*, etc.) (4 years). Note lines 16–17
396	20	3	25	5906	Rent of a field to grow sesame (IGI-3-GÁL.LA)
397	20	10	1	5911	Rent of a field (GÚ.UN) (fragment)
398	20	2(?)	16	5929	Rent of a field to grow barley and sesame (NAM.TAB.BA, IGI-3-GÁL, *mānaḫātum*)
399	20	12^2	29	6028	Record of work done by harvesters
400	20	12^2	25	4328	Donation of an É-KANKAL from the family estate to a sister. Note line 10
401	21			7743	Rent of an AB.SÍN-field (IGI-3-GÁL, *ana errēšūtim*, *maiarī gamārum*, *šakākum*, *erēšum*). Note lines 15–18
402	21	4	5	6671	Receipt for dates
403	21	6	26	5942	Rent of AB.SÍN and KANKAL-fields (fragment)
404	21	11	20	5884	Receipt for dates (DIRI)
405	21	(?)	9	6079	Rent of a date grove (GÚ.UN)
406	22	1	1	6437	Small cattle entrusted (*paqādum*) to a shepherd (*riābum*)
407	22	5	6	7643	Agreement concerning *ṣubbûm* (unique text) (IGI *ma-du-tim*^{MEŠ})

Text	*Year*	*Month*	*Day*	*YBC Number*	*Contents*
408	22	12	25	8359	The NU.BANDÀ-official (and the *mādūtum*) claim (*esērum*) stolen *unût ekallim* from a woman who is made to pay one shekel of silver
409	23	1	10	6095	Fragment of court proceedings
410	23	1	14	8208	Itemized record of barley
411	23	1	16	6101	Record of work done by harvesters
412	23	1	21	5952	Same
413	23	1	22	5893	Same
414	23	1	26	5875	Record of work done by carriers (*zābilum*)
415	23	1	28	8743	Same
416	23	1	29	6066	Same
417	23	2		4369	ŠU.TI.A-receipt for onions (*paqādum*)
418	23	2		4408	Same (*nadānum*)
419	23	2		4469	Same (fragment)
420	23	2	1	6110	Record concerning ERÉN-workers (*ša ši-pi-ir ka-la-ak-ki-im i-pu-šu*) (fragment)
421	23	2	1	4291	Hire of an oxdriver (*arki* GUD.ḪI.A) (*adi paṭār erēšim, iniātum*) with an obscure phrase (lines 9–10)
422	23	2	16	6060	Record concerning ERÉN-workers making bricks
423	23	3	5	8410	Rent of a house
424	23	4	1	5980	Loan (silver against barley)
425	23	4	20	8223	Receipt (*namḫartu*) of straw for 60 *e'iltu*-bundles
426	23	5	5	6057	Record concerning an amount of barley for which a PA.PA-official (NÍG.ŠU PN GAL. MAR.TU) had made out a tablet 12 years before the present document
427	23	5	6	6019	Expenditures (ZI.GA) of small amounts of barley
428	23	5	10	5888	Receipt (*namḫartu*) for GA.RAŠ.SAG.SAR
429	23	7	10	5970	Rent of a house
430	23	7	25	5652	Expenditure (ZI.GA) of barley (food for donkeys)
431	23	9	10(?)	6572	Receipt for dates
432	23	9	1	6108	Loan (silver)
433	23	10	11	6065	Itemized expenditures (*leqûm*) of silver for various purposes (line 6: *wilid bītim*, line 13: ŠE. GIŠ.Ì *pa-aḫ-ṣu-tim*, line 28: *tašpîtum*)
434	23	10	15(?)	6311	Duplicate of Grant, Haverford Symposium no. 9 (cf. also no. 126)
435	23	11	16	3321	Loan (silver)
436	23	12	1	4205	Rent of two fields (one: *ana* IGI-3-GÁL.LA, the other, a KANKAL-field: *ana teptîtim* for 3 years) to the same tenant. Note lines 14–16.

Text	Year	Month	Day	YBC Number	Contents
437	23	12	5	7225	Receipt (*namḫartu*) for dates (taxes of the preceding year)
438	23	12	10	8300	Record of dates delivered (MU.DU) to the MÁ.Ì.DUB of the palace
439	23	12	11	6046	Rent of a date grove held (*ṣabātum*) by the tenant from 5 persons; dates to be paid to the palace. Lines 13–15: *kīma ālik idišu*
440	23	12	30	5950	Rent of a date grove (*ana šākinūtim, ippal pīḫat rukkubi*, etc., *apālum*) and of a field therein (*puttûm* and *akālum*). Rent in sesame
441	23	12²	20(?)	5938	Record concerning work (*eṣēdum*) done by gardeners (GÌR PN *ù* EN₅.SI.ME) (fragment)
442	24	1	9	6981	Hire of 3 persons and the *paštum* of Shamash (x ŠE *kurummassu*) for one month and 3 days (unique document)
443	24	2	(?)	5880	Loan (sesame)
444	24	4	20	5863	Unusual document concerning a warranty (*qātāt* PN *leqûm*) (*qabâm šakānum*)
445	24	5	10	8353	*Šukunnû*-transaction. Cf. no. 49
446	24	5	21	5555	Same (cf. nos. 522, 541)
447	24	5	21	6348	A female calf entrusted for pasturing (*ana rē'īm paqādum*) (*pīḫat . . uzuzzu*)
448	24	5	30	8342	Loan (barley)
449	24	8	2	5971	Receipt for dates
450	24	8	19	5999	Loan (silver), creditor: Shamash (*ina balṭu u šalmu*). Design
451	24	8	17	8391	Same, creditor: Sin and Adad (*ina balṭu u šalmu*). Design
452	24	8	26	6038	Rent of a field (GÚ.UN) for one year
453	24	9	20	5878	Receipt for dates (MÁ.Ì.DUB.É.GAL)
454	24	9	20	6011	Same
455	24	11	1	5901	Rent of a field (*teptītum, ana* ITI MU-3-KAM). Rent
456	24	11	28	6044	Small cattle entrusted (*ana rē'ûtim paqādum*) for pasturing (*riābum, ana pīḫat pissātim izzaz*)
457	24	12	10	5935	Marriage contract (*ana kallūtim ḫârum, terḫatum*)
458	24	12	30	8682	Receipt (fragment)
459	24	7(?)	(?)	6053	Rent of a *ḫubtum*-field (*ana teptîtim ana* ŠE) (3 years). Rent. Note obscure clause in lines 12–14 (cf. no. 462)
460	25	1	7	8493	Record concerning 2 harvesters
461	25	1	10	6022	ŠU.TI.A-loan (30 GIŠ.SA.ḪIR for 5 days)

Text	Year	Month	Day	YBC Number	Contents
462	25	1	20	4308	Rent of a field for 2 years (specific rent for each year). The tenant is to dig an *ikum* and a *kalakkum* of prescribed dimensions (lines 13–18)
463	25	1	26	8718	Fragment (probably same type as nos. 506–511)
464	25	5	20	6094	Rent of a house
465	25	2	22	4884	Record of dates delivered (MU.DU)
466	25	5	1	6070	Rent of a person *itti ramānišu* as an oxherd (*ana kullizūtim*) (*iniātum*, *ēnā-qannu-ṣupru*-clause)
467	25	9	1	6644	Rent of a house
468	25	9	1	8281	Same
469	25	10	29	6816	A woman assumes the obligation to support (*qāt* PN *kullum*) her aunt, a LUKUR-priestess who "gives" her several lots of real estate
470	25	12	1	6091	Receipt (*maḫārum*) for silver (KÙ.BABBAR UGULA-NAM-10) by 5 persons (*u mādūtum*)
471	26	1	1	4267	Rent of a field . . . for 3 years (GÚ.UN)
472	26	3	20	8400	Loan (silver), creditor: Shamash (MÁŠ *ù ma-ka-lu* U_4.EBUR$_x$ . . . *utâr*)
473	26	6	5(?)	5960	Loan (silver)
474	26	8	26	6104	Receipt for large amounts of GI.SA
475	26(?)	9	1	8368	Promissory note for draff (unusual form)
476	26	11	3	8455	Rent of date grove (*ana šukunnê šûṣûm*) (1 year)
477	26	11	10	3389	Loan (oil against barley)
478	26	11	15	8279	Rent of a boat (10 KÙR) for "a month of 25 days"
479	26	12	(?)	6035	Receipt for dates (SAG.NÍG.GA, *madādum*, LÁ.NI)
480	26	12	10	5909	Rent of two fields (lines 1 and 10) to grow barley and sesame, owners and tenants identical (respectively: IGI-4-GÁL.LA.AM and IGI-3-GÁL.LA)
481	26	12	10	6617	Same type as no. 479
482	26	(?)	4	8739	Loan (silver) by 4 persons *u mâdūtum*
483	27	1	5	5403	Small cattle belonging to two persons (lines 1ff. and 13ff.) entrusted (*paqādum*) to one shepherd (*riābum*, *ana pissātim uzuzzu*)
484	27	1	10(?)	7666	Rent of a field to grow barley for 2 years ([ ], *šakākum*, *erēšum*)
485	27	1	30	3388	Receipt for silver (*qabâm šakānum*)
486	27	2	6	5892	Record concerning work done by harvesters
487	27	2	10	7665	Receipt (*maḫārum*) for barley (*ana qabê* PN)
488	27	2	15	8162	Record concerning work done by harvesters and carriers (*zābil šaḫarrî*)

Text	Year	Month	Day	YBC Number	Contents
489	27	2	15	8214	Record concerning work done by carriers (*zābil šaḫarrî*)
490	27	2	20	6073	Rent of an AB.SÍN-field to grow sesame (*maiarī maḫāṣum, marārum,* [ ] *epēšum*) (1 year)
491	27	2	20	6055	Exchange of donkeys (*ana pūḫtim nadānum*)
492	27	3	(?)	5907	Rent of a field to grow sesame (*ana šalustim, ana qabê* PN)
493	27	3	20	6075	Same
494	27	5	(?)	4290	Rent of a field (*ana teptītim*) for 3 years
495	27	5	20	7664	Rent of a house
496	27	8	18	6056	Rent of a field for one year (fragment)
497	27	11	12	4407	Receipt (*maḫārum*) for silver (part of rent of a house)
498	27	12	9	7833	Loan (silver against barley)
499	27	12	24	7688	Small cattle entrusted (*paqādum*) for pasturing (*a-na re-'u*$_5$*-tim*). Note lines 6 and 11
500	27	12	30(?)	4876	Loan (barley)
501	28	1	(?)	6447	Record concerning work done by carriers (*zābil šaḫarrîm*)
502	28	1	1	5986	Rent of a field to two tenants to grow sesame (*ana tappûtim,* IGI-3-GÁL, *mānaḫātum, nidi-aḫim*-clause). Seal without inscription
503	28	1	5	5858	Record of work done by harvesters
504	28	1	17	4255	Same
505	28	1	8	5900	Same
506	28	1	23	5981	Record of work done by carriers (*zābil šaḫar-rîm*)
507	28	1	27	6051	Same
508	28	1	30	5861	Same
509	28	1	25(?)	7918	Same
510	28	2	3	6640	Same
511	28	2	5	3361	Same
512	28	2	8	5869	Record concerning ERÉN-workers
513	28	2	21	5899	Same
514	28	3	1	3377	Loan (barley against dates)
515	28	3	1	8063	Loan (silver) (fragment)
516	28	3	4	5915	Rent of a Ú.SAL-field for one year (GÚ.UN)
517	28	3	16	6419	Record concerning beer in *pīḫu*-containers (DUG.Ú.SA.KA.DÙ)
518	28	3	19	5860	Expenditures (ZI.GA) of sesame
519	28	3	25	3367	Loan (silver against barley)
520	28	4	22	4923	Loan (barley and sesame)
521	28	4	25	3376	Loan (barley against sesame)
522	28	6	9	5940	*Šukunnû*-transaction (cf. nos. 446, 541)
523	28	8	1	6054	Rent of a house (*gadum rugbātim u* [ ])

Text	Year	Month	Day	YBC Number	Contents
524	28	5	22	5660	Receipt (*maḫārum*) for small cattle (given *ana šu-ku(?)-lim*)
525	28	10	20	8692	Loan (silver), creditor: Sin (*ina bulṭu u šalmu*). Design
526	28	(?)	12	7644	Loan (barley against sesame)
527	28	(?)	21	6063	Hire of a person *itti ramanišuma* for 3 months (*qātam ṣabātum* for 3 days each month)
528	28	(?)	14	6090	Record concerning work done by harvesters (fragment)
529	30	1	5	6092	Same
530	30	1	6	6738	Rent of a *šukūsu*-field (*errēšūtum, šakākum, širḫam šakānum*) (the tenant receives one tenth for his *mānaḫtu*)
531	30	2	1	5916	Hire of a person *itti ramānišu* for one month (*qātam ṣabātum*)
532	30	2	16	3353	Promissory note (creditor: Sin) for silver, an *ikribu* of the debtor (*ana ālim illakma kaspam inandin*)
533	30	2	20	4273	Rent of a house
534	30	3	1	6062	Rent of a field to grow sesame (*ana errēšūtim*, IGI-3-GÁL)
535	30	3	2	3318	Record concerning work done by "gatherers" (*ḫāmimum*)
536	30	8	(?)	4981	Exchange of houses (*puḫḫum*). Case
537	30	(?)	20	4222	Sale of a house (*šītat bītim ša innezbu*). Case and tablet
538	30	12	27	8695	Loan (dates against barley)
539	32	9	16	4937	Delivery (MU.DU) of oil
540	36	12	24	4871	Loan (barley)
541	(?)			8607	*Šukunnû*-transaction (fragment). Cf. nos. 446, 522
542	(?)	1	1	5908	Rent of a house
543	(?)	2	10(?)	6233	Rent of a *šukūsu*-field by two tenants (*ana šamaššammī epēšim*) (*ana* TAB.BA, *elītum, nēsipētim ana mānaḫtišunu ileqqû*)
544	(?)	3(?)	1	8269	Rent of a house
545	(?)	4	5	6699	Rent of an A.ŠÀ.KIRI$_6$ to grow sesame and barley on the field and *ana teptītim* (3 years).
546	(?)	4	25	7275	Rent of a boat (60 KÙR) and its skipper (*ana girri iabl[ia]*) (fragment)
547	(?)	5	5	6382	*Šukunnû*-transaction. Same type as no. 365
548				5883	Loan (sprouted grains[?]), *pa ra* x (x) *tum šu* (and flour against seeds)
549	(?)	6	6	4922	Loan (silver against GI.SA.ḪI.A)
550	(?)	10	20	6077	Rent of a field to grow barley and sesame (*ana errēšūtim*). Rent in silver

Text	*Year*	*Month*	*Day*	*YBC Number*	*Contents*
551	2	6	17	7601	Fragment of a court decision
552	(?)	12	2	7612	Sale of a Subarean slave girl
553	24	10	1	5946	Rent of a house (for ITI.MU-1-KAM)
554	24	11	15	5965	Rent of a field to grow barley and sesame (for ITI.MU-1-KAM) (MU.BAL)
555	(?)	12	25	4350	Warranty (ŠU.DÙ.A) for the availability of a person until a debt is paid
556	(?)	(?)	28	8643	Sale of a house(?) (fragment). Case and tablet
557	(?)	(?)	3	7595	Lawsuit concerning measurements of sold property (*izibtum, igar birītim*)
558	(?)	(?)	(?)	8696	Rent of a date grove (*rukkubum, pāḫat kirîm uzuzzu, libbi kirîm puttûm*) (fragment)
559	(?)	(?)	(?)	7581	Sale of a house (fragment)
560	(?)	4	1	4247	Rent of a field (*ana* [*teptītim*]) for 3 years (*maḫāṣum, parākum, širḫam šakānum*) (fragment)
561	24			6964	Date formula of the 24th year of Samsuiluna (repeated 4 times). Exercise tablet

INDICES

PERSONAL NAMES

Akkadian personal names have been transcribed as an aid to both onomastic and prosopographic studies. Significant variants and orthographies, however, have been transliterated in parentheses after the transcribed entry. Akkadian names whose analysis remains uncertain, as well as all Amorite and Sumerian names, are entered in transliteration only. Names that occur in both Akkadian and Sumerian have been listed under the Akkadian with a notation indicating passages in which the name is rendered in Sumerian. Personal names occurring only in Sumerian are listed under the Sumerian.

The following abbreviations are used: b., brother; d., daughter; f., father; gf., grandfather; gs., grandson; h., husband; m., mother; s., son; sis., sister; w., wife.

A-[. . .], s. of *Lipit*-[. . .], 116 seal.
A-ak-ka-lu-um, see *A-ka-lum*.
A-a-ma-dar, *A-ma-dar**, *Ḫa-ya-ma-dar*†, f. of *Aḫum*, 360:17†, seal; 390:21*.
A-ap-pa-[*a*], see *Ap-pa-a*.
A-ap-ta-a, GUDU$_4$, f. of ^{d}*Sîn-magir*, 69:7.
A-ba$^{?}$*-a*, 119:19.
Abatum, 432:4.
Abī-iddinam, f. of *Apil*-^{d}*Amurru*, 363:5.
Abī-ilī,
1. s. of ^{d}*Sîn-imguranni*, 559:21.
2. f. of *Apilšunu*, 225:19, case 17.
Abī-libūr, SAG.GEMÉ, m. of *Quttunum*, 322:3.
A-bi-sú-u[*m*], f. of *Erīb*-^{d}*Sîn*, 220 seal.
Abiyatum,
1. f. of *Awīl-Ištar*, 438 seal; 439 seal; 449 seal; 454 seal.
2. 80:4, 6, 9; 142:15; 268:5; 285:12; 354:10.
Abu-kīma-ilim, NAGAR, 338:2.
Abu-lalû(*m*), s. of ^{d}*Enlil-issu*, 185:46, case 48.
Abum-Ištar, f. of *Apil*-^{d}*Amurru*, 552 seal.
Abu(*m*)*-waqar*,
1. s. of *Abu-rabi*, 363:26.
2. s. of DUMU-HI.GAR^{ki}, 153:8, case 10.
3. f. of *Iddin*-^{d}*Sîn*, 29 seal; 343 seal.
4. f. of ^{d}*Sîn-aḫ-iddinam*, 61:29; 342 seal.
5. f. of ^{d}*Šamaš-liṭṭul*, 342:rev. 4.
6. f. of *Tarībatum*, 271:15.
7. ŠABRA, 27:8.
8. UGULA-NAM-5, 417:4.
9. (of) *Dunnum*^{ki}, 26:9.
10. 126.17; 268:9; 397:6; 398:2, 3; 439:4.
Abu-rabi, f. of *Abu-waqar*, 363:26.
^{d}*Adad-bāni*, f. of *Ubarum*, 457:1.
^{d}*Adad-bēl-ilī*, 85:3; 101:16; 159:6; 170:3.
^{d}*Adad-erībam*, 309:2.

^{d}*Adad-iddinam*,
1. f. of *Aḫum*, 322:27.
2. DAM.GÀR, 192:rev. 5.
3. 14:2; 119:8; 160:3; 296:5; 322:19.

^{d}*Adadma-ilī*,
1. f. of *Apil-Kūbi*, 323:14.
2. 59:16; 431:3.

^{d}*Adad-nāṣir*,
1. s. of ^{d}*Šamaš-abīšu*, 44:16, case 18, seal.
2. 22:4, 5, 12.

^{d}*Adad-rabi(m)*, ^{d}IŠKUR.GAL*, 11:4; 52:1, 10; 56:6*; 277:26; 434:11; 440:6.

^{d}*Adad-ri-*[. . .], f. of *Aḫum-waqar*, 153 seal.

^{d}*Adad-rīm-ilī*, 201:3, 7, 13.

^{d}*Adad-šar-ilī*, 190:25.

^{d}*Adad-šarrum*,
1. s. of *Sakkiya*, 376:6.
2. ŠANDAN, s. of *Šalim-kīnum*, 490:12, seal.
3. s. of *Ṭāb-balāṭum*, 217:13, seal.
4. s. of *Ṭāb-Ištar*, 482:4.
5. h. of *Sabītum*, 371:2, 4, 6, 11.
6. ^{LÚ}NIMGIR, 247:12.
7. ŠANDAN, 490:12, seal; 496:8.
8. 112:9; 126:7; 375:16; 393:15; 470:5.

^{d}*Adad-tayyār*, 333:1.

A-da-la-lum, 482:6.

Adān-^{d}*Sîn*, f. of *Ali-waqrum*, 95:14, seal.

Adaya,
1. f. of *Iddin-Ištar*, 46:3; 114 seal; 342:rev. 1.
2. 340:rev. 11.

Adayatum,
1. f. of *A-ka-lum*, 153:18, case 21, seal.
2. f. of *Iddin-*^{d}*Adad*, 309 seal.
3. f. of *Kunniyatum*, 227:24.

A-di-[. . .], 56:13.

Adīdum, 52:11; 56:57; 220:12; 393:13.

[*Adi*]*-mati-ilī*, f. of *Awīl-ili*, 274:23.

Adu-anniam, f. of ^{d}*Sîn-imguranni*, 286:18.

A-gu-ya, *A-gu-ú-a-a**, 130:3; 330:9*.

Aḫam-arši,
1. s. of *Iddin-*^{d}*Bunene*, b. of *Ali-talīmī*, *Iddin-*^{d}*Amurru*, *Ilīma-aḫī*, *Ilšu-abū-šū*, ^{d}*Sîn-rēmēni*, 556:8.
2. 56:18; 117:2, 3.

Aḫam-nirši,
1. s. of ^{d}*Sîn-magir*, 224:16.
2. f. of *Ibbi-*^{d}*Ilabrat*, 402 seal; 462 seal.
3. 496:7.

Aḫa(m)-nūta,
1. s. of *Ilī-erībam*, 373:2, seal.
2. 396:5; 474:3.

Aḫassunu,
1. m. of ^{d}*Ningizzida-abī*, w. of *Ištar-ilum*, 253:3, 9.
2. 372:16.

Aḫatum, d. of *Nūr-*^{d}*Sîn*, 141:5.

A-ḫa-tum, ^{d}*Na-na-a-*É.GAL, 92:3.

A-ḫi-[. . .], f. of *Ya-*x-[. . .], 321:rev. 2.

Aḫi-a(y)-amši,
1. f. of [*Ilīm*]*a-aḫī*, 277:29.
2. b. of ^{d}*Amurru-muballiṭ*, *Qurrudum*, *Ilīma-abī*, *Šumman-lā-*^{d}*Šamaš*, 102:8.
3. 2:4.

Aḫi-lūmur, h. of *Kurītum*, 408:5.

Aḫī-maraṣ, 300:3, 4.

A-ḫi-mar-ši
1. f. of ^{d}*Sîn-damiq*, 526:5.
2. 560:17.

Aḫī-šagiš, 112:34; 328:6.

Aḫī-wēdum, 177:20; 294:12.

Aḫīya,
1. s. of ^{d}*Sîn-uselli*, 48:4, 7, 21.
2. NU.BÀNDA, 307:19.
3. 177:18, case 17; 200:6; 238:6; 326:12; 347:3; 349:6; 512:1; 530:20.

Aḫīyama, f. of *Nūršu-e-li*, 379 seal.

A-ḫi-ya-šu, 396:10; 455:2, 3.

Aḫi-yû, 263:9.
Aḫu-kīnum,
1. s. of *Ya-am-nu-um*, b. of *Šū-ilišu*, 61:4, 9, 20; 62:4, 9.
2. f. of *Tarībatum*, 350 seal; 351 seal; 367 seal.
Aḫum,
1. s. of *A-a-ma-dar*, 360:17, seal; 390:21.
2. s. of ᵈ*Adad-iddinam*, 322:27.
3. s. of GÌRI.NI-Ì.SÀ, 186:rev. 11.
4. s. of *Ipquša*, 552:21.
5. s. of ᵈ*Šamšī-*ᵈ*Enlil*, b. of *Apil-*ᵈ*Kittim*, *Saniq-pî-*ᵈ*Šamaš*, *Ūṣi-nūrum*, 185:29, 35, case 33, 39.
6. s. of *Waqar-abūšu*, b. of ᵈ*Sîn-uselli*, 277:10; 297:4, 7.
7. 142:17; 147:3; 282:5; 313:4; 332:3, 4; 336:3, 4.
Aḫum-abī, 475:8.
Aḫu(m)-waqar,
1. s. of ᵈ*Adad-ri-*[. . .], h. of *Inbatum*, 153:4, 6, 7, case 5, 6, 8, seal.
2. s. of *Rabût-*ᵈ*Sîn*, 544:1, 2, seal; 553:1, 2, seal.
3. s. of *Samsu*, 308:3, seal.
4. s. of *Uqâ-ilam*, 421:11, seal.
5. f. of ᵈ*Marduk-zuqqip*, 380:15, seal; 401 seal.
6. f. of *Qaqqadum*, 556:22.
7. f. of *Rīš-*ᵈ*Šamaš*, 526:12.
8. f. of *Sāmum*, 200 seal.
9. SIPA, 353:27.
10. 56:27, 46; 118:19; 240:3; 339:3; 348:14; 375:14; 432:3; 446:14; 544:11.
Aḫūni, 55:2; 56:32; 101:21; 125:3, 4; 151:11; 178:3; 376:16; 385:16; 405:16(?); 467:11; 468:11; 546:3, 4, 9, 11, 18.
Aḫūšina, f. of *Qurrudum*, 559:23.
Aḫūšunu,
1. ŠANDAN, s. of *Siyatum*, 404:3, seal.
2. f. of ᵈ*Šamaš-muballiṭ*, 260 seal.
3. b. of ᵈ*Sîn-šamuḫ*, 301:6.
4. SIPA, 200:7.
5. UGULA, 486:3.
6. 177:6.
Aḫu-ṭābu(m), *Aḫḫu-ṭābu**,
1. *rabiānum*, s.(?) of [. . .]-*lim*, 390:18*, seal(?).
2. 401:21; 421:12*; 444:3, 4.
Aḫu-waqrum, 543:19.
Aḫuyatum,
1. f. of *Apil-ilišu*, 260 seal; 261 seal.
2. 434:19.
*A-ka-*x, f. of *Apil-*ᵈ*Amurru*, 473:4.
A-ka-lum, *A-ak-ka-lu-um**, s. of *Adayatum*, 153:18, case 21, seal*.
Aklatum, NIN.DINGIR, 105:4, 5.
ᵈ*Alammuš-ekallī*, 498:3.
ᵈ*Alammuš-nāṣir* (ᵈ*A-la-mu-uš-na-ṣir*), NAGAR, 475:3.
Ali-abūša, SAG.GEMÉ, 250:5, 11.
Ali-bānīšu,
1. f. of *Ipiq-Annunītum*, 536:34.
2. UGULA-MAR.TU, 325:7.
Ali-damqum, s. of *Zu-za-tum*, 102:23; 194: rev. 8.
Ali-ilī, s. of *Ṭāb-šār-ilī*, 559:25.
Ali-illatī, f. of *Apil-ilišu*, 242:6.
Ali-liwwir, s. of *Ana-panī-ili*, b. of [. . .]-x-*šar-ilī*, 102:25, seal; 194:rev. 6.
Ali-lūmur,
1. ENGAR, s. of *Ilum-damiq*, 492:9, seal.
2. s. of *Kurû*, 13:14, seal; 140 seal; 162:14.
3. UGULA, 501:3; 503:3; 504:3; 505:3; 506:5; 507:3; 508:3; 510:3; 511:3; 528:4; 529:3.

4. 1:14; 36:4; 119:6; 120:9; 147:9; 195:7; 290:44; 512:7; 513:2, 6.
A-li-ša?-ri, 188:7.
Ali-talīmī, s. of *Iddin-^{d}Bunene*, b. of *Aḫam-arši*, *Iddin-^{d}Amurru*, *Ilīma-aḫī*, *Ilšu-abūšu*, *^{d}Sîn-rēmēni*, 556:8.
Alittum, 107:3.
Ali-waqrum,
1. s. of *Adān-^{d}Sîn*, 95:13, seal.
2. (of) Nippur, f. of *^{d}Enlil-bāni*, 275:18.
3. f. of *Imgur-Ištar*, *Ātanaḫ-ilī*, 277:5, 15.
A-li-wu-um, 221:2.
Aliyatum, 448:8; 487:5.
Alûm (*A-lu-ú*, *A-lu-ú-um**, *A-lu-um*†),
1. s. of *Imgurum*, 225:21, case 19.
2. f. of *^{d}Šamaš-liwwir*, 121:10*.
3. 91:2*, case 2*; 125:17†.
A-ma-dar, see *A-a-ma-dar*.
Amat-bēltim, d. of *^{d}UTU-ša!-tum*, sis. of *Šāt-^{d}Marduk*, 469:12.
*Amat-^{d}*EN.[. . .], SAG.GEMÉ, 275:1.
Amat-^{d}Kabta, SAG.GEMÉ, 315:1.
Ammatum, *rabiānum*, 363:19.
Am-mi-da-nu, 485:6.
Āmur-ilūssa,
1. f. of *Erišam*, 157 seal.
2. f. of *Qištum*, 176 seal.
Āmur-narbīša, 92:8.
Āmur-rabūssa, 69:3.
^{d}Amur[ru. . .], 458:3.
^{d}Amurru-abī, SIPA, 447:3.
^{d}Amurru-ibbīšu,
1. s. of *^{d}Amurru-malik*, 312:17.
2. s. of DUMU-^{d}MAR.TU, 312:20.
^{d}Amurru-illassu, 225:6, case 6; 307:3.
^{d}Amurru-illatī, 307:10.
^{d}Amurru-[is]su, 253:14.
^{d}Amurru-liwwir, 370:15.
^{d}Amurru-malik, f. of *^{d}Amurru-ibbīšu*, 312:17.
^{d}Amurru-muballiṭ,
1. RÁ.GABA, s. of *Nūr-iliya*, 194:5, 8.
2. b. of *Aḫī-a(y)-amši*, *Qurrudum*, *Ilīma-abī*, *Šumman-lā-^{d}Šamaš*, 102:7, 13; 194:rev. 14.
3. 102:3; 263:3; 267:3.
^{d}Amurru-mudī, 78:20.
^{d}Amurru-mušallim, 457:11.
^{d}Amurru-nāṣir, 29:4; 543:18.
^{d}Amurru-šemi, f. of *Lipit-Ištar*, 385 seal.
^{d}Amurru-tayyār, 10:8; 281:6.
Ana-Ea-taklāku, 307:22; 395:2, 3.
Ana-Ištar-taklāku, GEMÉ, 320:1, 19.
Anāku-ša-Ištar, 92:18.
Ana-panī-ili, *Ana-pān-ili* (*Ap-pa-an-*DINGIR)*,
1. s. of *Palḫūya*, 559:22*.
2. f. of *Ali-liwwir*, [. . .]-x-*šar-ilī*, 102:25, seal; 194:rev. 6.
3. 368:11.
Ana-panī-^{d}Nusku, SUKKAL, f. of *Elmēšum*, 73:30, case 32.
Ana-panī-^{d}Sîn-nadi, 322:24.
Ana-^{d}Sîn-taklāku, SAG.ÌR, 250:4, 10.
Ana-ṣillīša-ēmid,
1. s. of *Ātanaḫ-[ilī]*, 559:19.
2. s. of *Lalûm*, b. of *Asīrum*, 194:rev. 11.
Ana-^{d}Šamaš-līṣi, 348:4.
Ana-^{d}Šamaš-takil, f. of *Ea-iddinam*, 533 *seal.*
A-na-tum,
1. s. of *Erībam*, 75:16.
2. s. of *Ti-in-gi*, 497:7.
3. DUB.SAR, 440:19.
Aḫ-NE-*ya*, 125:5.
Annaḫum, ŠU.I, 290:45.
*An-na-ka-la-^{d}*UTU, 485:9.

Annî, 56:12.
Annû, 411:9; 412:9; 413:9; 414:9; 416:9; 422:8; 463:11.
Annum-pî-Ea, s. of ^{d}*Sîn-ēriš*, 42:22.
Annum-pî-^{d}Ilabrat,
1. DUB.SAR, 537:25; 556:31.
2. 22:15; 536:40.
Annum-pî-Ištar, f. of MU.ZU.ŠÈ, 74:3, seal.
Annum-pîša,
1. s. of *Inbuša*, 520:4.
2. f. of *Imgur-^{d}Šamaš*, 48 seal.
Annum-pî-^{d}Šamaš, 204:3; 244:12.
Ap-[. . .], s. of ^{d}*Sîn-ēriš*, 323 seal.
A-pa-a, see *Ap-pa-a*.
Apil-[. . .],
1. f. of ^{d}*Šamaš-nāṣir*, 388 seal.
2. 311:1; 319:11.
Apil-^{d}[. . .], 26:17.
Apil-^{d}Adad,
1. f. of *Lā-qīpum*, 79 seal.
2. f. of *Nabi-ilišu*, 14:5.
3. 239:3.
Apil-^{d}Amurru,
1. s. of *Abī-iddinam*, 363:5, 9, 13.
2. s. of *Abum-Ištar*, 552 seal.
3. s. of *A-ka-*x, 473:3.
4. s. of *A-ap-pa-*[*a*], 120:33(?).
5. s. of ÌR-^{d}UTU and *Ina-pîša-lubluṭ*, 331:1.
6. s. of *Kurullum*, f. of *Idiyatum*, b. of *Nūr-Ištar*, 363:20.
7. s. of *Sāmum*, 37:5, seal.
8. ŠANDAN, s. of ^{d}*Sîn-imguranni*, 522:4, seal.
9. f. of *Ibni-^{d}Marduk*, 550:5.
10. f. of *Inbilišu*, 322:26.
11. f. of *Tarībatum*, 558:12.
12. AGA.UŠ-GAL-UKKIN.NA, 325:5.
13. DUB.SAR, 277:31.
14. NAR É-^{d}NIN.ŠUBUR, 353:24.
15. UGULA, 513:1, 5.
16. 49:12; 216:3; 280:17; 281:22; 291:4, 9; 322:20; 323:4; 325:26; 452:2, 3; 512:3; 538:3; 551:7.
Apil-^{d}Ašnan,
1. s. of *Tiz*[*qarum*], 228:17.
2. 202:3; 316:8.
Apil-Ea, 492:10; 518:8; 545:12.
Apil-erṣetim,
1. f. of *Ibni-^{d}Šērum*, *Kīma-aḫum*, *Kubbultum*, 95:4(?), 10(?).
2. SIPA, 203:24.
3. 148:9; 302:21.
Apil-ili,
1. s. of *Siyatum*, 457:9.
2. 112:29.
Apil-ilišu,
1. s. of *Aḫuyatum*, 260:10, seal; 261:9, seal.
2. s. of *Ali-illatī*, 242:5.
3. s. of *Ibbi-^{d}Sumuqan*, 226:9.
4. s. of *Ibni-^{d}Amurru*, 275:21.
5. s. of *Imgurum*, 342:6.
6. s. of ÌR-^{d}SUEN, 16:2, seal.
7. s. of *Lipit-Ištar*, 286:16.
8. s. of *Nūrum-līṣi*, 8:9, seal.
9. s. of ^{d}*Sîn-uselli*, b. of *Nabi-ilišu*, 353:4, 11.
10. s. of ^{d}UTU-DINGIR, 214:3, 7, 8, 16, seal.
11. s. of *Zikir-ilišu*, 279:14, seal.
12. f. of *Awīl-^{d}Nabium*, 493:12.
13. f. of *Ea-*[*šar*]*-ilī*, 274:22.
14. f. of ^{d}*Enlil-rabi*, 186:rev. 4.
15. f. of *Ibbi-^{d}Šamaš* and *Iddin-^{d}Nanâ*, 552:5.
16. AB.AB.DU$_{7}$, 552:26.
17. *kāṣirum*, 69:4.
18. SIPA, 103:19.

19. 111:5; 192:rev. 7; 273:10; 276:8; 344:11.

Apil-^{d}Irra
1. f. of *Ilum-gāmil*, 357:31.
2. 124:2; 252:3; 293:4.

Apil-^{d}Kabta, f. of *A-ap-pa-[a]*, 12:4.

Apil-^{d}Kittim, *Apil-^{d}Kittum**,
1. s. of ^{d}*Šamšī-^{d}Enlil*, b. of *Aḫum*, *Saniq-pî-^{d}Šamaš*, *Ūṣi-nūrum*, 185:10, 30, 36, case 11, 34, 40; 555:4*.
2. 68:4–5; 138:11; 306:4.

Apil-Kūbi,
1. s. of ^{d}*Adadma-ilī*, 323:13.
2. f. of *Mār-erṣetim*, 259:4.
3. 65:1; 82:2; 101:4; 112:6; 118:17; 125:13.

Apil-^{d}Lisi, GUDU$_4$, 290:36.

Apilliya, b. of ^{d}*Šamaš-gimlanni*, 97:5.

Apil-^{d}Sîn,
1. GUDU$_4$.ABZU, 295:11.
2. SIPA, 324:6.
3. 46:2, 5, 8.

Apilša,
1. f. of *Ṣillī-^{d}Amurru*, 444 seal(?).
2. LÚ *Ikūn-pî-^{d}Sîn*, 61:27; 62:16.
3. 148:8; 235:11.

Apil-^{d}Šamaš,
1. s. of *Lā-qīpum*, 552:22.
2. 424:4; 432:9; 445:9.

Apil-^{d}[Šēr]um, 267:9.

Apilšunu,
1. s. of *Abī-ilī*, 225:19, case 17.
2. KISAL.LUḪ, 383:22.

Aplatum,
1. d. of *Luštammar*, 135:13, seal.
2. d. of ^{d}*Marduk-kašid*, 377:rev. 2.
3. d. of *Mār-erṣetim*, 536:38; 556:29.
4. d. of *Warad-ilišu*, 217:14, seal.
5. 49:10.

Aplum,
1. s. of ^{d}EN.LÍL!.LE!, 60:1, 10, 14.
2. UGULA-NAM-5, s. of *Iddin-^{d}Sîn*, b. of *Bēletum*, *Ilī-iqīšam*, *Kalūmum*, 14:9, seal; 227:3, 7, 16.
3. Á.GÁL, s. of *I?-ir-bu-ni*, 227:33.
4. s. of ^{d}*Sîn-iddinam*, 552:27.
5. s. of *Šēp-^{d}Sîn*, b. of *Erībam-^{d}Sîn*, *Ilī-gimlanni*, *Ṣillī-^{d}Amurru*, 278:4.
6. s. of *Sînatum*, 226:8.
7. s. of [. . .]-^{d}*Ninurta*, 353:29(?).
8. (of) *Bad-tibira*, f. of *Ipquša*, 275:15.
9. f. of ^{d}*Sîn-iddinam*, 283:5.
10. f. of ^{d}*Šamaš-muballiṭ*, 244:2.
11. f. of *Tarībatum*, 227:31.
12. AGA.UŠ, 46:25.
13. GUDU$_4$, 28:18.
14. KÙ.DÍM, 253:15.
15. RÁ.GABA, 156:rev. 5.
16. 36:11; 164:7, 8, 22; 249:12, 14; 262:4; 280:4, 9; 365:4; 427:10.

Apluša, s. of *Issu-kabit*, 153:24, case 26, seal.

Ap-pa-a, *A-ap-pa-a**, *A-pa-a*†,
1. s. of *Apil-^{d}Kabta*, 12:5*.
2. SIMUG, s. of *Ḫabil-kīnu*, 245:9†, seal†; 286:15*.
3. f. of *Apil-^{d}Amurru*(?), 102:33*.
4. f. of *Ibašši-ilum*, 497:8.
5. f. of ^{d}*Šamaš-bē[l-ilī]*, 216 seal*.
6. 42 seal*; 201:5*, 8*; 305:8*; 385:15*.

*Ap-pa-an-*DINGIR, see *Ana-panī-ili*.

Ap?-pa-na-tum, 538:9.

Apparrûm,
1. f. of *Bāš-ilum*, 360:4.
2. 232:3.

Aqāl-ana-^{d}Šamaš, 93:3.

Arassa, 279:8.

Arbum, 38:3(?); 160:9.

*Arši-aḫum, Ar-še-ḫu-um**,
1. f. of *Awīl-*^{d}*Nabium*, 495:5.
2. 446:16*.
Arwium, f. of *Ya-gu-nu-um*, 542 seal.
^{d}*Asarluḫi-muballiṭ*, 28:1.
^{d}ASAR.LÚ.ḪI-ŠA$_{6}$.GA, 217:9.
Asīrum,
1. s. of *Lalûm*, b. of *Ana-ṣilliša-ēmid*, 194:4, rev. 10.
2. 108:rev. 4.
Aššumiya-libūr, SAG.GEMÉ, 185:23, case 27.
A-ta-li-im (perhaps genitive of *Atallûm*), f. of ^{d}*Nabium-malik*, 544 seal.
Ātanaḫ-ilī,
1. s. of *Ali-waqrum*, b. of *Imgur-Ištar*, 277:6, 716.
2. f. of *Ana-ṣilliša-ēmid*, 559:19.
3. 78:11.
A-ta-šu, 215:14.
At-ta-ḫa-aš-tu-uk, 387:5.
At-ta-ku?-zu?, *At-ta-ku?-zu?-ni**, s. of *Ipqu-*^{d}*Adad*, 72:5*, seal.
Attatum, 518:7.
Awāt-erṣetim (KA-*er-ṣe-tim*), 56:45.
Awīl-[. . .], 471:12.
Awīl-^{d}[. . .], 383:16.
Awīl-^{d}*Aya*, 207:12.
Awīl-^{d}*Adad*, LÚ-^{d}IŠKUR.RA*,
1. s. of *Gu-ur-ru-*[x], 27:3, seal.
2. s. of ÌR.X.[. . .], 5:3, seal.
3. 36:5; 190:29; 262:8; 430:4; 437:19*; 447:4*, 11; 533:1, 2; 553:4.
Awīl-^{d}*Amurru*, LÚ-^{d}MAR.TU*, 46:20*; 465:2, 6.
Awīl-Ea, LÚ-^{d}EN.KI.KA*,
1. f. of *Eridu*^{ki}*-liwwir*, 42:21*.
2. 77:19*; 106:3*; 203:25.
Awīl-ili,
1. s. of [*Adi*]*-mati-ilī*, 274:23.
2. s. of *Naplis-ilum*, 363:25.
3. f. of *Baliya*, 331:5.
4. *rabiānum*, 27:10 (URU *A-ka-nu*^{ki}); 60:2, 6, 13.
5. UGULA-DAG.GI$_{4}$.A, 227:38.
6. PA.PA, 491:3.
7. 287:5.
Awīl-[*ilī*]*šu*, 143:2.
Awīl-Ištar, see also LÚ.DINGIR.RA
1. ŠANDAN, s. of *Abiyatum*, 438:5, seal; 439:3, seal; 446:4, seal; 449:5, seal; 453:6, seal; 454:6, seal.
2. s. of *Ḫāzirum*, 320:5, 18, 20.
3. s. of *Purādānu*, 390:24.
4. 381:3; 476:3 (^{d}INANNA), 4 (^{d}MÚŠ).
Awīliya,
1. s. of *A-ya-ḫu-*[*nu*], 220:6, seal.
2. s. of *Sa-nu-ub-ti-*X, 246:4.
3. h. of *Ḫuzālatum*, 270:4.
4. MUḪALDIM, 209:3.
5. *rā'ibānum*, 246:3; 270:3.
6. 34:4; 163:16; 221:3; 223:3; 237:11; 240:2; 245:2; 254:3; 255:3; 259:5, 11; 265:3; 268:3; 269:3, 8; 286:5; 336:19; 380:4, 5; 478:5.
Awīl-^{d}*Nabium*, *Awīl-*^{d}*Na-bu-um**,
1. s. of *Apil-ilišu*, 493:12.
2. s. of *Arši-aḫum*, 495:4.
3. s. of DINGIR.DÙG-*ya*, 482:12.
4. s. of *Dan-ilišu*, 382:15.
5. 122:3*; 493:6.
Awīl-^{d}*Šamaš*,
1. b. of ^{d}*Sîn-iddinam*, 358:7.
2. *rabiānum*, 344:10.
3. 20:9; 22:18; 28:14; 290:40.
Awiyatum,
1. s. of *Iddin-*^{d}*Adad*, 77:13.
2. ŠÀ.TAM É-^{d}UTU, ŠÀ.TAM *ša* ^{d}UTU*, s. of *Na*[*bi*]*-ilišu*, 73:29, case 27*, seal.

3. f. of *Nūr-^{d}Amurru*, 186:1.
4. NU.$KIRI_6$, b. of *Ubarum*, 227:36.
5. $GUDU_4$.ABZU, 557:30.
6. 216:2.

Aya,
1. f. of *^{d}Išumuatum*, 177 seal.
2. f. of *^{d}Sîn-iqīšam*, 164:1, 10.
3. w. of *Ḫuzālum*, 249:10.
4. 229:8.

A-ya-ḫu-[nu], f. of *Awīliya*, 220 seal.

Ba-a-a-mu, 50:2; 248:12; 354:4; 356:4.

BA.AN.ZI.GE, f. of *^{d}Šamaš-gamil*, 161:3.

BA-^{d}INANNA.[. . .], 56:62.

Bal-a, *Bal-la-a**, 21:3; 35:10; 58:3*; 67:4; 72:4; 163:15; 177:2*, 3*; 258:4, 5, 15, 17; 347:2; 349:12; 357:19; 543:4.

BALA-^{d}IŠKUR, ENGAR, 179:7.

BALA-MU-NAM.ḪÉ,
1. s. of *Iddin-Ea*, 312:13.
2. 72:3; 152:18; 302:15; 334:4, 8.

Balāssu-ra[bi], f. of *Ḫuzālum*, 376:15, seal.

Baliya, s. of *Awīl-ili*, 331:5.

Bal-ilum (*Ba-li-lu-um*, *Ba-li-lum**, *Ba-li-*DINGIR†),
1. s. of *Iddin-^{d}Sîn*, 50:9.
2. *rabiānum*, s. of *^{d}Sîn-magir*, 153:17*, case 20*, seal*.
3. f. of *Keš^{ki}-iddinam*, 26:13†.

^{d}BARÁ.UL.E.GAR.RA-[. . .], f. of *Bitu-rabi*, 46 seal.

Bāṣirum, f. of *^{d}Sîn-iddinam*, 469:2.

Bāš-ilum (*Ba-aš-*DINGIR, *Ba-ši-*DINGIR*),
1. s. of *Apparrûm*, 360:4, 5.
2. 429:1*, 2*; 523:5*.

Baštī, 429:10.

Ba-ya-um, s. of *Ibni-^{d}Adad*, b. of *Paluḫ-rigimšu*, 536:37; 537:23, case 14; 556:23.

Ba-zi-ya, 270:9.

Be-[. . .], 26:41.

Be-el-ti-a-bi-it, 92:21.

Bēlānum,
1. s. of *Ibni-^{d}Adad*, 556:27.
2. s. of *Mār-erṣetim*, 75:22.
3. s. of *Šumum-libši*, 380:14(?).
4. f. of *Ibni-^{d}*[. . .], 540:9.
5. DUB.SAR, 63:4; 108:rev. 6; 425:9; 498:9.
6. SIPA, 499:17.
7. UGULA-MAR.TU, 444:8.
8. 36:6; 83:4; 98:7; 168:4; 179:12; 516:12; 544:12.

Bēlessunu,
1. LUKUR-^{d}UTU, d. of DUMU-ZIMBIR^{ki}, sis. of *Ilī-awīli* and *Ilšu-bāni*, 536:7, 8, 20, 24.
2. m. of DUMU-ḪI.GAR^{ki} 247:11.
3. 92:6.

Bēletum,
1. d. of *En-nu*, 141:18.
2. d. of *Iddin-^{d}Sîn*, sis. of *Aplum*, *Ilī-iqīšam*, *Kalūmum*, 227:5, 18.
3. 2:3.

Bēlī, f. of *^{d}Sîn-imguranni*, 236:3, 6; 250:16; 355:22.

Bēlī-āpilī, 246:9.

Bēlī-ēpirī, 365:9.

Bēlī-iddina(m),
1. s. of *^{d}Sîn-ēriš*, 74:4.
2. 248:11; 329:21.

Bēlī-imdī, 410:12.

Bēlī-libūr, b. of *Immer-ili*, 138:1.

Bēlī-lū-dāri,
1. s. of *^{d}Šamaš-nāṣir*, 552:23.
2. 453:8; 454:8.

Bēlī-mudī, RÁ.GABA, s. of *^{d}Šamaš-šadūša*, 111:19, seal.

Bēlšunu,
1. s. of *Būr-*^{d}*Adad*, 210:4, 6.
2. s. of *Ilum-wēdum*, 477:7.
3. UGULA-NAM-5, 437:21.
4. 28:15; 443:13; 447:12.

Bēltani,
1. d. of *Ilī-ippalsam*, 192:1(?).
2. d. of ^{d}*Sîn-muštēšir*, 469:9.
3. d. of *Nūr-*^{d}*Kabta*, sis. of *Šumum-libši*, 400:7.
4. 205:2.

Bēltiya, 345:3.
Bēltum-kīma-abī, 433:9.
Bēlum-muštāl, 353:6.
Bi-x-[. . .], f. of ^{d}*Sîn-iqīšam*, 214:28.
Bi-bi-x, f. of *Šarrum-bāni*, 243 seal.
Bitu-rabi, s. of ^{d}BÁRA.UL.E.GAR.RA-[. . .], 46:16, seal.
Bi-tu-ú-a, f. of [. . .]*-ba?-ši*, 277:28.
Bulluṭ-ilum, f. of ^{d}*Sîn-iddinam*, 559:20.
Bulluṭ-Ištar, 361:7.
^{d}*Bunene-abi* (^{d}*Bu-né-né-a-bi*), 442:3.
Būr-^{d}*Adad*, f. of *Bēlšunu*, 210:4.
Būr-Ištar, 365:8.
Būr-^{d}*Sîn*, f. of *Ilī-iddinam*, 74:14, case 2.
Bu-zu-[. . .], SAG.GEMÉ, 76:13.

Da-da, *Da-da-a**,
1. f. of ^{d}*Sîn-imgur*[*anni*] and ^{d}*Sîn-tukultī*, 228:20.
2. 7:12*, 20; 340:5*.

Dādušа, 397:10; 424:3; 448:7; 542:11.
^{d}*Dagan-bāni*,
1. s. of ^{d}*Sîn-abūšu*, 304:10, seal.
2. 241:8; 478:2, 3, 10.

DAM.GÀR, f. of *Saniq-pî-*^{d}*Šamaš*, 355:2.
Damiq-abum ($ŠA_6$*-a-bu-um*), 242:11.
Damiq-ilišu, see *Damqilišu*.
Damqilišu (sandhi for *Damiq-ilišu*),
1. s. of *Lalûm*, 306:6, case 7, seal; 555:3, seal.
2. 551:8.

Dan-^{d}*Adad*, f. of *Tarībum*, 149:4.
Dan-^{d}*Amurru*, 306:3.
Dan-i[*lišu*], f. of *Awīl-*^{d}*Nabium*, 382:16.
Dāpinum,
1. DUB.SAR, 214:30.
2. PA.PA, 381:16.
3. 38:9.

DINGIR*-bi-ni-šu*, s. of *Imguyatum*, 102:26.
DINGIR.DILI, see *Ilum-wēdum*.
DINGIR.DÙG*-ya*, f. of *Awīl-*^{d}*Nabium*, 482:13.
DINGIR*-mu*-[. . .], f. of *Iddin-*^{d}*Amurru*, 236 seal.
Du?-ba-bu, 516:11.
DUMU-ḪI.GAR^{ki}
1. s. of *Bēlessunu*, 247:11.
2. f. of *Abu*(*m*)*-waqar*, 153:8, case 10.

DUMU-^{d}IŠKUR, 480:5, 13.
DUMU-KÁ.DINGIR.RA^{ki},
1. ŠANDAN-URÍ^{ki}, s. of *Ilī-dādiya*, 378:6, seal.
2. ŠANDAN, 374:6; 384:6; 389:6; 405:2, 3.

DUMU.KI, see *Mār-erṣetim*.
DUMU-^{d}MAR.TU, see *Mār-*^{d}*Amurru*.
DUMU-^{d}UTU, 56:32(?); 434:7.
DUMU-ZIMBIR^{ki},
1. s. of ^{d}*Sîn-adallal*,
   f. of *Bēlessunu*, *Ilī-awīlim*, *Ilšu-bāni*, 536:4, 7, 8, 21, 24; 537:9.
2. 520:10.

Dumuq-^{d}*Šamaš*, s. of ^{d}*Šamaš-šemi*, 282:17.

É-x-[. . .], 316:rev. 1.
Ea-abūšu, 278:2.
Ea-bēl-ilī,

1. ŠU.I, 290:41.
2. 190:26.
Ea-erībam, s. of *Ibni-Ea*, 322:30.
Ea-gāmil,
1. s. of *Manniya*, 530 seal.
2. f. of *Ea-ṣulūlī*, 169 seal.
3. 50:8; 93:4; 212:15; 216:16.
Ea-ḫegallum, 474:5.
Ea-ibnīšu, UGULA-MUḪALDIM, s. of ^{d}*Sîn-rabi*, 119:18, seal.
Ea-iddinam,
1. SIPA-UDU(?).ḪI.A, s. of *Ana-*^{d}*Šamaš-takil*, 533:4, seal.
2. 212:3; 382:3, 7; 467:1, 2; 468:1, 2; 523:1, 3.
Ea-imitti (*É-a-*ZAG^{ti}), 246:10.
Ea-līdiš, 203:6.
Eama-ilī,
1. s. of *Iddin-*^{d}*Sîn*, 355:26.
2. 12:11; 358:12; 362:11.
Ea-massû, 216:14.
Ea-nāṣir, 73:2, 4, 14, 16, 18, case 2, 4, 13, 15, 16.
Ea-zānin, 158:2.
Ea-rībam-ṣēni, 349:10.
Ea-rīm-ilī, 22:2.
Ea-ṣillī,
1. f. of [. . .]-NI-*šu*, 357:27.
2. 349:19.
Ea-ṣulūlī (*E-a-ṣú-lu-li*, ^{d}EN.KI-AN.DÙL^{lí}*), s. of *Ea-gāmil*, 169:4, seal*.
Ea-ṣulūlšu, 182:16.
Ea-šar-ilī, *Ea-šarri-ilī**,
1. s. of *Apil-ilišu*, 274:22.
2. DUB.SAR, 278:22.
3. 530:16*, seal.
Ea-tukultī, 391:12.
Ea-tūram, s. of ^{d}*Šamaš-nāṣir*, 57:11, seal.
Ebabbar-tukultī, 53:5.
E-gi-bu-ni, *Igi-bu-ni**, s. of ^{d}*Sîn*-x-[. . .], 11:12*, seal.
E-gi-iš-x-*úḫ*, s. of *Maqtu-lizziz*(?), 515:11.
Ekur-nāṣir, h. of *Elmēštum*, 245:4.
Ela-^{d}*Šamaš-danni*, 442:4.
El-erissa, 423:4.
E-li-iš, NA.GADA, 276:4.
Elmēštum,
1. w. of *Ekur-nāṣir*, 245:3.
2. 198:5.
Elmēšum,
1. s. of *Ana-panī-*^{d}*Nusku*, 73:30, case 32.
2. 290:41.
Emūq-^{d}*Sîn*, 50:7.
^{d}*Enlil-abī*, 243 seal.
^{d}*Enlil-bāni*,
1. s. of *Ali-waqrum*, 275:18.
2. 254:10.
^{d}EN.LÍL-GAL.ZU, s. of ^{d}*Sîn-tayyār*, 186: rev. 5.
^{d}*Enlil-gāmil*, 144:1, 2.
^{d}*Enlil-issu*,
1. s. of *Mannum-kīma-*^{d}*Sîn*, 185:42, case 46, seal; 225:14, case 13, seal.
2. s. of ÌR-^{d}[. . .], 214:27.
3. f. of *Abu-lalûm*, 185:46.
^{d}*Enlil-ka-*[. . .], 317:17.
^{d}*Enlil-mālik*, 277:3.
^{d}*Enlil-nādā*, 141:1.
^{d}*Enlil-nīšu*, GUDU$_{4}$(?), 290:35.
^{d}*Enlil-rabi*, s. of *Apil-ilišu*, 186:rev. 4, 20.
^{d}*Enlil-šadūšu*, 328:4.
^{d}*Enlil-wa*[*qar*], 206:rev. 2.
En-nu, f. of *Bēletum*, 141:18.
Epēš-ilim,
1. LÚ.KAS$_{4}$.E, s. of *Ṣillī-*^{d}*Sîn*, 161:16, seal.
2. 482:7(?).
E-ri-[. . .], 115:4.

Erībam, f. of *A-na-tum*, 75:16.
Erībam-ilī,
1. UGULA-DAM.GÀR, s. of ^{d}*Sîn-iddinam*, 75:2, 8.
2. 351:4; 403:16.
Erība(m)-^{d}Sîn,
1. s. of *Šēp-^{d}Sîn*, b. of *Aplum*, *Ilī-gimlanni*, *Sillī-^{d}Amurru*, 278:7.
2. f. of *Tarībatum*, 355:8, 20.
3. 167:16; 190:24, seal; 254:4; 291:13; 322:22.
Erīb-^{d}Sîn,
1. s. of *A-bi-sú-u[m]*, 220:2, 10, seal.
2. s. of *Kurīya*, 526:9.
3. s. of ^{d}*Marduk-tayyār*, 75:17.
4. 271:13.
Eridu^{ki}-liwwir,
1. s. of *Iddin-Ea*, 312:19.
2. s. of LÚ-^{d}EN.KI.KA, 42:20.
3. b. of *Nabi-^{d}Damgalnunna*, 28:3, 10.
4. IŠIB-^{d}EN.KI, 57:12, case 11.
5. 344:12; 347:5; 349:8; 352:20, seal.
Eriša(m),
1. s. of *Āmur-ilūssa*, 157 seal.
2. 145:4; 146:1.
Erišti-^{d}Amurru, 27:15.
Erišti-ilim, 119:5.
Erṣeya, m. of *Ubarum*, w. of *Ipquša*, 363:3.
Eše'i-panī-^{d}Šamaš, 247:13.
E-tamši-^{d}Samas, 435:3; 459:6.
E-ta-wi-ra-ši-im, f. of *Itūr-ašdum*, 44, case 6.
Etel-pî, 337:3; 344:5; 530:4, 17.
Etel-pî-^{d}[. . .], 383:14.
Etel-pî-Ea,
1. f. of *Šēp-^{d}Šamaš*, 194:rev. 12.
2. 551:7.
Etel-pî-^{d}Ilabrat,
1. AGA.UŠ, 557:38.
2. 177:5.
Etel-pî-Ištar, 291:12.
Etel-pî-^{d}Marduk,
1. f. of *Etel-pî-^{d}Nabium*, 533:12.
2. 437:18.
Etel-pî-^{d}Nabium,
1. s. of *Etel-pî-^{d}Marduk*, 533:11.
2. 289:11; 373:14; 538:10.
Etel-pî-^{d}Nusku, 245:8.
Etel-pî-^{d}Sîn, 277:2; 278:19; 379:3; 402:3; 456:7; 487:4.
Etel-pîša,
1. AB.AB.DU_7, 307:16.
2. DI-KU_5, 274:18.
3. 27:13.
Etel-pî-^{d}Šamaš,
1. NU.BÀNDA, 59:21.
2. 6:3–4; 52:8; 136:2.
Etel-pîšu,
1. f. of *Ibni-Irra*, 224:11, seal.
2. b. of *Nūr-^{d}Šamaš*, 552:7, 15.
Eteya, f. of ^{d}*Šamaš-muballiṭ*, 194:6.
Eteyatum,
1. f. of *Ibbi-^{d}Ilabrat*, 437:23.
2. 437:17.
Ēṭerum, 480:6, 13.
Ezida-gāmil, 161:21.

Gamāl-ilī, f. of *Ilī-ippalsam*, 307 seal.
Gāmiltum, m. of *Ibbi-^{d}Ilabrat*, w. of *Naplus*, 206:3.
GAZ-^{d}EN.[. . .], 56:49.
GAZ-^{d}UTU, 91:3.
GEMÉ-^{d}X-X, 259:9.
GEMÉ-^{d}ASAR.LÚ.ḪI, 442:10.
GEMÉ-^{d}NIN.ŠUBUR, 92:13; 312:1.
GEMÉ-^{d}UTU, d. of *Ibbi-^{d}Šaḫan*, sis. of *Luštammar-Ea*, 469:15, 18.

Gimil-ili,
1. s. of *Nūrum*, 74:16, case 4, seal.
2. f. of *Imgur-*d*Šamaš*, 161 seal.
3. f. of *Imgurum*, 228:19.
4. f. of d*Sîn-uselli*, 161:7; 228:7, 13.
5. RÁ.GABA, 185:43, case 46.
6. PA.PA, 35:6.
7. 67:7; 277:27; 332:1.

Gimil-Ištar, 317:3, 11.
*Gimillat-*d*Sîn*, s. of *Lalâ*, 288:16.
Gimillatum,
1. DUMU-É.DUB.BA.A, 457:17.
2. 531:1.

Gimillum,
1. s. of *Iddin-Ea*, 177 seal; 530 seal.
2. f. of *Ilšu-nāṣir*, 533:14.
3. GUDU$_4$-DUB.LÁ.MAḪ, 297:20.
4. 217:5; 421:1.

*Gimil-*d*Marduk*,
1. s. of x-x-[. . .], 397:11.
2. 466:13; 471:5.

*Gimil-*d*Šamaš*, 559:29.
[*Gi*]*mil-*d*Šubula*, 98:4.
GÌRI.NI-Ì.SÀ, f. of *Aḫum*, 186:rev. 11.
d*Gula-gāmilat*, GEMÉ, 46:1, 6.
Guqqû, f. of *Nu-pa-tum*, 228:18.
Gurrurum, 52:12; 56:12; 65:10; 90:4; 207:1; 220:3, 7; 341:5.
Gu-ur-ru-[x], f. of *Awīl-*d*Adad*, 27 seal.

*Ḫa-*x-x(-x), f. of d*Sîn-iddinam*, 153:19.
Ḫa-am-ru-um?, 491:14.
Ḫa-an-da-tum, w. of *Nūr-Ištar*, 212:11.
*Ḫa-an-na-mi-*x-AN, f. of *Ilī-awīli*, 382 seal.
Ḫabil-aḫi, *Habil-aḫ**,
1. s. of *Ina-šamê-wussum*, 519:4*, seal.
2. 217:3; 456:15.

Ḫabil-kīnu(*m*),
1. f. of *A-ap-pa-a*, 286:15; 245 seal.
2. NU.KIRI$_6$, 393:3.
3. 462:6.

Ḫabiya, 7:23.
Ḫablum, 471:2, 3.
Ḫa-da-a, 57:4.
Ḫadannum, 247:14.
Ḫaliq-ilum, see *Ḫalqilum*.
Ḫalqilum (sandhi for *Ḫaliq-ilum*), s. of *Ši-du-la?*, 228:8.
Ḫalqum, 288:3.
Ḫammurapi, 10 seal; 46 seal; 142 seal; 203:19.
Ḫammurapi-ilī, 463:17.
Ḫammurapi-ša-takālim, 192:3, 5; 206:4, 9, 15; 552:31.
Ḫa-su-ri, 491:4.
Ḫa-ya-ma-dar, see *A-a-ma-dar*.
Ḫa-za-ne, f. of d*Sîn-bēl-apli*, 473:10.
Ḫāzirum,
1. s. of d*Sîn-iddinam*, 275:20.
2. f. of *Awīl-Ištar*, 320:3, 5, 9, 20.
3. 175:6.

Ḫidūtum,
1. d. of *Ubaya*, 141:4.
2. 328:14.

ḪI.LI.MA.AN.SUM, GUDU$_4$.ABZU, 42:19.
Ḫiššatum, NIN.DINGIR, 141:17.
Ḫu-ba-a-a, 328:13.
Ḫummurum, *Ḫummuri**,
1. f. of *Pirḫum*, 78:7*.
2. f. of d*Sîn-imguranni*, 392:6.

Ḫundultum, m. of *Šallūrum*, w. of UR-dNIN.URTA, 186:4, 12.
Ḫunzû, 80:5.
Ḫu-pa-tum, 179:14.
Ḫurāṣatum, 98:10; 274:2, 5.
Ḫurrurum, s. of d*Sîn-magir*, 556:28.
Ḫuzālatum, w. of *Awīliya*, 270:5.

Ḫuzālum,
1. s. of *Balāssu-rabi*, 376:15, seal.
2. s. of *Mār-ili*, 265:4.
3. s. of ᵈNANNA-DALLA, 218:rev. 7.
4. h. of *Aya*, 249:9.
5. ENGAR(?), 301:18(?).
6. 56:11; 140:rev. 4; 164:13; 555:11(?).

I-x-[. . .], f. of *Uselli*, 214:11.
Ib-[. . .], 558:1.
Iballuṭ, 368:9.
I-ba-šar-rum,
1. s. of ᵈ*Sîn-magir*, 95:18.
2. 396:9.
Ibašši-ilum, s. of *Ap-pa-a*, 497:8.
Ibbatum, 456:14.
Ibbi-ᵈ[. . .], 382:17.
Ibbi-ᵈ*Ilabrat*,
1. ŠANDAN, s. of *Aḫam-niršī*, 402:5, seal; 462:19, seal.
2. s. of *Eteyatum*, 437:22.
3. s. of *Hammurapi-ša-takālim*, 552:30.
4. s. of *Lištašīm-ilum*, 355:25.
5. s. of *Naplus* and *Gāmiltum*, 206:1, 8, 16.
6. LÚ.ŠAH.ŠUM.MA, 10:1.
7. ŠANDAN, 431:5.
8. 56:55; 65:7; 104:5; 208:8(?); 379:9; 411:4; 412:4; 413:4; 414:4; 415:4; 416:4; 420:4; 422:4; 441:4; 458:5; 469:35; 470:6.
Ibbi-ilum, *rabiānum*, 496:15.
Ibbi-Irra, 179:5.
Ibbi-ᵈ*Li*[*si*], 329:20.
Ibbi-ᵈ*Na*[*bium*], f. of *Ku*-[. . .], 219 seal.
Ibbi-ᵈ*Nisaba*, 78:2.
Ibbi-ᵈ*Sîn*,
1. s. of ᵈ*Sîn-ašarid*, 500:4.
2. s. of UD-*ba-nu-um*, 210:10, seal; 265:10, seal.
3. DAM.GÀR, 521:10.
4. 30:6; 72:17; 195:2; 272:4; 285:14; 322:25; 343:4; 399:2.
Ibbi-ᵈ*Sumuqan*,
1. f. of *Apil-ilišu*, 226:10.
2. 137:9.
Ibbi-ᵈ*Šaḫan*, f. of GEME-ᵈUTU and *Luštammar-Ea*, 469:15.
Ibbi-ᵈ*Šamaš*,
1. s. of *Apil-ilišu*, b. of *Iddin*-ᵈ*Nanâ*, 552:3.
2. s. of ᵈNANNA-ŠU.MU, 536:36; 537:21, case 12.
3. s. of *Rīm*-ᵈ*Nunu*, 227:32.
4. DI.KU₅, s. of ᵈ*Šamaš-muballiṭ*, 142:12, seal.
5. 30:3.
Ibbiya,
1. s. of *Ú-ri-ya*, 274:20.
2. f. of *Ipquatum*, 559:26.
3. NU.BÀNDA, 60:17.
Ibbiyatum, 560:13.
I-bi-AN.NA, 325:2, 4.
Ibnatum,
1. f. of ᵈ*Sîn-magir*, 376:22.
2. 112:15; 215:13; 379:7; 397:5; 470:7; 482:5; 494:13.
Ibni-ᵈ[. . .],
1. s. of *Bēlānum*, 540:8.
2. 443:2.
Ibni-ᵈ*Adad*,
1. f. of *Ba-ya-um* and *Paluḫ-rigimšu*, 536:37; 537:23; 556:24.
2. f. of *Bēlānum*, 556:27.
3. f. of *Ilī-tūram*, 258:22.
4. f. of *Rīš*-ᵈ*Šubula*, 442:19.
5. *na-ṣi-ri*-UM, 355:21(?).
6. UGULA-NAM-5-KA, 236:4, 7, 8.
7. PA.PA, 325:28.
8. 16:7; 77:16; 174:2, 3; 261:4; 290:6; 498:4.

Ibni-^{d}Amurru,
1. s. of *^{d}Šamaš-rabi*, 321:6, case 8; 536:10, 15, 17, 18, 23; 537:3, 11.
2. f. of *Apil-ilišu*, 275:21.
3. 256:3; 364:1, 2, 9; 519:3; 521:3.

Ibni-Ea,
1. s. of *Ṣillī-^{d}Amurru*, 363:27.
2. f. of *Ea-erībam*, 322:31.
3. 177:16; 373:15(?).

Ibni-Irra,
1. s. of *Etel-pīšu*, 224:10, seal.
2. f. of *Šum-erṣetim*, 75:19.

Ibni-^{d}Lisi, 222:3.

Ibni-^{d}Marduk,
1. s. of *Apil-^{d}Amurru*, 550:5.
2. 466:1; 545:2, 3.

Ibni-^{d}Sîn,
1. s. of *Ubar-^{d}Šamaš*, 355:24.
2. LÚ.Ì.[DU$_8$], 433:16.
3. 444:18; 542:10.

Ibni-^{d}Sumuqan,
1. s. of *Iddin-^{d}Šamaš*, 227:10, 19.
2. DUB.SAR, 156:rev. 10; 322:32.
3. 57:case 12; 364:14.

Ibniša, 551 seal.

Ibni-^{d}Šērum, s. of *Apil-erṣetim*(?), b. of *Kīma-aḫum* and *Kubbultum*, 95:3, 9.

Iddin-^{d}[. . .], f. of *Gimillum*, 530 seal.

Iddin-^{d}Adad,
1. s. of *Adayatum*, 309:3, seal.
2. f. of *Awiyatum*, 77:14.
3. f. of x-x-*im*, 380:19.
4. 32:14; 101:31; 118:23; 262:7; 386:13; 492:5, 7.

Iddin-^{d}Amurru,
1. s. of DINGIR-*mu*-[. . .], 236 seal.
2. s. of *Iddin-^{d}Bunene*, b. of *Aḫam-arši*, *Ali-talīmī*, *Ilīma-aḫī*, *Ilšu-abūšū*, *^{d}Sîn-rēmēni*, 556:9.
3. *rabiānum*, s. of *^{d}Sîn-aḫam-[iddinam]*, 457:8, seal.
4. [. . .]-MÁ.BÀNDA, 46:19.
5. 55:4; 65:13; 101:17; 112:8; 118:8, 24; 123:4; 125:1, 11; 173:7; 210:11; 542:12.

Iddin-AN.DÙL(?)-*lā-maḫar*, 429:4; 434:12.

Iddin-^{d}Bunene, s. of *Šū-^{d}Damkina*, f. of *Aḫam-arši*, *Ali-talīmī*, *Iddin-^{d}Amurru*, *Ilīma-aḫī*, *Ilšu-abūšu*, *^{d}Sîn-rēmēni*, 556:3, 5, 6, 7.

Iddin-Ea,
1. s. of *Ipqu-Ištar*, 186:rev. 8.
2. f. of BALA-MU-NAM.ḪÉ, 312:13.
3. f. of *Eridu^{ki}-liwwir*, 312:19.
4. f. of *Gimillum*, 177 seal.

Iddin-^{d}Gu[la], s. of *Ilum-damiq*, b. of *Ilī-awīli*, 559:3.

Iddin-Irra,
1. s. of *Ši-mu*-x-[x], 63:1, seal.
2. 43:3; 84:14; 165:9; 166:8.

Iddin-Ištar,
1. s. of *Adaya*, 46:3, 10; 114:5, seal; 342:rev. 2.
2. f. of *^{d}Adad-šarrum*, 482:4.
3. 16:8; 162:3; 167:19; 175:2; 207:4; 290:43; 315:4; 345:8; 434:9; 494:2, 3; 526:13.

Iddin-^{d}Išum, 226:4; 276:9; 298:6.

Iddin-^{d}Nabium, f. of *Irra-muballiṭ*, 440:18.

Iddin-^{d}Nanâ,
1. s. of *Apil-ilišu*, b. of *Ibbi-^{d}Šamaš*, 552:4.
2. s. of *Ilī-iddinam*, 323:5, seal.
3. LÚ.TÚG, 332:15.
4. 336:18.

Iddin-^{d}Ninsikilla, 282:18.

Iddin-^{d}Sîn,
1. s. of *Abum-waqar*, 29:7, seal; 343 seal.

2. s. of *Ipqu-Ištar*, 196:rev. 8.
3. s. of *ᵈŠamaš-ḫegallum*, 557:33.
4. s. of *Za-a-zum*, 227:23; 557:32.
5. f. of *Aplum*, *Bēletum*, *Ilī-iqīšam*, *Kalūmum*, 14 seal; 227:4.
6. f. of *Bal-ilum*, 50:9.
7. KÙ.DÍM, f. of *Eama-ilī*, 355:26.
8. f. of *ᵈSîn-iqūlam*, 442:11.
9. 212:14; 248:10; 307:20.

Iddin-ᵈŠamaš,
1. f. of *Ibni-ᵈSumuqan*, 227:10.
2. f. of *Ipqu-ᵈŠala*, 312:16.
3. f. of *Nidnuša*, 224:13.
4. 98:3.

Iddiyatum,
1. s. of x(-x)-x-*ra*, 194:rev. 5.
2. s. of NÌ.SI.SÁ.NI-A.AB.DIRI, 275:14.
3. f. of *Tarībatum*, 549:11.
4. s. of *Apil-ᵈAmurru*, gs. of *Kurullum*, nephew of *Nūr-Ištar*, 363:22.
5. ZABAR.DAB, 35:5.
6. 67:6.

I-di-a-lim-ma, 406:5.
Igi-bu-ni, see *E-gu-bu-ni*.
I-gi-gi-tu-ni-iš, 444:5.
I?-ir-bu-ni, f. of *Aplum*, 227:33.
Ikūn-pî-[. . .], 227:9.
Ikūn-pî-Ištar, 357:12, 22; 559:28.
Ikūn-pî-ᵈSîn,
1. GUDU₄-ᵈNIN.URTA, f. of *Ilīma-ilum*, 354 seal.
2. 61:27; 62:16; 71:3.

ᵈIlabrat-abī, 92:11.
ᵈIlabrat-ṣillī, ŠU.I-ᵈNIN.ŠUBUR, 353:25.
Ilam-dugul, 102:2.
Ilam-ēriš,
1. f. of *Simtī-Ištar*, 17 seal; 23 seal.
2. 73:2, 4, 7, 11, 19, case 2, 4, 7, 11, 17; 77:12; 203:36.

Ilam-nīšu, 49:11.
Ì-lí-[. . .],
1. f. of *ᵈMarduk-nāṣir*, 430 seal.
2. 26:25.

Ilī-amtaḫar, 36:8–9; 121:3; 386:12.
Ì-lí-a-[. . .]*-ši-im*, NIMGIR, 2:5.
Ilī-awīli(m),
1. s. of DUMU-ZIMBIR^ki^, b. of *Bēlessunu* and *Ilšu-bāni*, 536:3; 537:8.
2. s. of *Ilum-damiq*, b. of *Iddin-ᵈGula*, 559:14.
3. s. of *Ḫa-an-na-mi*-x-AN, 382:12, seal.
4. 440:16; 444:17.

Ilī-awīli-rabi (*Ì-lí-*LÚ*-ra-bi*), 348:12.
Ilī-bāni,
1. s. of *Nabi-ilišu*, 389:3.
2. 143:6; 176:rev. 5; 350:5; 367:5; 374:4; 403:15; 439:6; 453:3; 522:5.

Ilī-dādiya, f. of DUMU-KÁ.DINGIR.RA^ki^, 378 seal.
Ì-lí-du-x, 314:1.
Ilī-dūrī, 92:7.
Ilī-eraḫ, 390:4, 6, 7.
Ilī-erība(m),
1. s. of *Lipit-Ištar*, 376:19.
2. f. of *Aḫam-nūta*, 373 seal.
3. 26:7, 32; 66:3; 125:12; 133:3; 307:24; 368:8.

Ilī-ē-taddianni, f. of *ᵈSîn-iddinam*, 192 seal.
Ilī-gimlanni, s. of *Šēp-ᵈSîn*, b. of *Aplum*, *Erībam-ᵈSîn*, *Ṣillī-ᵈAmurru*, 278:3.
Ilī-ibbīšu, f. of *Ipiq-ilišu*, 394 seal.
Ilī-ibnīšu, 484:15.
Ilī-iddinam,
1. s. of *Būr-ᵈSîn*, 74:14, case 2.
2. DUMU-É.DUB.BA, s. of *Nawram-šarūr*, 135:10, seal.
3. s. of *ᵈSîn-uselli*, 102:31.
4. f. of *Iddin-ᵈNanâ*, 323 seal.

5. f. of *Ilī-iqīšam*, 74:18, case 6.
6. NAR.GAL-^{d}UTU, 227:39.
7. 76:15, 19; 105:8; 184:1; 190:27; 198:4; 235:12; 320:31; 462:2; 517:10.
Ilī-ile'e, 252:5.
Ilī-ippalsa(m),
1. s. of *Gamāl-ilī*, 307:21, seal.
2. s. of *Imgurum*, 73 case 33.
3. s. of [. . .]-^{d}*Šamaš*, 146:13, seal.
4. f. of *Bēltani*, 192:2.
5. 2:13; 25:6–7; 26:31; 201:15; 290:40; 328:7; 405:15; 439:7; 459:2.
Ilī-ippašra, 260:40.
Ilī-iqīšam,
1. s. of *Iddin-*^{d}*Sîn*, b. of *Aplum*, *Bēletum*, *Kalūmum*, 227:3, 6, 16.
2. s. of *Ilī-iddinam*, 74:18, case 6.
3. s. of ^{d}*Išumatum*, 225:16, case 15, seal.
4. s. of *Ú-da-an-*DINGIR, 552:24.
5. s. of ^{d}UTU-DINGIR, 177:19, seal.
6. *rabiānum*, 258:25.
7. 26:29; 138:12; 207:2; 306:8, case 10; 336:16; 381:19; 437:20; 485:7.
Ilī-išmeanni,
1. DUMU-É.DUB.BA, 127:8.
2. 280:16; 281:21.
Ilī-kimtī, 126:2.
Ilī-luṭṭul, s. of *Mannum*, 457:13.
Ilīma, 152:9; 348:3; 370:2, 3.
Ilīma-abī,
1. UGULA-NAM-5, s. of ^{d}*Šaḫan-šemi*, 419:4, seal.
2. b. of *Aḫī-ay-amši*, ^{d}*Amurru-muballiṭ*, *Qurrudum*, *Šumman-lā-*^{d}*Šamaš*, 102:7, 10, 11, 18; 194:rev. 14.
3. 65:2; 101:4–5; 111:2; 112:6; 118:18; 267:4; 527:3, 9, 17.
Ilīma-aḫī,
1. s. of *Aḫī-ay-amši*, 277:29(?).
2. s. of *Iddin-*^{d}*Bunene*, b. of *Aḫam-arši*, *Ali-talīmī*, *Iddin-*^{d}*Amurru*, *Ilšu-abūšu*, ^{d}*Sîn-rēmēni*, 556:10.
3. s. of *Itūram*, 277:30.
4. 292:3; 560:15.
Ilīma-ilum,
1. s. of *Ikūn-pî-*^{d}[. . .], 354 seal.
2. GUDU$_4$-^{d}INANNA, 290:39.
3. 493:14.
*Ì-lí-pu-*x*-ya*, 516:5.
*Ilī-*AN.DÙL*-lí*, 483:16.
Ilī-šūma, 125:6; 151:9.
Ilī-tappê, 154:3; 407:1.
Ilī-tanattī (*Ì-lí-ta-a-na-ti*), 215:11.
Ilī-tukultī,
1. ŠÀ.TAM, 26:42.
2. 92:9, 25.
Ilī-tūram,
1. s. of *Ibni-*^{d}*Adad*, 258:22.
2. f. of ^{d}*Sîn-*[. . .]*-lim*, 560 seal.
3. A.ZU.IŠIB-^{d}EN.LÍL.LÁ (or: ÍD-^{d}EN.LÍL.LÁ?), 383:7.
4. GUDU$_4$(?), 162:13.
5. 201:16; 352:7, 9, 14; 560:14.
Ilī-unnennī, 383:18.
Ilī-u-^{d}*Šamaš*,
1. s. of ^{d}*Nergal-mu-*[. . .], 227:34.
2. f. of *Kezrum*, 258:6.
3. f. of ^{d}*Šamaš-iddinam*, 135 seal; 415 seal; 416 seal.
4. LÚ.SILA$_4$, 78:8.
5. 117:13; 142:14; 307:17; 478:13.
*Ì-lí-*WA*-ri*, 548:4.
Ilī-wēdima, 152:16.
Ì-lí-ya-bu-ki, 233:9.
Iliyatum, 3:3; 111:4.
Ilī-yûm, 493:13.
Il-lu-lu, 258:26.
Ilšu-abūšu,
1. s. of *Iddin-*^{d}*Bunene*, b. of *Aḫam-arši*,

Ali-talīmī, *Iddin-^{d}Amurru*, *Ilīma-aḫī*, *^{d}Sîn-rēmēni*, 556:10.
2. s. of *Waqar-awīlum*, 556:21.
3. DUB.SAR, 360:18.
Ìl-šu-ba-[. . .], 317 seal.
Ilšu-bāni,
1. s. of DUMU-ZIMBIR^{ki}, b. of *Bēlessunu*, *Ilī-awīlim*, 536:3; 537:8.
2. f. of *Nabi-^{d}Šamaš*, 495:14.
3. f. of *^{d}Šamaš-napširum*, 75:20.
4. 23:14, case 11.
Ilšu-ibbi,
1. f. of [*Man*]*num*, 457:10.
2. f. of *Munawwirum*, 236:19.
3. 158:rev. 2; 357:18.
Ilšu-ibbīšu,
1. UGULA-NAM-5, s. of *Nūr-ilišu*, 236:13, seal.
2. MUḪALDIM, 153:3, case 3.
3. 19:3; 26:3, 40; 320:26; 543:4.
Ilšu-ibnīšu,
1. s. of *Mār-erṣetim*, 536 seal; 537:22, case 13.
2. s. of *Nūr-^{d}Šamaš*, 322:4, seal.
3. DAM.GÀR, 514:9.
4. *rabiān Kār-^{d}Šamaš^{ki}*, 536:33.
5. ŠÀ.TAM, 46:22.
6. 56:49; 59:6; 109:5; 142:16; 323:16; 358:11; 477:2; 514:3.
Ilšu-illassu, 102:29; 267:8.
Ilšu-muballiṭ, DAM.GÀR-AKŠAK^{ki}, 433:8, 29.
Ilšu-nāṣir,
1. s. of *Gimillum*, 533:13.
2. s. of *Itūr-ašdum*, 557:2, 5, 15.
3. DUB.SAR, 289:12.
4. MÁ(?).LAḪ$_{x}$(DU.DU), 383:21.
5. 79:10; 157:25; 275:5; 318:4; 320:4, 8, 16; 326:4; 330:3; 386:3; 484:5.
Iltāni,
1. w. of *^{d}Sîn-liwwir*, 162:9.
2. 46:5, 9; 341:3.
Ilum-bāni, s. of *Nidnat-^{d}Sîn*, 277:24.
Ilum-damiq,
1. f. of *Ali-lūmur*, 492 seal.
2. f. of *Iddin-^{d}Gula* and *Ilī-awīli*, 559:4.
Ilum-dān, 494:15.
Ilum-gamil,
1. s. of *Apil-Irra*, 357:31.
2. f. of *^{d}Sîn-iddinam*, 74:15, case 3.
Ilu(*m*)*-ḫabil* (*I-lu-ḫa-bil*, DINGIR^{lum}*-ḫa-bil**, DINGIR*-ḫa-bil*†),
1. s. of *Šū-ilišu*, 95:15†.
2. 266:4*; 493:8; 534:6†.
Ilum-kīnam-i[*di*], s. of *^{d}Sînma-ilum*, 559:6.
Ilum-liṭṭul,
1. f. of *Rīm-^{d}Nunu*, 227:25.
2. 16:9.
Ilum-mālik, s. of *Ubar-^{d}Ninazu*, 161:4, 18; 228:4(?).
Ilum-mušallim, 363:23.
Ilum-nāṣir,
1. UGULA-NAM-5, s. of *Nūr-^{d}Kabta*, 236:14, seal.
2. s. of *^{d}Sîn-bāni*, 299 seal.
Ilum-rabi, f. of *Ubar-^{d}Nergal*, 185:44.
Ilum-rība, 268:10.
Ilum-šagiš, f. of *Tir-zum-na-tu-tu*, 515:6.
Ilum-tayyār, 15:3.
Ilum-wēdum (DINGIR-DILI), f. of *Bēlšunu*, 477:8.
*I-*x*-ma*, 196:4.
Im[*gur*]-^{d}x-x-x, 484:18.
Imgur-Ištar, s. of *Ali-waqrum*, b. of *Āta-naḫ-ilī*, 277:5, 7, 15.
Imgur-^{d}Sîn, 100:4; 112:30; 394:2.
Imgur-^{d}Šamaš,
1. s. of *Annum-pîša*, 48 seal (48:24 *Im-gur-ru?-um?*)

2. s. of *Gimil-ili*, 161 seal.
3. f. of ^{d}*Marduk-mušallim*, 428 seal.
4. f. of *Munawwirum*, 105:16.
Imgurum,
1. s. of *Gimil-ili*, 228:19.
2. s. of *Tarībum*, 186:rev. 9, 19.
3. f. of *Alû*, 225:case 19.
4. f. of *Apil-ilišu*, 342:6.
5. KUŠ$_x$(IŠ) ŠA ^{d}INANNA, f. of *Ilī-ippal-sam*, 73:case 33.
6. f. of *Narām-ilišu*, 95:17.
7. f. of ^{d}*Sîn-iddinam*, 225:15, case 14; 283:4.
8. 86:4; 112:2; 133:4; 216:15; 411:10; 412:10; 413:10; 414:10; 416:10; 420:10; 422:9; 463:13.
9. Cf. *Im-gur-ru?-um?* 48:24 with 48 seal *Im-gur-*^{d}*Šamaš*.
Imgutum, see also *Imguyatum*.
1. f. of *Ipqu-*^{d}*Enlil*, 186:rev. 12.
2. f. of *Ipqu-Ištar*, 186:rev. 10.
Imguya, 102:24.
Imguyatum, f. of DINGIR-*bi-ni-šu*, 102:26; see also *Imgutum*.
Immer-ili,
1. b. of *Bēlī-libūr*, 138:2.
2. 235:5; 310:3.
Imtagar-ilum, 31 seal.
Imtagar-^{d}*Šamaš*, f. of *Saniq-pî-*^{d}*Šamaš*, 352 seal.
In-x-[. . .], 38:7.
I-na-bal?-[. . .], 203:8.
Ina-libbi-eršet, LUKUR-^{d}UTU, d. of *Luštam-mar-Ea*, sis. of ^{d}*Šamaš-iddinam*, 469:16, 24, 26.
I-na-me-at-ì-lí, 288:5.
^{d}INANNA-DINGIR.MU, see *Ištar-ilī*.
Ina-pîša-lubluṭ, w. of ÌR-^{d}UTU, m. of *Apil-*^{d}*Amurru*, 331:3, 10.
Ina-qabêša, 313:9.
Ina-qabêša-abluṭ, 92:4.
Ina-qabê-^{d}*Šamaš*, f. of *Zi-zi-e*, 141:3.
Ina-šamê-wussum,
1. f. of *Ḫabil-a-ḫi*!, 519:5, seal.
2. 551:9.
Inbatum, w. of *Aḫu-waqar*, 153:6, 7, case 7, 9.
Inbili (sandhi for *Inib-ili*), 319:4; 541:15.
Inbilišu (sandhi for *Inib-ilišu*),
1. s. of *Apil-*^{d}*Amurru*, 322:26.
2. DUMU-É.DUB.BA.A, 329:4, 18; 412:12; 413:12; 414:12; 415:12; 416:12; 420:12; 422:11.
3. 26:8; 234:5; 463:16.
Inbištar (sandhi for *Inib-Ištar*),
1. s. of *Tizqarum*, 275:19.
2. 278:21; 320:30; 326:11; 330:8.
Inbum, 167:18.
Inbuša,
1. s. of ÌR-^{d}MAR.TU, 321 seal; 556:33.
2. f. of *Annum-pîša*, 520:4.
3. f. of *Ka-ap-la-lum*, 285:3.
4. UGULA-MAR.TU, 176:3.
Inib-ili, see *Inbili*.
Inib-ilišu, see *Inbilišu*.
Inib-Ištar, see *Inbištar*.
Inib-^{d}*Šamaš*, 99:1.
INIM-^{d}UTU, 57:10; 65:16; 112:1.
Ipiq-^{d}*Adad*, see *Ipqu-*^{d}*Adad*.
Ipiq-^{d}*Alla*, see *Ipqu-*^{d}*Alla*.
Ipiq-^{d}*Amurru*, see *Ipqu-*^{d}*Amurru*.
Ipiq-Annatum, see *Ipqu-Annatum*.
Ipiq-Annunītum,
1. s. of *Ali-bānīšu*, 536:34.
2. 298:7; 375:4.
Ipiq-Antum, s. of *Zi?-mu*-[. . .], 75:21.
Ipiq-^{d}*Araḫtum*, 49:4; 215:6; 452:5.
Ipiq-^{d}*Aya*, s. of ^{d}*Šamaš-tappâšu*, 536:35.
Ipiq-^{d}*Baba*, see *Ipqu-*^{d}*Baba*.
Ipiq-Ea, *Ipqu-Ea**,

1. DAM.GÀR, 108:rev. 5.
2. b. of *Nūr-Ištar*, 212:10*.
3. 78:6*; 90:13(ᵈ*E-a*); 233:10; 333:11.
Ipiq-ᵈEnlil, see *Ipqu-ᵈEnlil*.
Ipiq-erṣetim, *Ipqu-erṣetim**,
1. s. of LUGAL-*ma*-DINGIR, 186:rev. 6*.
2. 196:9.
Ipiq-ᵈIlabrat,
1. f. of ᵈ*Sîn-imguranni*, 363:24.
2. UGULA-NAM-5, 236:15.
Ipiq-ilīša, see *Ipqu-ilīša*.
Ipiq-ilīšu, PA.PA, s. of *Ilī-ibbīšu*, 394:7, seal.
Ipiq-Ištar, *Ipqu-Ištar**,
1. s. of x-*ni-it?-ḫi-ri*, 274:25.
2. s. of *Imgutum*, 186:rev. 10*.
3. f. of *Iddin-Ea*, 186:rev. 8*.
4. SIMUG, 295:4.
5. 31:4*; 56:30; 112:26; 196:3; 201:4*; 239:4; 279:7; 313:3.
Ipiq-ᵈLisi, see *Ipqu-ᵈLisi*.
Ipiq-ᵈNabium, *Ipqu-ᵈNabium**, 383:10*; 424:10*; 444:19*; 480:16; 492:17*.
Ipiq-ᵈNingal, see *Ipqu-ᵈNingal*.
Ipiq-ᵈSîn, see *Ipqu-ᵈSîn*.
Ipiq-ᵈŠala, see *Ipqu-ᵈŠala*.
Ip-pu-qá-am, 56:46; 82:3; 101:20; 112:27; 125:5; 151:8; 173:8; 193:2.
Ipqatum,
1. s. of *Tarībum*, 514:4.
2. f. of KUR-*tum*, 556:30.
3. LÚ.KURUN.NA, LÚ.KURÚN.NA*, 153:26*, case 27*; 227:26.
4. 143:5; 351:4; 378:4; 384:4; 446:3; 531:10; 557:32.
Ipqu-ᵈAdad,
1. f. of *At-ta-ku?-zu?*, 72 seal.
2. f. of DUMU-ᵈMAR.TU, 312:15, seal.
Ipqu-ᵈAlla, f. of *Iš-la?-a*, 141:2.
Ipqu-ᵈAmurru, f. of *Rīš-ᵈMarduk*, 360:3.
Ipqu-Annatum, 432:10.
Ipqu-ᵈBaba,
1. RÁ.GABA, 3:6.
2. 28:17; 258:23.
Ipqu-Ea, see *Ipiq-Ea*.
Ipqu-ᵈEnlil, s. of *Imgutum*, 186:rev. 12.
Ipqu-erṣetim, see *Ipiq-erṣetim*.
Ipqu-ilīša, ŠITIM, 302:18.
Ipqu-Ištar, see *Ipiq-Ištar*.
Ipqu-ᵈLisi,
1. KISAL.LUH (*ša*) ᵈUTU, 73:27, case 30.
2. 42:17; 53:6; 156:7; 206:rev. 3; 290:36; 305:4; 353:7, 13; 552:9.
Ipqu-ᵈNabium, see *Ipiq-ᵈNabium*.
Ipqu-ᵈNingal, s. of *Nawirtum*, 359:3, 5, 10.
Ipqu-ᵈSîn,
1. s. of ÌR-ᵈSUEN, 370:14, seal; 396:2, 3, seal.
2. ŠU.I, 466:12.
Ipquša,
1. s. of *Aplum*, 275:15.
2. f. of *Aḫum*, 552:21.
3. f. of *Tappâ-wēdim*, 556:26.
4. f. *Ubarum*, h. of *Erṣeya*, 363:2.
5. 56:10; 551:6.
Ipqu-ᵈŠala, s. of *Iddin-ᵈŠamaš*, 312:16.
Ipquyatum, s. of *Ibbiya*, 559:26.
ÌR-[. . .], f. of *Awīl-ᵈAdad*, 5 seal.
ÌR-ᵈ[. . .],
1. s. of *I*-[x]-*wa*-[. . .], 153 seal.
2. f. of ᵈ*Enlil-issu*, 214:27.
3. 254:12.
ÌR-É.[. . .], UM.MI.A, 355:27.
ÌR-ᵈEN.LÍL, 394:3.
I-ri-b[*a*. . .], 317:15.
I-ri-ri, s. of ᵈ*Sin-rēmēni*, 238:5, seal.
ÌR-ᵈLAL, 56:60.
Ir-ma?-am-mu, s. of *Ul-li-gi*, 390:19.
ÌR-ᵈMAR.TU,

1. f. of *Inbuša*, 321 seal; 556:33.
2. 302:22.
ÌR-^{d}NIN.ŠUBUR, 92:17.
ÌR-^{d}PA.LÀL, 65:17; 87:3; 101:7; 118:20.
[Ir]ra-gāmil, 555:14.
Irra-muballiṭ, s. of *Iddin-^{d}Nabium*, 440:17.
Irra-šadî, 381:6.
ÌR-SIG$_4$, s. of [. . .]-^{d}*Asnan*, 161:8.
ÌR-^{d}SUEN, see *Warad-^{d}Sin*.
ÌR-^{d}SU.NIR, see *Warad-^{d}Šurinni*.
ÌR-^{d}UTU,
1. f. of *Apil-^{d}Amurru*, h. of *Ina-pîša-lublut*, 331:2.
2. f. of ^{d}*Sîn-magir*, 224:15.
3. f. of *Sutûm*, 44:17, case 20.
4. 56:48; 193:1; 391:6.
Isiq-ilišu, see *Isqilišu*.
Isqilišu (sandhi for *Isiq-ilišu*), 58:4; 312:2, 11; 345:5.
Issu-arik, 135:2; 505:7.
Issu-kabit,
1. s. of ^{d}*Sîn-rēmēni*, 242:3.
2. f. of *Aplusa*, 153:24, case 26.
Išar-ilī, 302:20.
Išar-palûšu, 152:7.
Išgum-^{d}Adad, 155:5.
^{d}IŠKUR.GAL, see ^{d}*Adad-rabi(m)*.
^{d}IŠKUR(.RA*)-MA.AN.SUM,
1. DUMU-É.DUB.BA, 55:12*.
2. 59:22.
Iš-la?-a, d. of *Ipqu-^{d}Alla*, *ša* ^{d}NIN.SI.AN.NA, 141:2.
Išme-^{d}Adad, *Iš*-WI-^{d}*Adad**, 92:15*, 137:3.
Išmeanni, PA.PA, s. of ^{d}*Šamaš-illatī*, 187:3, seal.
Išme-^{d}Sîn,
1. s. of *Nabi-ilišu*, 559:18.
2. PA.PA(?), 274:19.
3. 169:2.
Išmeya, f. of ^{d}*Sîn-pilaḫ*, 129 seal; 133 seal.
^{d}*Ištaran-mušallim*, 183:10.
Ištar-ēpirī, 56:24; 81:8; 82:1; 90:8; 101:12; 112:21; 118:13; 173:3.
Ištar-ilī (*Es$_4$dar*-DINGIR, ^{d}INANNA-DINGIR.MU*),
1. s. of ^{d}NANNA-É.MAḪ, b. of *Nūr-^{d}Kabta*, 42:3*, 5*.
2. f. of LÚ-^{d}UTU, 194:rev. 4.
3. f. of ^{d}*Ningizzida-abī*, h. of *Aḫassunu*, 253:2, 8.
4. UGULA-MÁ.LAH$_x$(DU), 334:6, 10.
5. 141:19; 155:4*; 218:7*; 320:27; 543:2, 3, 5.
Ištar-kīma-iliya, 35:13; 363:28.
Ištar-muballiṭ, SAG.GEMÉ, 74:1.
Ištar-naplisim, GEMÉ, 157:1.
Ištar-NIN.[. . .], SAG.GEMÉ, 552:1.
Ištar-šemi, 173:6.
Ištar-tayyārat, 92:2.
^{d}*Išum-abī*, 491:15.
^{d}*Išumatum*, ^{d}*Išumuatum**, ^{d}*Išumutum*†,
1. s. of *Aya*, 177:17*, case 18†, seal*.
2. f. of *Ilī-iqīšam*, 225:16, case 15, seal.
^{d}*Išum-ḫāzir*, s. of *Iddin-^{d}Išum*, 226:5.
^{d}*Išum-qarrād*, 340:10.
^{d}*Išumu(a)tum*, see ^{d}*Išumatum*.
I-tu?-a-lim-ma, w. of *Lipit-Ištar*, 457:3.
Itūr-ālī (cf. *Litūr-ālī*), 56:59; 112:25.
Itūr-ašdum,
1. s. of *E-ta-wi-ra-ši-im*, 44:4, case 5.
2. f. of *Ilšu-nāṣir*, 557:2.
3. 412:7; 413:7; 414:7; 415:7; 416:7; 422:7.
Itūrum,
1. f. of *Ilīma-aḫī*, 277:30.
2. 531:3.
I-ya-gu-nu-um, *I-ya-gu-nim*, see *Ya-gu-nu-um*.
Iz-bu-na, SIMUG, 372:5.

Ka-ap-la-lum, s. of *Inbuša*, 285:3.
Kabbārum, 286:2, 3.
Kabīya, 233:4.
ᵈ*Kabta-bāni*,
  1. SIPA, 499:14.
  2. 126:16.
ᵈ*Kabta-illatī*, 121:4.
ᵈ*Kalkal-tillassu*, 26:27.
KAL.LA.MU, 243:4, seal.
Kalūmtum, d. of ᵈ*Sîn-rēmēni*, 469:11.
Kalūmum,
  1. s. of *Iddin-ᵈSîn*, b. of *Aplum*, *Bēletum*, *Ili-iqīšam*, 227:4, 8, 17.
  2. 290:7.
Kamû, 491:13.
Karānatum, 249:18.
Kārum-mušallim, b. of *Ṣillī-Ebabbar*, ᵈ*Šamaš-idī*, *Uri*ᵏⁱ*-līšir*, 190:5.
Kasap-ᵈSîn, s. of ᵈ*Sîn-li-ta*-x, 73 seal.
*Keš*ᵏⁱ*-iddinam*,
  1. s. of *Balilum*, 26:13.
  2. s. of *Ma-ru-ša*, 26:14.
  3. 94:8; 262:9.
Kezrum, DAM.GÀR, s. of *Ilī-u-ᵈŠamaš*, 258:6, 19.
Kīma-aḫum, s. of *Apil-erṣetim*(?), b. of *Ibni-ᵈŠērum*, *Kubbultum*, 95:2, 8.
Kî-maruṣ, s. of *Palâ-Irra*, 556:36.
Ki?-ni-ik-x, f. of *Rašub-bītum*, 194:rev. 9.
Kīnum-ḫabil, s. of ᵈ*Sîn-mupaḫḫir*, 521:4.
Ku-[. . .], s. of *Ibbi-ᵈN*[*abium*], 219 seal.
Kubbultum, s. of *Apil-erṣetim*(?), b. of *Ibni-ᵈŠērum*, *Kīma-aḫum*, 95:4, 10.
Kubbulum,
  1. *ša* MÁ.LAḪₓ (DU.DU), 112:11.
  2. 56:33; 65:14.
Kubburu, 338:4.
Kubbutum,
  1. DUB.SAR, 515:13.
  2. 163:13; 304:4.
Ku-du-ú, 197:5; 240:7; 289:1, 2; 464:1, 2.
Kukkum, s. of ᵈ*Sîn-nūrka*, 177 seal.
Kûm, 550:15.
Kunna, 421:4; 436:4, 10; 459:3, 4; 462:1, 5; 466:3.
Kunniyatum,
  1. s. of *Adayatum*, 227:24.
  2. 336:17.
Kurītum,
  1. w. of *Aḫī-lūmur*, 408:4.
  2. 518:11.
Kurīya, f. of *Erīb-ᵈSîn*, 526:10.
KUR-tum, s. of *Ipqatum*, 556:30.
Kurû, *Kurrû*(*m*)*,
  1. s. of ᵈ*Šamaš-ummatī* and *Unnubtum*, 307:5*.
  2. f. of *Ali-lūmur*, 13 seal; 140 seal; 162:14*.
  3. GUDU₄, 160:10*.
  4. 530:21*.
Kurullum, f. of *Apil-ᵈAmurru* and *Nūr-Ištar*, gf. of *Idiyatum*, 363:20.
Ku-um-ḫu-ba-al, 390:2, 9.
Ku-za-ri, f. of ᵈ*Sîn-ēriš*, 63:3.
Ku-zu-[. . .], f. of ᵈ*Sîn-šamuh*, 63 seal.

Lalâ, f. of *Gimillat-ᵈSîn*, 288:17.
Lalê,
  1. s. of *Nūr-ilišu*, 61:30.
  2. 62:19.
Lā-enī-pîšu, LÚ *E-mu-ut-ba-lum*, 433:7.
Lalûm,
  1. s. of *Sînatum*, 559:24.
  2. f. of *Asīrum*, b. of *Ana-ṣillīša-ēmid*, 194:4, rev. 10.
  3. f. of *Damqilišu*, 306 seal; 555 seal.
Lalûtum, 290:1, 22, 24, 27, 29, 30, 31.
Lamassum,
  1. d. of *Tizqaru*, 141:7.

2. 164:5; 284:4; 448:3.
Lā-qīpum,
1. s. of *Apil-*^{d}*Adad*, 79:3, seal.
2. f. of *Apil-*^{d}*Šamaš*, 552:22.
3. 152:20.
Larsûm, f. of *Pirḫum*, 183 seal.
Lipit-[. . .], f. of *A-*[. . .], 116 seal.
Lipit-^{d}*Adad*, 102:27.
Lipit-Ea, 176:5; 530:19.
Lipit-^{d}*Enlil*, s. of MU.ḪÉ.GÁL, 222 seal.
Lipit-Ištar,
1. s. of ^{d}*Amurru-šemi*, 385:3, 4, 12, seal.
2. s. of *Šunuma-ilum*, 102:30.
3. f. of *Apil-ilišu*, 286:16.
4. f. of *Ilī-erībam*, 376:20.
5. f. of ^{d}*Sîn-aḫ-iddinam*, 228:22.
6. f. of ^{d}*Ši-mu-ut-ṣillī*, 197 seal.
7. f. of *Ubayatum*, 127:4, seal.
8. h. of *I-tu-a-lim-ma*, 457:2.
9. b. of *Šū-ilišu*, 140:1.
10. DUB.SAR, 353:30; 377:rev. 6.
11. 97:10; 139:8; 144:14; 157:29; 212:5, 18; 239:8; 243:3; 280:2; 333:13; 356:7; 362:4; 390:3.
Lisâtum, ŠU.I (*ša*) ^{d}UTU, 73:26, case 28.
^{d}*Lisi-qarrād*, 27:4.
^{d}*Lisi-tayyār*, 78:9.
Lištašīm-ilum, f. of *Ibbi-*^{d}*Ilabrat*, 355:25.
Litūr-ālī (cf. *Itūr-ālī*), 65:15.
Liwwir-[. . .], 518:6.
Liwwir-Bābilum, 549:13.
Liwwir? (ERÉN)*-ya-ku-nu-um*, 203:12.
LÚ-^{d}ASAR.LÚ.ḪI, 302:17.
Lubluṭ-ilum, 202:4.
Lū-dāri, 221:7.
LÚ-DINGIR.RA, 222:9. See also *Awīl-ili*.
LÚ-^{d}DUMU.ZI(-DA*),
1. AB.A.AB.DU, 297:18*, seal*.
2. 42:18.
LÚ-^{d}EN.KI.KA, see *Awīl-Ea*.
LUGAL-*ma*-DINGIR, f. of *Ipqu-erṣetim*, 186:rev. 6.
LUGAL-^{d}UTU, DAM.GÀR, 46:18.
LÚ-^{d}IŠKUR.RA, see *Awīl-*^{d}*Adad*.
LÚ-[^{d}LI]SI, 191:3.
LÚ-^{d}MAR-TU, see *Awīl-*^{d}*Amurru*.
Lūmur-ša-^{d}*Marduk*, UGULA, 411:3; 412:3; 413:3; 414:3; 415:3; 416:3; 420:3; 422:3; 437:10; 441:3; 486:4; 509:4.
LÚ*-na-tum*, 28:16; 163:11.
LÚ*-ni-i*, s. of *Ú-ri-ya*, 355:3, 23; 358:14.
LÚ-^{d}NIN.IN.SI.NA, 206:rev. 6.
LÚ-^{d}NIN.ŠUBUR, 335:16.
LÚ-^{d}NIN.URTA, 524:3.
*Lu?-pa-*x*-qí-bi-*[x] f. of *Ṭāb-wašāb*[*šu*], 142 seal.
Lū-šalim, LÚ *E-mu-ut-ba-lum*, 433:5.
Luštammar,
1. s. of *Muḫaddûm*, b. of *Ubarum*, 42:24.
2. s. of ^{d}*Sîn-napšerum*, 556:25.
3. f. of *Aplatum*, 135 seal.
4. 47:9.
Luštammar-Ea, s. of *Ibbi-*^{d}*Šaḫan*, f. of *Ina-libbi-eršet* and ^{d}*Šamaš-iddinam*, 469:17.
Luštammar-^{d}*Ilabrat*, 249:17(!).
Luštammar-^{d}*Šamaš*, 29:6; 225:5, case 5.
Lu-ub-ti-ya, 270:10.

Mād-gimil-^{d}*Šamaš*,
1. GUDU$_{4}$.ABZU, 557:29.
2. 411:8; 412:8; 413:8; 414:8; 415:8; 416:8; 422:8; 463:12.
Maqtu-lizziz(?) (*Ma-aq!-tu-li?-zi-zu*), f. of *E-gi-iš-*x*-úḫ*, 515:12.
^{d}MA.LÚ.TI, 78:12.
Mannium, 108:2.
Manniya,

1. f. of Ea-gāmil, 530 seal.
2. 336:20; 337:5; 348:13.

Mannum,
1. s. of Ilšu-ibbi, 457:10(?).
2. f. of Ilī-luṭṭul, 457:14.
3. f. of ^{d}Sîn-uselli, 76:5.
4. 237:5(?).

Mannum-kīma-abim (AD), 547:4.

Mannum-kīma-^{d}Sîn, f. of ^{d}Enlil-issu, 185:42, seal; 225 seal.

Mannu(m)-kīma-^{d}Šamaš, Ma-an-nu-um-ma-ki-^{d}UTU*,
1. f. of ^{d}Šamaš-liwwir, 272:3.
2. SIMUG, 332:14.
3. 31:3; 53:7*; 294:2, 3.

Mannum-libluṭ, 92:14.

Mannu-^{d}Šamaš, 546:7.

Mār-A-am-ma-a, wilid-bītim, 433:6.

Mār-^{d}Adad, see DUMU-^{d}IŠKUR.

Mār-^{d}Amurru, Ma-ri-^{d}MAR.TU*,
1. s. of Ipqu-^{d}Adad, 312:15, seal.
2. s. of Wa-ra-a-a, 312 seal*.
3. f. of ^{d}Amurru-ibbīšu, 312:20.
4. 234:11; 302:4, 13.

Mār-^{d}Araḫtum, DUMU-^{i_7}A-ra-⟨aḫ⟩-ti*,
1. ŠU.I-LUGAL, 373:1, 11.
2. 411:11; 412:11; 413:11; 414:11; 415:11; 416:11; 420:11; 422:11; 434:2*; 463:15.

Mārat-^{d}Araḫtum, 187:4.

Mār-Bābilim, see DUMU-KÁ.DINGIR.RA^{ki}.

Mār-dādi, 183:6.

^{d}Marduk-[. . .], 529:6.

^{d}Marduk-abī, 484:2, 3; 495:15.

^{d}Marduk-dayyān,
1. s. of ^{d}Nabium-tillatī, 104:2, seal.
2. NU.KIRI$_{6}$, 217:15.
3. 79:2; 135:5; 256:10; 299:2.

^{d}Marduk-e-le-el, 401:3, 5.

^{d}Marduk-ḫāzir, 550:2, 3.

^{d}Marduk-iddinam, 464:12.

^{d}Marduk-kāšid, f. of Aplatum, 377:rev. 3.

^{d}Marduk-mālik, NU.BÀNDA, 383:20.

^{d}Marduk-mušallim,
1. s. of Imgur-^{d}Šamaš, 428:4, seal.
2. b. of ^{d}Sîn-iddinam, 409:10.
3. ŠA$_{x}$.DUB.BA, 486:5; 501:6; 503:7; 504:7; 505:6; 507:6; 508:6; 509:5; 510:7; 511:6; 528:7.
4. GAL.UKKIN.NA, 422:5.
5. GAL.UKKIN.NA-ERÍN.KÁ.É.GAL, 411:5; 412:5; 415:5; 416:5; 420:5.
6. ZABAR.DAB, 399:4.
7. 413:5; 414:5; 441:6; 463:5; 464:4; 506:8; 517:6; 534:10.

^{d}Marduk-nāṣir,
1. AB.AB.DU$_{7}$, s. of Ì-lí-[. . .], 430 seal.
2. DUMU-ŠAGINA$_{x}$(GÌR.NITÁ), 182:9.
3. s. of ^{d}Nabium-tappê, 153:22, case 24.
4. s. of ^{d}Sîn-šar-ilī, 540:3.
5. NU.BÀNDA, 408:1.
6. rabiān Kār-^{d}UTU^{ki}, 537:20, case 10.
7. 152:6; 153 seal; 247:6; 409:5; 436:19; 445:3, 10; 461:3.

^{d}Marduk-nīšu,
1. ŠU.I-LUGAL, 500:3; 520:3; 526:3.
2. 534:3, 4.

^{d}Marduk-pa-ri-ni, ^{d}Marduk-pa-li-ni*, s. of ^{d}Sîn-šemi, 436:1, 2, 7, 8, 16, seal*.

^{d}Marduk-rēmēni, 104:3.

^{d}Marduk-tayyār, f. of Erīb-^{d}Sîn, 75:18.

^{d}Marduk-zuqqip, ^{d}Marduk-zunqip*, s. of Aḫu-waqar, 380:15, seal; 401:19*, seal.

Mār-erṣetim (DUMU-er-ṣe-tim, DUMU.KI*, Ma-ri-er-ṣe-tim†),
1. s. of Apil-Kūbi, 259:3.
2. s. of Palâ-Irra, 321:3.
3. s. of ^{d}Šamaš-massû, 556:34.
4. s. of ^{d}Šamaš-rabi, 549:3.
5. f. of Aplatum, 536:38; 556:29*.

6. f. of *Bēlānum*, 75:22*.
7. f. of *Ilšu-ibnīšu*, 536 seal; 537:22*.
8. f. of *Ṣillī-dDamkina*, 408 seal.
9. ENGAR, 64:10*.
10. SIPA-U8.UDU.ḪI.A, 203:23*.
11. 56:9*; 88:2*; 101:35*; 112:13, 26*; 118:1; 174:10; 304:11; 330:4†; 364:3; 381:18; 386:5; 392:3; 465:11; 540:2.
Mār-ḪI.GAR^{ki}, see DUMU-ḪI.GAR^{ki}.
Mār-ili, f. of *Ḫuzālum*, 265:5.
Mār-Ištar, *Ma-ri-Eš$_4$-dar**,
1. f. of *Pirḫum*, 536 seal; 556:35.
2. 94:7*; 198:9*; 429:9; 435:4; 448:2.
Mār-^{d}Šamaš, see DUMU-^{d}UTU.
Mār-Sippar^{ki}, see DUMU-ZIMBIR^{ki}.
Mār-^{d}Tašmetum, NU.BÀNDA, 273:14.
Mārti-iltim (*Ma-ar-ti-il-tim*), 315:2.
Mār-tizqarum, 47:1, 2.
Ma-ru-ša, f. of *Keš^{ki}-iddinam*, 26:14.
Mār-wardiya, 101:18; 178:6.
Mār-^{i_7}Zi-la-ku, 217:8.
Ma-šu, 385:2.
Mati-ilum, 361:2.
Me-AB-[. . .], f. of ^{d}*Sîn-ēriš*, 551:rev. 4.
Me-in-bu-ša, 183:3, 4.
Me-ni-ḫu-um, *Mi-ni-ḫu-um**, 81:4*; 90:6; 100:2; 101:22; 109:2, 9; 118:3(?).
MES?.^{d}EN.[. . .], f. of *Nūr-^{d}Kabta*, 286 seal.
Mi-ni-ḫu-um, see *Me-ni-ḫu-um*.
MU.DINGIR.MU, 515:3.
Muḫaddītum,
1. d. of ^{d}UTU-DINGIR, 141:6.
2. 205:3; 230:3; 333:2.
Muḫaddû(m),
1. s. of *Šū-Ištar*, 153 seal.
2. f. of *Luštammar* and *Ubarum*, 42:23, seal.
3. UGULA-DAG.GI.A, 214:29.
4. 97:11; 234:10; 381:9.
MU.ḪÉ.GÁL,
1. f. of *Lipit-^{d}Enlil*, 222 seal.
2. 349:21; 532:3, 4; 543:17.
Munawwirum,
1. s. of *Ilšu-ibbi*, 236:19.
2. s. of *Imgur-^{d}Šamaš*, 105:16.
3. f. of ^{d}*Sîn-bēl-aplim*, 390:23.
4. PA.PA, 277:22.
5. 5:4; 23:15, case 12; 105:7, 11; 271:12; 294:11; 392:4.
Murrûm, 517:2.
Mutī-ḫuršānī (*Mu-ti-ḫu-ur-ša-ni*, *Mu-ti-ḫur-ša-ni**, *Mu-ti-ḫu-ur-ša*†, *Mu-ut-ḫu-ur-ša*‡, *Mu-ti*-ḪUR.SAG§), 503:11; 504:15*, 505:16; 508:16; 510:14†; 516:16‡; 519:13§; 527:22†.
MU.ZU.ŠÈ, s. of *Annum-pî-Ištar*, 74:3, 10, seal.

Nabi-^{d}Damgalnunna,
1. b. of *Eridu^{ki}-liwwir*, 28:2, 7.
2. 249:16; 258:24; 302:6; 312:4; 337:4; 344:3; 347:4; 352:6, 10; 530:8; 543:16.
Nabi-^{d}Damkina, 349:7.
Nabi-^{d}Ilabrat, 206:16.
Nabi-ilišu,
1. s. of ^{d}[. . .], 559:27.
2. s. of *Apil-^{d}Adad*, 14:4.
3. s. of ^{d}*Sîn-uselli*, b. of *Apil-ilišu*, 353:3, 10.
4. f. of *Awiyatum*, 73 seal.
5. f. of *Ilī-bāni*, 389:4.
6. f. of *Išme-^{d}Sîn*, 559:18.
7. 26:12; 39:3; 129:3; 148:4; 209:2; 224:3, 8; 355:5; 446:13; 495:12; 502:5.
Nabi-^{d}Sîn, 16:3; 20:3; 144:4; 148:3; 234:4; 235:4; 292:2; 317:5.

Nabi-[d]*Šamaš*,
1. s. of *Ilšu-bāni*, 495:13.
2. f. of [d]*Sîn-imguranni*, 161:6; 228:6.
3. 167:17; 216:5; 241:4; 255:9; 296:4; 332:5; 336:5.

[d]*Nabium-abī*, LÚ.TÚG, 433:2.

[d]*Nabium-mālik*, [d]*Na-bu-um-ma-lik**,
1. s. of *A-ta-li-im*, 544:10, seal.
2. *rabiānum*, 496:16.
3. 135:3, 4; 192:7, rev.12; 279:6*; 383:11; 439:17; 495:11; 548:3.

[d]*Nabium-mušallim*,
1. SANGA, 98:6.
2. 380:20.

[d]*Nabium-nāṣir*, 535:1.

[d]*Nabium-tappê*, f. of [d]*Marduk-nāṣir*, 153:22, case 24.

[d]*Nabium-tillatī*, f. of [d]*Marduk-dayyān*, 104 seal.

Nabiyatum, 357:11.

Na-x-*da*-[. . .], f. of [d]*Sîn-erība*, 549:12.

Namārša-lūmur, SAG.GEMÉ, 185:14, case 15.

Namra(m)-šarūr (*Nam-ra(-am)-ša-ru-ur*, *Na-am-ra-ša-ru-ur**, *Nam-ra-am-ši-ru-ur*†, ZALAG-*ša-ru-ur*‡, *Nam-ra-aš-ša-ru-ur*§, *Nam-ra-ša-ru-ur*§§), see also *Nawra(m)-šarūr*,
1. f. of *Nūr-*[d][. . .], 314 seal*.
2. DAM.GÀR, 192:rev. 1.
3. 36:2*; 52:2†; 56:51‡; 59:10; 81:5†; 90:11†; 101:27–28; 109:7, 10†; 112:16–17; 117:4§; 118:27; 150:4; 178:5; 215:12§§; 314:3; 320:25.

Namru-ilī, s. of [d]*Šamšī-*[d]*Enlil*, 280:15; 281:20, seal.

NAM.TI, $GUDU_4$-[d]NIN.GAL, 297:19.

[d]NANNA-[. . .], ŠÀ.TAM.$GURU_7$, 557:31.

[d]NANNA-AN.DÙL, 27:7.

[d]NANNA-A.RÁ.MU, URUDU.NAGAR, 278:18.

[d]NANNA-DALLA, f. of *Ḫuzālum*, 218:rev. 7.

[d]NANNA-DÙG?, f. of [. . .]-*balāṭi*, 218:rev. 9.

[d]NANNA-É.MAḪ, [d]NANNA-Ì.MAḪ*,
1. f. of [d]INANNA-DINGIR.MU and *Nūr-*[d]*Kabta*, 42:6, 8.
2. DUB.SAR, 324:12*.

[d]NANNA-ḪÉ.GÁL, s. of [d]*Sîn-iddinam*, b. of *Erībam-ilī*, 75:7.

[d]NANNA-Ì.MAḪ, see [d]NANNA-É.MAḪ.

[d]NANNA-MA.AN.SUM, see [d]*Sîn-iddinam*.

[d]NANNA-SAG.KAL, see [d]*Sîn-ašarid*.

[d]NANNA-ŠU.MU,
1. f. of *Ibbi-*[d]*Šamaš*, 536:36; 537:21.
2. x - x, 257:5.

Naplis-ilum, f. of *Awīl-ili*, 363:25.

Naplus-[. . .], f. of *Ibbi-*[d]*Ilabrat*, h. of *Gamiltum*, 206:2.

Naplus-Ea, RÁ.GABA, 192:rev. 6.

Narām-ilišu,
1. s. of *Imgurum*, 95:16.
2. DUB.SAR, 301:21.
3. 7:24; 546:6.

Narām-[d]*Sîn*, 34:3; 59:7.

Narubtum,
1. m. of *Ṭāb-qabâša*, w. of *Ti-im-gu*, 307:8.
2. 410:4.

Nawir-Akšak, 72:18.

Nawirtum, m. of *Ipqu-*[d]*Ningal*, 359:2.

Nawra(m)-šarūr, see also *Namra(m)-šarūr*,
1. f. of *Ilī-iddinam*, 135 seal.
2. 298:12.

Nawrum-ilī, f. of [. . .]-*iqīšam*, 218:rev. 10.

Nēpešet-[d]*Sîn*, 212:7; 333:12.

[d]*Nergal*-[. . .], $ŠA_x$.DUB.BA, 273:9.

[d]*Nergal-ḫāzir*, 181:12; 208:7(?); 263:10.

[d]*Nergal-illassu*, 59:17.

[d]*Nergal-mu*-[. . .], f. of *Ilī-u-*[d]*Šamaš*, 227:34.

Nidin-[. . .], f. of ^{d}*Sîn-a-ḫ*[*u*-. . .], 71 seal.
Nidnat-^{d}Sîn,
1. f. of *Ilum-bāni*, 277:24.
2. KA.KI, 227:37.
3. UGULA-MAR.TU, 425:7.
4. 198:10; 203:11; 316:7; 440:2, 3.
Nidnatum,
1. s. of ^{d}*Sîn-šamuḫ*, 387:6; 470:3; 482:3.
2. *kaparrum*, 7:18.
3. 108:rev. 3(?); 462:20; 473:8; 518:2; 522:16.
Ni-id-ni-in-^{d}Sîn, f. of ^{d}*Sîn-ša-takāli*, 225:18.
Nidnuša,
1. s. of *Iddin-^{d}Šamaš*, 224:12.
2. 78:5; 385:6, 11; 393:2; 398:6; 401:7.
Níg-gi$_4$-ya, *Níg-gi-ya**, *Ni-gi-i-ya*†, *Ni-in-ki-ya*‡,
1. s. of ^{d}*Sîn-magir*, 312:18; 530:18*, seal‡.
2. DAM.GÀR, 290:37.
3. 1:8*; 13:11*; 23:case 13*; 117:14†; 140:rev. 3*; 352:18*.
NÌ.GI.NA, 78:17.
NÌ.GI.NA.NI.ḪÉ-DU, s. of ^{d}NANNA-MA.AN.SUM, 148 seal.
^{d}*Ninazu-gāmil*, f. of *Takil-ilišu*, 277:23.
^{d}*Ningizzida-abī*, s. of *Ištar-ilī* and *Aḫas-sunu*, 253:1.
^{d}*Ningizzida-gāmil*, 161:21.
^{d}*Ningublam-abī*, 512:4.
Ninnû, 222:6, seal; 239:7.
^{d}*Ninsianna-nāṣir*, 26:10.
^{d}NIN-SUN-ME.A.TUM, 205:5, 9.
^{d}*Ninurta-atpalam*, Ì.DU$_8$ É EN-^{d}UTU, 142:4.
NÌ.SI.SÁ.NI A.AB.DIRI, f. of *Iddiyatum*, 275:14.
Nūḫam-ilī, [x] AD-KID, 377:rev. 4.
Nunnû, 2:12.
Nu-pa-tum, s. of *Guqqû*, 228:18.
Nūr-^{d}[. . .],
1. f. of *Namra-šarūr*, 314 seal.
2. 192 seal.
Nūr-^{d}Alla, 50:10.
Nūr-^{d}Amurru, s. of *Awiyatum*, 186:1.
Nūratum,
1. m. of *Tarībum*, 186:rev. 7.
2. 57:9; 225:3, case 3; 260:8; 261:8.
Nūr-^{d}Ilabrat,
1. ŠÀ.TAM, 332:13.
2. 119:21; 163:8.
Nūr-ili,
1. f. of ^{d}*Šamaš-muballiṭ*, 156:rev. 9.
2. 295:10.
Nūr-ilišu,
1. f. of *Ilšu-ibbīšu*, 236 seal.
2. f. of *Lalê*, 61:30.
3. f. of *Rāmatum*, 44:case 4.
4. f. of ^{d}UTU-AN.DÙL, 123 seal.
5. LÚ.ŠU.I, 433:10.
6. 149:3; 173:2.
Nūr-iliya, f. of ^{d}*Amurru-muballiṭ*, 194:9.
Nūr-Ištar,
1. s. of *Kurullum*, b. of *Apil-^{d}Amurru*, uncle of *Idiyatum*, 363:21.
2. s. of *Šumum-libši*, 48:3, 10, 19, 22.
3. b. of *Ipqu-Ea*, h. of *Ḫa-an-da-tum*, 212:1, 9, 11.
4. 365:5; 547:8.
Nūr-^{d}Kabta,
1. *rabiānum*, s. of MES?.^{d}EN.[. . .], 286:14, seal.
2. s. of ^{d}NANNA-É.MAḪ, b. of ^{d}INANNA-DINGIR.MU, 42:7.
3. s. of ^{d}*Sîn-iddinam*, 275:16.
4. f. of *Ilum-nāṣir*, 236 seal.
5. f. of *Šumum-libši* and *Bēltani*, 400:6.
6. 75:3; 192 seal; 218:6, seal; 387:8; 555:15(?).
Nūr-kî-^{d}Šamaš, 525:4.

*Nūr-ᵈ*MAḪ, f. of *ᵈŠamaš-muballiṭ*, 227:2, 29.
Nūr-ᵈSîn, f. of *Aḫātum*, 141:5.
Nur-ᵈŠala, f. of *Šumman-lā-ᵈŠamaš*, 74:17, case 5.
Nūr-ᵈŠamaš,
1. f. of *Ilšu-ibnīšu*, 322:4, seal.
2. f. of *Saniq-qabûšu*, 380:17.
3. b. of *Etel-pîšu*, 552:8, 16.
4. 13:4; 47:3; 56:53; 76:10; 83:5; 99:6; 112:10; 210:9; 294:15(?); 300:6; 453:7; 454:7.
Nūršu-e-li,
1. s. of *Aḫīyama*, 379:8, seal.
2. 470:8.
Nūrum,
1. f. of *Gimil-ili*, 74:16, case 4, seal.
2. 344:4.
Nūrum-līṣi,
1. f. of *Apil-ilišu*, 8 seal.
2. 348:10.
Nūr-ᵈWēdum, 479:4.

Palâ-Irra,
1. f. of *Mār-erṣetim*, 321:4.
2. f. of *Kî-maruṣ*, 556:36.
Palḫūya,
1. f. of *Ap-pa-an-ilum*, 559:22.
2. NAGAR, 54:5.
Paluḫ-rigimšu,
1. s. of *Ibni-ᵈAdad*, b. of *Ba-ya-um*, 556:23.
2. 536:6; 537:6.
Palûšu-līrik, 501:5; 503:5; 504:5; 505:5; 506:7; 507:5; 508:5; 510:5; 511:5; 513:8; 528:6; 529:5.
Pí-ir-ḫa-il-lu?-ša, 56:10.
Pilaḫ-ᵈAdad, f. of ᵈUTU-DINGIR, 549:4.
Pirḫilišu (sandhi for *Piriḫ-ilišu*),
1. f. of *Tarībum*, 285:2.
2. 26:20; 65:3.
Pirḫum,
1. s. of *Ḫummuri*, 78:7.
2. s. of *Larsûm*, 183:11, seal.
3. s. of *Mār-Ištar*, 536:39, seal; 556:35.
4. s. of *Si-na-ti-ia*, 400:13.
5. s. of x-*ta*-x-x-*ik*, 102:32.
6. NU.BÀNDA, 181:13.
7. SIMUG, 98:2.
8. 1:13; 3:4; 4:4; 6:5; 9:5; 13:12; 14:11; 16:10; 17:4, case 3; 18:7; 23:3, case 3, 9; 36:3, 12; 40:4; 41:5; 53:4; 54:4; 107:2; 114:6; 119:4; 120:3; 123:3; 124:3; 136:3; 137:4; 140:4; 145:5; 146:3; 162:12; 181:3, 9; 191:4; 203:34; 208:3; 213:2; 244:3; 253:4; 290:3, 8, 10, 28, 32; 305:2; 315:12; 342:5; 555:12(?).
Piriḫ-ilišu, see *Pirḫilišu*.
Pūḫum, 56:48; 275:13.
Purādānu, f. of *Awīl-Ištar*, 390:24.
PÚZUR.[. . .], 319:10.
PÚZUR-(ᵈ)A.BA, 76:3; 355:5.
Puzur-ili, SUKKAL, 323:9.
Puzur-ilišu?, 152:3.
Puzur-ᵈMarduk, 26:41.
PÚZUR-ᵈNANNA, 152:19.
PÚZUR-ᵈNIN.GAL, s. of *ᵈSîn-šemi*, 228:23.
PÚZUR-ᵈUTU, 295:3.

Qaqqadum, s. of *Aḫu-waqar*, 556:22.
Qīš-ᵈBaba,
1. AB.AB.DU_7, 353:8.
2. 175:3.
Qīš-ᵈŠamaš, 158:rev. 1.
Qīšti-ᵈDamkina, NA.GADA, 324:7.
Qīšti-ᵈEnlil, 3:8.
Qīšti-Irra, NA.GADA, 25:5.

Qīštum, s. of *Āmur-ilūssa*, 176 seal.
Qulālum, f. of ^{d}*Šamaš-magir*, 195:10.
Qurdišu?, 327:8.
Qurdiya, s. of the NU.BÀNDA-UGULA, 290:38.
Qurrudum,
1. s. of *Aḫūšina*, 559:23.
2. NAGAR, b. of *Aḫī-a(y)-amši*, ^{d}*Amurru-muballiṭ*, *Ilīma-abī*, *Šumman-lā-*^{d}*Šamaš*, 102:6.
3. 126:6.
Quttunum, SAG.ÌR, *wilid bītim*, s. of *Abī-libūr*, 322:1.
Qù-ur-ru-[x], see *Gu-ur-ru-*[x].

Ra-bi-a?-nu?-u[*m*], f. of [. . .]-*tum*, 555:16.
Rabi-^{d}*Ištaran*, 319:14.
Rabûm, 211:10.
Rabūt-^{d}*Sîn*,
1. f. of *Aḫum-waqar*, 544 seal; 553 seal.
2. 101:29–30; 112:22; 172:3.
Rāmatum, LUKUR-^{d}UTU, d. of *Nūr-ilišu*, 44:3.
Rašub-bītum,
1. s. of *Ki?-ni-ik-*x, 194:rev. 9.
2. f. of *Ubar-*^{d}*Mama*, 323:12.
Rēmanni-^{d}*Adad*, 338:3.
Rēmanni-ilum, $GUDU_4$, 290:35.
Rē'ûšu-qarrād, 27:14.
Rībam-ilī,
1. $GUDU_4$-^{d}UTU, 73:23, case 23.
2. 407:2; 438:3; 454:3.
Rīm-^{d}*Adad*, 257:11.
Rīm-Ištar, 535:4.
Rīm-^{d}*Nunu*,
1. s. of *Ilum-liṭṭul*, 227:25.
2. f. of *Ibbi-*^{d}*Šamaš*, 227:32.
Rīm-^{d}*Sîn*, LUGAL, 307:2.
Rīš-^{d}*Dumuzi*, 78:15.
Rīš-Ea, 547:7.
Rīš-^{d}*Marduk*, s. of *Ipqu-*^{d}*Amurru*, 360:2, 5.
Rīš-^{d}*Šamaš*,
1. s. of *Aḫum-waqar*, 526:11.
2. SIMUG, s. of ^{d}*Sîn-tukultī*, 153:20, case 23.
3. s. of *Zikir-Kūbi*, 400:14.
4. 116:2; 130:5; 301:2, 3; 406:6; 526:11; 553:13.
Rīš-^{d}*Šubula*,
1. s. of *Ibni-*^{d}*Adad*, 442:18.
2. 98:4.

Sabītum,
1. d. of ^{d}*Sîn-šamuḫ*, 371:1, 6, 12.
2. d. of *Waqar-aḫum*, 469.3.
Sadīdum, RÁ.GABA, 393:1.
Sakkiya, f. of ^{d}*Adad-šarrum*, 376:6.
Sakkum, f. of ^{d}*Šamaš-nīšu*, 556:12.
Sak-ku-pu, *ša panī*, 401:20.
Salīmu, 119:22.
Samsi-erâḫ, 92:10.
Samsu, f. of *Aḫu-waqar*, 308 seal.
Samsu-ilūna, date formula; 29 seal; 46 seal; 113 seal; 123 seal; 142 seal; 173 seal; 343 seal; 388 seal; 430 seal.
Sāmum,
1. s. of *Aḫu-waqar*, 200:12, seal.
2. f. of *Apil-*^{d}*Amurru*, 37 seal.
3. 325:27.
Saniq-pî-^{d}*Šamaš*,
1. s. of *Imtagar-*^{d}*Šamaš*, 352:17, seal.
2. s. of DAM.GÀR, 355:2.
3. s. of ^{d}*Šamaš-muballiṭ*, 552:29.
4. s. of ^{d}*Šamšī-*^{d}*Enlil*, b. of *Aḫum*, *Apil-*^{d}*Kittim*, *Ūṣi-nūrum*, 185:8, 27, 37, case 9, 31, 41, 42, seal.
5. f. of ^{d}*Sînatum*, 490 seal.

6. GUDU$_4$-^{d}UTU, 73:24, case 25.
7. 185: case 13; 319:5; 383:17; 403:3, 4; 405:14.
Saniq-qabûšu, *Saniq-qabûša**,
1. s. of *Nūr-^{d}Šamaš*, 380:16.
2. s. of *Zammukku*, 211:3*, seal.
Sāniqu, f. of *Tarību*, 56:7.
Saniyatum, 445:8; 455:12; 475:4; 554:11.
Sanqum,
1. s. of *Šar-ru-na?-^{d}Sîn*, 156: rev. 8.
2. GALA.MAḪ, 325:25.
3. 185:2.
*Sa-nu-ub-ti-*x, f. of *Awīliya*, 246:5.
Sa-nu-um, 320:28.
Sa-ra-mu-um, 265:11.
Sarrum, f. of *Siyatum*, 303:4.
Sartiya, 518:1.
Si-im-da-an-da-ni-im, 436:17.
Si-im-me, 387:3; 491:6.
Silīlum, *Si-li-lum* GAL, 65:5; 101:8, 37; 112:3.
Simtī-ilum, NU.ÈŠ, 390:5.
Simtī-Ištar, *Šimtī-Ištar**, s. of *Ilam-ēriš*, 17:3, 7, case 2,. 7, seal; 23:4*, case 4, 8, seal.
^{d}*Sîn-*[. . .],
1. f. of ^{d}*Sîn-iddinam*, 214:26.
2. f. of ^{d}*Šamaš-ummatī*, 230 seal.
3. 469:31.
^{d}*Sîn-abūšu*,
1. f. of ^{d}*Dagan-bāni*, 304 seal.
2. f. of ÌR-^{d}SUEN, 153 seal.
3. f. of ^{d}*Sîn-erībam*, 537:24.
4. 468:4.
^{d}*Sîn-adallal*,
1. f. of DUMU-ZIMBIR^{ki}, 536:4.
2. f. of ^{d}*Šamaš-gamil*, 320:29.
3. 56:13(?); 216:13; 320:23.
^{d}*Sîn-aḫam-iddinam*,
1. f. of *Iddin-^{d}Amurru*, 457 seal.
2. 56:47; 90:7; 101:15; 112:19; 118:26; 125:9; 151:3; 173:5; 179:13; 294:5; 434:9; 517:7.
^{d}*Sîn-a-ḫi-i-din-nam*,
1. s. of *Abu(m)-waqar*, 61:29, seal.
2. s. of *Lipit-Ištar*, 228:22.
3. 62:18; 326:10; 379:4.
^{d}*Sîn-a-ḫ[u- . . .]*, s. of *Nidin-*[. . .], 71 seal.
^{d}*Sîn-apil-*GÚ.DU$_8$.A, 211:9.
^{d}*Sîn-asû*, 78:3.
^{d}*Sîn-ašarid*, ^{d}NANNA-SAG.KAL*,
1. f. of *Ibbi-^{d}Sîn*, 500:5.
2. BUR.GUL, 313:8.
3. DUB.SAR, 95:19*.
Si-na-ti-ya, f. of *Pirḫum*, 400:13.
Sînatum (^{d}SUEN-*na-tum*, *Sí-na-tum*†, *Si-na-tum*‡, ^{d}NANNA-*tum*§)
1. s. of *Saniq-pî-^{d}Šamaš*, 490 seal.
2. s. of *Sînatum*, 400:15‡.[1]
3. f. of *Aplum*, 226:8†.
4. f. of *Sînatum*, 400:15§.
5. DAM.GÀR, f. of *Lalûm*, 559:24†.
6. GUDU$_4$, 290:34†.
7. GUDU$_4$-^{d}UTU, 73:23†, case 22†.
8. 285:13§; 368:10; 494:14‡; 527:1, 10.
^{d}*Sîn-bāni*, (^{d}ŠEŠ$_x$.KI-*ba-ni**)[2]
1. f. of ^{d}*Sîn-šamuḫ*, 376:18*.
2. f. of *Ilum-nāṣir*, 299 seal.
3. 223:2; 382:8.
^{d}*Sîn-bēl-apli(m)*, ^{d}*Sîn-bēl-aplum**,
1. s. of *Ḫa-za-ne*, 473:9.
2. s. of *Munawwirum*, 390:22*.
3. s. of ^{d}*Sîn-šemi*, 394:8.
4. 12:10; 316:6; 476:7; 487:2; 524:6.
^{d}*Sîn-bēl-ilī*, f. of *Ibbi-^{d}Enlil*, 322 seal.
^{d}*Sîn-damiq*, s. of *A-ḫi-mar-ši*, 526:4.

[1] Father and son with the same name?
[2] ŠEŠ$_x$ = 6!

^{d}*Sîn-emūqī*, 212:16.
^{d}*Sîn-erībam*,
1. s. of *Na*-x-*da*-[. . .], 549:12.
2. s. of ^{d}*Sîn-abūšu*, 537:24.
3. s. of ^{d}*Sîn-muballiṭ*, 218:rev. 8(?).
4. s. of ^{d}*Šamaš-bāni*, 556:20.
5. s. of ^{d}*Šamaš-muttabbil*, 322:29.
6. s. of *Ṭāb-šār-Ištar*, 457:15.
7. f. of ^{d}*Šamaš-itūram*, 275:17.
8. DAM.GÀR, 433:14.
9. DUB.SAR, 74: case 7; 186:rev. 14; 228:24.
10. GALA.MAḪ, 297:22.
11. ŠITIM, 75:23.
12. 7:22; 254:11; 288:4.

^{d}*Sîn-ēriš*,
1. s. of *Ku-za-ri*, 63:2.
2. s. of *Me*-AB-[. . .], 551:4.
3. s. of ^{d}*Šamaš-mušēzib*, 334:13.
4. f. of *Annum-pî-Ea*, 42:22.
5. f. of *Ap*-[. . .], 323 seal.
6. f. of *Bēlī-iddinam*, 74:4.
7. f. of ^{d}SUEN-MAŠ.MAŠ, 337 seal.
8. RÁ.GABA, b. of *Ṣillī*-^{d}*Šamaš*, 227:35.
9. LÚ.É.SILÁ, 357:2, 10, 20.
10. 300:12; 349:20.

^{d}*Sîn-gāmil*, 96:2; 139:5; 185:1, 11, case 1, 12; 274:21; 294:13; 357:13, 23.
^{d}*Sîn-gimlanni*, UGULA-NAM-5, 236:17; 418:4.
Sîn-ḫāzir, 271:3.
^{d}*Sîn-ibnīšu*, 207:11.
^{d}*Sîn-iddinam*, ^{d}NANNA-MA.AN.SUM*,
1. s. of *Aplum*, 283:5.
2. s. of *Bāṣirum*, 469:2.
3. s. of *Bulluṭ-ilum*, 559:20.
4. s. of *Ḫa*-x-x-(x), 153:19.
5. s. of *Ilī-ē-taddianni*, 192 seal.
6. s. of *Ilum-gamil*, 74:15, case 3.
7. UGULA-NAM-5, s. of *Imgurum*, 225:15, case 14, 23; 283:3.
8. s. of ^{d}*Sîn*-[. . .], 214:26.
9. s. of *Šallūrum*, 186:rev. 3*, 20*.
10. f. of *Aplum*, 552:27.
11. f. of *Erībam-ilī*, 75:9.
12. f. of *Ḫāzirum*, 275:20.
13. f. of NÌ.GI.NA.NI.ḪÉ.DU, 148 seal*.
14. f. of *Nūr*-^{d}*Kabta*, 275:16.
15. f. of ^{d}*Sîn-šemi*, 417 seal*.
16. b. of *Awīl*-^{d}*Šamaš*, 358:8.
17. b. of ^{d}*Marduk-mušallim*, 409:2, 7.
18. DUB.SAR, 153:19, case 28; 185:47*, case 48*.
19. GUDU$_{4}$-^{d}UTU, 192:rev. 2.
20. KA.GURU$_{7}$, 357:3*, 15*, 17*.
21. SIPA, 456:8.
22. ŠÀ.TAM (?), 94:3.
23. 3:9; 56:54; 65:4; 94:8; 108:3; 119:20; 153:19; 190:30; 197:4; 211:4; 219:3; 274:4; 289:4; 315:13; 403:6; 404:4; 434:7; 439:16; 467:4; 494:5; 518:10; 531:11*; 541:14; 554:2.

^{d}*Sîn-ilum*, see ^{d}SUEN-DINGIR.
^{d}*Sîn-imgur*,
1. x - x, s. of *Da-da*, b. of ^{d}*Sîn-tukultī*, 228:20.
2. 32:7.

^{d}*Sîn-imguranni*,
1. s. of *Adu-anniam*, 286:17.
2. s. of *Bēlī*, 236:3, 6, 11; 250:15; 355:22.
3. s. of *Ḫummurum*, 392:5.
4. s. of *Ipiq*-^{d}*Ilabrat*, 363:24.
5. s. of *Nabi*-^{d}*Šamaš*, 161:5; 228:5.
6. f. of *Abī-ilī*, 559:21.
7. of *Apil*-^{d}*Amurru*, 522 seal.
8. f. of ^{d}*Šamaš-bēl-ilī*, 227:30.
9. f. of *Šū-Ea*, 334:14.
10. AGA.UŠ, 192:rev. 11.

11. Ì.DU$_8$-^{d}UTU, 192:rev. 8.
12. 28:13; 32:15; 35:9; 94:4; 97:4; 119:7; 142:13; 294:14; 314:2; 315:11; 340:9; 434:20.
^{d}*Sîn-imnanni*, RÁ.GABA, 274:3, 6, 7, 11, 14.
^{d}*Sîn-ippalsam*, s. of ^{d}*Sîn-tukultī*, 156:rev. 6.
^{d}*Sîn-iqīšam*,
1. s. of *Aya*, 164:3.
2. s. of *Bi*-x-[. . .], 214:28.
3. f. of ^{d}*Sîn-magir*, 236:2.
4. 51:3; 118:31; 142:18; 167:2, 4; 185:21, case 25.
^{d}*Sîn-iqūlam*,
1. s. of *Iddin-*^{d}*Sîn*, 442:11.
2. DUB.SAR, 48:25.
^{d}*Sîn-išmeanni*, ^{d}*Sîn-išmêni**,
1. s. of ^{d}*Sîn*-[. . .], 552:28.
2. KÙ.DÍM, 288:15.
3. SIPA, 483:7, 17.
4. 78:19; 92:23*; 111:17; 243:8*; 248:2, 3; 282:7*, 13*; 293:7*; 329:19; 354:2*, 3*; 356:6*; 439:5; 449:3.
^{d}*Sîn-itâšu*, 78:10.
^{d}*Sîn-itūram*, DAM.GÀR, 225:20, case 18.
^{d}*Sîn-kīma-ilišu*, 436:18.
^{d}*Sîn-kīma-iliya*, ŠU.I *ša* ^{d}UTU, 73:case 29.
^{d}*Sîn-līdiš*, 185:21, case 24; 379:6.
^{d}*Sîn*-[. . .]-*lim*, s. of *Ilī-tūram*, 560 seal.
^{d}*Sîn-li-ta*-x, f. of *Kasap-*^{d}*Sîn*, 73 seal.
^{d}*Sîn-liwwir*, 162:1.
^{d}*Sîn-ludlul*, 214:2.
^{d}*Sîn-magir*,
1. s. of *A-ap-ta-a*, 69:7.
2. s. of *Ibnatum*, 376:21.
3. s. of ÌR-^{d}UTU, 224:14, 21.
4. s. of ^{d}*Sîn-iqīšam*, 236:2, 12.
5. s. of ^{d}*Sîn-muballiṭ*, 355:6, 7.
6. s. of *Warad-*^{d}*Sîn*, 153:25, case 22.
7. f. of *Aḫam-nirši*, 224:16.
8. f. of *Balilum*, 153 seal.
9. f. of *Ḫurrurum*, 556:28.
10. f. of *I-ba-šar-rum*, 95:18.
11. f. of *Níg-gi$_4$-ya*, 312:18.
12. f. of ^{d}*Sîn-muštāl*, 113 seal; 167 seal.
13. NU.KIRI$_6$, 483:6.
14. *rabiānum*, 277:21.
15. 167:1, 3; 190:28; 207:13(?); 551:9.
^{d}*Sînma-ilum*,
1. s. of *Akšak*^{ki}*-iddinam*, 168 seal.
2. f. of *Ilum-kīnam-idi*, 559:7.
^{d}*Sîn-muballiṭ*,
1. f. of ^{d}*Sîn-erībam*(?), 218:rev. 8.
2. f. of ^{d}*Sîn-magir*, 355:6, 7 (^{d}SUEN-*mu*! (text *ú*)-*ba-li-iṭ*).
3. f. of [. . .]-^{d}*Sîn*, 277:25.
4. 27:9; 251:7.
^{d}*Sîn-mudammiq*, RÁ.GABA, 282:16.
^{d}*Sîn-mupaḫḫir*, s. of ^{d}*Sîn-mušallim*, f. of *Kīnum-ḫabil*, 521:5, seal.
^{d}*Sîn-mušallim*,
1. f. of ^{d}*Sîn-mupaḫḫir*, 521 seal.
2. UGULA-DAM.GÀR, 250:7; 290:5.
3. 56:29; 76:6.
^{d}*Sîn-muštāl*, s. of ^{d}*Sîn-magir*, 113:10, seal; 167:6, seal.
^{d}*Sîn-muštēšer*, f. of *Bēltani*, 469:9.
^{d}*Sîn-nabi-ilī*, GUDU$_4$-DUB.LÁ.MAḪ, 297:21.
^{d}*Sîn-nādin-šumi*, 388:7; 423:1, 2; 492:4, 6.
^{d}*Sîn-napšeram*,
1. f. of *Luštammar*, 556:25.
2. DUB.SAR, 465:12.
3. 59:4; 65:19; 101:14; 112:9; 220:11; 271:2; 300:13; seal, 311:8–9.
^{d}*Sîn-nāṣir*, LÚ.KÁ.GAL, s. of [. . .]-*a-a*, 48:23, seal.
^{d}*Sîn-nāši*, 557:1, 6, 12, 27.
^{d}*Sîn-ni-i*, 181:4, 10; 208:2; 356:5.
^{d}*Sîn-nūrka*, f. of *Kukkum*, 177 seal.

^{d}*Sîn-pa-la*-x, 469:8.
^{d}*Sîn-pāṭir*, 42:16; 235:10.
^{d}*Sîn-pilaḫ*,
1. s. of *Išmeya*, 129 seal; 133 seal.
2. 56:31; 81:6; 101:24–25; 112:20; 118:14; 125:8; 151:10.
^{d}*Sîn-puṭra*, 11:11; 377:1(?).
^{d}*Sîn-rabi*,
1. f. of *Ea-ibnīšu*, 119 seal.
2. 333:10.
^{d}*Sîn-rēmēni*,
1. s. of *Iddin-*^{d}*Bunene*, b. of *Aḫam-arši, Ali-talīmī, Iddin-*^{d}*Amurru, Ilīma-aḫi, Ilšu-abūšu*, 556:9.
2. f. of *I-ri-ri*, 238 seal.
3. f. of *Issu-kabit*, 242:4 (^{d}*Sin-re-me-an-ni*).
4. f. of *Kalūmtum*, 469:11.
5. b. of ^{d}*Sîn-uselli*, 138:4.
6. GAL.UKKIN.NA, 428:3.
7. ŠÀ.TAM, 55:11.
8. 20:2; 225:4, case 4, 23; 251:8; 255:4; 455:5 (^{d}*Sin-re-me-a-ni*).
^{d}*Sîn-rē'ûm*, see ^{d}SUEN-SIPA.
^{d}*Sîn-rība*, 366:3.
^{d}*Sîn-rīmanni*, ŠU.I, 258:27.
^{d}*Sîn-ṣulūlī*, see ^{d}NANNA-AN.DÙL.
^{d}*Sîn-*^{d}*Šamaš*, 281:3.
^{d}*Sîn-šamuḫ*,
1. s. of *Ku-zu-*[. . .], 63 seal.
2. s. of ^{d}*Sîn-bāni*, 376:17.
3. ŠANDAN, s. of *Siyatum*, 51:4, seal; 371 seal.
4. f. of *Nidnatum*, 387:7; 470:3; 482:3.
5. f. of *Sabītum*, 371:1.
6. ŠANDAN, b. of *Aḫūšunu*, 301:5.
7. 7:11; 95:5, 7; 189:13; 370:5; 371:16; 373:4, 12; 375:6; 376:4; 380:6; 551:6.
^{d}*Sîn-šar-ilī*,
1. f. of ^{d}*Marduk-nāṣir*, 540:4.
2. 64:13; 278:6.
^{d}*Sîn-šar-mātim*, 180:9; 278:17.
^{d}*Sîn-ša-takāli*, DAM.GÀR, s. of *Ni-id-ni-in-*^{d}*Sîn*, 225:17, case 16.
^{d}*Sîn-šemi*,
1. s. of ^{d}NANNA-MA.AN.SUM, 417 seal.
2. f. of ^{d}*Marduk-pa-li-ni*, 436 seal.
3. f. of PÚZUR-^{d}NIN.GAL, 228:23.
4. f. of ^{d}*Sîn-bēl-aplim*, 394:8.
5. *rabiānum*, 3:5.
6. ZABAR.DAB, 21:1; 67:2, 5; 297:8.
7. 77:15; 522:17; 543:15.
^{d}*Sîn-tayyār*, f. of ^{d}EN.LÍL-GAL.ZU, 186:rev. 5.
^{d}*Sîn-tamkārī*, 78:13–14.
^{d}*Sîn-tappâ-wēdi(m)*, 224:2, 5, 20.
^{d}*Sîn-tukultī* (^{d}SUEN-*tu-kul-ti*, ^{d}SUEN-^{tu}*tukul-ti**, 30-^{tu}*tukul-ti*†),
1. s. of *Da-da*, b. of ^{d}*Sîn-imgur*, 228:21.
2. f. of *Rīš-*^{d}*Šamaš*, 153:21†, case 23*, seal*.
3. f. of ^{d}*Sîn-ippalsam*, 156:rev. 7.
4. 57 seal.
^{d}*Sîn-uballissu*, 12:12; 278:20.
^{d}*Sîn-ublam*, f. of *Waqartum*, 3:11.
^{d}*Sîn-uselli*,
1. s. of *Gimil-ili*, 161:7, 13; 228:7, 13.
2. s. of *Mannum*, 76:5.
3. s. of *Šēp-*^{d}*Sîn*, 185:45, case 47; 283:2.
4. s. of *Waqar-abūšu*, b. of *Aḫum*, 297:3, 6, 14.
5. f. of *Aḫīya*, 48:4.
6. AB.AB.DU_7, f. of *Apil-ilišu* and *Nabi-ilišu*, 353:5, 12.
7. f. of *Ilī-iddinam*, 102:31.
8. b. of ^{d}*Sîn-rēmēni*, 138:3.
9. DAM.GÀR, 290:37.
10. $GUDU_4$, 290:34.
11. LÚ URU *A-ḫa-ka*, 227:27.
12. *rabiānum*, 102:22.

13. 26:26; 40:3; 50:3; 68:3; 147:2; 202:6; 212:8; 225:2, case 2; 251:3; 282:4, 12; 287:6; 306:9; 437:16.

ᵈ*Sîn-ya-zu*, GAL(?)-MAR.TU, 426:3.

Siyatum (*Si-ya-tum*, *Si-ya-tim**),
1. s. of *Sarrum*, 303:3, 8.
2. f. of *Aḫūšunu*, 404 seal.
3. f. of [. . .]-*ili*, 457:9*.
4. f. of ᵈ*Sîn-šamuḫ*, 51 seal.
5. 118:6; 125:10; 151:4; 173:9; 193:5.

ᵈSUEN-DINGIR, f. of ÌR-ᵈSUEN, 552:20.

ᵈSUEN-MAŠ.MAŠ, s. of ᵈ*Sîn-ēriš*, 337:6, seal.

ᵈSUEN-NÌ.BA, 56:61; 65:9; 88:1.

ᵈSUEN-NÌ.ŠU, 56:64.

ᵈSUEN-SIPA, GUDU$_4$-ᵈUTU, 73:24, case 21.

ᵈSUEN-ᵈUTU, see ᵈ*Sin*-ᵈ*Šamaš*.

Sukkukum, 112:14.

ᵈ*Sumuqan-ḫabil*, 266:4.

Sutûm, s. of ÌR-ᵈUTU, 44:17, case 19.

Ṣalīlu(m),
1. f. of *Tarībum*, 302:16; 312:14.
2. 557:33.

Ṣaprum,
1. f. of ᵈ*Šamaš-bāni*, 142:3.
2. GUDU$_4$-ᵈUTU, 73:23, case 24; 160:5.

Ṣillī-[. . .], 26:18; 317:16; 546:26.

Ṣillī-ᵈ[. . .], 509:3.

Ṣillī-ᵈ*Adad*,
1. s. of [. . .]-ᵈ*Nin*-[. . .], 25:4(?), seal(?).
2. 26:4; 56:42; 59:2; 65:8; 81:7; 90:5; 101:13; 112:18; 118:11; 151:6; 193:4; 220:13; 271:1; 356:9; 502:2, 3; 553:12.

Ṣillī-ᵈ*A-ḫu-ú-a*,
1. f. of *Šumī-aḫiya*, 61:28.
2. 386:4.

Ṣillī-ᵈ*Amurru*,
1. s. of *Apilša*, 444:13, 15, seal.
2. s. of *Šēp*-ᵈ*Sîn*, b. of *Aplum*, *Ilī-gimlanni*, *Erībam*-ᵈ*Sîn*, 278:8.
3. f. of *Ibni-Ea*, 363:27.
4. 476:13; 527:16.

Ṣillī-ᵈBÁRA.⟨PA$_4$⟩.NIGÌN.GAR.RA, 26:30.

Ṣillī-ᵈ*Damkina*,
1. ŠANDAN, s. of *Mār-erṣetim*, 408:12, seal.
2. ŠANDAN, 428:5; 470:4; 479:5; 481:6.
3. 375:10; 437:9; 499:13.

Ṣillī-Eanna, 370:13.

Ṣillī-Ebabbar (-É.BABBAR, -É.BABBAR$_x$ (UD.UD)-*ri**),
1. b. of *Kārum-mušallim*, ᵈ*Šamaš-idī*, *Uri*ᵏⁱ-*līšir*, 190:20*).
2. 326:13.

Ṣillī-Emaḫ, 215:10.

Ṣillī-ᵈ*Gula*, h. of *Unnubtum*, 156:5.

Ṣillī-Ištar, (-EŠ$_4$-DAR,-ᵈINANNA*,-ᵈMÚŠ†),
1. s. of *Šumištar*, 134:3†, seal*.
2. DUB.SAR, 192:rev. 10.
3. NA.GADA, 551:5.
4. 76:8*; 100:3*; 101:38*; 118:5†; 201:17.

Ṣillī-ᵈ*Marduk*, 485:4; 490:13; 518:4.

Ṣillī-ᵈPA$_4$.NIGÌN.GAR.RA, *Ṣillī*-ᵈPA$_4$.⟨NIGÌN⟩.GAR.RA*,
1. s. of *Šūpîm*, 304:1.
2. 473:2(?); 476:6; 490:5(?); 554:4*.

Ṣillī-ᵈ*Saḫan*, 445:4.

Ṣillī-ᵈ*Sîn*, f. of *Epēš-ilim*, 161:17, seal.

Ṣillī-ᵈ*Šamaš*,
1. b. of ᵈ*Sîn-ēriš*, 227:35.
2. DAM.GÀR, 290:42.
3. UGULA-UN(?).ÍL, 557:34.
4. 4:3; 13:3; 73:31, case 35; 157:28; 164:15; 295:9; 326:3; 395:4; 485:3; 497:4; 544:4; 553:14.

Ṣillī-ᵈ*Šubula*, 518:3.

Ṣīssu-namrat, 59:18.
Ṣur-ru-ru-tum, 518:5.

Ša-bu-lum,
1. LÚ *a-ki-a-tim*, LÚ *a-ki-tim**, *ša a-ki-tum*†, *ša a-ki-a-tim*‡, 56:58; 89:3†; 112:5‡; 433:4*.
2. 56:41.

Šalim-kīnum, f. of ^{d}*Adad-šarrum*, 490 seal.
Šalim-SAG.[ÍL], f. of ^{d}*Šamaš-nāṣir*, 173 seal.
Šallūrum,
1. s. of *Ḫundultum*, 186:6, 11.
2. f. of ^{d}NANNA-MA.AN.SUM, 186:rev. 3.
3. cf. *Mārat-Šallūrum*.

Ša-ma-ḫum, 189:14.
^{d}*Šamaš*-[. . .],
1. f. of ^{d}*Šamaš-dayyān*, 120 seal.
2. 117:12; 317:14; 410:9.

^{d}*Šamaš-a*-[. . .], 56:31.
^{d}*Šamaš-abī*,
1. f. of *Warad-Ištar*, 227:27; 353:28.
2. ŠANDAN, 70:13; 182:15; 417:7; 418:7; 419:6.
3. 41:2, 4; 530:2, 6.

^{d}*Šamaš-abīšu*, f. of ^{d}*Adad-nāṣir*, 44 seal.
^{d}*Šamaš-ašarid*, see ^{d}UTU-SAG.KAL.
^{d}*Šamaš-ay-aḫâš*, SAG.ÌR, 317:2.
^{d}*Šamaš-bāni*,
1. s. of *Ṣaprum*, 142:3; 160:4.
2. f. of ^{d}*Sîn-erībam*, 556:20.

^{d}*Šamaš-ba-ri*, 115:2; 119:2.
^{d}*Šamaš-bēl-ilī*,
1. NU.BÀNDA, s. of *A-ap-pa-a*, 216:4, seal.
2. s. of ÌR-^{d}SUEN, 153:23, case 25.
3. s. of ^{d}*Sîn-imguranni*, 227:30.
4. 83:2.

^{d}*Šamaš-dayyān*,
1. s. of ^{d}*Šamaš*-[. . .], 120:4, seal.
2. 114:9; 140:rev. 2; 145:7; 146:14; 208:6.

^{d}*Šamaš-ēpirī*, $GUDU_4$, 210:13.
^{d}*Šamaš-gāmil*,
1. s. of BA.AN.ZI.GE, 161:3.
2. s. of ^{d}*Sîn-adallal*, 320:29.
3. 47:10; 53:3; 200:13; 226:3; 260:3; 261:3; 276:3; 343:3; 443:11.

^{d}*Šamaš-gimlanni*, b. of *Apilliya*, 97:6.
^{d}*Šamaš-ḫāzir*,
1. DI.KU_5, 358:10.
2. SIPA, 103:18.
3. 22:3; 196:8; 555:13(?).

^{d}*Šamaš-iddinam*,
1. s. of *Ilī-u-*^{d}*Šamaš*, 135 seal; 411:7; 412:8; 413:8; 414:8; 415:8, seal; 416:8, seal; 422:7.
2. s. of *Luštammar-Ea*, b. of *Ina-libbi-eršet*, 469:27.
3. ENSÍ, 371:17; 375:15.
4. *rabiānum*, 371:18; 375:15.
5. 393:14.

^{d}*Šamaš-idī*, b. of *Kārum-mušallim*, *Ṣillī-Ebabbar*, *Uri*^{ki}*-līšir*, 190:10.
^{d}*Šamaš-ilī*, see ^{d}UTU-DINGIR.
^{d}*Šamaš-il-ilī*, 22:17; 119:3.
^{d}*Šamaš-illatī*,
1. f. of *Išmeanni*, 187 seal.
2. 307:4.

^{d}*Šamaš-itūram*, s. of ^{d}*Sîn-erība*, 275:17.
^{d}*Šamaš-kabtī*, 179:16.
^{d}*Šamaš-kīma-ilišu*, RÁ.GABA, 102:28.
^{d}*Šamaš-liqūl*, 327:9.
^{d}*Šamaš-liṭṭul*, s. of *Abu-waqar*, 342:rev. 3.
^{d}*Šamaš-liwwir*,
1. s. of *Alûm*, 121:9.
2. s. of *Mannu-kīma-*^{d}*Šamaš*, 272:2.
3. s. of *Ṭāb-šār-ilī*, 335:4.

4. RÁ.GABA, 192:rev. 4.
5. UGULA-NAM-5, 213:4; 236:16.
6. 32:13; 93:10; 111:3; 121:9; 206:rev. 5; 291:3, 10; 314:10; 315:14; 320:32; 322:6; 323:3; 335:3.

^{d}*Šamaš-māgir*,
1. s. of *Qulālum*, 195:9.
2. f. of ^{d}*Šamaš-tukultī*, 73:28, case 31.
3. 125:17; 139:9; 488:4.

^{d}*Šamaš-massû*, f. of *Mār-erṣetim*, 556:34.

^{d}*Šamaš*-x-*mu*-x-[. . .], s. of *Tutub*-[. . .], 257 seal.

^{d}*Šamaš-muballiṭ*,
1. s. of *Aḫūšunu*, 260 seal.
2. s. of *Aplum*, 244:1.
3. s. of *Eteya*, 194:6, rev. 13.
4. s. of *Nūr-ili*, 156:rev. 9.
5. s. of *Nūr*-^{d}MAḪ, 227:2, 29.
6. s. of *Ubar*-^{d}*Šamaš*, 250:1.
7. f. of *Ibbi*-^{d}*Šamaš*, 142 seal.
8. f. of *Saniq-pî*-^{d}*Šamaš*, 552:29.
9. DAM.GÀR-LARSA^{ki}, f. of *Šēp*-^{d}*Sîn*, 10 seal; 46 seal; 182:7.
10. DAM.GÀR, 192:rev. 9.
11. GALA, 78:21.
12. GALA-^{d}NIN.ŠUBUR, 353:23.
13. 16:11; 139:10; 144:15; 146:15, seal; 164:16; 325:24; 348:11.

^{d}*Šamaš-mušallim*, ŠABRA, 461:4.

^{d}*Šamaš-mušēzib*,
1. f. of ^{d}*Sîn-ēriš*, 334:13.
2. ŠÀ.TAM-^{d}UTU, 46:21.
3. 174:5.

^{d}*Šamaš-muttabbil*, f. of ^{d}*Sîn-erībam*, 322:29.

^{d}*Šamaš-naḫrārī*, 92:19.

^{d}*Šamaš-napširum* (^{d}UTU-*na-ap-še-rum*), s. of *Ilšu-bāni*, 75:20.

^{d}*Šamaš-naṣir*,
1. s. of *Apil*-[. . .], 388 seal.
2. s. of *Šalim*-SAG.[ÍL], 173:11, seal.
3. f. of *Bēlī-lū-dāri*, 552:23.
4. f. of *Ea-tūram*, 57 seal.
5. ŠANDAN, 237:4; 273:5.
6. (of) URU.ANŠE.ḪI.A, 171:3.
7. 56:34; 101:10; 112:28, 34; 118:30; 128:3; 210:3; 256:2; 257:4; 464:11.

^{d}*Šamaš-nīšu*, s. of *Sakkum*, 556:12.

^{d}*Šamaš-pāṭir*, AGA.UŠ, 320:33.

^{d}*Šamaš-qūlam*, DAM.GÀR, 3:7.

^{d}*Šamaš-rabi*,
1. f. of *Ibni*-^{d}*Amurru*, 321:2, 7, case 9; 536:10, 15, 18, 19, 23, seal; 537:3, 11.
2. f. of *Mār-erṣetim*, 549:3.

^{d}*Šamaš-rīmanni*, 27:12.

^{d}*Šamaš-rīm-ilī*, 49:3.

^{d}*Šamaš-sà-ḫi?-ri*, 307:23.

^{d}*Šamaš-ṣulūlī*, see ^{d}UTU-AN.DÙL.

^{d}*Šamaš-šadûšu*, f. of *Bēlī-mudī*, 111 seal.

^{d}*Šamaš-ša-takāli(m)*,
1. s. of *I*-[. . .], 214:25.
2. ENSÍ, 411:10; 422:10.
3. 412:10; 413:10; 414:10; 415:10; 416:10; 420:10; 463:14; 535:2.

^{d}*Šamaš-šemi*,
1. *kuzallum*, s. of *Šamayatum*, 328:12, seal.
2. f. of *Dumuq*-^{d}*Šamaš*, 282:17.
3. RÁ.GABA, 167:15(?).
4. 47:11.

^{d}*Šamaš*-[. . .]-x-*ta-ni*, 38:4.

^{d}*Šamaš-tappâšu*, f. of *Ipiq*-^{d}*Aya*, 536:35.

^{d}*Šamaš-tappê*,
1. SAG.ÌR, 225:1.
2. 56:9; 81:9 (TAB.BA$^{pé=e}$); 90:2; 101:11; 112:13; 118:4, 28; 178:4; 548:5.

^{d}*Šamaš-tillatī*, RÁ.GABA, 449:6.

^{d}*Šamaš-tukultī*,
1. ŠANDAN, s. of ^{d}*Šamaš-magir*, 73:28, case 31.

2. 231:1.
^{d}*Šamaš-ummatī*,
1. s. of ^{d}*Sîn-*[. . .], 230:4, seal.
2. f. of *Kurûm*, h. of *Unnubtum*, 307:5 (*-um-*⟨*ma*⟩*-ti*).
^{d}*Šamaš-ummeānī*, 444:2, 7.
Šamayatum,
1. f. of ^{d}*Šamaš-šemi*, 328 seal.
2. 260:9; 261:10.
Šamšatum,
1. f. of *Amat-bēltim* and *Šāt-*^{d}*Marduk*, 469:12.
2. 302:19.
^{d}*Šamšī-*^{d}*Enlil* (^{d}UTU-^{d}EN.LÍL.LÁ, ^{d}UTU^{ši}-^{d}EN.LÍL.LÁ*),
1. f. of *Aḫum*, *Apil-*^{d}*Kittim*, *Saniq-pî-*^{d}*Šamaš*, *Ūṣi-nūrum*, 185 seal; 555:5.
2. f. of *Namru-ilī*, 281 seal*.
Šamur-ezessa, *wilid bītim*, 302:1.
Šār-Ištar, see *Ṭāb-šār-Ištar*.
Šarru(*m*)*-bāni*, s. of *Bi-bi-x*, 243:9, seal.
Šarrum-kīma-ili, 501:4; 503:4; 504:4; 505:4; 506:6; 507:4; 508:4; 510:4; 511:4; 513:7; 528:5; 529:4.
Šar-ru-na-^{d}*Sîn*, f. of *Sanqum*, 156:rev. 8.
Šāt-^{d}*Marduk*, d. of *Šamšatum*, sis. of *Amat-bēltim*, 469:13.
Šāt-^{d}*Nanâ*, 345:6; 347:6; 349:14, 15.
Šāt-^{d}*Sîn*,
1. NIN.DINGIR *ša* ^{d}NIN.GIŠ.ZI.DA, 141:13.
2. 164:6, 17.
Šēlibum,
1. f. of *Warad-Ištar*, 174 seal; 298 seal.
2. 241:3; 489:3; 495:1, 2.
Šēp-erṣetim, 52:13(?).
Šēp-Ištar (*Še-ep-*, GÌR-*),
1. RÁ.GABA, 203:13.
2. 56:56*; 65:6*.
Šēp-^{d}*Sîn* (*Še-ep-*, *Ši-ip-**, GÌR†),
1. s. of ^{d}*Šamaš-muballiṭ*, 182:7.
2. DI.KU$_5$, s. of ^{d}*Šamaš-muballiṭ*, 10:7*, seal; 46:15, seal*.
3. f. of *Aplum*, *Erībam*, *Ilī-gimlanni*, *Ṣillī-*^{d}*Amurru*, 278:4*, 9*.
4. f. of ^{d}*Sîn-uselli*, 185:45; 283:2.
5. UGULA-DAM.GÀR, 417:6; 418:6; 419:5.
6. UGULA-MAR.TU, 46:17.
7. PA.PA, 381:17.
8. 36:7*; 61:18*; 62:7*; 70:12, 15; 76:16*; 78:22*; 106:4; 110:7*; 127:3; 157:30; 158:1; 249:18*; 250:3; 273:11†; 275:3*, 11*; 290:6; 307:18*; 326:9; 357:8*.
Šēp-^{d}*Šamaš*, s. of *Etel-pî-Ea*, 194:rev. 12.
Šērum-ilī, 65:16; 82:4; 101:19; 112:1; 125:2; 151:7.
Šērum-šar-ilī, s. of *Ana-panī-ili*, b. of *Ali-liwwir*, 194:rev. 7.
Ši-bu-ša-[. . .], 26:11.
Ši-du-la?, f. of *Ḫalqilum*, 228:3, 8.
Ši-ir-pa-la, 401:2, 4.
Šimat-Ištar, 18:6.
*Šimat-*SAG.ÍL, d. of *Šū-*^{d}*Damkina*, 376:3.
Šimat-^{d}*Sîn*, 157:26.
Šimat-^{d}*Šala*, 341:4.
Šimtī-Ištar, see *Simtī-Ištar*.
*Ši-mu-*x-[x], f. of *Iddin-Irra*, 63:1, seal.
^{d}*Ši-mu-ut-ṣillī*, s. of *Lipit-Ištar*, 197 seal.
Šū-^{d}*Damkina*,
1. f. of *Iddin-*^{d}*Bunene*, 556:6.
2. f. of *Šimat-*SAG.ÍL, 376:3, 11.
Šū-Ea, s. of ^{d}*Sîn-imguranni*, 334:14.
Šū-^{d}*Gula*, 319:13; 530:5.
Šū-ilišu,
1. s. of *Ya-am-nu-um*, b. of *Aḫu-kīnum*, 61:2, 7, 12, 19, seal; 62:2, 8.
2. f. of *Ilum-ḫabil*, 95:15.
3. b. of *Lipit-Ištar*, 140:2.
4. 26:2; 152:16.

Šū-Ištar, f. of *Muḫaddûm*, 153 seal.
ᵈŠulpae-bāni, *ᵈŠulpaea-bāni**,
1. s. of *Šulpaema-ilī*, 147:11*, seal*.
2. UGULA-ŠU.ḪA.MEŠ, 46:23.
3. 244:11.
ᵈŠulpaema-ilī, f. of *ᵈŠulpaea-bāni*, 147 seal.
ᵈŠulpae-nāṣir, 218:rev. 5.
Šūma-aḫum, 242:10.
Šumi-erṣetim (*Šu-mi-er-ṣe-tim*, *Šu-mi-*KI*),
1. s. of *Ibni-Irra*, 75:19*
2. 497:5.
Šumī-aḫiya,
1. s. of *Ṣillī-ᵈA-ḫu-ú-a*, 61:28.
2. DAM.GÀR, 60:16; 127:7.
3. 32:3, 5; 62:17; 76:7; 322:23; 386:11.
Šumištar (sandhi for *Šum-Ištar*), f. of *Sillī-Ištar*, 134 seal.
Šumma-ilum, 167:14; 493:5(?).
Šumma-lā-ᵈŠamaš-mannu, 92:12.
Šumman-lā-ᵈŠamaš,
1. s. of *Nūr-ᵈŠala*, 74:17, case 5.
2. b. of *Aḫī-a(y)-amši*, *Ilīma-abī*, *ᵈAmurru-muballiṭ*, *Qurrudum*, 102:8.
Šum-mi?-il, 9:4.
Šumum-libši,
1. s. of *Nūr-ᵈKabta*, b. of *Bēltani*, 400:5.
2. f. of *Bēlānum*, 380:14.
Šunuma-ilī,
1. f. of *Lipit-Ištar*, 102:30.
2. 126:8; 217:7; 434:8; 452:5; 541:13.
Šu-nu-uḫ-ᵈŠamaš, 60:3, 8.
Šūpîm, f. of *Ṣillī-ᵈ*PA$_4$.NIGÌN.GAR.RA, 304:2, 3.
Šū-pu-ša-[. . .], 26:11.
Šū-ᵈŠamaš, 531:9.
ᵈŠušinak-ilī, 491:5.
Šu-ta-mi-rum, 203:28.
Ta-ga-ki-im, 266:3.
Takil-ilišu, s. of *ᵈNinazu-gāmil*, 277:23.
Tappâ-wēdim, s. of *Ipquša*, 556:26.
Tappûm, *rabiānum*, 135:12.
Tarībatum,
1. s. of *Aḫu-kīnum*, 350:7, seal; 351:6, seal; 367:6, seal.
2. s. of *Apil-ᵈAmurru*, 558:11.
3. s. of *Aplum*, 227:31.
4. s. of *Erībam-ᵈSîn*, 355:8.
5. s. of *Iddiyatum*, 549:10.
6. d. of *Abum-waqar*, 271:14.
7. SAG.GEMÉ, 185:4, case 5.
8. ŠU.I, 27:5.
9. 8:2; 12:3; 76:4; 77:10, 17; 93:11; 145:8; 215:2, 3; 320:24; 338:5; 340:4; 352:19; 358:9; 362:3; 382:14; 405:4; 434:8; 439:1, 8; 460:2; 477:3; 525:9.
Tarību(m),
1. s. of *Dan-ᵈAdad*, 149:4.
2. s. of *Nūratum*, 186:rev. 7.
3. s. of *Pirḫilišu*, 285:1.
4. s. of *Ṣalīlum*, 302:16; 312:14.
5. s. of *Sāniqu*, 56:7.
6. f. of *Ipqatum*, 514:5.
7. f. of *Imgurum*, 186:rev. 9.
8. f. of *Ubar-ᵈŠamaš*, 186:rev. 15.
9. AGA.UŠ, 290:44.
10. (LÚ)-ŠU.I, 56:54; 112:12; 118:29; 131:3; 173:10.
11. *ša* LUGAL, 56:51; 59:9; 109:10; 118:15; 151:5; 178:2.
12. *nāgirum*, 118:25.
13. NU.KIRI$_6$, 256:11.
14. SIPA, 287:3.
15. 52:3; 90:10; 101:6, 26; 112:16, 23; 150:3; 195:8; 263:4; 401:22; 523:12.
Ti-im-gu, f. of *Ṭāb-qabâša*, h. of *Narubtum*, 307:7.

Ti-in-gi, f. of *A-na-tum*, 497:7.
Tir-zum-na-tu-tu, s. of *Ilum-šagiš*, 515:5.
Tizqaru(m),
1. f. of *Apil-*ᵈ*Ašnan*, 228:17.
2. f. of *Inbištar*, 275:19.
3. f. of *Lamassum*, 141:7.
4. 26:5; 290:43.
Tūlissa, 205:4.
Tūram-ilī, 383:15.
Tutub-[. . .], f. of ᵈ*Šamaš-*x-*mu-*x-[. . .], 257 seal.
Tutub-magir, *Tutummagir**, 88:3; 100:1*; 101:36*; 118:2.

Ṭāb-balāṭum, f. of ᵈ*Adad-šarrum*, 217:13, seal.
Ṭāb-Ištar, f. of ᵈ*Adad-šarrum*, 482:4.
Ṭāb-qabâša, d. of *Ti-im-gu* and *Narubtum*, 307:7.
Ṭāb-ṣillum, 1:7; 448:9.
Ṭāb-šār-ilī,
1. f. of *Ali-ilī*, 559:25.
2. f. of ᵈ*Šamaš-liwwir*, 335:5.
Ṭāb-šār-Ištar, f. of ᵈ*Sîn-erībam*, 457:16.
Ṭāb-wašāb[*šu*], PA.PA, s. of *Lu?-pa-*x-*qí-bi*, 142:11, seal.

Ubar-[. . .], 560:4.
*Ubar-*ᵈ[. . .], 319:12.
*Ubar-*ᵈ*Adad*, 22:16; 405:13.
Ubar-Ea, 381:7.
*Ubar-*ᵈ*Mama*, s. of *Rašub-bītum*, 323:11.
*Ubar-*ᵈ*Nergal*, s. of *Ilum-rabi*, 185:44, case 47.
*Ubar-*ᵈ*Ninazu*,
1. f. of *Ilum-malik*, 161:4, 18.
2. 228:4.
*Ubar-*ᵈ*Ninurta*, 26:28.
*Ubar-*ᵈ*Šamaš*,
1. s. of *Tarībum*, 186:rev. 15.
2. f. of *Ibni-*ᵈ*Sîn*, 355:24.
3. f. of ᵈ*Šamaš-muballiṭ*, 250:2.
4. 280:1; 281:1, 5, 18.
Ubaršunu, 310:rev. 2.
Ubartum, 544:5.
Ubarum,
1. s. of ᵈ*Adad-bāni*, 457:4.
2. s. of *Ipquša* and *Erṣeya*, 363:1, 8, 14.
3. s. of *Muḫaddûm*, b. of *Luštammar*, 42:23, seal.
4. b. of *Awiyatum*, 227:36.
5. UGULA-I_7.DA, 37:3.
6. 364:13; 411:9; 412:9; 413:9; 414:9; 415:9; 416:9; 422:9; 534:11.
Ú-ba-ú, f. of ᵈUTU-DINGIR, 214:5.
Ubaya, f. of *Ḫidūtum*, 141:4.
Ubayatum,
1. s. of *Lipit-Ištar*, 127:4, seal.
2. SIPA, 78:16.
*Ú-da-an-*DINGIR, f. of *Ilī-iqīšam*, 552:24.
UD-*ba-nu-um*, f. of *Ibbi-*ᵈ*Sîn*, 265 seal.
Ú-ḫi-li-a-tum, 13:13.
Ù-ku-la-tum, 173:1.
Ú-li-li, f. of *Warad-Kūbi*, 360:16.
Ul-li-gi, f. of *Ir-ma?-am-mu*, 390:20.
Ú-ma-na-nu, 358:13.
Ummī-waqrat, 410:3.
U-na-ba-tum, 480:2, 3, 11, 12.
ᵈ*Un-*x-*ba-ni*, RÁ.GABA, 231:8.
Unnubtum,
1. m. of *Kurûm*, w. of ᵈ*Šamaš-ummatī*, 307:6.
2. w. of *Ṣillī-*ᵈ*Gula*, 156:6.
3. NIN.DINGIR *ša* ᵈGUŠKIN-ᵈBÀN.DA, 141:15.
Uqâ-ilam, f. of *Aḫum-waqar*, 421 seal.
UR-ᵈBA.BA_6, 98:5.

Uri[ki]*-līšir*,
1. b. of *Kārum-mušallim*, *Ṣillī-Ebabbar*, [d]*Šamaš-idī*, 190:15.
2. 57:3; 212:17; 248:4; 333:4.

Ú-ri-ya,
1. f. of LÚ-*ni-i*, 355:3, 23.
2. f. of *Ibbiya*, 274:20.

UR-[d]NIN.URTA, h. of *Ḫundultum*, 186:5.

UR-[d]ŠUL.PA.È,
1. RÁ.GABA, 192:rev. 3.
2. 206:rev. 4.

Uselli, s. of *I*-[. . .], 214:11.

Ūṣi-nūrum, s. of [d]*Šamšī*-[d]*Enlil*, b. of *Aḫum*, *Apil*-[d]*Kittim*, *Saniq-pî*-[d]*Šamaš*, 185:7, 19, 31, case 8, 20, 22, 35, 42, seal.

[d]UTU-AN.DÙL,
1. s. of *Nūr-ilišu*, 123:2, seal.
2. 240:8; 290:5.

[d]UTU-DINGIR,
1. s. of *Pilaḫ*-[d]*Adad*, 549:4.
2. s. of *Ú-ba-ú*, 214:5.
3. f. of *Apil-ilišu*, 214:4, 7, 8, 17, seal.
4. f. of *Ilī-iqīšam*, 177 seal.
5. f. of *Muḫaddītum*, 141:6.
6. 203:7.

[d]UTU-ḪÉ.GÁL,
1. f. of *Iddin*-[d]*Sîn*, 557:33.
2. 22:7.

[d]UTU-*ma?-dan-nu*, 144:13.

Utul-Mami, 493:2, 3.

[d]UTU-SAG.KAL, IŠIB-[d]EN.KI-ERIDU[ki].GA.KE₄, 57 seal.

Waqar-abūšu, f. of *Aḫum* and [d]*Sîn-uselli*, 277:10; 297:5.

Waqar-aḫum, f. of *Sabītum*, 469:3.

Waqar-awīlum, f. of *Ilšu-abūšu*, 556:21.

Waqartum, d. of [d]*Sîn-ublam*, 3:10, seal.

Wa-ra-a-a, f. of *Māri*-[d]*Amurru*, 312 seal.

Warad-[d]*Amurru*, see ÌR-[d]MAR.TU.

Warad-[d]*Enlil*, see ÌR-[d]EN.LÍL.

Warad-ilišu,
1. f. of *Aplatum*, 217:14, seal.
2. DAM.GÀR, 250:17.
3. 237:10; 548:10.

Warad-Ištar,
1. s. of [d]*Šamaš-abī*, 227:27; 353:28.
2. s. of *Šēlibum*, 174:1, 9, seal; 298:3, 4, seal.
3. AGA.UŠ, 186:rev. 13.
4. 52:4; 56:63; 81:3; 90:3; 101:23; 109:3, 12; 112:7; 118:12; 151:1; 193:3; 273:7; 383:13.

Warad-Kūbi, s. of *Ú-li-li*, 360:16.

Warad-[d]*Marduk*, 548:9.

Warad-[d]*Sîn* (ÌR-[d]SUEN, ÌR.30*),
1. s. of [d]*Sîn-abūšu*, 153 seal.
2. s. of [d]*Sîn-ilum*, 552:20.
3. f. of *Apil-ilišu*, 16 seal.
4. f. of *Ipqu*-[d]*Sîn*, 370 seal; 396 seal.
5. f. of [d]*Sîn-magir*, 153:25*, case 22.
6. f. of [d]*Šamaš-bēl-ilī*, 153:23, case 25.
7. 401:23; 443:12; 469:30*; 541:16; 550:16.

Warad-Šērum,
1. DAM.GÀR, 433:12(?).
2. 132:3.

Warad-šigāri, 147:4.

Warad-[d]*Šurinni* (ÌR-[d]ŠU.NIR, ÌR-[d]*Šu-ri-ni**), 398:5; 440:5*.

Wardiya, 55:3; 82:5; 86:3; 112:2.

Wa-ri-sà-ḫi-su?, 138:13.

Watar-[d]*Šamaš*, 29:5; 32:2, 4; 326:8.

[d]*Wēdum-ilum*, DUB.SAR, 490:14.

WI-*lu-li-ya*, 78:18.

Wussumtum, 19:4; 346:4.

Ya-x-[. . .], s. of *A-ḫi*-[. . .], 321:rev. 1.
Ya-a, 369:6.
Ya-ab-ki-rum, 210:12; 265:12.
Ya-aḫ-su-ub-DINGIR, 203:27.
Ya-am-nu-um, f. of *Aḫu-kīnum* and *Šū-ilišu*, 61:19, seal; 62:8.
Ya-da-aḫ-li-im, 45:4; 49:9.
Ya-da-ḫu-um, 215:5.
Ya-di-a-bu(-um), *Ya-du-a-bu-um**, 503:11; 504:15; 505:16; 508:16; 510:14; 512:10; 516:15*; 519:12; 527:21.
Ya-gu-nu-um, *I-ya-gu-nu-um**, *I-ya-gu-nim*†,
 1. s. of *Arwium*, 542:1†, 2†, seal.
 2. 269:4; 444:6*, 11*; 450:4; 451:3; 523:11.
 3. cf. *Liwwir* (ZALAG)*-ya-ku-nu-um*.
Ya-ḫa-bu-um, 194:rev. 3.
Ya-ḫa-ti-lum, 258:2.
Ya-ḫi-ḫu-um, 11:1, 2.
Yaraḫtum, 416:11.
Ya-si-a-ra-aḫ, 434:2.
Ya-si?-ni, 397:2, 3.
Yûm, 8:4.
Za-a-zum, f. of *Iddin-*ᵈ*Sîn*, 227:23; 557:32.
ᵈ*Zababa-nāṣir*,
 1. DUB.SAR, 486 seal; 513 seal.
 2. 501:10; 504:9; 505:9; 507:10; 508:9; 510:10; 511:10; 528:11; 529:8.
Za-la-gu, 35:12.
Zammukku, f. of *Saniq-qabûšu*, 211 seal.
Zi-a-tum, see *Siyatum*.
Zi-ga-ša-ar, 487:8.
ZI-*ḫa*-AN, 96:4.
Zikir-ilišu,
 1. f. of *Apil-ilišu*, 279 seal.
 2. DUMU-É.DUB.BA, 197:7; 209:8; 241:9; 286:19; 298:13.
 3. 26:6, 15; 202:7; 254:13; 472:3; 481:4.
Zikir-Kūbi, f. of *Rīš-*ᵈ*Šamaš*, 400:14.
Zikrum, 103:12.
*Zimri-*ᵈ*Šamaš*, 370:12; 443:3.
Zi?-mu-[. . .], f. of *Ipiq-Antum*, 75:21.
Zi-zi-e, d. of *Ina-qabî-*ᵈ*Šamaš*, 141:3.
Zu-uz-zu, 251:4.
Zu-za-tum, f. of *Ali-damqum*, 102:23; 194:rev. 8.

DEITIES

ᵈ*Aya* (ᵈ*A-a*)
 1. as witness: 44:15, case 17; 442:17.
 2. in oath formulas: 400:11; 469:28; 536:31; 537:17, case 7.
 3. seal inscriptions: 13; 225.
ᵈ*Adad* (ᵈIM)
 1. as witness: 45:11; 309:7.
 2. as contractant: 451:2, 7.
 3. seals dedicated to: 44; 72; 73; 79; 114; 153; 174; 298; 354; 376.
 4. KASKAL *ša* ᵈIM: 48:1.
ᵈ*Amurru* (ᵈMAR.TU)
 1. seals dedicated to: 11; 37; 73; 111; 210; 211; 217; 236; 238; 265; 350; 351; 367; 373; 417; 421; 490; 522; 536; 551.
ᵈAN.MAR.TU
 1. seal inscription: 158.
 2. seals dedicated to: 16; 61; 153; 161; 168; 192; 197; 220; 238; 243; 260; 261; 307; 312; 321; 322; 323; 385; 436; 444; 521; 536; 552.
ᵈ*Ašratum* (ᵈ*Aš-ra-tum*)
 1. seals dedicated to: 402; 462.
 2. $GUDU_4$: 353:26.

^{d}*Baba* (^{d}*Ba-ba*$_{6}$)
1. MAR.ZA É-^{d}BA.BA$_{6}$: 282:1; 329:2.

^{d}*Dagan* (^{d}*Da-gan*)
1. seals dedicated to: 233; 304.

^{d}*Damgalnunna* (^{d}DAM.GAL.NUN.NA)
1. seal inscription: 288.

^{d}*Dumuzi* (^{d}DUMU.ZI)
1. UD-*um ki-mi-it* ^{d}DUMU.ZI: 427:12.

Ea (*É-a*)
1. as witness: 334:11.

^{d}*Enki* (^{d}EN.KI)
1. in oath formula: 218:rev. 3.
2. seal inscription: 288.
3. seals dedicated to: 17; 23; 119; 169; 352; 419.
4. IŠIB ^{d}EN.KI-ERIDU^{ki}.GA.KE$_{4}$: 57:13, case 11, seal.

^{d}*Enlil* (^{d}EN.LÍL)
1. seal inscription: 124.
2. seals dedicated to: 185; 222; 225; 260.

^{d}*Guškin-banda* (^{d}KÙ.GI-^{d}BÀN.DA)
1. NIN.DINGIR *ša*: 141:16.

^{d}*Ilabrat* (^{d}NIN.ŠUBUR)
1. as witness: 76:2; 362:10.
2. seals dedicated to: 42; 74; 243; 279; 299; 382; 402; 462.
3. (females) *ša* ^{d}NIN.ŠUBUR: 141:3, 8.
4. GALA: 353:23.
5. MAR.ZA NAM.[KISAL.LUḪ] *ša* É: 353:2, 14.
6. NAR-É: 353:24.
7. ŠU.I: 353:25.

^{d}*Inanna*
1. as witness: 231:7.
2. in oath formula: 559:16.
3. GUDÚ$_{4}$: 290:39.
4. KISAL: 212:12.
5. KUŠ$_{x}$ (IŠ) *ša*: 73: case 34.

^{d}*Išar-kidiššu* (^{d}*I-šar-ki-di-šu*)
1. seals dedicated to: 428.

^{d}*Ištaran* (^{d}KA.DI)
1. seal inscription: 384.
2. seals dedicated to: 127; 378.

^{d}*Išum* (^{d}*I-šum*)
1. seals dedicated to: 13; 140; 225; 337.

^{d}*Kalkal* (^{d}KAL.KAL)
1. seal inscriptions: 174; 197.

^{d}LUGAL-[. . .]
1. seal dedicated to: 224.

^{d}LUGAL-GÚ.D[U$_{8}$.A^{ki}]
1. seal dedicated to: 217.

^{d}*Marduk* (^{d}AMAR.UTU)
1. as witness: 39:8; 45:10; 209:7; 223:8; 284:9; 296:12; 435:9; 450:10; 451:9; 452:11; 476:12; 502:15.
2. in oath formulas: 73:20, case 18; 153:15; 156:rev. 2; 214:20; 274:16; 277:19; 278:14; 290:33; 331:15; 353:20; 355:17; 360:14; 390:16; 400:11; 469:28; 491:11; 536:31; 537:17, case 7; 556:18; 559:16.
3. seal inscription: 384.
4. A.ŠÀ: 379:2.
5. measuring vessels:
   a. GIŠ.BA.AN: 417:2.
   b. GIŠ.BÁN: 129:2 passim.
   c. GIŠ.BÁN.EŠ: 70:2, 9 and passim; 419:2.
   d. GIŠ.BA.RÍ.GA: 26:34 and passim.

^{d}*Nabium* (^{d}*Na-bi-um*)
1. seal inscription: 197.

2. seals dedicated to: 102; 135; 376; 394; 415; 416; 428; 486; 513.

^{d}*Nanna* (^{d}ŠEŠ.KI), (^{d}*Na-an-na**)
1. as witness: 231:7*.
2. in oath formulas: 73:20, case 18; 156:rev. 2; 214:20; 218:rev. 3; 277:19; 278:14; 288:13; 290:33; 353:20; 355:17.
3. *qá-qá-ar*: 75:5.

^{d}*Nergal* (^{d}*Nè.iri*$_{11}$*.gal*)
1. seal inscriptions: 124; 158.
2. seals dedicated to: 27; 134; 158; 177; 200; 260; 261; 342; 438; 439; 446; 449; 453; 454.

^{d}*Ninazu* (^{d}NIN.A.ZU)
1. É: 356:3.

^{d}NIN.É.NI.[GA]
1. GUDU$_4$: 297:1.

^{d}*Ningal* (^{d}NIN.GAL)
1. GUDU$_4$: 297:19.

^{d}*Ningizzida* (^{d}NIN.GIŠ.ZI.DA)
1. NIN.DINGIR: 141:12, 14.

^{d}*Ninsianna* (^{d}NIN.SI.AN.NA, ^{d}NIN.SI$_4$.AN.NA*)
1. seals dedicated to: 8; 51; 73; 74; 209; 219*; 236; 257; 286; 300*; 314*; 322; 323; 371; 404; 408; 446.
2. (females) *ša*: 141:2, 10.

^{d}*Ninurta* (^{d}NIN.URTA)
1. GUDU$_4$: 354 seal.

^{d}*Sa-*[. . .]
1. seals dedicated to: 380; 401.

^{d}*Sa-am-su-*[. . .]
1. seal dedicated to: 116.

^{d}*Sîn* (^{d}EN.ZU)
1. as witness: 15:11; 45:9; 155:10; 450:9.
2. as contractant: 39:2; 296:2; 451:2, 7; 525:2, 3, 8; 532:5.
3. in oath formula: 153:15.
4. seals dedicated to: 129; 133; 153; 183; 192; 220; 436.
5. BÁRA: 194:3.
6. É: 69:9; 102:2; 517:3.
7. ÍD: 348:6.
8. UD: 475:6.

^{d}*Šaḫan* (^{d}MUŠ)
1. seal dedicated to: 419.

^{d}*Šamaš* (^{d}UTU)
1. as witness: 1:12; 8:8(?); 39:7; 44:15, case 17; 72:16; 76:1; 93:9; 155:11; 209:7; 223:7; 284:7(?); 296:11; 298:11; 314:9; 334:12; 362:9; 435:8; 451:8; 452:10; 502:14.
2. as contractant: 1:8; 15:4; 30:4; 45:3; 234:3; 235:3; 284:2, 3; 450:2, 3, 8; 472:2, 8.
3. in oath formulas: 46:12; 73:20, case 18; 156:rev. 2; 214:20; 277:19; 278:14; 290:33; 353:20; 355:17; 400:11; 469:28; 491:11; 536:31; 537:17, case 7; 556:18.
4. seal inscriptions: 225; 323.
5. seals dedicated to: 31; 187; 192; 216; 560.
6. É: 290:8, 10, 23, 30; 307:10; 557:14, 15, 28.
7. EZEN: 469:22.
8. GIŠ.BÁN: 44:8, case 10; 135:8; 442:13; 520:2; 526:1.
9. GUDU$_4$: 73:25, case 26, seal; 192:rev. 2.
10. ḪAR.MUŠEN.NA, *ḫuḫāru**, 73:9–10, case 9–10; 325:11*.
11. Ì.DU$_8$: 192:rev. 8.
12. KÁ: 73:8–9, case 8–9; 358:3.
13. KISAL.LUḪ: 73:27, case 30.

14. LUKUR: 44:case 3; 469:32–34; 536:7, 8, 20, 24.
15. *maḫar* ^{d}*Šamaš nikkassam epēšum*: 16:4.
16. NAR.GAL: 227:39.
17. ^{na_4}ŠEN.TAB.BA, *paštum**: 73:9, 10, case 9, 10; 442:1*.
18. SANGA(?): 469:31.
19. SILA.DAGAL.LA: 214:6.
20. ŠÀ.TAM: 46:21; 73:29, case 27.
21. ŠU.I: 73:26, case 28, 29.

^{d}*Šî-labbat* (^{d}*Ši-la-ba-at*)
1. as witness: 309:8.

^{d}*Šulpae* (^{d}ŠUL.PA.È)
1. seals dedicated to: 147, 153.

^{d}ŠU.NI.IR
1. seal dedicated to: 230.

^{d}*Ta-*[. . .]
1. seal dedicated to: 153.

^{d}*Timua* (^{d}TI.[MÚ].A)
1. seal inscription: 12.

^{d}*Wēdum*
1. seal dedicated to: 490.

TITLES AND OCCUPATIONS

Á.GÁL, (*mu'erru*) see under GAL-UKKIN.NA 227:33.

AB.AB.DU$_7$, AB.A.AB.DU*, (*ababdû*) "an administrative temple official," 297:18*; 307:16; 353:8, 12; 430 seal; 552:26.

AD.KID, (*atkuppu*) "a craftsman making objects of reeds," 357:1; 377:rev. 5.

AGA.UŠ, (*redû*) "soldier,"
1. AGA.UŠ, 46:25; 186:rev. 13; 192:rev. 12; 290:44; 301:13; 320:33; 557:38.
2. AGA.UŠ GAL-UKKIN.NA, 325:6.

BUR.GUL, (*purkullu*) "stonecutter," 313:8.

DAM.GÀR, (*tamkāru*) "merchant,"
1. DAM.GÀR, 3:7; 46:18; 60:16; 108:rev. 5; 127:7; 192:rev. 1, 5, 9; 225:17, 20, case 16, 18; 250:17; 258:19; 290:37, 42; 433:12, 14; 514:9; 521:10; 559:24.
2. DAM.GÀR AKŠAK^{ki}, 433:8.
3. DAM.GÀR LARSA^{ki}, 182:8, 274:23–24.
4. UGULA-DAM.GÀR, see under UGULA.

DI.KU$_5$, (*dayyānu*) "judge," 46:15; 73:5,6; 142:12; 192:7; 274:18; 320:6, 14; 358:10.

DUB.SAR, (*ṭupšarru*) "scribe," 48:25; 63:4; 74:case 7; 95:19; 108:rev. 6; 153:19, case 28; 156:rev. 10; 185:47, case 48; 186:rev. 14; 192:rev. 10; 214:30; 228:24; 277:31; 278:22; 289:12; 301:21; 322:32; 324:12; 353:30; 360:18; 377:rev. 6; 425:9; 440:19; 465:13; 486 seal; 490:14; 498:9; 513 seal; 515:13; 537:25; 556:31.

DUMU-É.DUB.BA(.A*), "a member of the scribal school," 55:13; 127:8; 135:11; 197:8; 209:9; 241:10; 286:19; 298:14; 329:5; 412:12; 413:12; 414:12*; 415:12*; 416:12*; 420:12*; 422:12; 457:17*.

DUMU.ŠAGINA (GÌR.NITÁ), 182:9.

EN ^{d}UTU, (*ēnu ša ^{d}Šamaš*) "high-priest of Šamaš," 142:5.

ENGAR, (*ikkaru*) "farm laborer," 64:10; 179:7; 301:18(?); 492:9.

ENKU (ZAG.KU$_6$), (*mākisu*) "tax collector," 211:8.

ENSÍ, (*iššakku*) "a member of a class of privileged farmers," 371:17; 375:13; 411:10; 422:10.

ERÍN.KÁ.É.GAL, see under GAL-UKKIN.NA.

ERÍN.ŠE.GUR$_{10}$.KUD.MEŠ, see under LÚ.ŠE.GUR$_{10}$.KUD.

ERÍN *za-bi-lu*^{meš}, "porter(s)," 414:1; 415:1; 416:1.

GALA, (*kalû*) "lamentation singer,"
1. GALA, 78:21.
2. GALA.MAḪ, 297:22; 325:25.
3. GALA ^{d}NIN.ŠUBUR, 353:23.

GAL(?)-MAR.TU, 426:3 (perhaps to be read UGULA!-MAR.TU).

GAL-UKKIN.NA, (*mu'erru*) "an official in charge of personnel or the collection of agricultural products,"
1. AGA.UŠ GAL-UKKIN.NA, 325:6.
2. GAL-UKKIN.NA, 422:5; 428:3.
3. GAL-UKKIN(.NA*)-ERÍN.KÁ.É.GAL, 411:5; 412:5; 415:5*; 416:5*; 420:5*.

GUDU$_4$, (*pašīšu*) "a priestly official,"
1. GUDU$_4$, 28:18; 69:7; 160:10; 162:13(?); 210:13; 290:34–36.
2. GUDU$_4$ ^{d}*Aš-ra-tum*, 353:26.
3. GUDU$_4$ DUB.LÁ.MAḪ, 297:20, 21.
4. GUDU$_4$ ^{d}INANNA, 290:39.
5. GUDU$_4$ ^{d}NIN.É.NI.[GA], 297:1.
6. GUDU$_4$ ^{d}NIN.GAL, 297:19.
7. GUDU$_4$ ^{d}NIN.URTA, 354 seal.
8. GUDU$_4$ ^{d}UTU, 73:25, case 26; 192:rev. 2.

GUDU$_4$.ABZU, (*gudapsû*) "a priest of high rank," 42:19; 295:11; 557:29, 30.

Ì.DU$_8$, (*atû*) "doorkeeper,"
1. Ì.DU$_8$ (-É EN*) ^{d}UTU, 142:5*; 192: rev. 8.
2. LÚ.Ì.[DU$_8$], 433:16.

IŠIB ^{d}EN.KI(-ERIDU^{ki}.GA.KE$_4$*), "purification priest of Enki (of Eridu)," 57:12, case 11, seal*.

KA.GURU$_7$, (*kagurrû*) "an official in charge of grain stores," 357:3, 15.

KA.KI, (*kakikku*) "an official recording and witnessing transactions concerning real estate and slaves," 227:37.

ka-pa-ru, "shepherd of low rank," 7:18.

ka-ṣi-rum, "a craftsman producing textiles by a special technique," 69:4.

KISAL.LUḪ, (*kisalluḫḫu*) "courtyard sweeper,"
1. KISAL.LUḪ, 383:22.
2. KISAL.LUḪ (*ša**) ^{d}UTU, 73:27, case 30*.

KÙ.DÍM, (*kutimmu*) "silversmith," 253:15; 288:15; 355:26.

KUŠ$_x$ (IŠ) *ša* ^{d}INANNA, (*kizû ša ^{d}Ištar*) "equerry of Ištar," 73: case 34.

ku-za-lu, "shepherd," 328:12.

LÚ *a-ki-a-tim*, LÚ *a-ki-tim**, *ša a-ki-tum*†, *ša a-ki-a-tim*‡, 56:58; 89:3†; 112:5‡; 433:4*.

LÚ.É.SILA$_4$, 357:2, 10; see also LÚ.SILA$_4$.

LUGAL, (*šarru*) "king,"
1. LUGAL, 307:2.
2. *ša* LUGAL, 56:51(?); 59:9; 109:10; 118:15; 151:5; 178:2.
3. ŠU.I-LUGAL, see under ŠU.I.

LÚ *ḫa-mi-mu*, "gatherer(s)," 535:6.

LÚ.Ì.DU$_8$, see under Ì.DU$_8$.

LÚ.KÁ.GAL, (*ša abulli*) "gatekeeper," 48:23, seal.

LÚ.KAS$_4$.E, (*lāsimu*) "courier," 161:16.

LÚ.KURUN.NA, LÚ.KURÚN.NA*, (*sabû*) "innkeeper," 153:case 27*; 227:26.

LUKUR ^{d}UTU, (*nadītu ša ^{d}Šamaš*) "female votary of Šamaš," 44:3; 469:24; 536:7, 8, 20, 24.

LÚ.NIMGIR, see NIMGIR.

LÚ.SILA$_4$, 78:8; see also LÚ.É.SILA$_4$.

LÚ.ŠAḪ.ŠUM.MA, (*ṭābiḫu*) "hog butcher," 10:2.

LÚ.ŠE.GUR$_{10}$.KUD, ERÍN.ŠE.GUR$_{10}$.KUD*, ERÍN.ŠE.GUR$_{10}$.KUD.MEŠ†, ŠE.GUR$_{10}$.KUD‡, (*ēṣidu*) "harvester(s)," 411:1*; 412:1‡; 413:1*; 488:1; 503:1*; 504:1†; 505:1*; 528:1†; 529:1†.

LÚ.TÚG, (*ašlāku*) "fuller," 332:15.

LÚ *za-bi-il ša-ḫa-ar-ri*, ERÍN *za-bi-il ša-ḫa-rum**, ERÍN *za-bi-il ša-ḫar-ri*†, ERÍN *za-bi-il ša-ḫar-ri-im*‡, "carrier(s) of bundle(s) of straw," 488:2–3; 489:1–2; 501:1(?)*; 506:1*; 507:1*; 508:1†; 509:1*; 510:1‡; 511:1*.

MÁ.LAH$_4$, (*malāḫu*) "sailor,"
1. MÁ.LAḪ$_4$.LAH$_4$, 178:1.
2. MÁ.LAḪ$_x$ (DU.DU), 308:4; 383:21(?).
3. *ša* MÁ.LAḪ$_x$ (DU.DU), 112:11.
4. UGULA-MÁ.LAḪ$_x$ (DU), 334:6.

MUḪALDIM (MU), (*nuḫatimmu*) "cook,"
1. MUḪALDIM, 153:3, case 3; 209:3.
2. UGULA-MUḪALDIM, 119:18.

NA.GADA, (*nāqidu*) "shepherd," 25:6; 276:4; 324:7; 551:5.

NAGAR, (*naggāru*) "carpenter," 54:6; 102:6; 338:2; 475:3.

na-gi-rum, see NIMGIR.

NAR, (*nāru*) "singer,"
1. NAR É-^{d}NIN.ŠUBUR, 353:24.
2. NAR.GAL ^{d}UTU, 227:39.

na-ṣi-ri-UM?, "guard," 355:21.

NIMGIR, LÚ.NIMGIR*, *na-gi-rum*†, "herald," 2:5; 118:25†; 247:12*.

NIN.DINGIR, (*ēntu, ugbabtu*) "priestess,"
1. NIN.DINGIR, 105:4, 5; 141:17.
2. NIN.DINGIR *ša* ^{d}GUŠKIN-^{d}BÀN.DA, 141:15.
3. NIN.DINGIR *ša* ^{d}NIN.GIŠ.ZI.DA, 141:14.

NU.BÀNDA, (*laputtû*) "overseer,"
1. NU.BÀNDA, 59:21; 60:17; 181:13; 216:4; 273:14; 307:19; 383:20; 408:1.
2. NU.BÀNDA-UGULA, 290:38.

NU.ÈŠ, (*nêšakku*) "priest," 390:5.

NU.KIRI$_6$, (*nukaribbu*) "gardener", 217:15; 227:36; 256:11; 393:4; 411:2; 412:2; 413:2; 414:2; 415:2; 416:2; 483:6; 486:2; 501:2; 504:2; 506:4; 507:2; 508:2; 509:2; 510:2; 511:2; 528:3; 529:2.

PA.PA (*ša ḫaṭṭātim?*) "captain," 35:6; 142:11; 187:3; 274:19(?); 277:22; 325:28; 381:16, 17; 394:7; 491:3.

ra-bi-a-nu-um, *ra-bi-a-nu**, *ra-bi-a-an*†, *ra-bi-nim*‡, "chief magistrate of a town or tribe,"
1. *rabiānum*, 3:5; 60:2; 102:22; 135:12*; 153:17, case 20; 258:25*; 277:21*; 286:14; 344:10*; 363:19†; 371:18; 375:15*; 390:18; 457:8‡; 496:15, 16.
2. *ra-bi-a-an Kar-^{d}Šamaš^{ki}*, 536:33; 537:20, case 11.
3. *ra-bi-a-an* URU *A-ka-nu^{ki}*, 27:11.

RÁ.GABA, (*rakbu*) "rider," 3:6; 102:28; 111:19; 156:rev. 5; 167:15; 185:43, case 46; 192:rev. 3, 4, 6; 194:8; 203:13;

227:35; 231:9; 274:6; 282:16; 393:1; 449:6.

ra-i-ba-ni, "deputy?," 246:3; 270:3.

SANGA, (*šangû*) "priest,"
  1. SANGA, 98:6.
  2. SANGA(?) ^{d}UTU, 469:31.

SIMUG, (*nappāḫu*) "smith," 98:1, 2; 153:20; 245:9; 295:4; 332:14; 372:5.

SIPA, (*rē'û*) "shepherd,"
  1. SIPA, 78:16; 103:18, 19; 200:7; 203:24; 287:3; 324:6; 353:27; 447:4; 456:8; 483:7; 499:14, 17.
  2. SIPA-UDU(?).ḪI.A, 533:4.
  3. SIPA-U_8.UDU.ḪI.A, 203:23.

SUKKAL, (*sukkallu*) "messenger," 73:30, case 32; 323:9.

ša a-ki-tum, see under LÚ *a-ki-a-tim*.

ŠABRA, (*šabrû*) "prefect of an estate or temple," 27:8(?); 461:4.

$ŠA_x$ (GÁ).DUB.BA, (*šandabakku*) "archivist," 273:9; 486:6; 501:7; 503:7; 504:7; 505:6; 507:7; 508:6; 509:6; 510:7; 511:7; 528:8.

ŠAGINA (GÌR.NITÁ), (*šakkanakku*) "military governor," 281:4.

ša LUGAL, see under LUGAL.

ša MÁ.$LAḪ_x$ (DU.DU), see under MÁ.LAH_4.

ša-ma-le-e, "apprentice to a merchant," 281:4.

ŠANDAN (GAL.NI), (*šandanakku*) "head gardener,"
  1. ŠANDAN, 51:4(?); 70:13; 73:28, case 31; 182:15; 237:4; 273:5; 301:5; 374:6; 384:7; 389:6; 404:3; 405:2, 3; 408:12; 417:7; 418:7; 419:6; 428:6; 431:5; 438:5; 439:3; 446:4; 449:5; 453:6; 454:6; 470:4; 479:5; 481:6; 490:12; 496:8; 522:4.
  2. ŠANDAN $URUK^{ki}$, 378:6.

ša pa-ni, 401:20.

ŠÀ.TAM, (*šatammu*) "accountant,"
  1. ŠÀ.TAM, 26:42; 46:22; 55:11; 65:12; 94:3(?); 332:13.
  2. ŠÀ.TAM-É-^{d}UTU, ŠÀ.TAM *ša* ^{d}UTU*, ŠÀ.TAM ^{d}UTU†, 46:21†; 73:29, case 27*.
  3. ŠÀ.TAM $GURU_7$, 557:31.

ŠITIM, (*itinnu*) "builder," 75:23; 302:18.

ŠU.ḪA, see under UGULA.

ŠU.I, (*gallābu*) "barber,"
  1. LÚ*.ŠU.I, 27:6; 56:54; 112:12*; 118:29*; 131:3*; 173:10; 258:27; 290:41, 45; 433:10*; 466:12.
  2. ŠU.I-LUGAL, 373:1; 500:3; 520:3; 526:3.
  3. ŠU.I ^{d}NIN.ŠUBUR, 353:25.
  4. ŠU.I (*ša**) ^{d}UTU, 73:26, case 28*, 29*.

TIBIRA, (URUDU.NAGAR), (*gurgurru*) "metalworker," 278:18.

UGULA, (*waklu*) "overseer,"
  1. NU.BÀNDA-UGULA, 290:38.
  2. UGULA, 486:3; 501:3; 503:3; 504:3; 505:3; 506:5; 508:3; 510:3; 511:3; 513:5; 528:4; 529:3.
  3. UGULA-DAG.GI_4.A, UGULA-DAG.GI.A*, 214:29*; 227:38.
  4. UGULA.DAM.GÀR, 75:8; 250:7; 290:5; 417:6; 418:6; 419:5.
  5. UGULA-UN(?).IL, 557:34.
  6. UGULA-ÍD.DA, 37:3.
  7. UGULA-MÁ.$LAḪ_x$ (DU), 334:6.
  8. UGULA-MAR.TU, 46:17; 176:4; 325:7; 425:8; 426:3; 444:8.
  9. UGULA-MUḪALDIM (MU), 119:18.

10. UGULA-NAM-5(-KA*), 14:10; 213:5; 236:4*, 13–17; 283:3; 417:5; 418:5; 419:4; 437:21.
11. UGULA-ŠU.ḪA.MEŠ, 46:24.
UM.MI.A, (*ummiānu*) "master (of the school)" or "creditor," 355:27.
ZABAR.DAB, (*zabardabbû*),
1. ZABAR.DAB, 21:1; 35:5; 297:8; 399:5.
2. ZABAR.DAB URI^{ki}, 67:2, 5.

GEOGRAPHICAL NAMES*

TOWNS

Adab	UD.NUN.KI	77:5
A-ḫa-ka	PN LU URU *A-ḫa-ka*	227:28
Ak-[. . .]	PN LÚ *Ak-*[. . .]	555:2
Akanu	PN *ra-bi-a-an* URU *A-ka-nu*^{ki}	27:11
Akšak	DAM.GÀR ÚH.KI	168 seal; 433:8
āl-Abisarê	É *ša* URU^{ki} *A-bi-sa-re-e*	73:1, case 1
āl-Rababa'i	URU *Ra-ba-ba-a-i*^{ki} MEŠ	434:4
	LÚ *Ra-ba-bi-i*^{ki} MEŠ	126:5
āl-Summa'il	*i-na* URU^{ki} *Su-um-ma-ìl*	48:2
ālum ša Idi-Ninurta	URU *ša I-di-*^{d}NIN.URTA^{ki}	163:3
ālum ša malāḫī	URU *ša* MÁ.LAḪ$_4$.LAḪ$_4$	178:1
	URU *ša* MÁ.LAḪ$_x$ (DU.DU)	308:4
ālum ša Saba'a	URU *ša Sa-ba-a-a*	13:2
Bābili	KÁ.DINGIR.RA.KI	21:3; 59:20; 67:9; 77:4; 250:6; 264:7; 388:5; 535:3.
Bāb-ṣērim(?)	URU KÁ.EDIN(?).NA.KI	163:5
Bad-tibira	(URU*) BÀD.TIBIRA.KI	77:7; 275:15*
Barsipa	GIŠ.MÁ-É(?)-Ì.DUB *Bar-si-pa*^{ki}	273:13
	GIŠ.MÁ-Ì.DUB *Bar-zi-pa*^{ki}	383:19
Batrum	A-ŠÀ URU *Ba-*AD*-rum*^{ki}	414:6; 415:6; 416:6; 420:6.
Bikasû	*i-na Bi-ka-si-i*^{ki}	271:8
Bulum	PN LÚ URU *Bu-lum*^{ki}	274:26
Dunnum	PN *Du-un-nu-um*^{ki}	26:9
Eridu	PN IŠIB ^{d}EN.KI-NUN.KI-GA.KE$_4$	57 seal
Ešnunna	URU *Éš-nun-na*^{ki}	325:2
Girsu	ZABAR.DAB *ša* GÍR.SU^{ki} ŠIR+BUR.LA.KI *ù* UNU×ḪA.KI	35:3
Ḫarmatum	URU *Ḫar-ma-tum*	56:50
	URU *Ḫar-ma-tum* (*ša**) URU *Kiš*^{ki}	56:52*, 65
Ḫurra'i	*i-na Ḫu-ur-ra-a-i*	381:4

*Those occurring in date formulas are excluded. See also the index of personal names *sub* Akšak-, DUMU-, Eridu-, Keš-, *Larsûm*, *Liwwir-* and *Uri-*.

Isin	*Ì-si-in*^{ki}, *I-ši-in*^{ki}*	26:33; 122:8*
Iškun-Nergal	URU(^{ki}*) *Iš-ku-un*-^{d}NÈ.IRI$_{11}$.GAL	552:6,25*
Kār-Šamaš	*Kar*-^{d}UTU^{ki}	80:3; 166:5; 536:13, 14; 537:2.
	PN *ra-bi-a-an Kar*-^{d}UTU^{ki}	536:33; 537:20, case
Kisurra	*Ki-sur-ra*^{ki}	77:6
Kiš	*Kiš*^{ki}	476:2
	URU *Ḫar-ma-tum* (*ša**) URU *Kiš*^{ki}	56:52*, 65
	BÀD *Kiš*^{ki}	425:5
Kubatānu	*i-na* URU *Ku-ba-ta-a-nu*	64:11–12
Kunnum	URU *Ku-un-nu-um*^{ki}	55:7
Lagaš	ŠIR+BUR.LA.KI	26:36
	ZABAR.DAB *ša* GÍR. SU^{ki} ŠIR+BUR.LA.KI *ù* UNU×ḪA.KI	35:3
	GÚ-ÍD-ŠIR+BUR.LA.KI	35:4
Larsa	UD.UNU.KI	344:8
	DI.KU$_{5}$ (-MEŠ) UD.UNU.KI	73:5, 6; 192:7; 320:6, 14.
	DAM.GÀR UD.UNU.KI	182:8; 274:24
	kar UD.UNU.KI	8:6
	La-ar-sà	1:10
Luḫaya	BÀD *Lu-ḫa-a-ya*	26:38
Ma-aḫ(?)-*bu*-[. . .]^{ki}		77:2
Malgium	NU.KIRI$_{6}$ SIG$_{4}$(.A*).KI	399:1; 411:2; 414:2; 415:2; 416:2; 420:2; 422:2; 437:8*; 486:2; 509:2.
Medûm	URU *Mi-du-ú*^{ki}	280:3
Nabrarâ	URU *Na-ab-ra-ra-a*	103:20
Nina	ZABAR.DAB *ša* GÍR.SU^{ki} ŠIR+BUR.LA.KI *ù* UNU×HA.KI	35:3
Nippur	URU EN.LÍL.KI	275:16, 18
Puš	BÀD *Pu-uš*^{ki}	469:1, 6
Rabum	*i-na Ra-bi-im*^{ki}	8:3
Sippar	UD.KIB.NUN(.KI*)	56:2, 43*, 64*; 61:5*
	kar UD.KIB.NUN.KI	442:15
Ur	ŠEŠ.UNÚG.KI	48:5, 8, 10; 141:1
	ZABAR.DAB ŠEŠ.UNÚG.KI	67:2, 5
Uruk	ERÍN UNU.KI	503:2
	kar UNU.KI	437:6
	NU.KIRI$_{6}$ UNU.KI	501:2; 504:2; 506:4; 507:2; 508:2; 510:2; 511:2; 513:4; 529:2.

URU.ANŠE.ḪI.A		171:3
URU(?) x-*am*-x[ki]	DUMU.MEŠ URU(?) x-*am*-x[ki]	203:18
Yabliya	*a-na gi-ir-ri-i Ya-ab-l[i-a]*	546:8
Yaḫrurum	KIRI$_6$(.MEŠ) *Ya-(aḫ*)-ru-rum* KI.TA	273:4*; 437:7

COUNTRIES

Elam	PN LÚ NIM.MA	380:18
Emutbalum	PN LÚ *E-mu-ut-ba-lum*	433:5, 7
Mutiabalum	*Mu-ti-* ⸢*a*⸣ *-ba-lu-um*	52:9
Šubarûm	GEME.MÍ SU.BIR$_4$.KI	552:2
	SAG.GEMÉ PN *Šu-ba-ri-tum*	76:13
Turukkū	ERÍN(.MEŠ LÚ*) *Tu-ru-kum*	51:7; 55:8*

CANALS AND RIVERS

ÍD *Amatim*	ÍD *A-ma-tim*	411:6; 412:6; 413:6; 422:6; 486:7; 501:8; 507:8; 508:7; 509:7; 511:8
ÍD [d]EN.LÍL-x-x-x		492:2
ÍD *Idiglat*		469:4
ÍD *Ka*-x-[. . .]	A.ŠÀ GÚ . . .	360:1
ÍD *Ki(?)-sí(?)-ir(?)-tim*	A.ŠÀ GÚ . . .	397:1
ÍD *Kudurmabuk*	ÍD *Ku-du-ur-ma-bu-uk*	238:2
ÍD *Lagaš*	ÍD ŠIR+BUR.LA.KI	35:4
ÍD *Me-Enlilla*	ÍD *me-*[d]*En-líl-lá*	383:8
ÍD *Naqab-nuḫši*	ÍD *Na-qá-ab-nu-⟨uḫ⟩-ši*	434:6
ÍD *Purattum*	[ÍD] UD.KIB.NUN.KI	469:5
ÍD *Suen*	*i-na* KIRI$_6$. . .	348:6
ÍD *Ūbil-nuḫša*	ÍD *Ú-bi-il-nu-uḫ-ša*	298:2; 440:1; 516:2
ÍD *Uri*[ki]	ÍD ŠEŠ.UNÚG.KI	352:12

SEAL INSCRIPTIONS

OWNER OF SEAL	FATHER OF OWNER	DEDICATED TO	SEAL NO.
A-[. . .]	Li-pí-it-[. . .]	^{d}Sa-am-su-[. . .]	116
A-ak-ka-lu-um	A-da-ya-tum	^{d}IŠKUR	153
[A-ap]-pa-a	[Ḫa]-bil-ki-nu	[. . .]	245
A-ḫa-am-[nu-ta]	Ì-lí-i-ri-[ba-am]	^{d}MAR.TU	373
[A]-ḫu-šu-[nu]	Sí-ya-tum	^{d}NIN.SI.AN.[NA]	404
A-ḫu?-[ṭà]-bu-um	[. . .mu]-ša-lim	[. . .]	390
A-ḫu-[um]	A-a-ma-[dar]	[. . .]	360
A-ḫu-um-wa-[qar]	^{d}IŠKUR-ri-[. . .]	^{d}[. . .]	153
A-ḫu-um-wa-qar	Ra-bu-ut-^{d}SUEN	^{d}[. . .]	544, 553
A-ḫu-um-wa-qar	Ú-qá-a-DINGIR	^{d}MAR.TU	421
A-ḫu-wa-qar	Sa-am-su	^{d}[. . .]	308
A-lí-li-wi-ir	A-na-[pa-ni-DINGIR]	^{d}Na-bi-um	102
A-li-lu-mur	DINGIR-da-mi-iq	^{d}[. . .]	492
A-lí-lu-mu-ur	Ku-ru-ú	^{d}I-šum	13, 140
A-lí-wa-aq-ru-um	[A-da-an]-^{d}SUEN	[. . .]	95
Ap-[. . .]	^{d}SUEN.URU$_4$	^{d}AN.MAR.TU	323
A-pil-ì-lí-šu	A-ḫu-ya-tum	^{d}NÈ.IRI$_{11}$.GAL ù ^{d}AN.MAR.TU	260, 261
A-pil-ì-lí-šu	ÌR-^{d}SUEN	^{d}AN.MAR.TU	16
A-pil-ì-lí-šu	Nu-rù-um-li-ṣi	^{d}NIN.SI.AN.NA	8
A-pil-ì-lí-šu	^{d}UTU-DINGIR	[. . .]	214
A-pil-ì-lí-šu	Zi-ki-ir-ì-lí-šu	^{d}NIN.ŠUBUR	279
A-pil-^{d}MAR.TU	A-bu-um-Eš$_4$-dar	^{d}AN.MAR.TU	552
A-pil-^{d}MAR.TU	Sa-mu-[um]	^{d}MAR.[TU]	37
A-pil-^{d}MAR.TU	^{d}SUEN-im-gur-an-[ni]	^{d}MAR.TU	522
Ap-la-[tum]	ÌR-ì-[lí-šu]	^{d}MAR.[TU]	217
Ap-la-[tum]	Lu-uš-ta-mar	^{d}Na-[bi-um]	135
Ap-[lu-ša]	Is-sú-ka-[bi-it]	^{d}ŠUL.PA.È	153
Ap-lu-um	I-din-^{d}SUEN	^{d}[. . .]	14
At-ta-ku?-zu?	Ip-qú-^{d}IŠKUR	^{d}IŠKUR	72
A-[wi-ya]-tum	Na-[bi]-ì-lí-šu	^{d}IŠKUR	73
A-wi-il-Eš$_4$-dar	A-bi-ya-tum	^{d}NÈ.IRI$_{11}$.GAL	438, 439, 446, 449, 453, 454
A-wi-il-[^{d}IŠKUR]	Gu-ur-ru-[x]	^{d}NÈ.IRI$_{11}$.GAL	27
[A]-wi-il-[^{d}IŠKUR]	ÌR-[. . .]	^{d}[. . .]	5
[A]-wi-li-ya	A-ya-ḫu-[nu]	^{d}AN.MAR.[TU]	220
Ba-li-lum	^{d}SUEN-ma-[gir]	^{d}AN.MAR.TU	153
Be-li-mu-di	^{d}UTU-ša-du-šu	^{d}MAR.TU	111

OWNER OF SEAL	FATHER OF OWNER	DEDICATED TO	SEAL NO.
^{d}*Da-gan-ba-ni*	^{d}SUEN-*a-bu-šu*	^{d}*Da-gan*	304
Dam-qí-ì-lí-šu	*La-a-lum*	^{d}X-X	306, 555
DINGIR-*ma*-DINGIR	*I-ku-un-pi*$_{4}$-^{d}SUEN GUDÚ$_{4}$-^{d}NIN.URTA	^{d}IŠKUR	354
DINGIR-[*na*]-*ṣi-ir*	*Nu-úr*-^{d}*Kab-ta*	[^{d}NIN].SI.AN.NA	236
DINGIR-*na-ṣi-ir*-X	^{d}SUEN-*ba-ni*	^{d}*Nin*.[. . .]	299
DINGIR-*šu-ba*-[. . .]	[. . .]	[. . .]	317
DINGIR-*šu-i-bi-šu*	*Nu-úr-ì-lí-šu*	^{d}[. . .]	236
DINGIR-*šu-ib-ni*-[*šu*]	DUMU-*er-ṣe*-[*tim*]	^{d}[. . .]	536
DINGIR-*šu-ib-ni-šu*	*Nu-úr*-^{d}UTU	^{d}X-X-X	322
DUMU-KÁ.DINGIR.RA^{ki}	DINGIR-*da-di-ya*	^{d}KA.DI	378
[DUMU]-^{d}MAR.TU	*Ip-qú*-^{d}IŠKUR	^{d}AN.MAR.TU	312
[*É-a*]-*ga-mil*	[*Ma*]-*an-ni-ya*	[. . .]	530
^{d}*É-a-i-din*-[*nam*]	*A-na*-^{d}UTU-*ta-ki-il*	[X]-*nu*-^{d}[. . .]	533
É-a-šar-ì-lí	[. . .]	[. . .]	530
É-a-tu-[*ra-am*]	^{d}UTU-*na-ṣi*-[*ir*]	^{d}EN.[. . .]*ú*^{d}[. . .]	57
E-gi-bu-ni	^{d}SUEN-[. . .]	^{d}MAR.[TU]	11
^{d}EN.KI-AN.DÙL-*lí*	^{d}EN.KI-*ga-mil*	^{d}EN.KI	169
^{d}EN.KI-*ib-ni-šu*	^{d}SUEN-*ra-bi*	^{d}EN.KI	119
^{d}*En-líl-is*-[*sú*]	*Ma-an-nu-um-ki-ma*-^{d}SUEN	^{d}EN.LÍL	185, 225
[*E*]-*pe-eš*-DINGIR	*Ṣi-lí*-^{d}SUEN	^{d}AN.MAR.TU	161
É-ra-[*bi*]	^{d}BARÁ.UL.E.GAR.RA.[. . .]	*Sa-am-su-i-lu*-[*na*]	46
E-ri-ib-^{d}SUEN	*A-bi-sú-u*[*m*]	^{d}SUEN	220
[*E*]-*ri-ša-am*	*A-mur-i-lu-ut-sà*	^{d}[. . .]	157
Gi-mi-il-lum	[. . .]	[. . .]	530
Gi-mil-ì-lí	*Nu-ru-um*	^{d}NIN.SI.AN.NA	74
Gi-mi-lum	*I-din*-^{d}EN.KI	[. . .]	177, 530
Ḫa-bil-[*a-aḫ*]	*I-na-ša-me*-[*wu-súm*]	^{d}[. . .]	519
Ḫu-za-[*lum*]	*Ba-la-sú-ra*-[*bi*]	^{d}IŠKUR Ù ^{d}*Na-bi-um*	376
I-X-[. . .]-X	^{d}SUEN-*ri-me-ni*	^{d}AN.MAR.TU	238
I-bi-^{d}*En-líl*	^{d}SUEN-*be-el-ì-lí*	^{d}NIN.SI.AN.[NA]	322
I-bi-^{d}NIN.ŠUBUR	*A-ḫa-am-nir-ši*	^{d}NIN.ŠUBUR	402, 462
I-bi-[^{d}UTU]	^{d}UTU-*mu-ba-li*-[*iṭ*]	*Ḫa-am-mu*-[*ra-pí*]	142
I-bi-^{d}SUEN	UD-*ba-nu-um*	^{d}MAR.[TU]	210, 265
Ib-ni-[*Ìr-ra*]	*E-tel*-[*pi*$_{4}$-*šu*]	^{d}LUGAL-[. . .]	224
[*Ib-ni*-^{d}MAR.TU]	^{d}UTU-*ra-bi*	^{d}EN.[. . .]*ù* ^{d}AN.MAR.TU	536

OWNER OF SEAL	FATHER OF OWNER	DEDICATED TO	SEAL NO.
I-din-Eš$_4$*-dar*	*A-da-a*	^{d}IŠKUR	114
I-din-^{d}*Ìr-ra*	*Ši-mu-*[. . .]	[. . .]	63
I-din-^{d}IŠKUR	*A-da-ya-tum*	[. . .]	309
I-din-^{d}MAR.TU	DINGIR-*mu-*[. . .]	^{d}MAR.TU	236
I-din-^{d}MAR.TU	^{d}SUEN-*a-ḫa-am-* [*i-din-nam*]	[. . .]	457
I-din-^{d}*Na-na-a*	*Ì-lí-i-din-nam*	[^{d}NIN.SI].AN.NA	323
I-din-^{d}SUEN	*A-bu-um-wa-qar*	*Sa-am-su-i-lu-na*	29, 343
Ì-lí-a-wi-[*li*]	*Ḫa-an-na-mi-*x-AN	^{d}NIN.ŠUBUR	382
Ì-lí-i-din-[*nam*]	*Na-*WI*-ra-am-*[*ša*]*-ru-*[*ur*]	^{d}*Na-bi-um*	135
Ì-lí-ip-pa-[*al-sà-am*]	*Ga-ma-al-ì-lí*	^{d}AN.MAR.TU	307
Ì-lí-ip-pa-al-sà-am	[. . .]-^{d}UTU	[. . .]	146
Ì-lí-i-qí-ša-am	^{d}*I-šum-*[*a-tum*]	^{d}*I-šum*	225
Ì-lí-i-qí-ša-am	^{d}UTU-DINGIR	^{d}[. . .]	177
Ì-lí-[*ma-a-bi*]	^{d}MUŠ-*še-mi*	^{d}EN.KI *ù* ^{d}MUŠ	419
Im-gur-^{d}UTU	DINGIR-*pi*$_4$*-ša*	[. . .]	48
Im-gur-^{d}UTU	*Gi-*[*mil*]-DINGIR	[. . .]	161
In-[*bu-ša*]	ÌR-^{d}MAR.TU	^{d}AN.MAR.TU	321
Ip-qú-^{d}SUEN	ÌR-^{d}SUEN	^{d}[. . .]	370, 396
ÌR.^{d}[. . .]	*I-*[x]*-wa-*[. . .]	^{d}EN.[x] *u* ^{d}AN.MAR.TU	153
ÌR-^{d}INANNA	*Še-li-bu-um*	^{d}IŠKUR	174, 298
I-[*ri-ri*]	^{d}SUEN-*ri-me-ni*	^{d}AN.MAR.TU	238
ÌR-^{d}SUEN	^{d}SUEN-*a-bu-*[*šu*]	[. . .]	153
^{d}IŠKUR-*na-ṣi-*[*ir*]	^{d}UTU-*a-bi-šu*	^{d}IŠKUR	44
^{d}IŠKUR-*šar-*[*rum*]	*Ša-lim-*GI	^{d}*We-du-*[*um*]	490
^{d}IŠKUR-*šar-rum*	*Ṭà-ab-ba-la-*[*ṭu*(*m*)]	^{d}LUGAL-GÚ.D[U$_8$.A]^{ki}	217
Iš-me-a-ni	^{d}UTU-ILLAT-*ti*	^{d}UTU	187
^{d}*I-šum-ú-a-*[*tum*]	*A-a*	^{d}NÈ.IRI$_{11}$.GAL	177
⌜*Ka*⌝*-bi-ya*	[. . .]	^{d}*Da-gan*	233
KAL.LA.MU	[. . .]	[. . .]	243
Ka-sà-ap-^{d}SUEN	^{d}SUEN-*li-ta-*x	^{d}NIN.SI.AN.NA	73
*Ki-*x-[. . .]	*A-di-ya-*[. . .]	^{d}[. . .]	176
Ku-[. . .]	*I-bi-*^{d}*Na-*[*bi-um*]	^{d}NIN.SI$_4$.[AN.NA]	219
Ku-ku-um	^{d}SUEN-*nu-úr-ka?*	[. . .]	177
La-qí-pu-um	*A-píl-*^{d}IŠKUR	^{d}IŠKUR	79
Li-pí-it-^{d}*En-líl*	MU.ḪÉ.GÁL	^{d}EN.LÍL	222
Li-pí-it-Eš$_4$*-*[*dar*]	^{d}MAR.TU-*še-mi*	^{d}AN.MAR.TU	385
LÚ-^{d}DUMU.ZI.DA	[. . .]	[. . .]	297
^{d}*Marduk-*[*da*]*-ya-an*	^{d}*Na-bi-um-ti-la-ti*	^{d}EN.[x]	104

OWNER OF SEAL	FATHER OF OWNER	DEDICATED TO	SEAL NO.
^{d}*Marduk-mu-ša-lim*	*Im-gur-*^{d}UTU	^{d}*I-šar-ki-di-šu ù* ^{d}*Na-bi-um*	428
^{d}*Marduk-na-ṣi-[ir]* AB.AB.DU$_{7}$	*Ì-lí-[. . .]*	*Sa-am-su-[i-lu-na]*	430
^{d}*Marduk-pa-li-ni*	^{d}SUEN-*še-me-e*	^{d}SUEN *ù* ^{d}AN.MAR.TU	436
^{d}*Marduk-zu-uq-qí-ip*	*A-ḫu-um-wa-qar*	^{d}*Sa-[am-su-i-lu-na]*	380, 401
Ma-ri-^{d}MAR.TU	*Wa-ra-a-a*	[. . .]	312
Mu-ḫa-du-um	*Šu-Eš*$_{4}$*-dar*	^{d}*Marduk-na-ṣi-ir*	153
MU.ZU.ŠÈ	AN-*pi*$_{4}$-*Eš*$_{4}$-*dar*	^{d}NIN.ŠUBUR	74
[*Na*]*-am-ra-ša-*[*ru-ur*]	*Nu-úr-*^{d}[. . .]	^{d}NIN.SI$_{4}$.AN.NA	314
^{d}*Na-bi-um-ma-lik*	*A-ta-li-im*	[. . .]	544
NÌ.GI.NA-ḪÉ.DU	^{d}NANNA-MA.AN.SUM	[. . .].KI	148
Ni-in-ki-ya	^{d}SUEN-*ma-gir*	[. . .]	530
Ni-[in-nu]-ú	[. . .]	[. . .]	222
NUN.KI-*li-wi-ir*		^{d}EN.KI	352
Nu-[úr]-^{d}*Kab-ta*	[. . .]	[. . .]	218
Nu-úr-^{d}*Kab-ta*	MES.^{d}EN.[. . .]	^{d}NIN.SI.AN.[NA]	286
Nu-úr-šu-e-li	*A-ḫi-ya-ma*	^{d}NIN.[. . .]	379
Pí-ir-ḫu-um	*La-ar-su-um*	^{d}SUEN	183
Pir-ḫu-[um]	DUMU-[*Eš*$_{4}$*-dar*]	^{d}AN.[MAR.TU]	536
Qi-iš-tum	*A-mur-i-lu-sà*	^{d}[. . .]	176
[*Ri-iš-*^{d}UTU]	^{d}SUEN-^{tu}*tukul-ti*	^{d}NIN.[. . .] *ù* ^{d}*Ta-*[. . .]	153
Sà-mu-[um]	*A-ḫu-wa-qar*	^{d}NÈ.IRI$_{11}$.GAL	200
Sà-ni-iq-pi$_{4}$-^{d}UTU	*Im-ta-ga-ar-*^{d}UTU	[. . .]	352
Sà-ni-iq-pi$_{4}$-^{d}UTU	^{d}UTU-^{d}EN.LÍL.LÁ	^{d}NIN.[. . .]	185
Sa-ni-iq-[qá-bu-ša]	*Sà-an-qú-[um]*	^{d}MAR-TU	211
SIG-^{d}*A-a*	^{d}UTU-TAB.BA-*šu*	É-UD-*ra*	536
SIG-*ì-lí-[šu]*	*Ì-lí-i-bi-[šu]*	^{d}*Na-[bi-um]*	394
Si-im-ti-^{d}NANNA	DINGIR-*lam*-URU$_{4}$	^{d}EN.KI	17, 23
^{d}SUEN-*a-ḫi-i-din-nam*	*A-bu-wa-qar*	^{d}NÈ.IRI$_{11}$.GAL	342
^{d}SUEN-*a-ḫu-[. . .]*	*Ni-di-in-[. . .]*	^{d}[. . .]	71
^{d}SUEN-*i-dí-nam*	*Ì-lí-e-ta-di-a-[ni]*	^{d}AN.MAR.[TU]	192
^{d}SUEN-[. . .]-*lim*	*Ì-lí-tu-ra-am*	^{d}UTU	560
^{d}SUEN-*ma*-DINGIR	ÚḪ^{ki}-*i-dí-nam*	^{d}AN.MAR.TU	168
^{d}SUEN.MAŠ.MAŠ	^{d}SUEN.URU$_{4}$	^{d}*I-šum*	337
^{d}SUEN-*mu-pa-ḫi-ir*	^{d}SUEN-*mu-ša-lim*	^{d}AN.MAR.TU	521
^{d}SUEN-*mu-uš-ta-[al]*	^{d}SUEN-*ma-gir*	*Sa-am-su-i-lu-na*	113, 167
^{d}SUEN-*na-ap-še-ra*		^{d}NIN.SI$_{4}$.AN.NA	300

OWNER OF SEAL	FATHER OF OWNER	DEDICATED TO	SEAL NO.
[^{d}SUEN-na-ṣi-ir]	[. . .]-a-a LÚ.KÁ.GAL		48
^{d}SUEN-na-tum	Sà-ni-iq-pi$_{4}$-^{d}UTU	^{d}MAR.TU	490
^{d}SUEN-pí-la-aḫ	Iš-me-ya	^{d}SUEN	129, 133
^{d}SUEN-ša-mu-[uḫ]	Ku-zu-[. . .]	^{d}[. . .]	63
^{d}SUEN-ša-mu-uḫ	Sí-ya-tum	^{d}NIN.SI.AN.NA	51, 371
^{d}SUEN-še-me-i	^{d}NANNA-MA.AN.SUM	^{d}MAR.TU	417
Ṣi-lí-^{d}[. . .]	[. . .]-^{d}NIN.[. . .]	[. . .]	25
Ṣíl-lí-^{d}Dam-[ki-na]	DUMU-er-ṣe-[tim]	^{d}NIN.SI.[AN.NA]	408
Ṣíl-lí-^{d}INANNA	Šu-mi-Eš$_{4}$-dar	^{d}NÈ.IRI$_{11}$.GAL	134
Ṣíl-lí-^{d}MAR.TU	A-pil-ša	^{d}AN.MAR.TU	444
Šar-ru-um-ba-[ni]	Bi-bi-x	^{d}AN.MAR.TU	243
Ši-ip-^{d}SUEN	^{d}UTU-mu-ba-[li-iṭ]	Ḫa-am-mu-[ra-pí]	10, 46
^{d}Ši-mu-ut-ṣíl-lí	Li-pí-it-Eš$_{4}$-dar	^{d}AN.MAR.TU	197
Šu-ì-lí-šu	Ya-am-nu-um	^{d}AN.MAR.TU	61
^{d}ŠUL.PA.È-ba-[ni]	^{d}ŠUL.PA.È-ma-DINGIR	^{d}ŠUL.PA.[È]	147
Ta-ri-ba-tum	A-ḫu-ki-nu-um	^{d}MAR.TU	350, 351, 367
Ṭà-ab-wa-ša-ab-[šu]	Lu?-x-pa-x-qí-bi	Sa-am-su-i-lu-[na]	142
Ú-ba-ya-tum	Li-pí-it-^{d}INANNA	^{d}KA.[. . .]	127
[U-ba]-ru-[um]	[Mu]-ḫa-du-um	^{d}GU$_{4}$?.TAB?.BA?.ḪÉ. UM	42
Ur-^{d}[. . .]	[. . .]-šu	É-UD.UD-ra	536
U-ṣi-nu-ru-um	^{d}UTU-^{d}EN.LÍL.LÁ	^{d}NIN.[. . .]	185
^{d}UTU-x-[. . .]	[. . .]	[. . .]	146
^{d}UTU-AN.DÙL	Nu-úr-ì-lí-šu	Sa-am-[su-i-lu-na]	123
^{d}UTU-be-el-ì-lí	A-ap-pa-a	^{d}UTU	216
^{d}UTU-da-ya-an	^{d}UTU-[. . .]	^{d}[. . .]	120
^{d}UTU-i-dí-nam	Ì-lí-ù-^{d}UTU	^{d}Na-bi-um	135, 415, 416
^{d}UTU-x-mu-x-[. . .]	Tu-tu-ub-[. . .]	^{d}NIN.SI.AN.NA	257
^{d}UTU-mu-[ba-li-iṭ]	[. . .]	[. . .]	146
^{d}UTU-mu-ba-li-iṭ	A-ḫu-šu-nu	^{d}EN.LÍL	260
^{d}UTU-na-ṣi-ir	A-pil-[. . .]	Sa-am-[su-i-lu-na]	388
^{d}UTU-na-ṣi-[ir]	Ša-lim-SAG.[ÍL]	Sa-am-su-i-[lu-na]	173
^{d}UTU-še-mi	Ša-ma-a-a-tum	^{d}Nin-[. . .]	328
^{d}UTU-[tu-kul-ti]	^{d}UTU-ma-gir	^{d}MAR.TU	73
^{d}UTU-um-[ma-ti]	^{d}SUEN-[. . .]	^{d}ŠU.NI.IR	230
Wa-qar-ar-tum	Sin-ub-lam	^{d}[. . .]	3

OWNER OF SEAL	FATHER OF OWNER	DEDICATED TO	SEAL NO.
Ya-gu-nu-um	*Ar-wi-ú-um*	[. . .]	542
^{d}*Za-ba$_4$-ba$_4$-na-ṣi-ir* DUB.SAR		^{d}*Na-bi-um*	486, 513
[. . .]	*Nu-úr-*^{d}*Kab-ta*	^{d}SUEN *ù* ^{d}UTU	192
[. . .] GUDU$_4$-^{d}UTU		^{d}NIN.SI.AN.NA	73
[. . .]	[. . .]	^{d}NIN.SI.AN.NA	202
[. . .]	[. . .]	^{d}NIN.SI.AN.NA	209, 446
[. . .^{d}]MAR.TU		^{d}AN.MAR.TU	312
[. . .]	^{d}*En-líl-a-bi*	^{d}NIN.ŠUBUR	243
[. . .]	[. . .]	*Sa-am-su-i-lu-na* LUGAL	461
[. . .]	*Ib-ni-ša*?-[. . .]	^{d}MAR.TU	551

text 12:
^{d}TI.[MÚ].A
DINGIR.ME.KÙ.GA
DINGIR.ME.TI

text 158:
x-^{d}[. . .]
ÌR-^{d}[. . .]
^{d}AN.MAR.TU
^{d}NÈ.[IRI$_{11}$.GAL]

text 174:
^{d}KAL.KAL[. . .]

text 184:
^{d}[. . .]
DUMU AN.[NA]
GIŠ.KUD.UR ŠU.DU$_8$

text 197:
^{d}*Na-bi-[um]*
^{d}KAL.KAL-AŠ-X
^{d}KAL.KAL-AŠ-X
^{d}KAL.KAL-AŠ-X

text 225:
^{d}UTU ^{d}*A-a*

text 288:
^{d}EN.KI
^{d}DAM.GAL.NUN.NA

text 323:
^{d}UTU

text 384:
DUMU *É*-^{d}x-[. . .]
DUMU ^{d}x-[. . .]
[. . .] ^{d}KA.[. . .]
[. . .] ^{d}*Da-[gan]*
[. . .] ^{d}Ka. [. . .]

TEXTS WITH SEAL INSCRIPTIONS

Text	*Text*	*Text*	*Text*
3	133	233	376
5	134	236	378
8	135	238	379
10	140	243	380
11	142	245	382
12	146	257	384
13	147	260	385
14	148	261	388
16	153	265	390
17	157	279	394
23	158	286	396
25	161	288	401
27	167	297	402
29	168	298	404
37	169	299	408
42	173	300	415
44	174	304	416
46	176	306	417
48	177	307	419
51	183	308	421
57	184	309	428
61	185	312	430
63	187	314	436
71	192	317	438
72	197	321	439
73	200	322	444
74	202	323	446
79	209	328	449
95	210	337	453
102	211	342	454
104	214	343	457
111	216	350	461
113	217	351	462
114	218	352	486
116	219	354	490
119	220	360	492
120	222	367	513
123	224	370	519
127	225	371	521
129	230	373	522

Text	*Text*	*Text*	*Text*
530	542	552	555
533	544	553	560
536	551		

CONCORDANCE OF MUSEUM NUMBERS

YBC	*Text*	*YBC*	*Text*	*YBC*	*Text*	*YBC*	*Text*
3315	168	4273	533	4463	127	5367	212
3316	241	4290	494	4464	207	5371	282
3318	535	4291	421	4469	419	5376	354
3321	435	4296	332	4472	76	5388	329
3330	272	4303	317	4479	321	5397	167
3332	174	4304	162	4495	183	5403	483
3345	16	4308	462	4868	291	5410	228
3353	532	4313	224	4871	540	5429	333
3358	200	4319	75	4876	500	5433	252
3361	511	4328	400	4882	84	5435	324
3367	519	4330	331	4884	465	5440	50
3368	264	4331	138	4890	64	5491	144
3376	521	4334	13	4897	166	5502	306
3377	514	4341	231	4907	2	5507	201
3380	30	4345	315	4922	549	5510	343
3388	485	4350	555	4923	520	5523	313
3389	477	4352	261	4931	169	5524	47
3393	392	4356	190	4937	539	5525	226
3396	188	4357	307	4948	80	5531	170
4197	227	4358	31	4952	199	5536	171
4199	281	4359	175	4953	165	5537	178
4205	436	4361	276	4957	8	5542	230
4206	61	4369	417	4959	96	5545	97
4209	186	4373	336	4961	147	5546	202
4214	323	4377	251	4963	94	5548	283
4221	274	4379	260	4967	239	5551	68
4222	537	4380	279	4981	536	5553	196
4226	250	4407	497	5095	43	5555	446
4231	182	4408	418	5103	204	5564	46
4232	70	4410	318	5177	335	5577	325
4239	10	4419	193	5196	262	5652	430
4242	360	4421	128	5208	176	5657	287
4245	322	4423	150	5209	327	5660	524
4246	225	4425	159	5337	98	5775	18
4247	560	4426	149	5338	48	5830	302
4254	280	4427	133	5342	248	5858	503
4255	504	4428	129	5347	293	5860	518
4257	217	4429	151	5349	297	5861	508
4260	1	4430	154	5350	69	5863	444
4263	328	4441	132	5358	141	5865	235
4267	471	4443	131	5359	356	5869	512
4269	286	4444	130	5362	288	5870	383
4272	62	4459	32	5366	243	5875	414

YBC	*Text*	*YBC*	*Text*	*YBC*	*Text*	*YBC*	*Text*
5876	60	5975	266	6069	215	6317	278
5878	453	5979	245	6070	466	6318	125
5880	443	5980	424	6072	382	6319	72
5882	51	5981	506	6073	490	6320	67
5883	548	5982	233	6075	493	6321	339
5884	404	5986	502	6076	301	6322	334
5888	428	5993	172	6077	550	6323	338
5891	143	5994	211	6079	405	6324	349
5892	486	5999	450	6083	300	6327	77
5893	413	6000	374	6088	52	6328	109
5899	513	6001	391	6090	528	6329	164
5900	505	6003	219	6091	470	6333	35
5901	455	6008	296	6092	529	6337	25
5906	396	6011	454	6094	464	6348	447
5907	492	6016	255	6095	409	6353	100
5908	542	6019	427	6099	299	6359	33
5909	480	6022	461	6100	173	6360	4
5910	236	6023	378	6101	411	6373	137
5911	397	6024	126	6104	474	6375	341
5915	516	6025	394	6108	432	6376	249
5916	531	6026	139	6110	420	6377	337
5928	385	6028	399	6112	345	6381	116
5929	398	6035	479	6149	177	6382	547
5933	367	6038	452	6150	55	6383	107
5935	457	6039	220	6173	372	6387	40
5937	350	6040	373	6174	289	6388	229
5938	441	6041	380	6183	39	6390	110
5940	522	6043	134	6184	191	6410	82
5942	403	6044	456	6185	303	6412	295
5943	95	6045	210	6186	361	6419	517
5944	7	6046	439	6193	369	6420	66
5945	298	6047	135	6194	308	6424	181
5946	553	6051	507	6227	45	6431	86
5947	393	6053	459	6232	153	6432	316
5950	440	6054	523	6233	543	6436	37
5952	412	6055	491	6235	376	6437	406
5957	65	6056	496	6236	258	6442	83
5960	473	6057	426	6239	42	6443	85
5965	554	6060	422	6242	161	6444	87
5966	242	6061	375	6248	102	6445	263
5967	384	6062	534	6310	163	6446	89
5969	79	6063	527	6311	434	6447	501
5970	429	6065	433	6312	347	6448	81
5971	449	6066	416	6313	152	6449	20
5973	104	6068	273	6315	122	6450	99

YBC	*Text*	*YBC*	*Text*	*YBC*	*Text*	*YBC*	*Text*
6478	352	7252	56	7930	17	8342	448
6523	189	7275	546	7966	213	8344	198
6531	136	7581	559	7970	49	8347	311
6547	6	7595	557	7972	123	8353	445
6556	59	7599	157	7978	29	8359	408
6572	431	7601	551	7991	257	8368	475
6617	481	7603	214	8029	342	8372	12
6628	346	7605	118	8037	205	8377	379
6640	510	7612	552	8038	340	8378	209
6644	467	7621	363	8043	304	8390	244
6654	344	7639	319	8045	256	8391	451
6656	106	7643	407	8058	197	8398	3
6671	402	7644	526	8062	364	8400	472
6672	368	7645	246	8063	515	8401	54
6683	271	7646	386	8064	223	8410	423
6699	545	7647	389	8068	11	8413	358
6701	22	7654	185	8082	208	8430	330
6709	92	7664	495	8162	488	8447	362
6710	105	7665	487	8164	232	8455	476
6712	90	7666	484	8166	24	8457	377
6714	371	7673	355	8167	265	8459	326
6725	312	7686	370	8178	53	8482	124
6734	247	7688	499	8208	410	8487	234
6738	530	7725	357	8214	489	8493	460
6744	74	7739	142	8223	425	8506	270
6746	113	7740	180	8227	5	8510	146
6757	314	7743	401	8230	121	8515	58
6758	351	7759	119	8232	310	8520	145
6767	195	7760	156	8233	240	8521	91
6787	216	7767	140	8238	284	8524	14
6816	469	7790	275	8257	63	8525	36
6821	192	7791	320	8269	544	8528	114
6964	561	7793	111	8279	478	8532	120
6972	44	7794	28	8281	468	8540	305
6981	442	7816	365	8295	115	8556	21
7055	184	7819	292	8296	254	8569	15
7066	112	7823	88	8298	148	8581	194
7075	101	7830	366	8300	438	8585	390
7079	203	7833	498	8305	387	8607	541
7081	73	7865	9	8318	160	8642	353
7160	285	7890	93	8326	179	8643	556
7204	78	7912	359	8330	187	8644	222
7219	26	7918	509	8332	41	8664	348
7220	218	7927	267	8336	395	8672	238
7225	437	7928	23	8340	38	8673	259

YBC	*Text*	*YBC*	*Text*	*YBC*	*Text*	*YBC*	*Text*
8676	268	8698	221	8743	415	9095	57
8679	108	8708	71	8767	206	9096	117
8681	237	8718	463	8773	253	9097	34
8682	458	8720	158	8777	290	9098	19
8692	525	8726	388	9092	277	9099	103
8694	269	8733	294	9093	27	9100	381
8695	538	8739	482	9094	155	9101	309
8696	558						

1

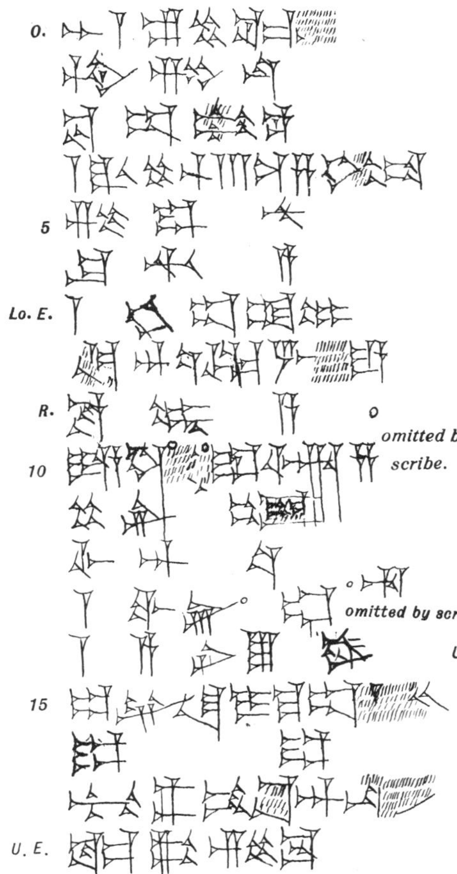

Indistinct seal impressions.

2

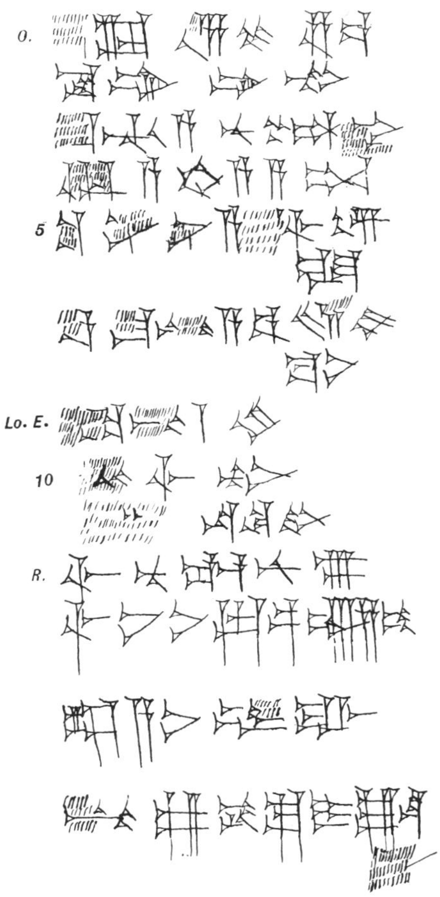

Indistinct seal impressions.

3

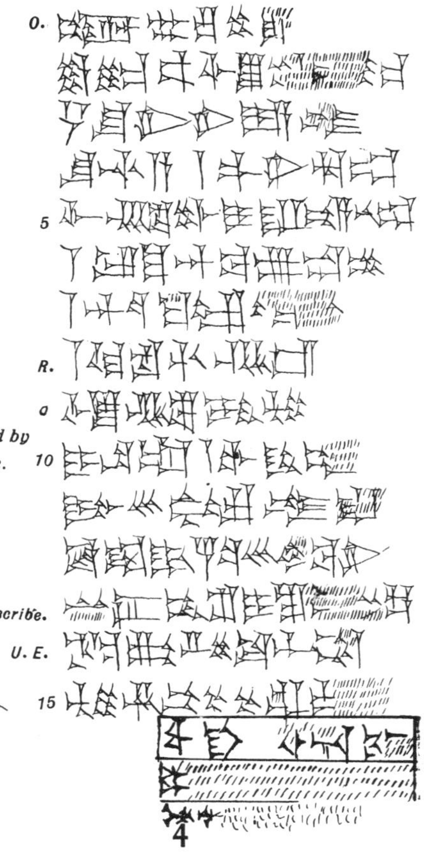

4

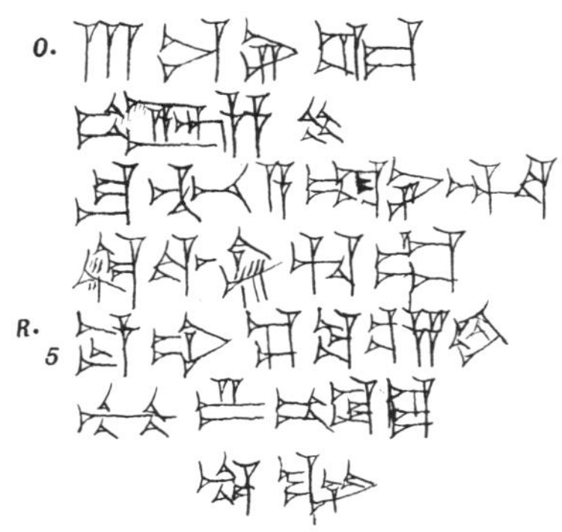

5

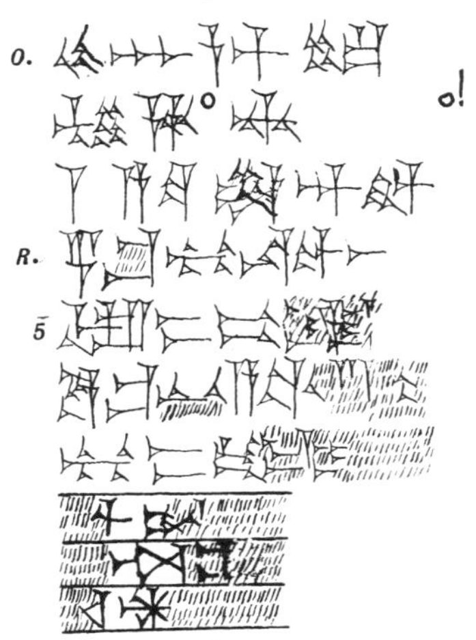

6

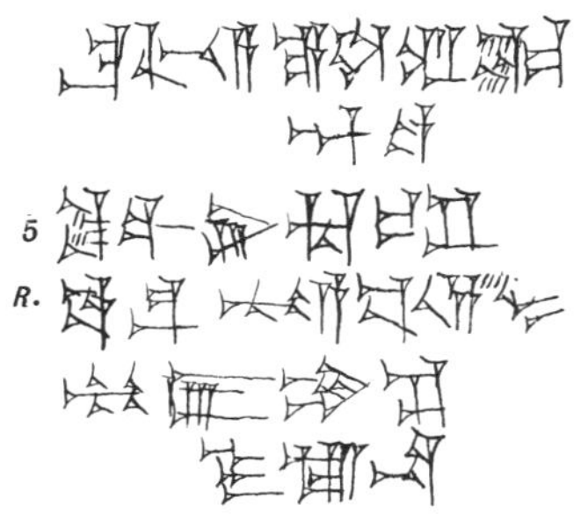

Indistinct seal impressions.

7

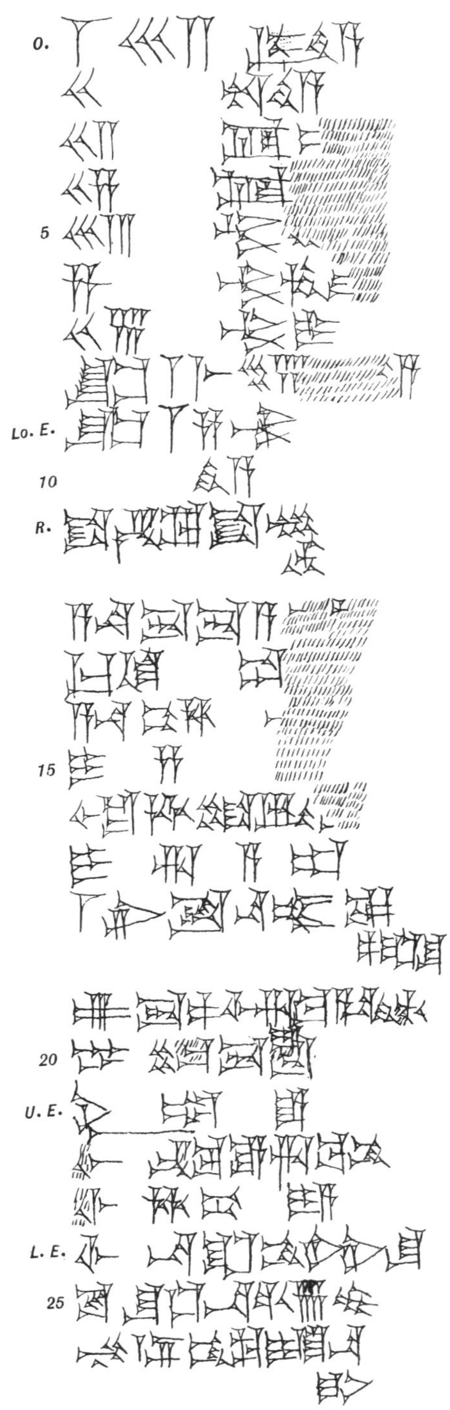

Indistinct seal impressions.

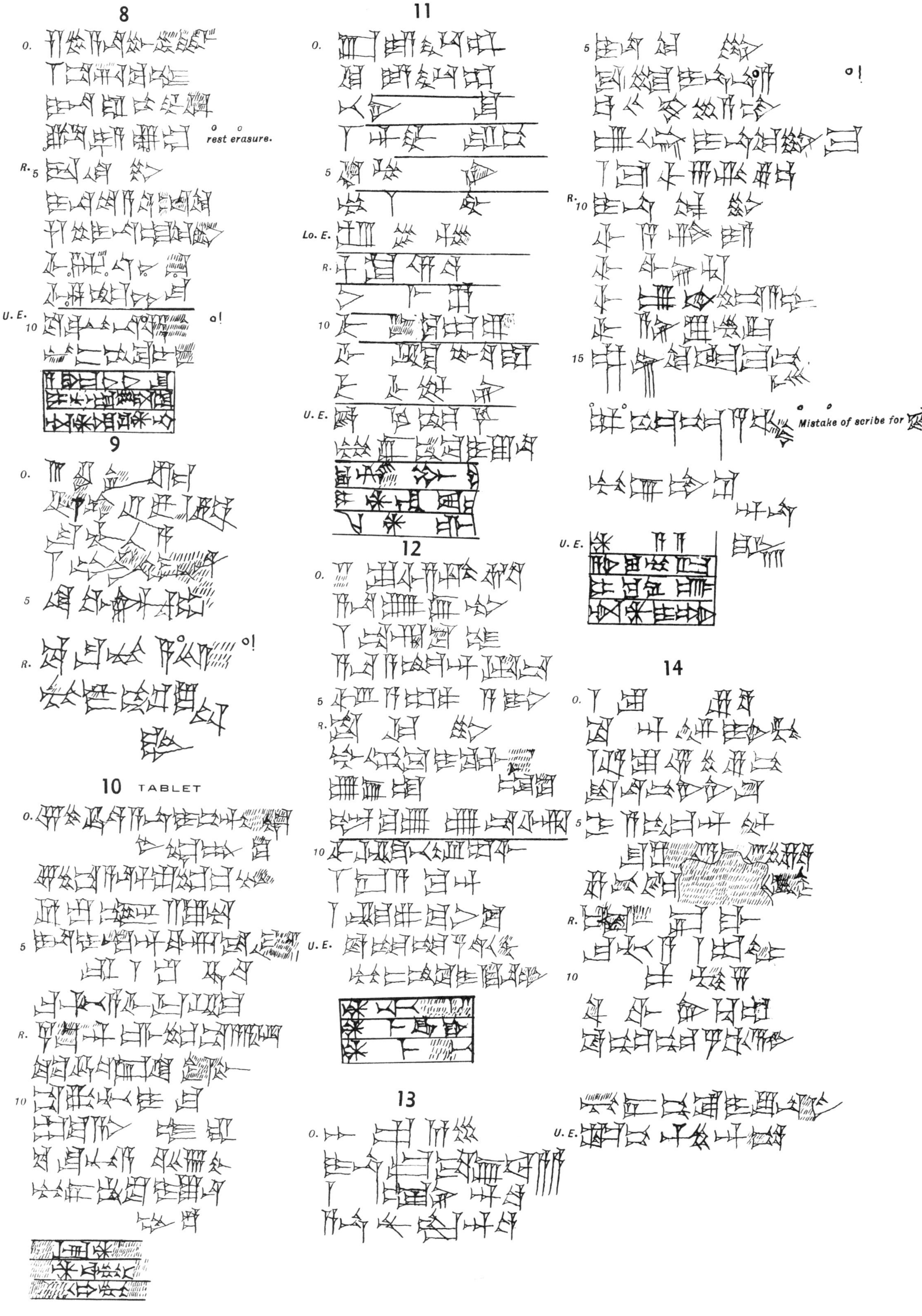
8
O.
rest erasure.
R. 5
U. E. 10
9
O.
5
R.
10 TABLET
O.
5
R.
10
11
O.
5
Lo. E.
R.
10
U. E.
12
O.
5
R.
10
U. E.
13
O.
5
R. 10
15
Mistake of scribe for
U. E.
14
O.
5
R.
10
U. E.

15

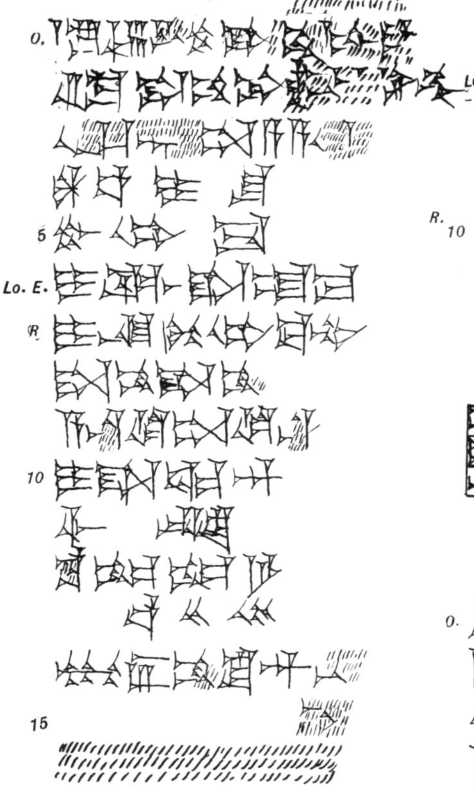

16

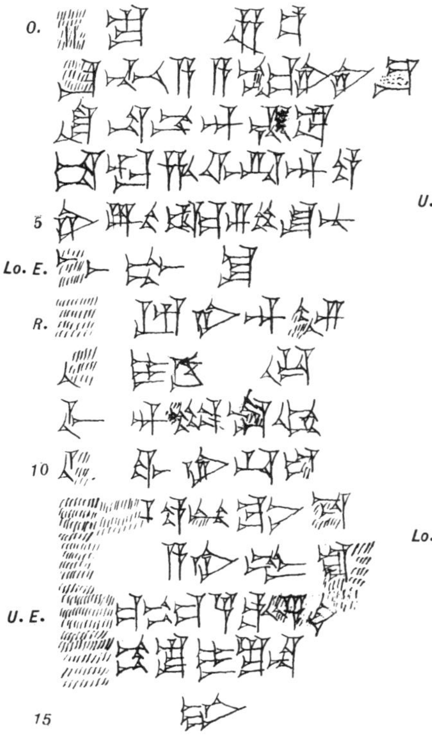

Indistinct seal impressions.

17 CASE

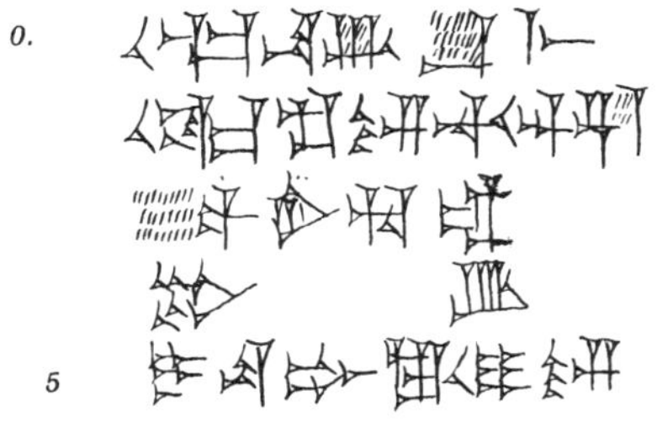

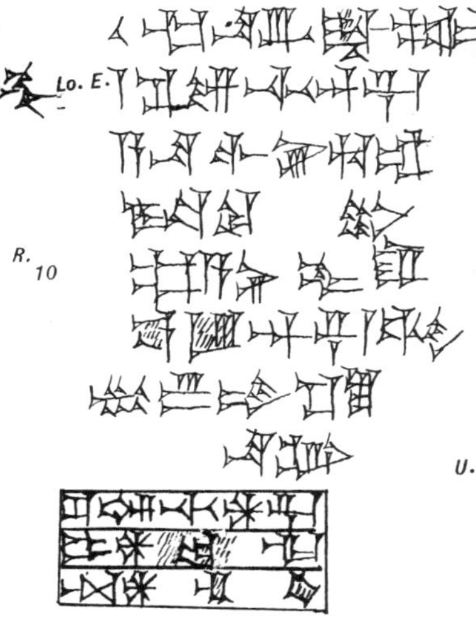

18

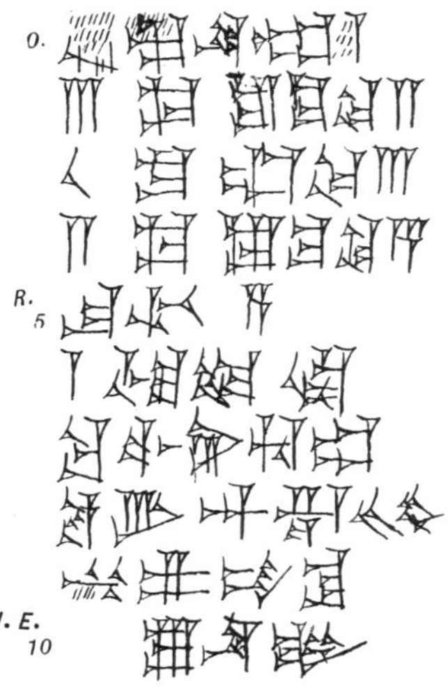

19

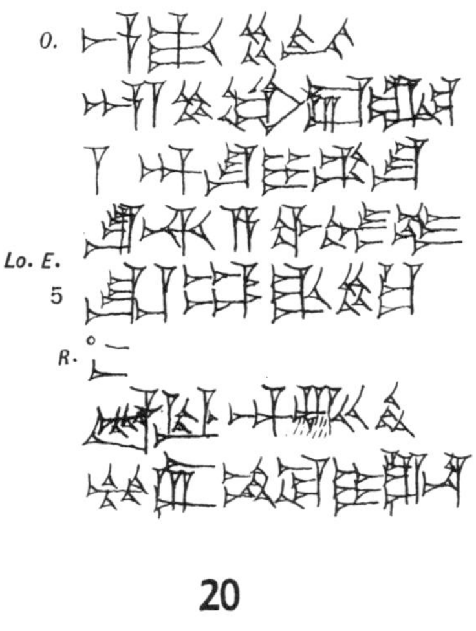

20

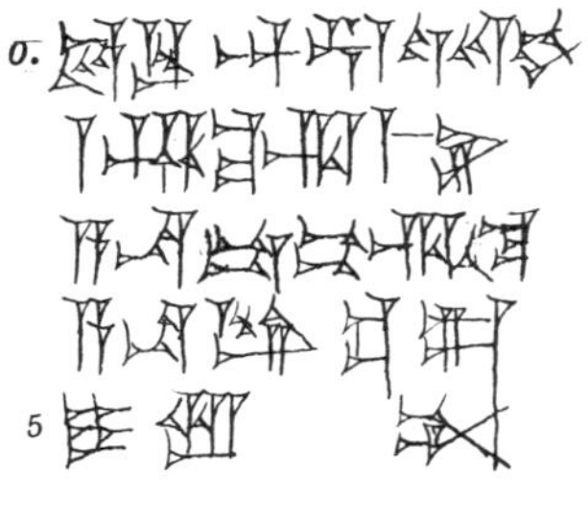

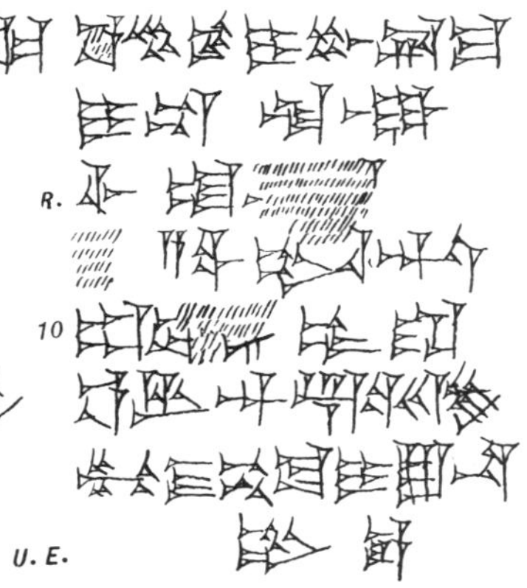

Indistinct seal impressions.

21

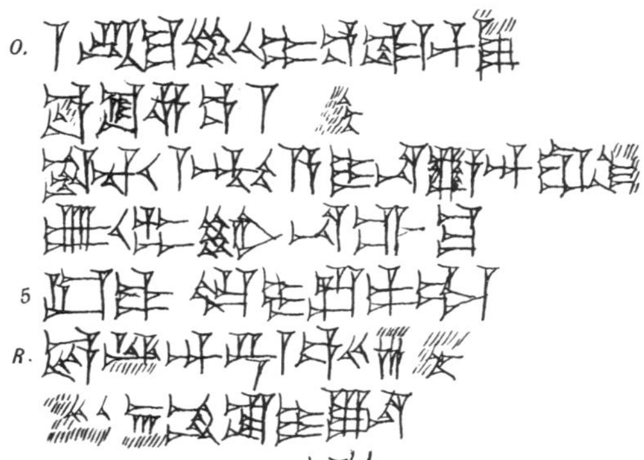

Indistinct seal impressions.

22

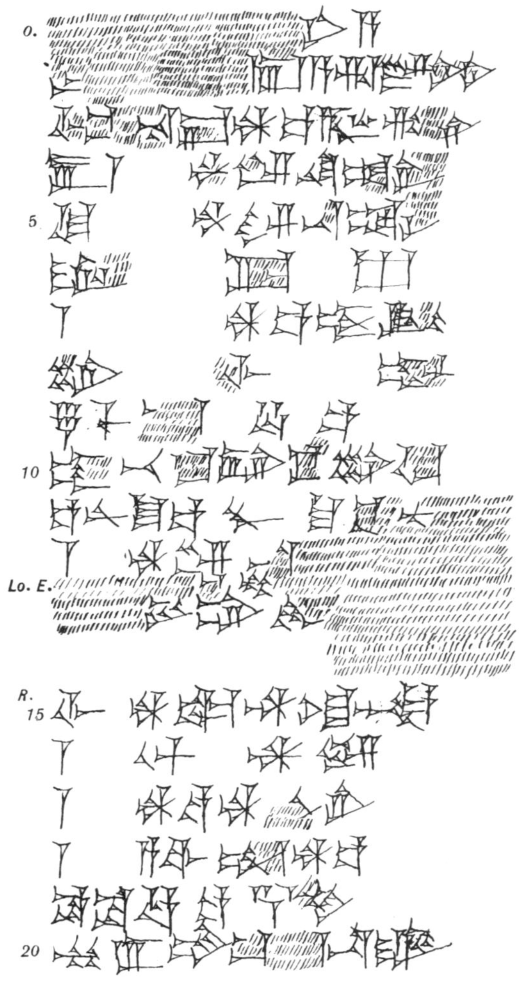

23 CASE

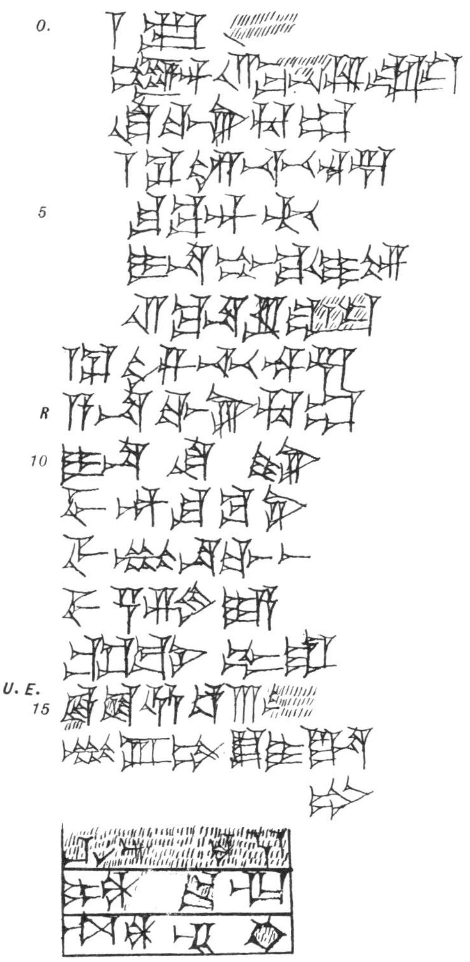

24

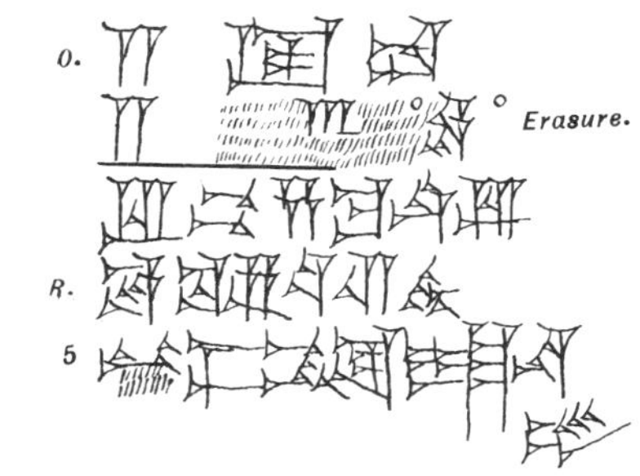

25

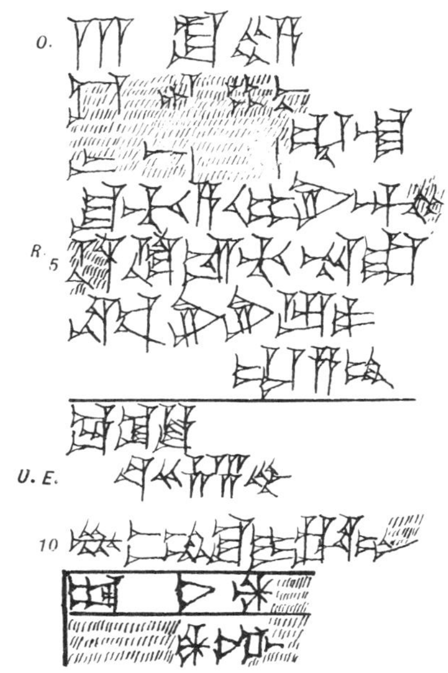

26

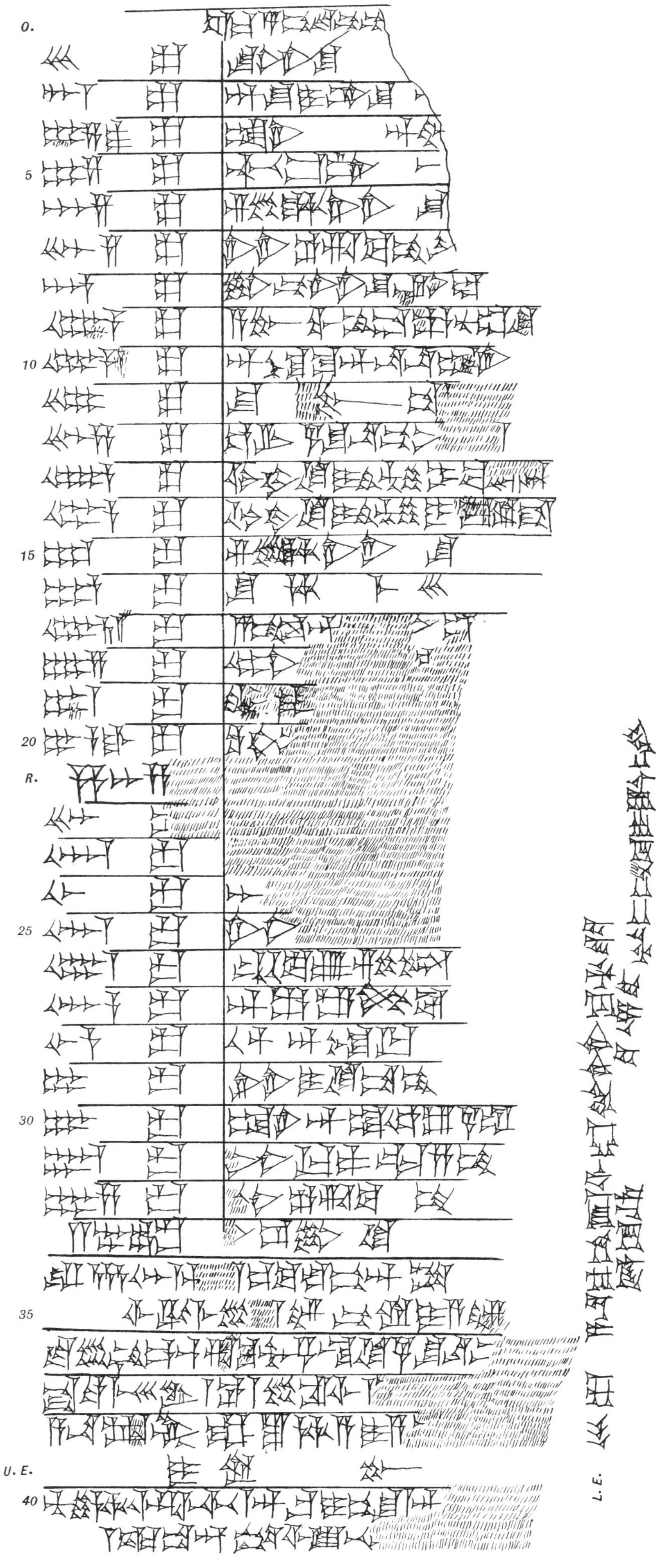

27

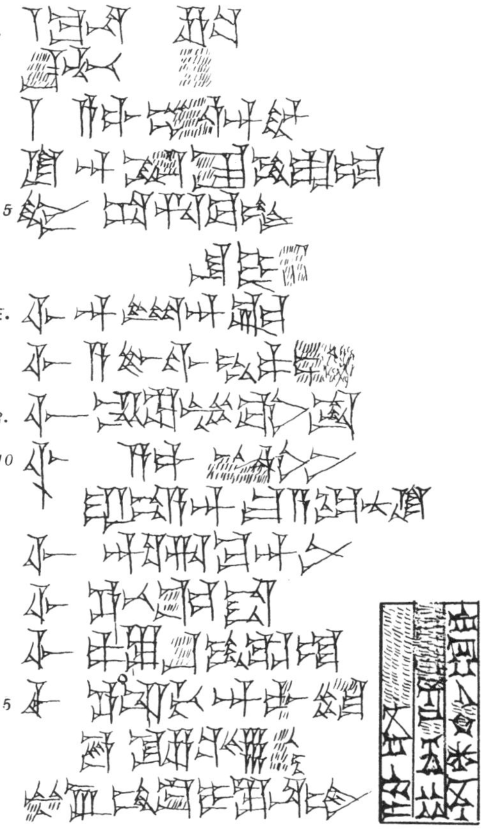

28

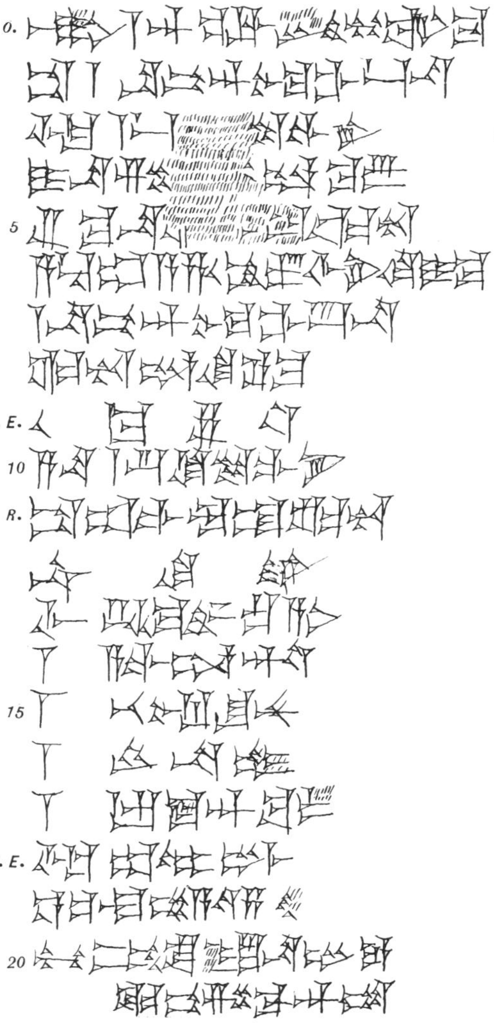

Indistinct seal impressions.

29

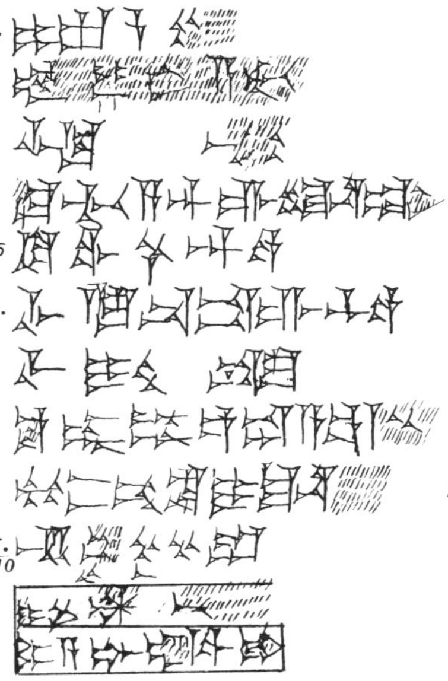

30

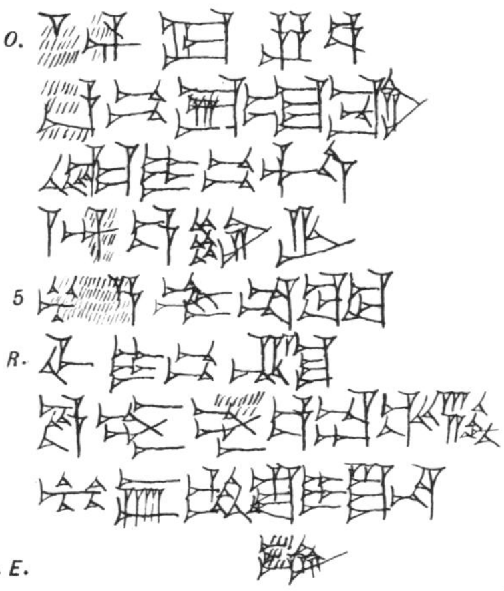

31

TABLET

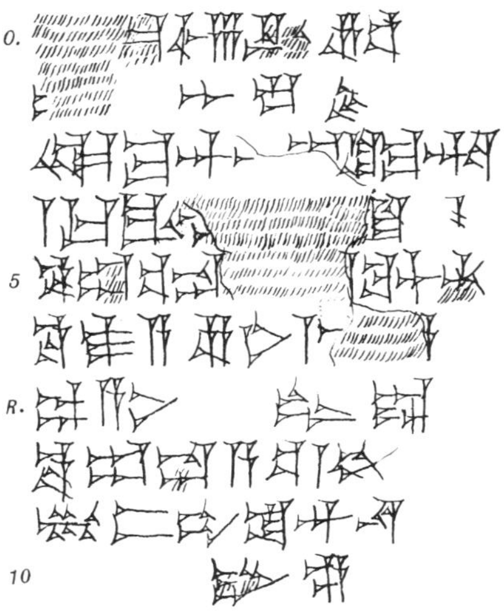

CASE

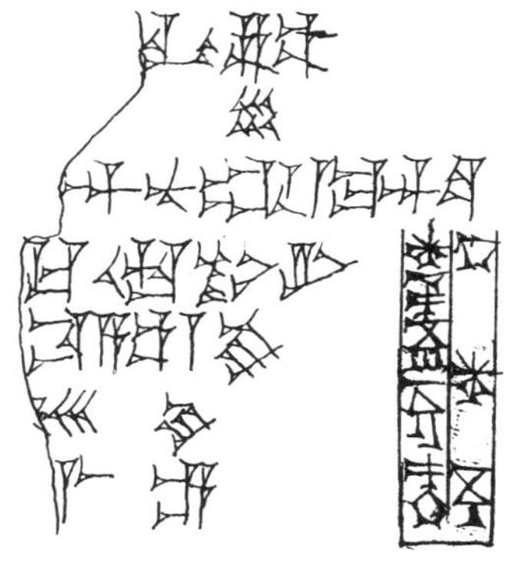

32

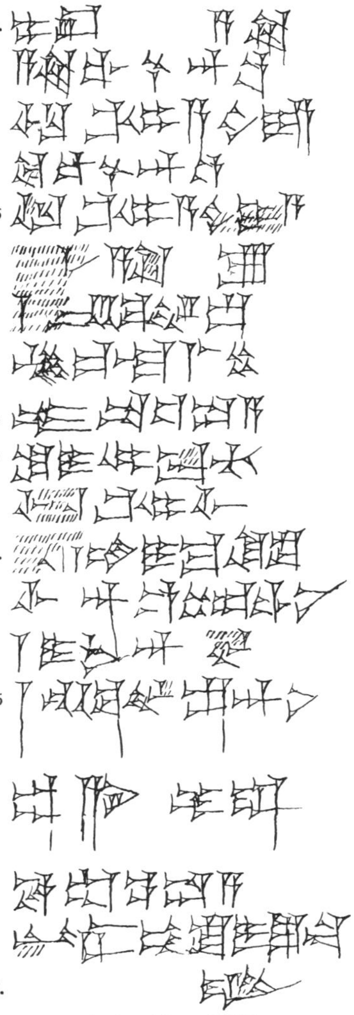

Indistinct seal impressions.

33

34

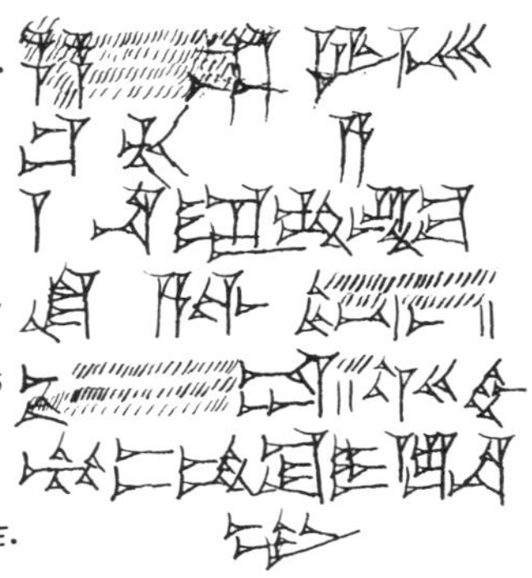

PLATE VI

35

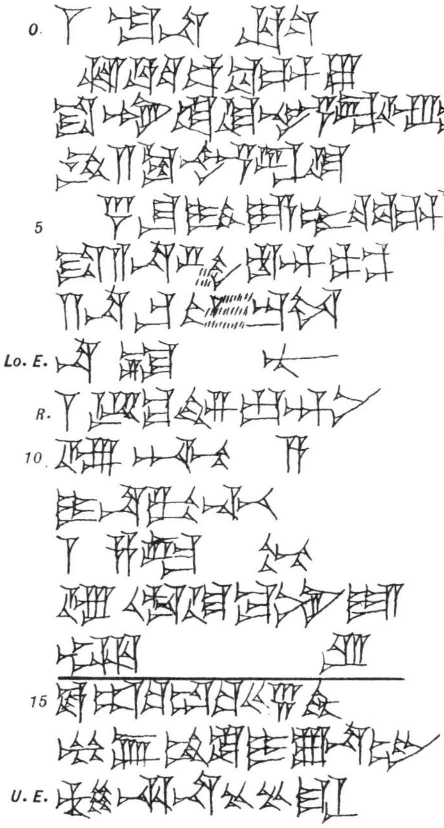

Indistinct seal impressions.

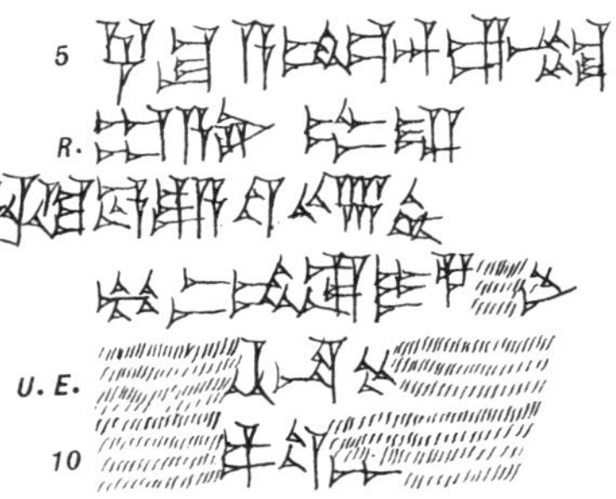

36

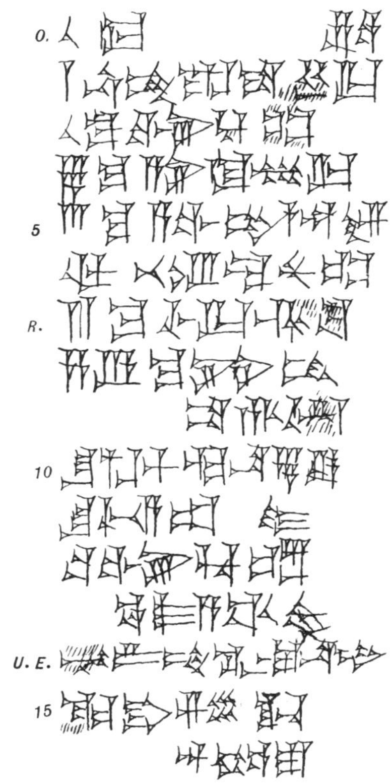

37

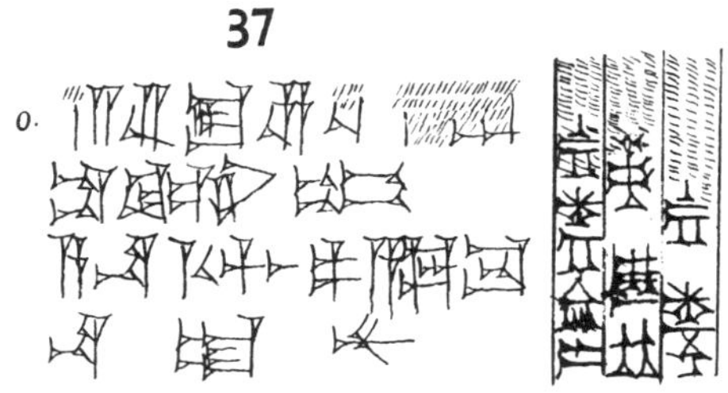

38

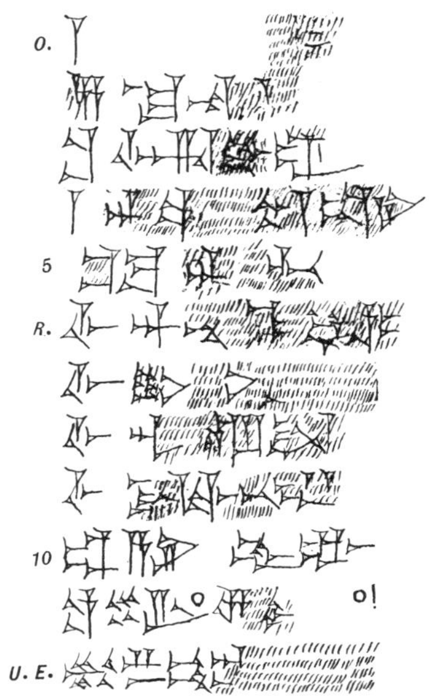

39

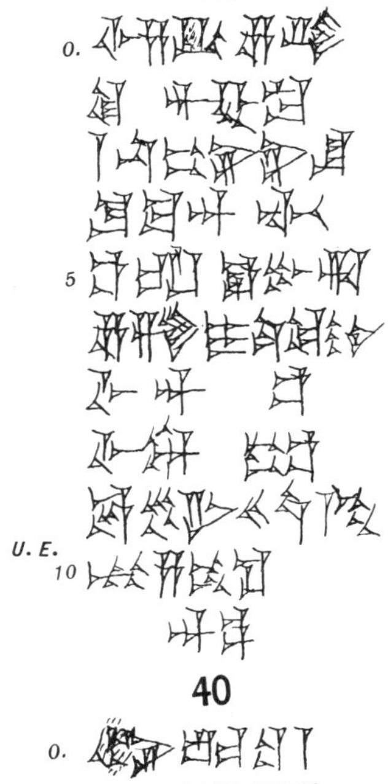

40

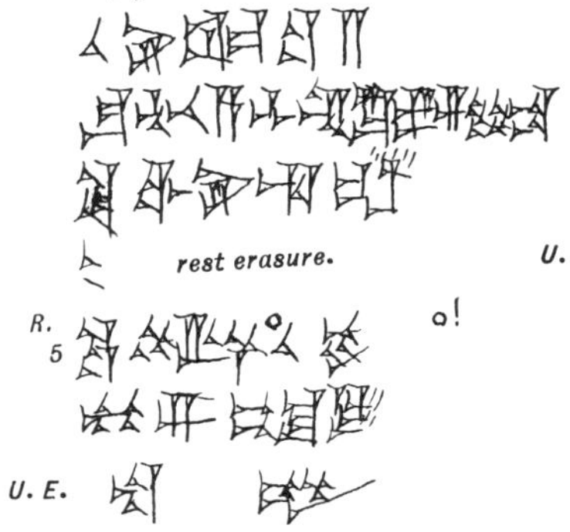

rest erasure.

41

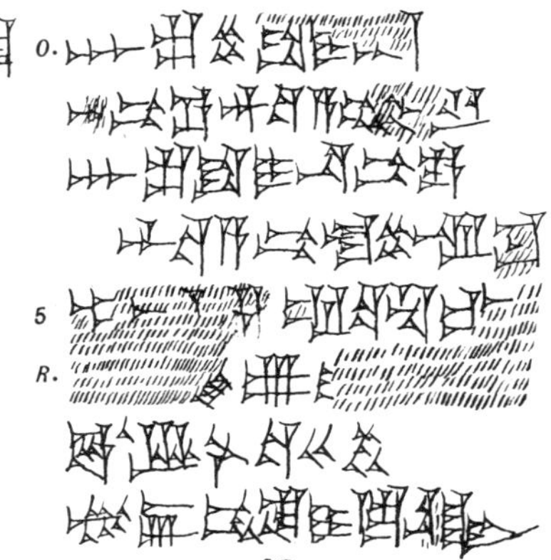

42

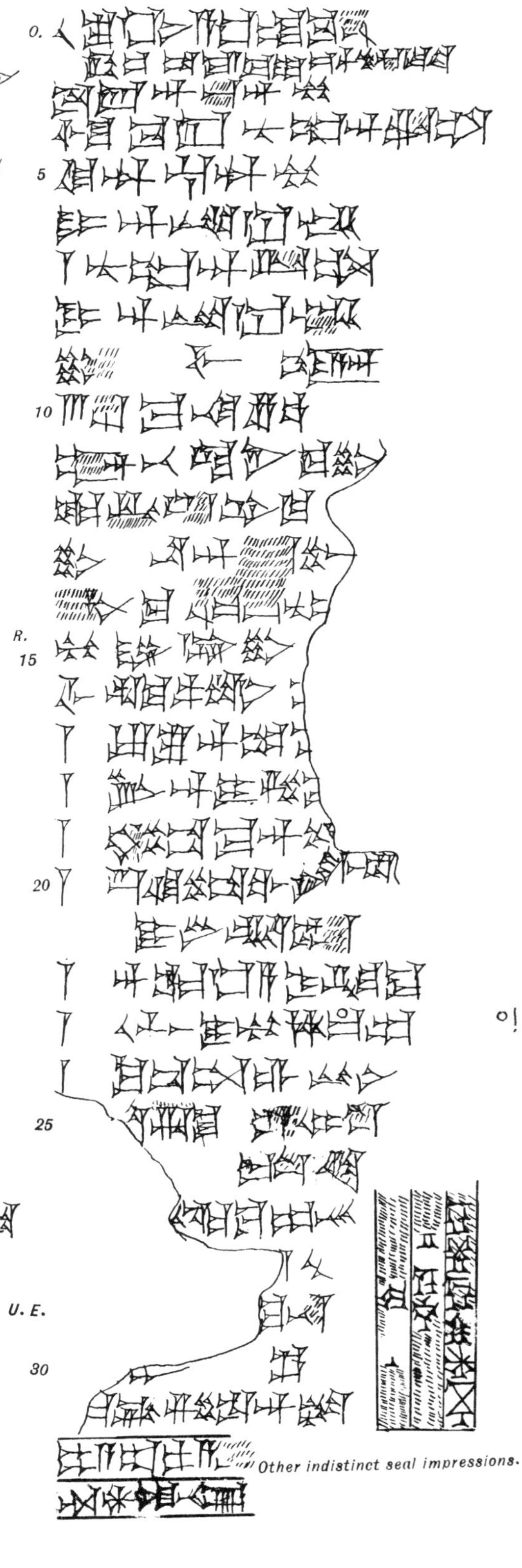

Other indistinct seal impressions.

43

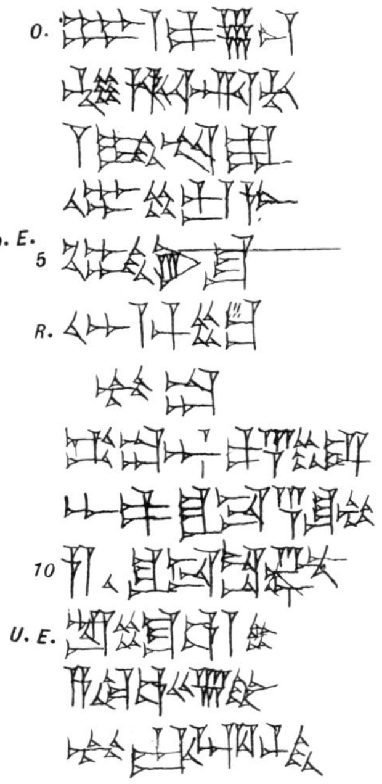

44 CASE

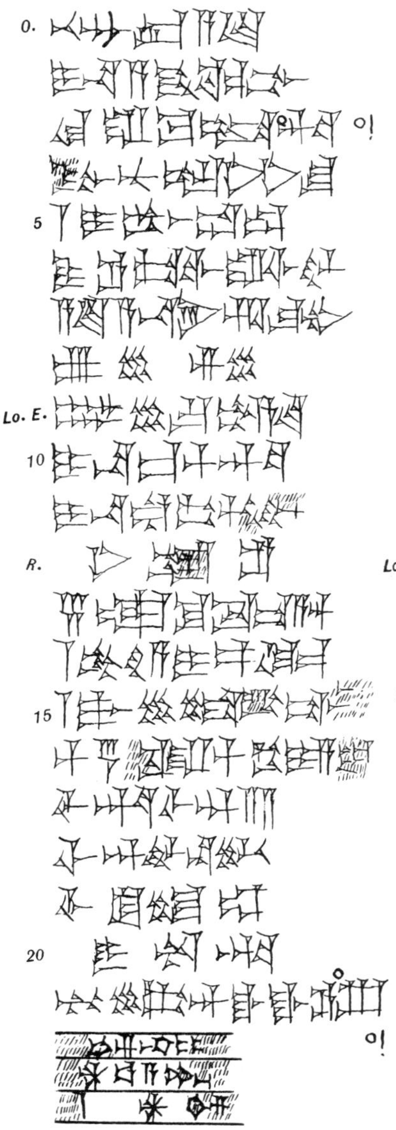

45

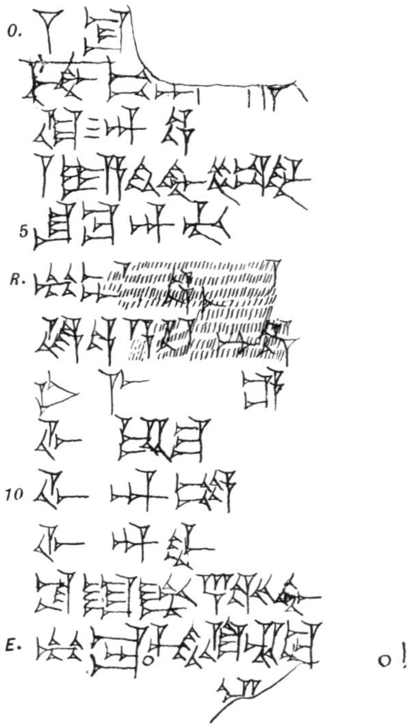

46

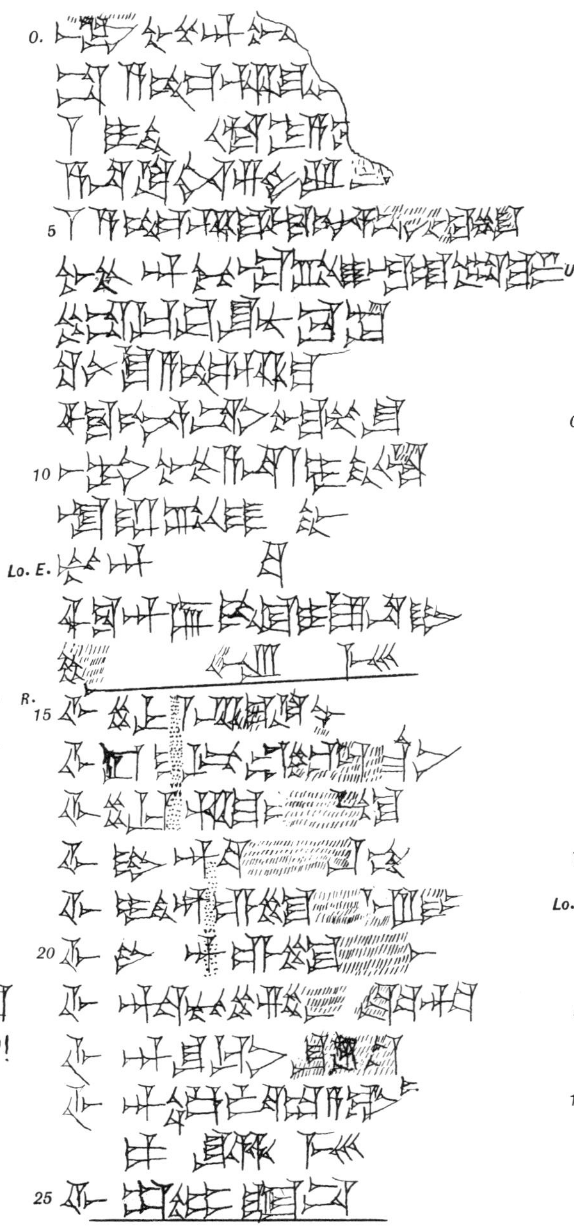

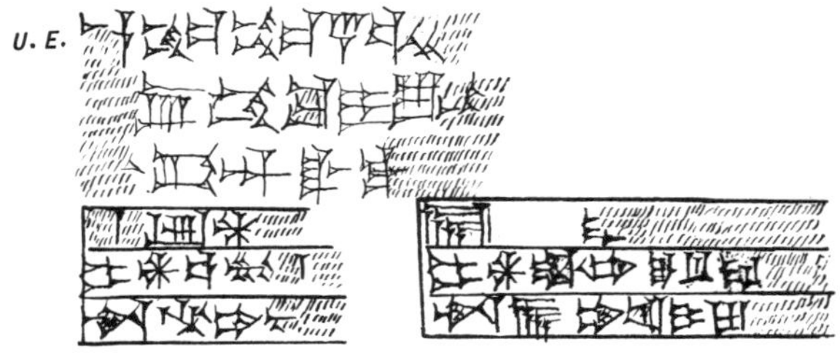

47

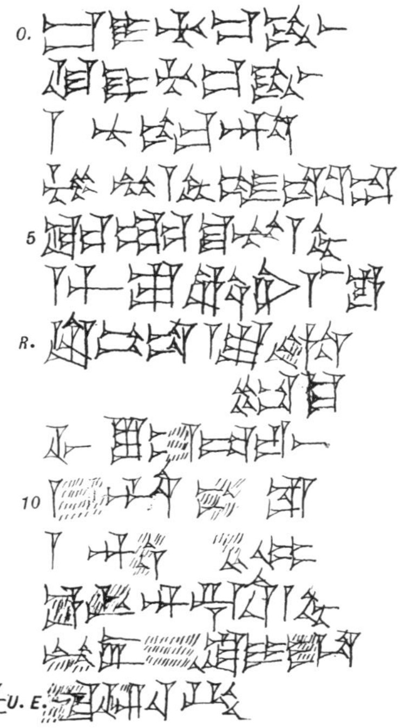

48

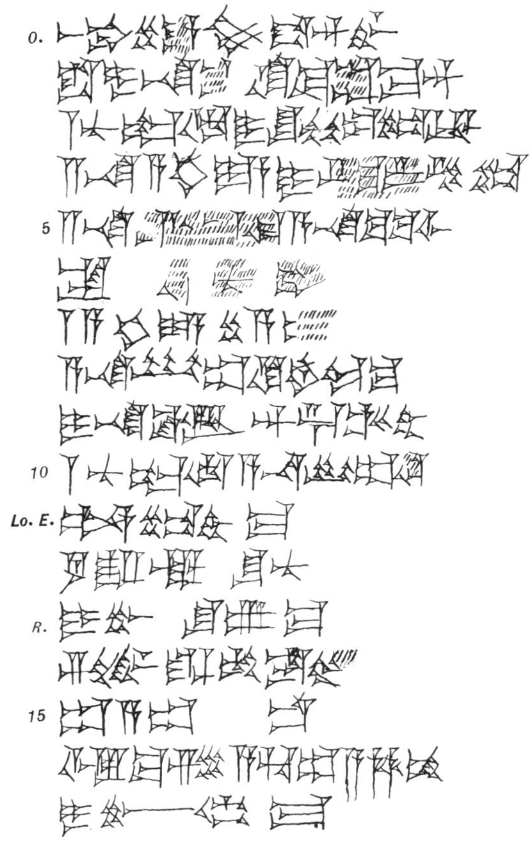

CONTINUED

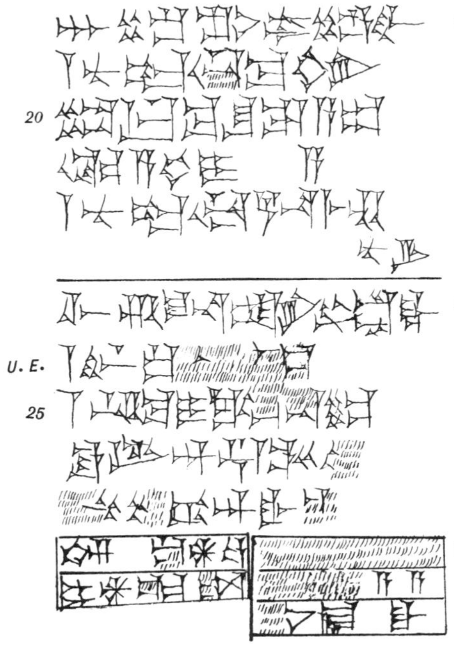

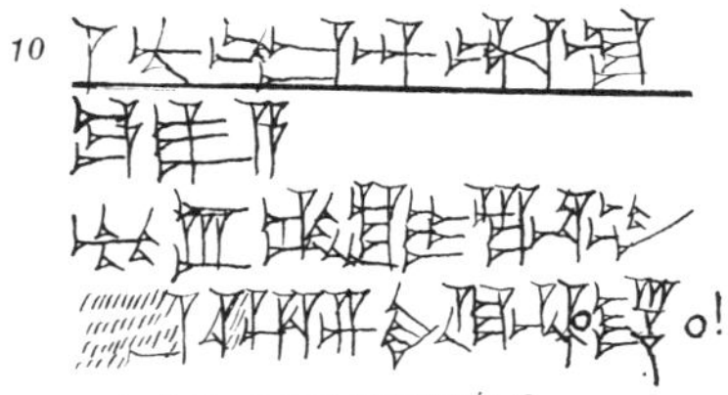

Indistinct seal impressions.

49

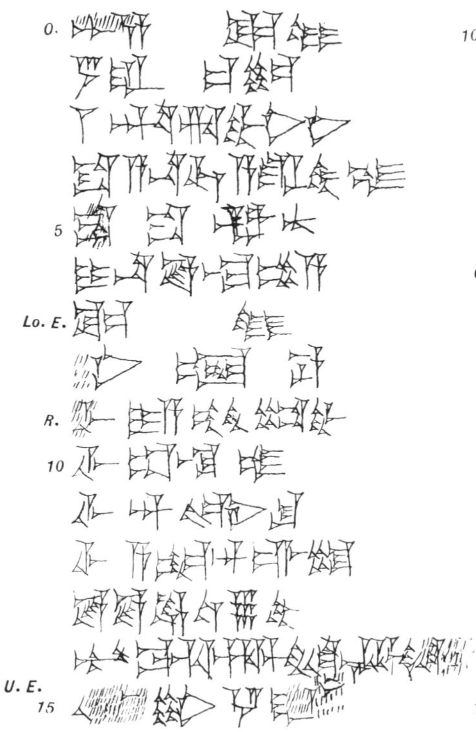

50

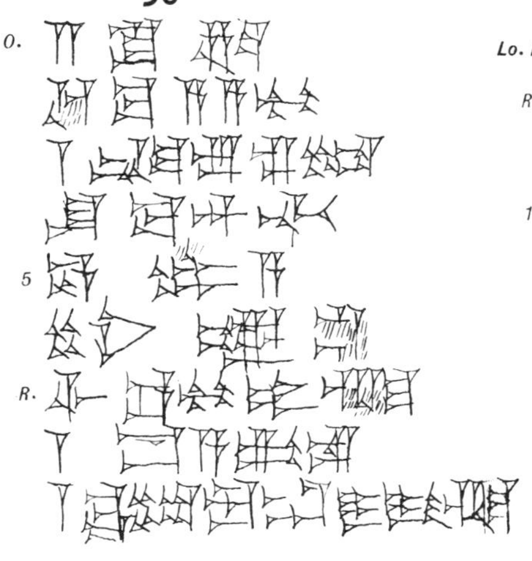

51

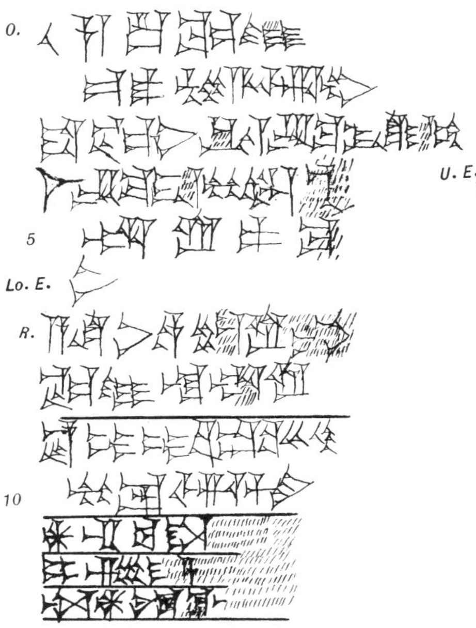

52

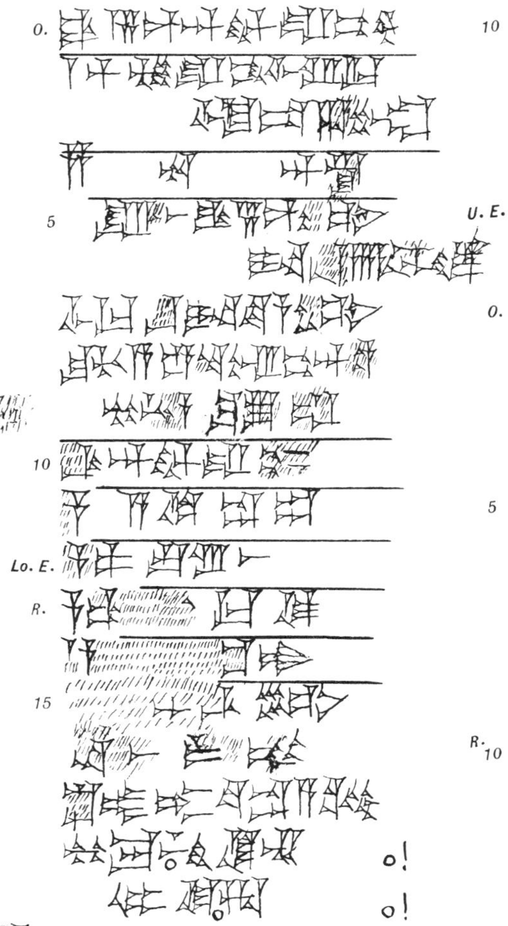

53

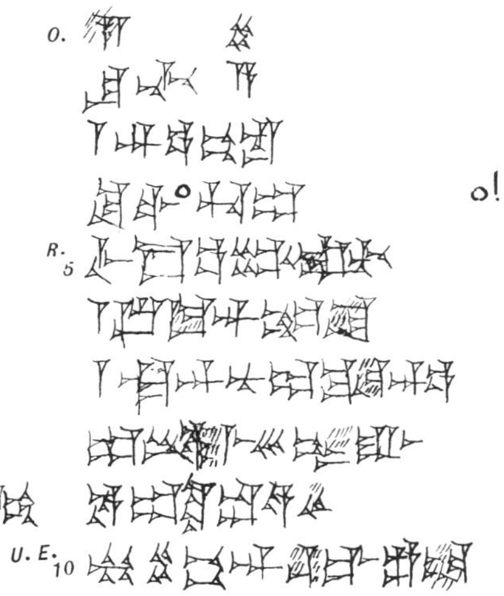

54

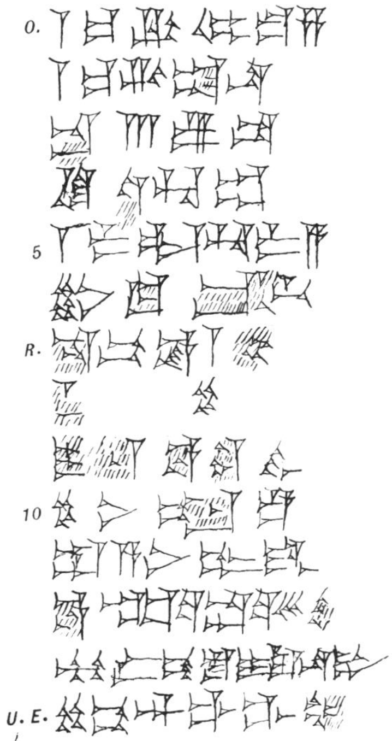

55

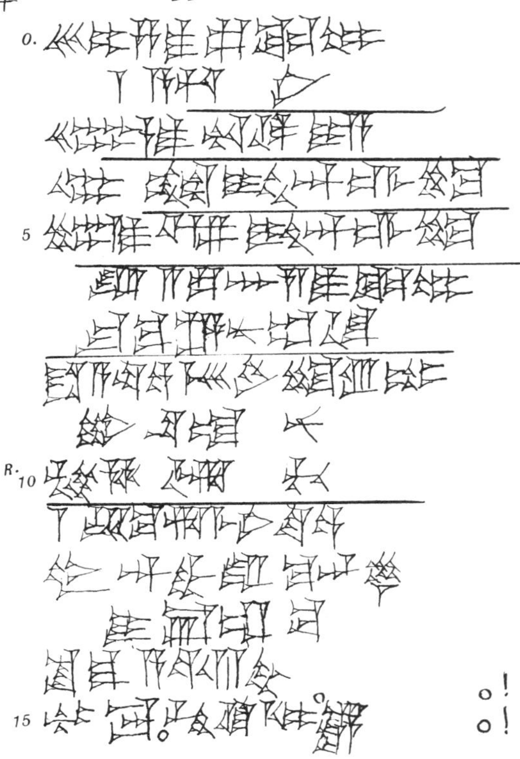

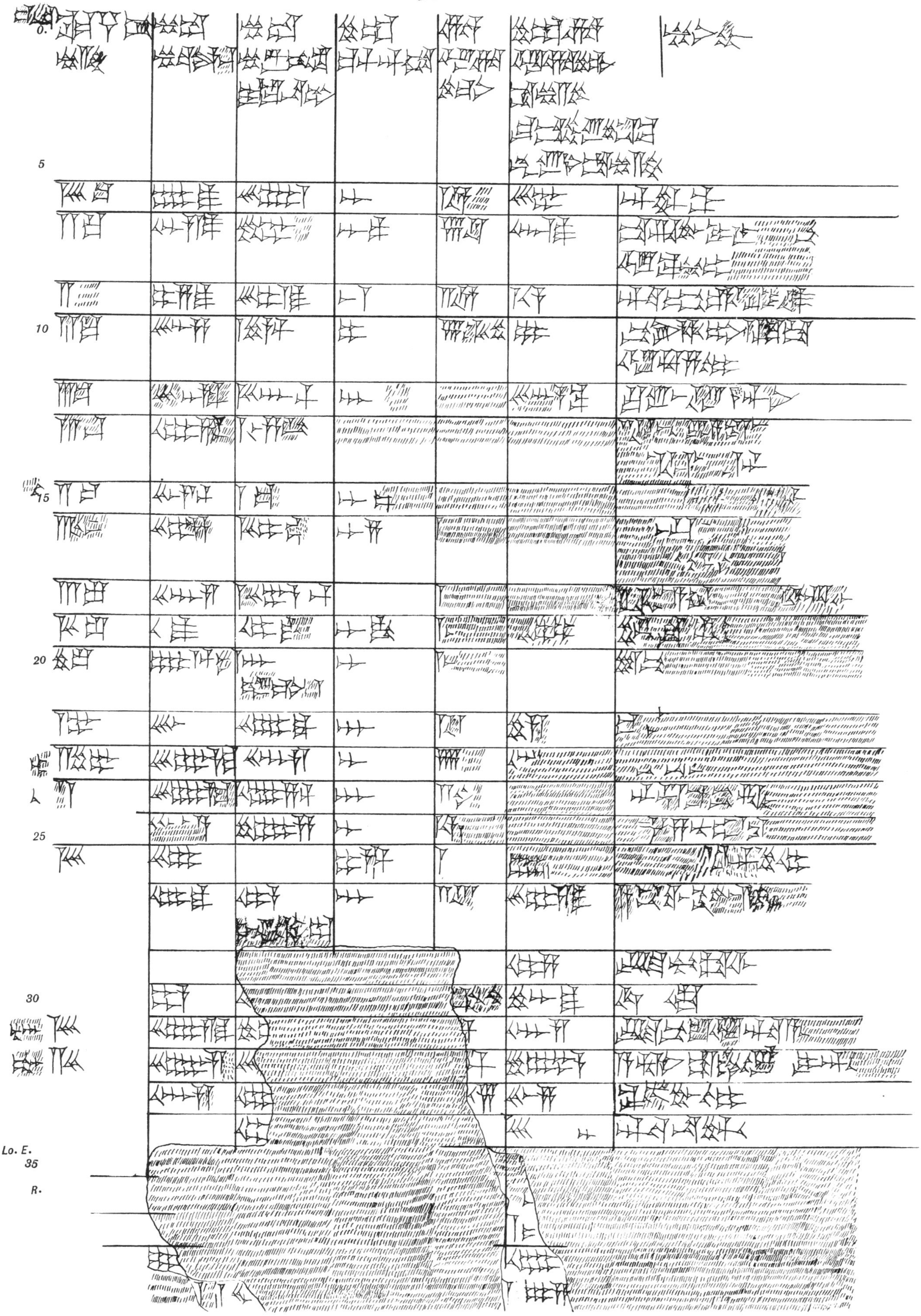

CONTINUED

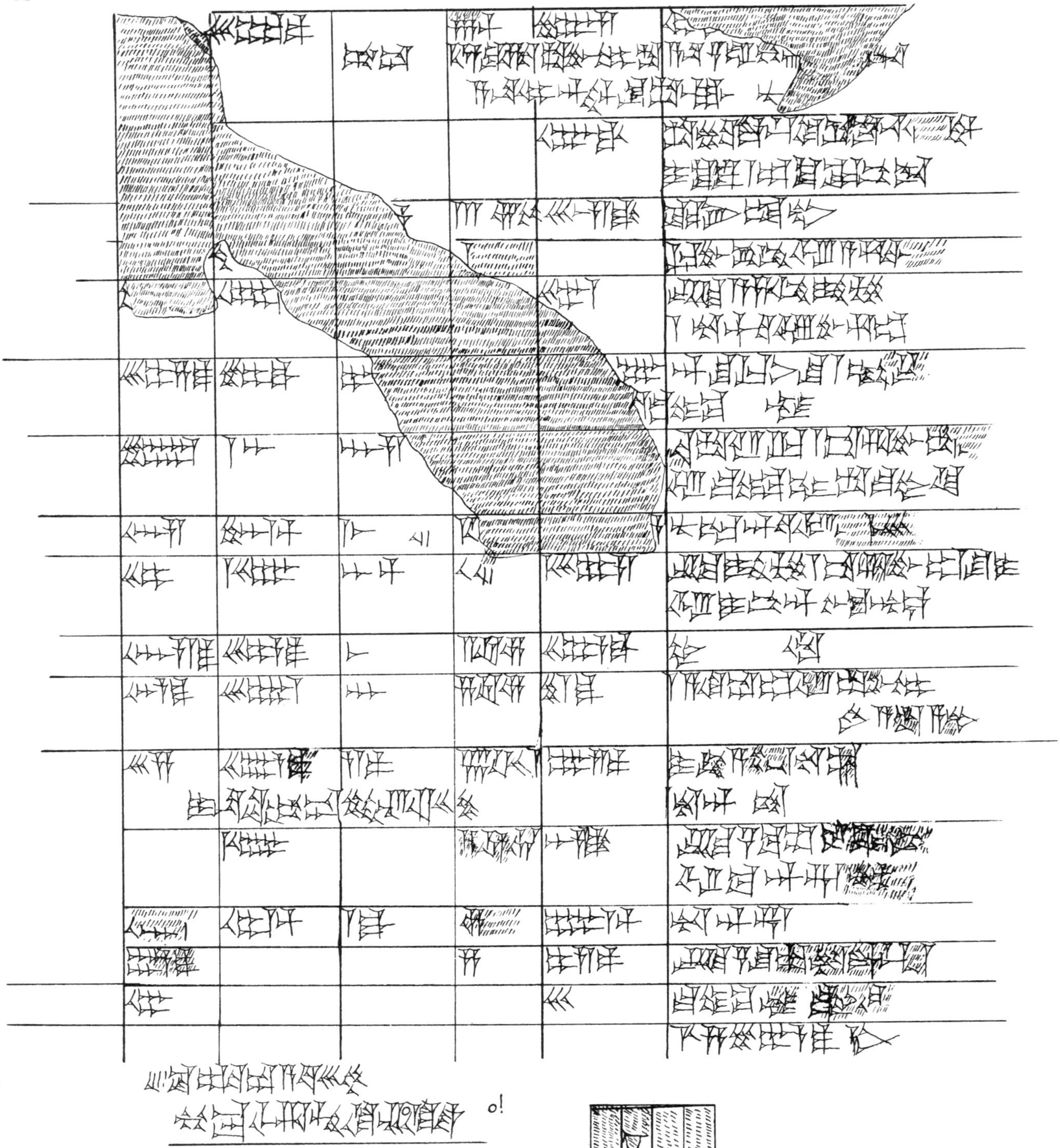

U. E.

57 CASE

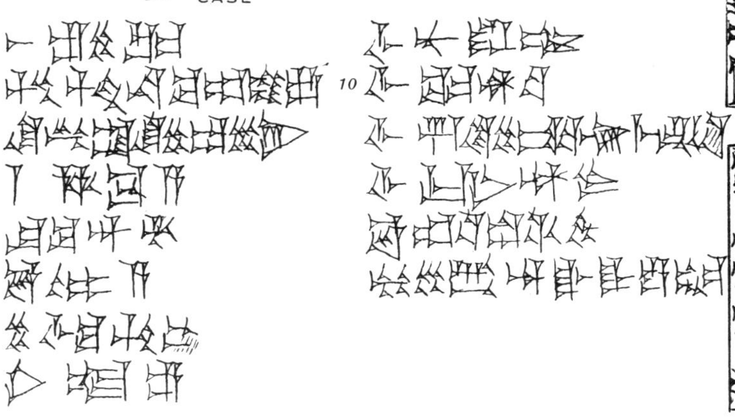

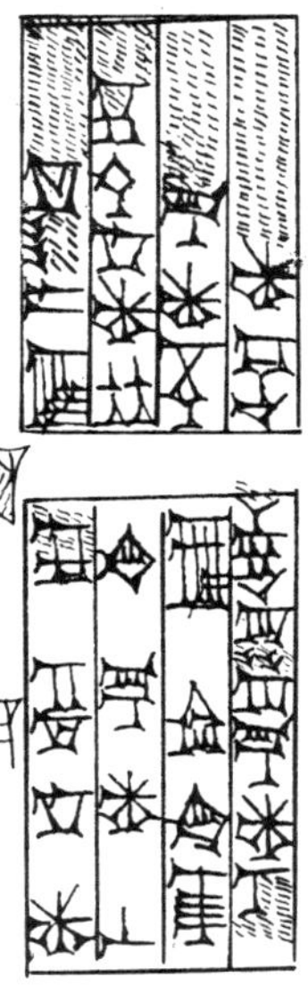

58

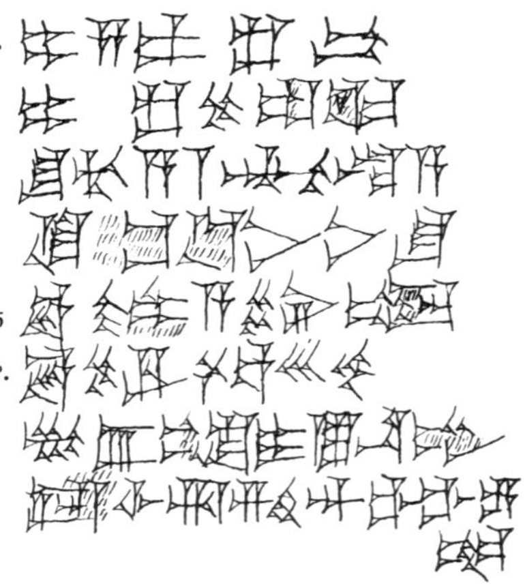

59

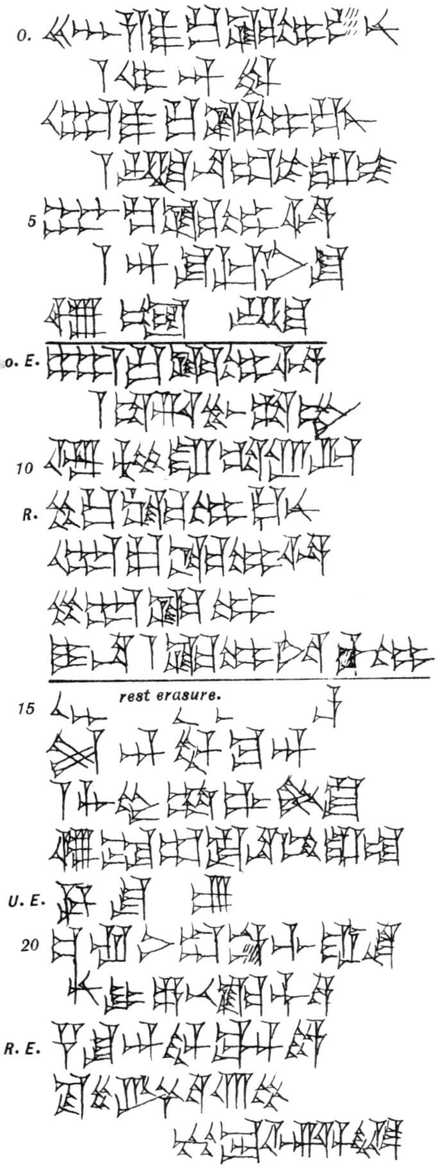

rest erasure.

60

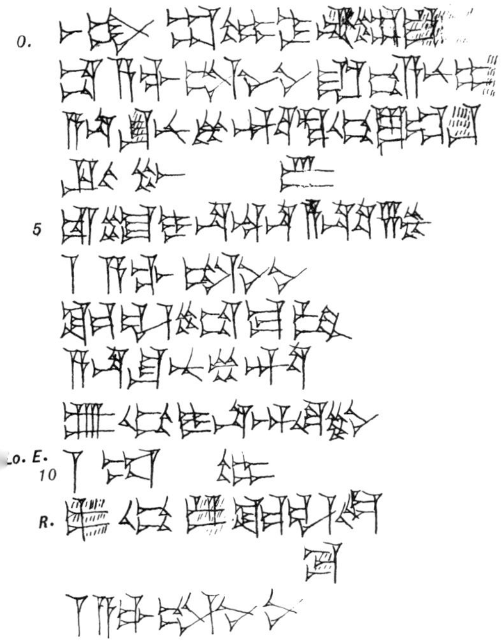

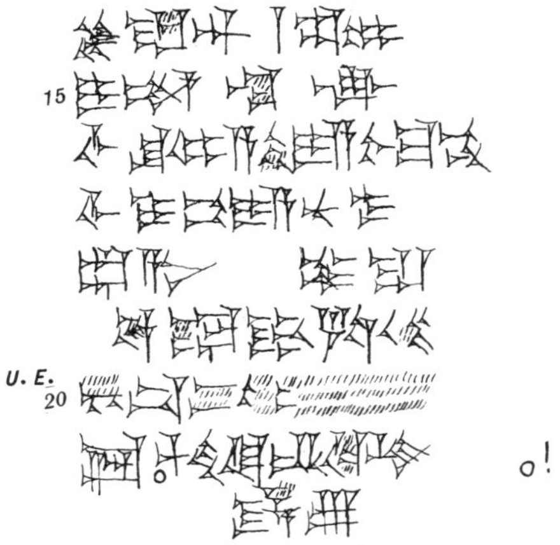

Indistinct seal impressions.

61

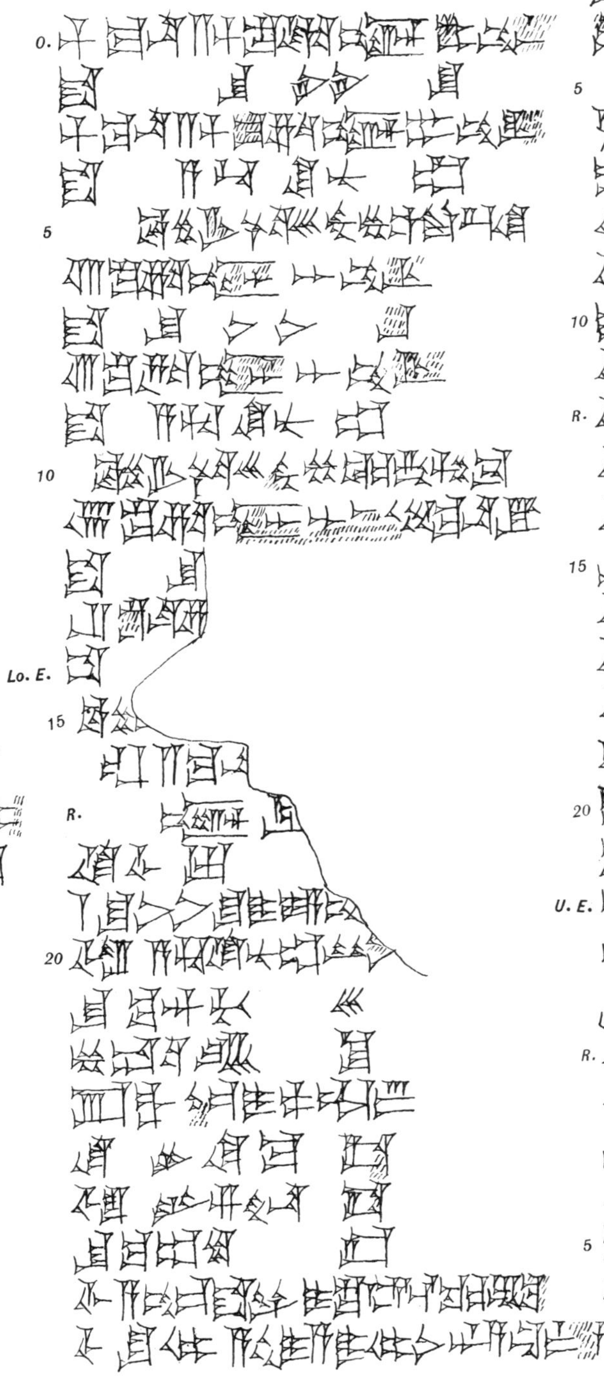

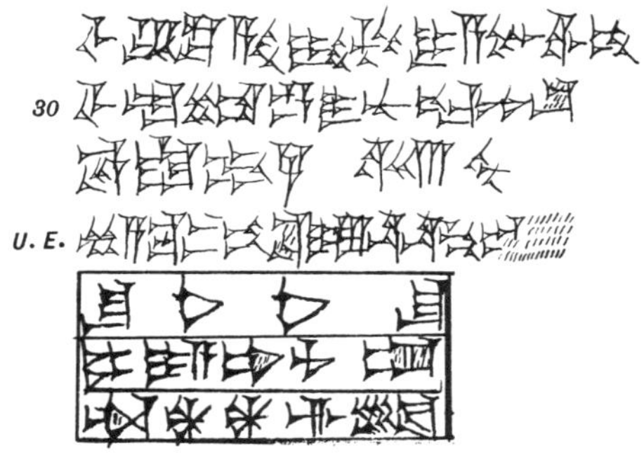

62

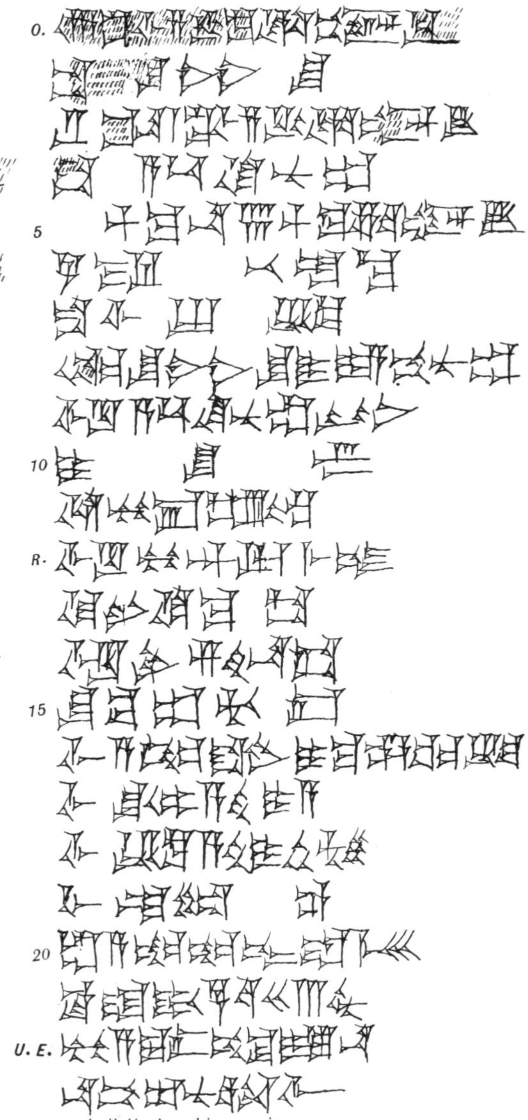

Indistinct seal impressions.

63

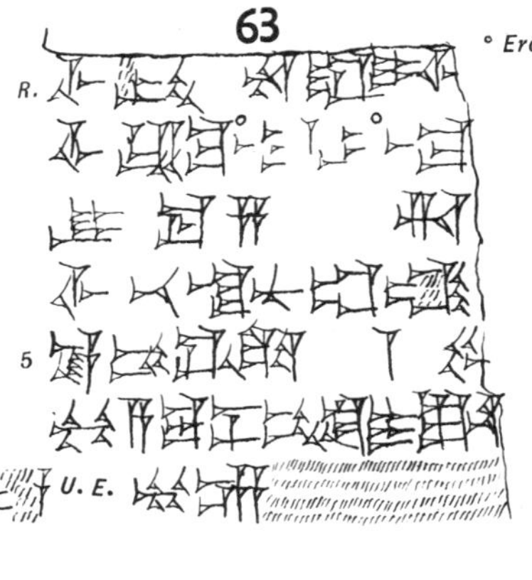

° Erasure.

64

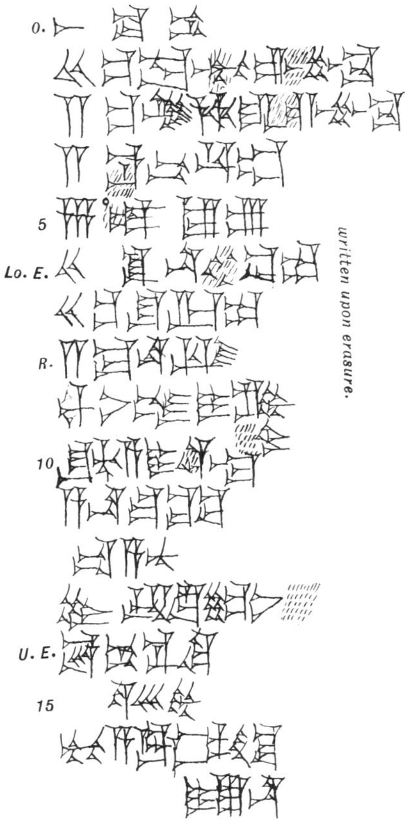

65

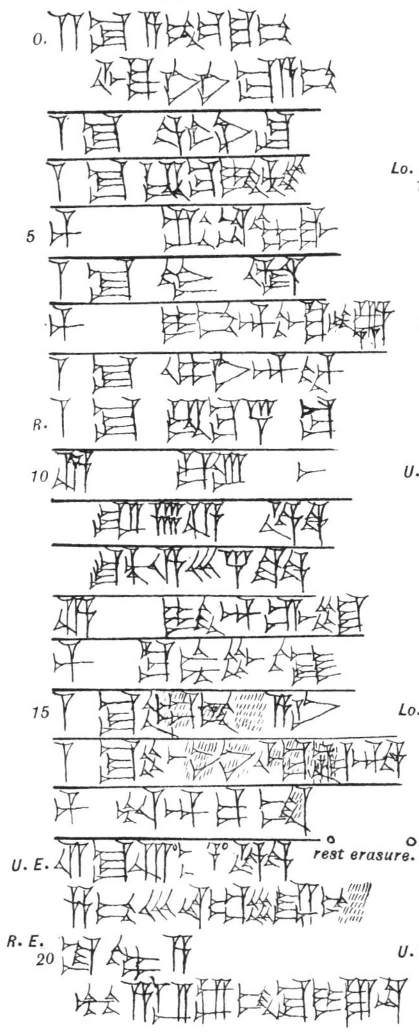

66

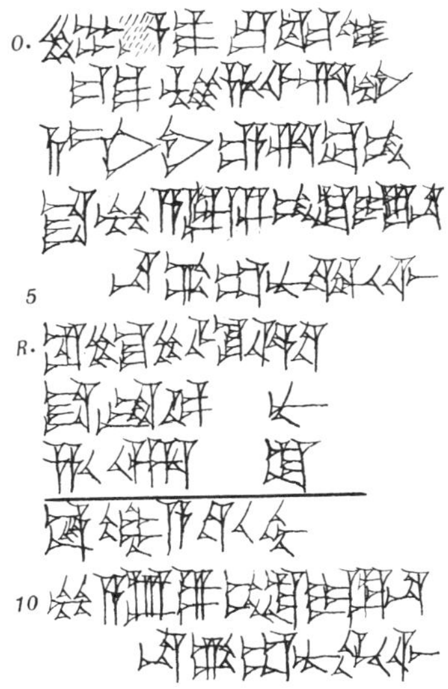

67

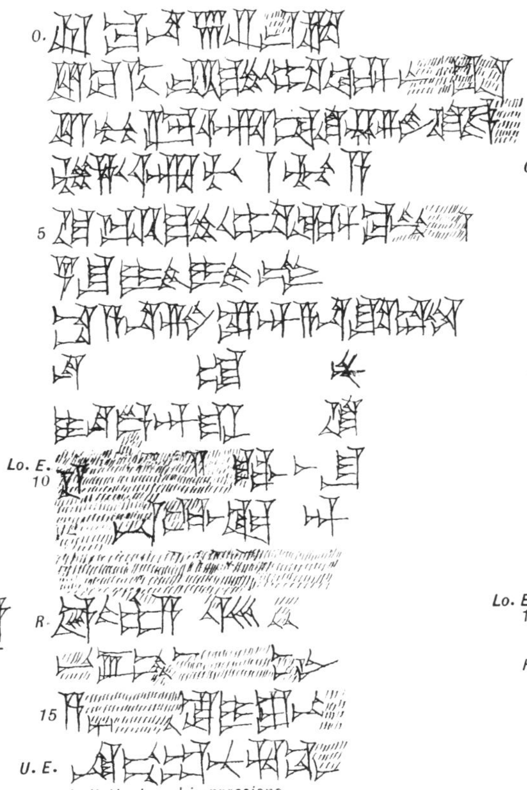

Indistinct seal impressions.

68

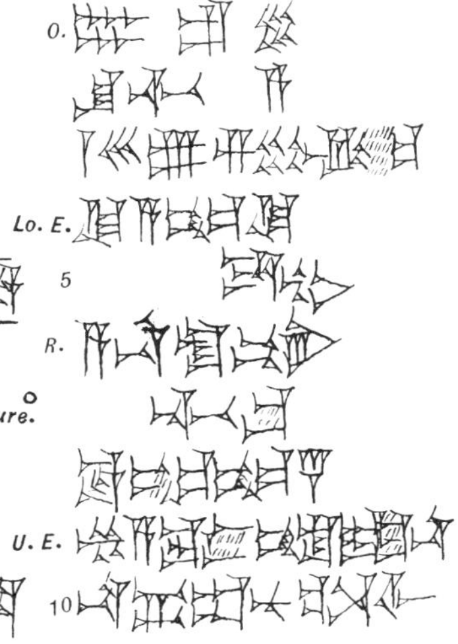

69

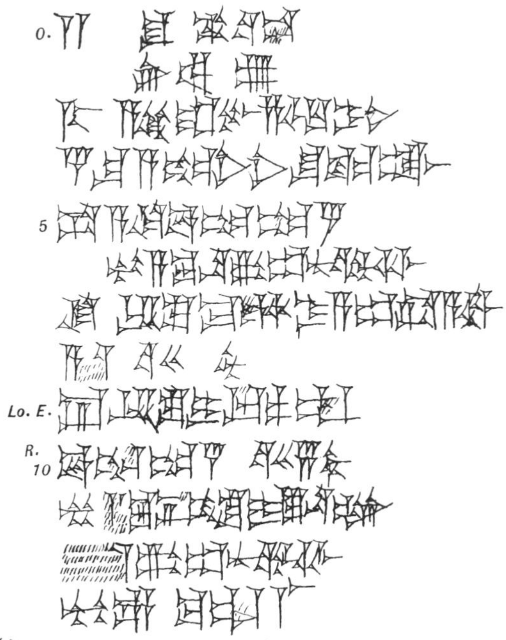

Indistinct seal impressions.

70

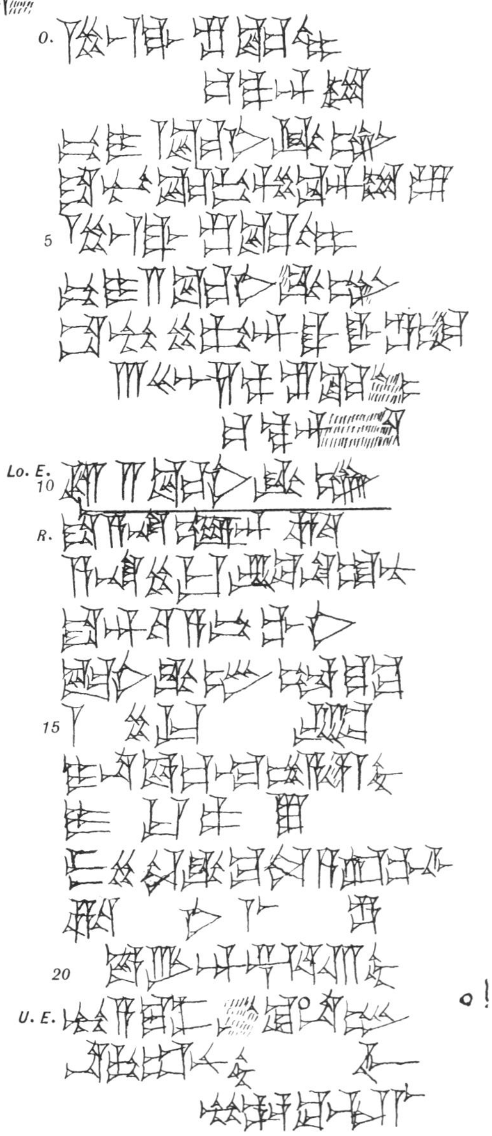

Indistinct seal impressions.

71

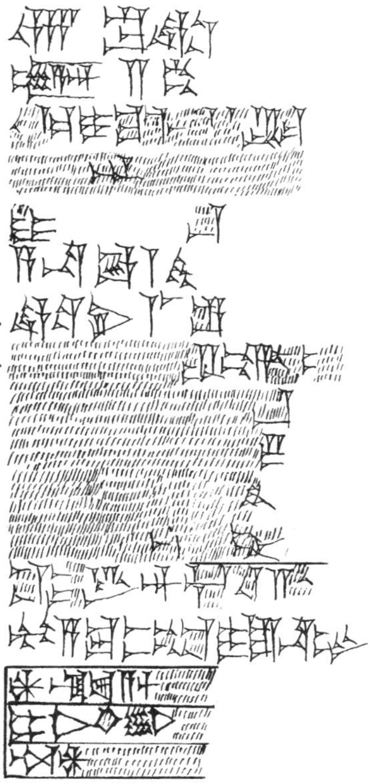

72

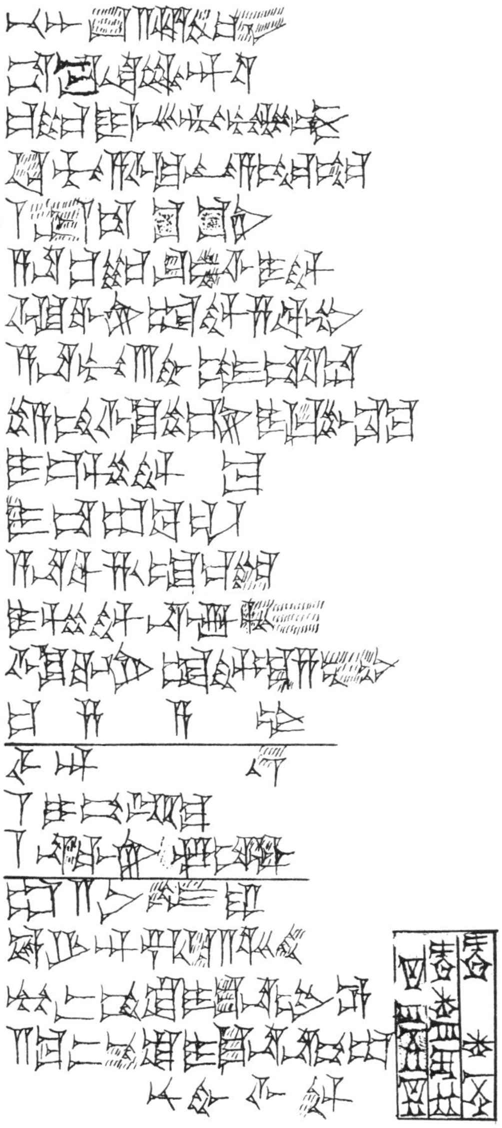

Other indistinct seal impressions.

73

CASE

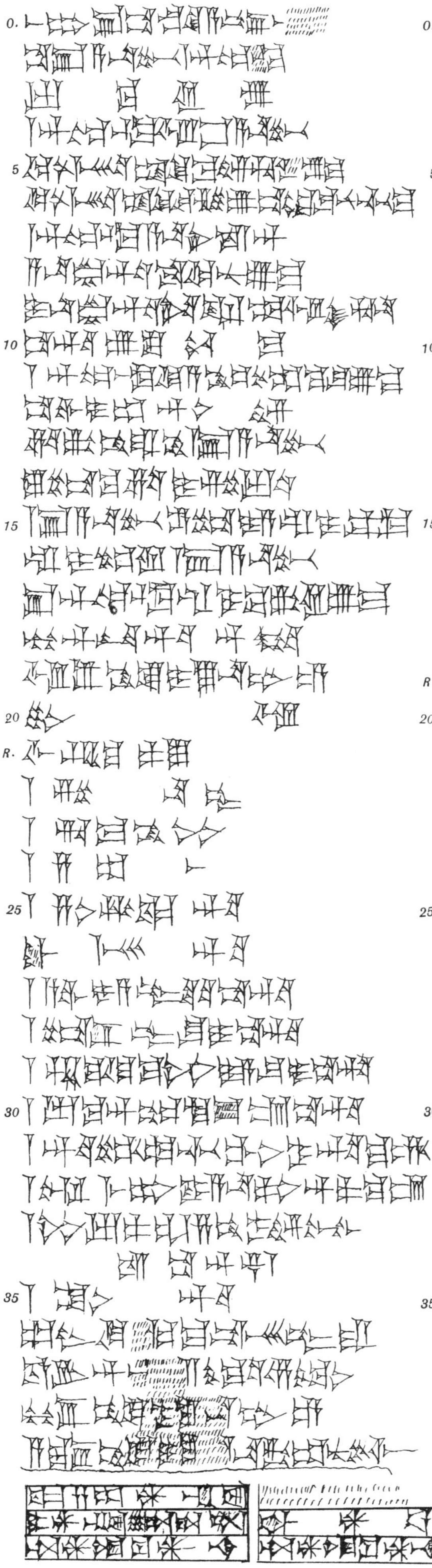

TABLET

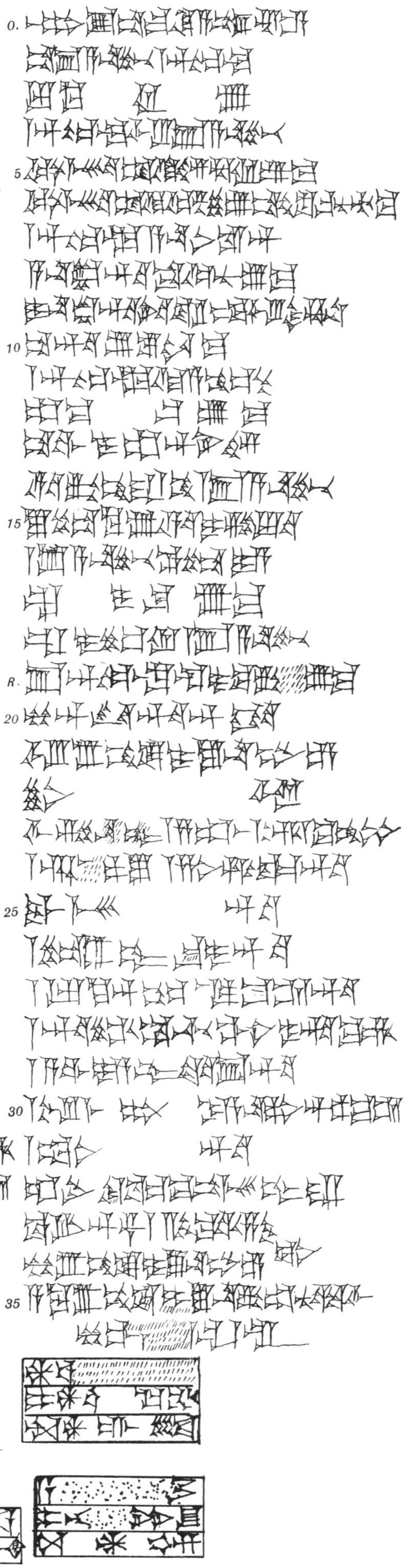

PLATE XIV

74

CASE

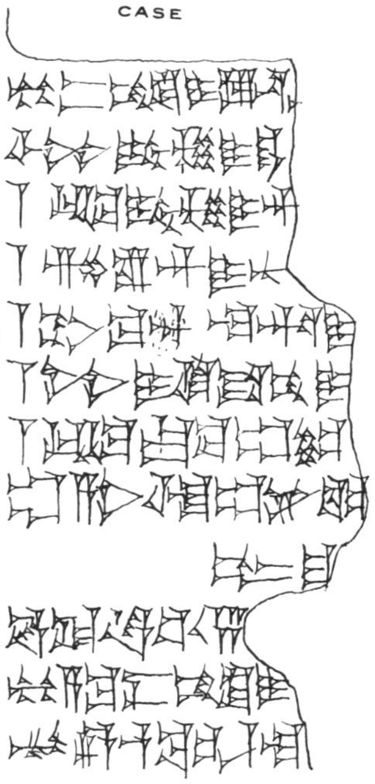

TABLET

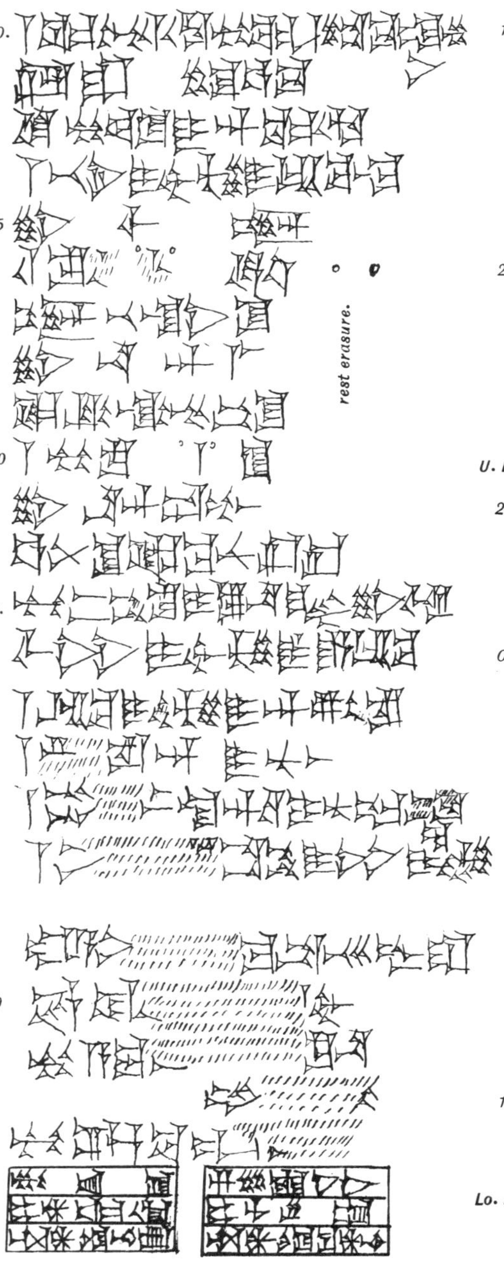

75

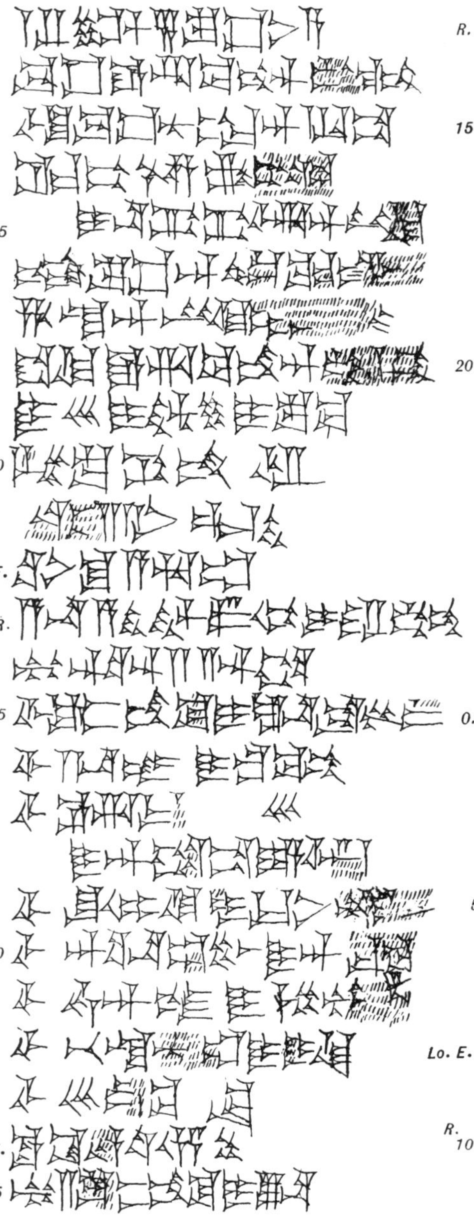

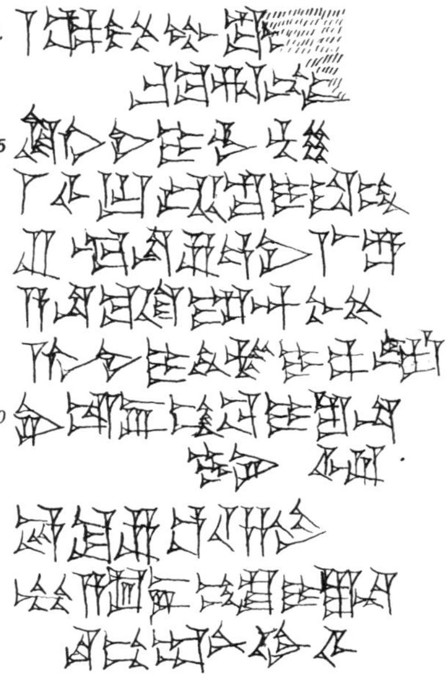

76

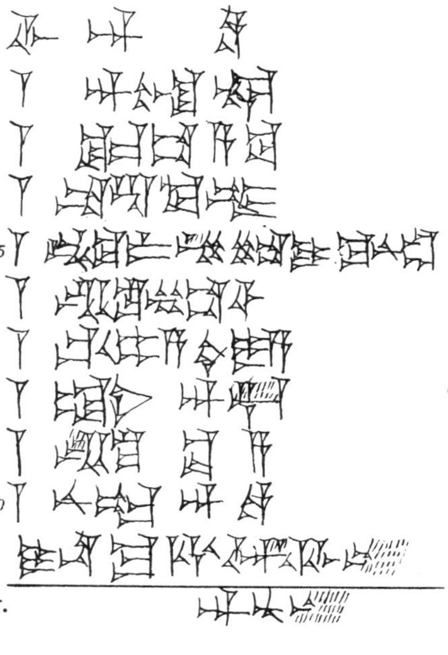

77

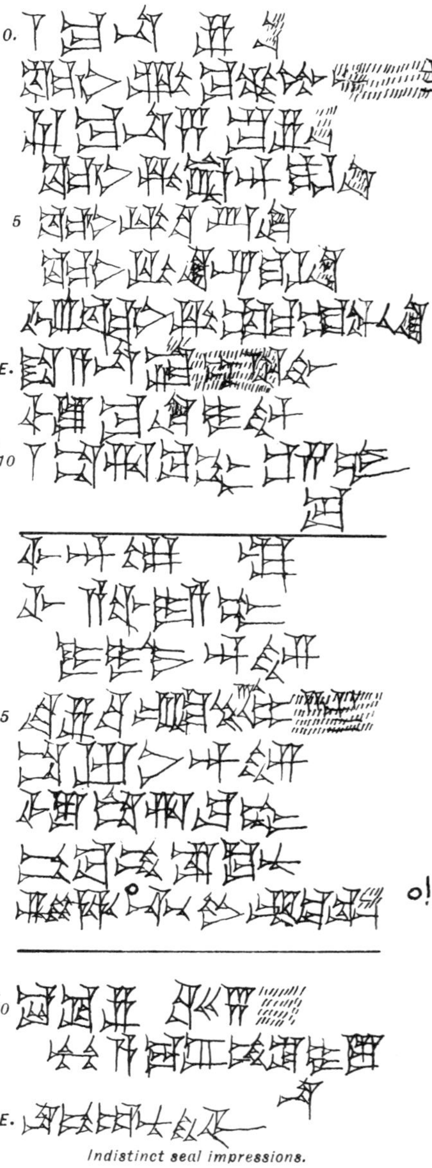

Indistinct seal impressions.

78

79

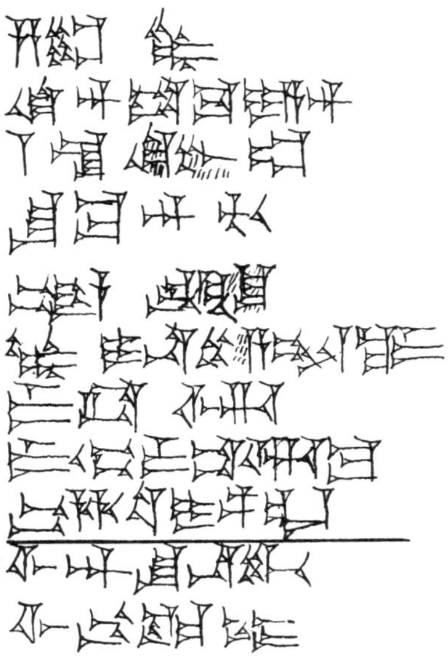

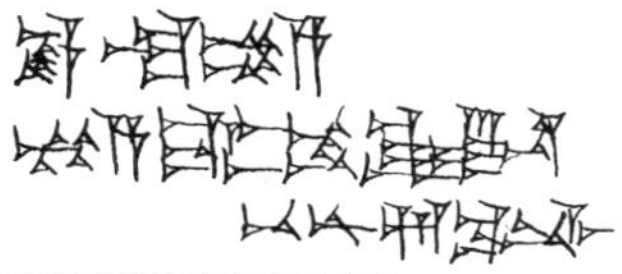

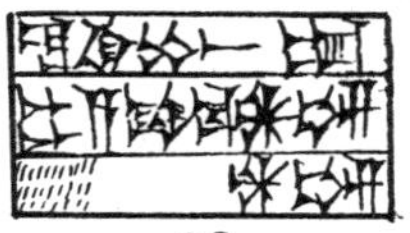

80

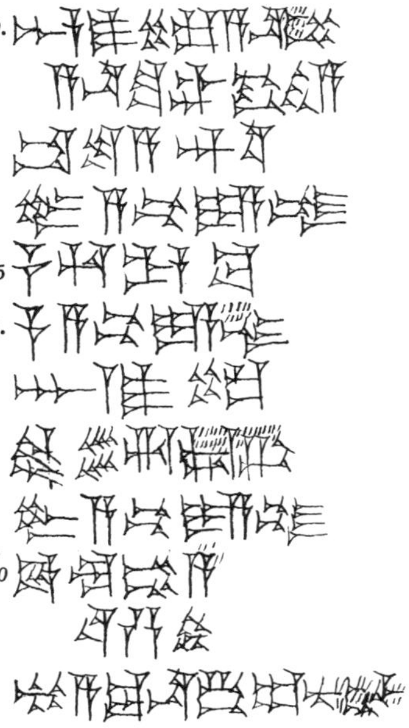

81

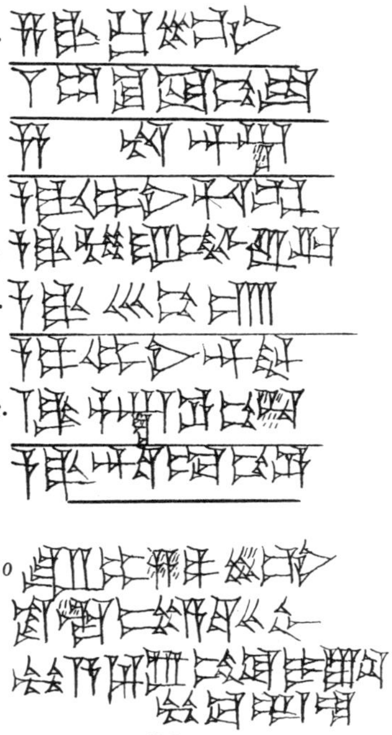

82

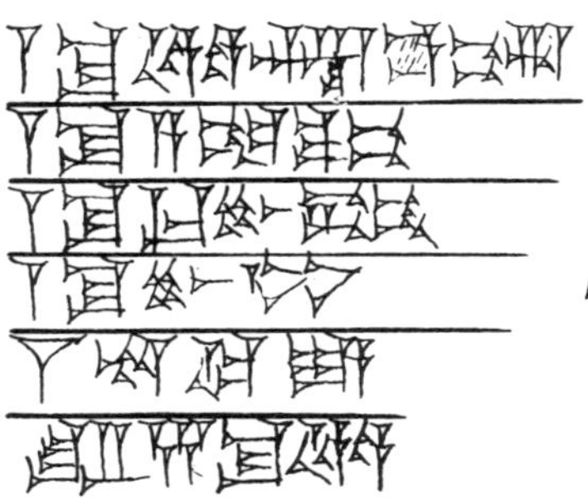

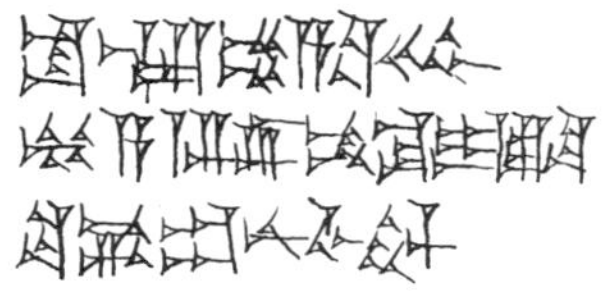

83

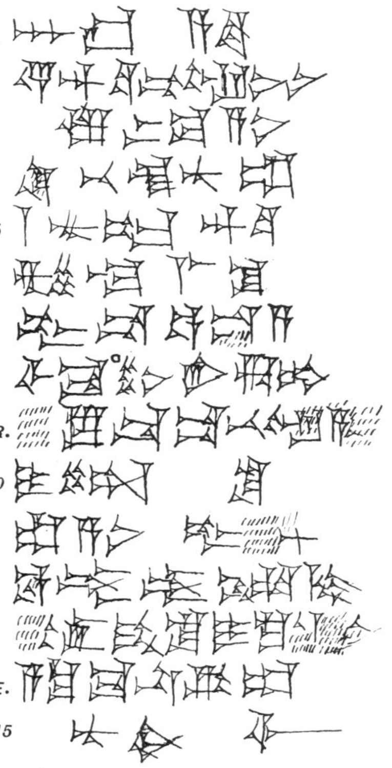

Indistinct seal impressions.

84

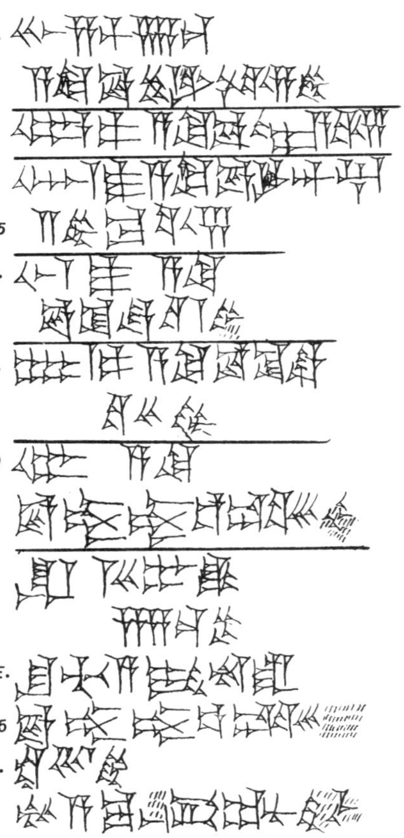

85

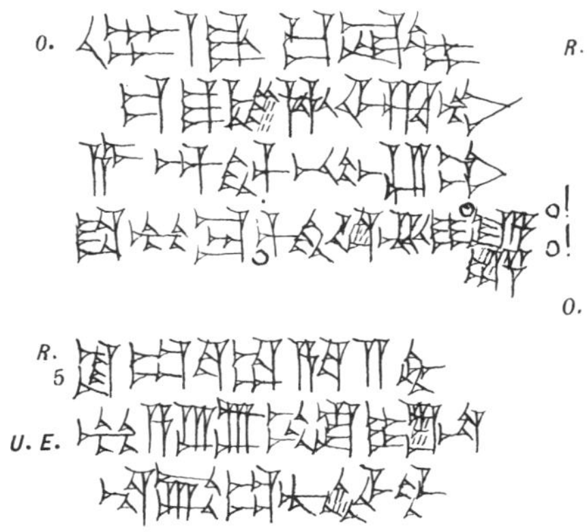

86

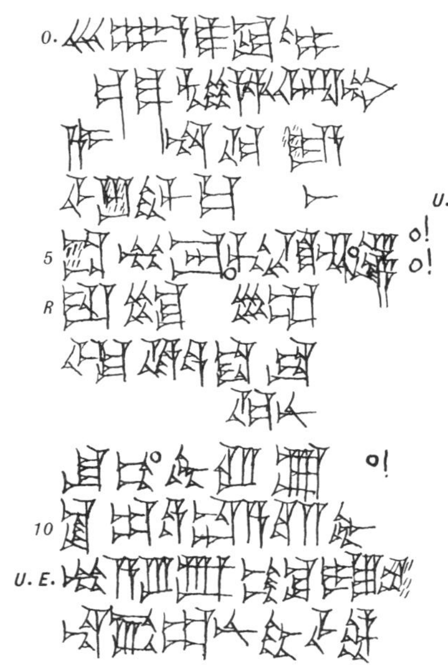

87

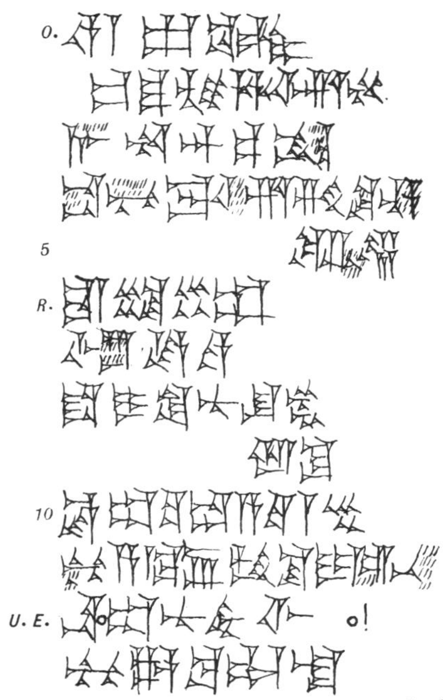

88

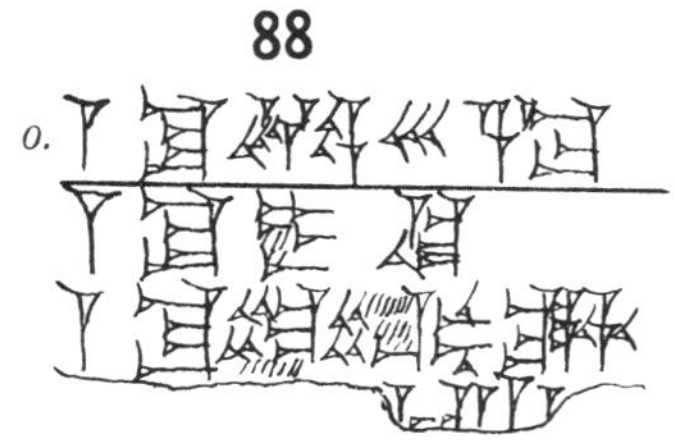

89

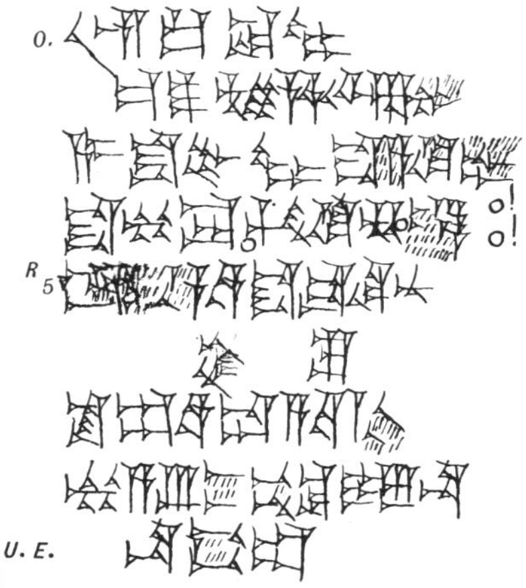

90

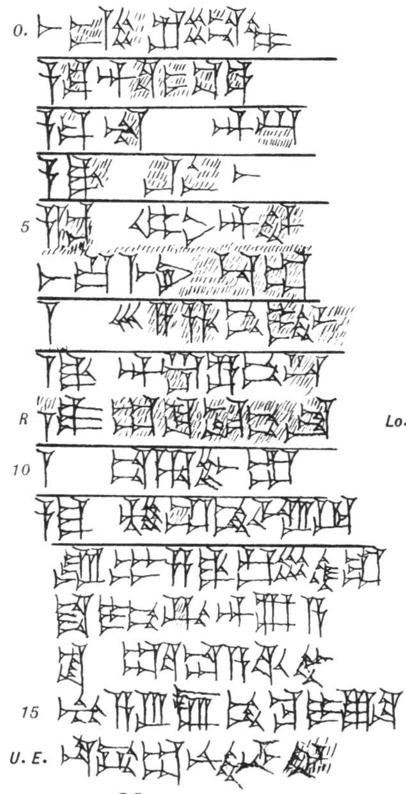

91 CASE

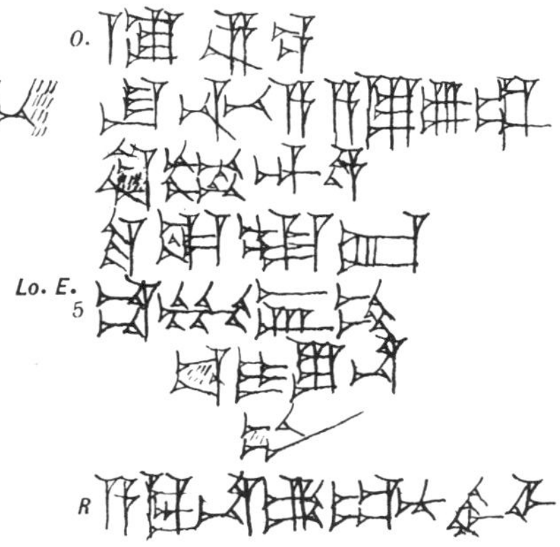

Indistinct seal impressions.

92

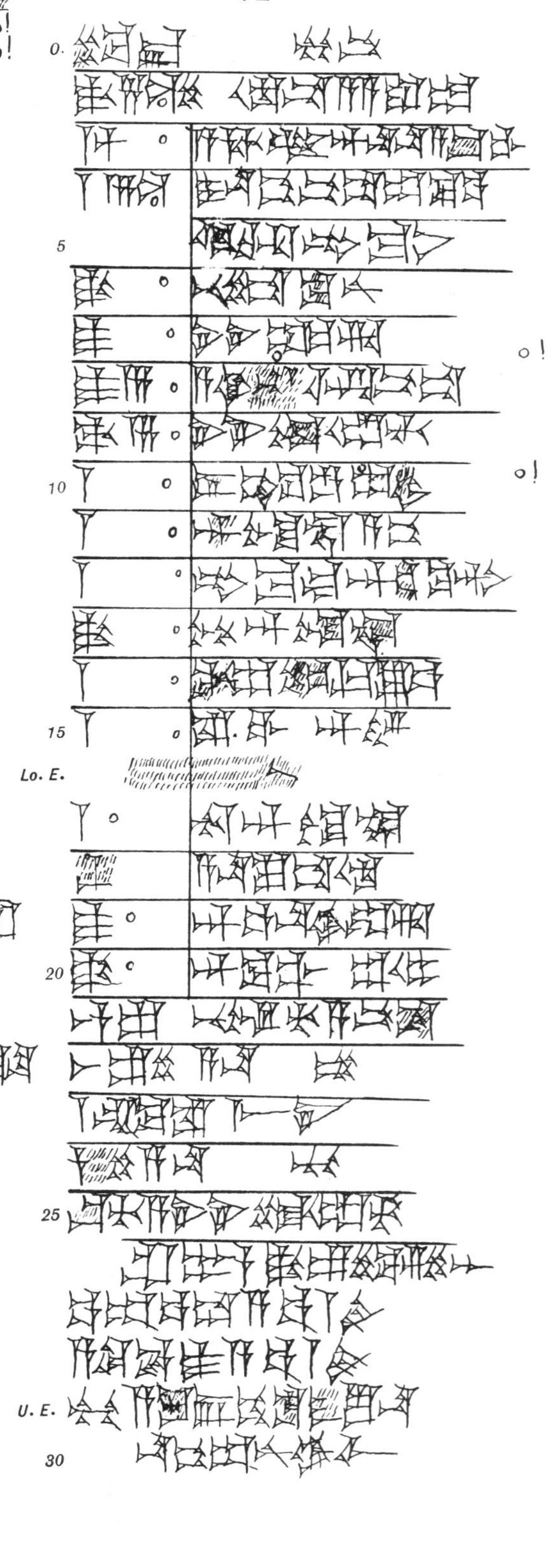

93

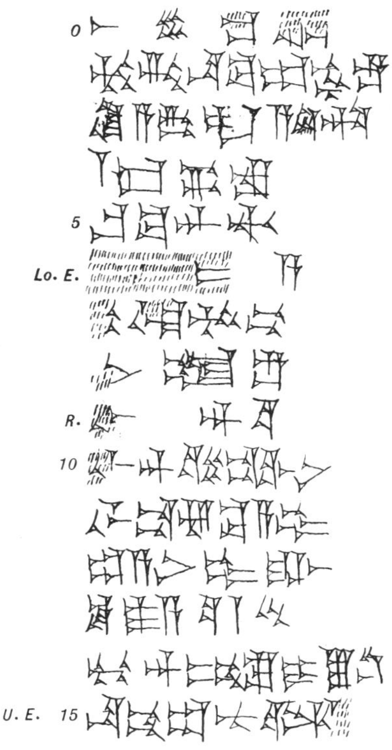

Indistinct seal impressions.

94

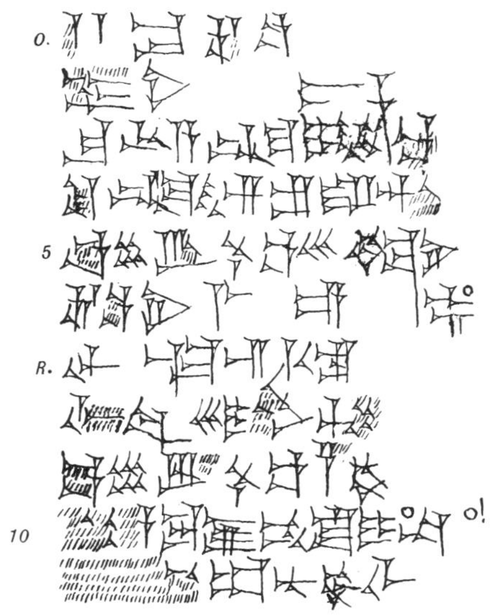

Indistinct seal impressions.

95

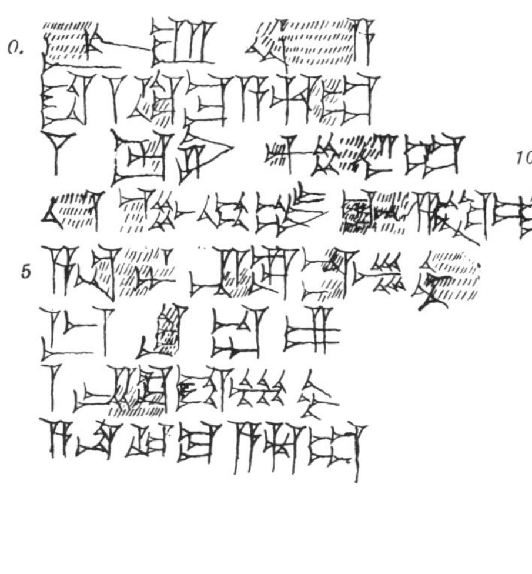

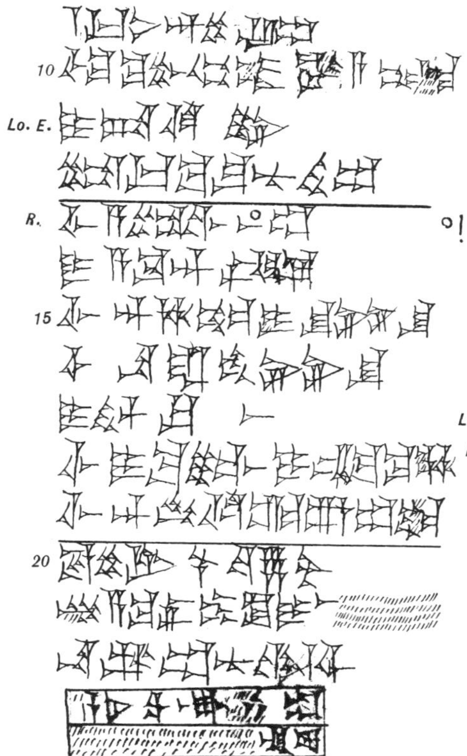

96

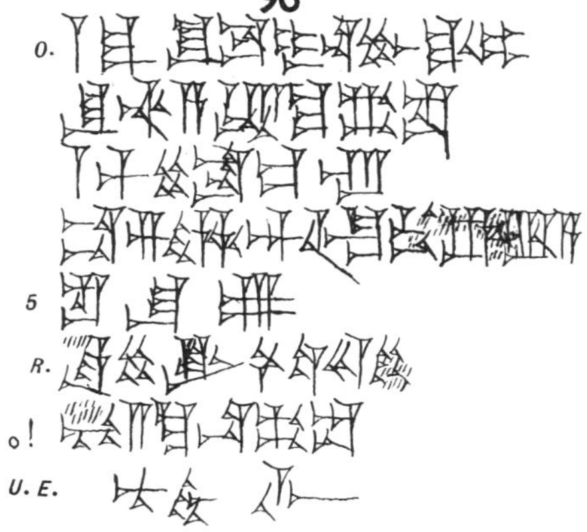

97

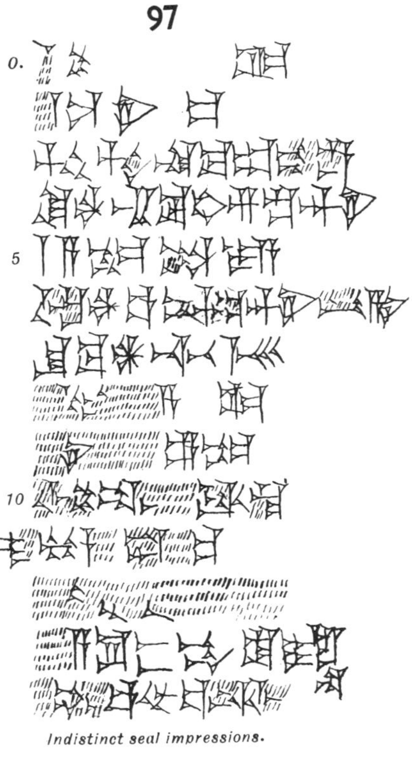

Indistinct seal impressions.

98

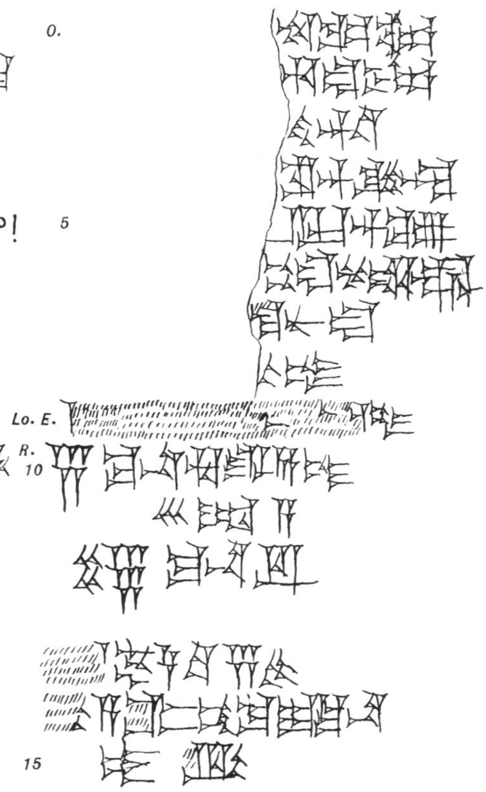

99

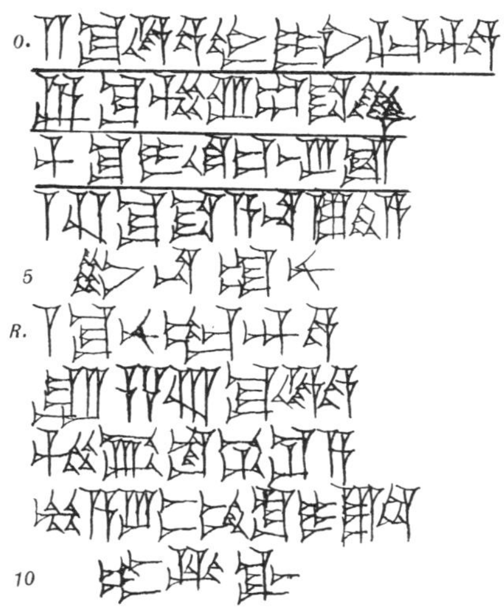

100

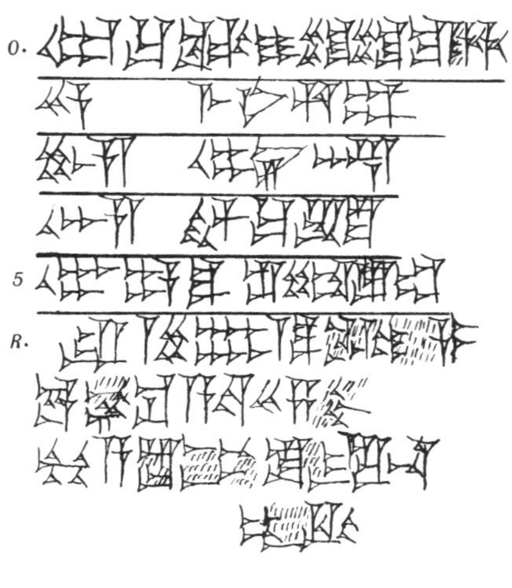

101

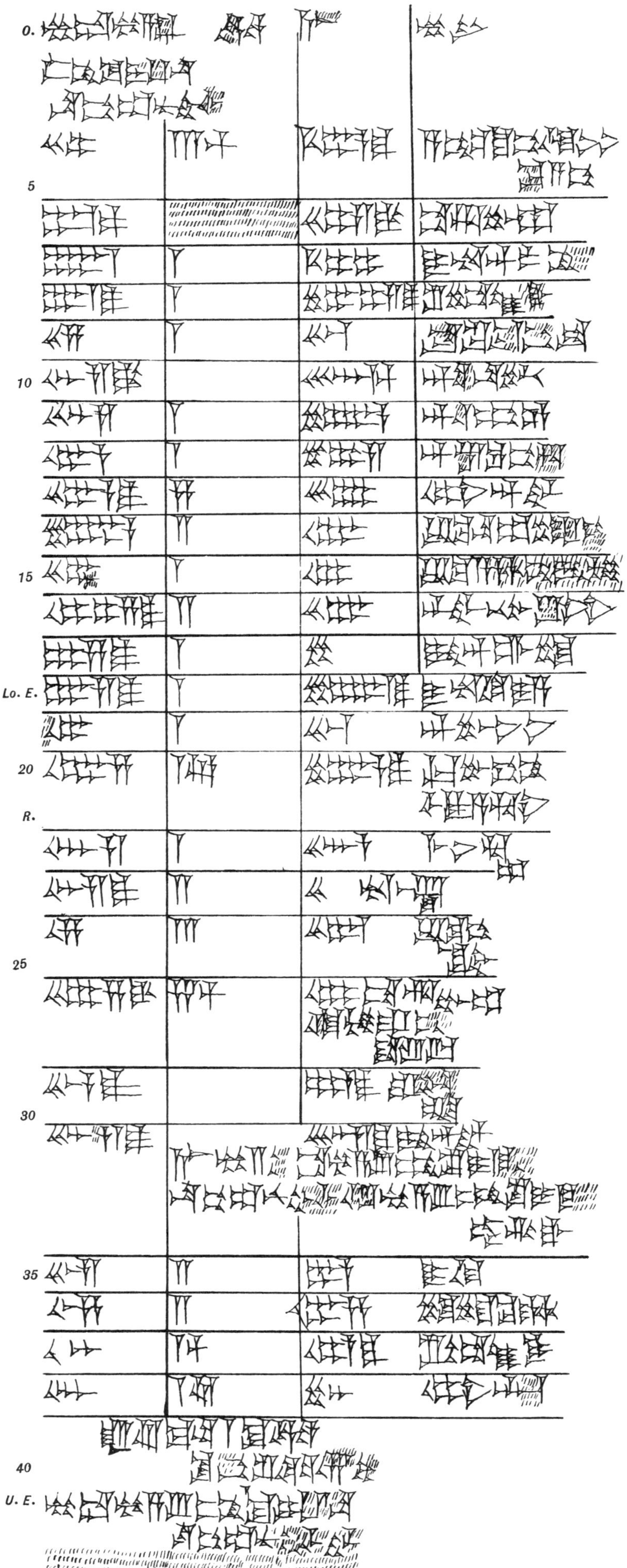

102

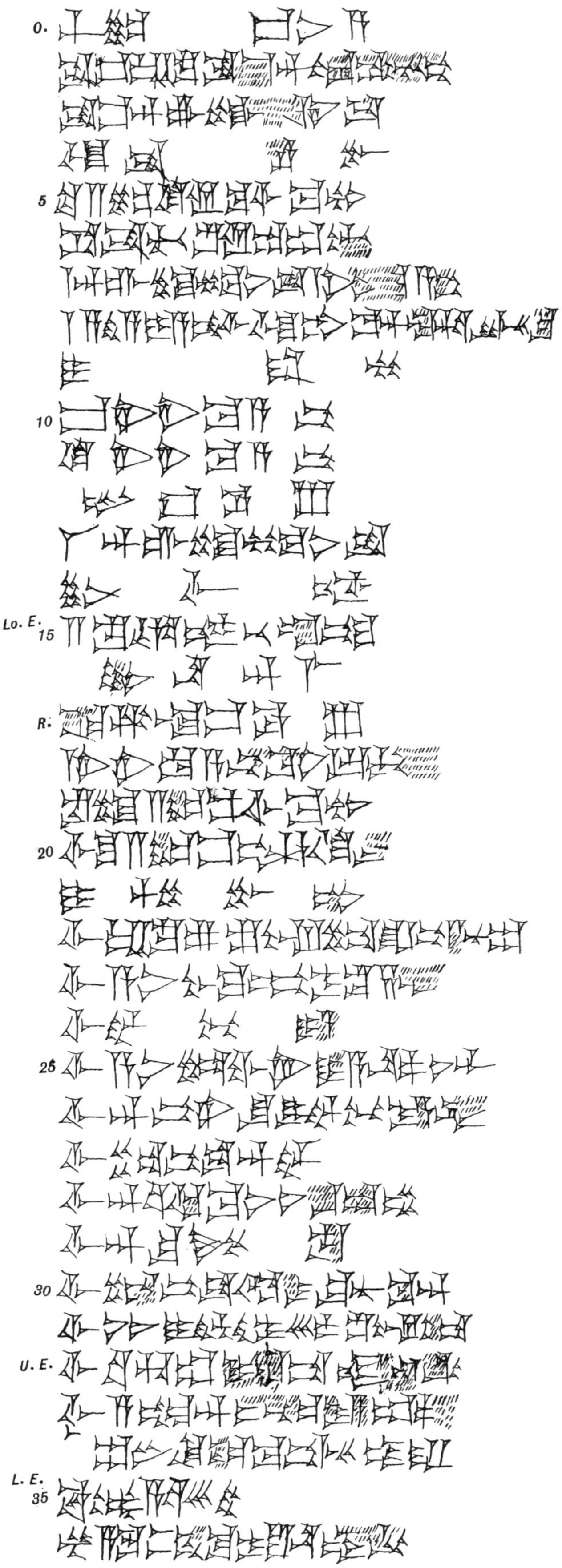

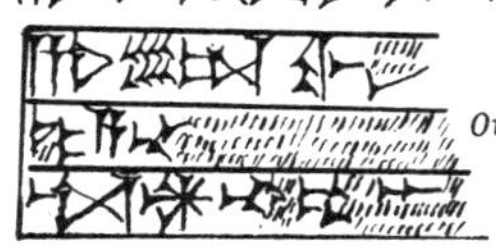

Other indistinct seal impressions.

103

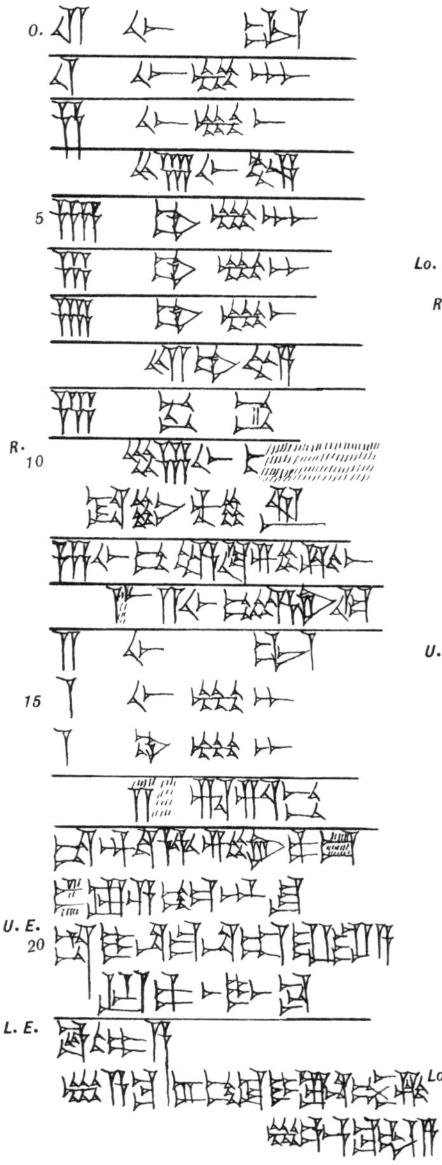

104

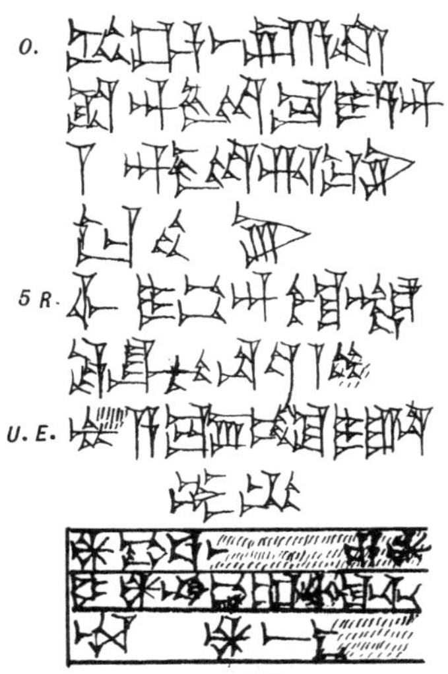

105

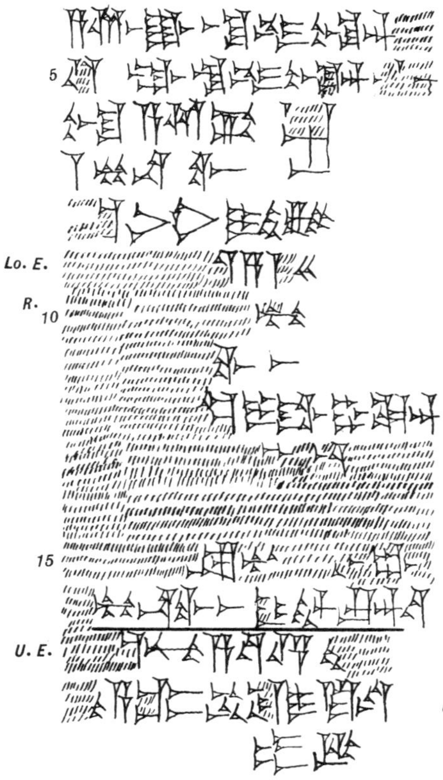

Indistinct seal impressions

106

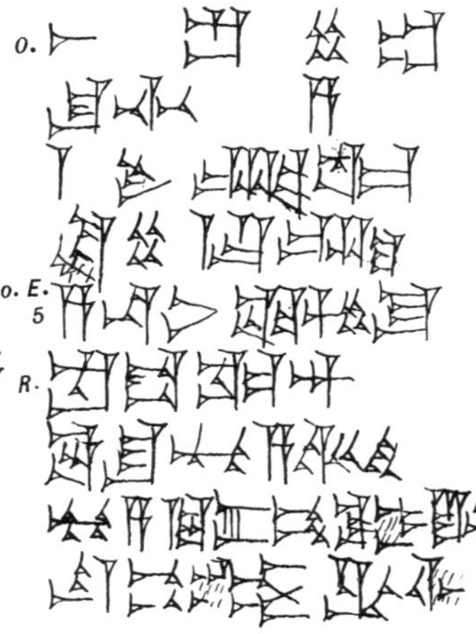

Indistinct seal impressions

107

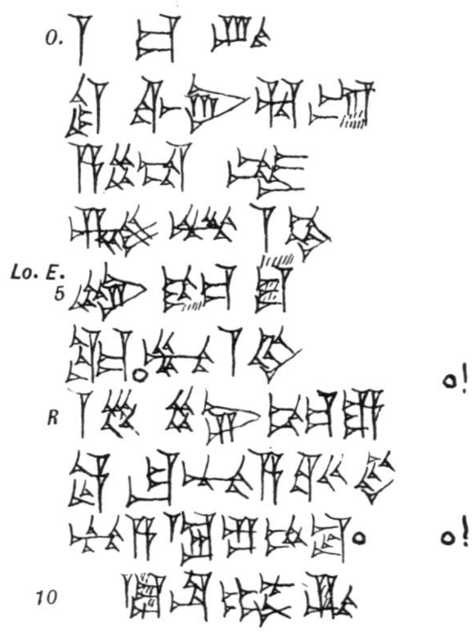

108

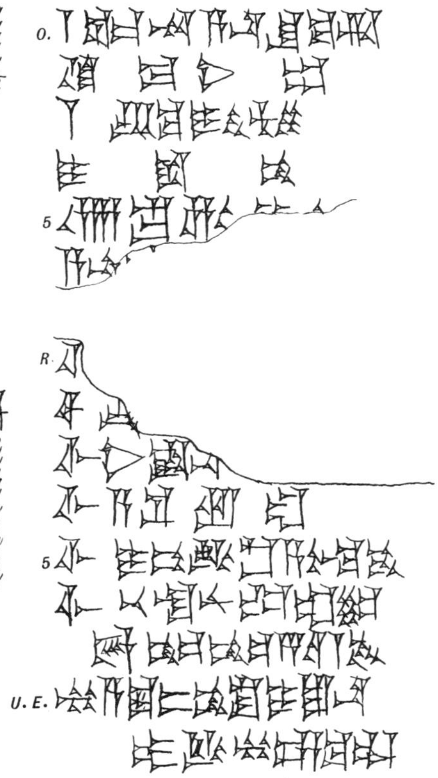

Indistinct seal impressions.

109

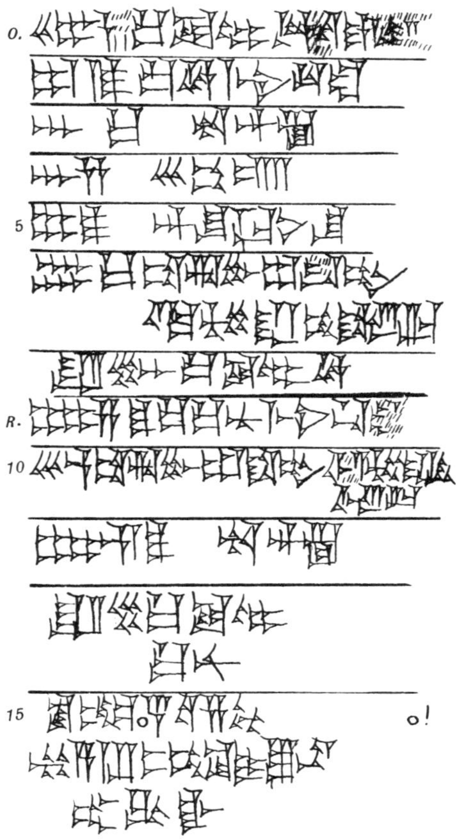

110

CONTINUED

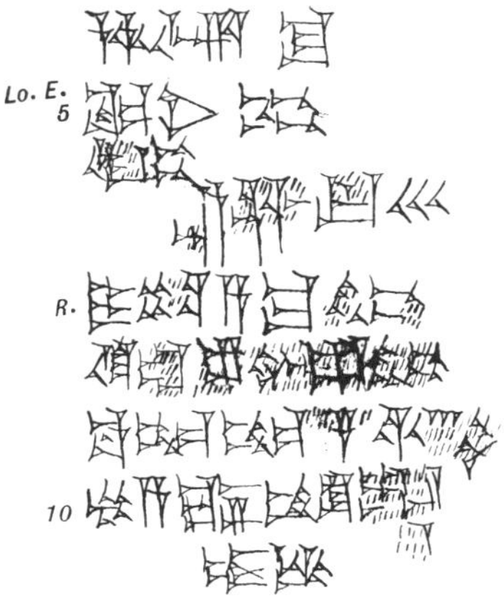

Indistinct seal impressions.

111

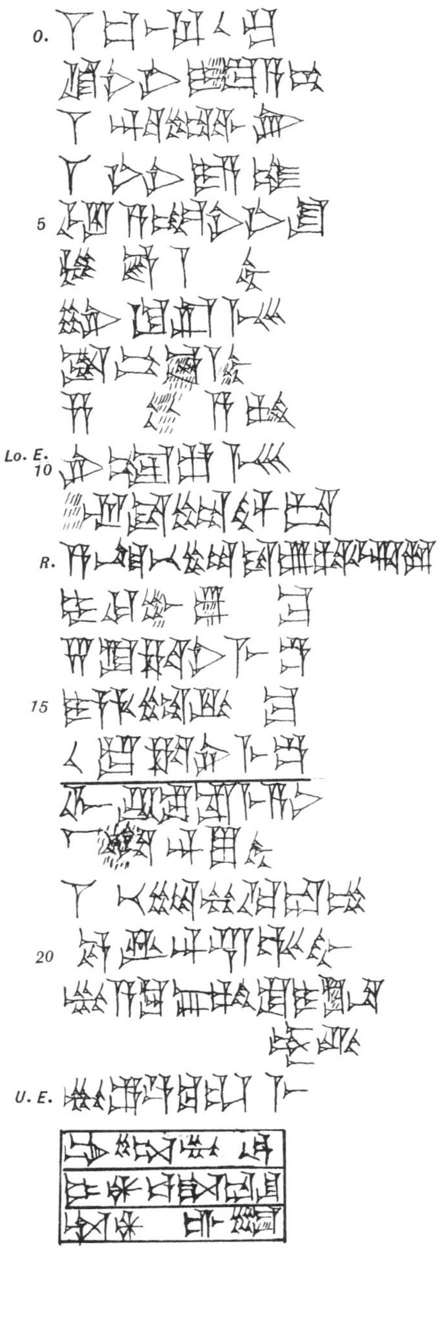

112

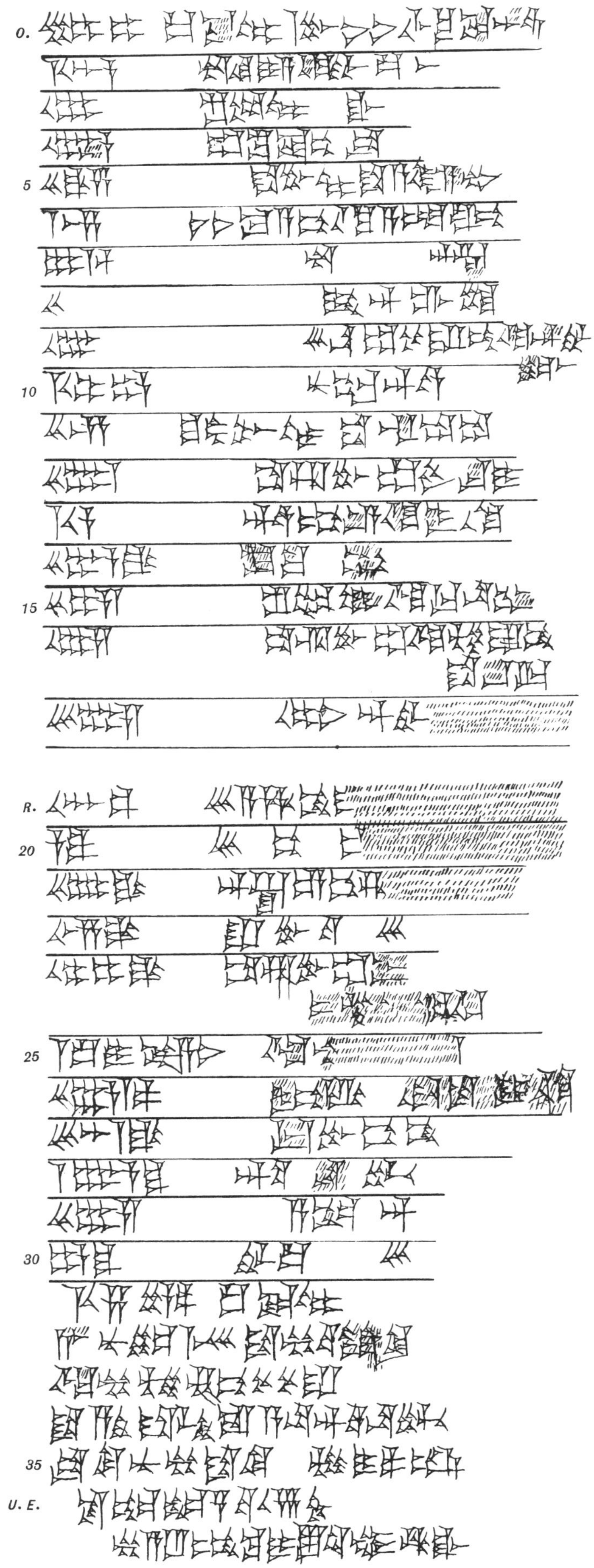

113

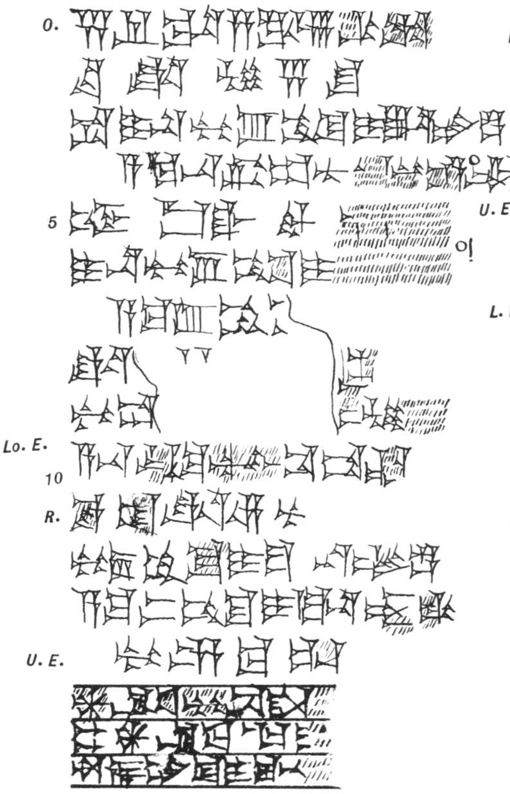

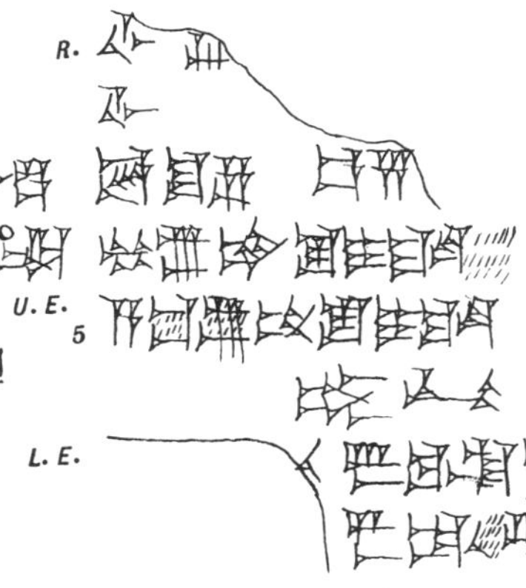

Indistinct seal impressions.

114

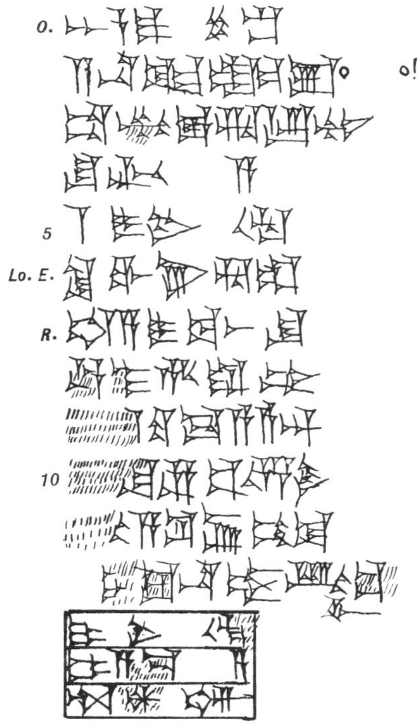

115

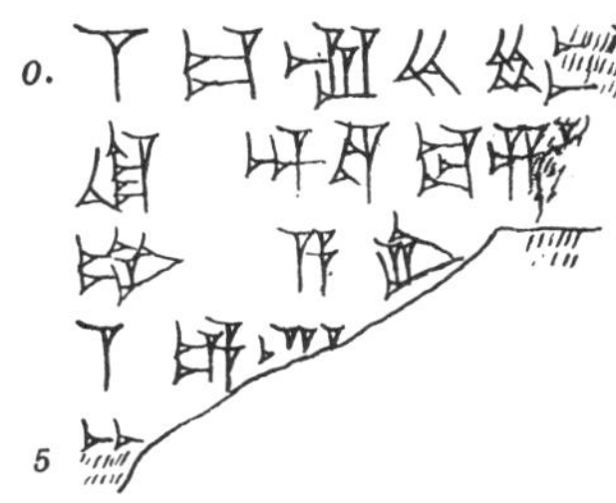

116

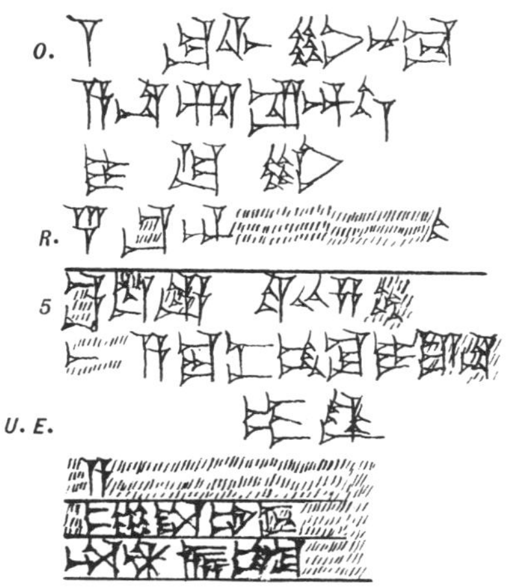

117

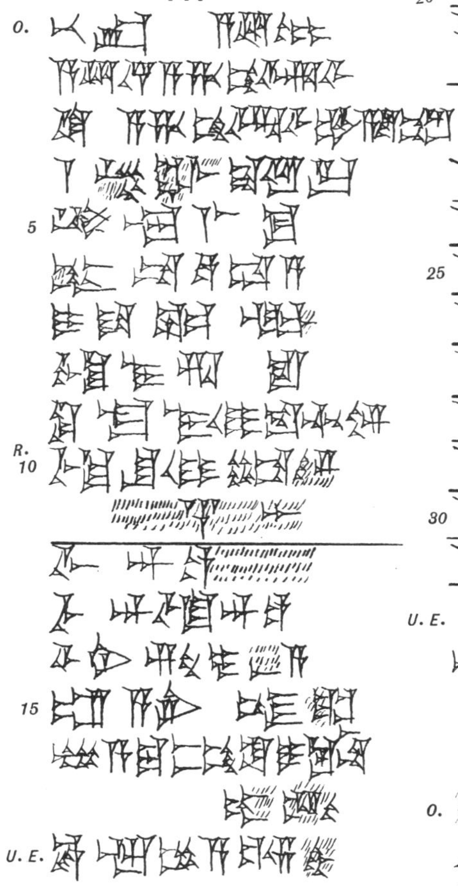

Indistinct seal impressions.

118

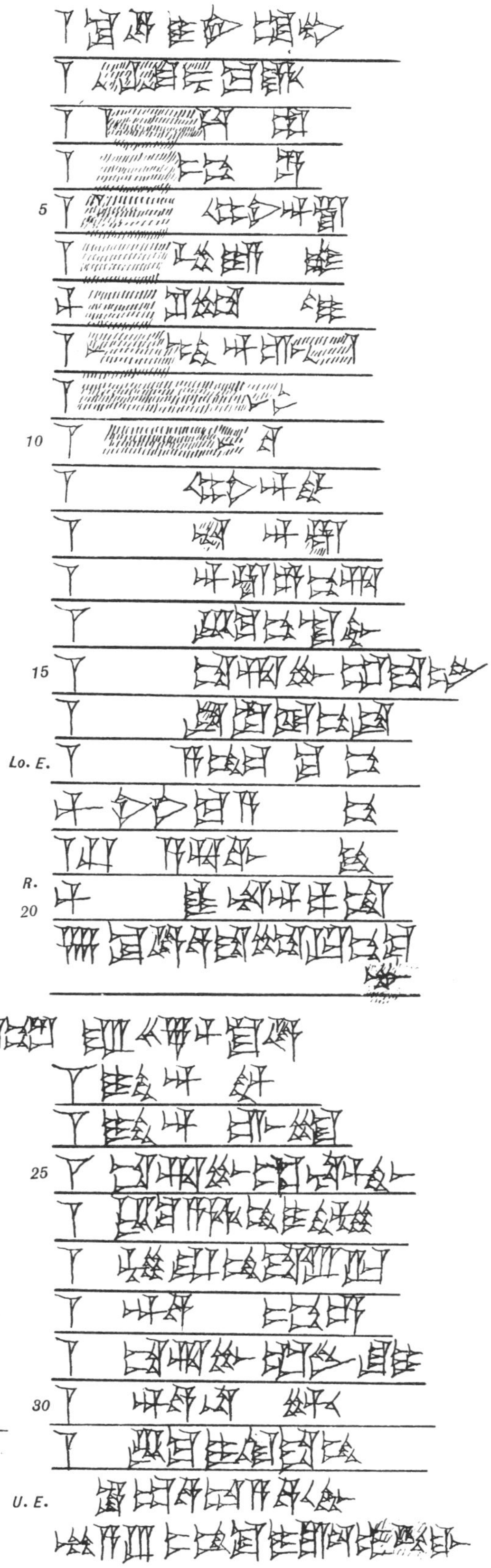

119

PLATE XXII

CONTINUED

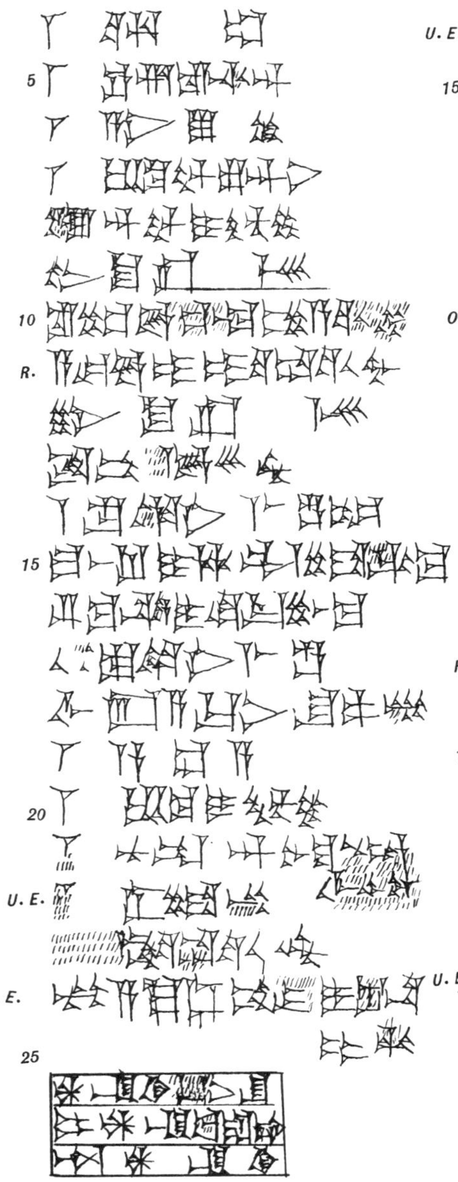

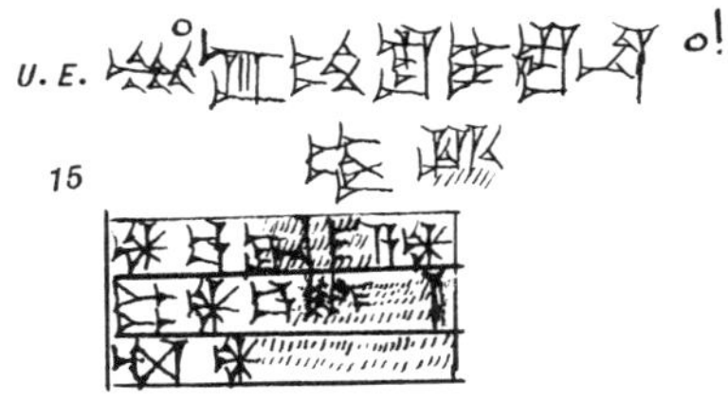

121

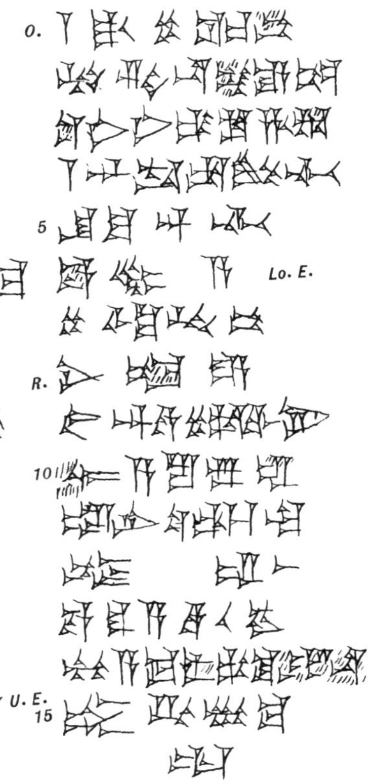

120

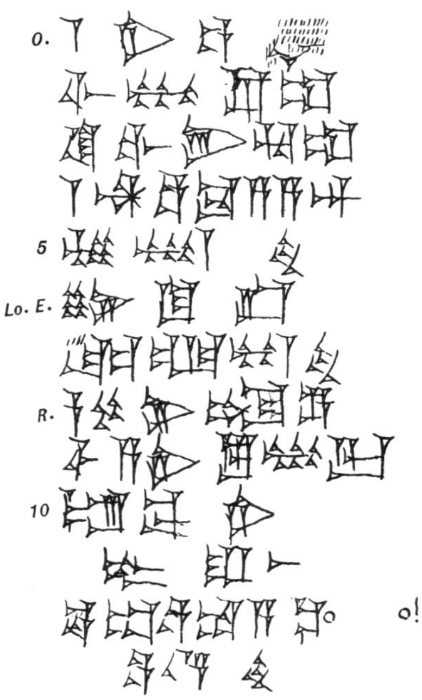

122

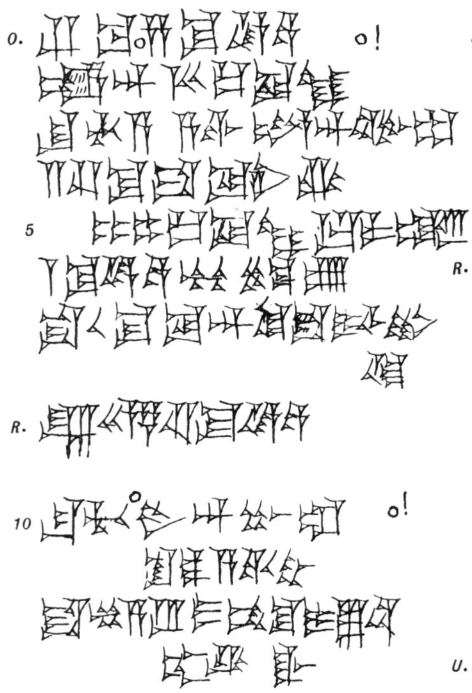

123

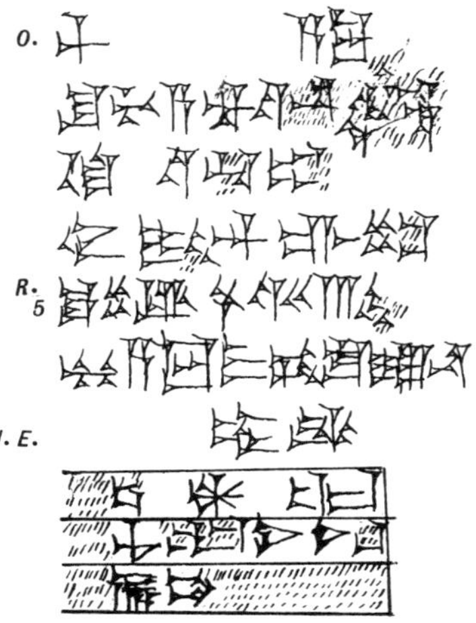

124

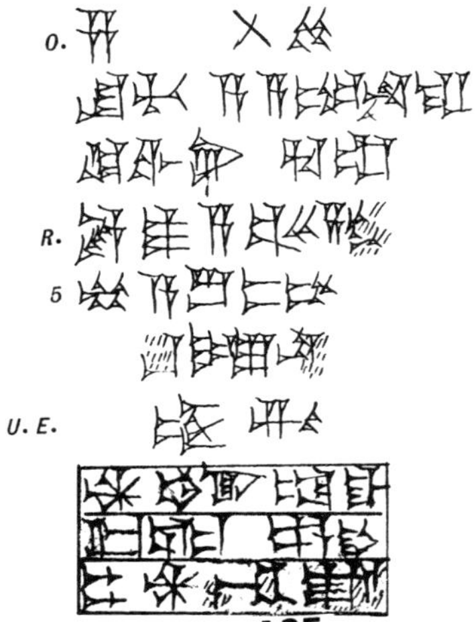

125

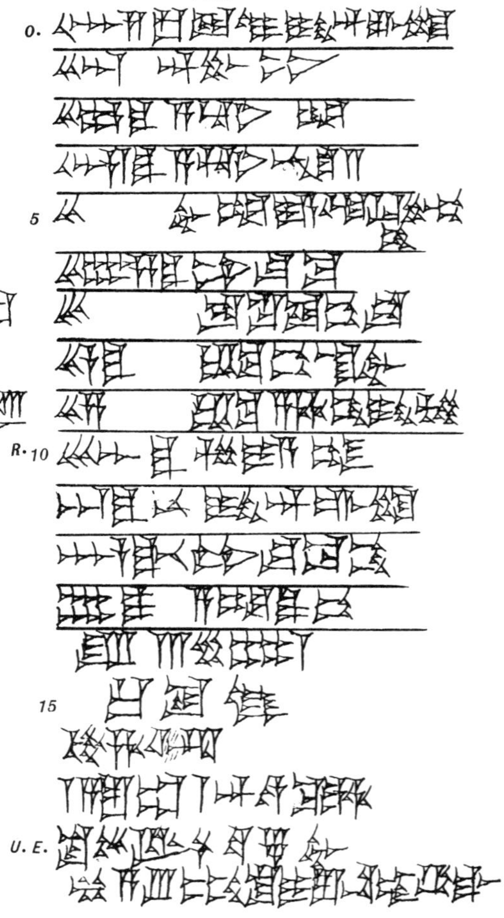

126

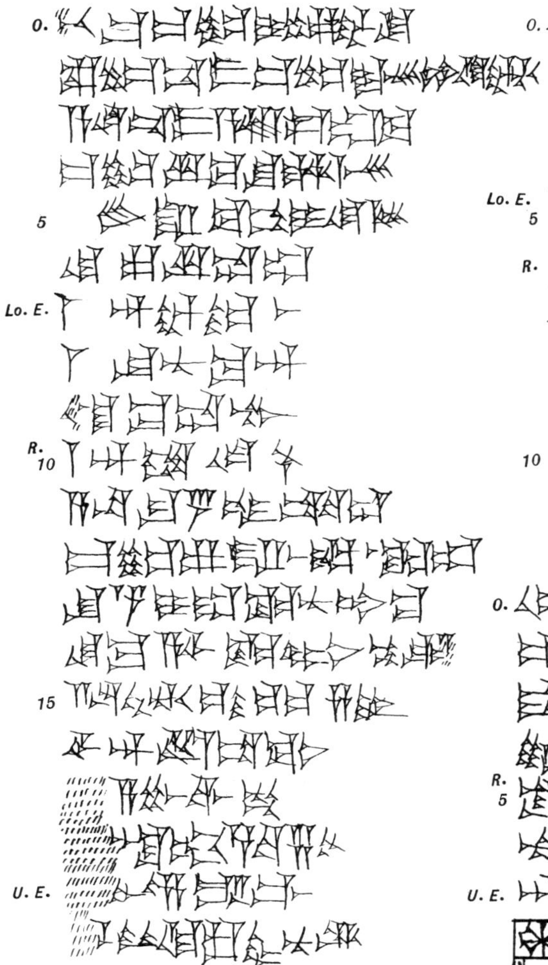

Indistinct seal impressions.

127

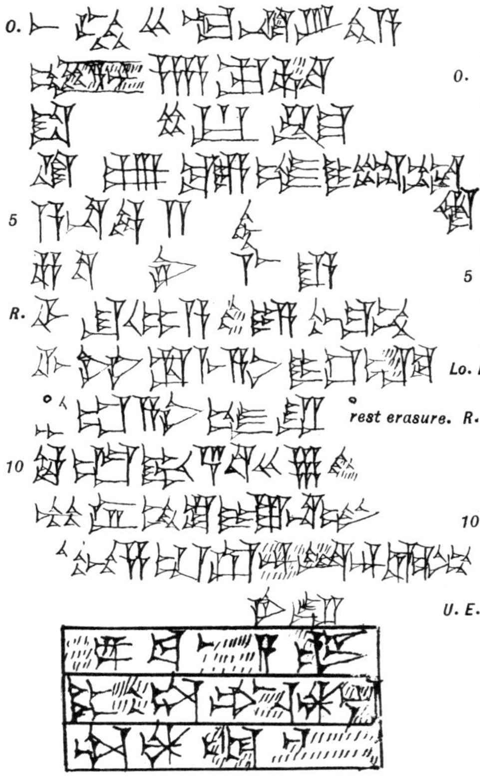

128

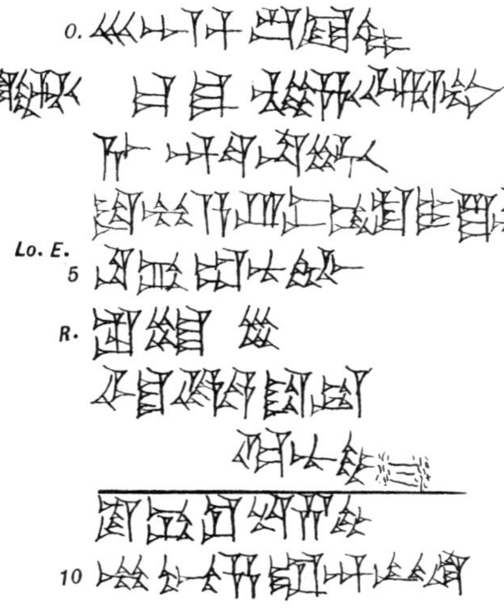

129

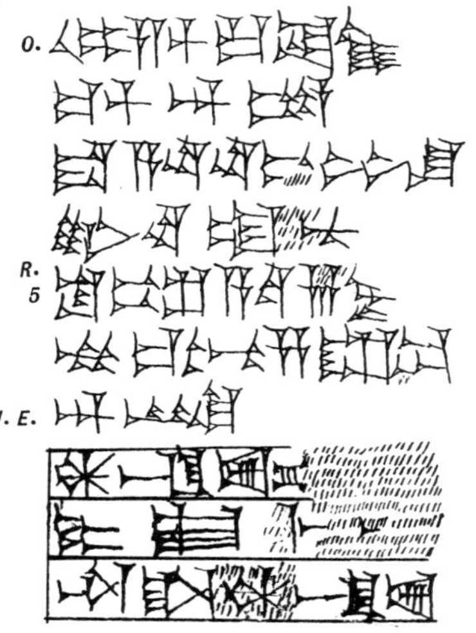

130

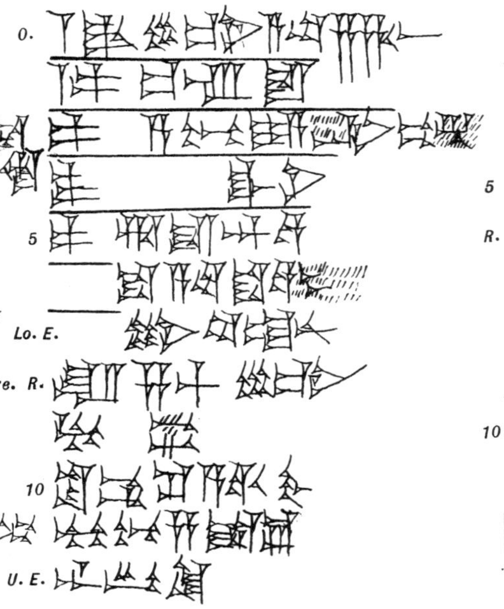

131

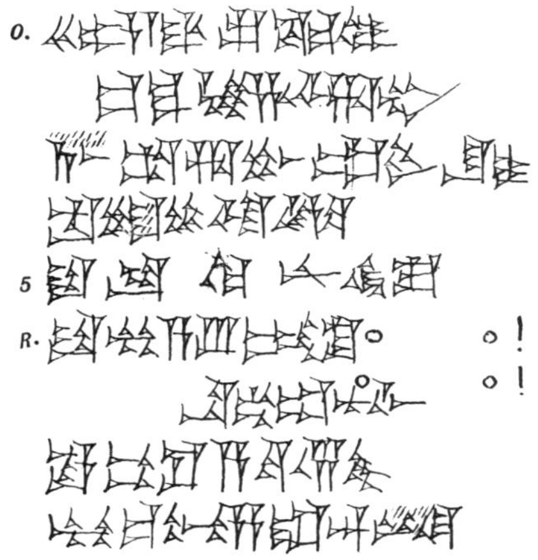

132

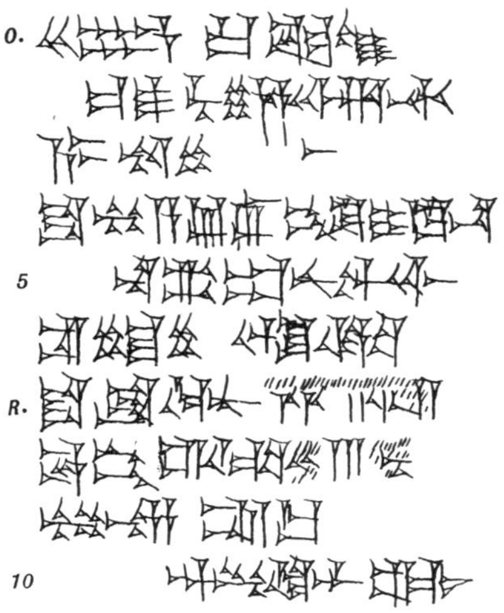

133

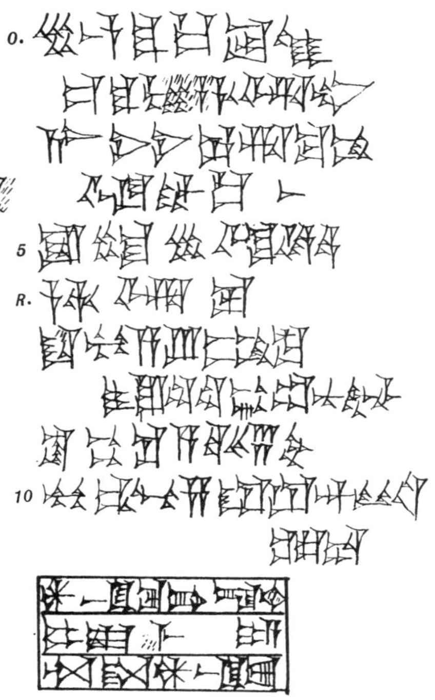

134

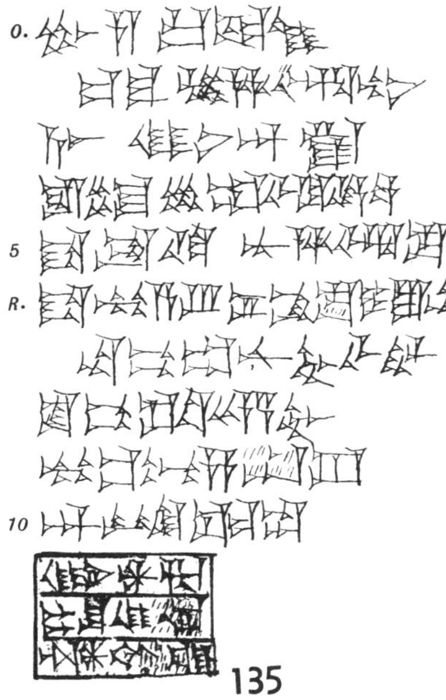

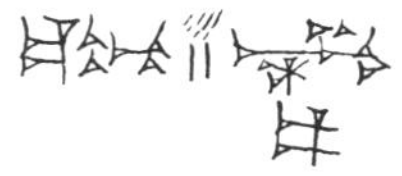

Indistinct seal impressions.

135

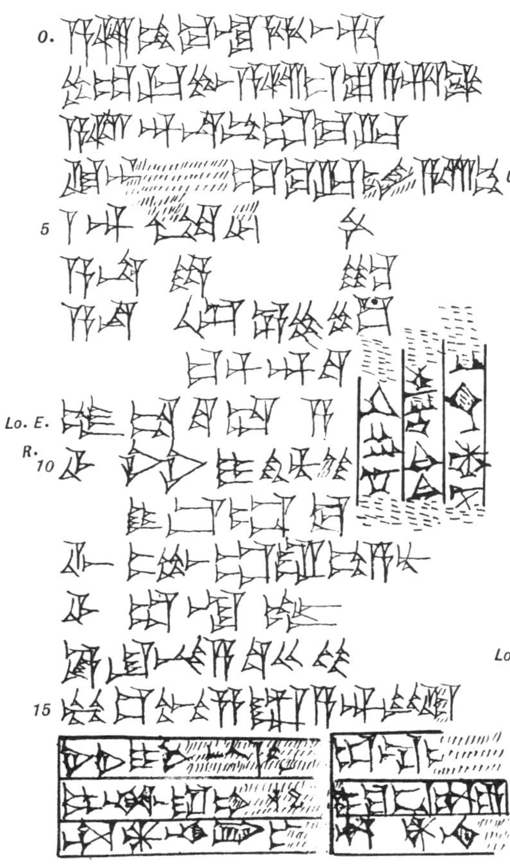

136

137

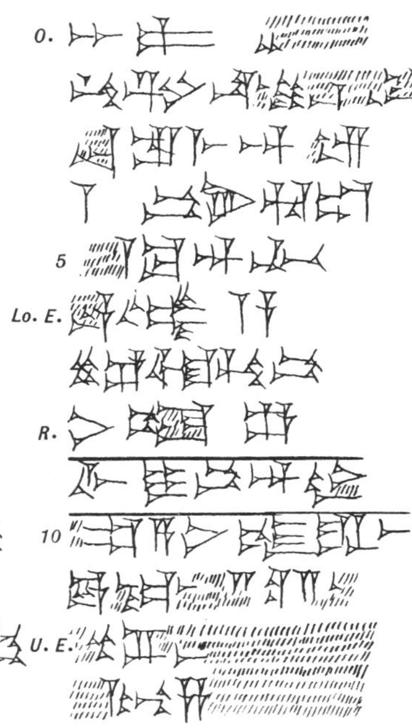

Indistinct seal impressions.

138

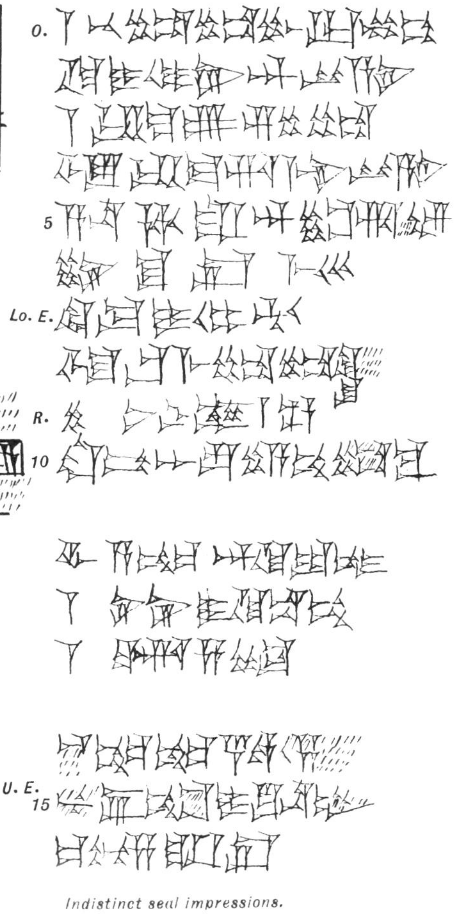

Indistinct seal impressions.

139

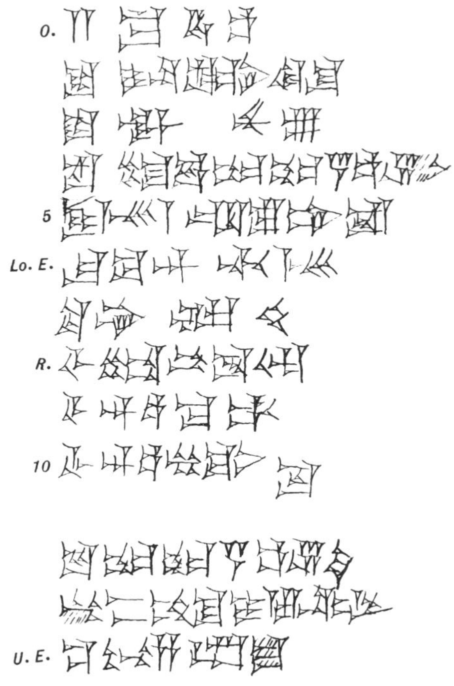

Indistinct seal impressions.

140

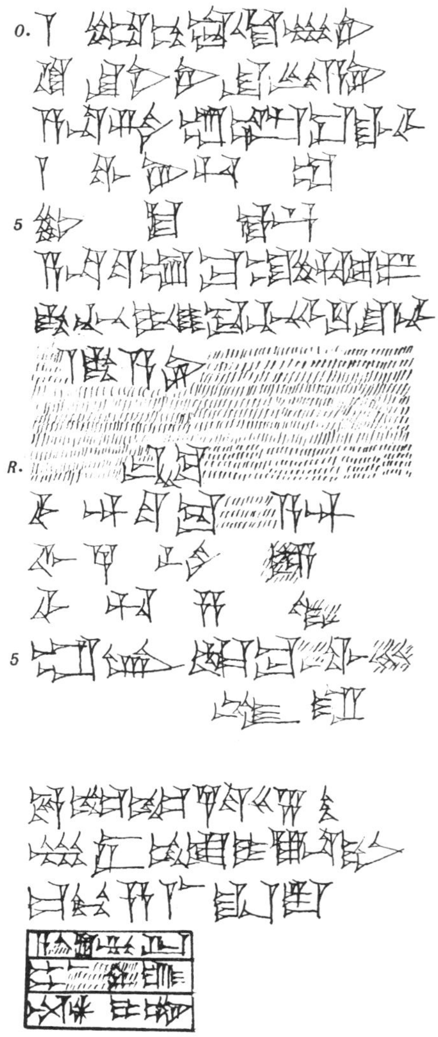

141

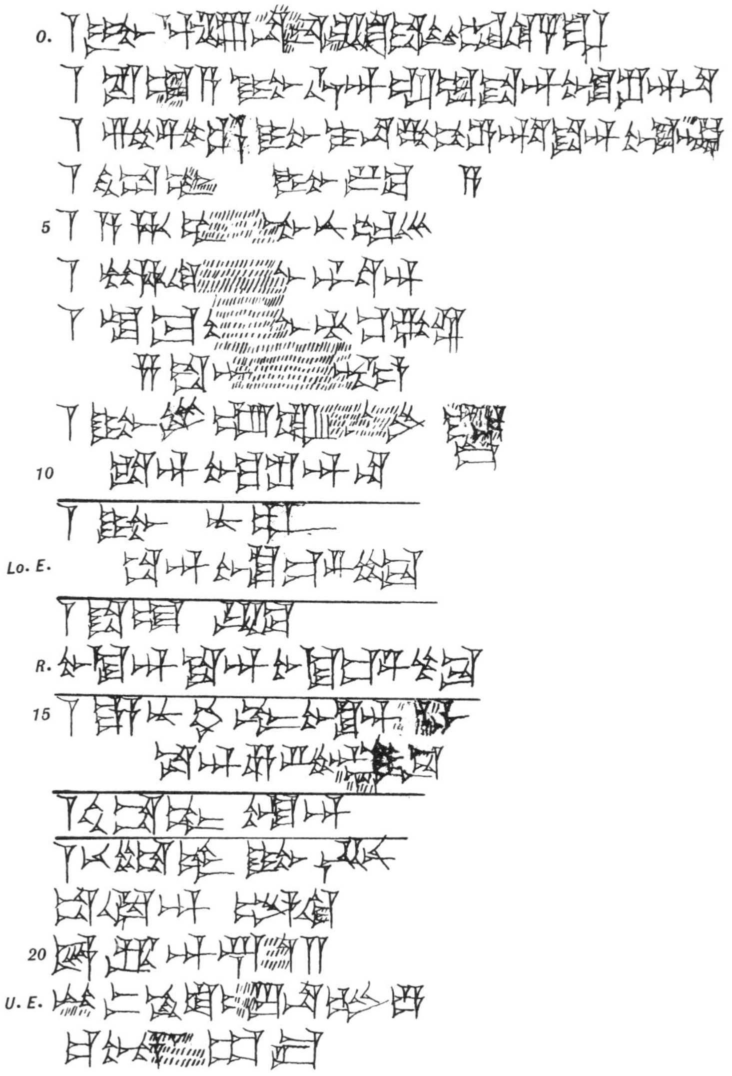

142

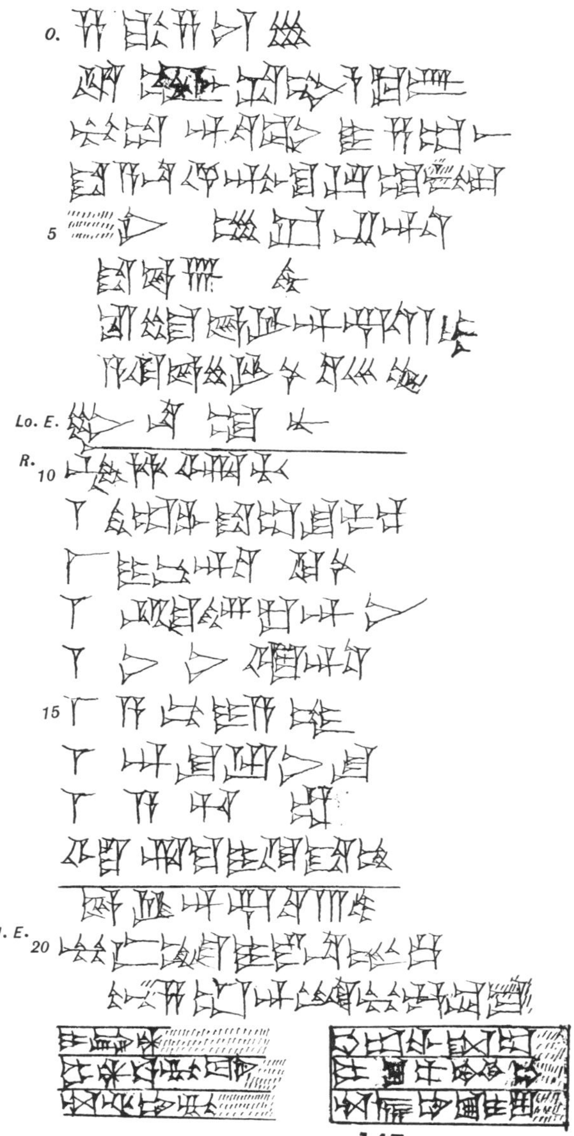

143

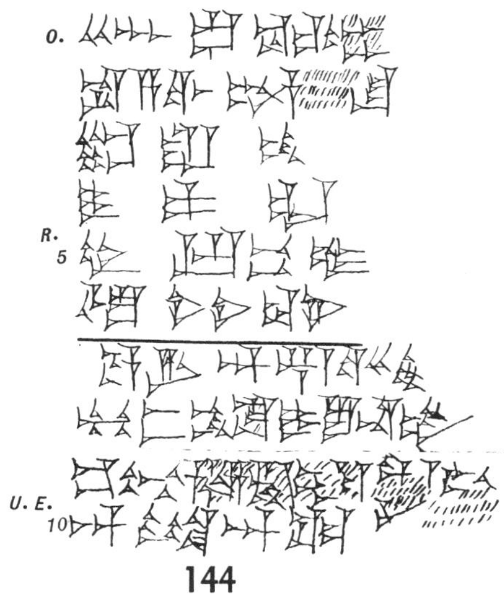

144

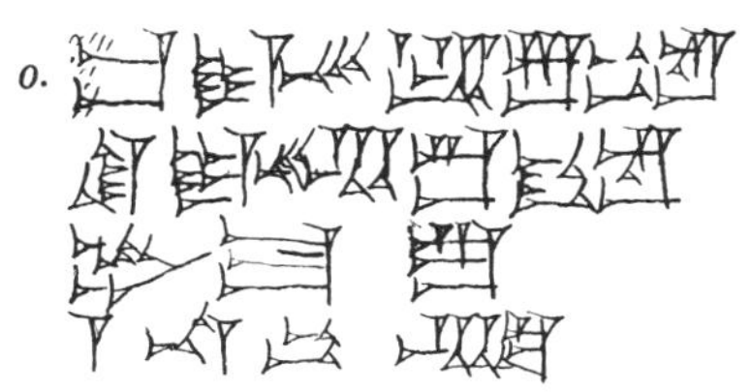

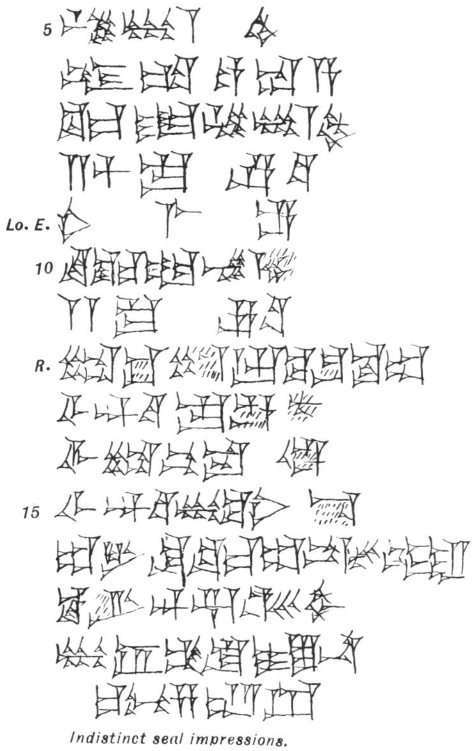

Indistinct seal impressions.

145

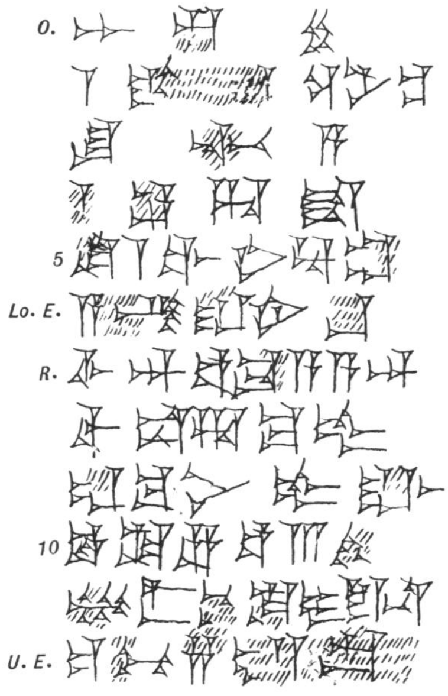

Indistinct seal impressions.

146

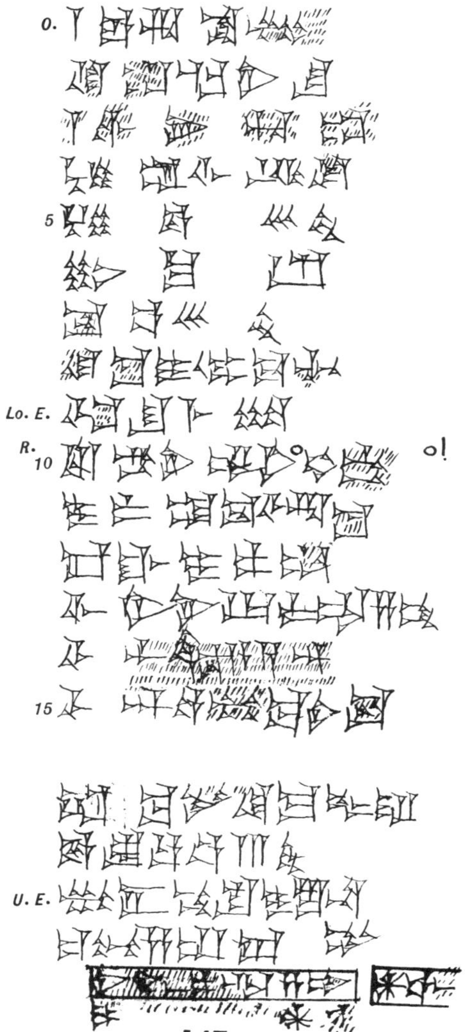

147

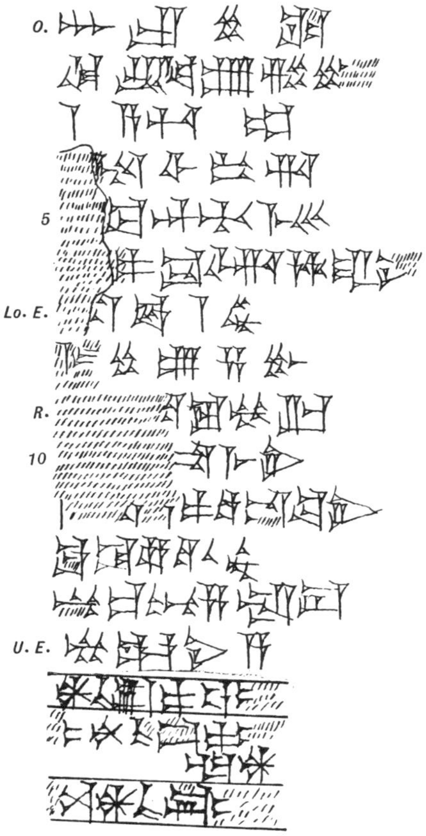

148

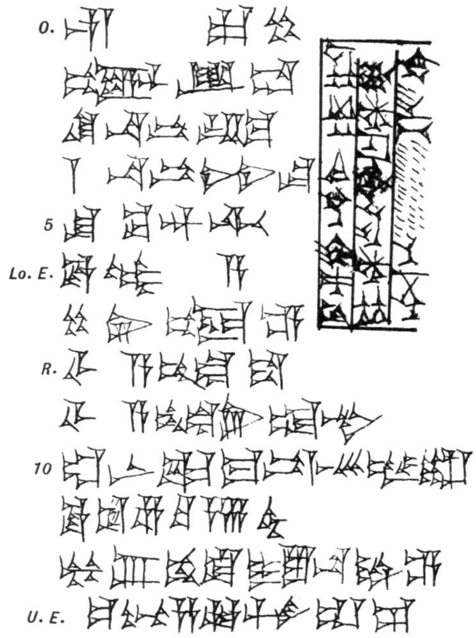

Indistinct seal impressions.

149

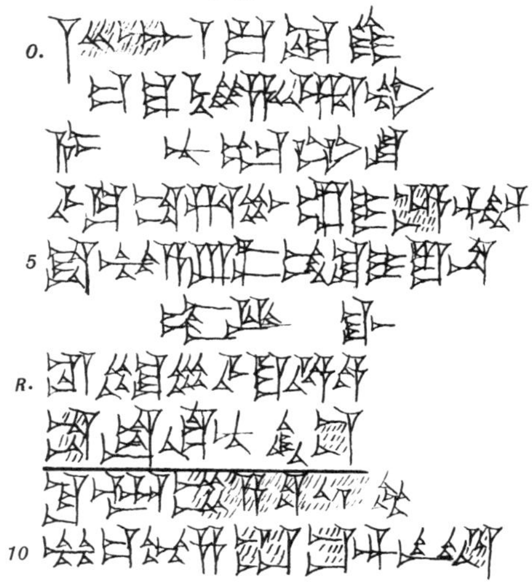

150

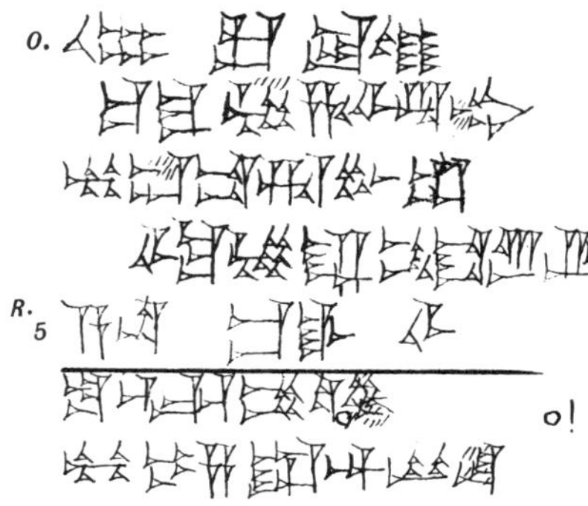

Indistinct seal impressions.

151

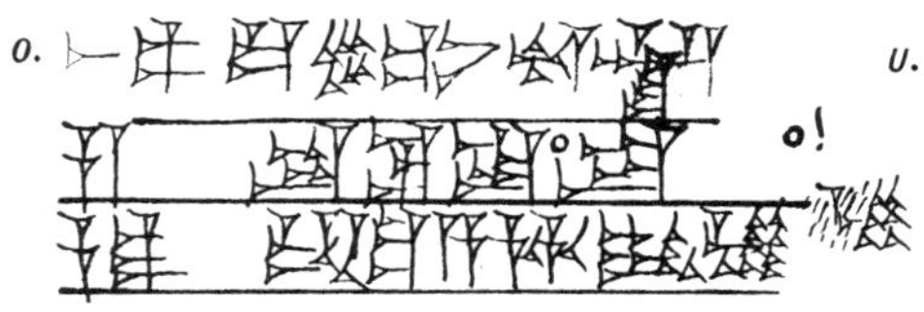

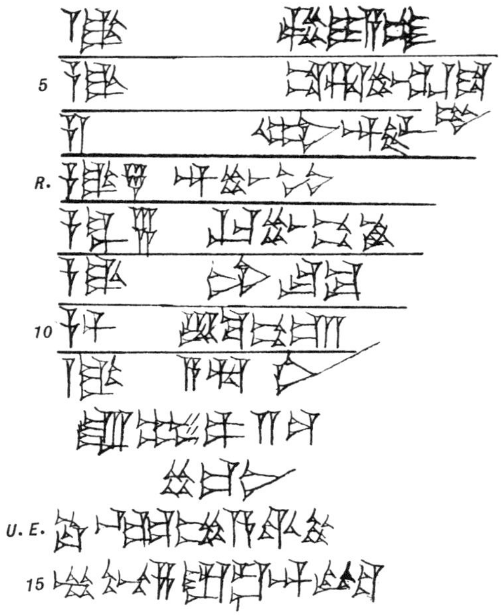

152

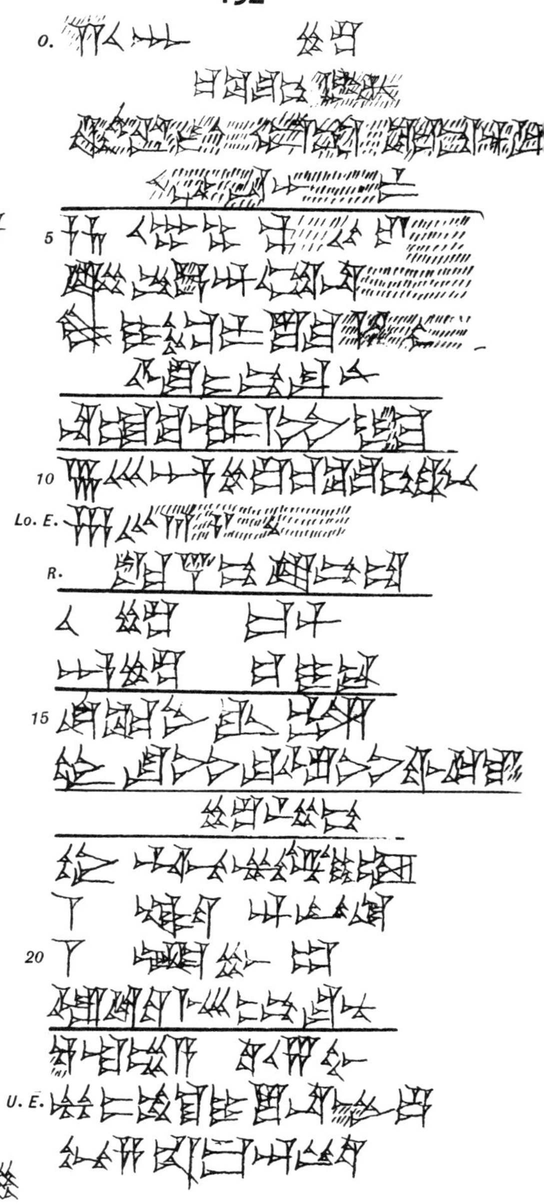

153

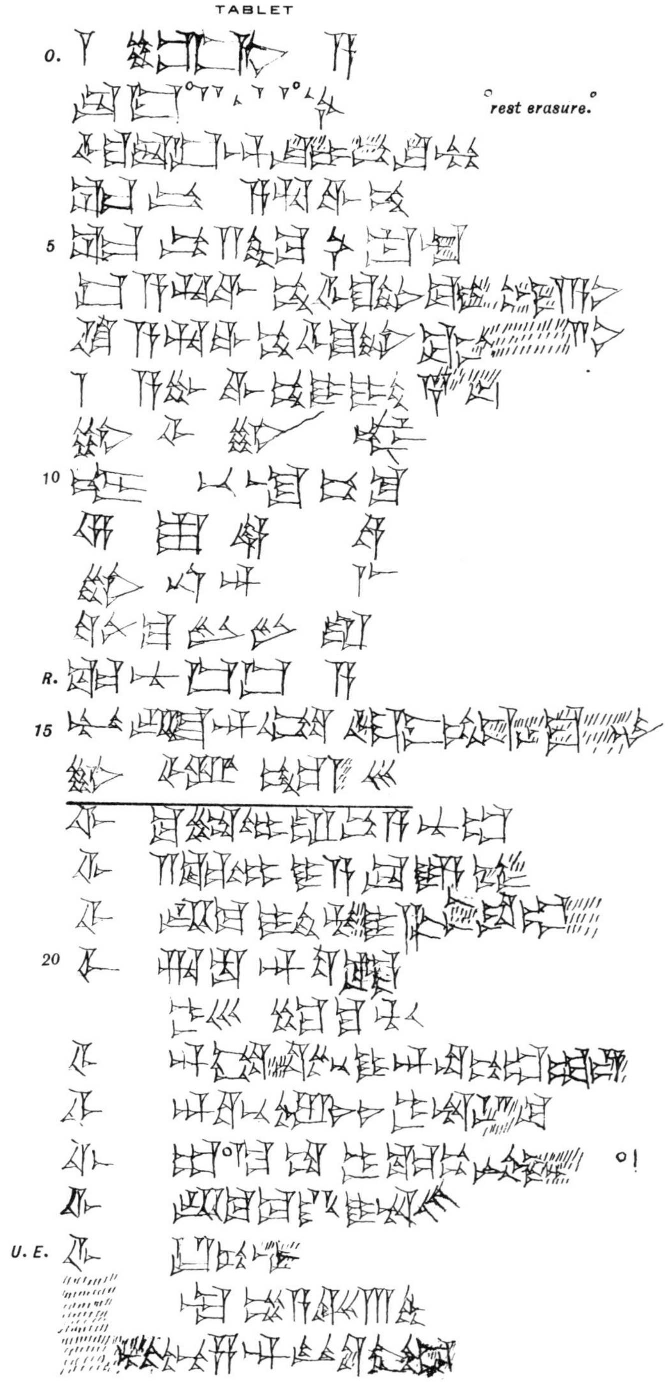

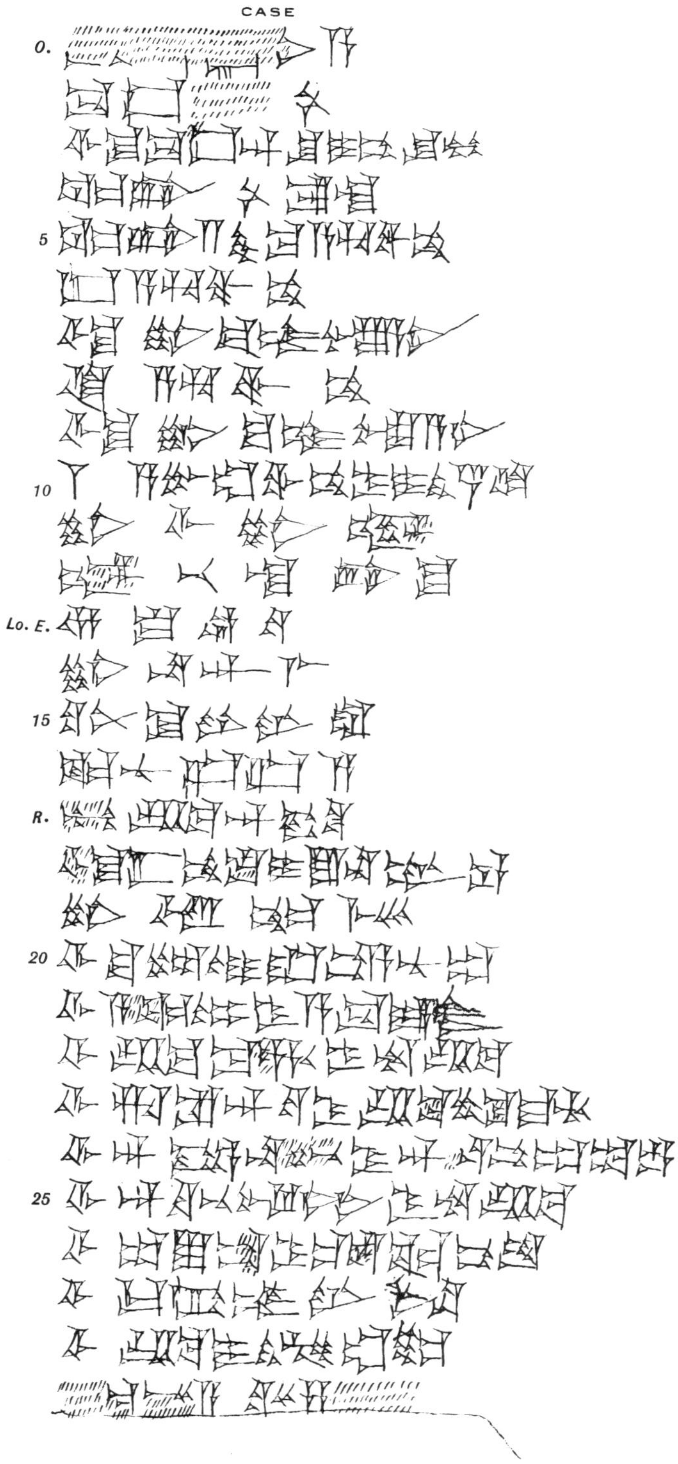

154

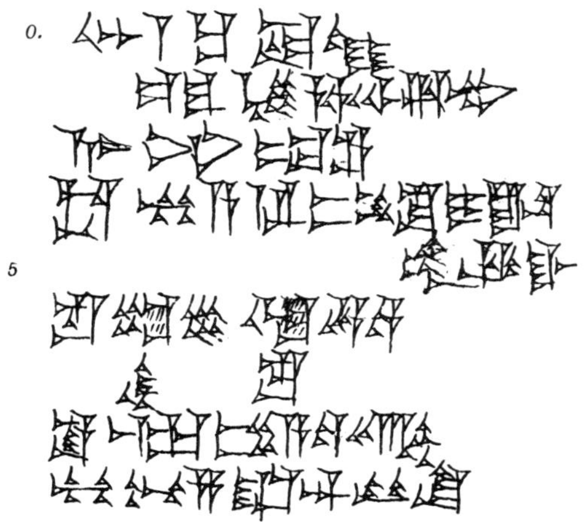

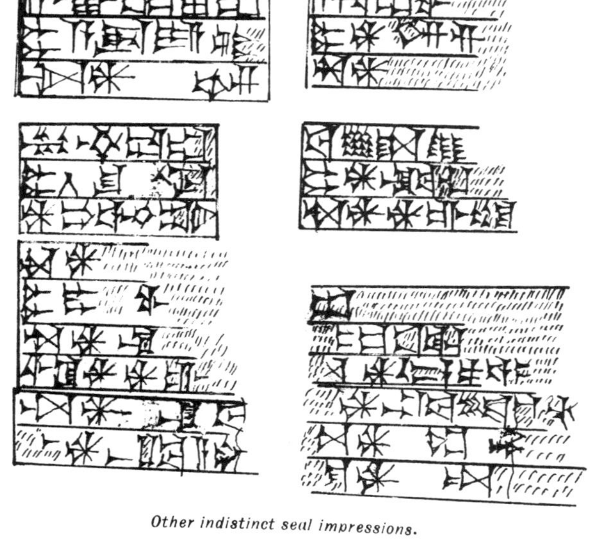

Other indistinct seal impressions.

155

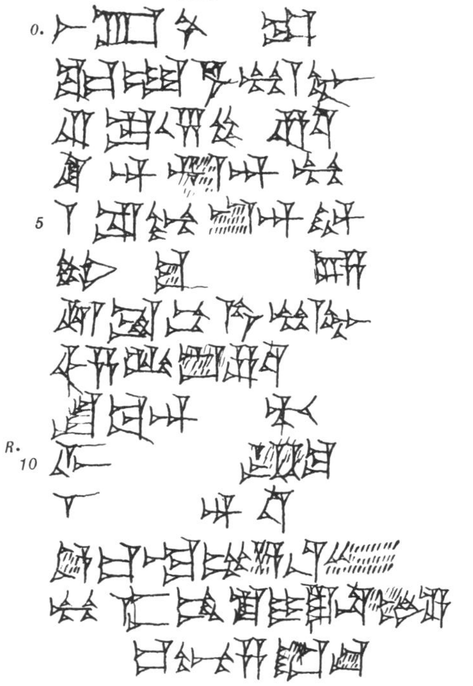

156

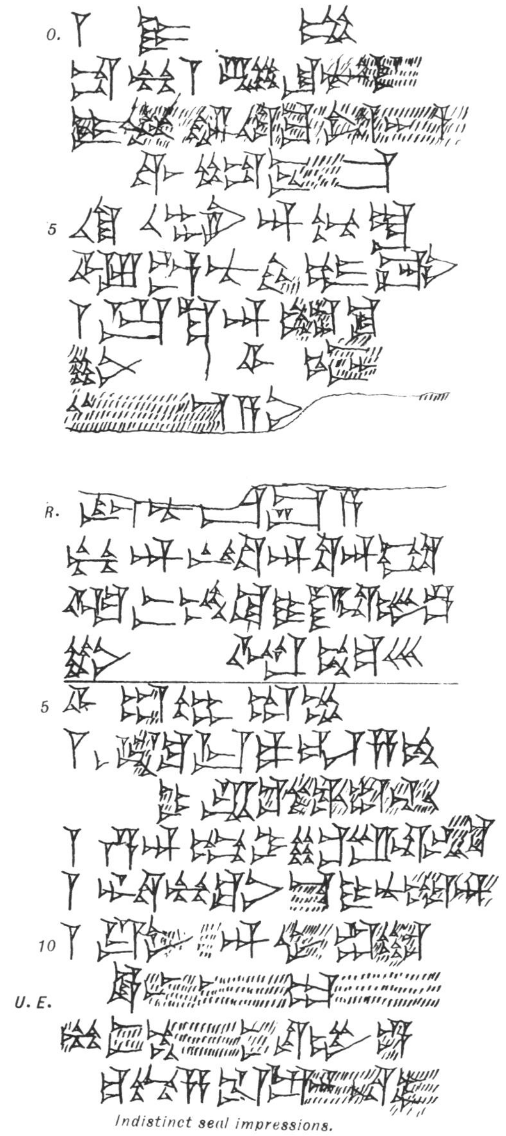

Indistinct seal impressions.

157

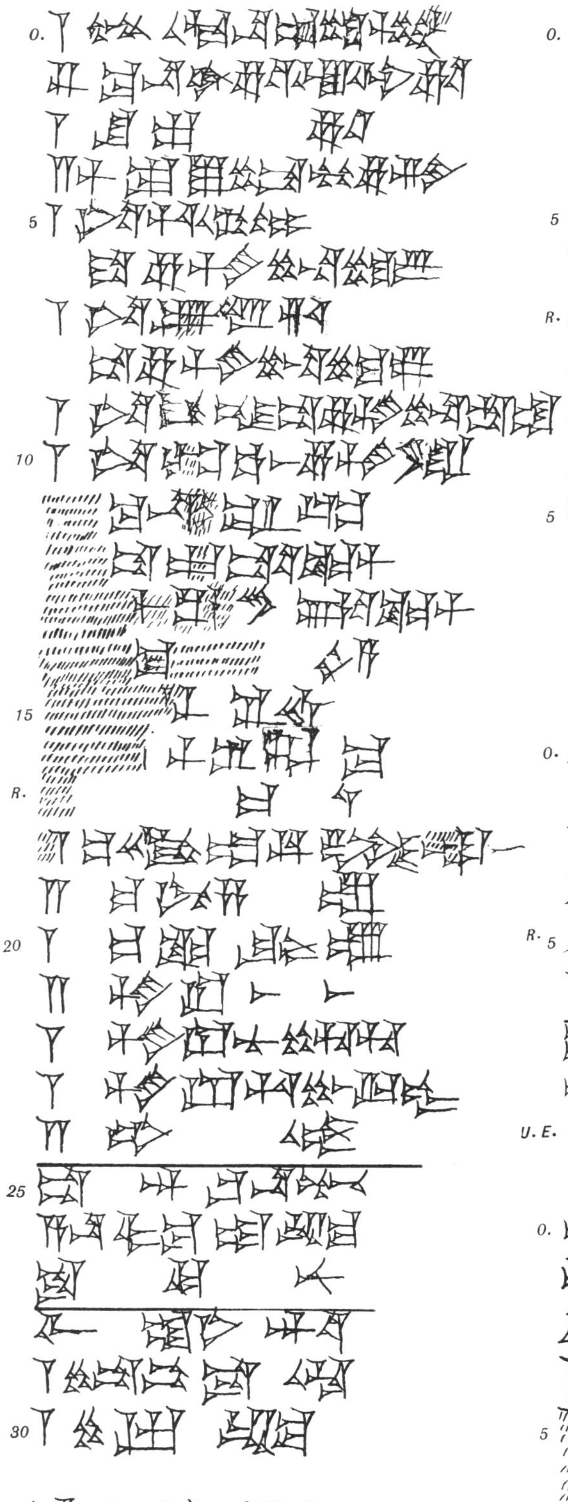

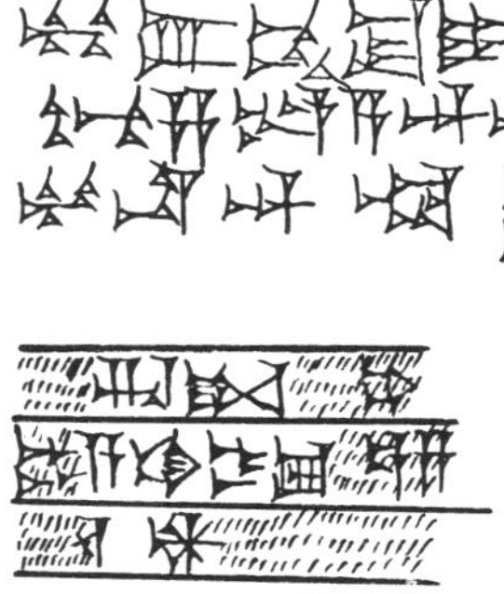

158

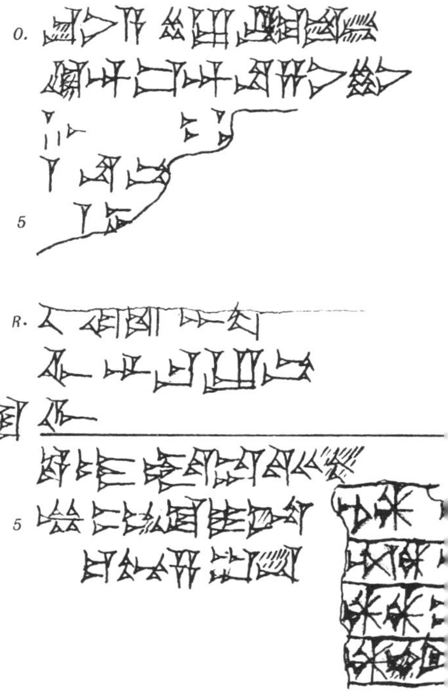

159

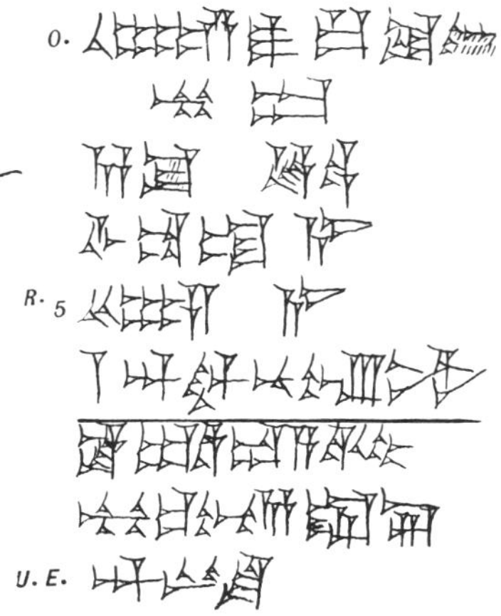

160

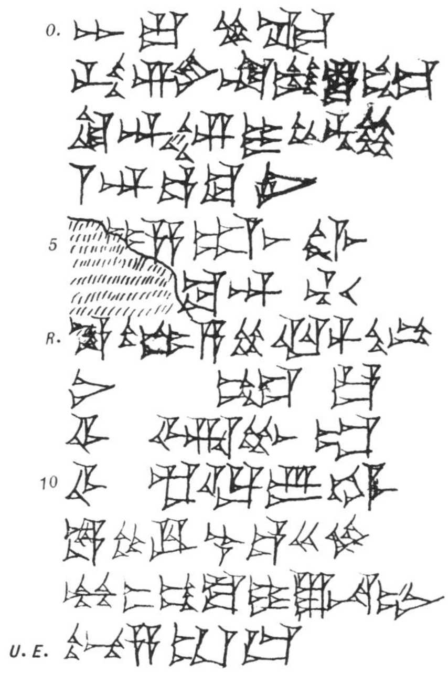

Indistinct seal impressions

161

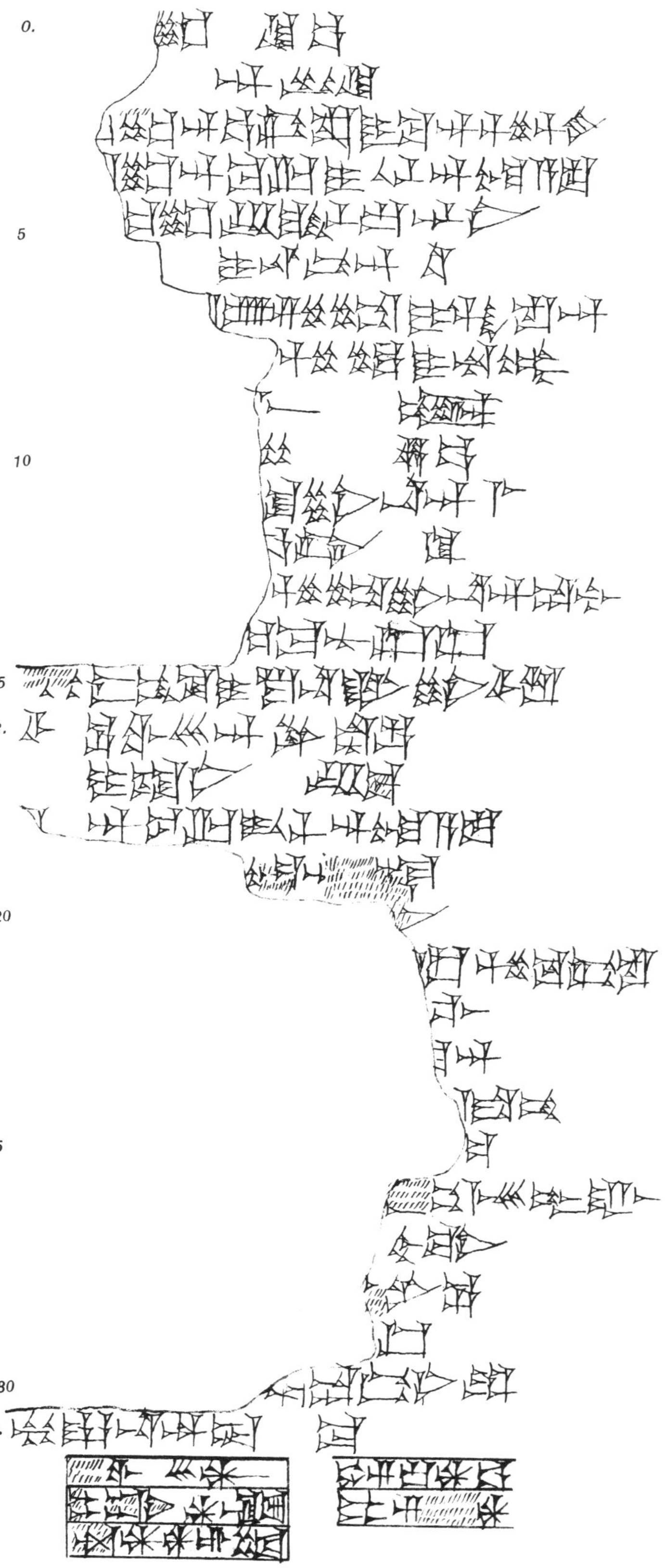

162

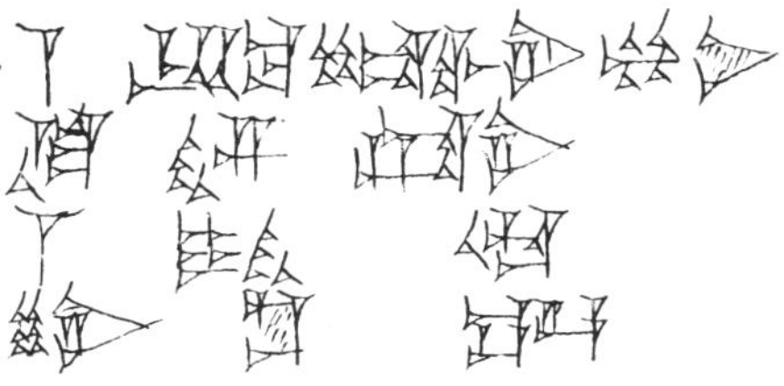

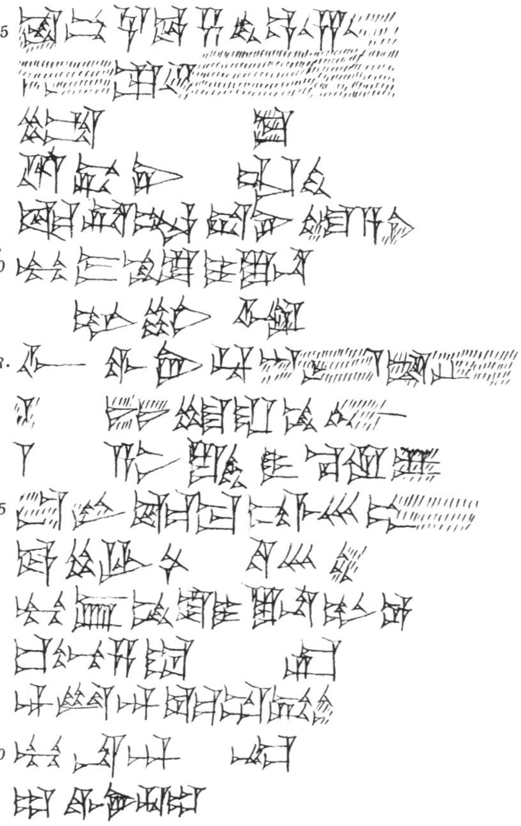

Indistinct seal impressions.

163

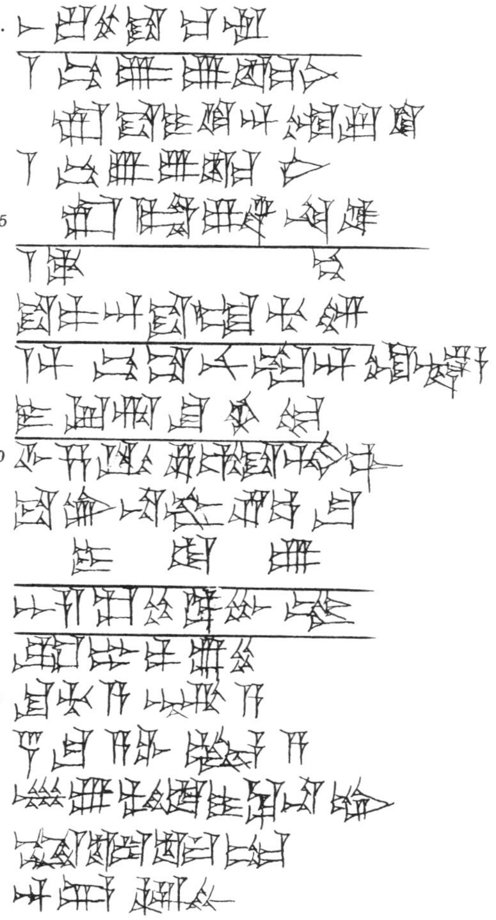

164

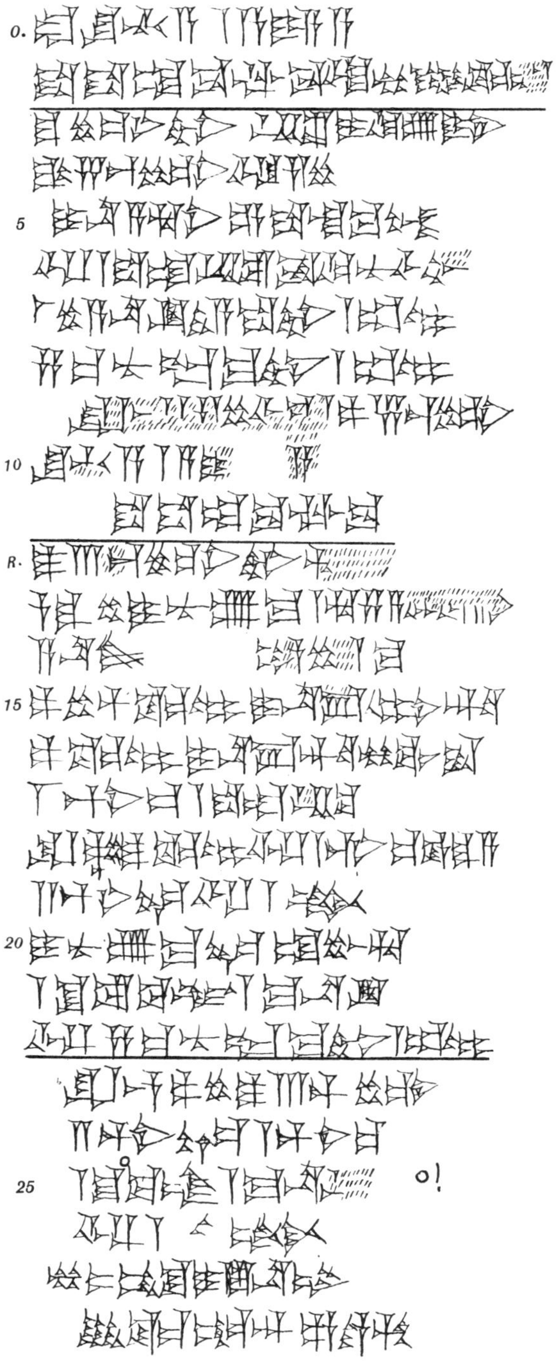

165

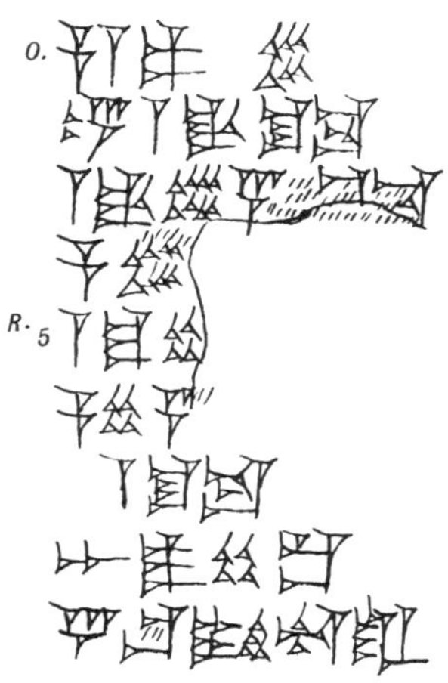

166

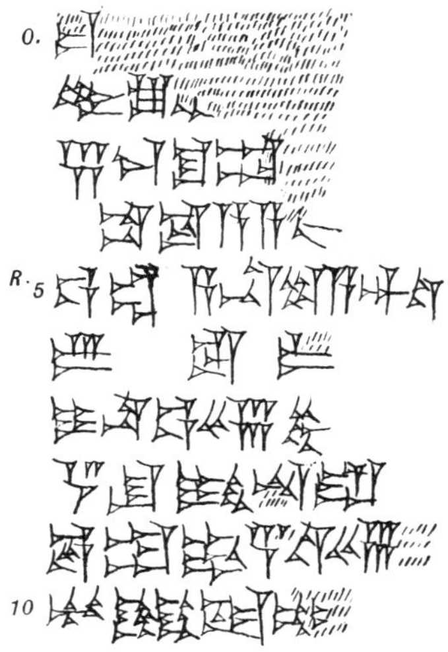

167

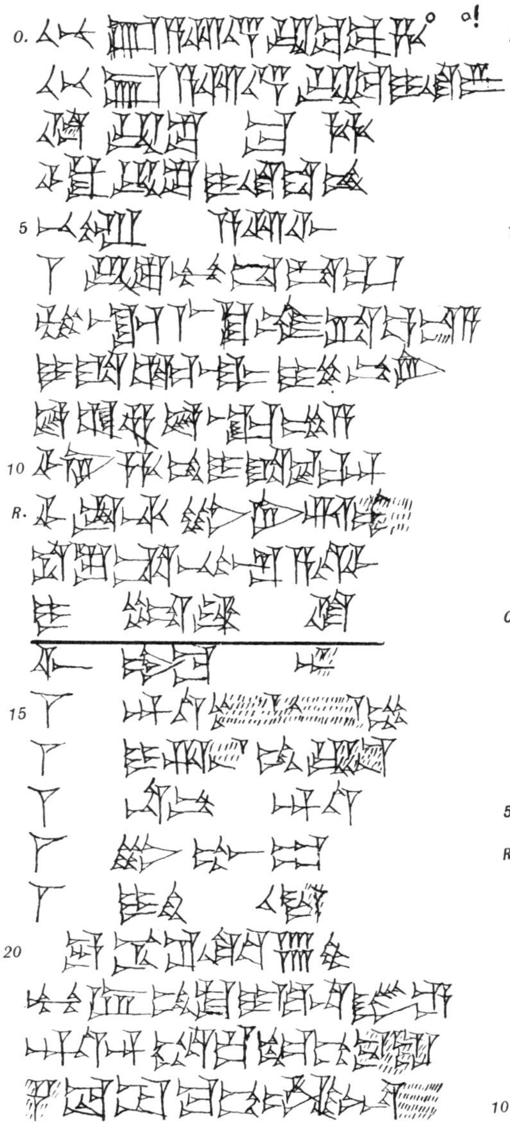

168

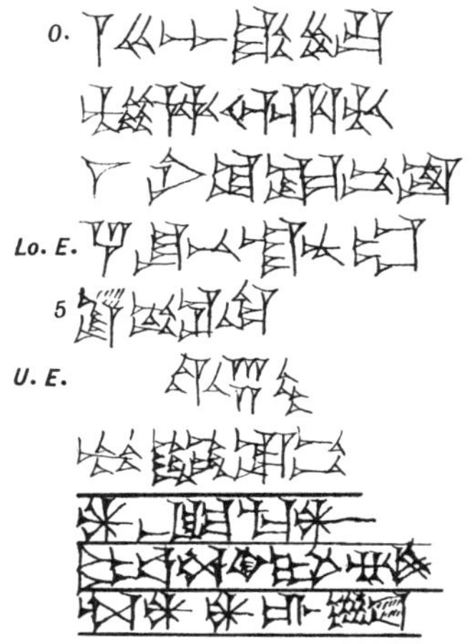

169

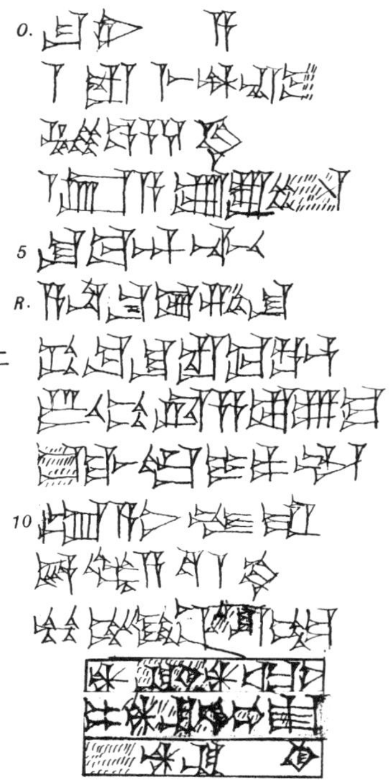

170

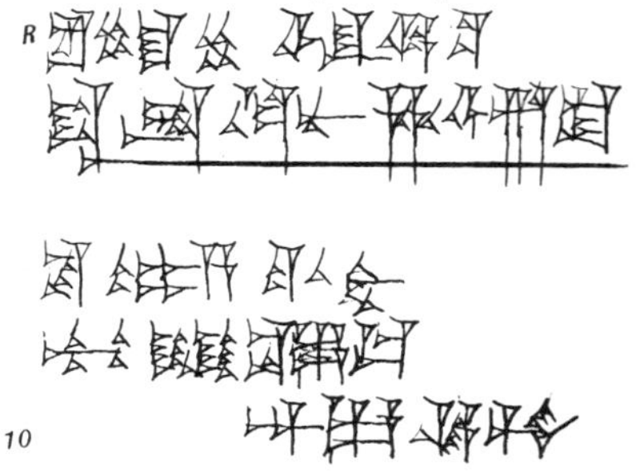

171

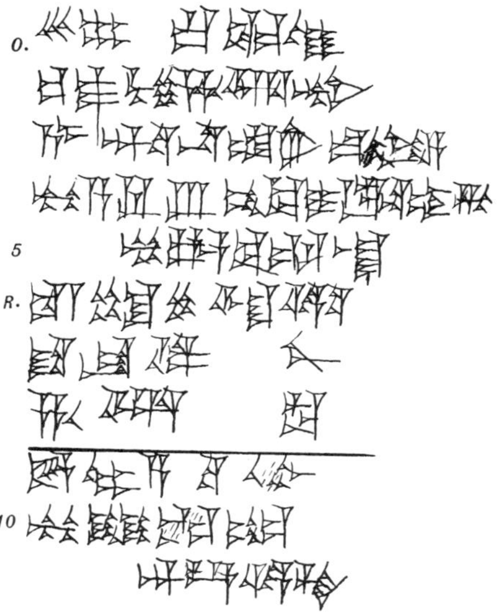

172

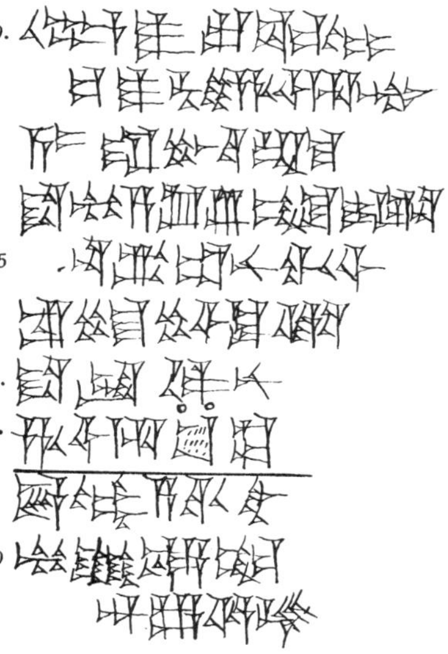

173

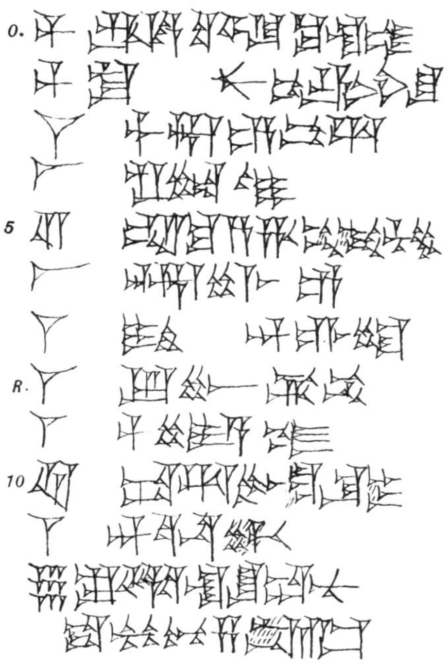

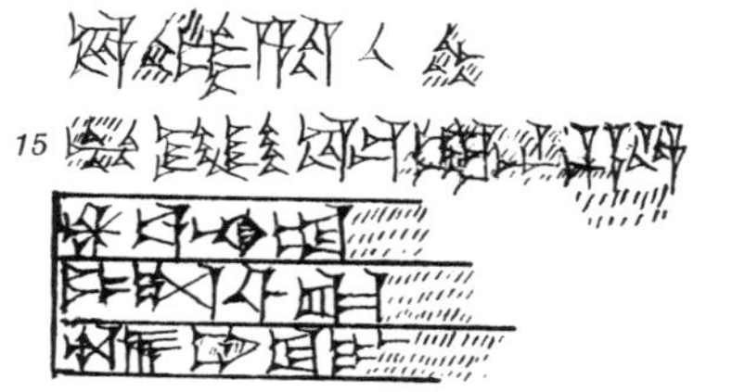

174

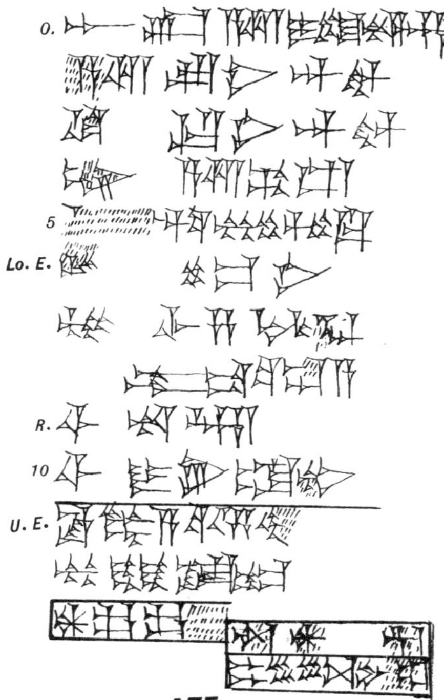

175

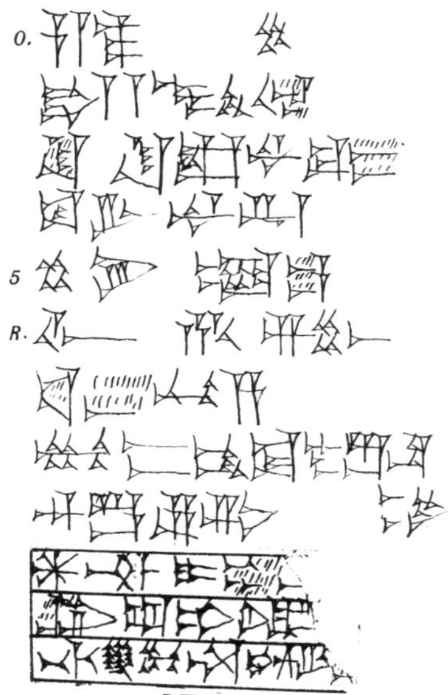

176

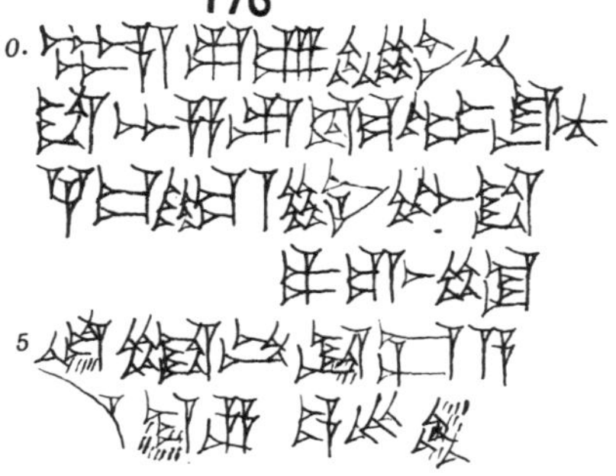

177 TABLET

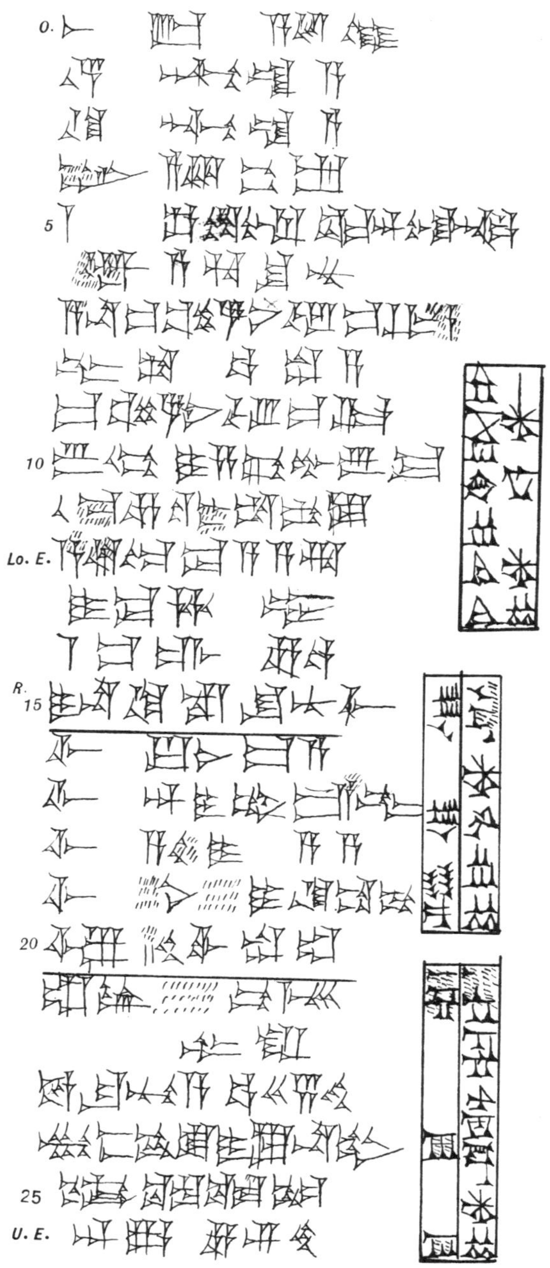

178

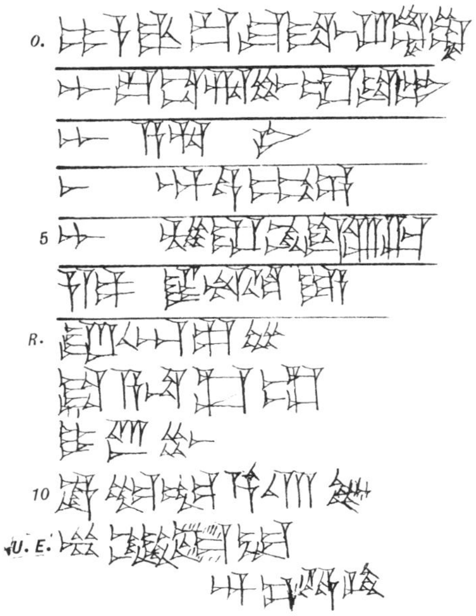

179

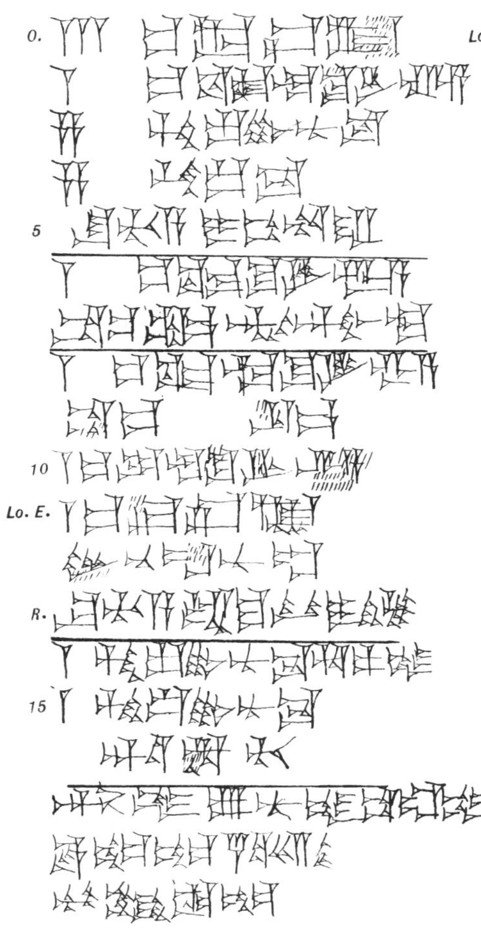

180

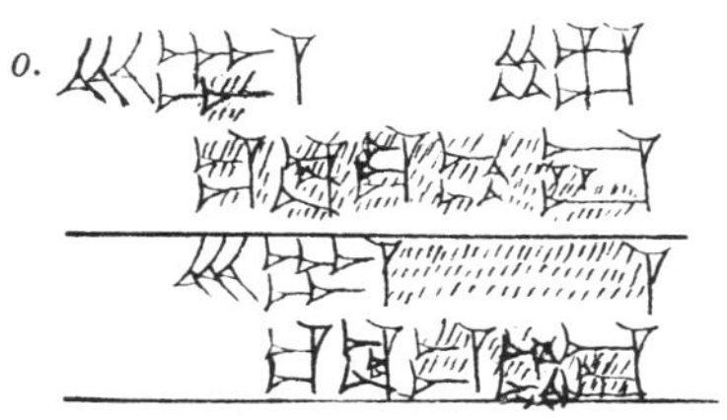

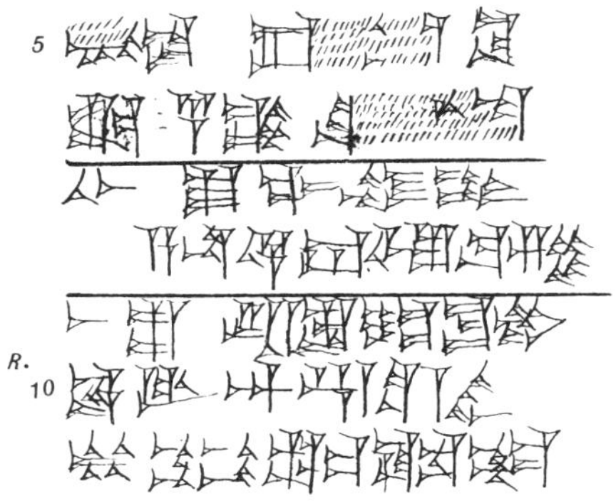

181

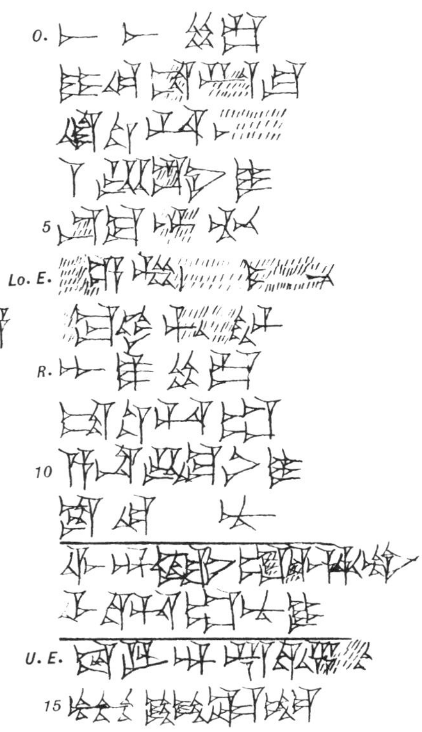

Indistinct seal impressions.

182

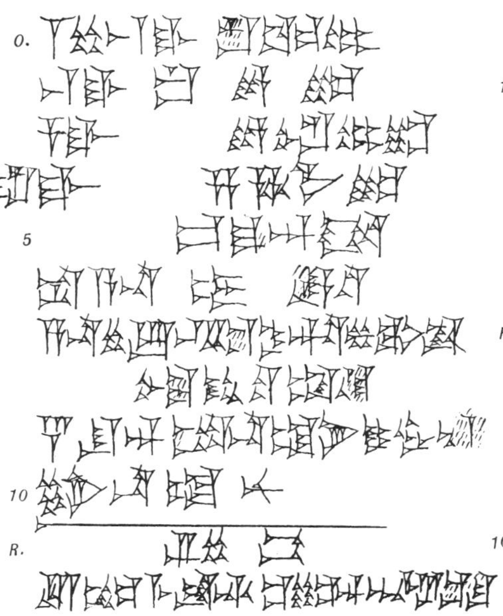

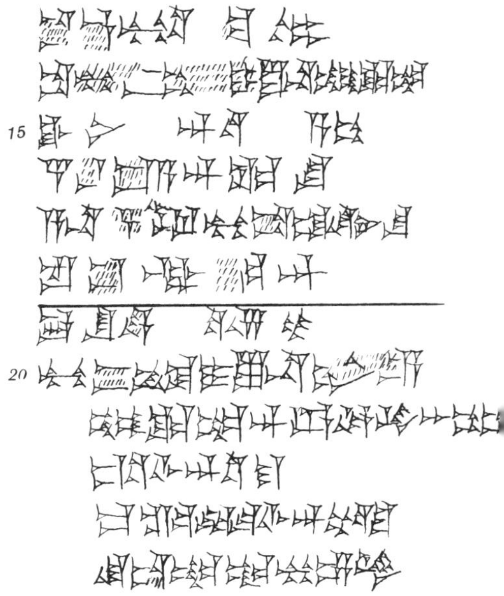

Indistinct seal impressions.

183

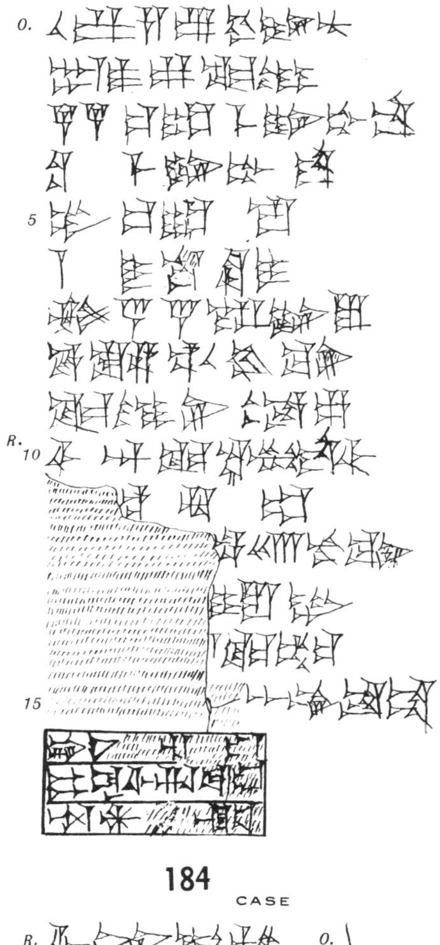

184

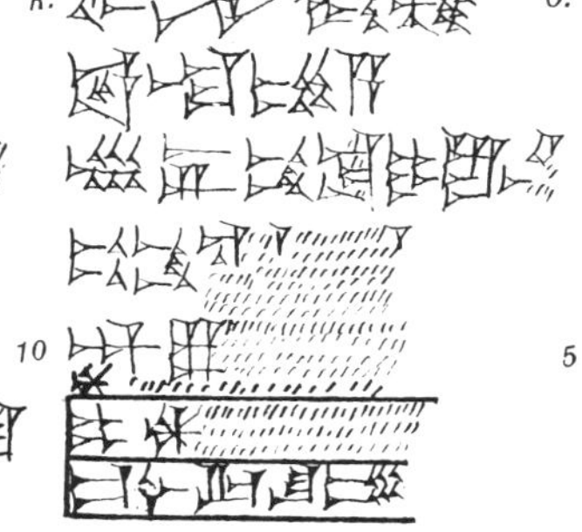

CASE

CASE

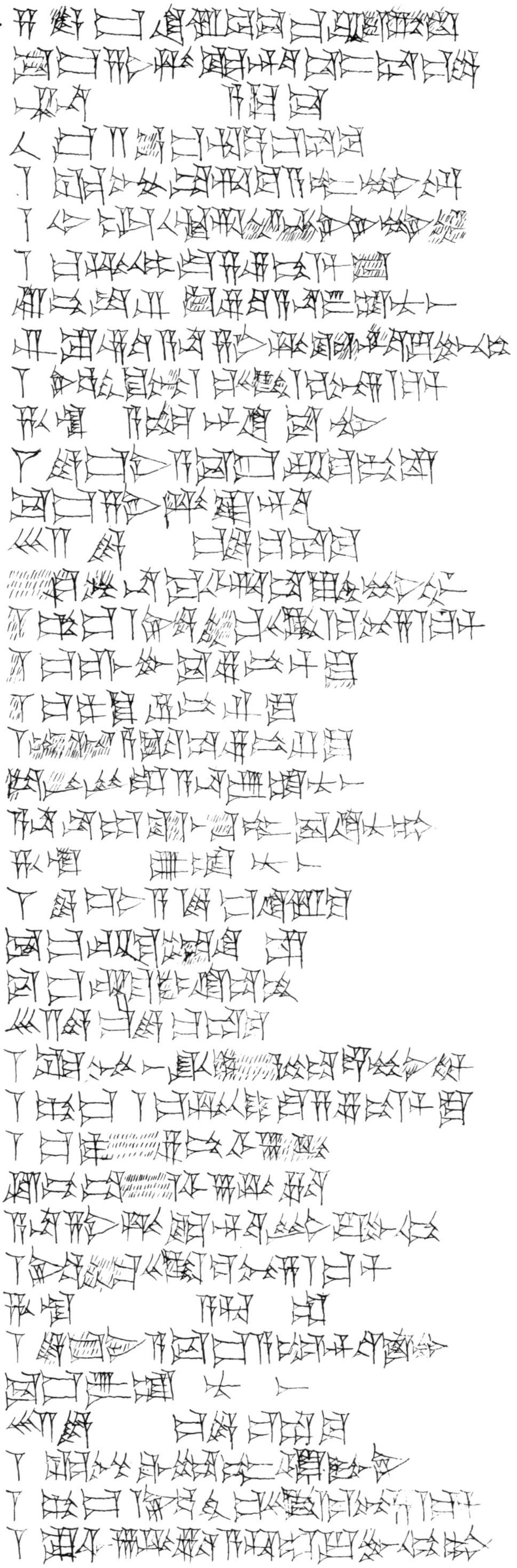

TABLET

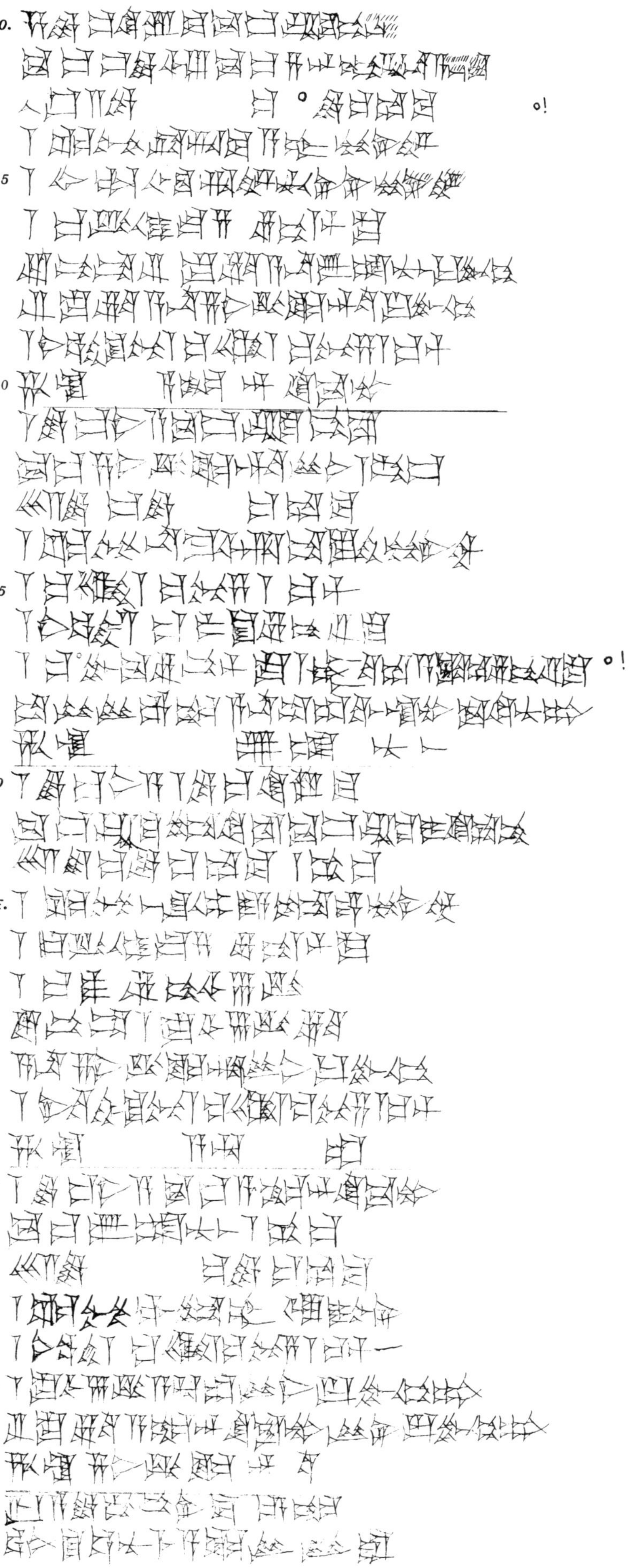

CONTINUED

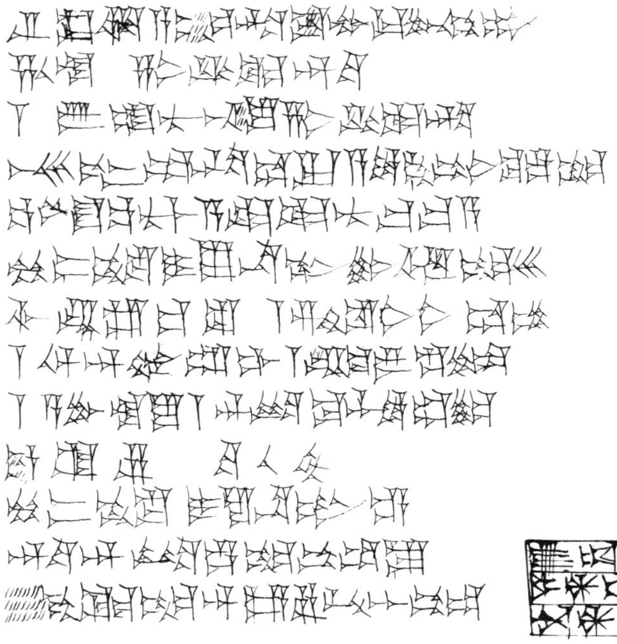

U. E.

CONTINUED

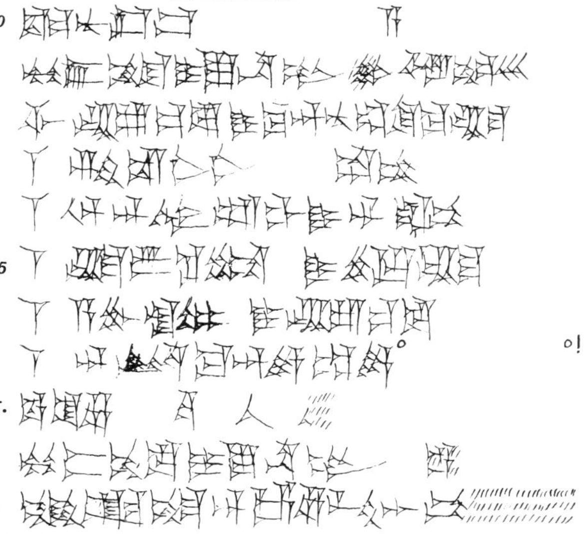

U. E.

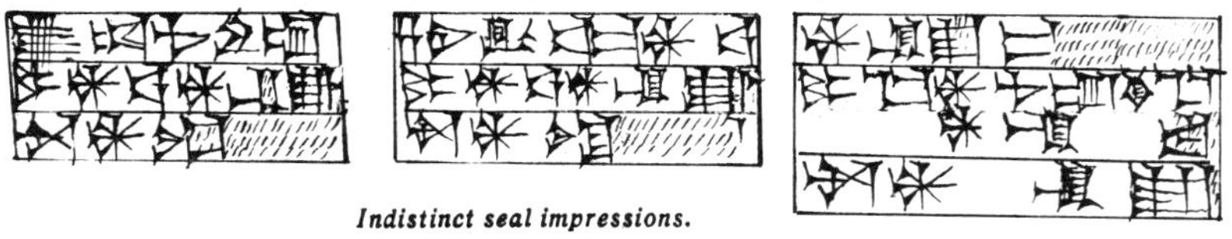

Indistinct seal impressions.

186

O.

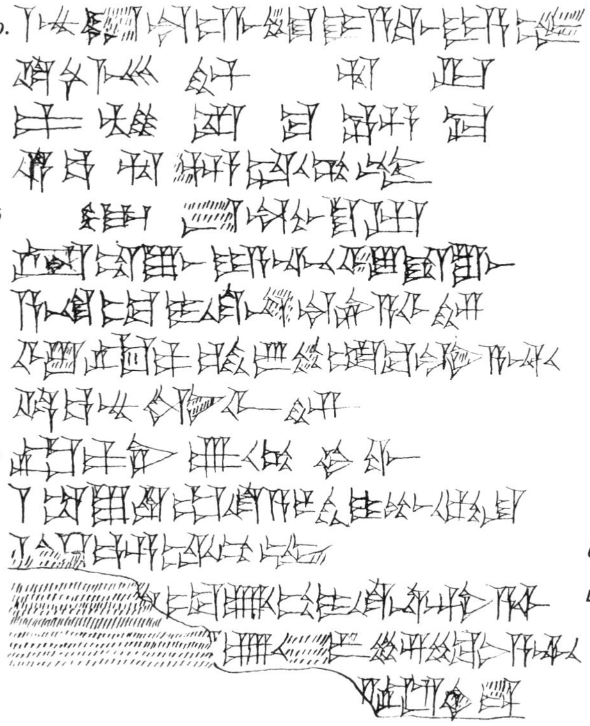

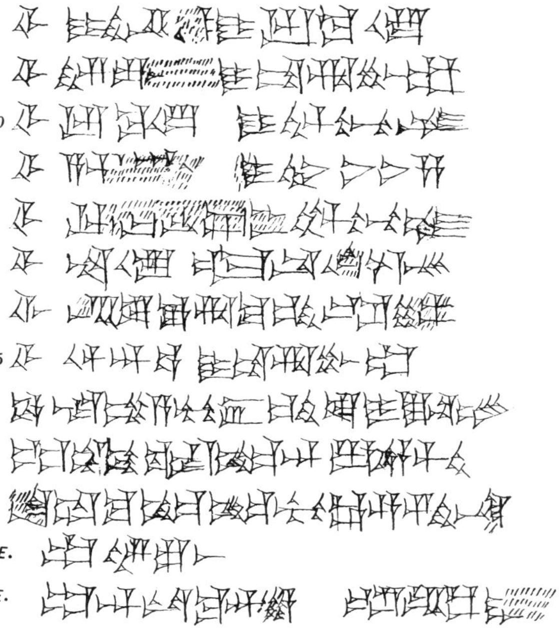

U. E.

L. E.

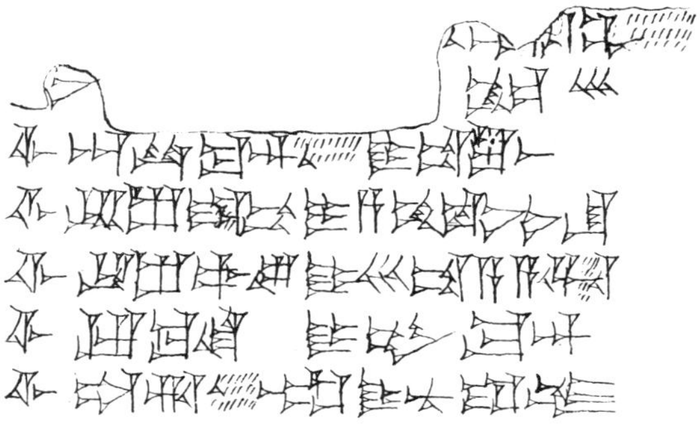

187

O.

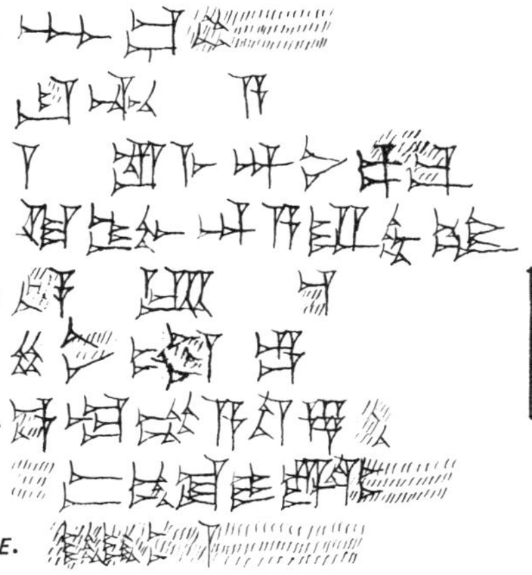

Lo. E.

R.

U. E.

188

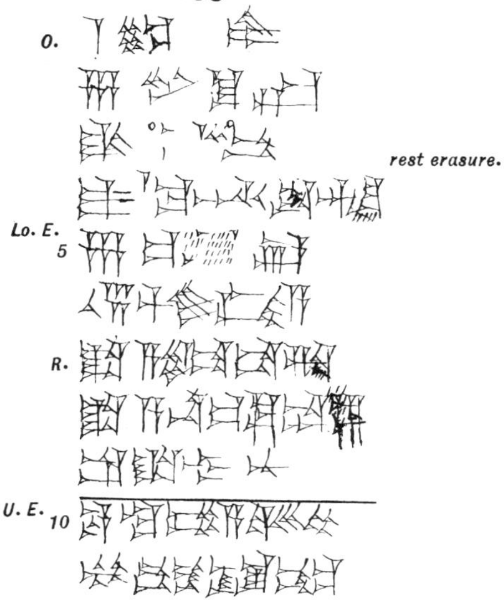

189

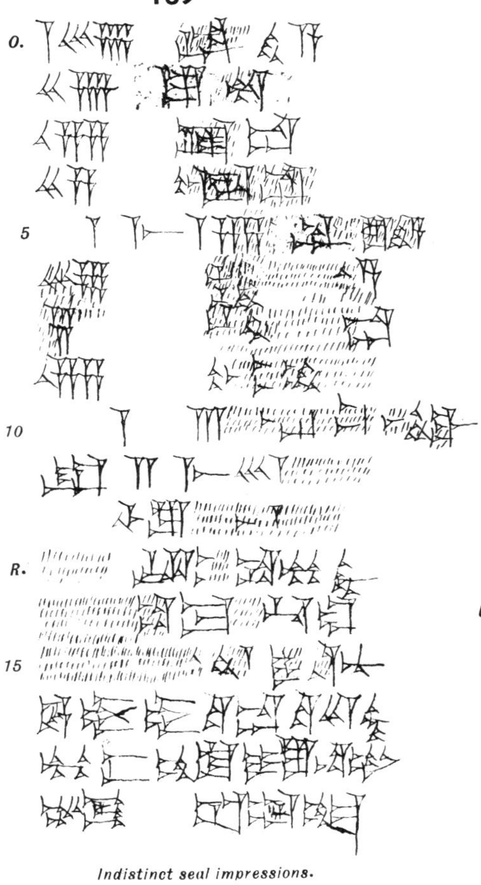

Indistinct seal impressions.

190

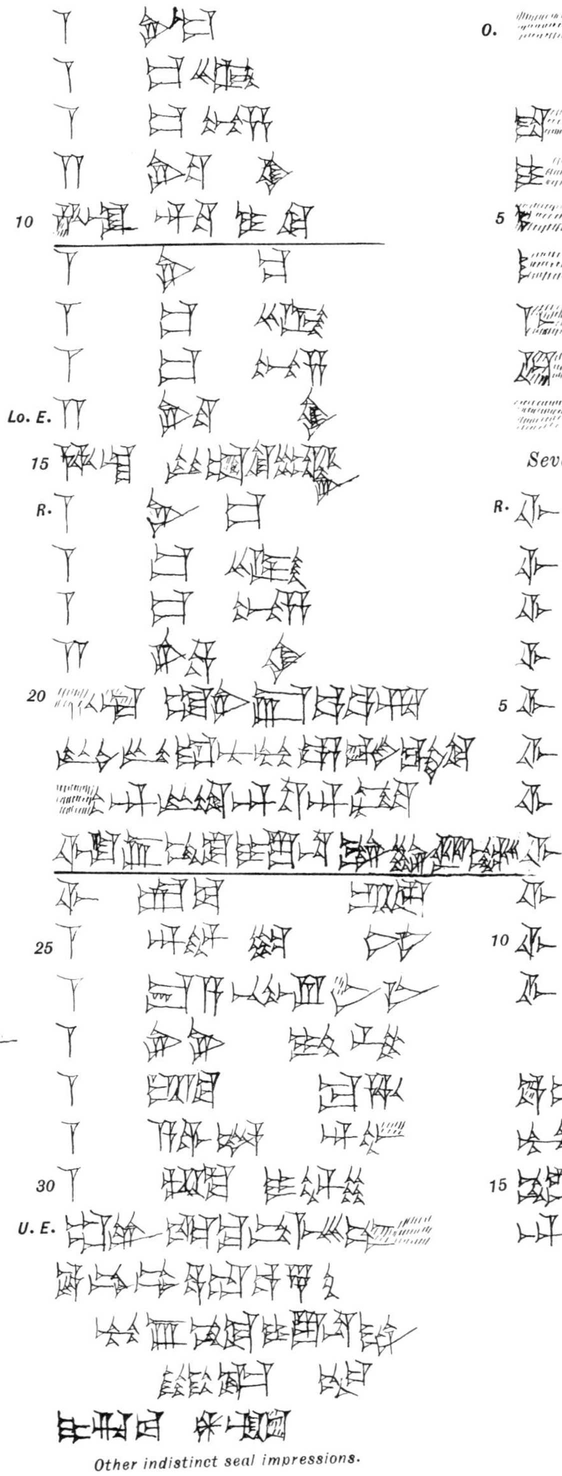

Other indistinct seal impressions.

191

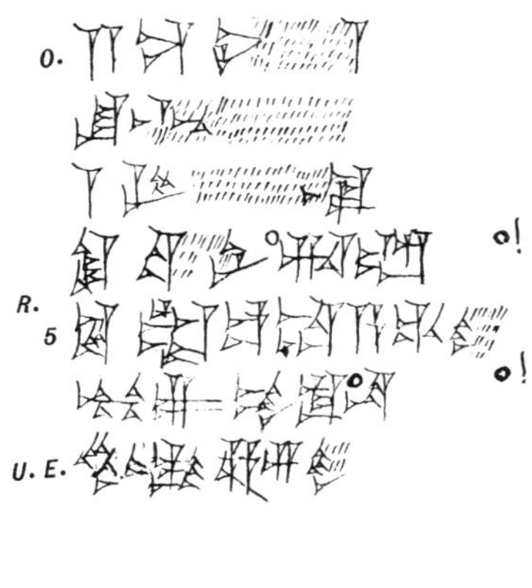

192

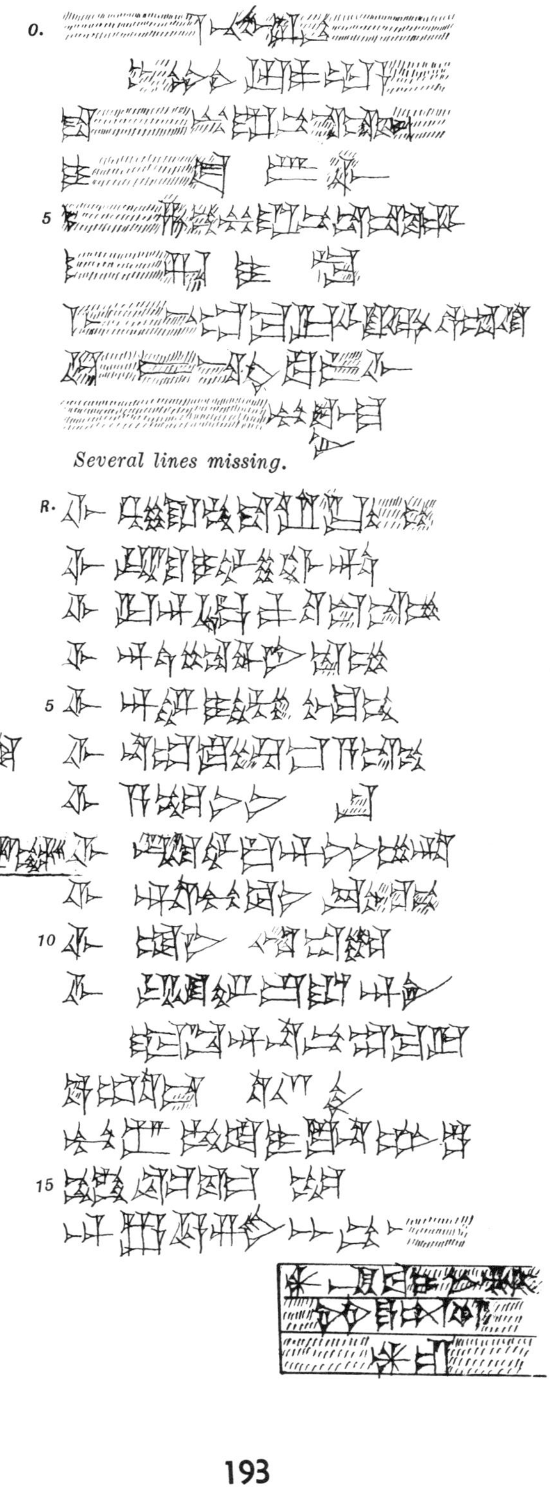

193

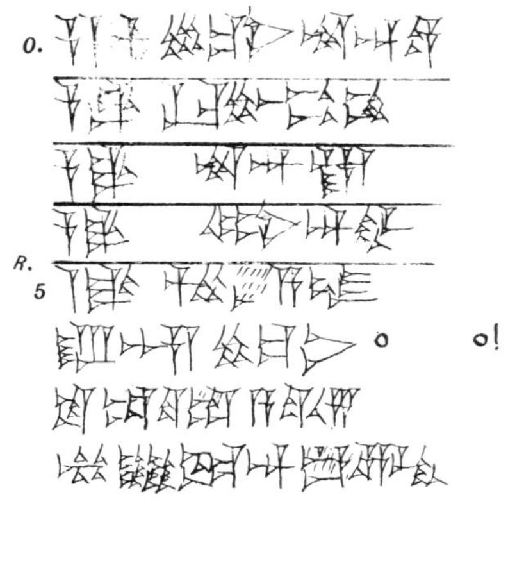

194

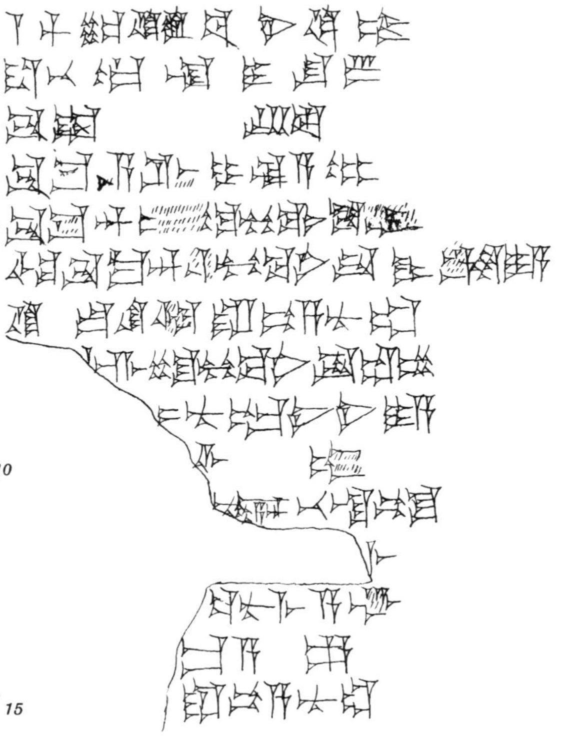

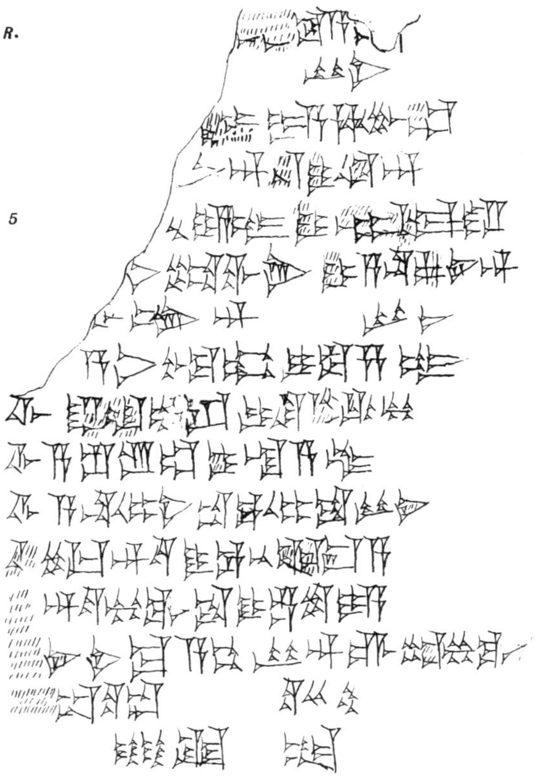

Indistinct seal impressions.

195

Indistinct seal impressions.

196

Indistinct seal impressions.

197

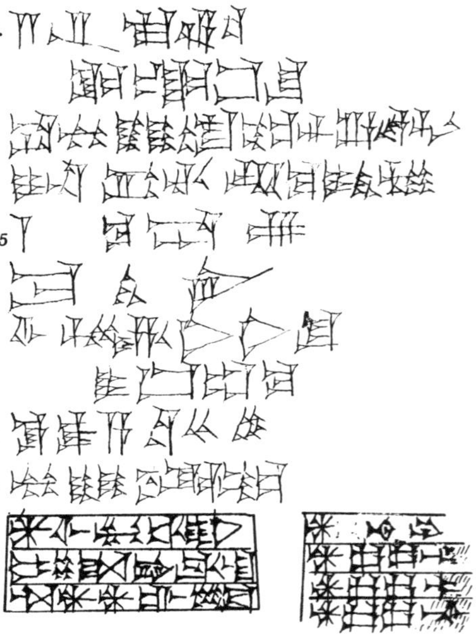

198

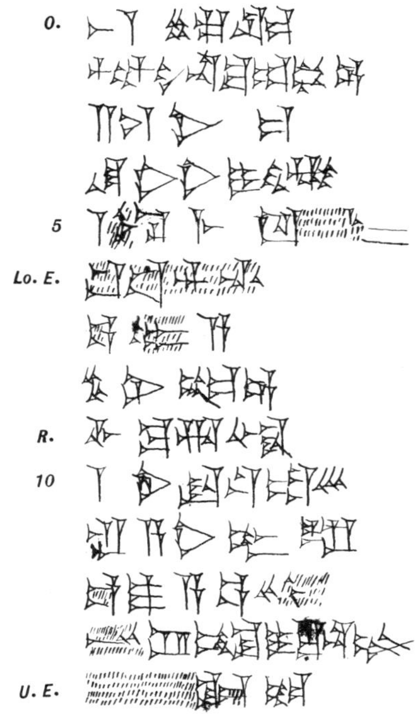

Indistinct seal impressions.

199

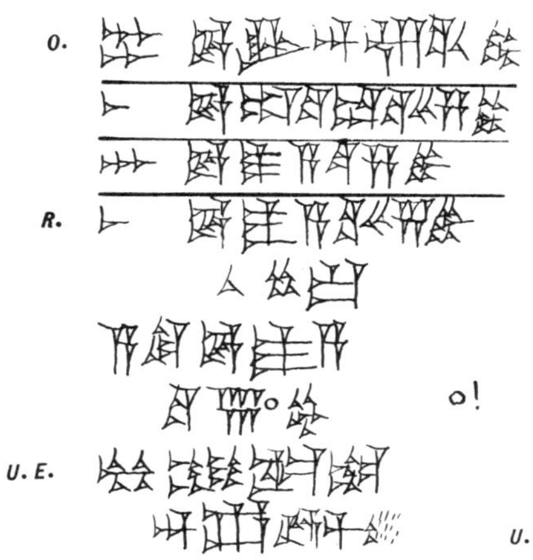

200

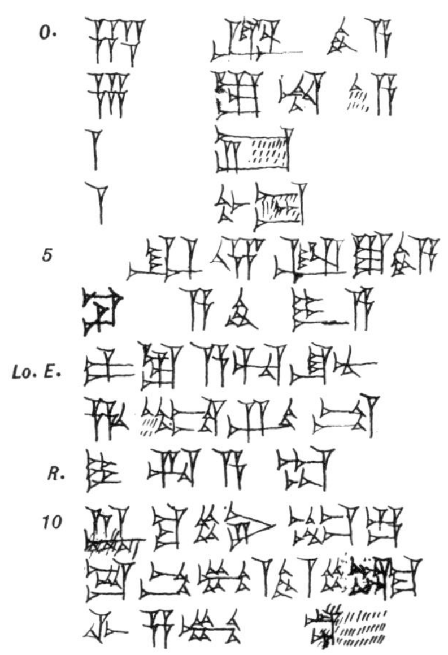

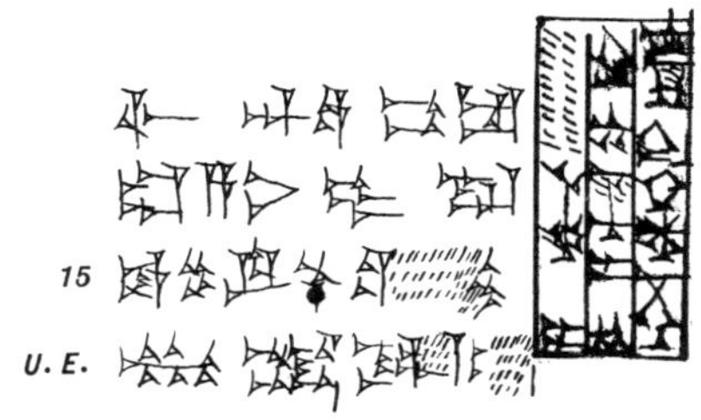

201

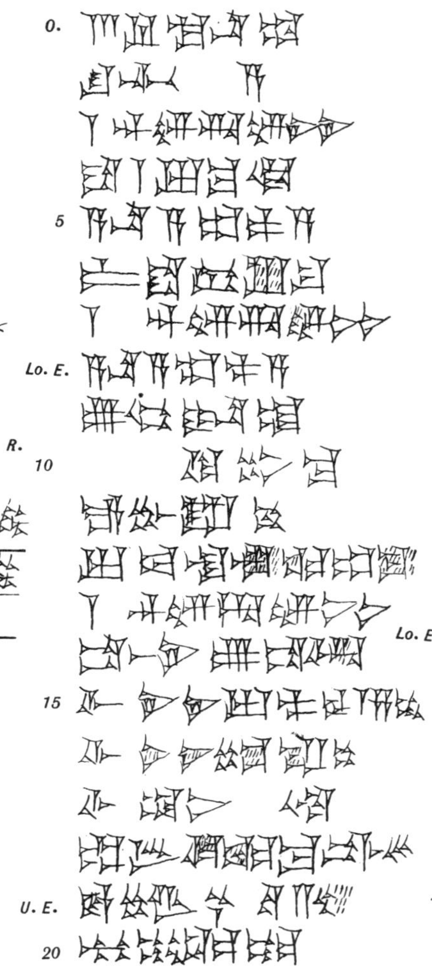

Indistinct seal impressions.

202

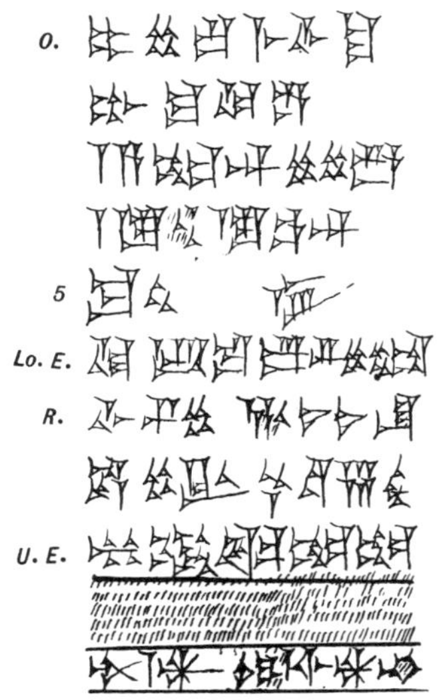

203

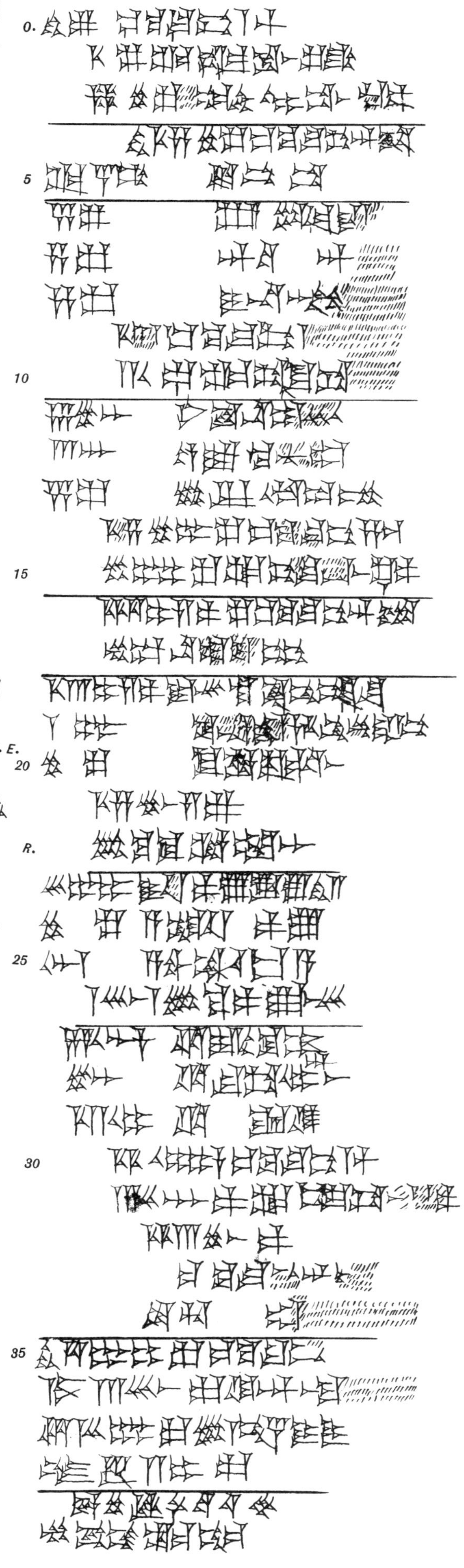

PLATE XXXVIII

204

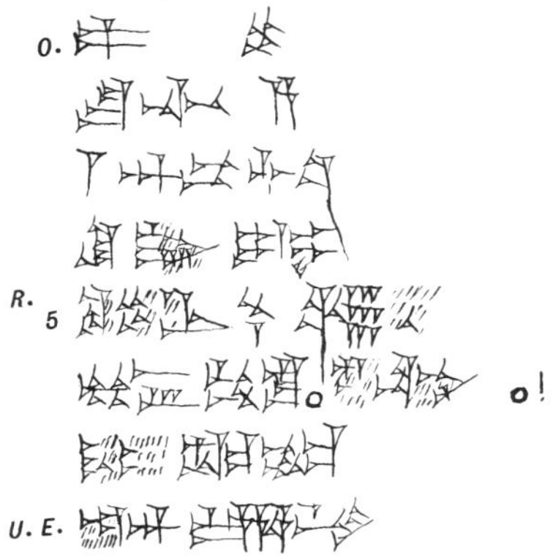

Indistinct seal impressions.

205

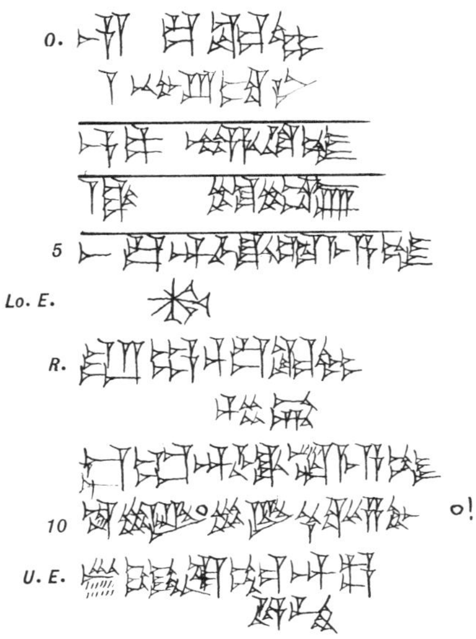

207

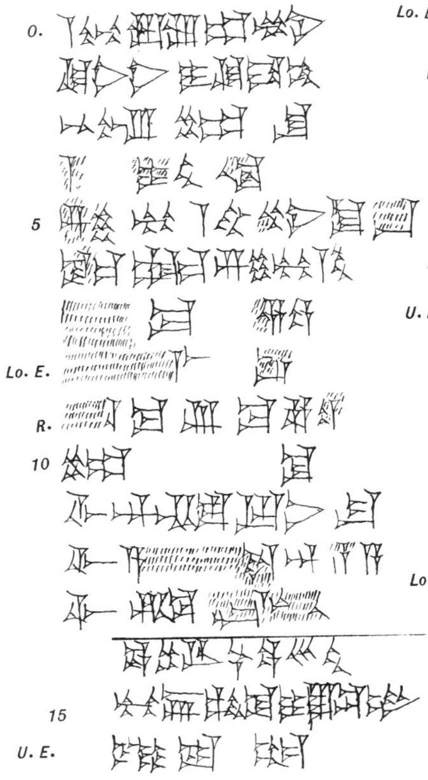

Indistinct seal impressions.

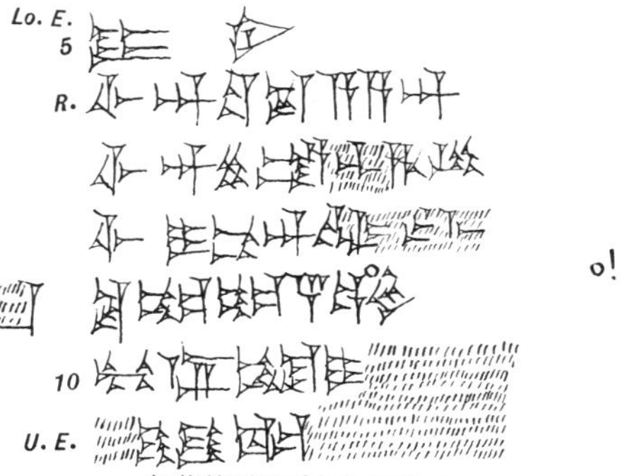

Indistinct seal impressions.

208

209

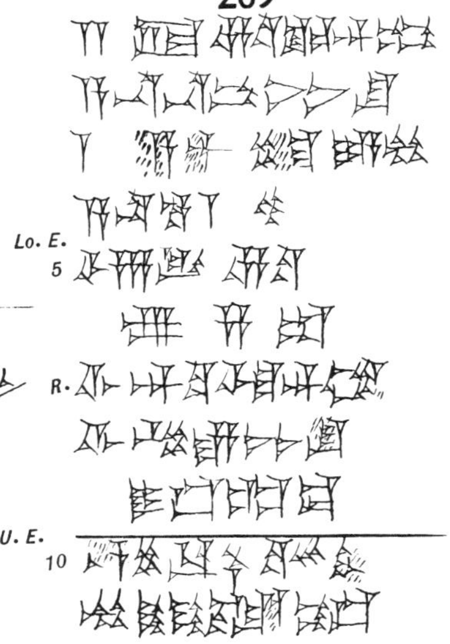

Indistinct seal impressions.

206

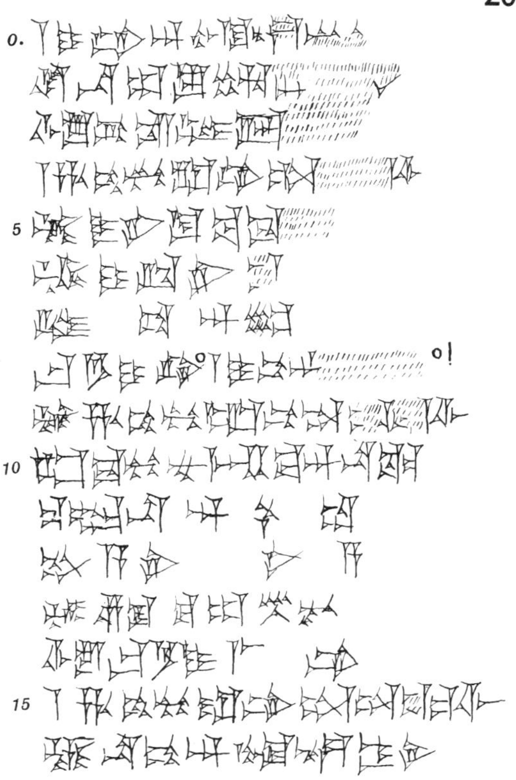

Several lines missing.

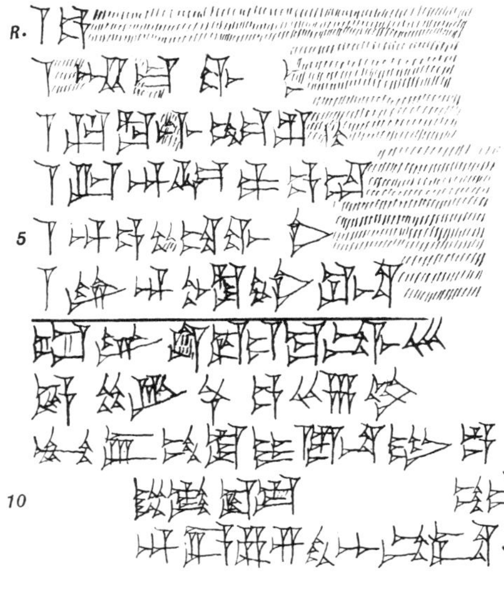

210

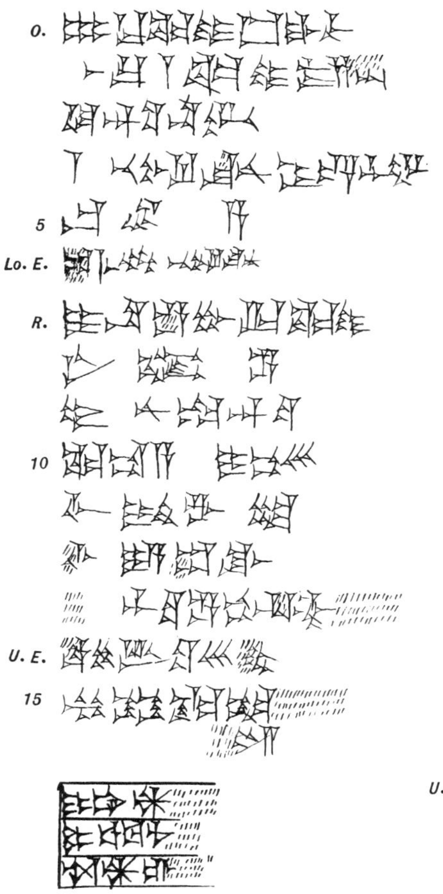

211

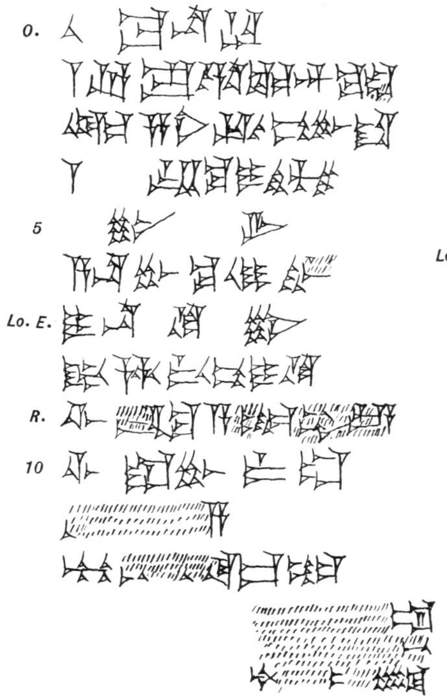

212

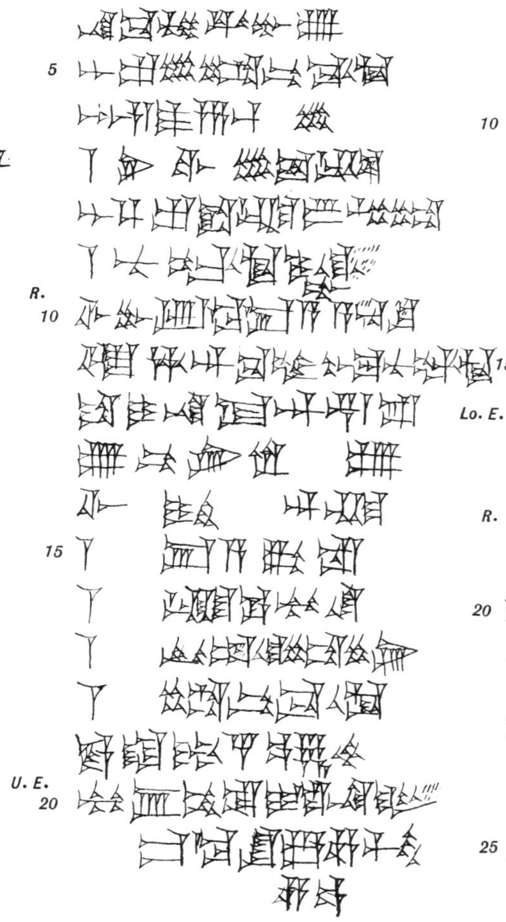

213

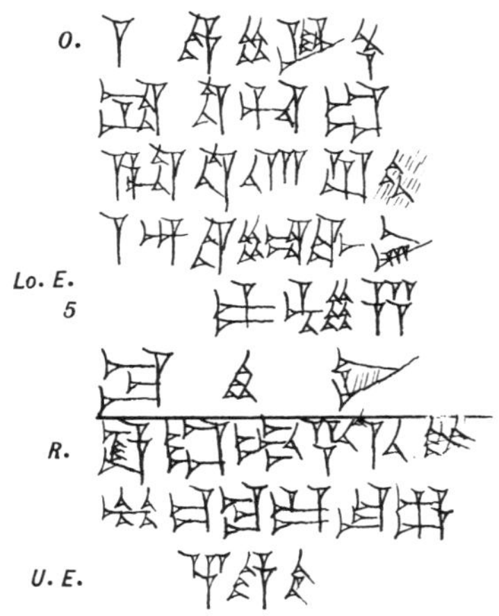

214

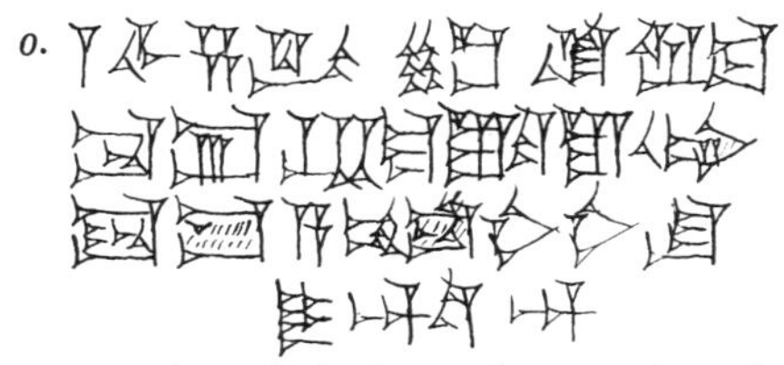

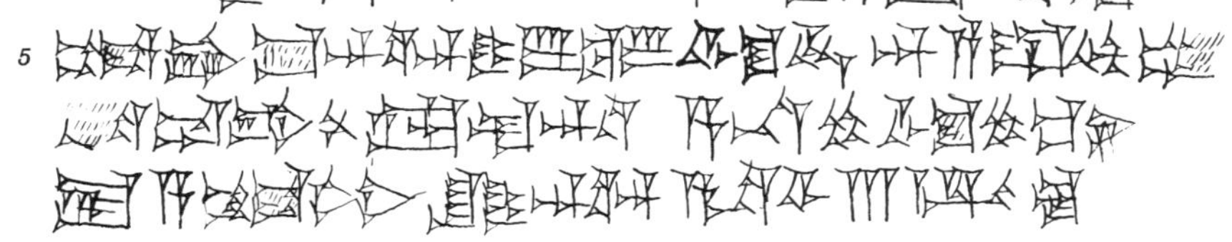

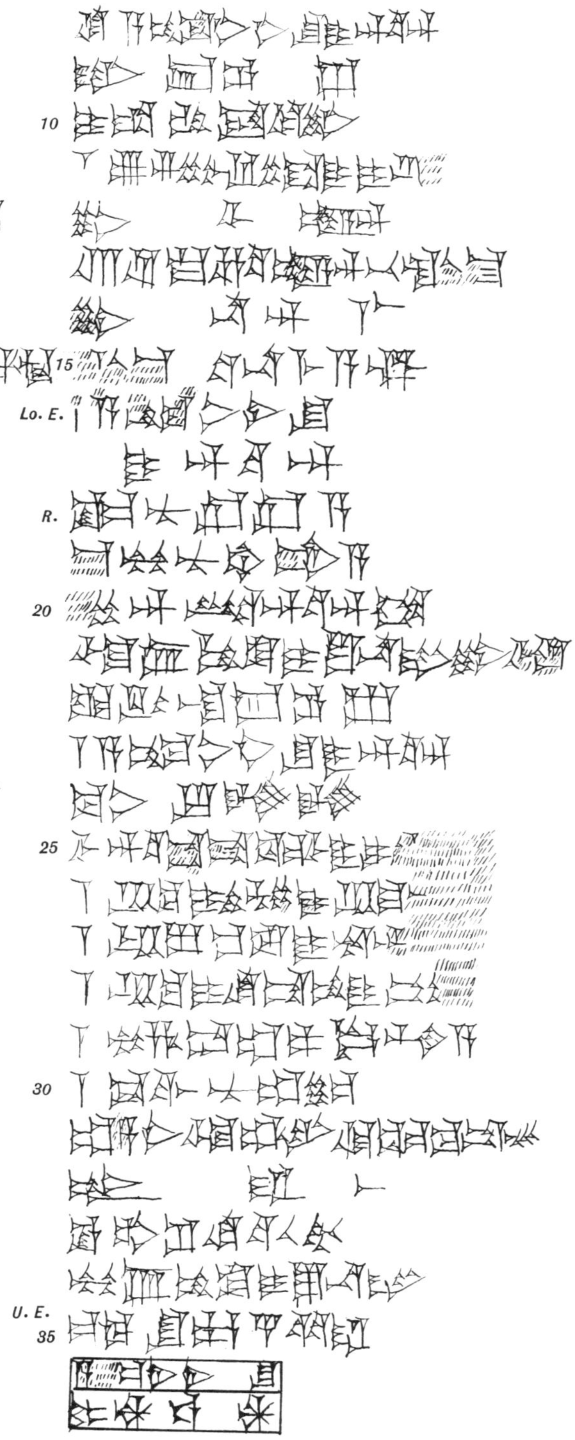

215

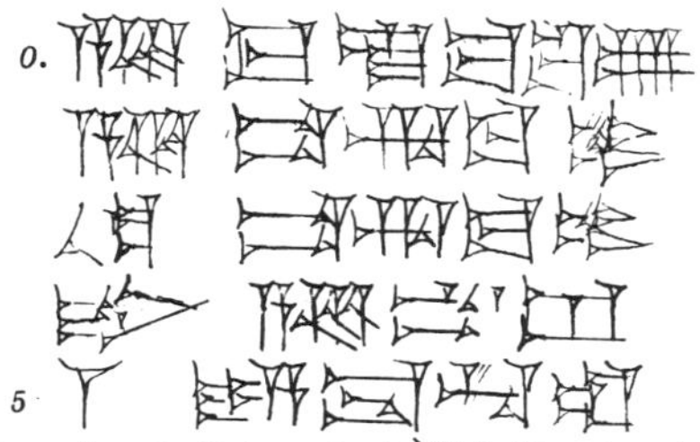

215

CONTINUED

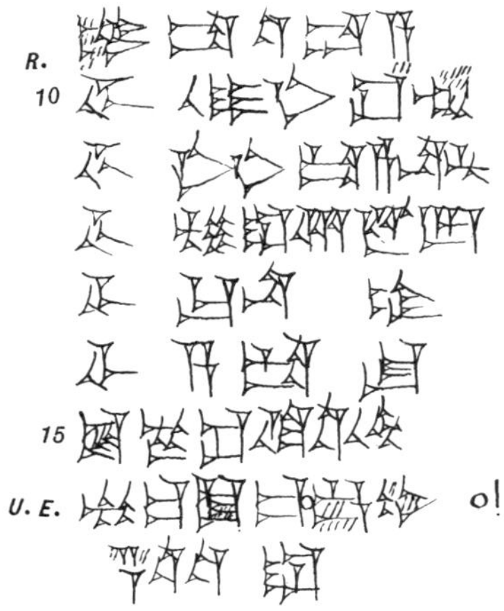

Indistinct seal impressions.

216

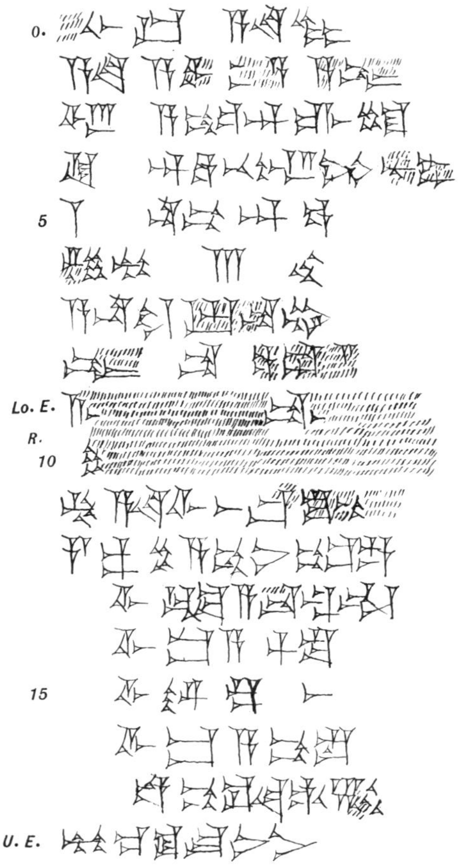

217

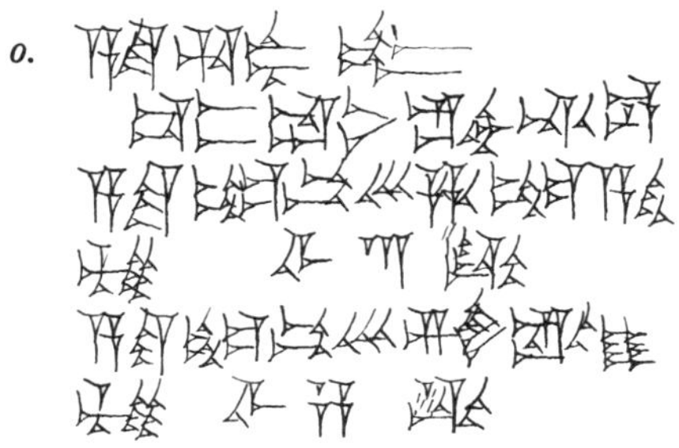

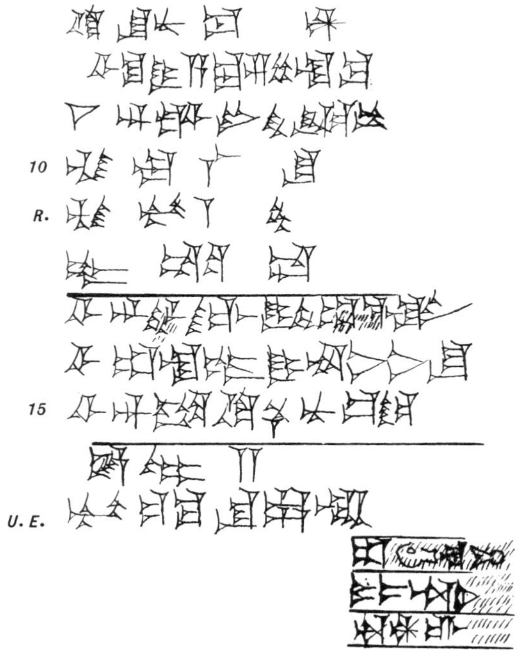

218

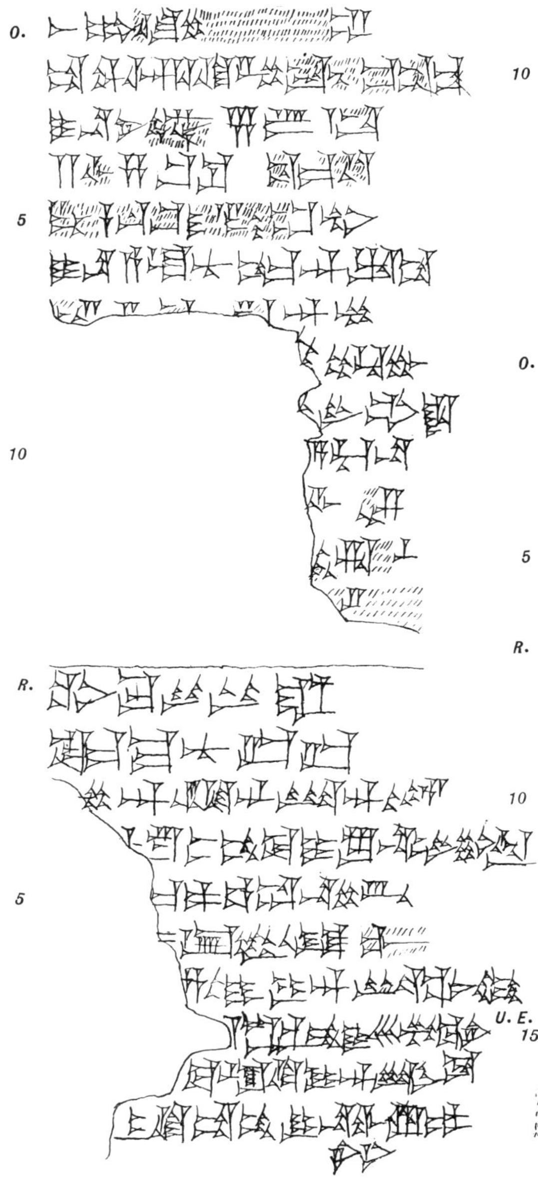

219

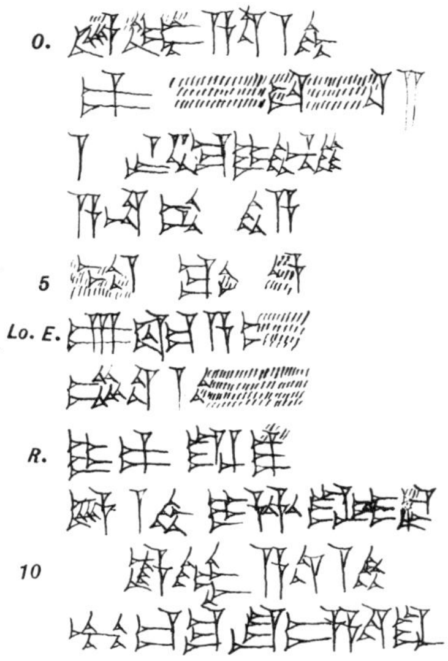

220

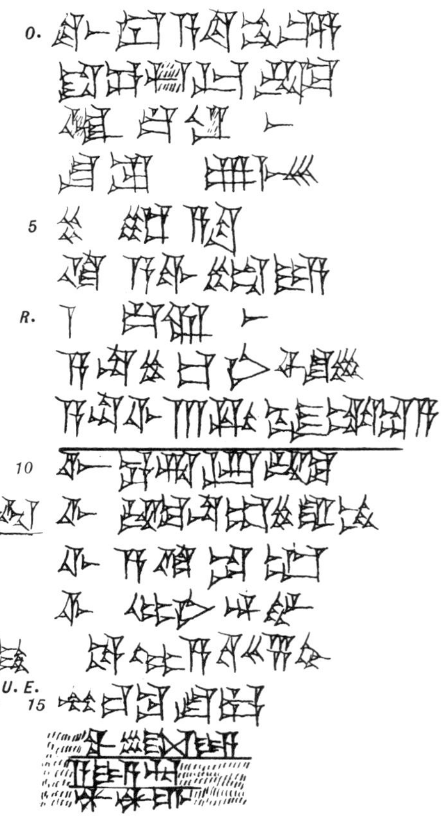

221

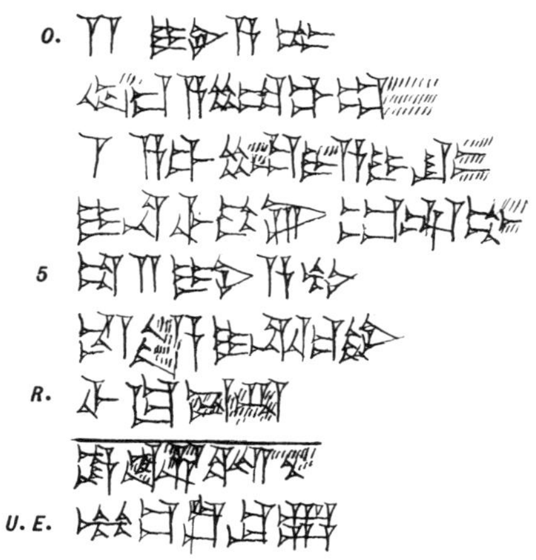

Indistinct seal impressions.

222

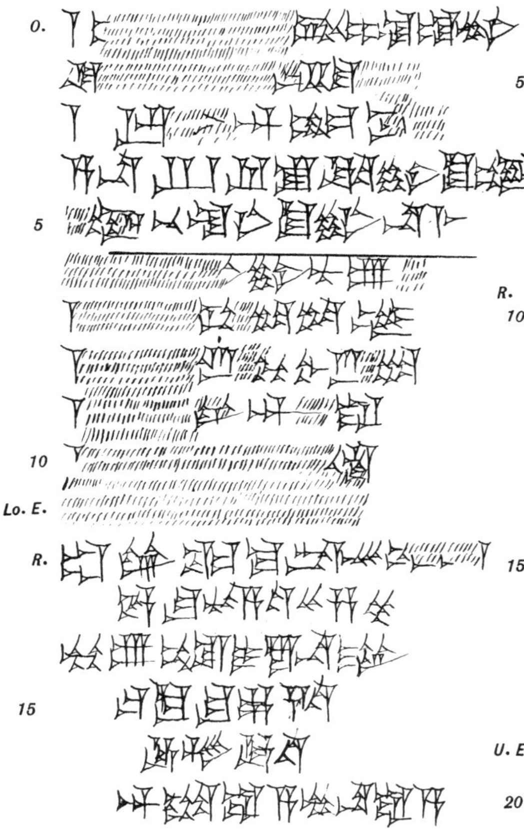

223

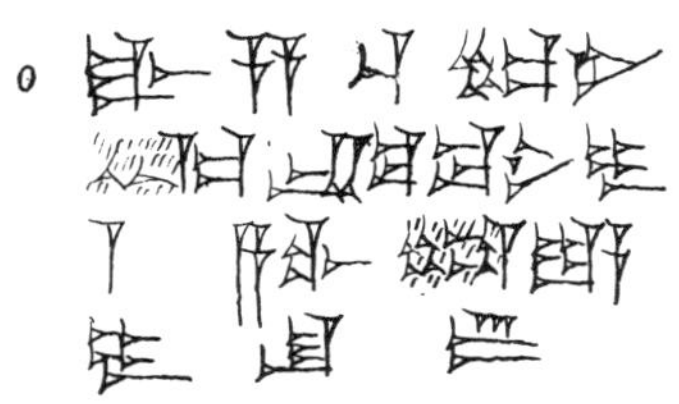

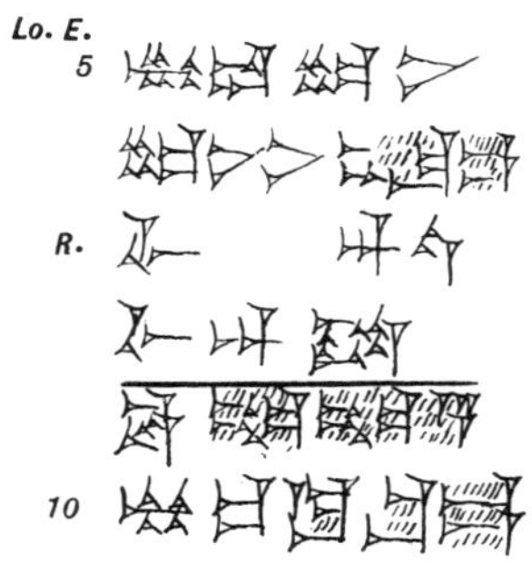

Indistinct seal impressions.

224

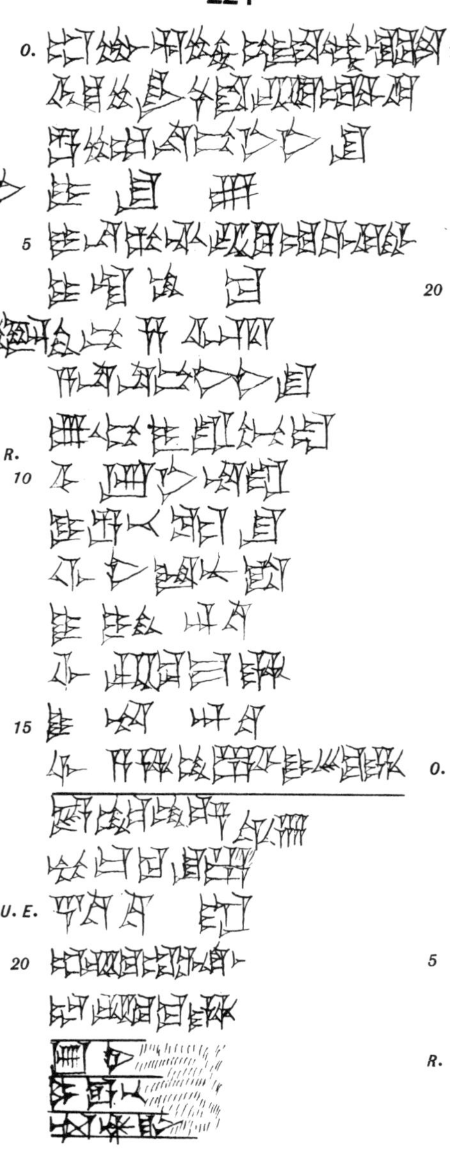

Other indistinct seal impressions.

CASE

225

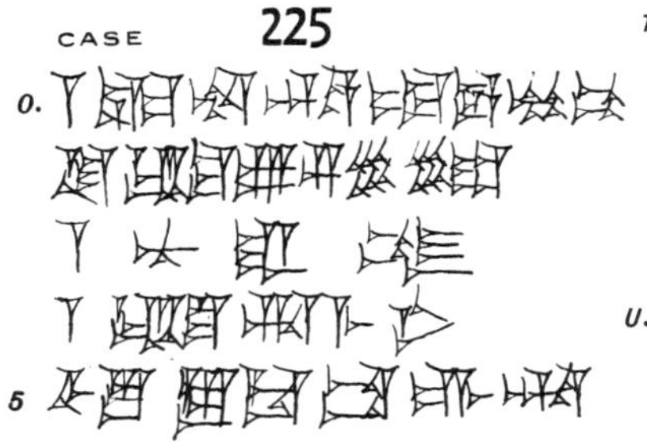

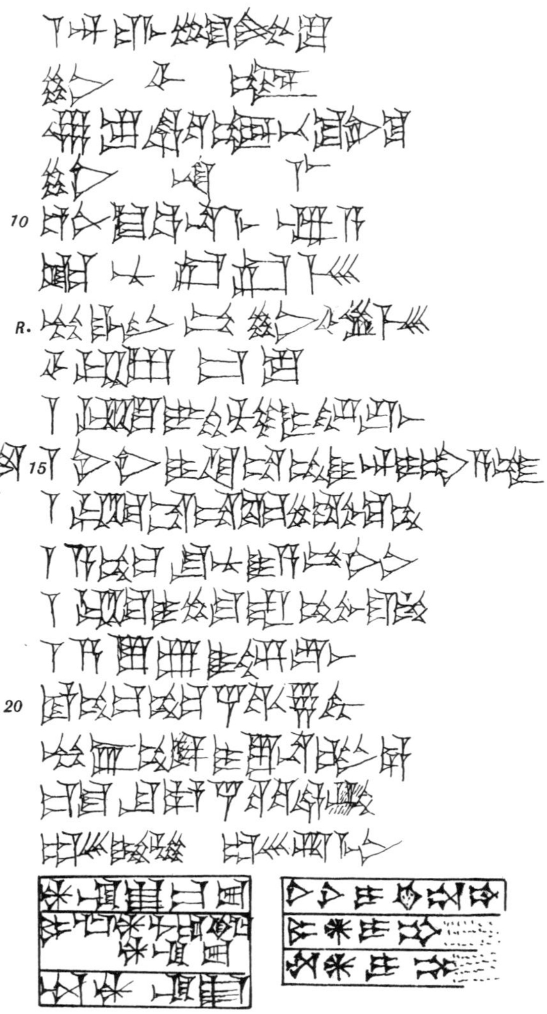

Other indistinct seal impressions.

226

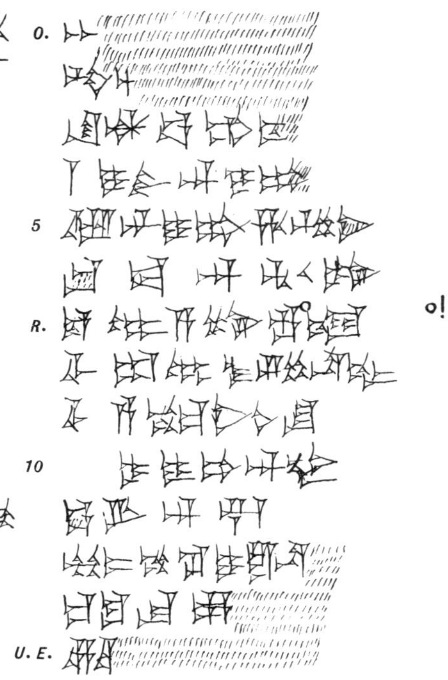

Indistinct seal impressions.

227

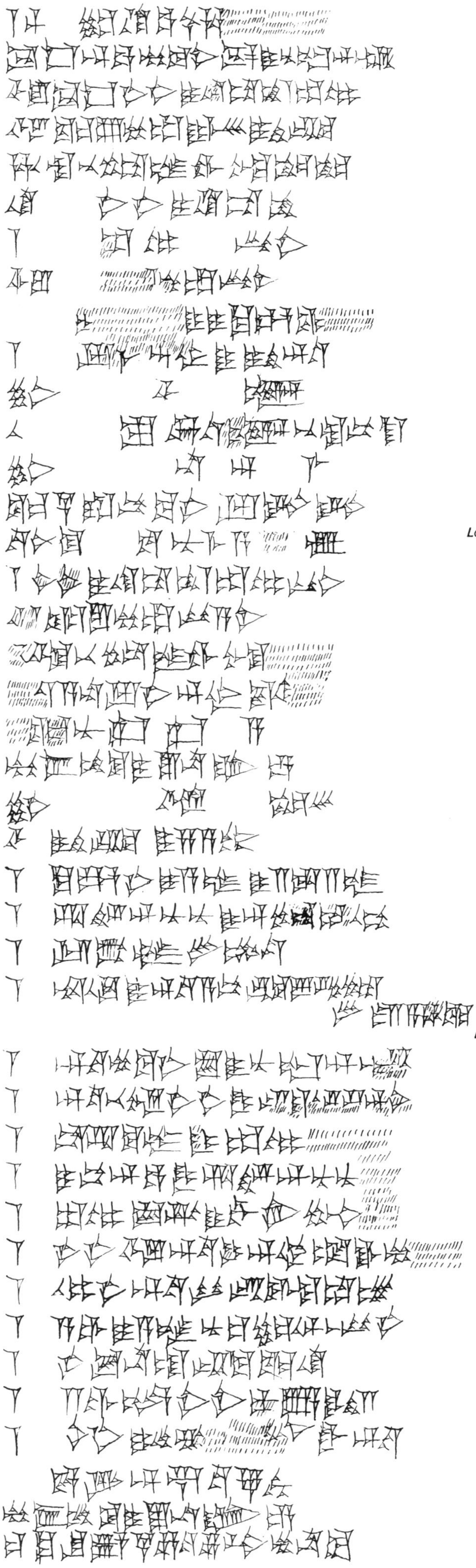

228

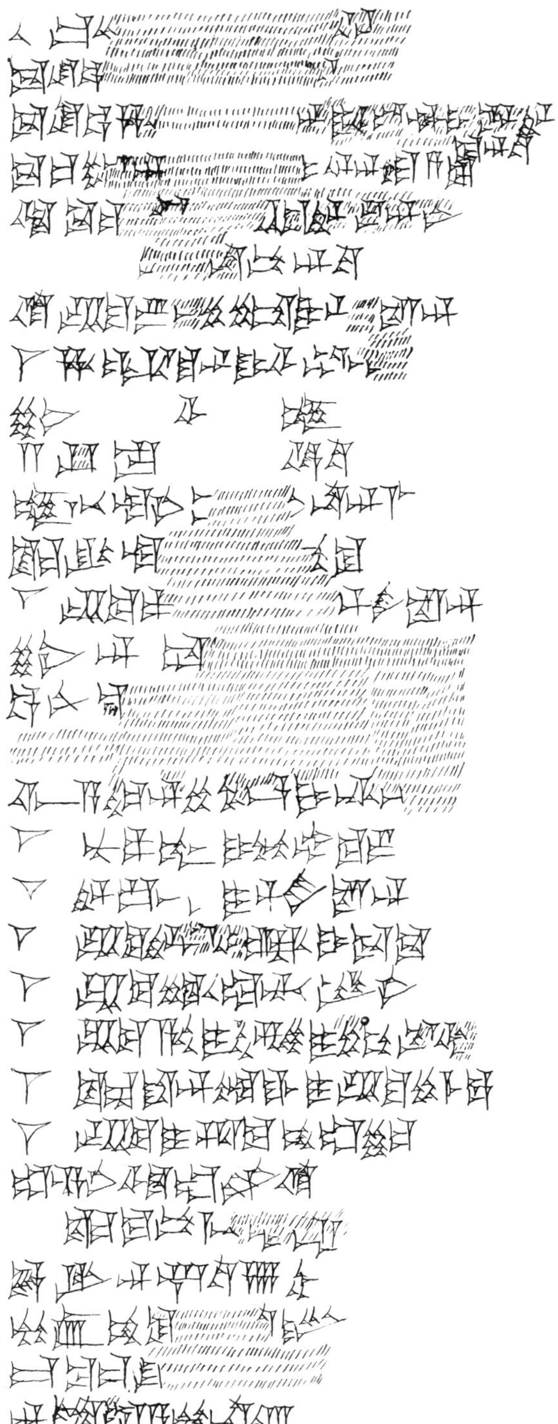

229

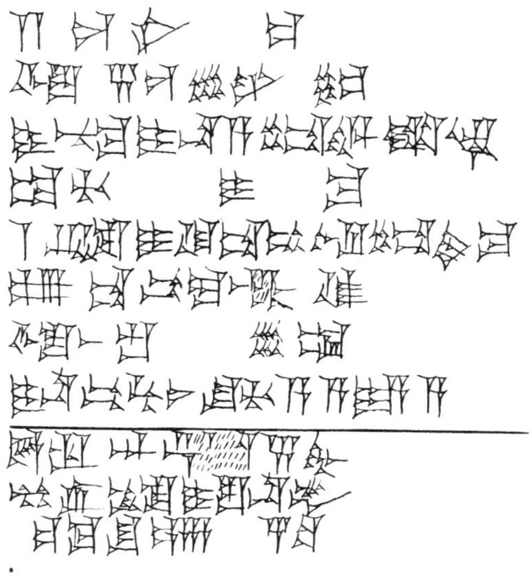

230

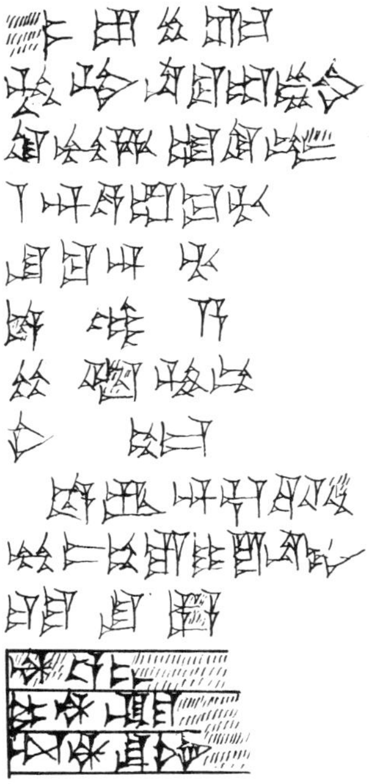

231

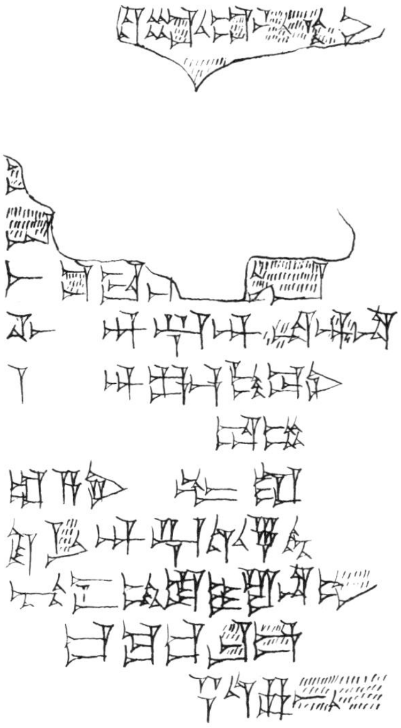

Indistinct seal impressions.

232

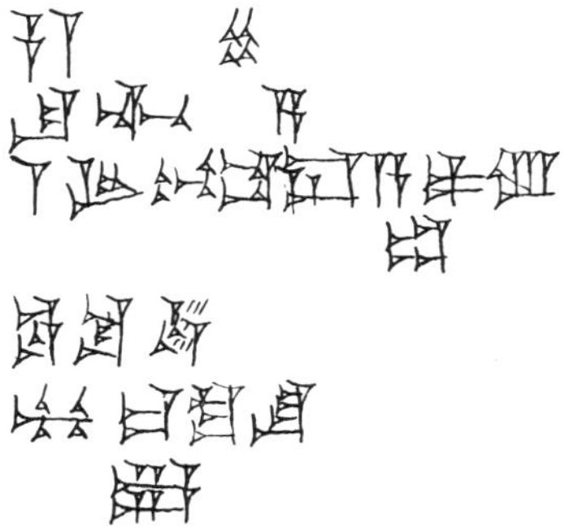

233

234

Indistinct seal impressions.

235

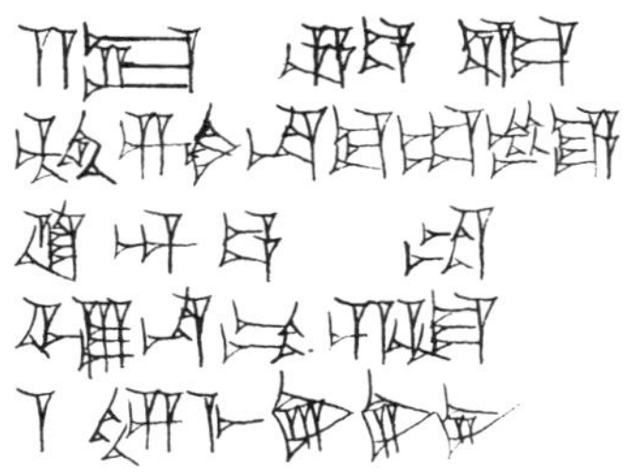

236

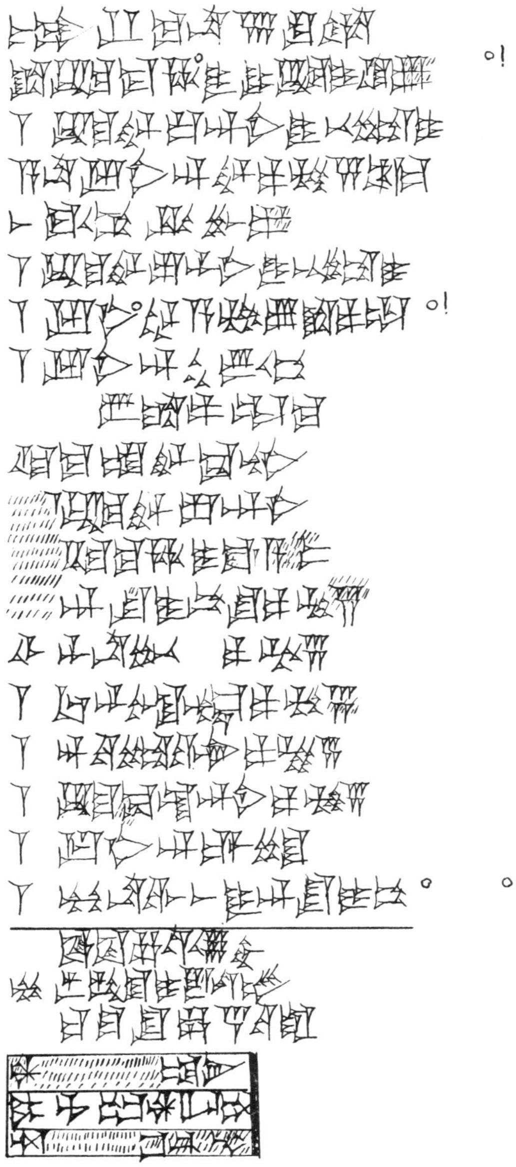

237

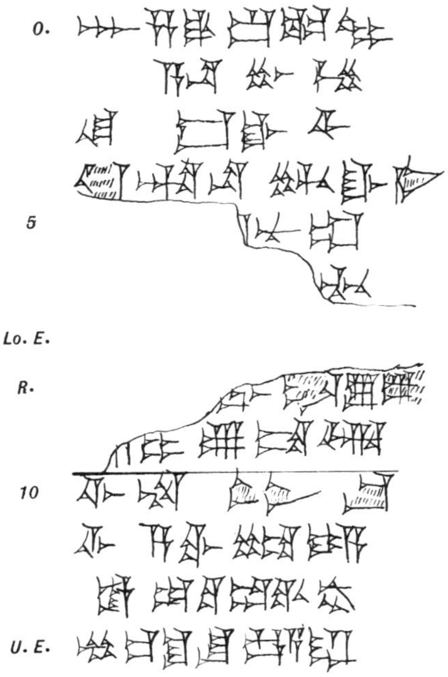

Indistinct seal impressions.

238

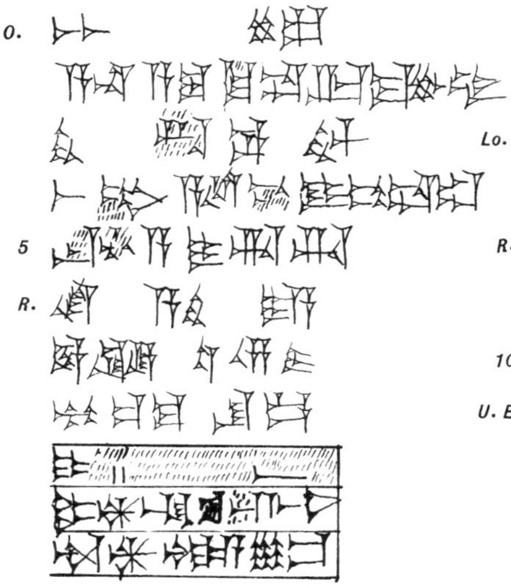

239

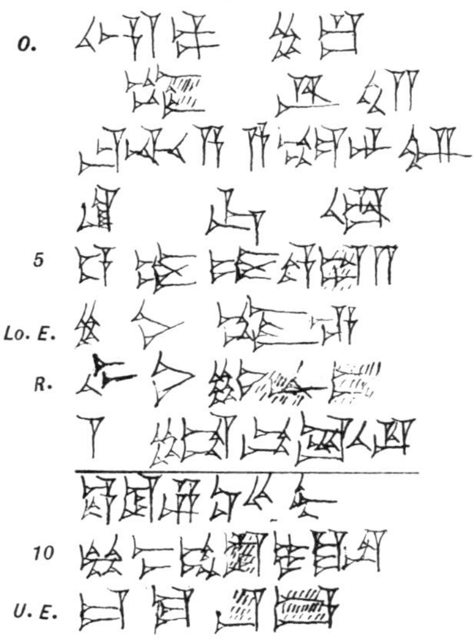

Indistinct seal impressions.

240

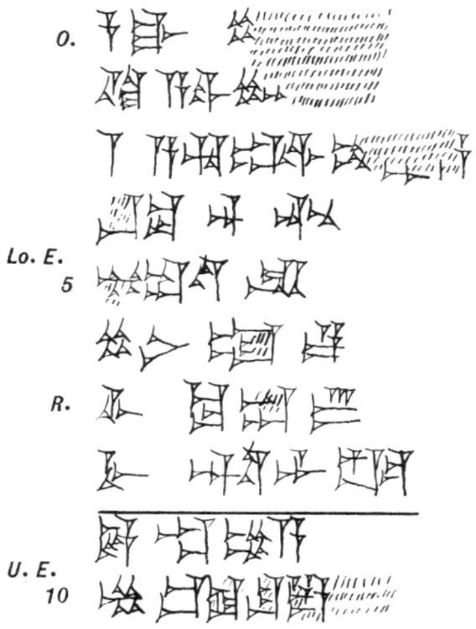

Indistinct seal impressions.

241

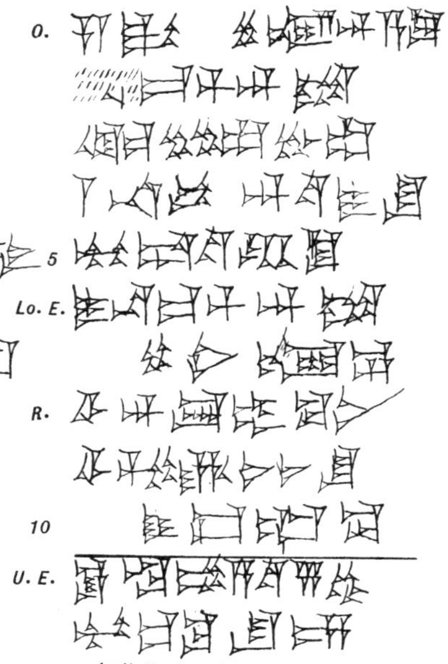

Indistinct seal impressions.

242

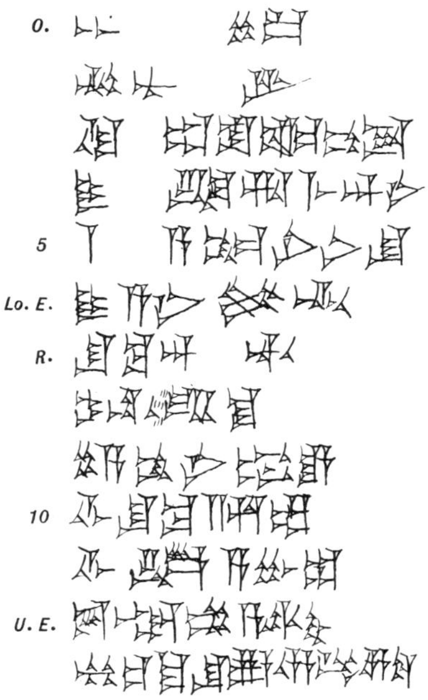

243

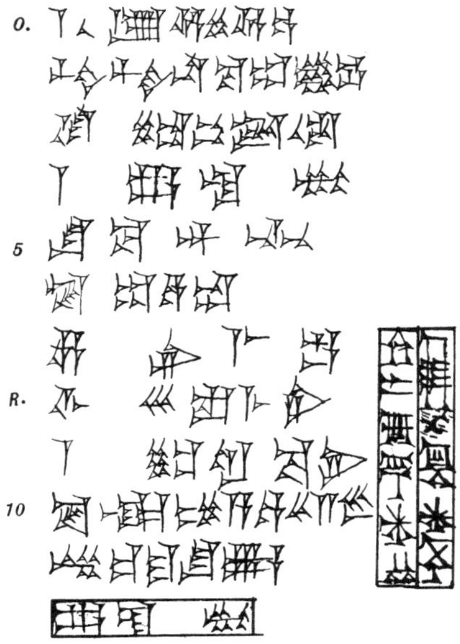

244

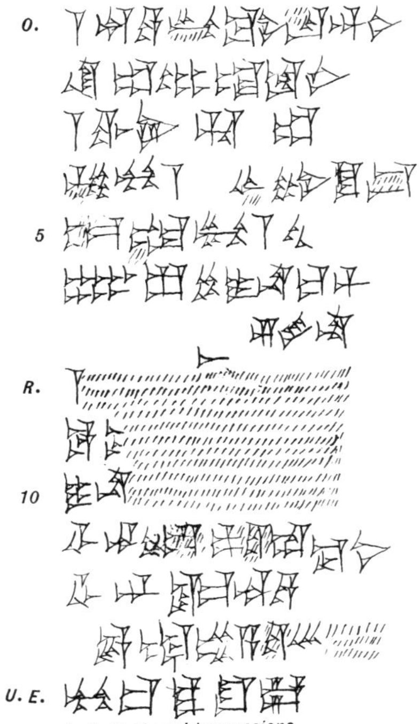

Indistinct seal impressions.

245

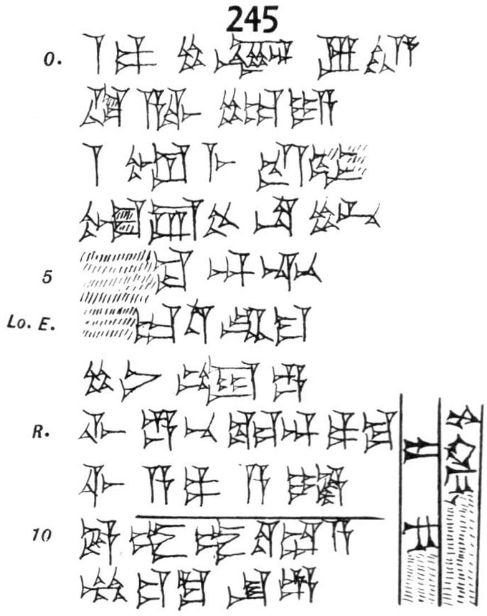

246

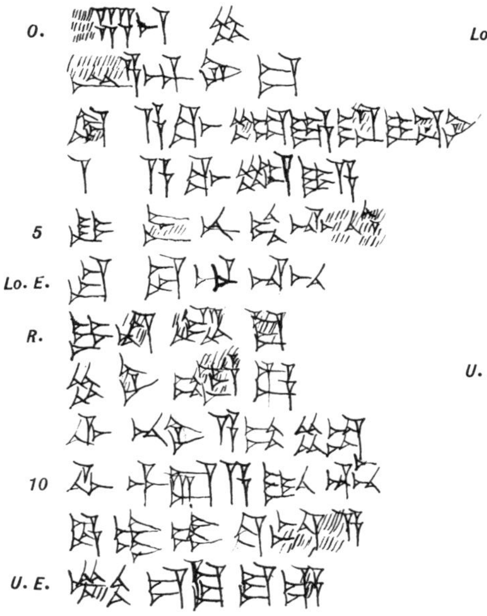

247

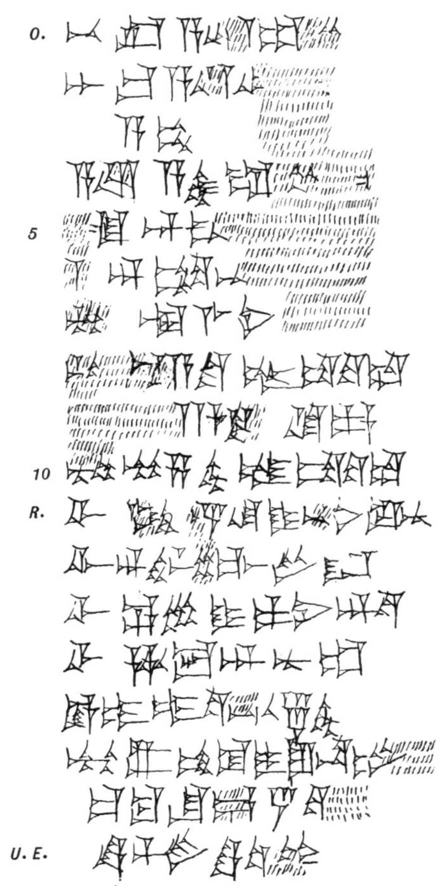

Indistinct seal impressions.

248

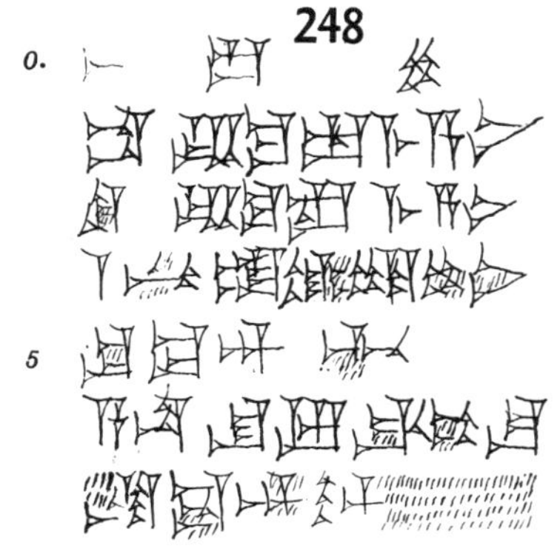

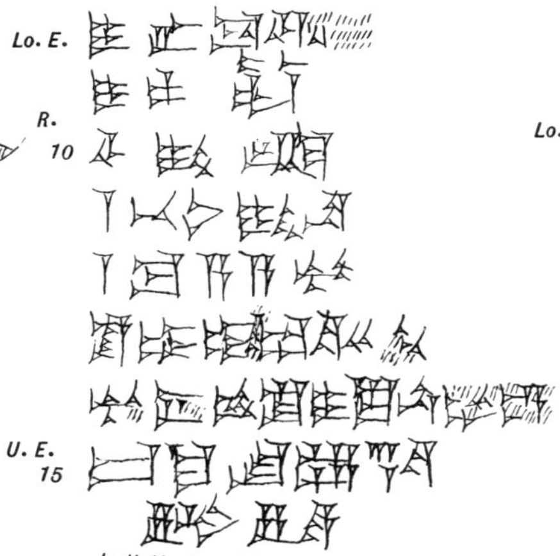

Indistinct seal impressions.

249

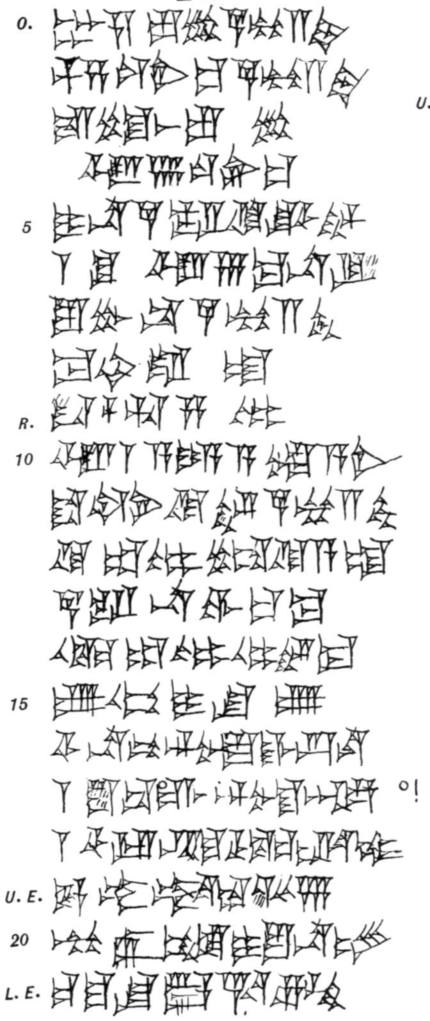

250

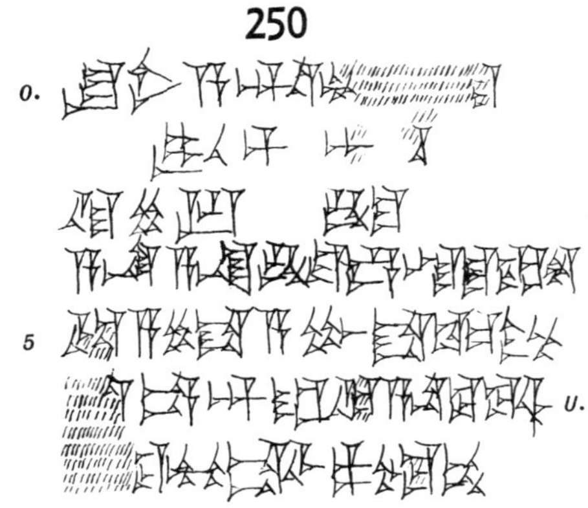

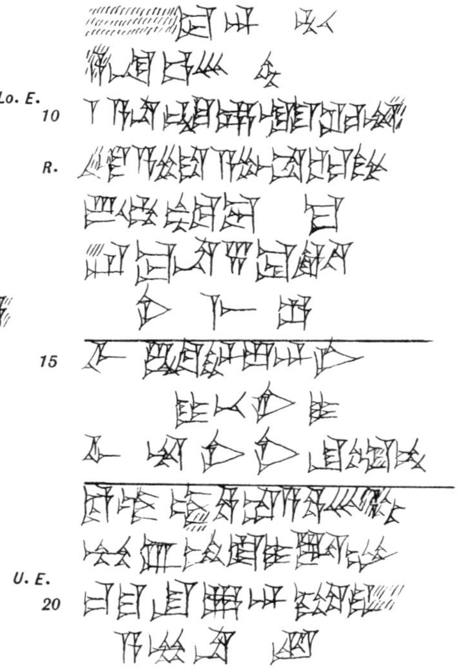

Indistinct seal impressions.

251

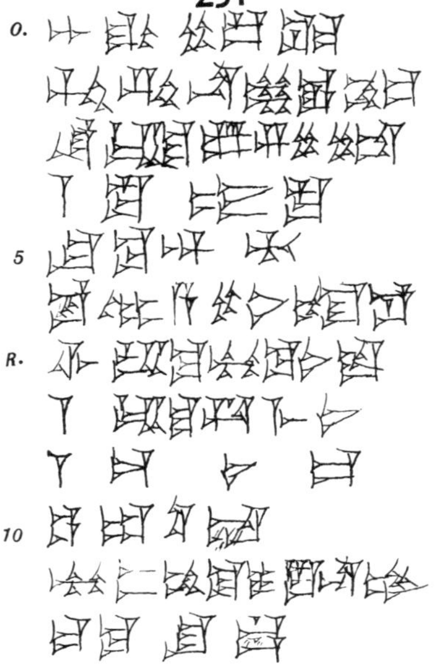

Indistinct seal impressions.

252

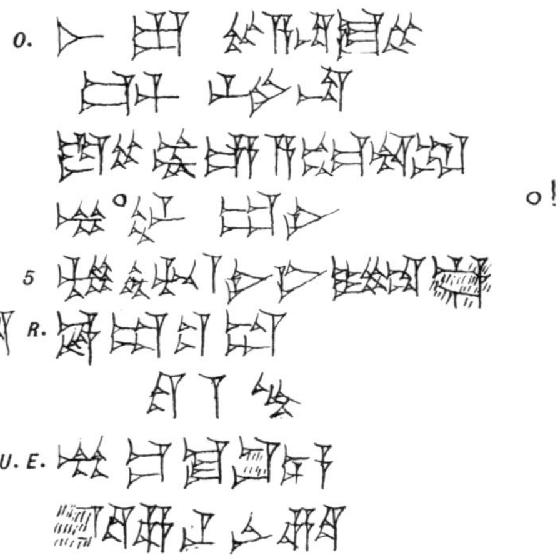

253

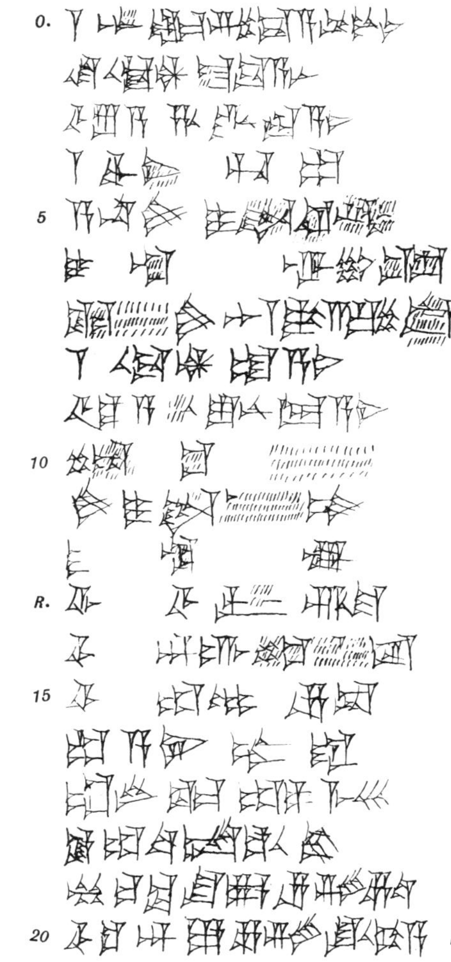

Indistinct seal impressions.

254

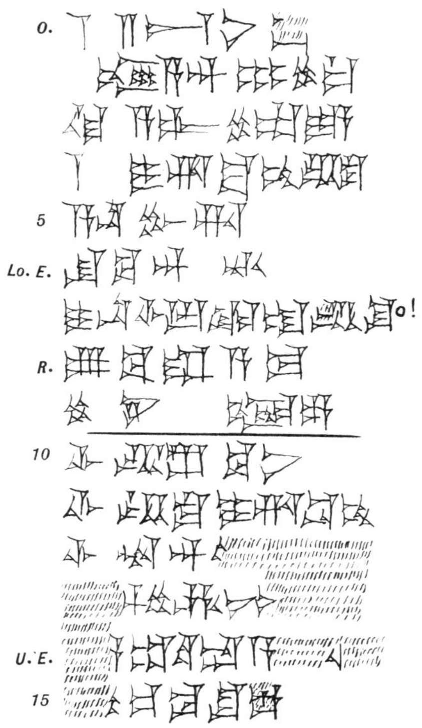

Indistinct seal impressions.

255

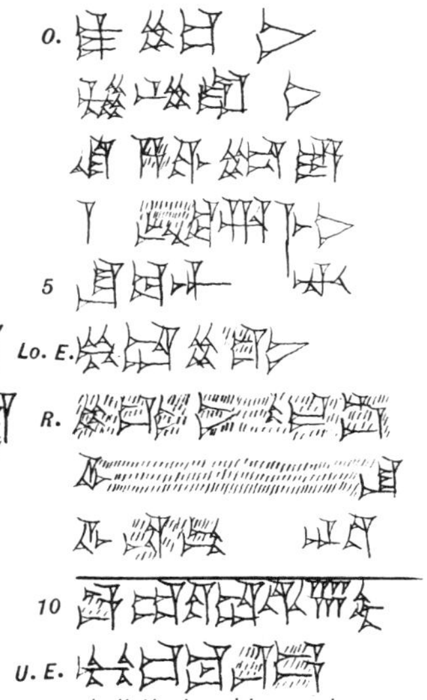

Indistinct seal impressions.

256

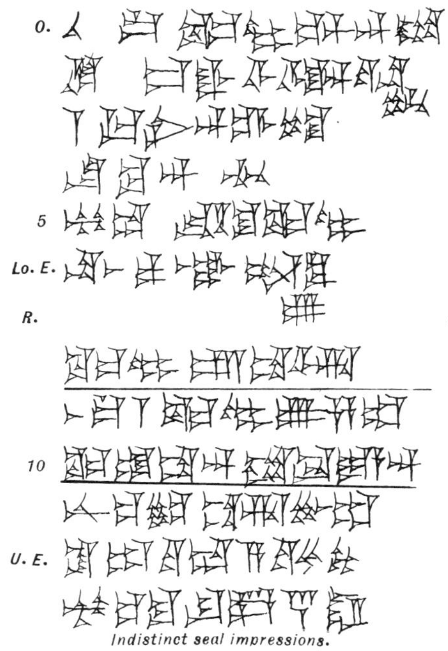

Indistinct seal impressions.

257

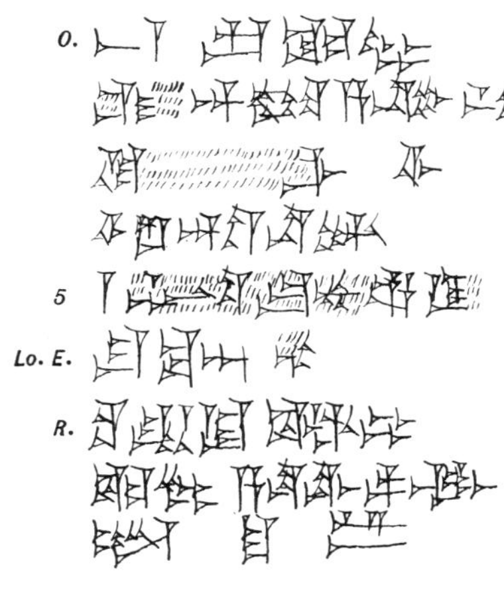

258

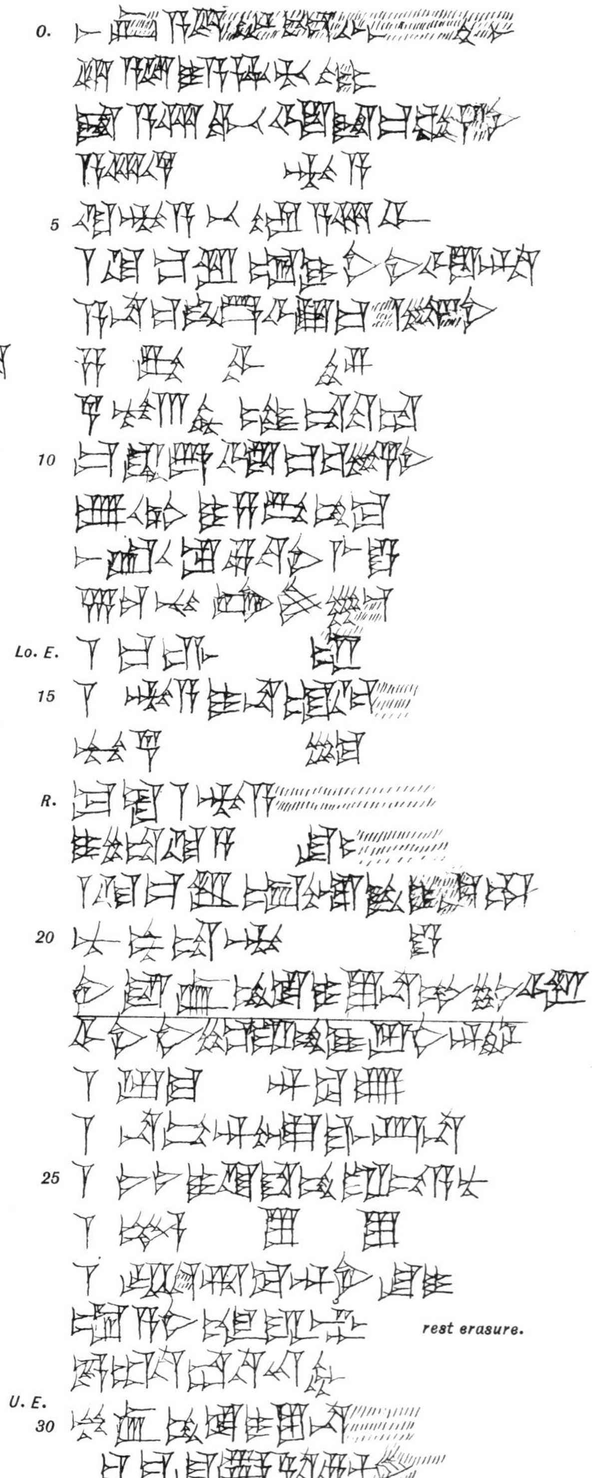

rest erasure.

Indistinct seal impressions.

259

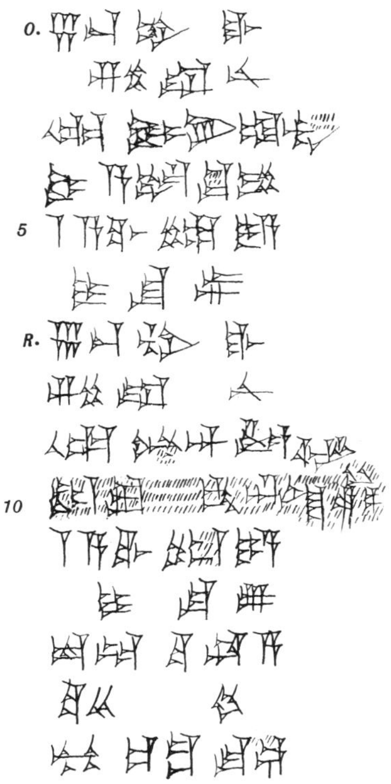

260

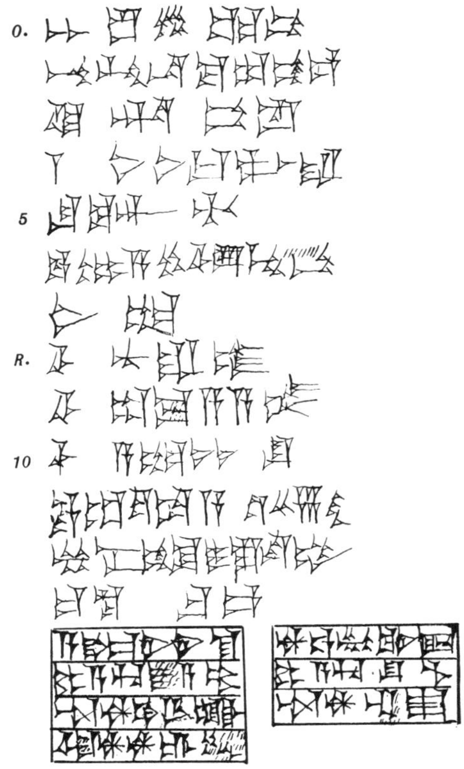

261

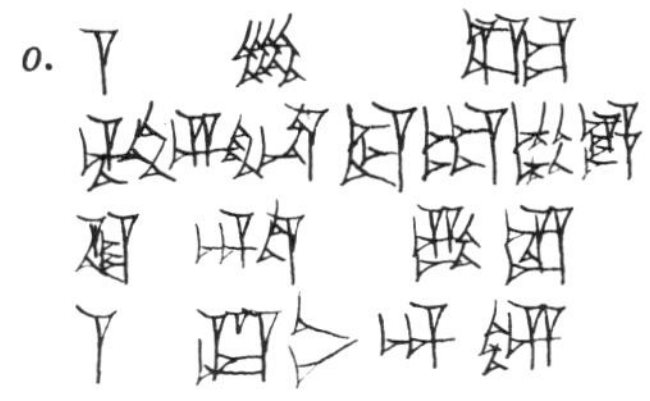

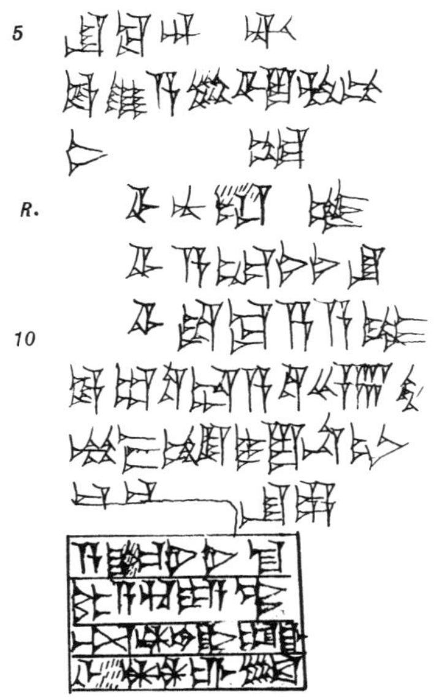

262

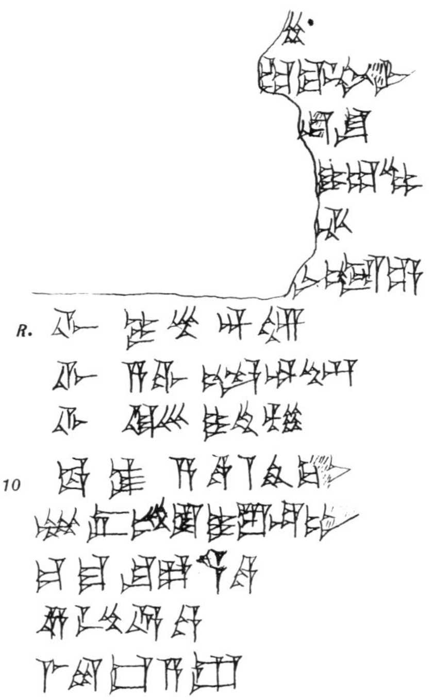

263

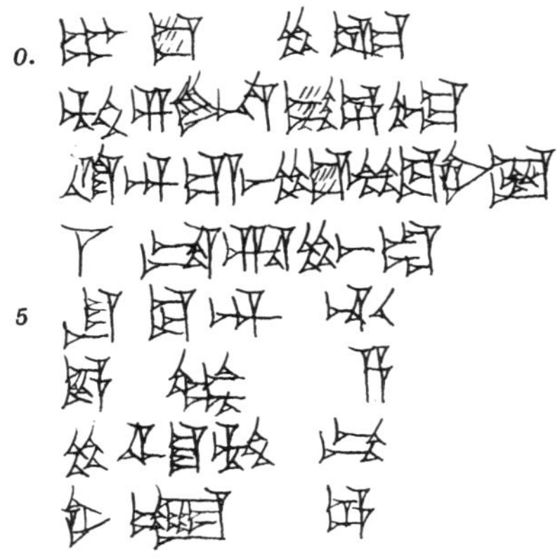

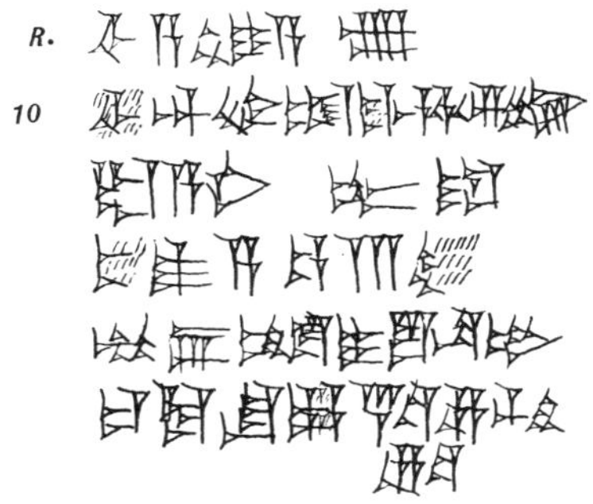

264

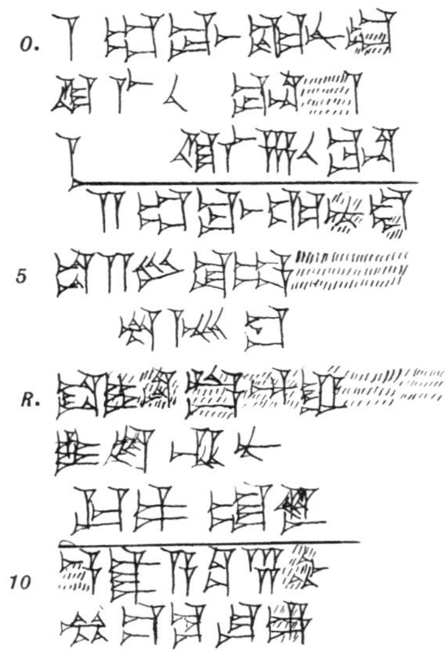

265

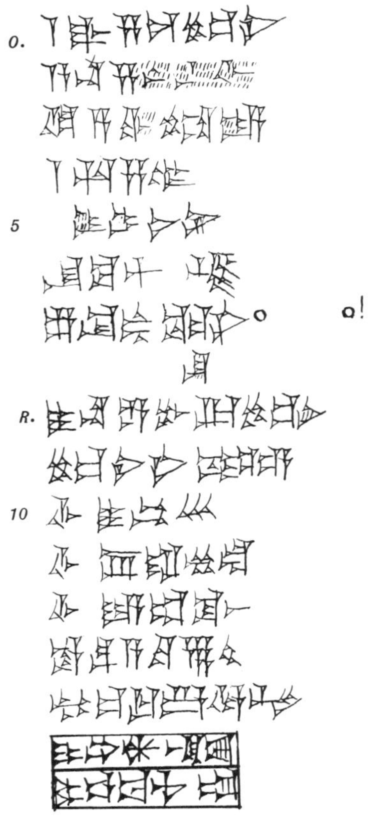

266

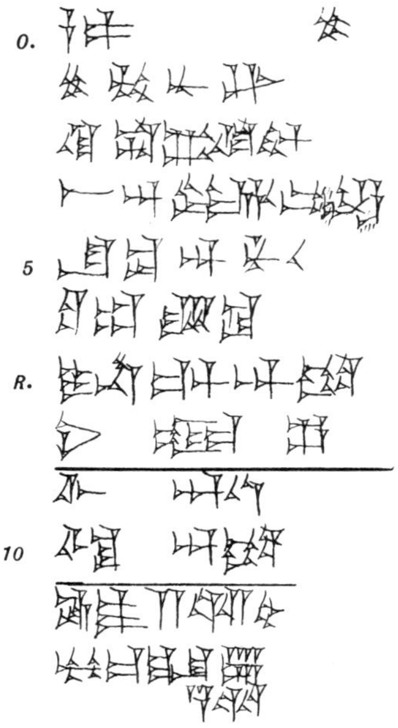

267

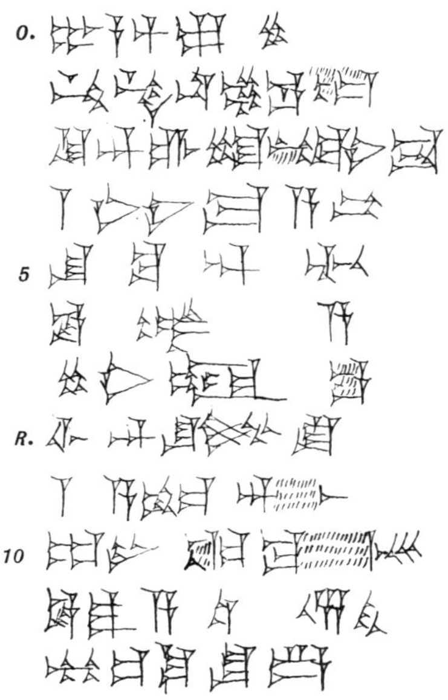

268

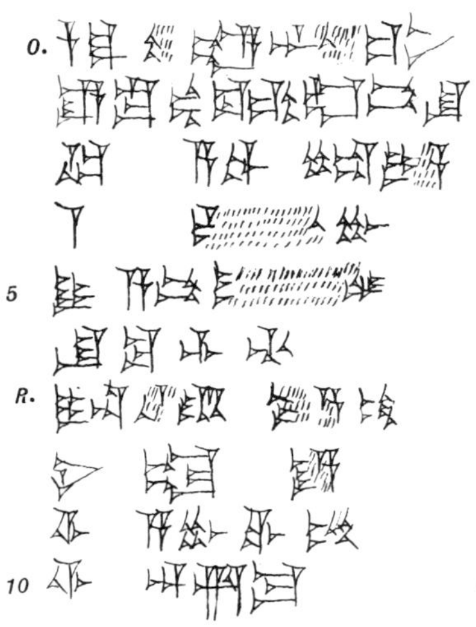

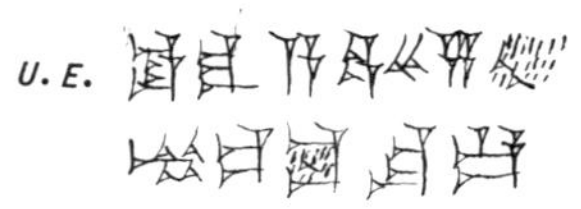

269

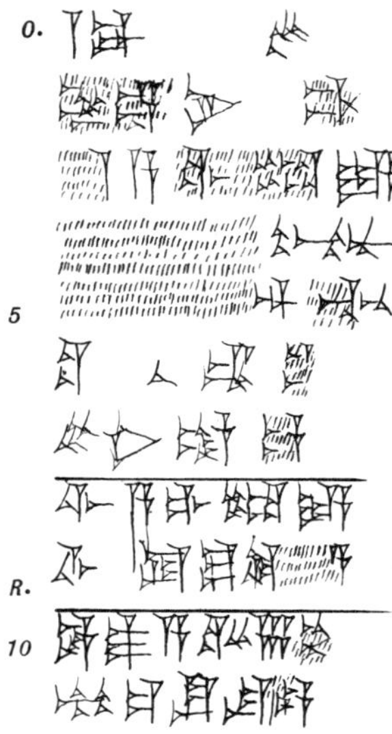

270

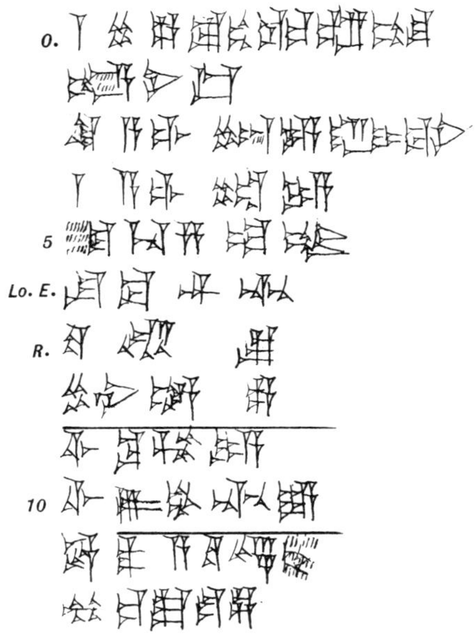

271

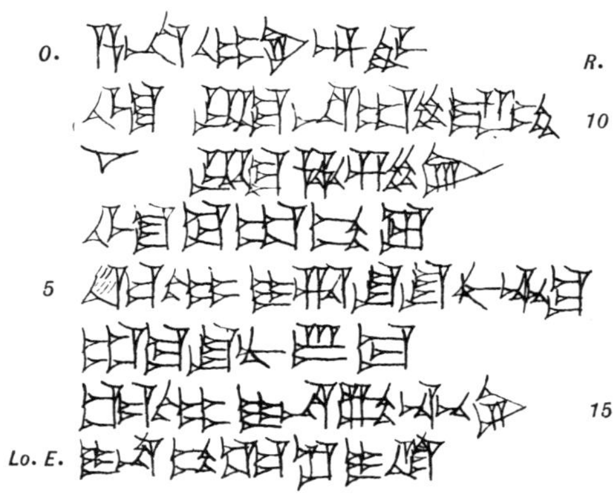

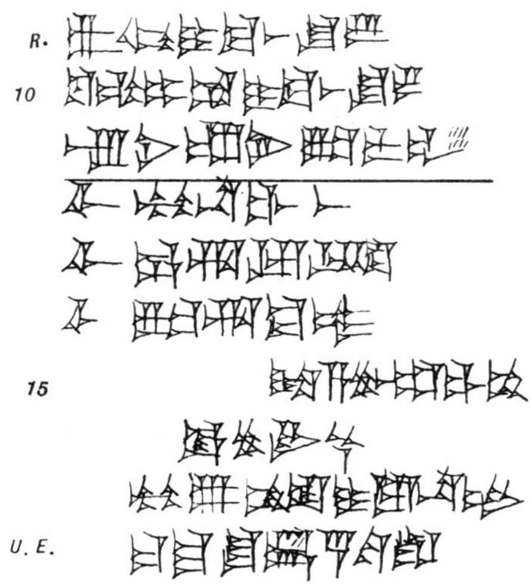

272

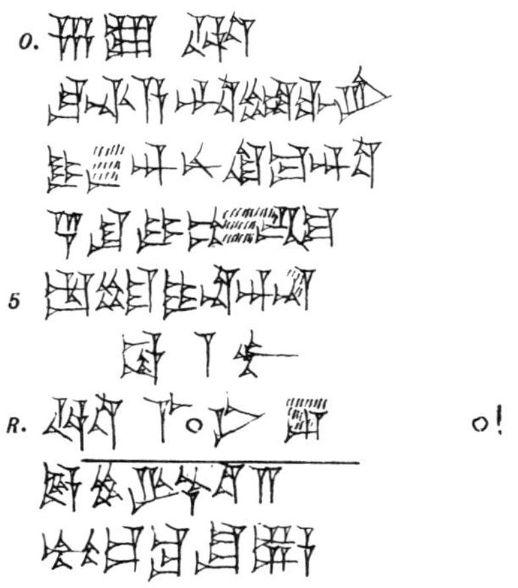

273

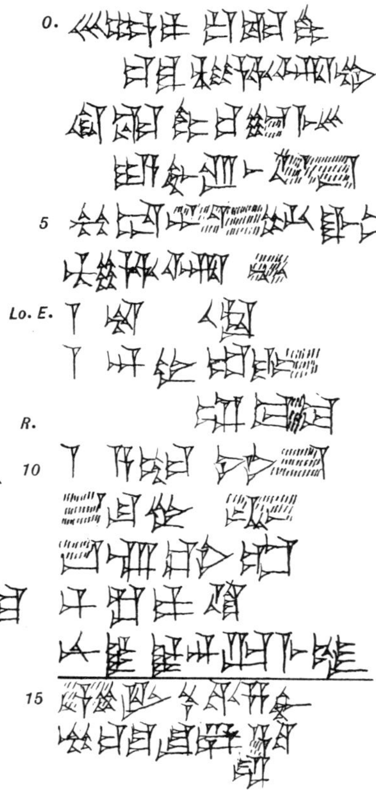

274

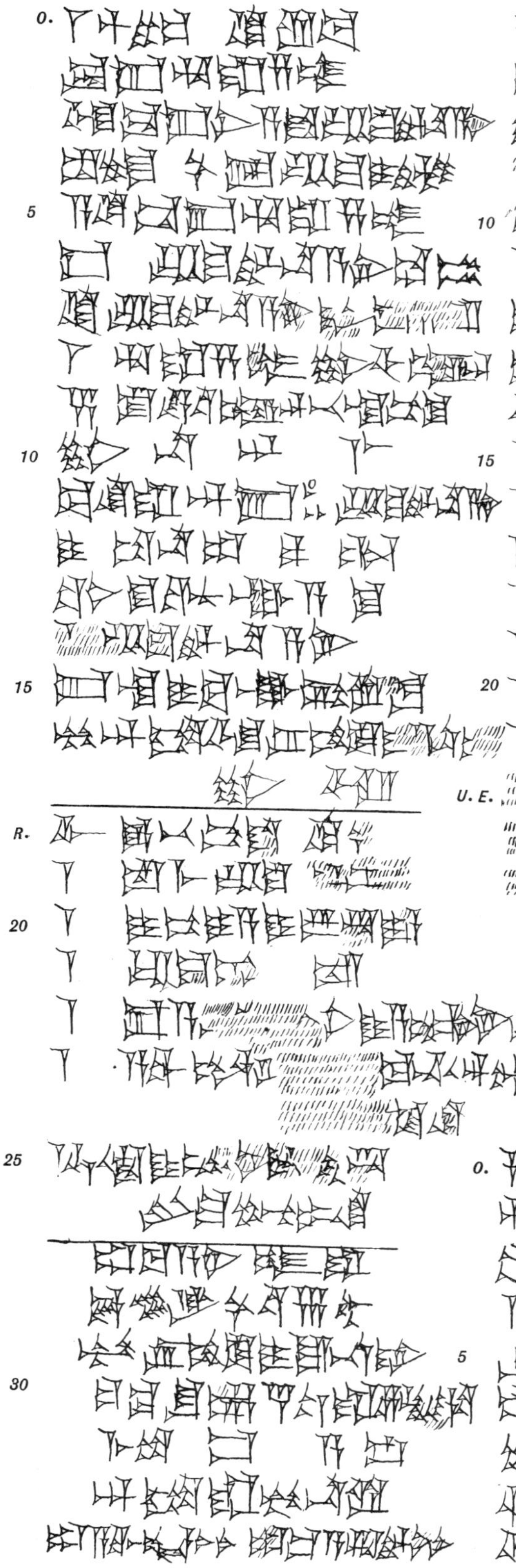

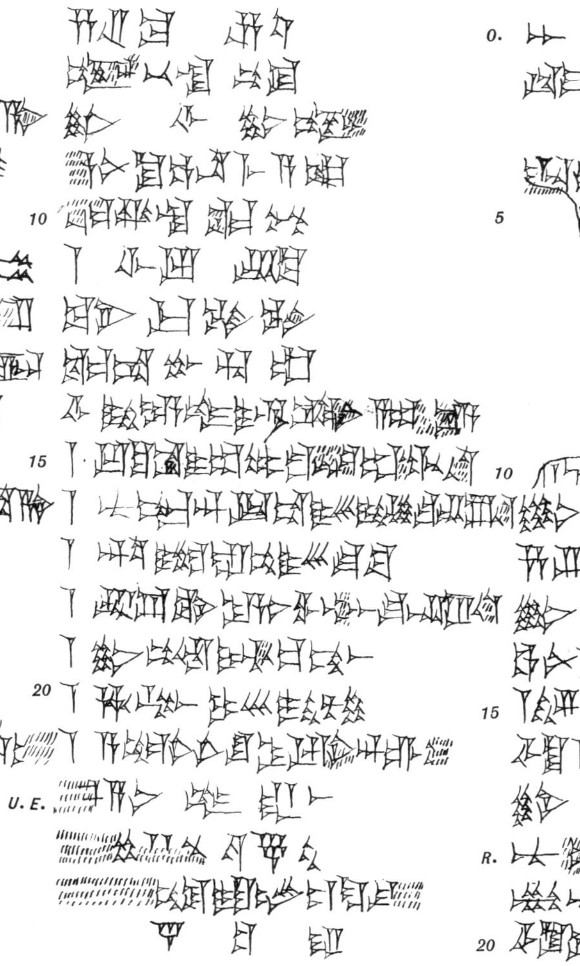

Indistinct seal impressions.

277

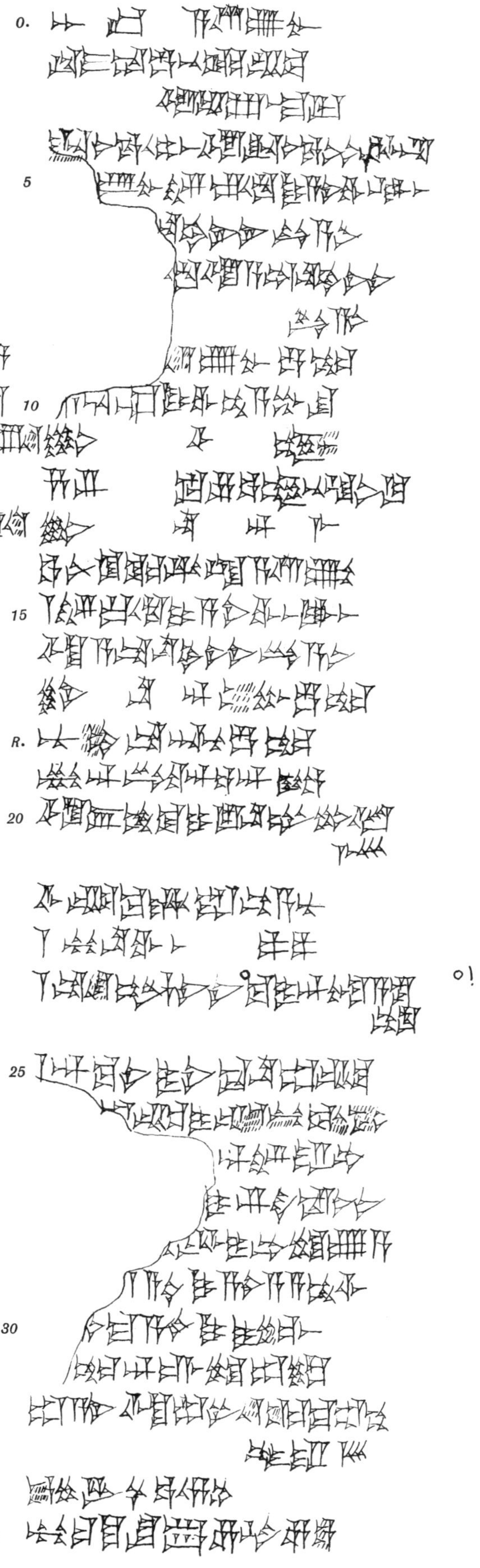

276

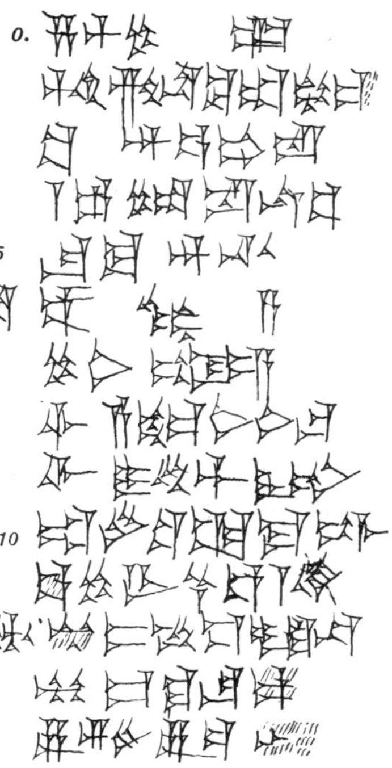

275

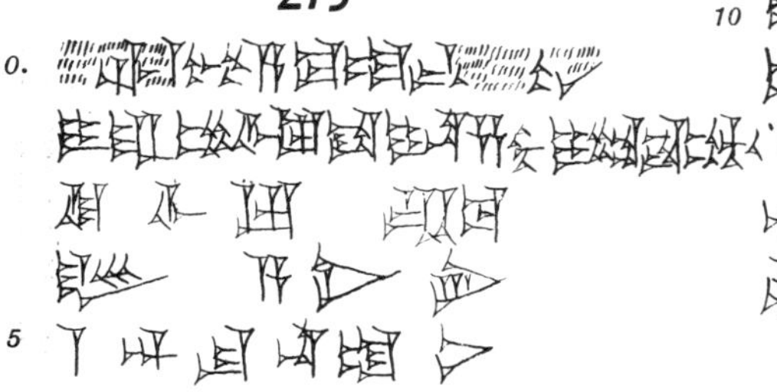

278

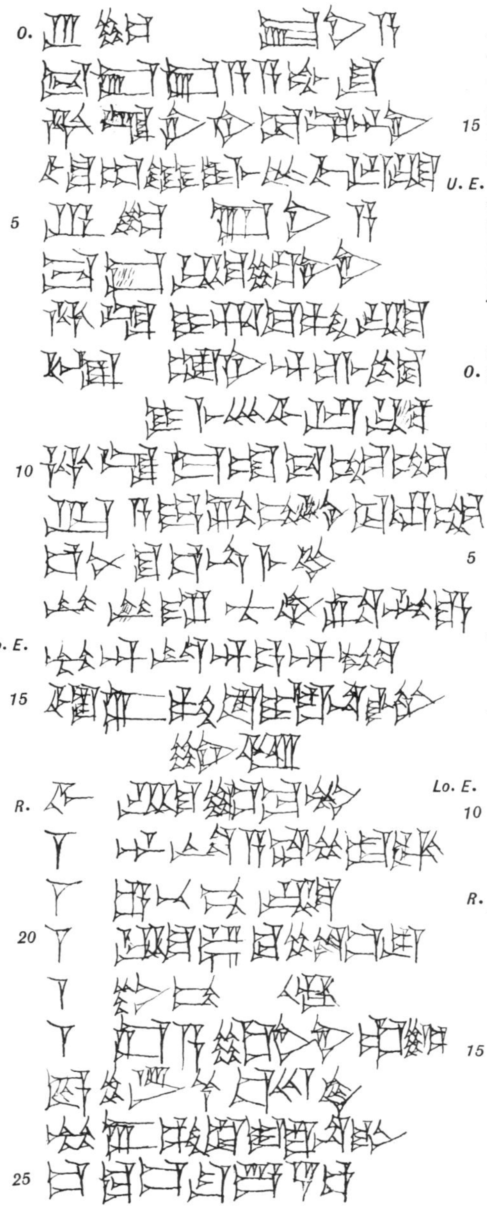

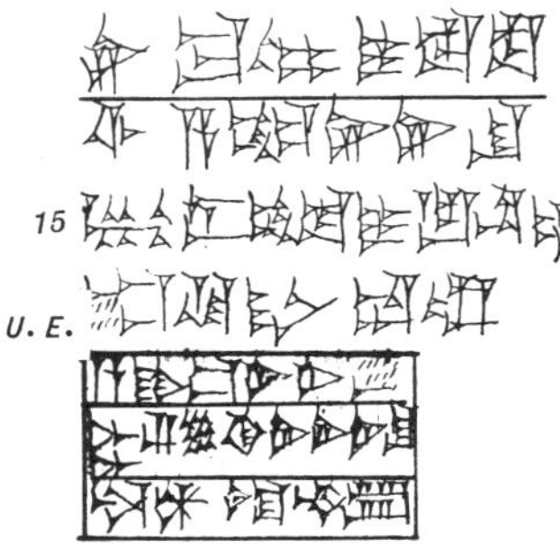

Indistinct seal impressions.

279

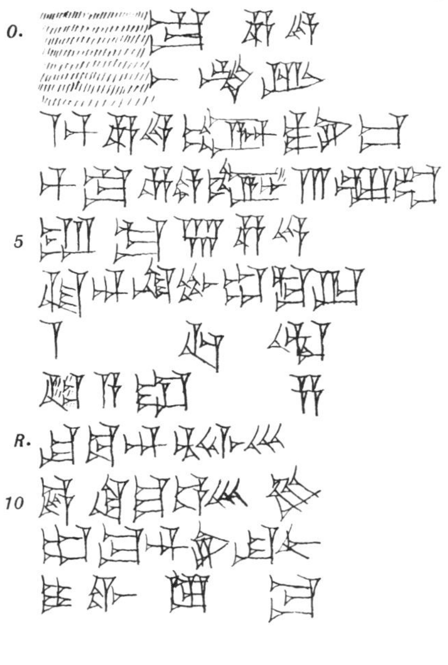

280

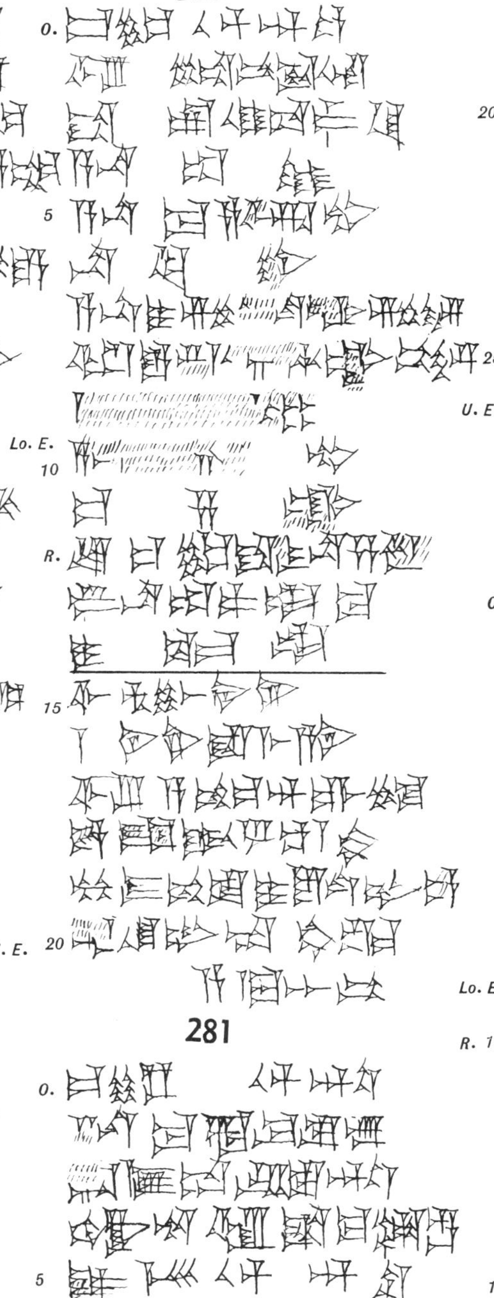

281

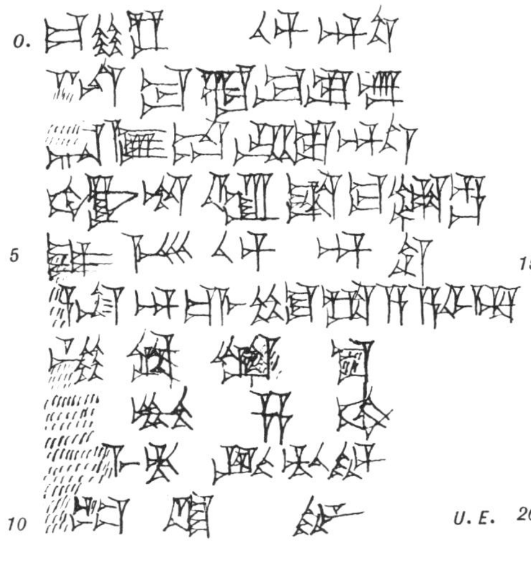

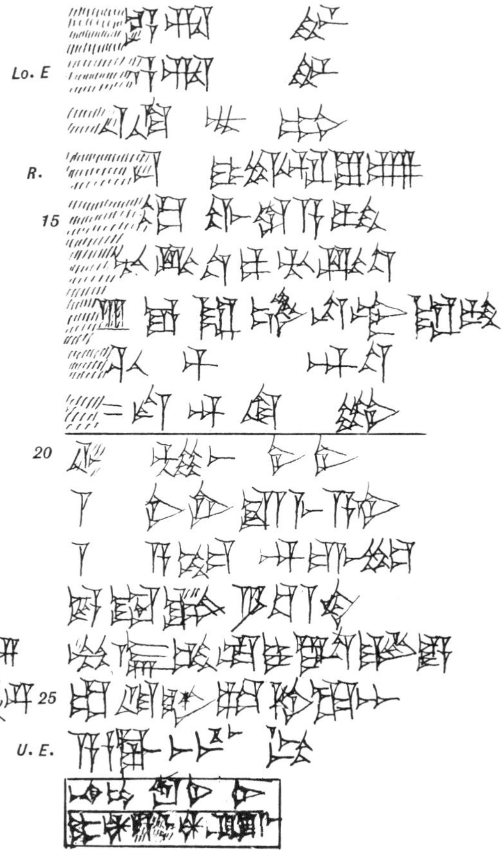

282

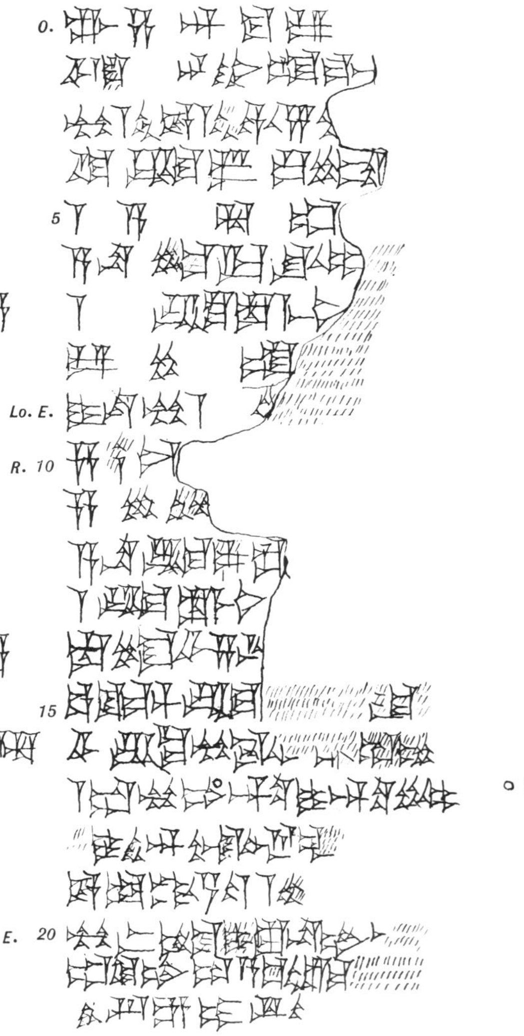

283

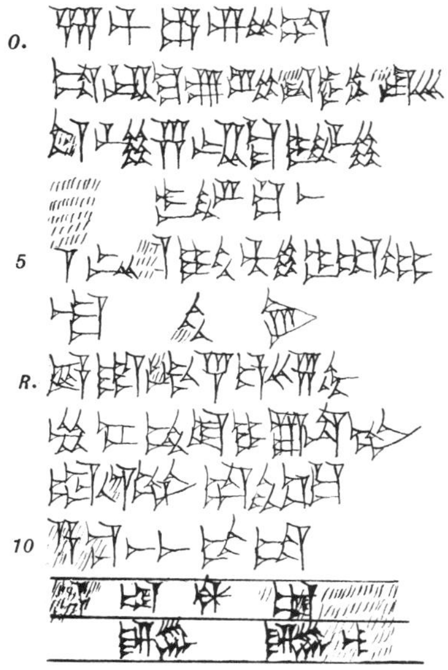

284

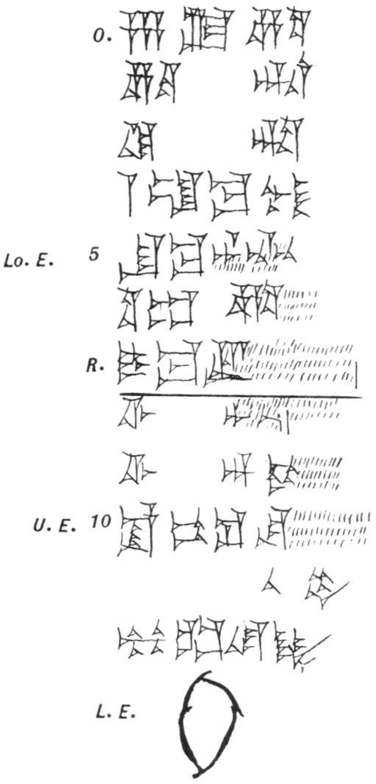

285 CASE

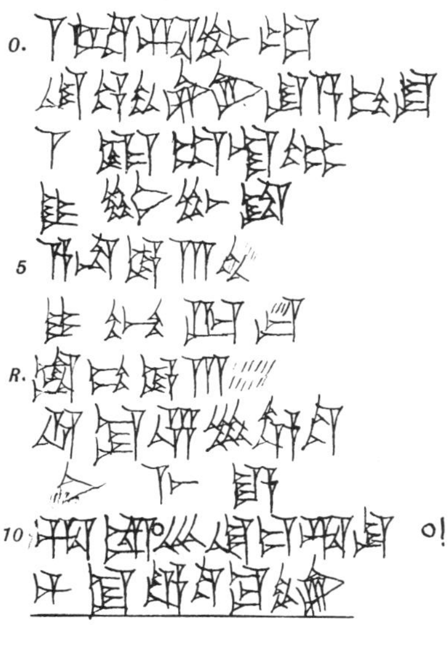

286

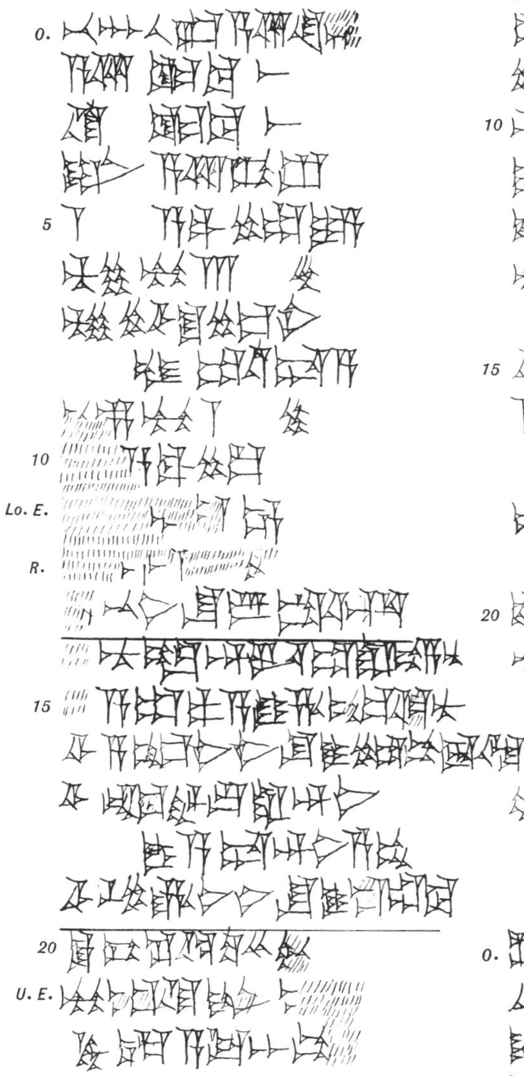

287

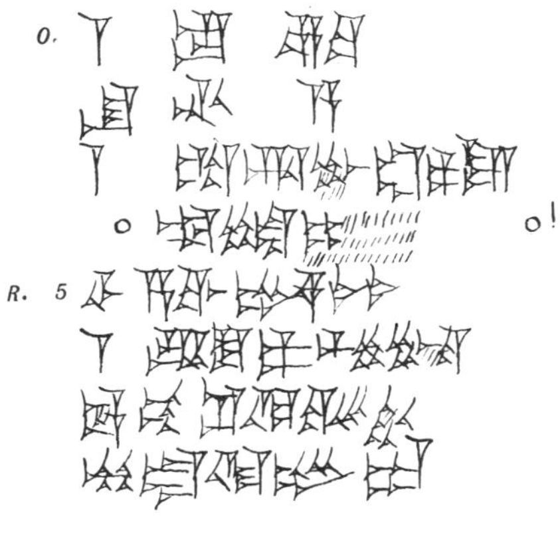

288

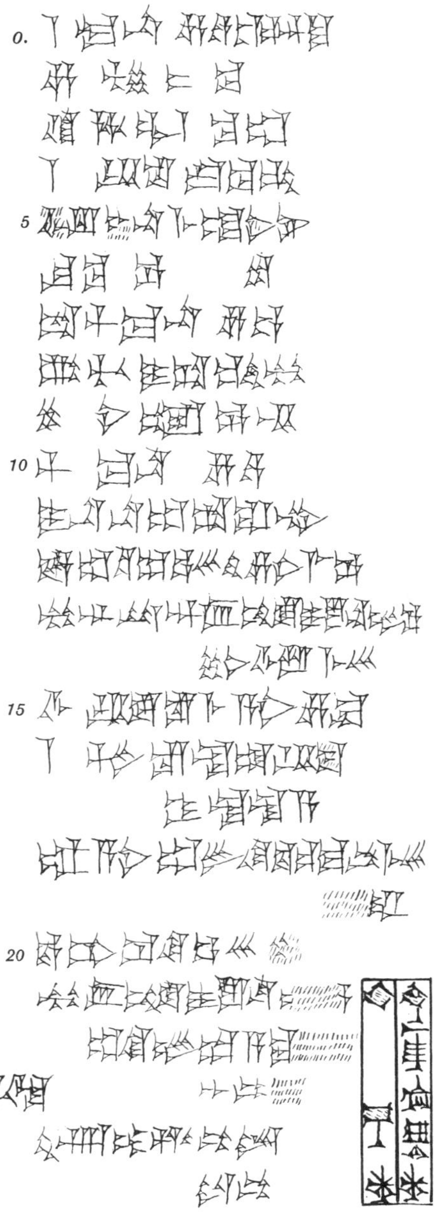

289

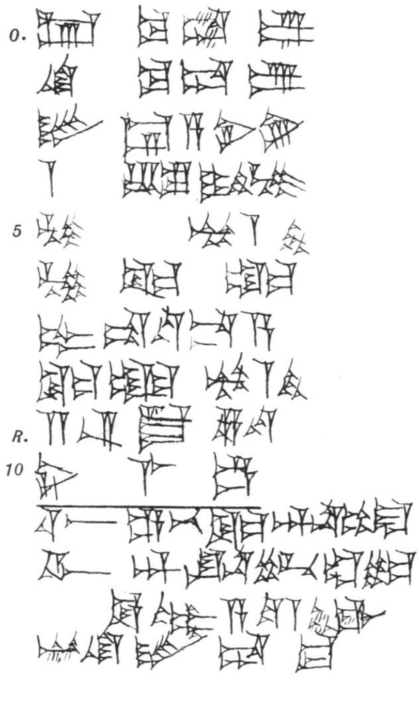

290

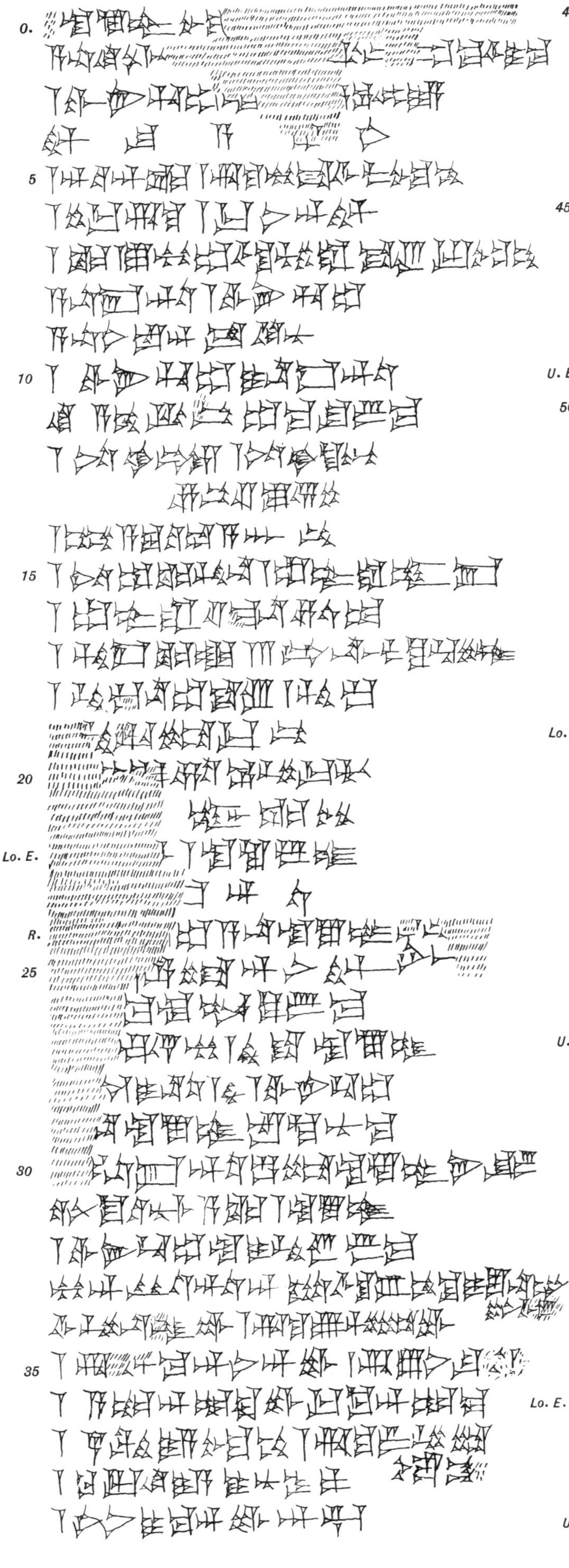

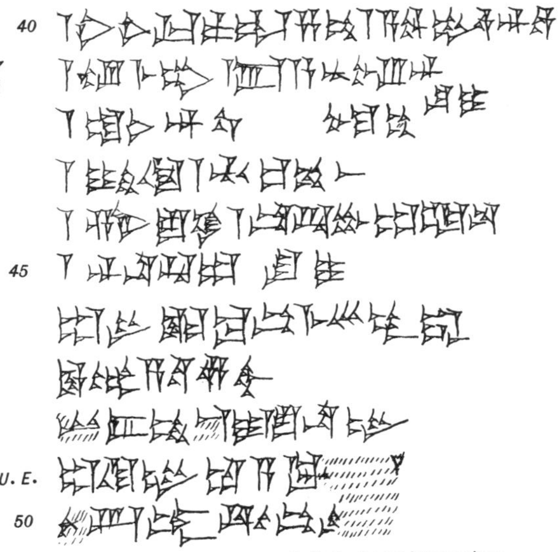

Indistinct seal impressions.

291

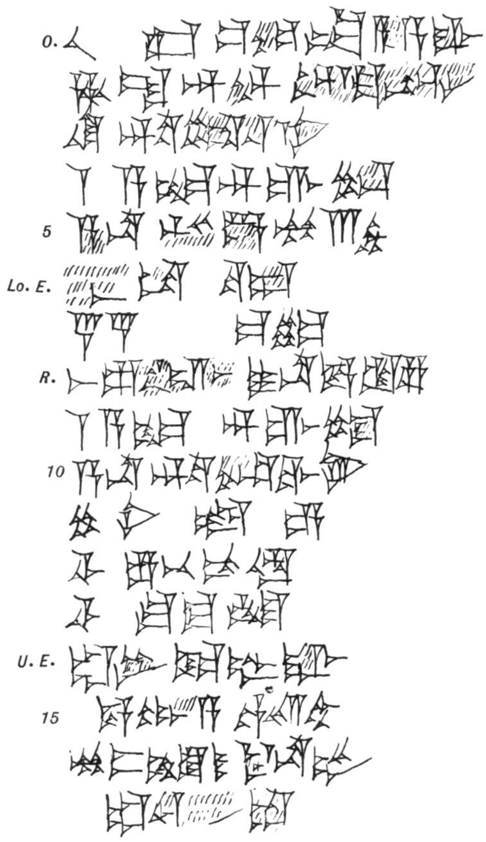

292

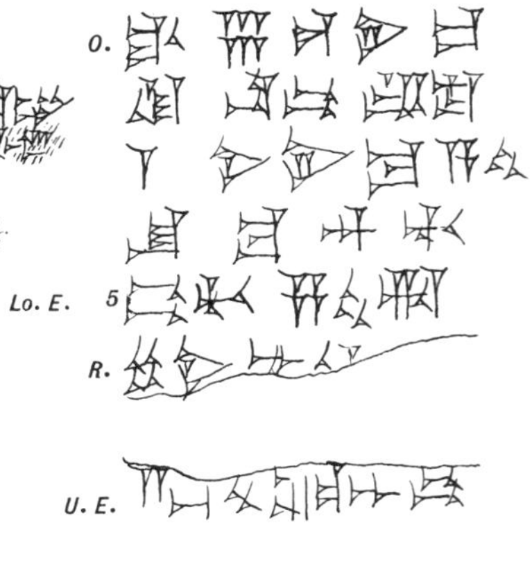

293

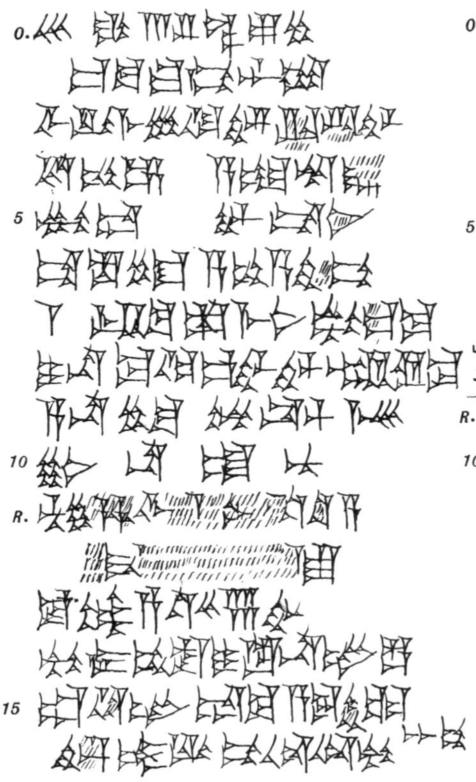

Indistinct seal impressions.

294

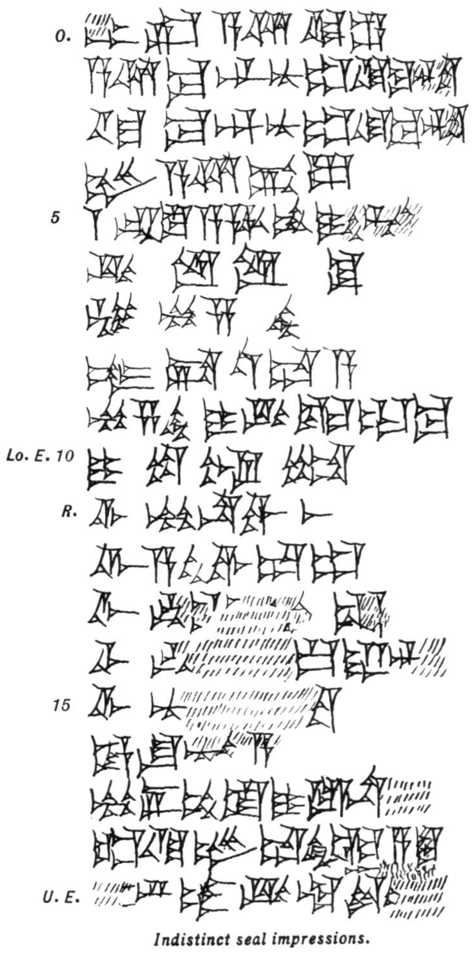

Indistinct seal impressions.

295

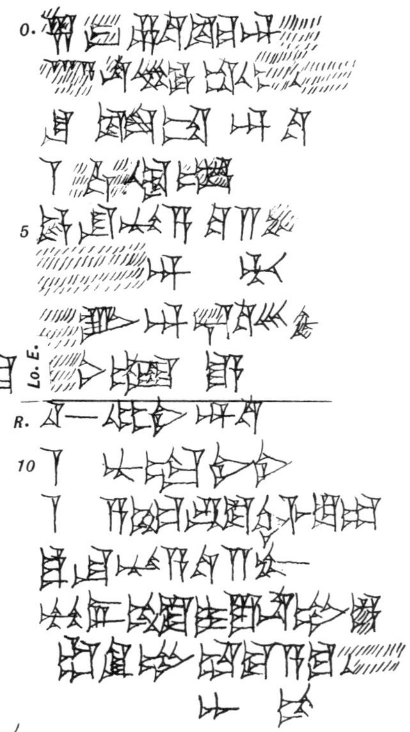

296

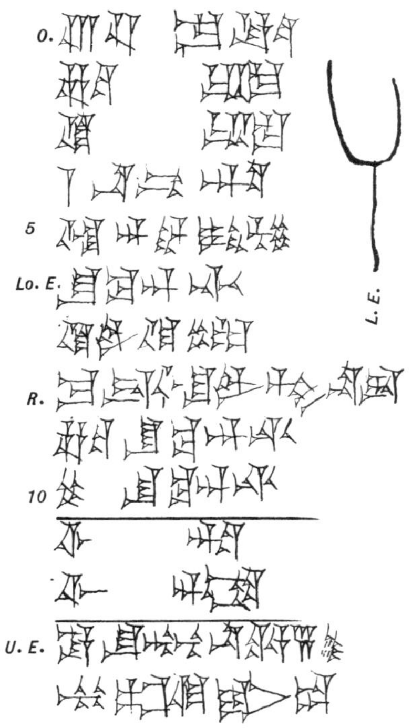

297

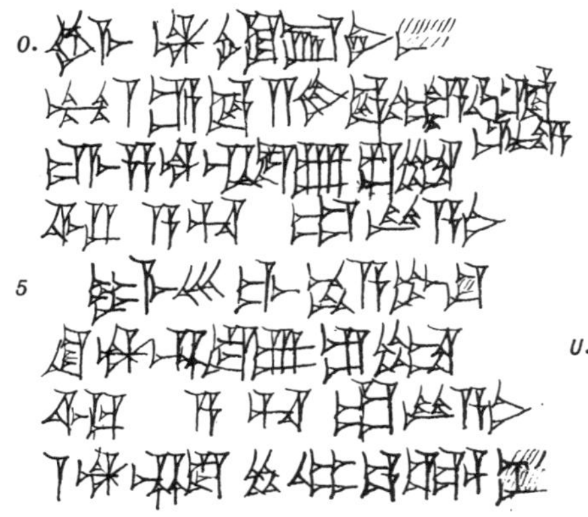

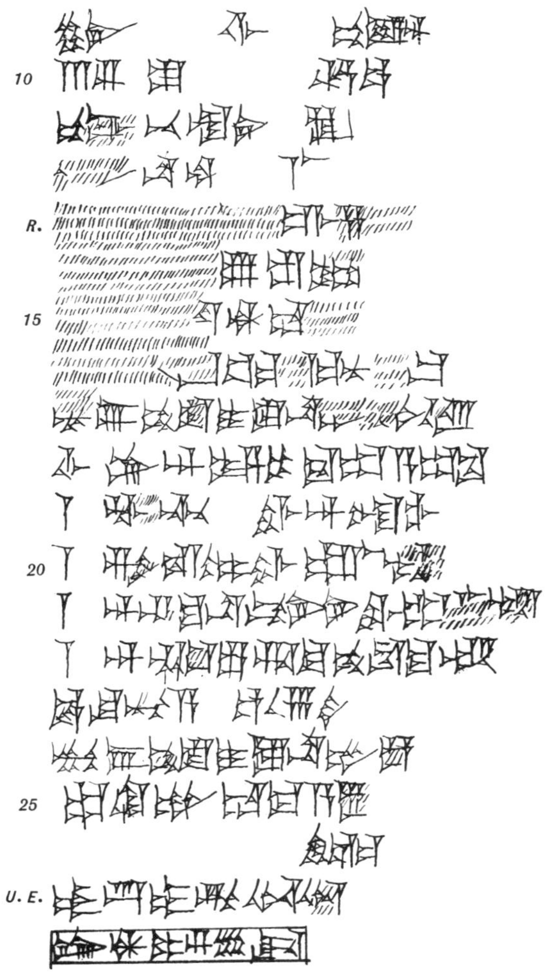

298

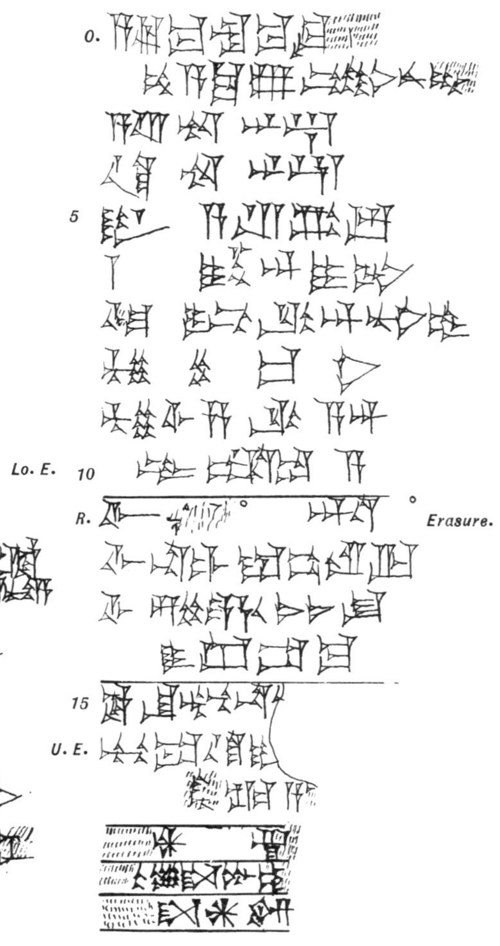

299

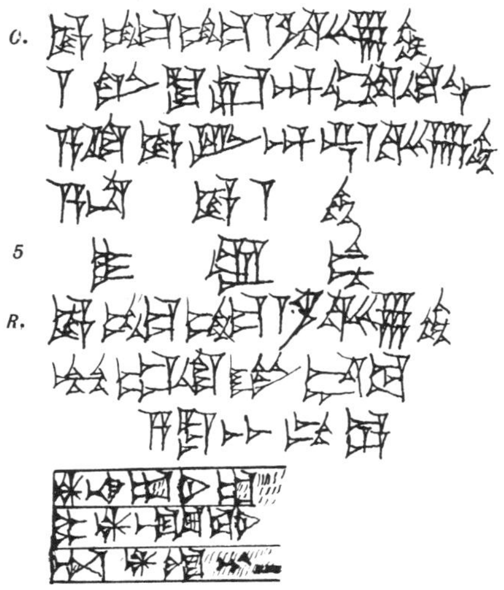

300

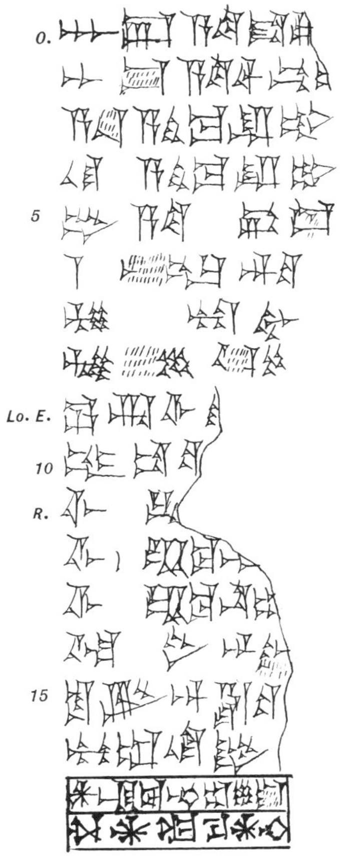

301

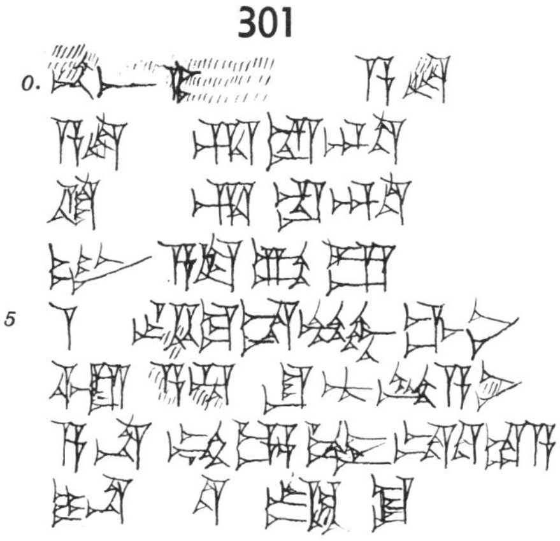

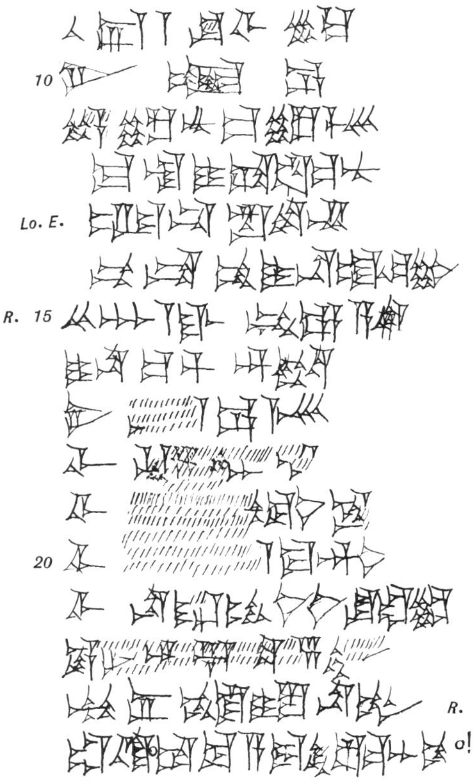

Indistinct seal impressions.

* *Erasure.*

302

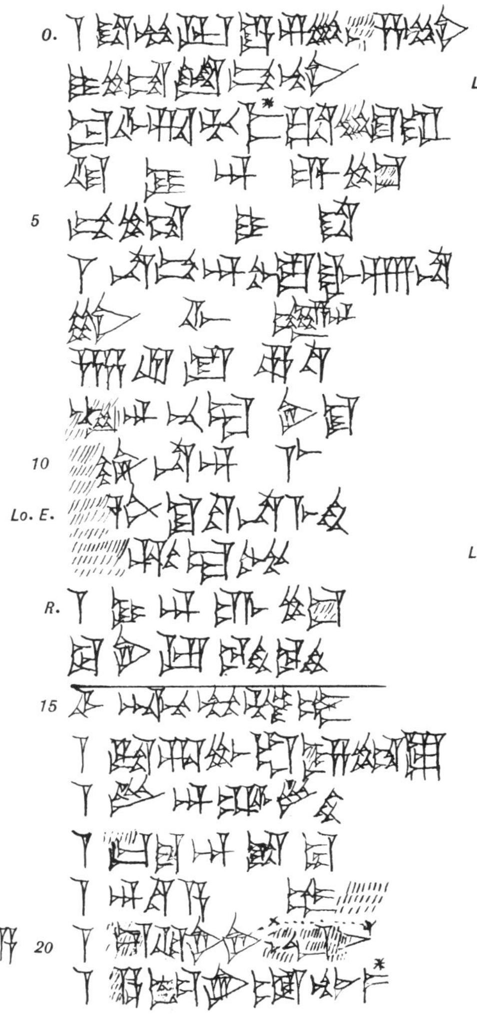

303

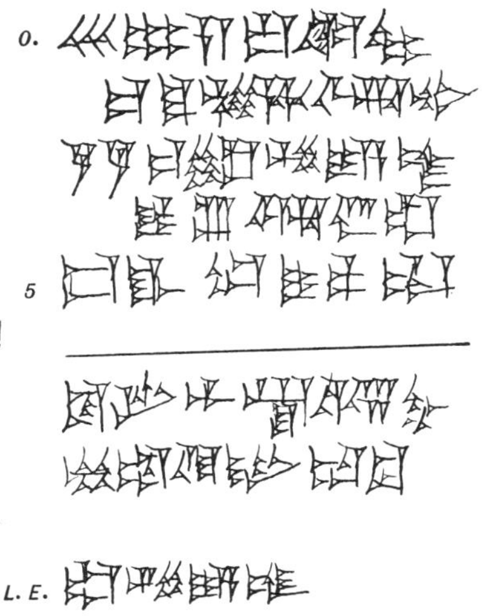

304

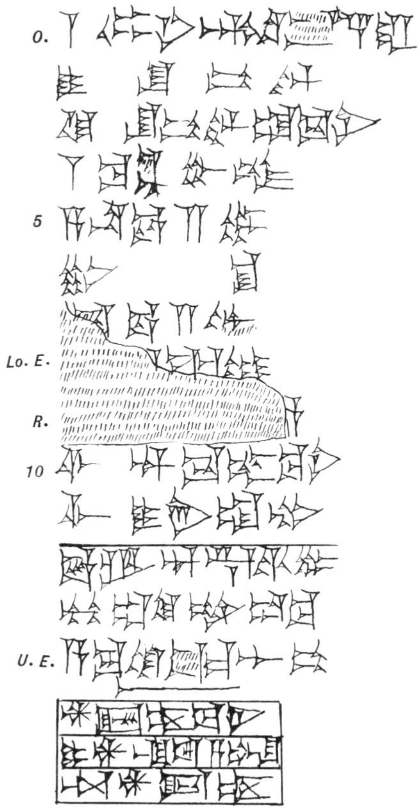

305

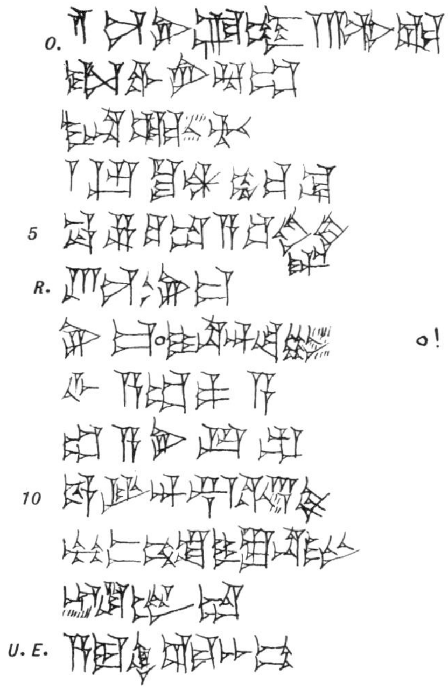

306 CASE

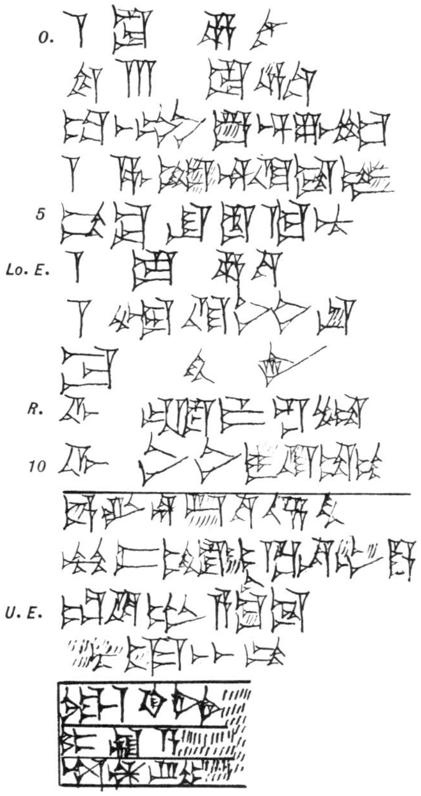

306 TABLET

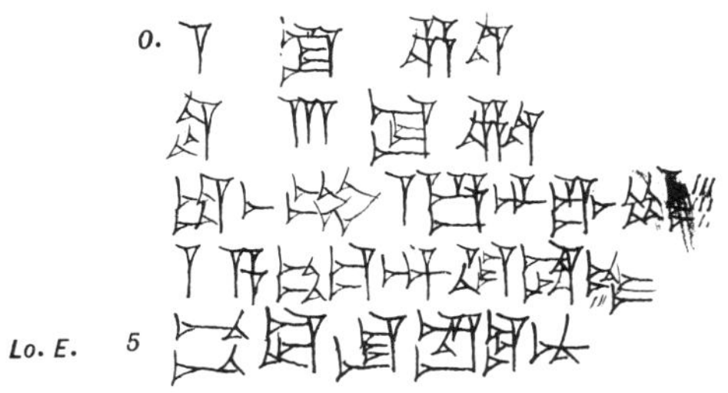

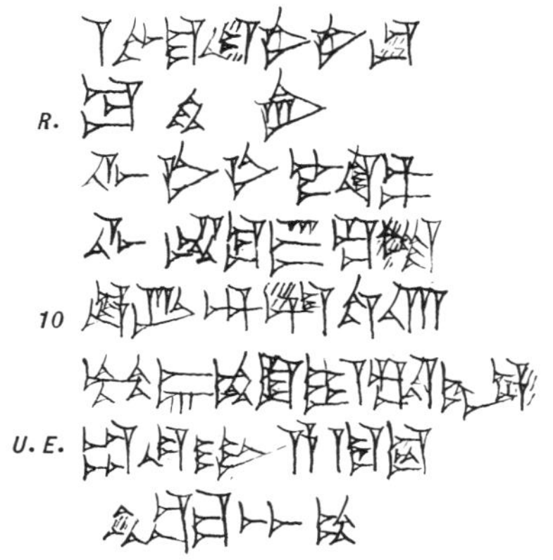

307

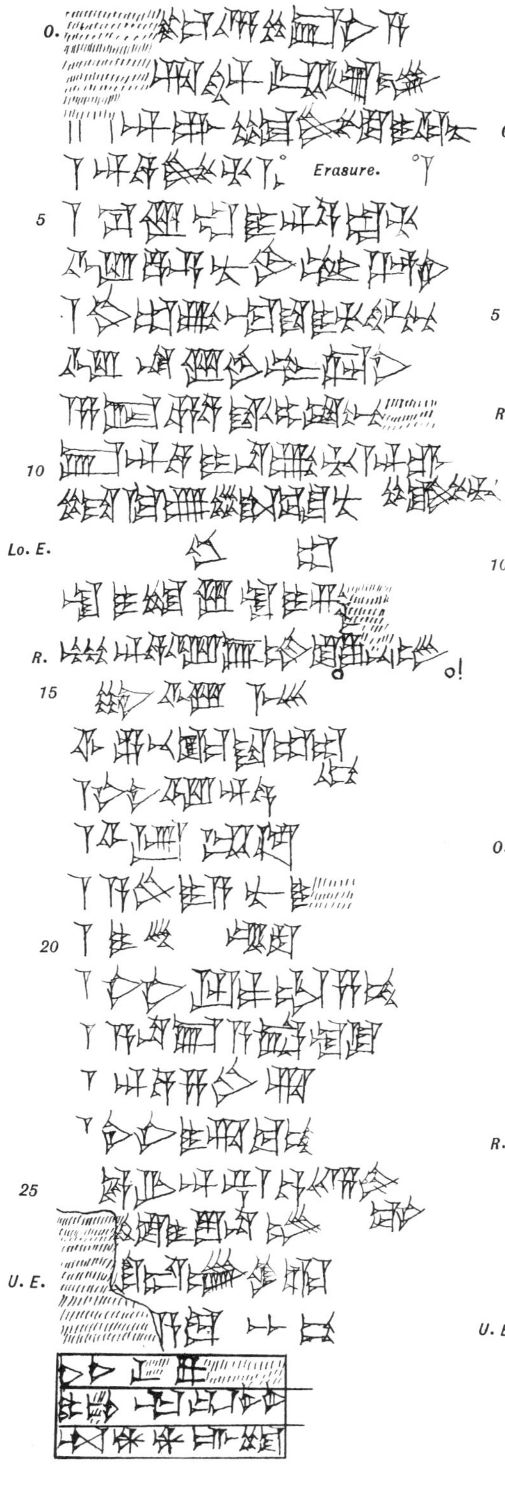

308

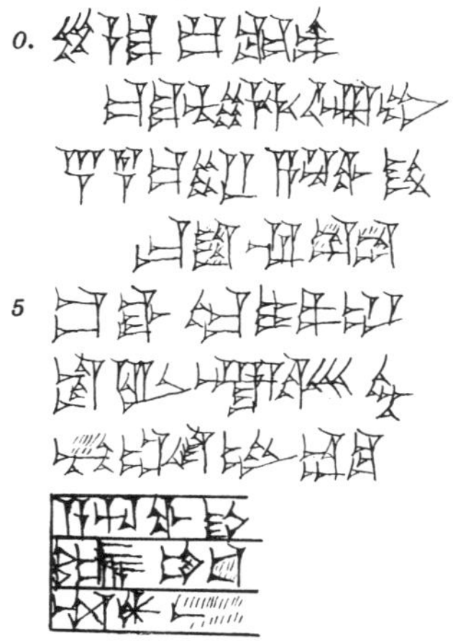

309

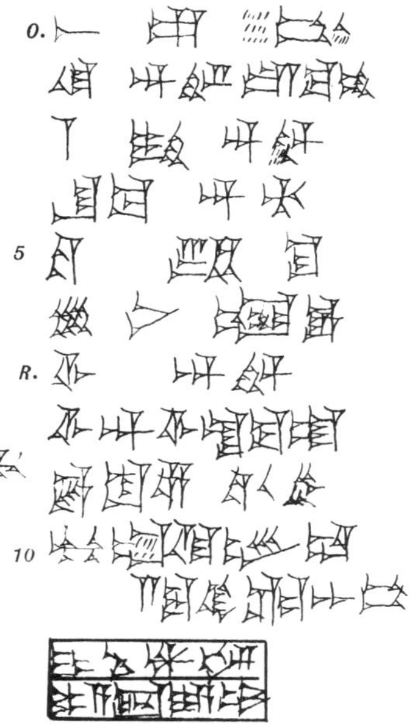

310

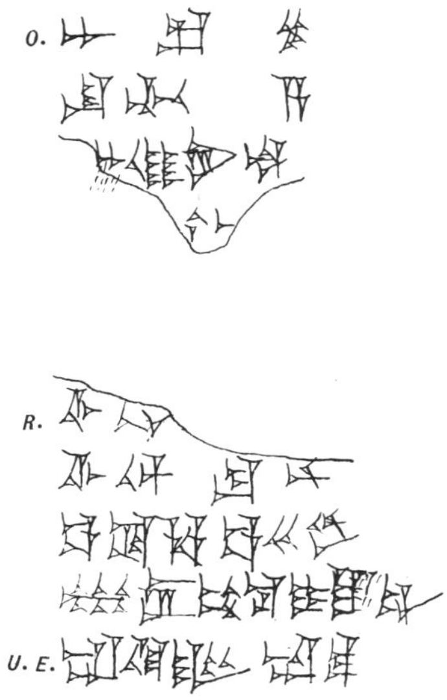

311

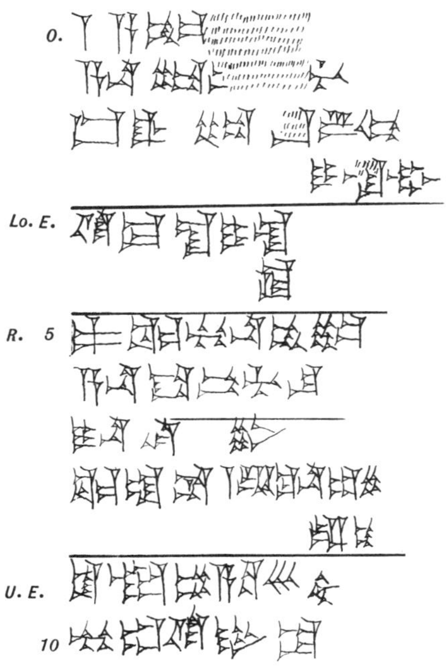

313

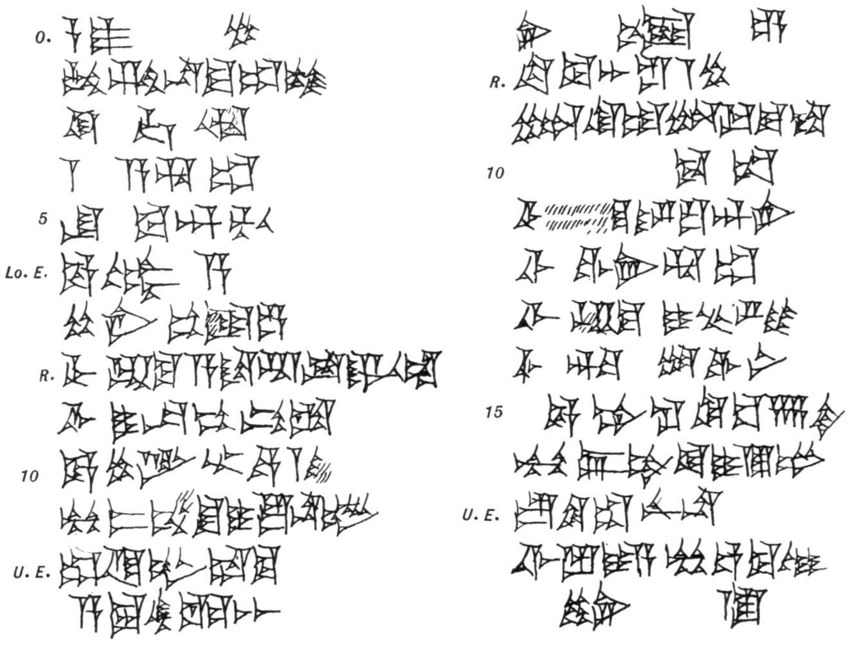

312

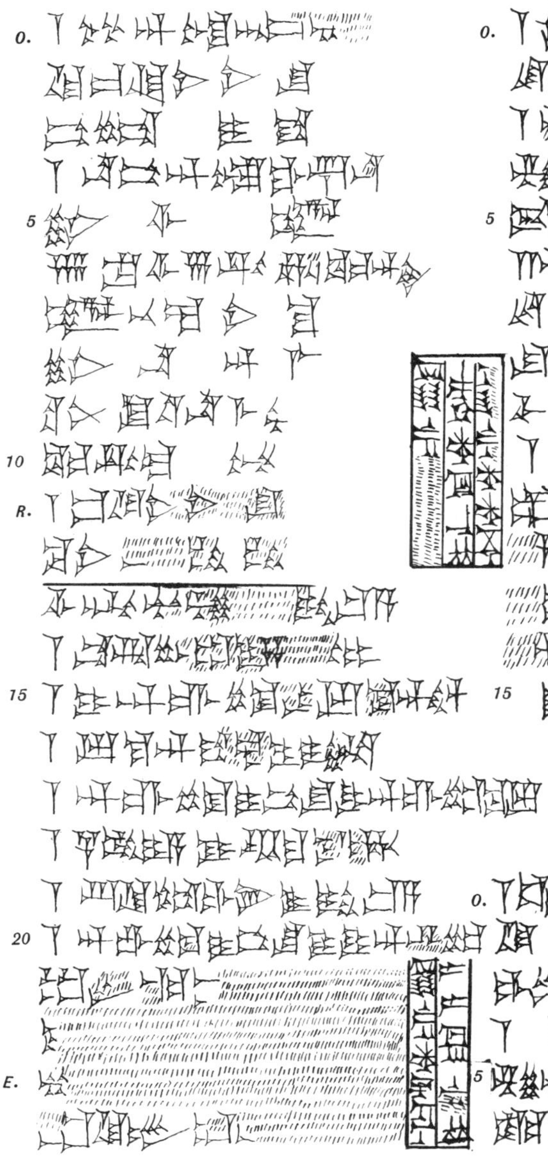

314

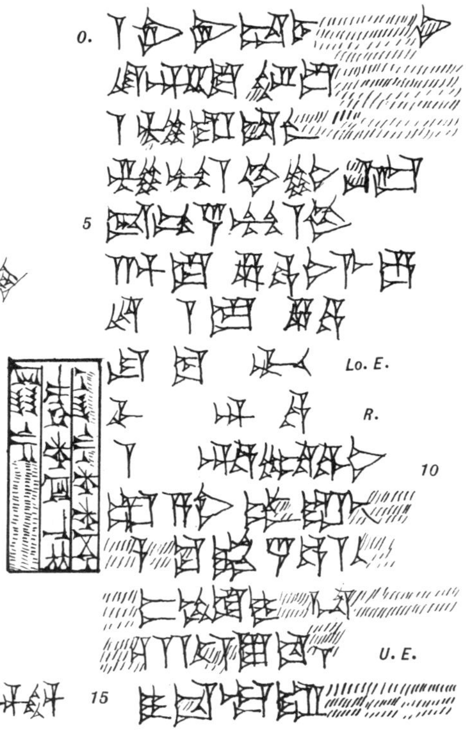

Indistinct seal impressions.

315

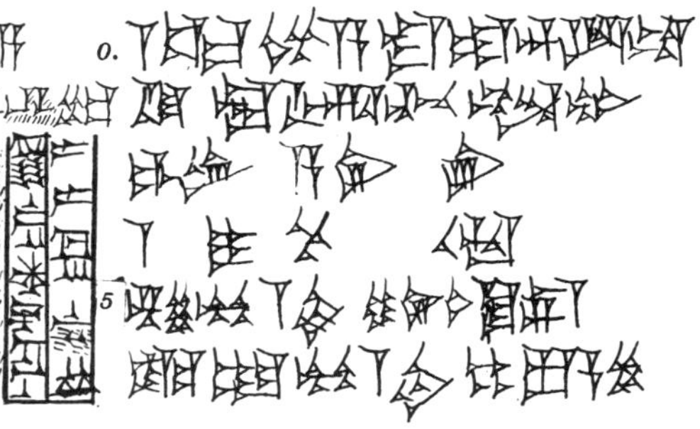

316

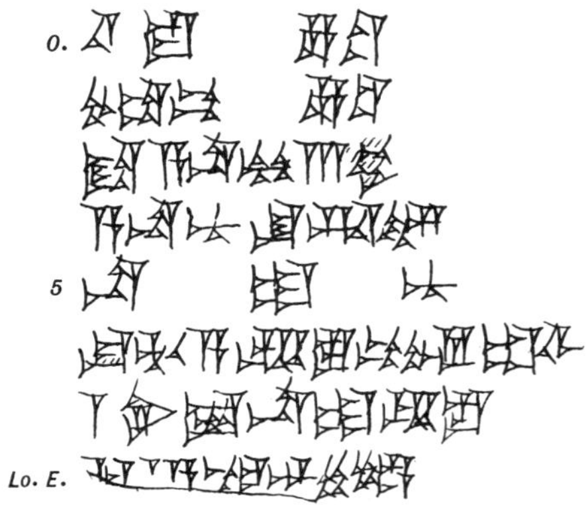

About 3 lines missing.

Indistinct seal impressions.

317

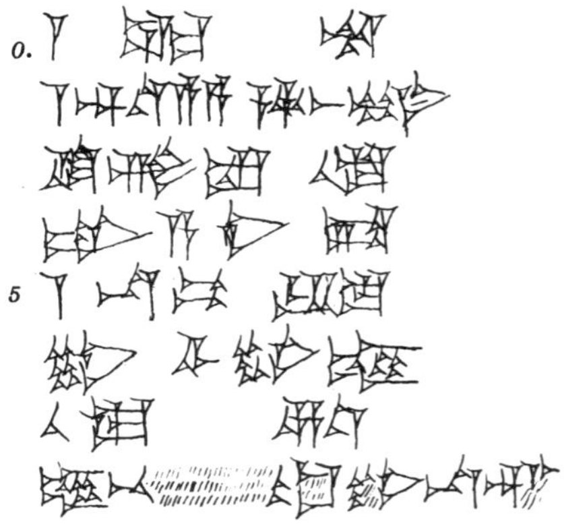

317 CONTINUED

Lo. E. R. U. E.

written upon erasure.

318

O. R.

319

O. Lo. E. R.

U. E.

320

O. R. U. E. L. E.

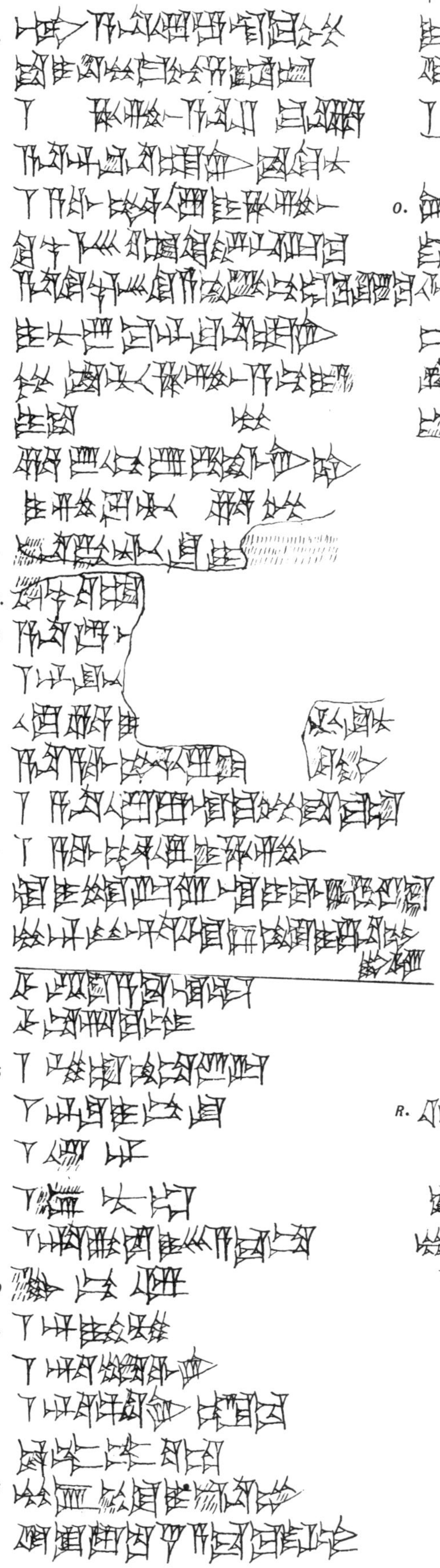

321

O. TABLET

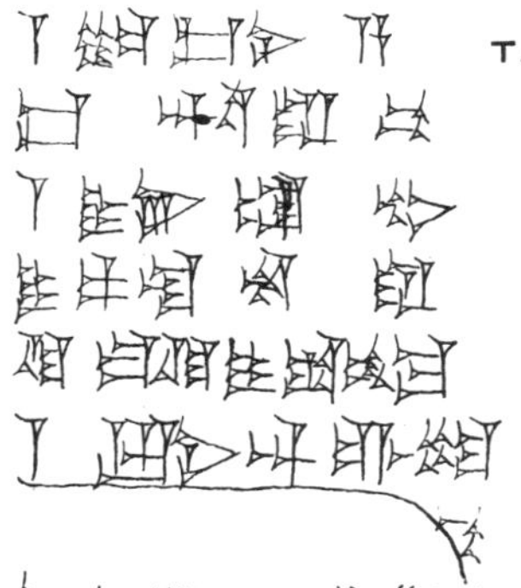

O. CASE

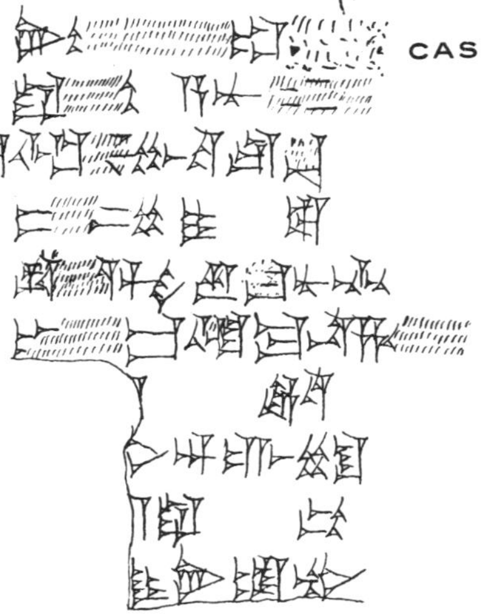

R. CASE

Indistinct seal impressions.

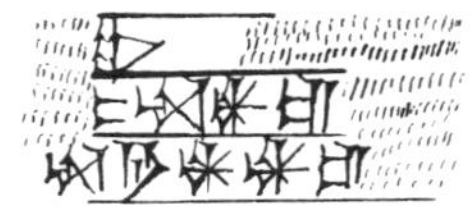

R. TABLET

322

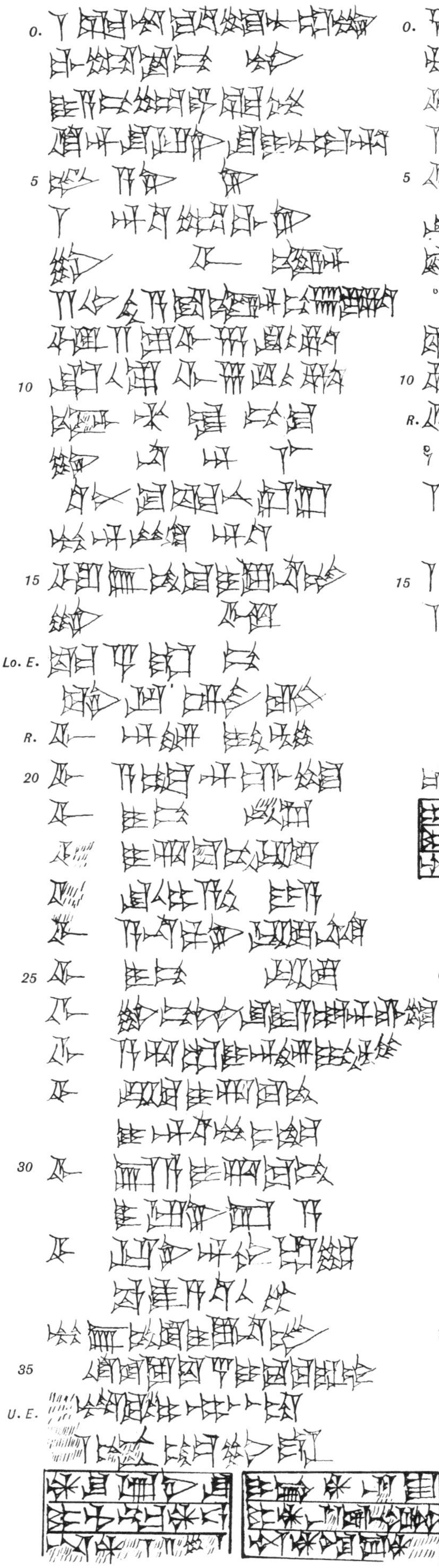

323

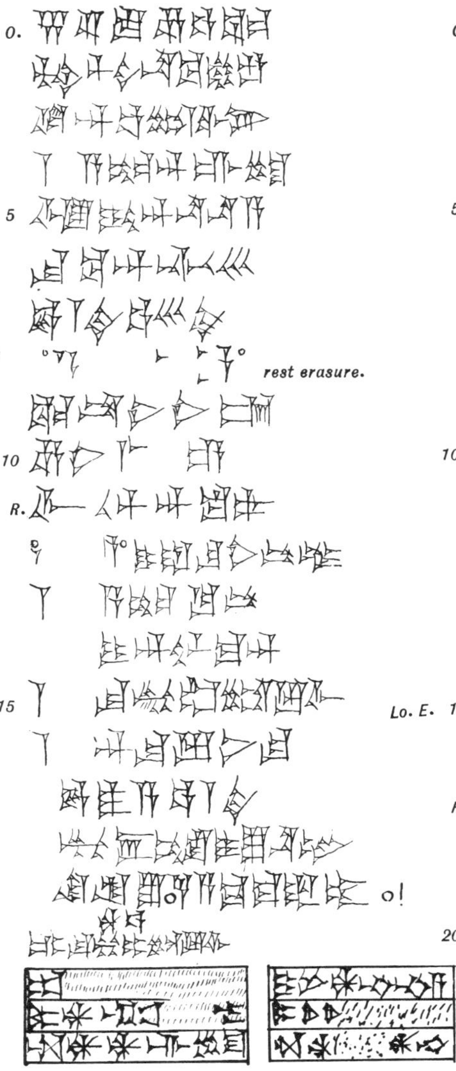

324

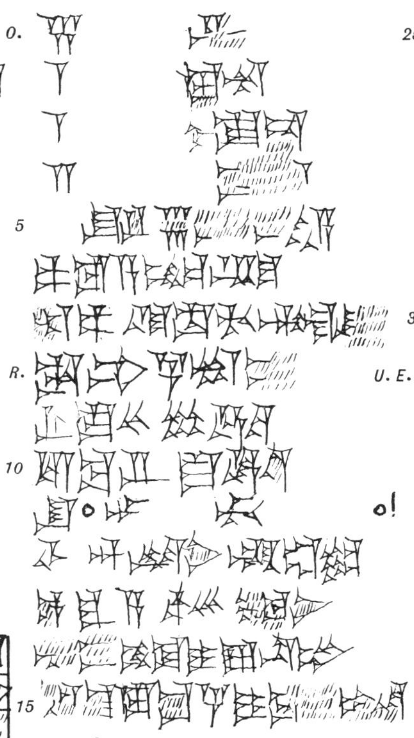

Indistinct seal impressions.

325

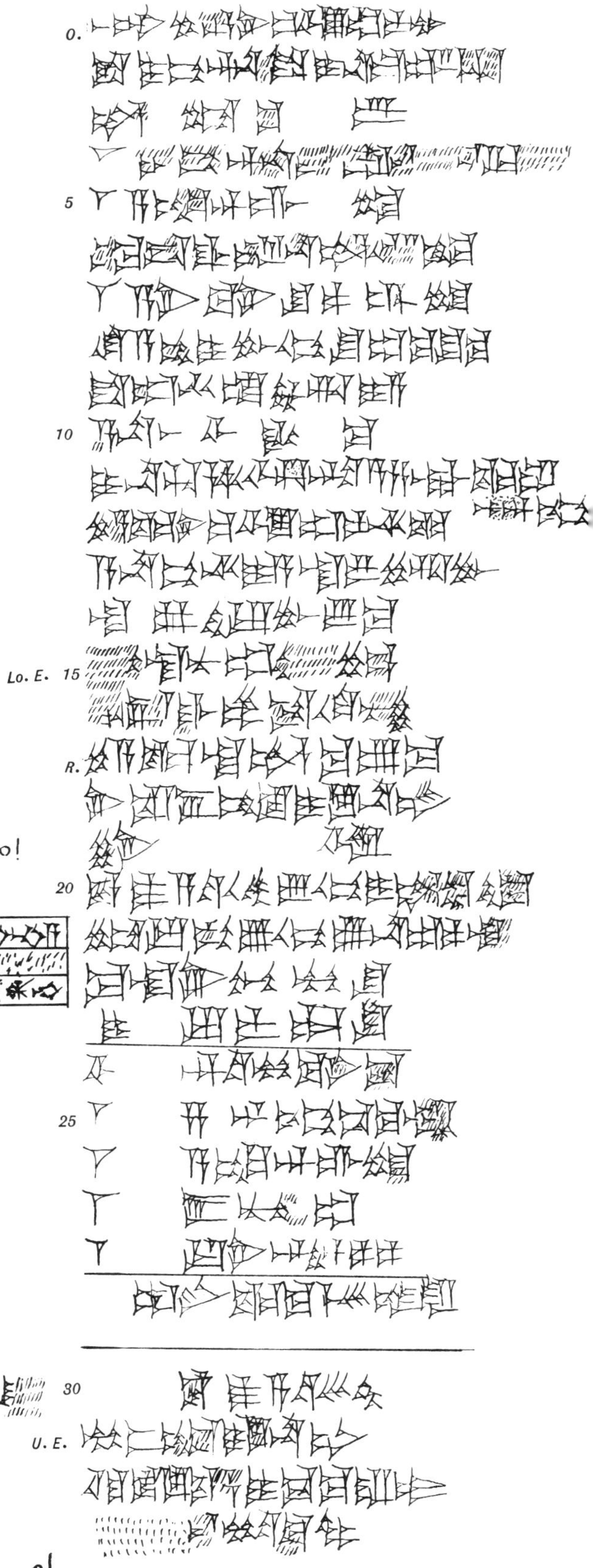

Indistinct seal impressions.

326

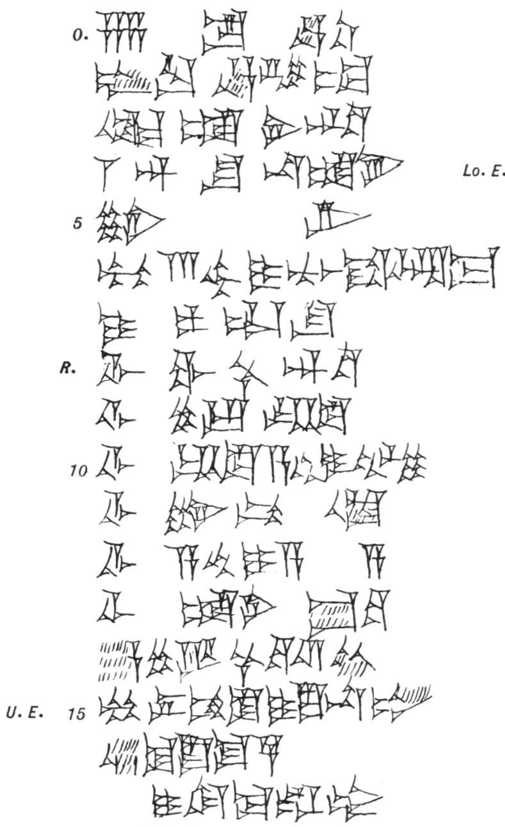

Indistinct seal impressions.

327

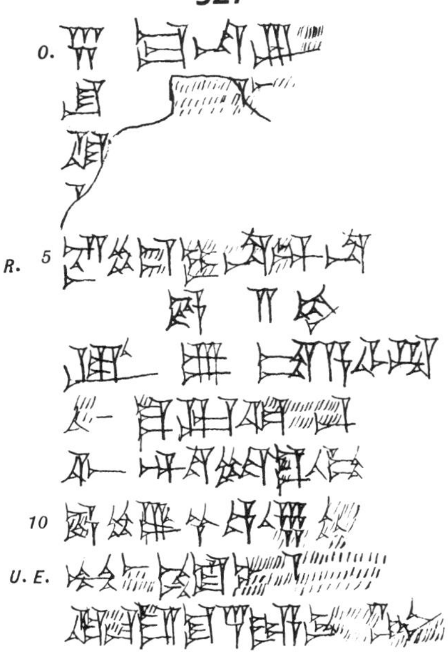

Indistinct seal impressions.

328

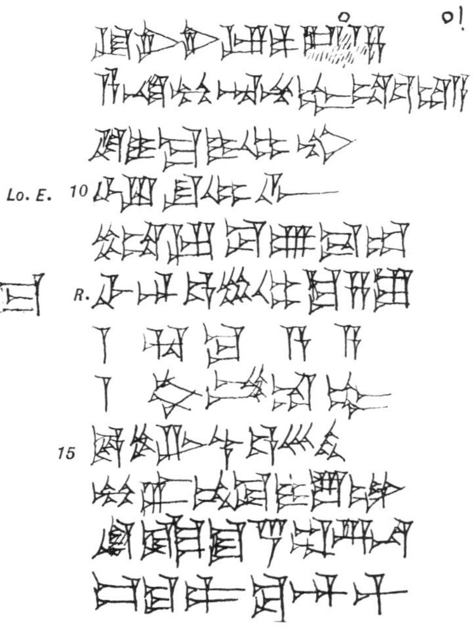

329

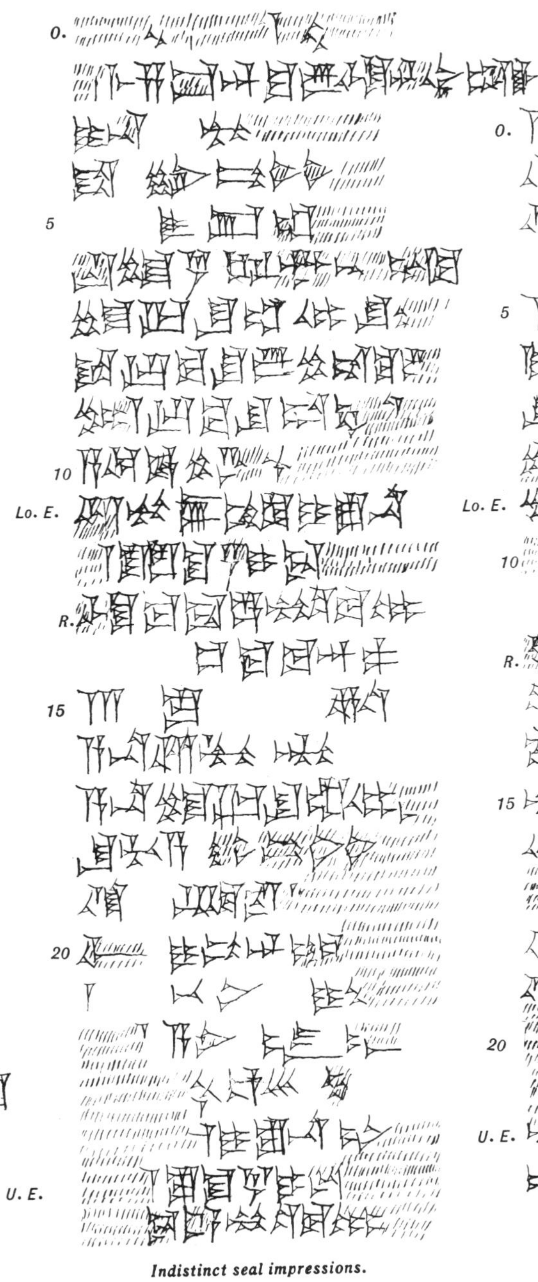

Indistinct seal impressions.

330

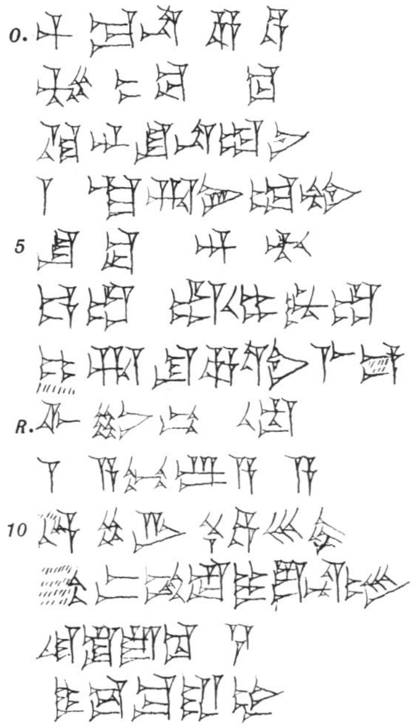

Indistinct seal impressions.

331

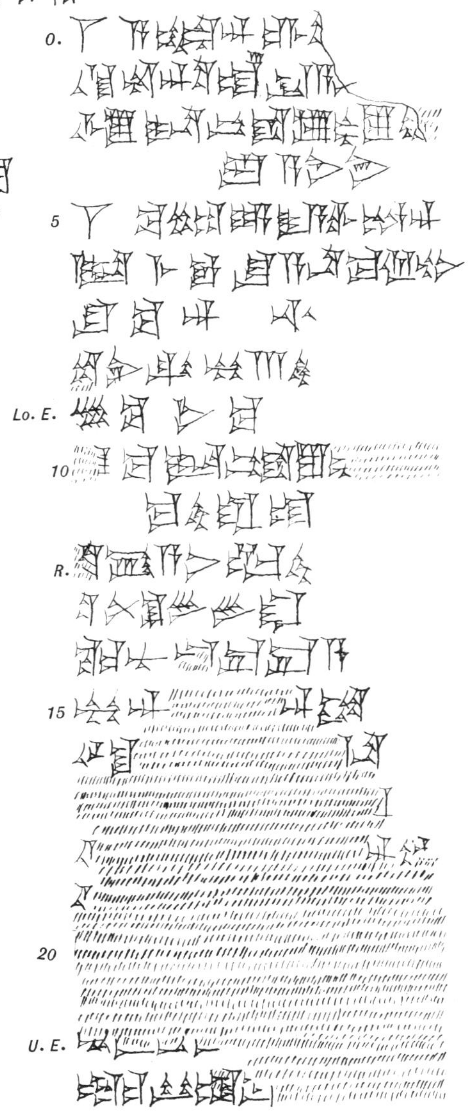

332

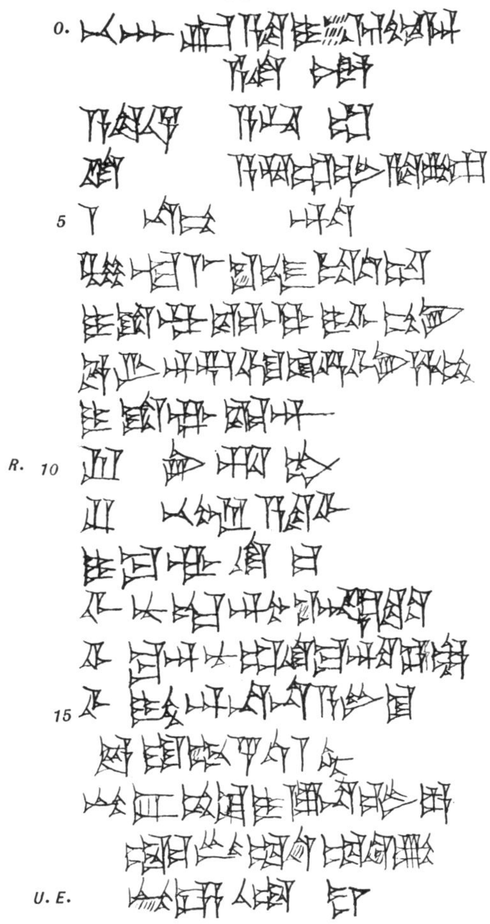

Indistinct seal impressions.

334

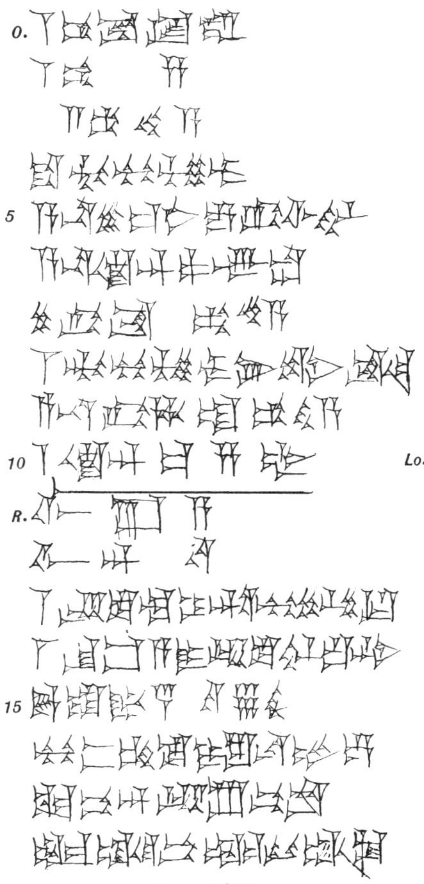

Indistinct seal impressions.

336

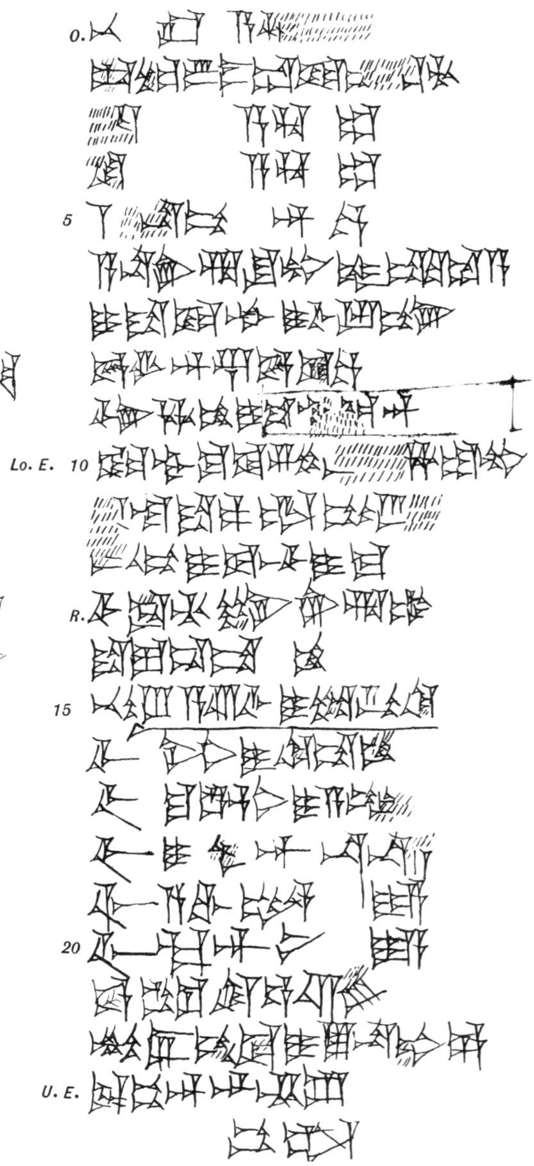

Indistinct seal impressions.

333

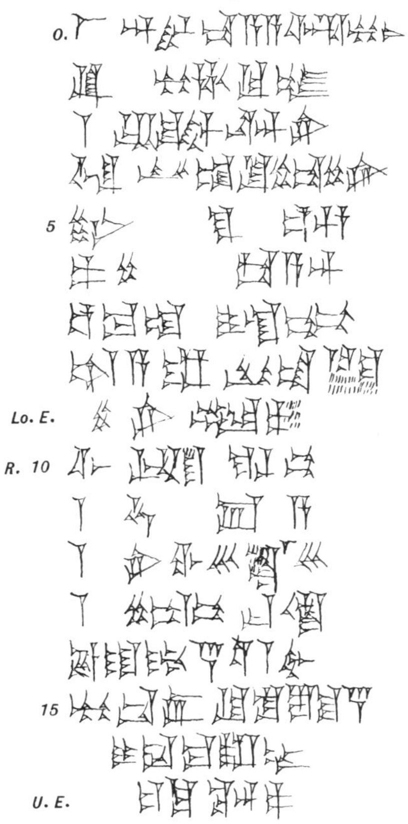

Indistinct seal impressions.

335

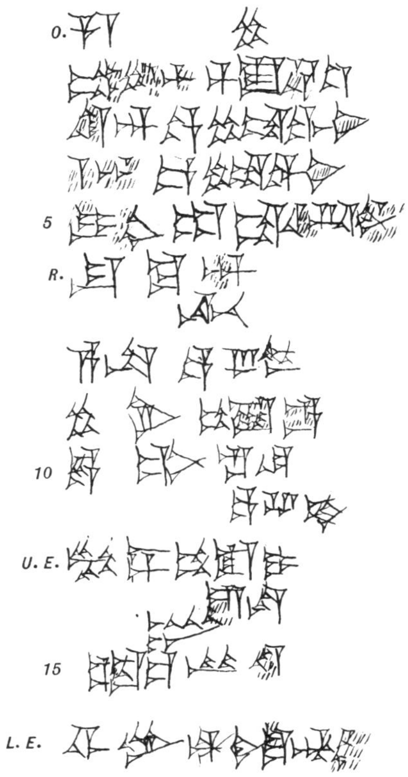

337

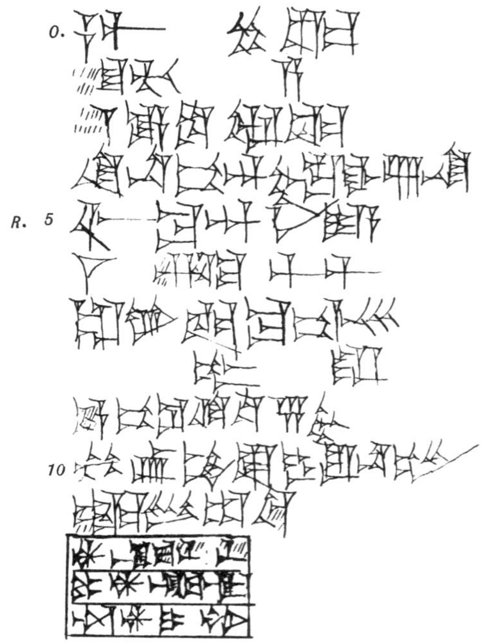

338

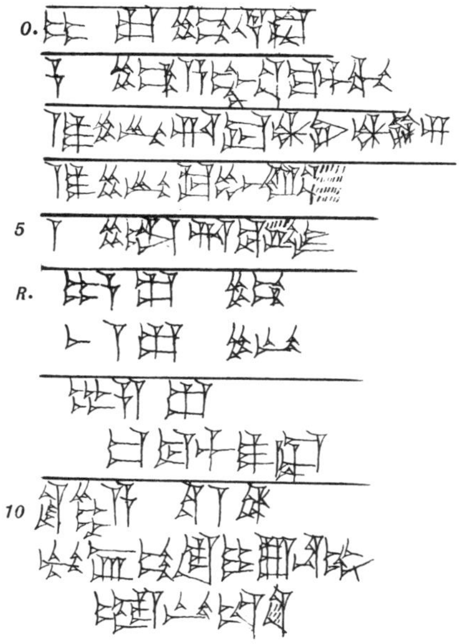

339

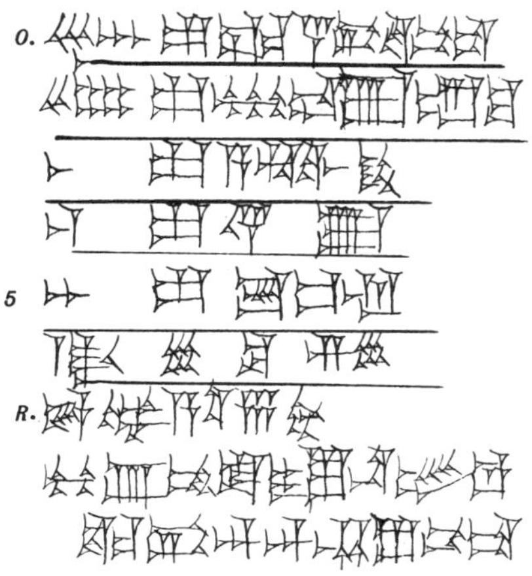

340

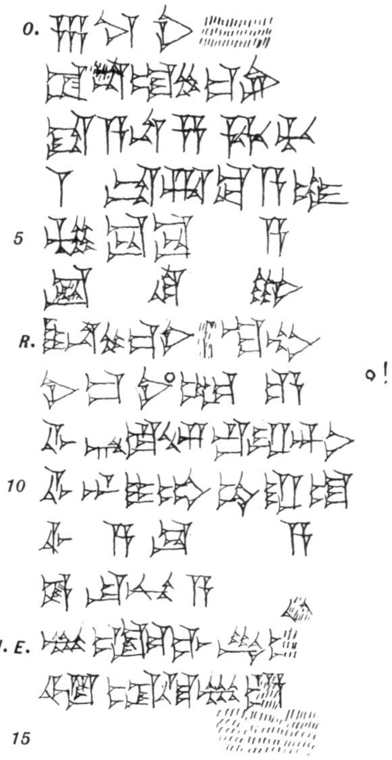

Indistinct seal impressions.

341

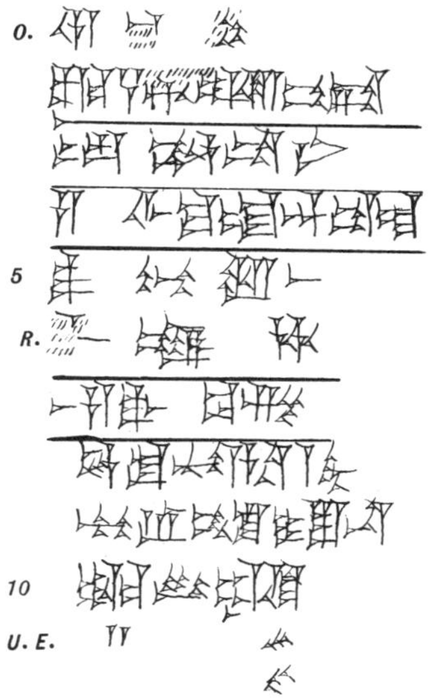

342

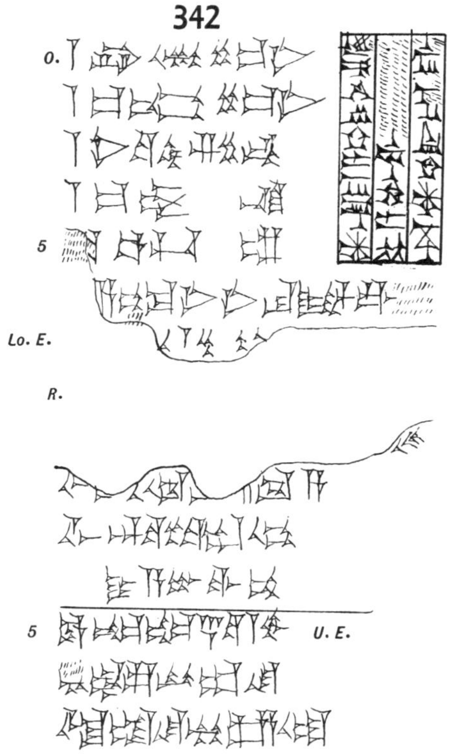

343

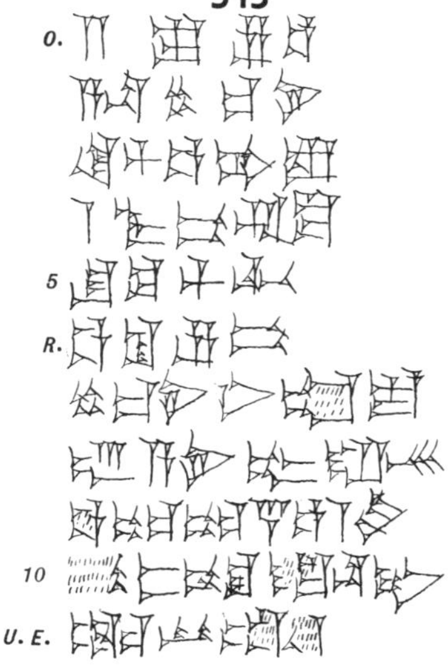

344

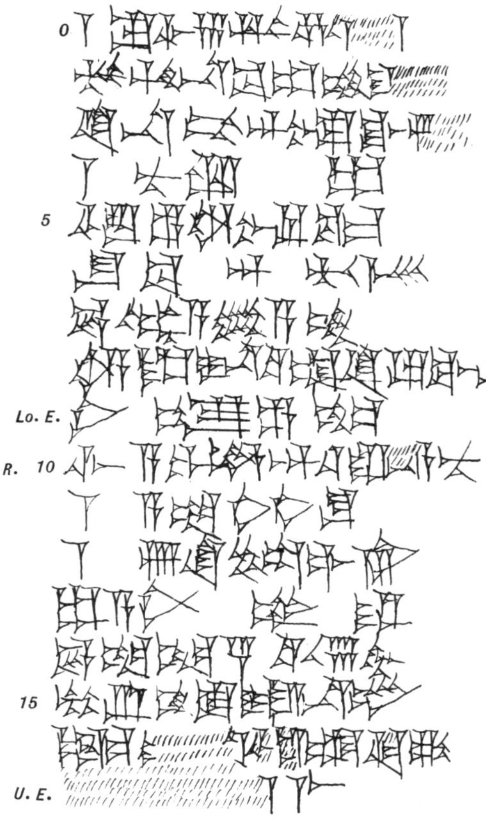

345

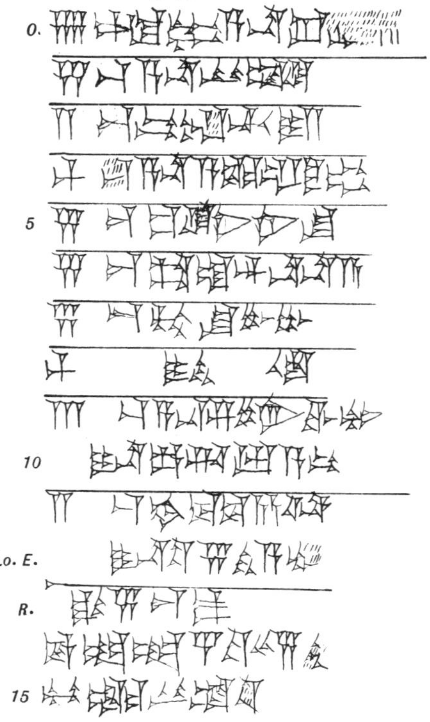

346

347

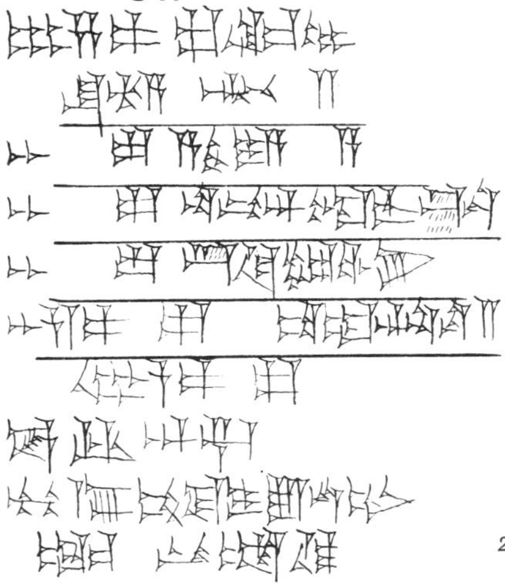

348

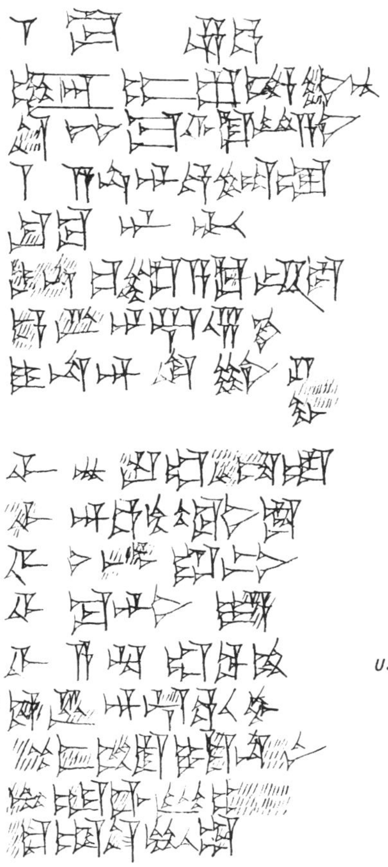

349

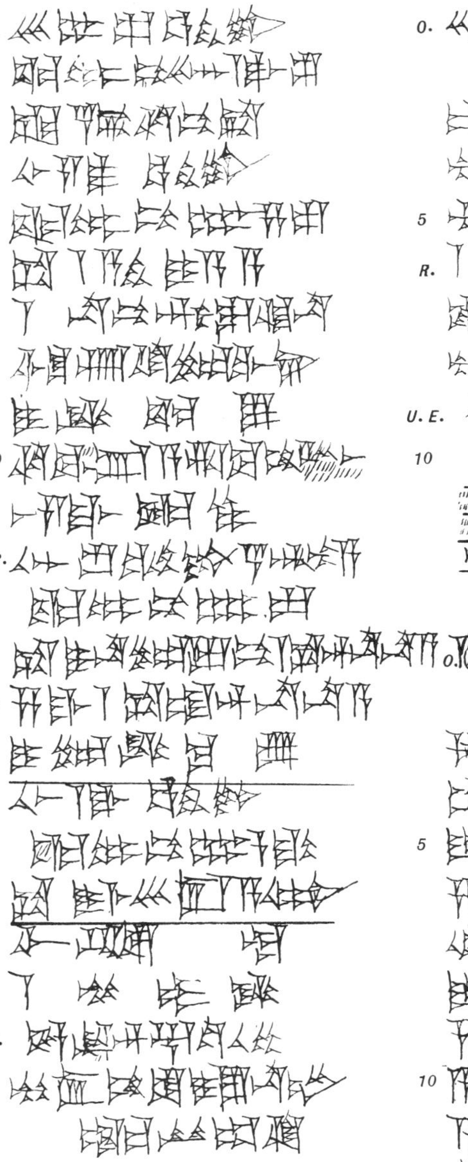

Indistinct seal impressions.

350 CASE

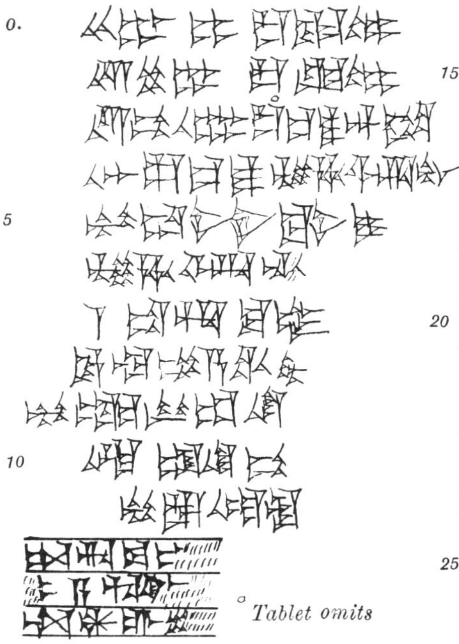

° *Tablet omits*

351

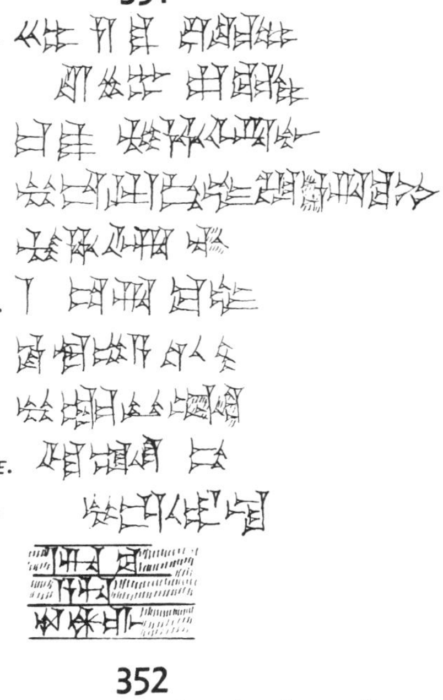

352

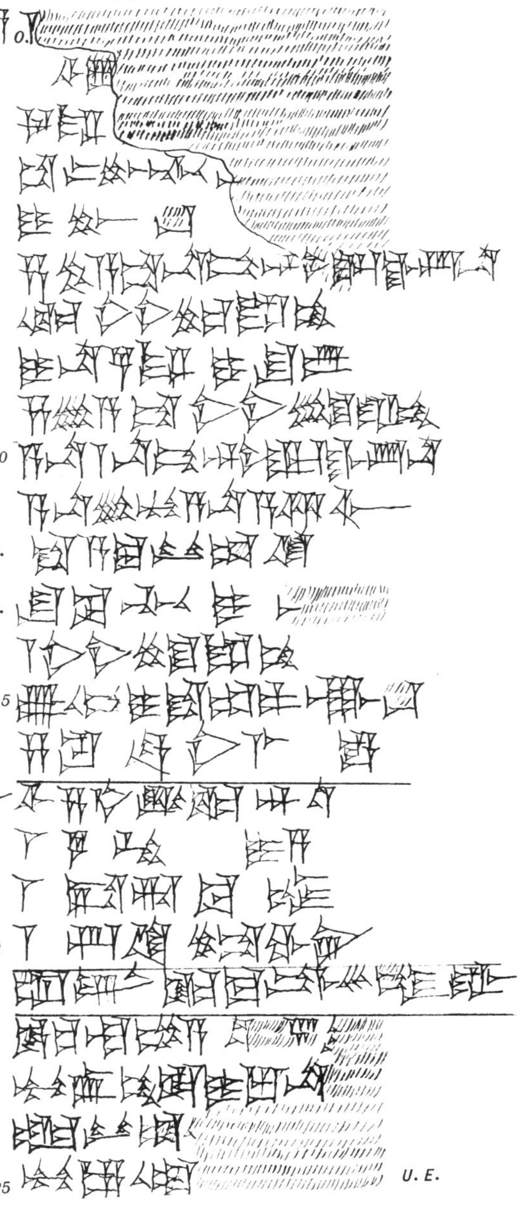

353

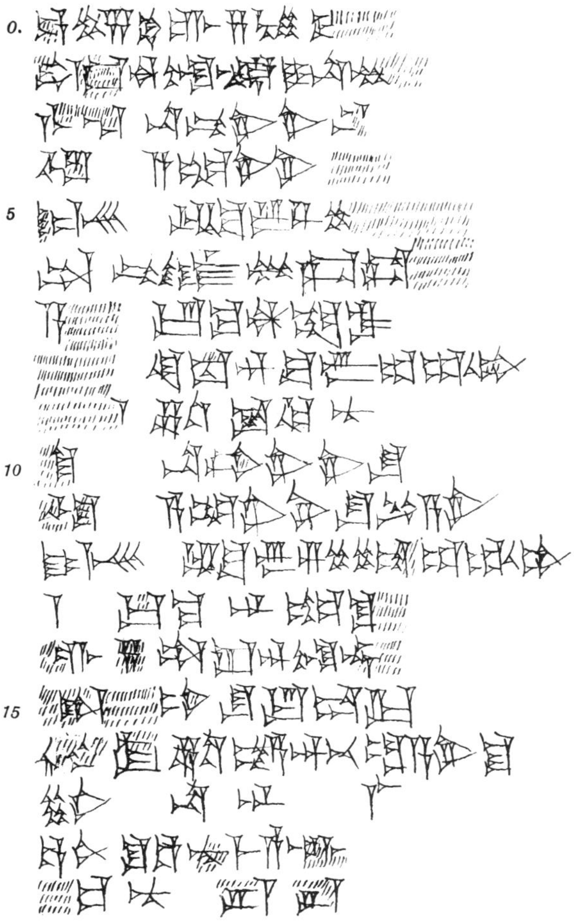

353 CONT

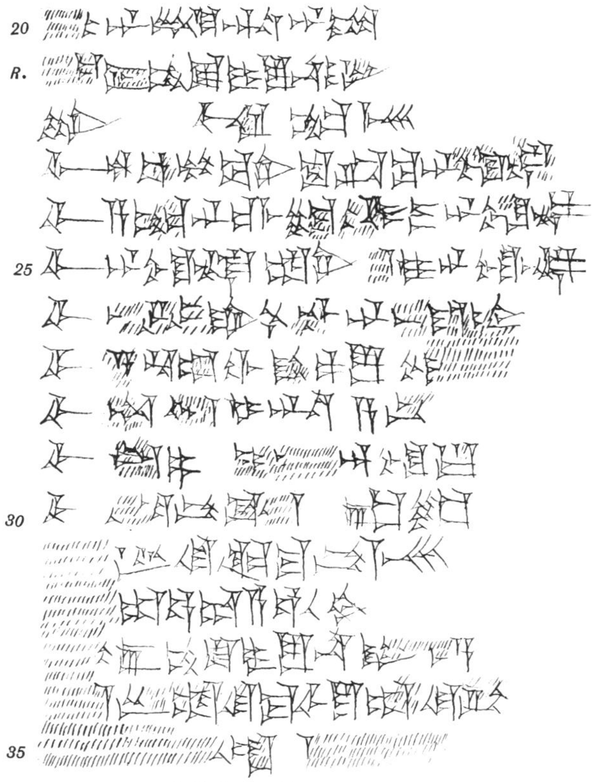

Indistinct seal impressions.

354

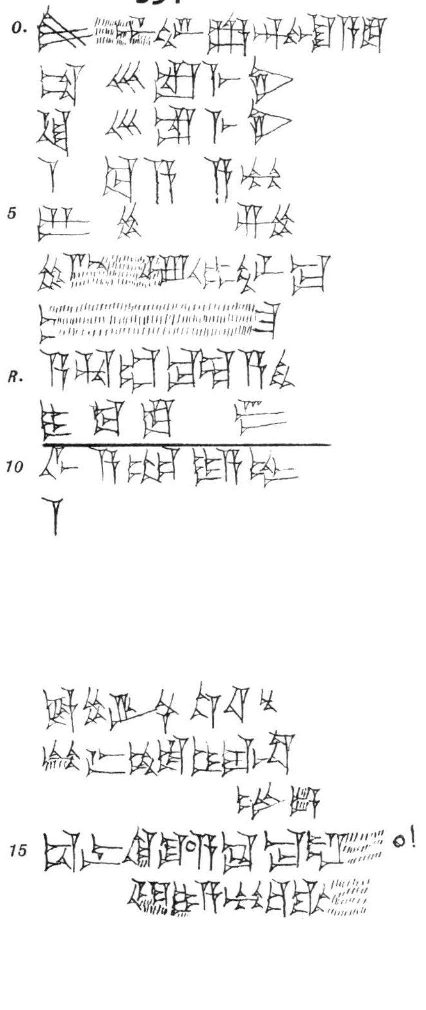

355

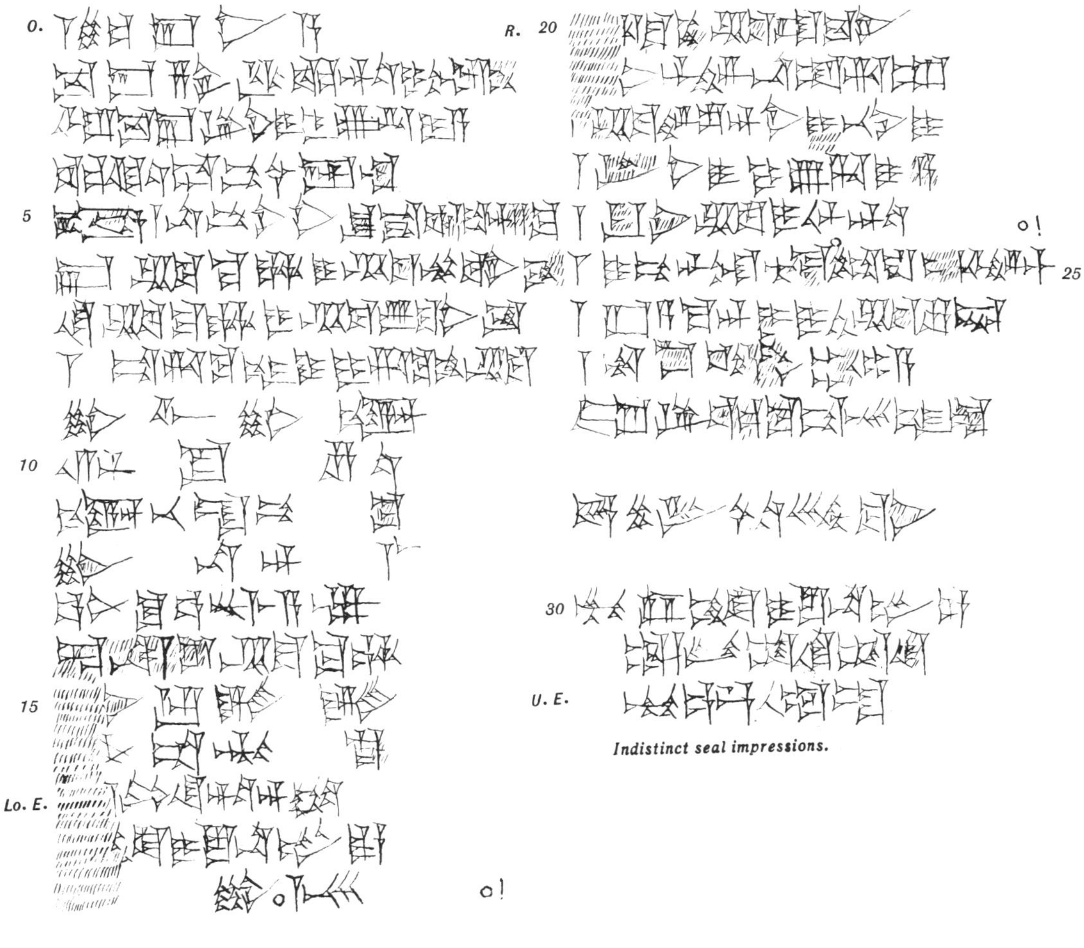

Indistinct seal impressions.

356

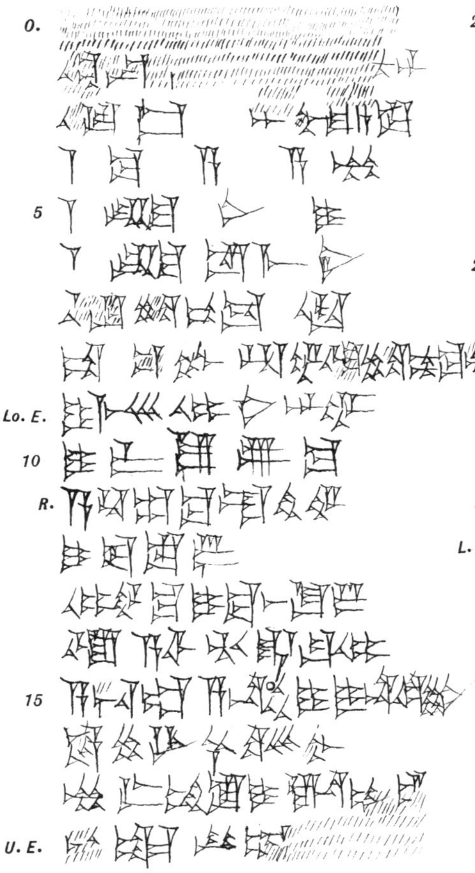

Indistinct seal impressions.

357

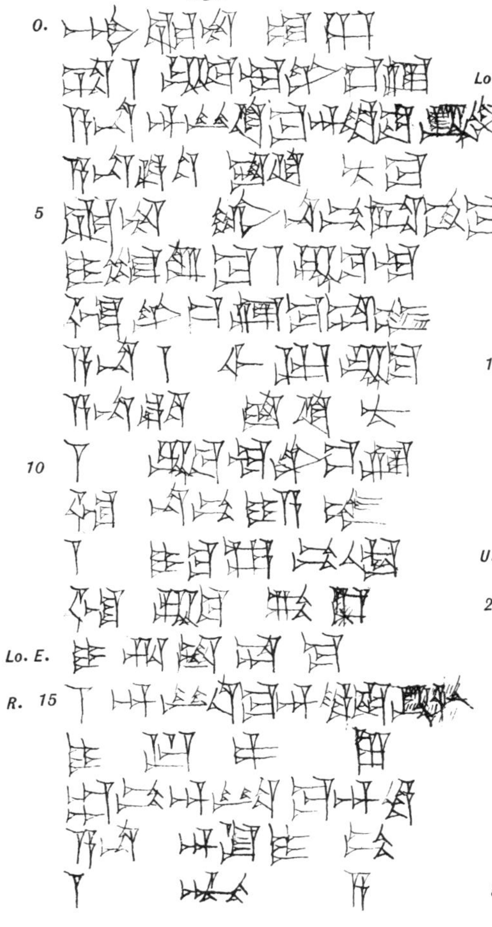

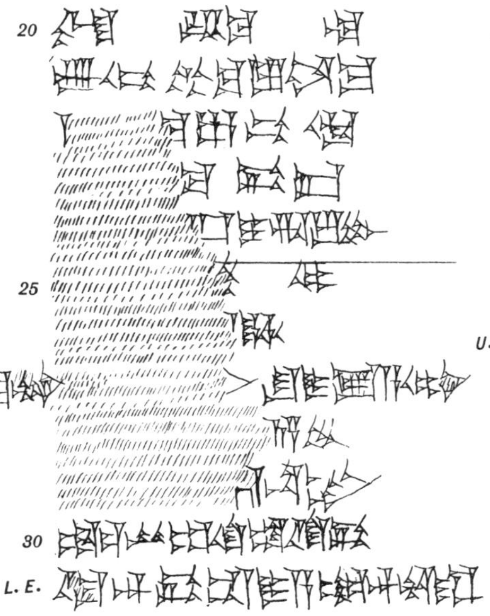

358

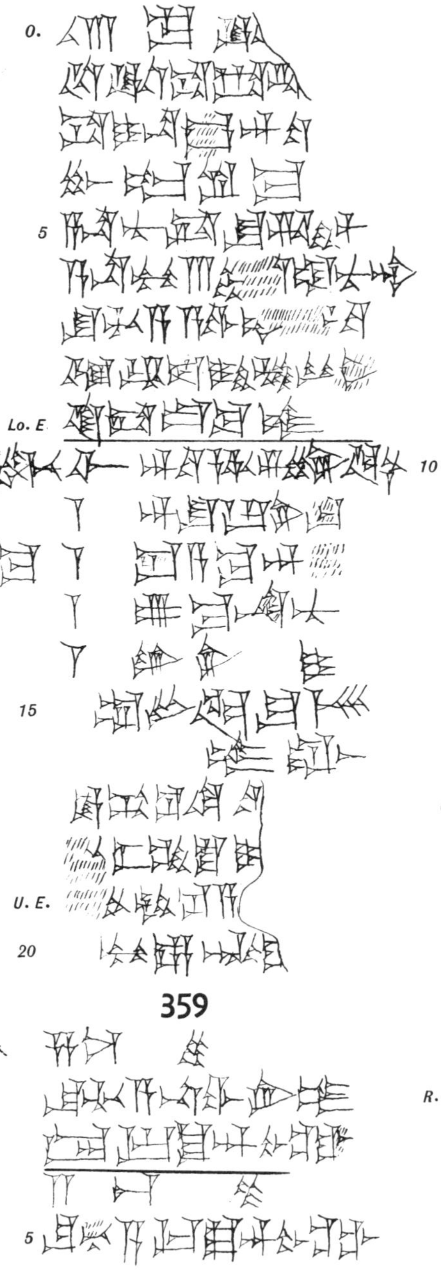

359

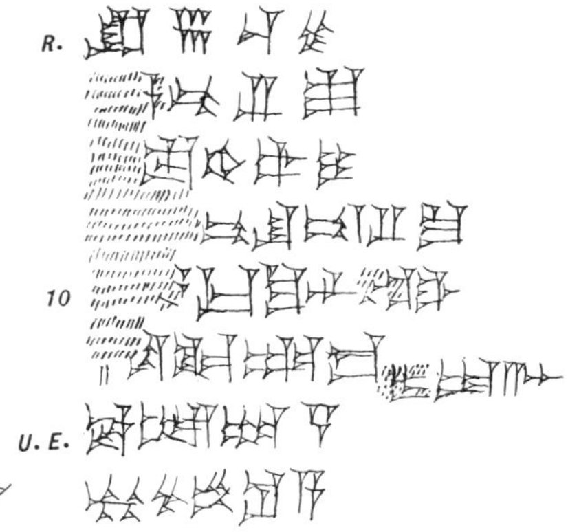

360

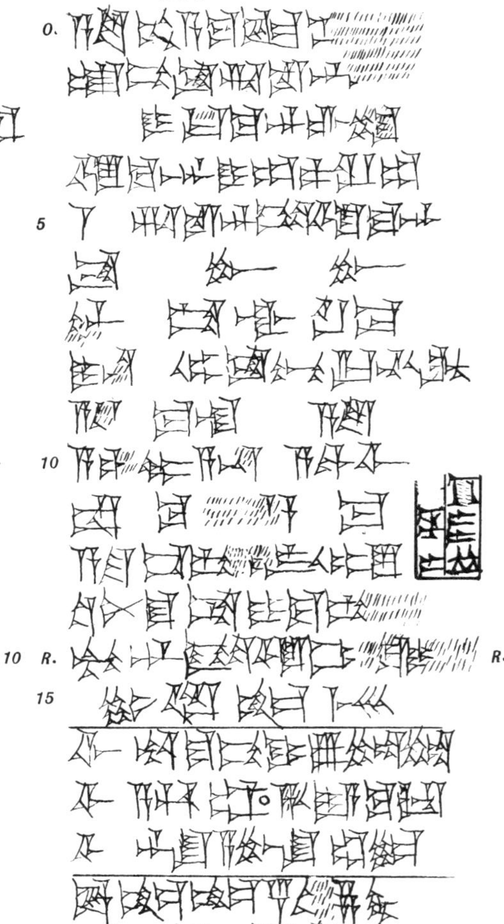

361

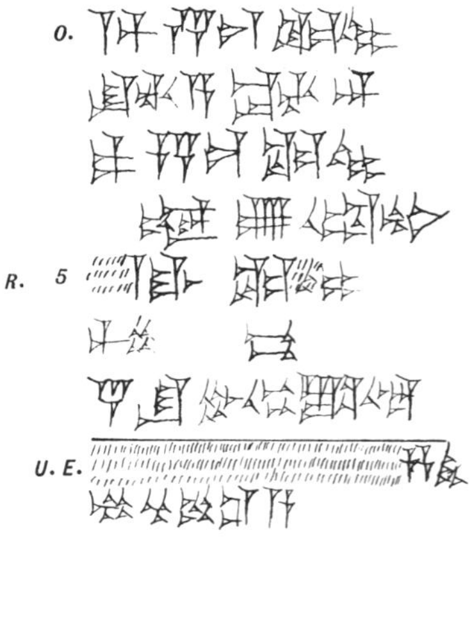

362

363

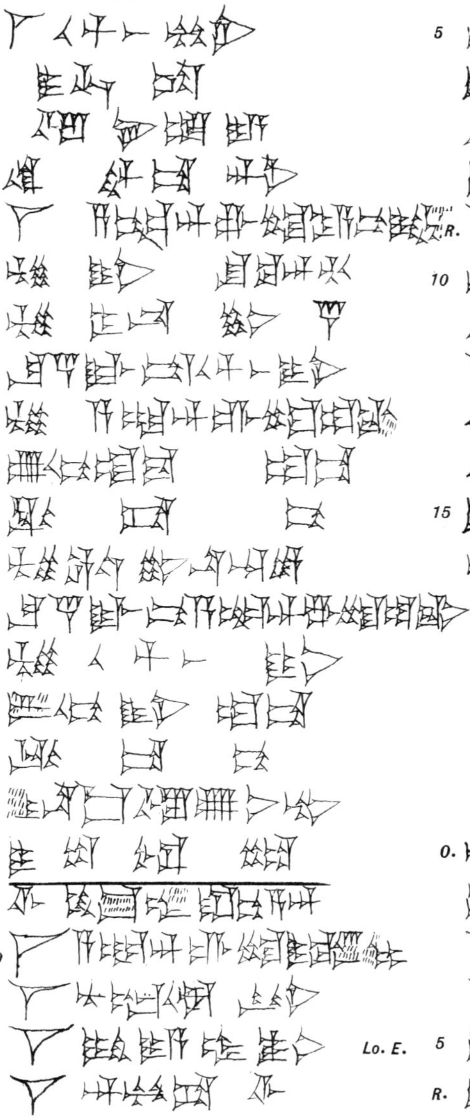

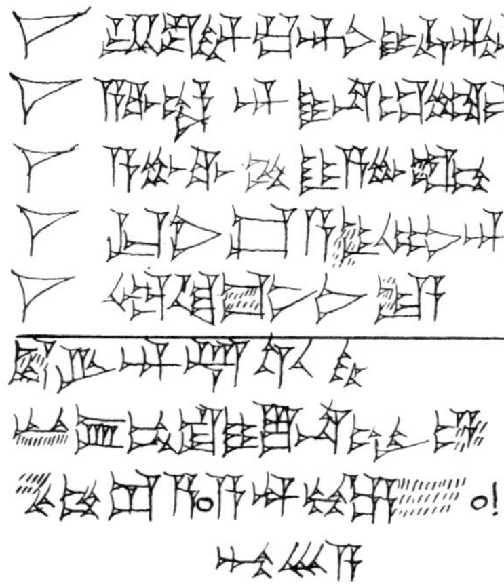

Indistinct seal impressions.

364

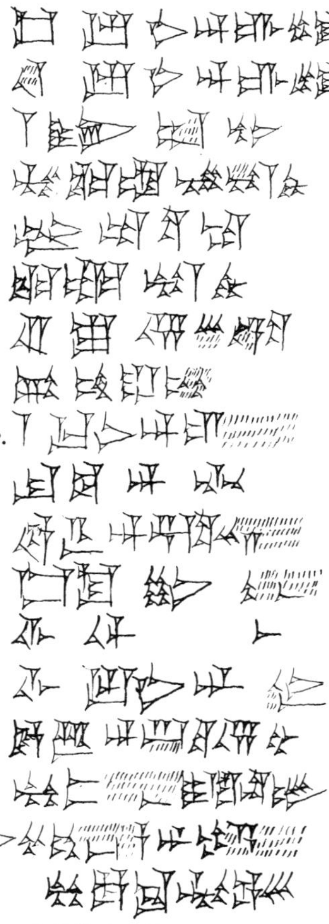

Indistinct seal impressions.

365

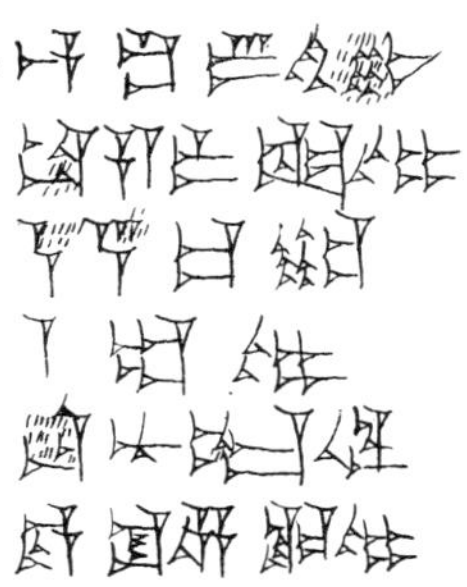

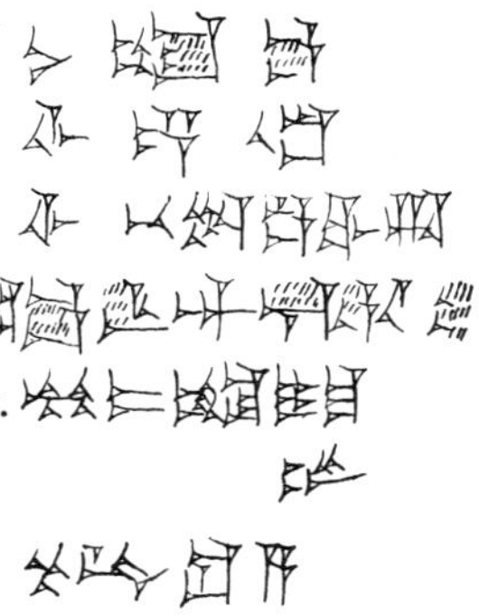

Indistinct seal impressions.

366

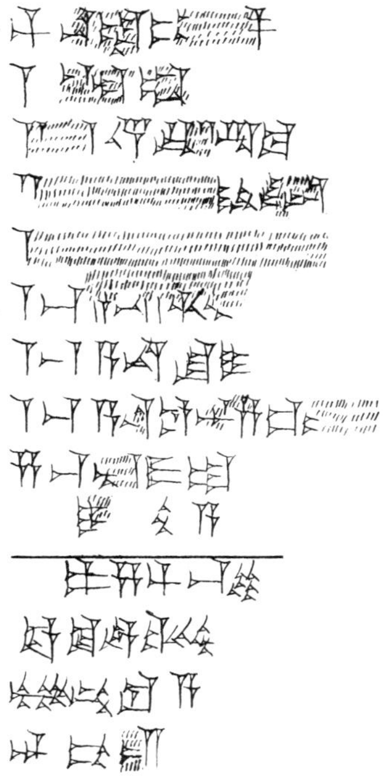

367 CASE

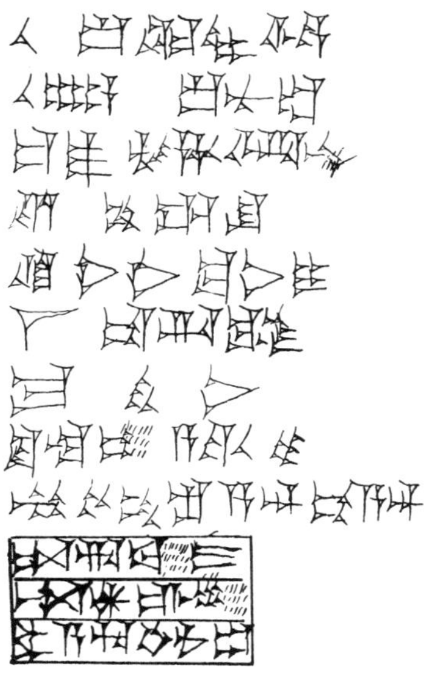

368

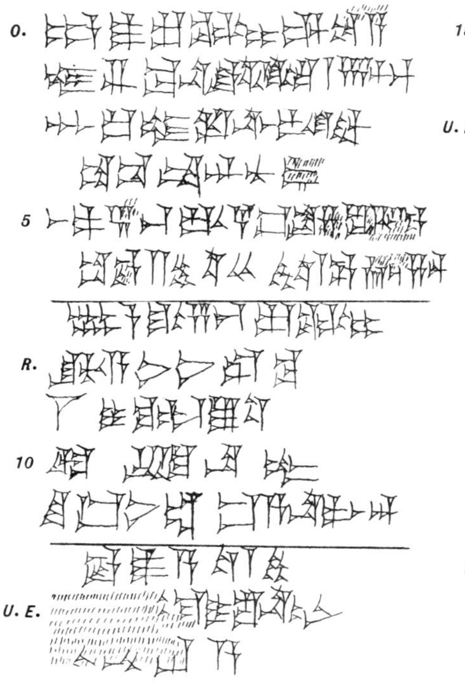

369

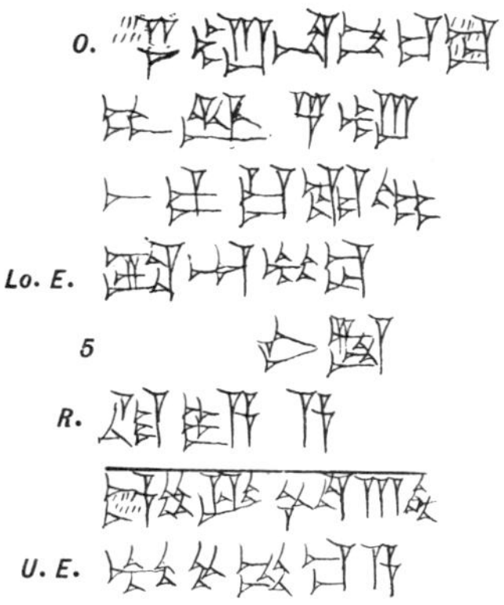

370

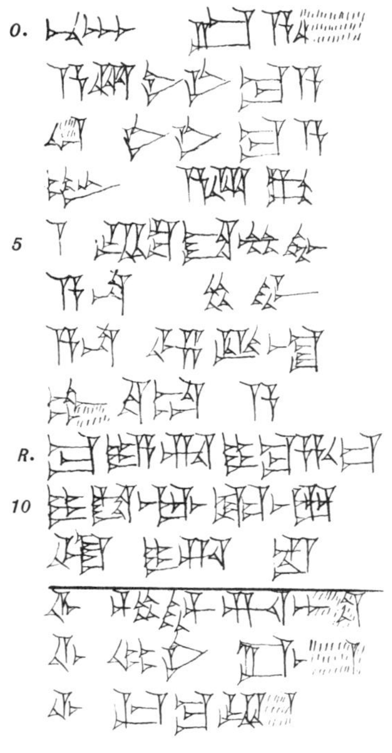

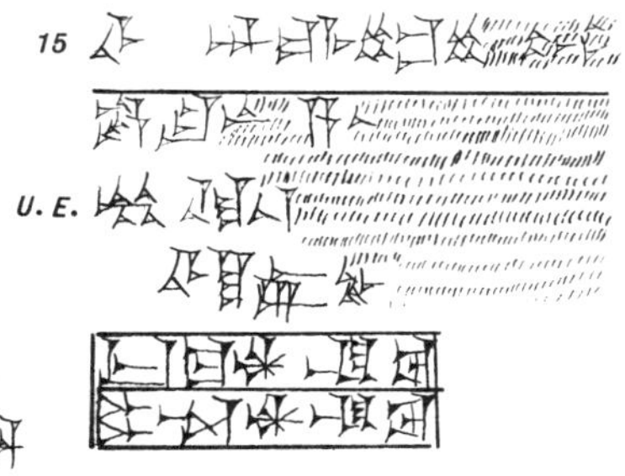

371

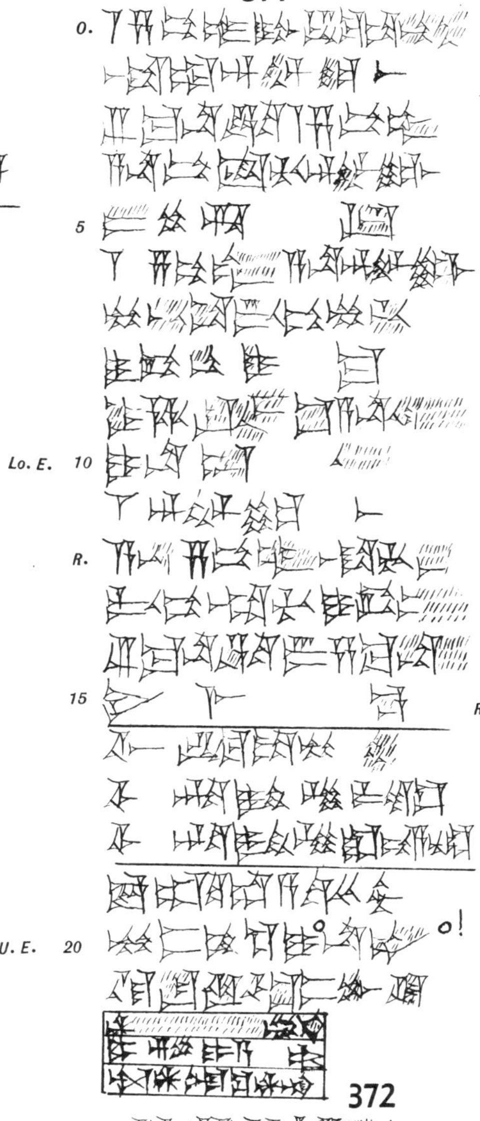

372

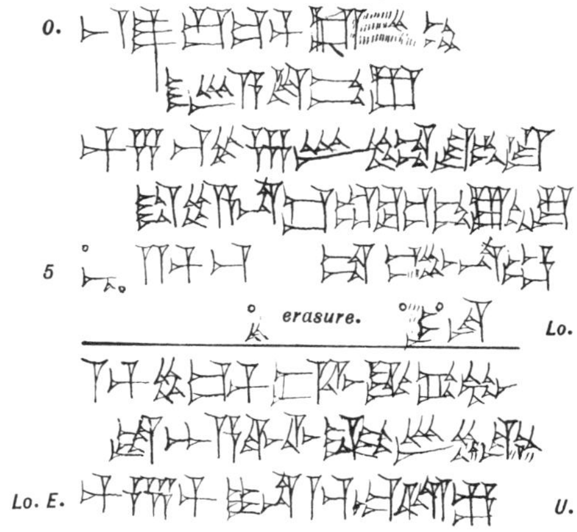

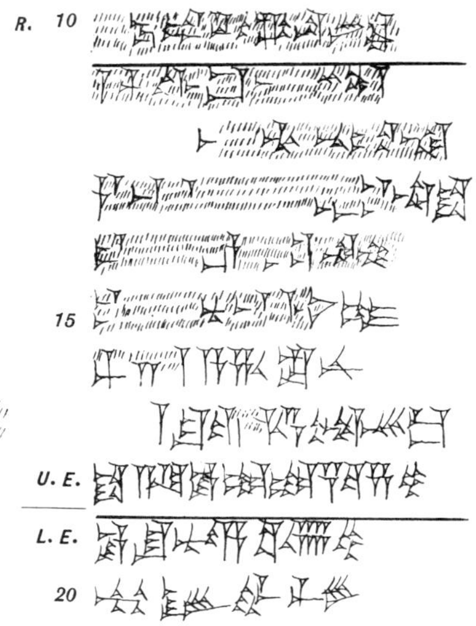

373

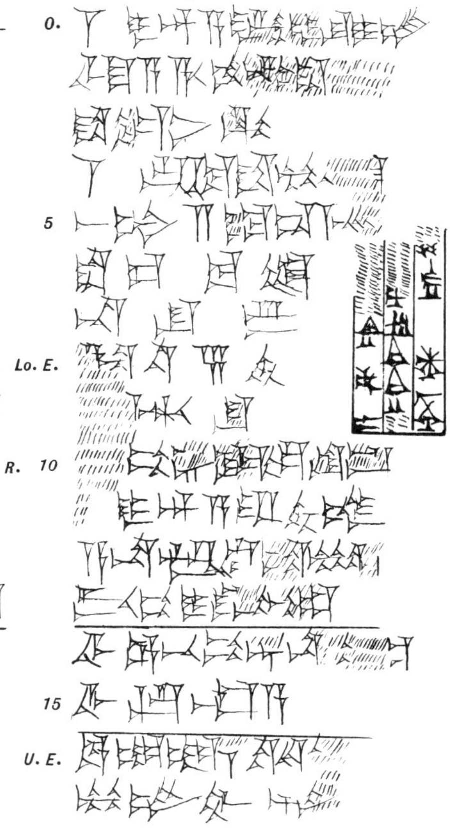

374

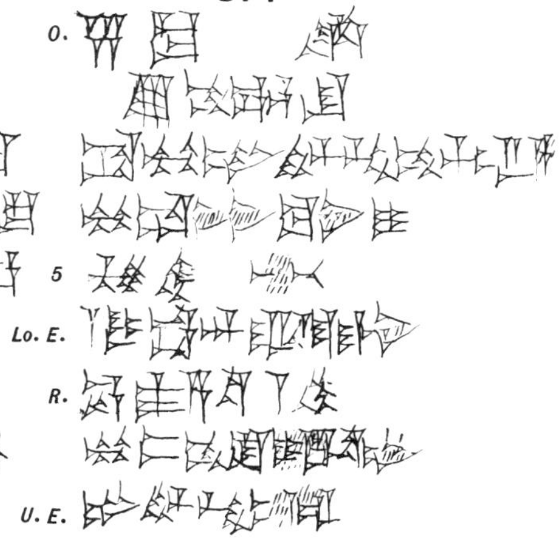

375

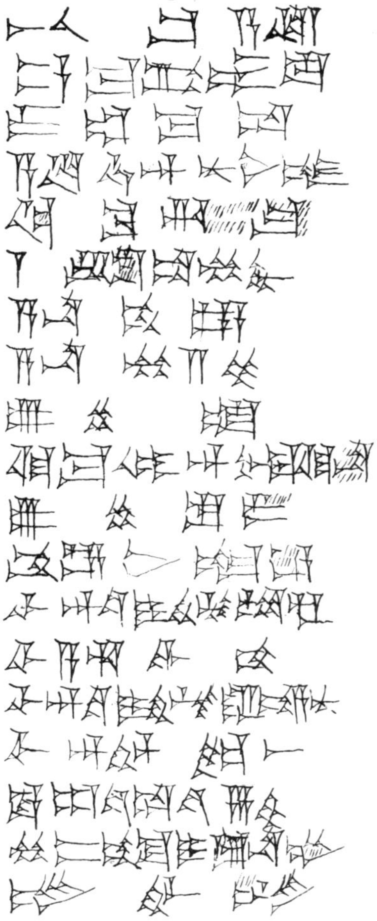

Indistinct seal impressions.

376

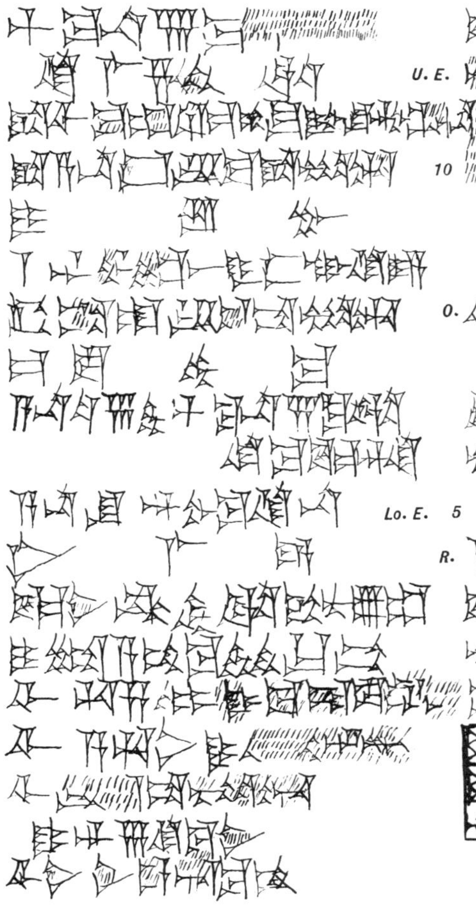

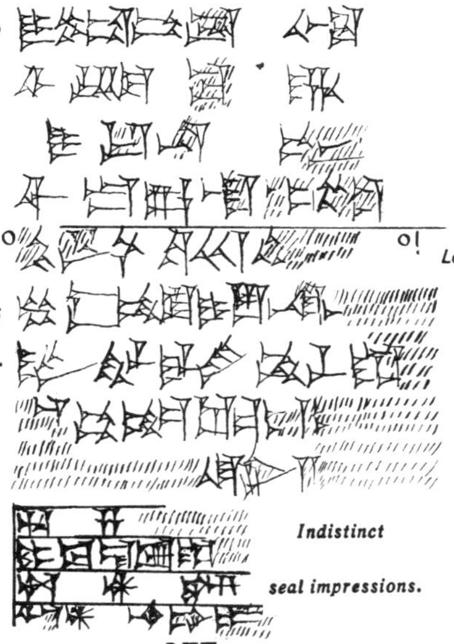

Indistinct seal impressions.

377

Several lines missing.

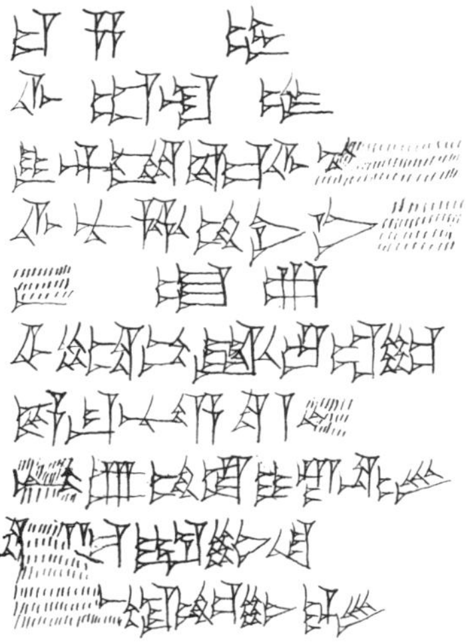

378

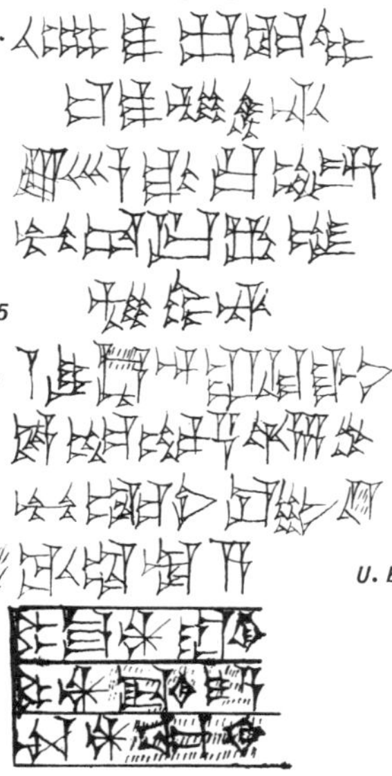

379

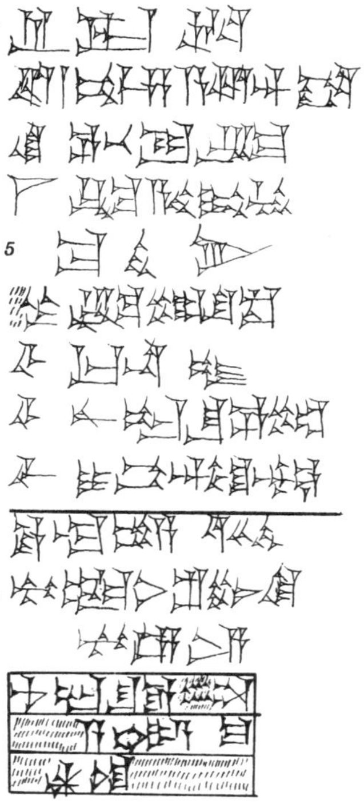

380

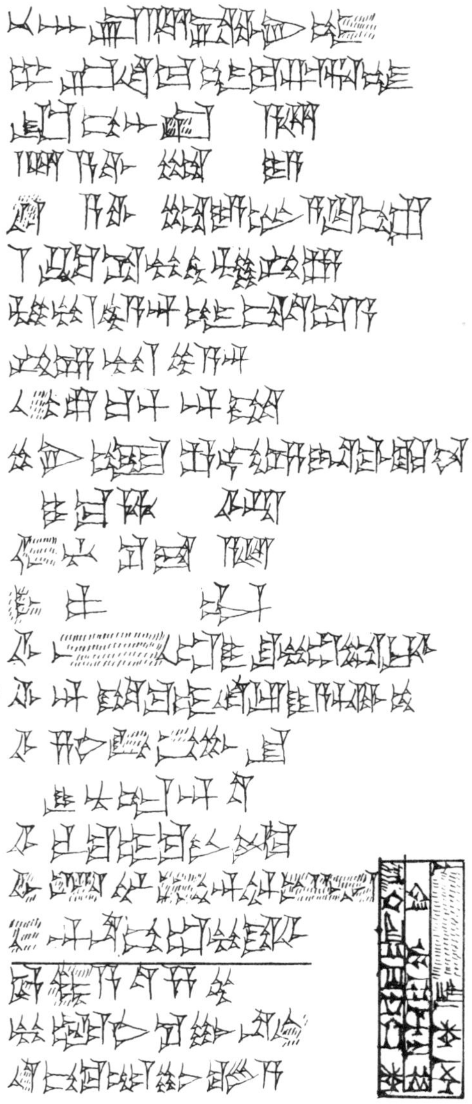

381

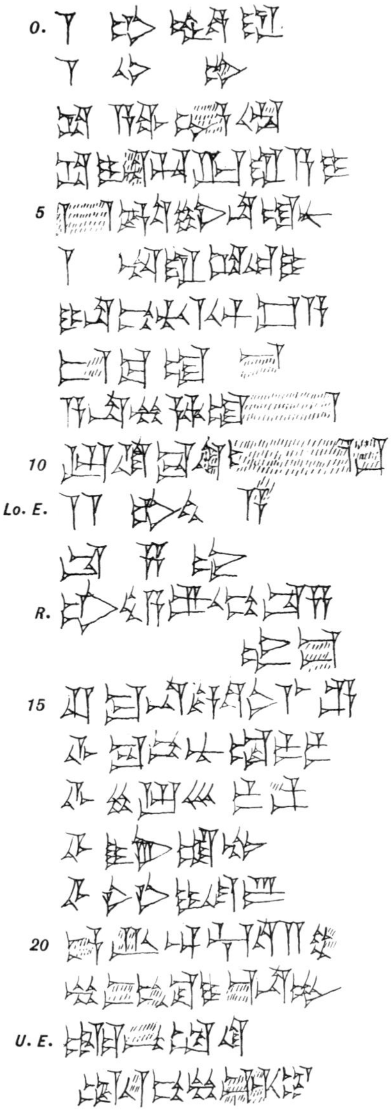

Indistinct seal impressions.

382

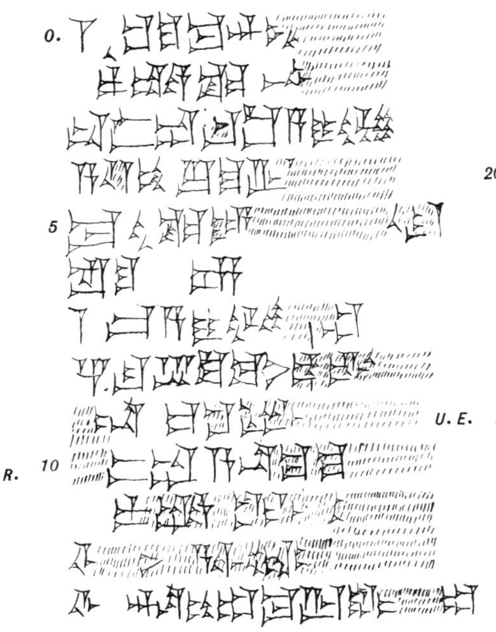

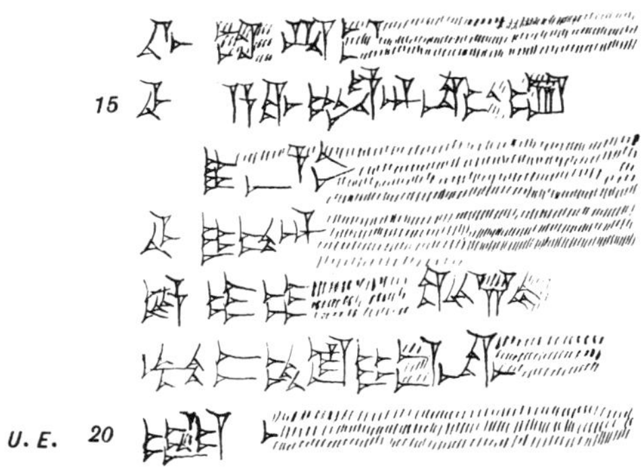

383

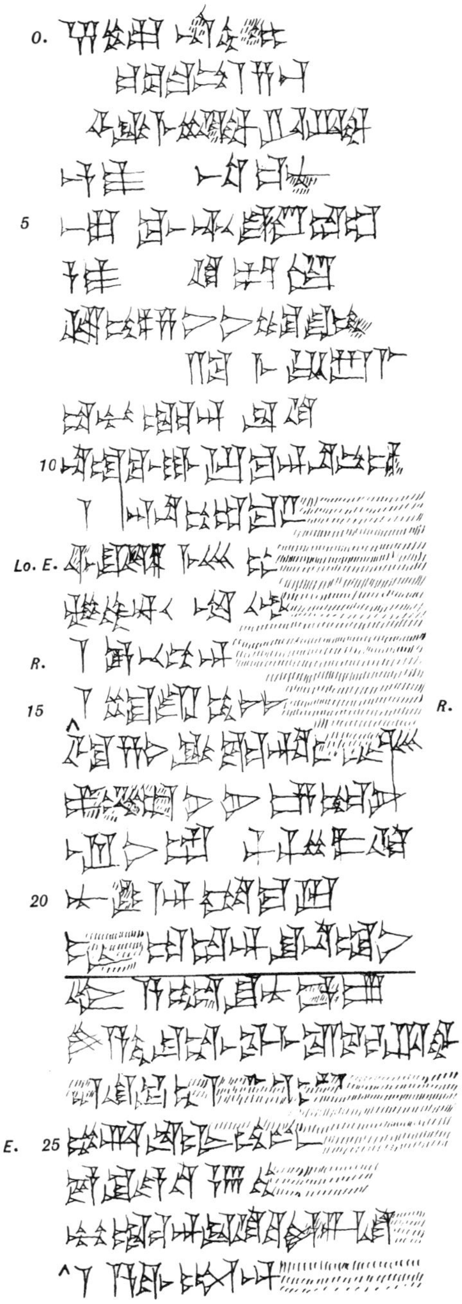

384

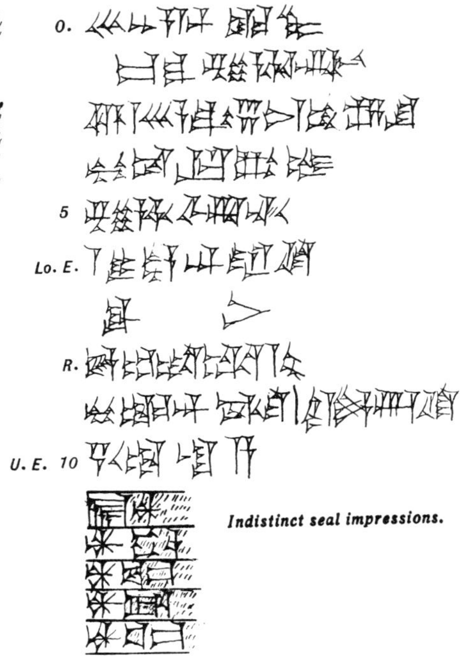

Indistinct seal impressions.

385

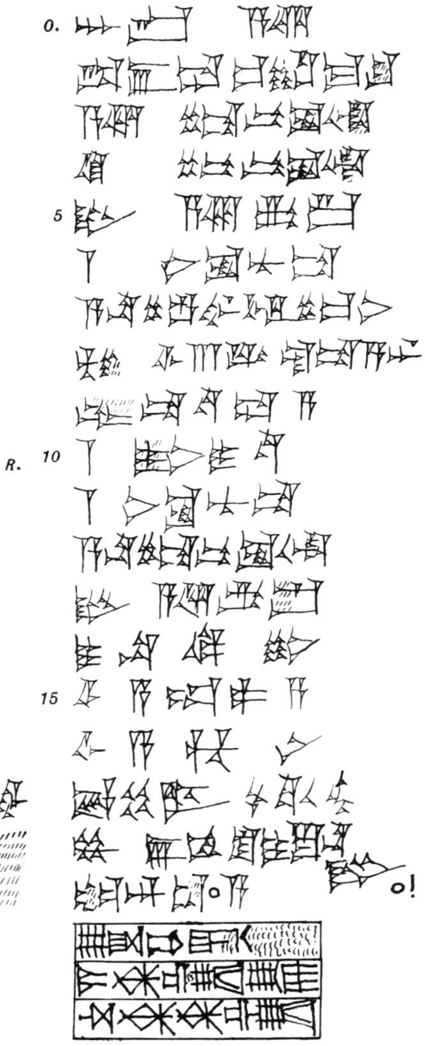

386

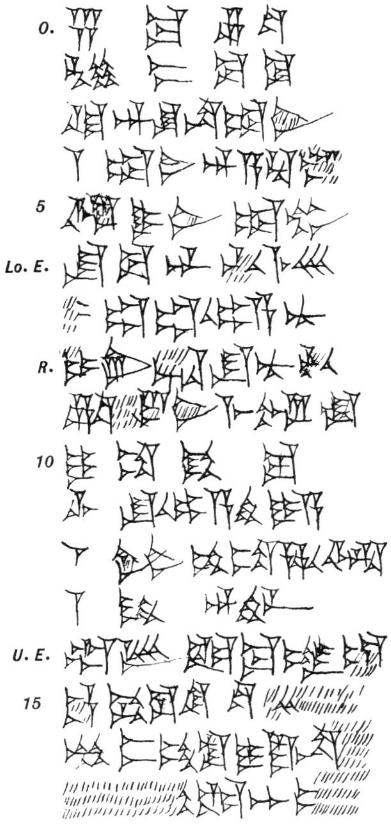

387

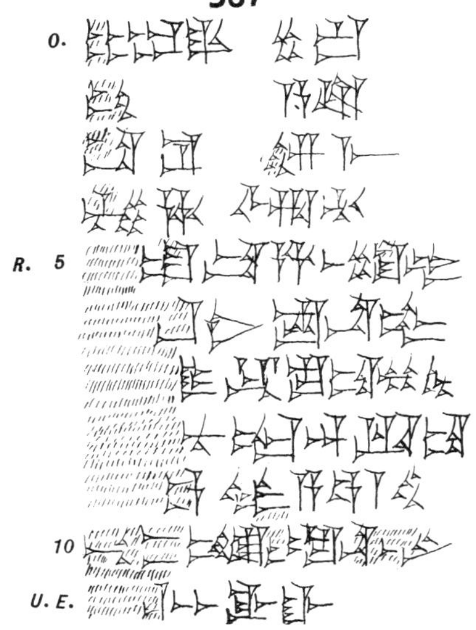

Indistinct seal impressions.

388

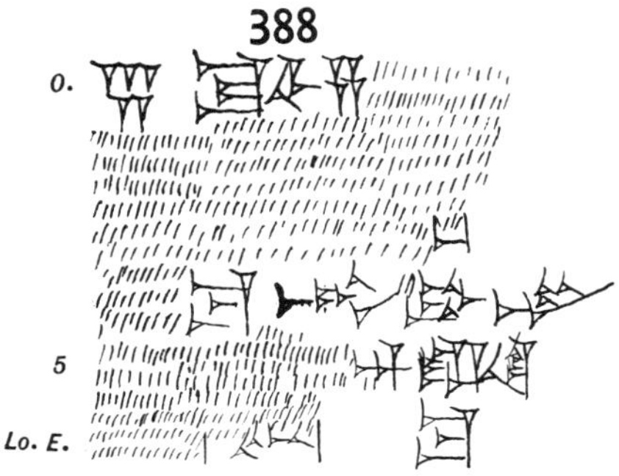

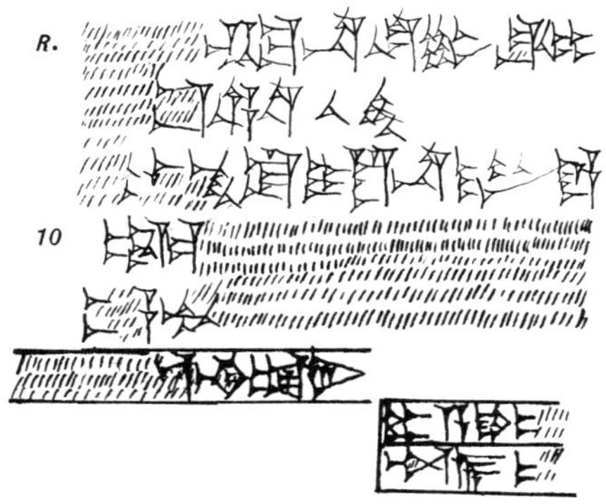

389

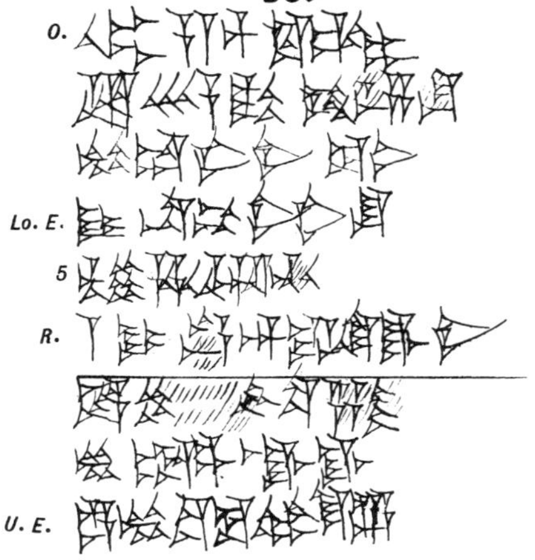

390

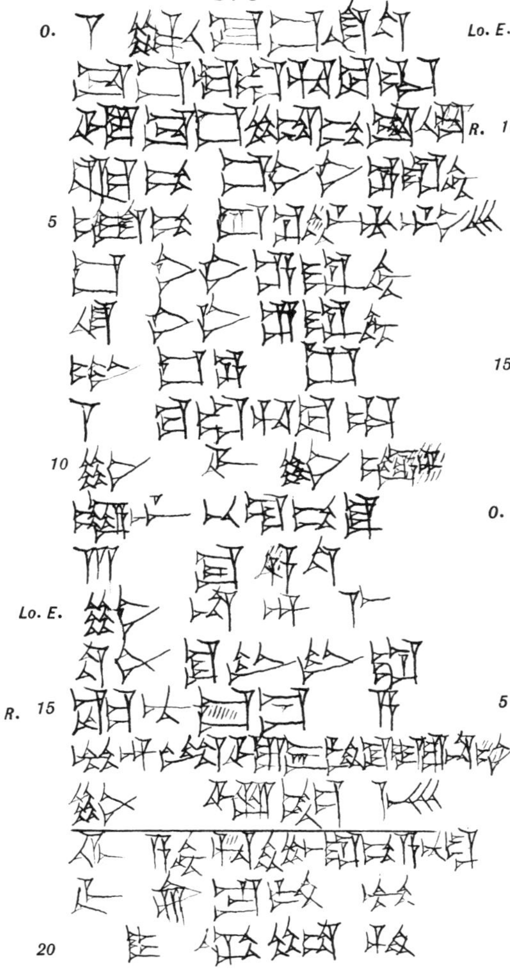

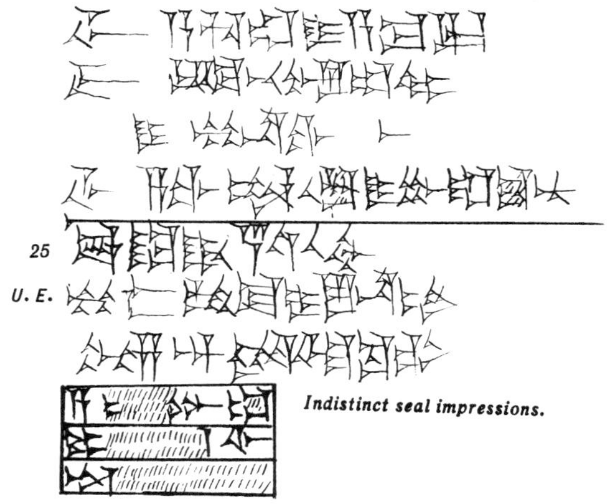

Indistinct seal impressions.

391

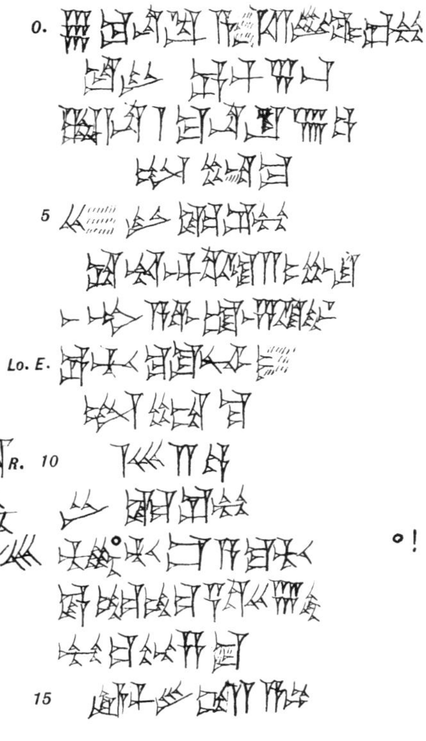

392

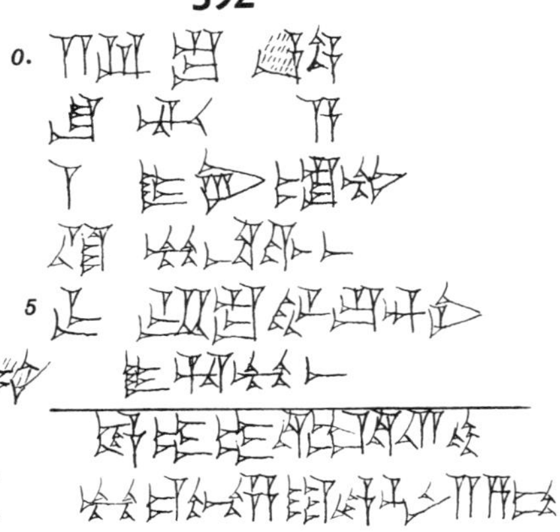

Indistinct seal impressions.

393

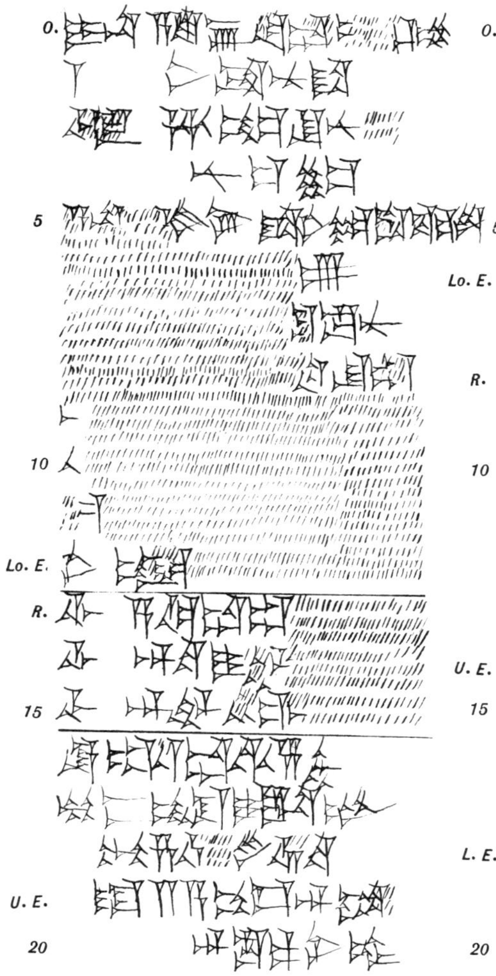

Indistinct seal impressions.

394

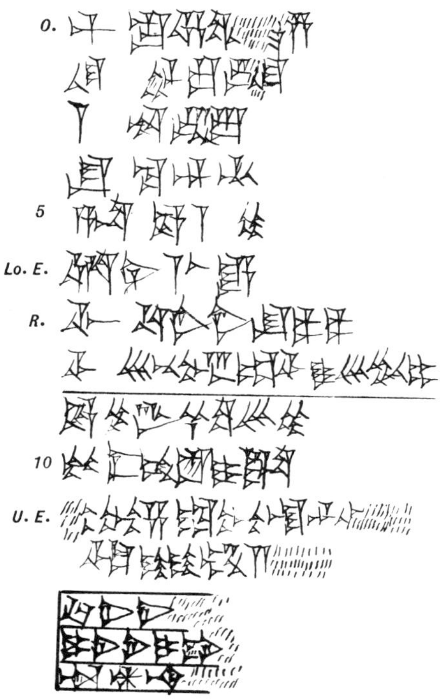

395

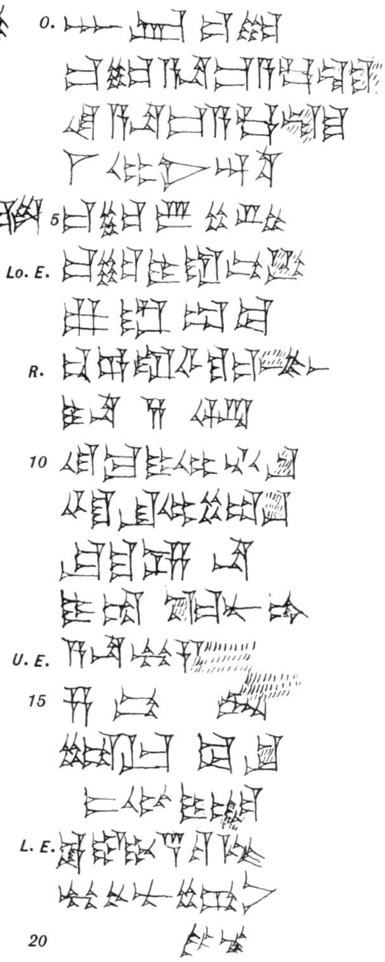

396

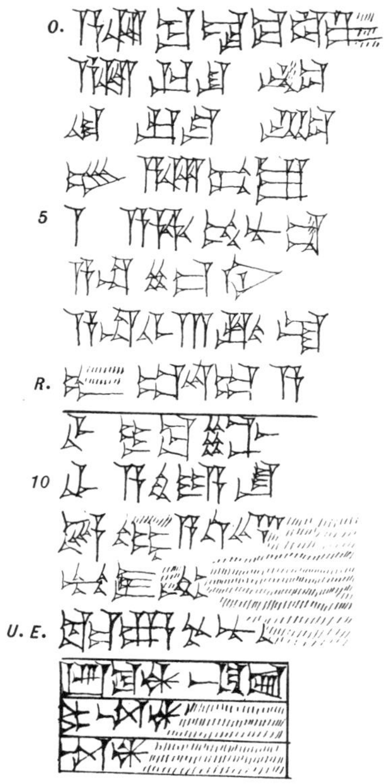

397

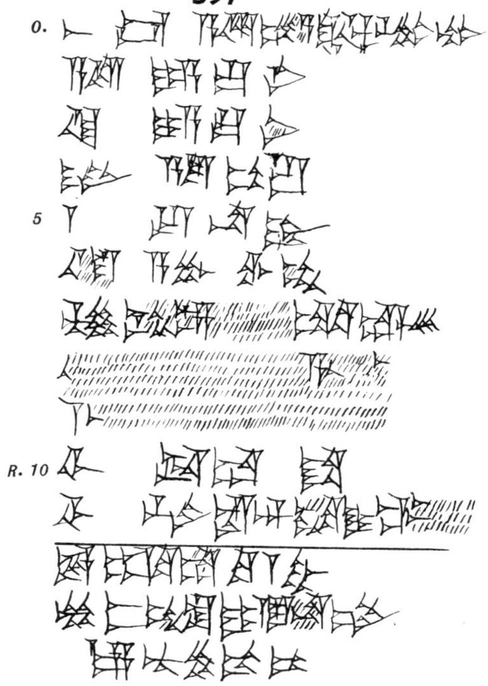

Indistinct seal impressions.

398

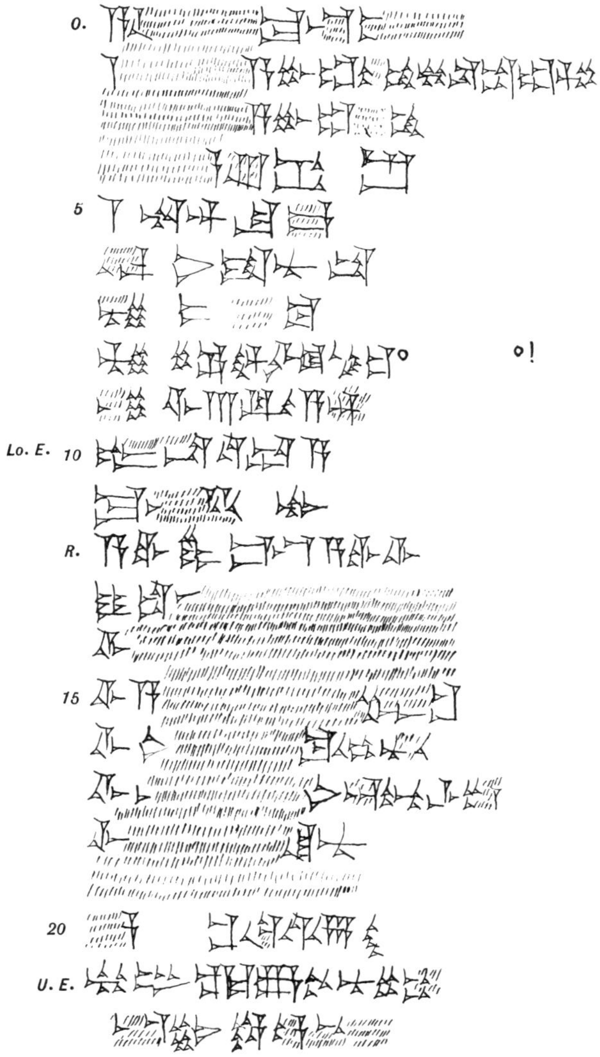

Indistinct seal impressions.

399

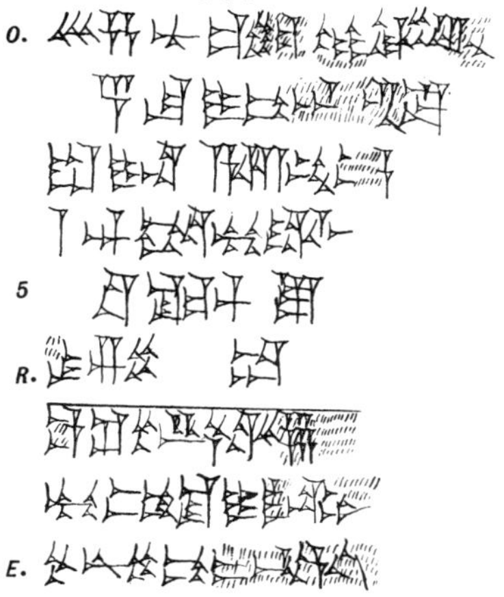

400

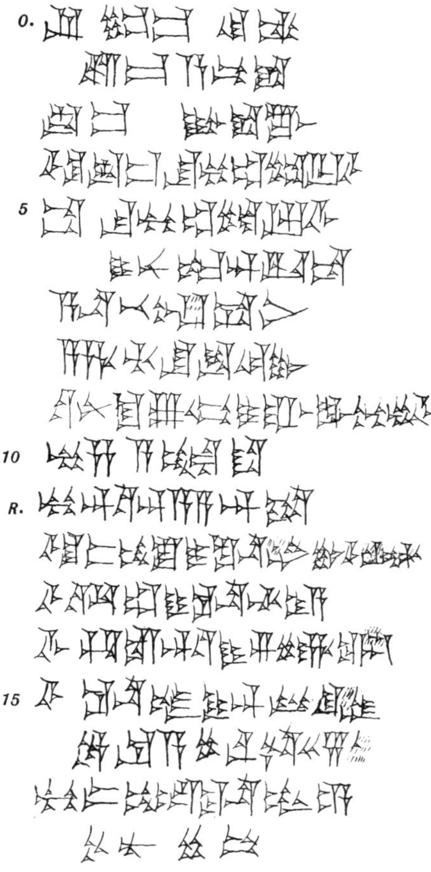

401

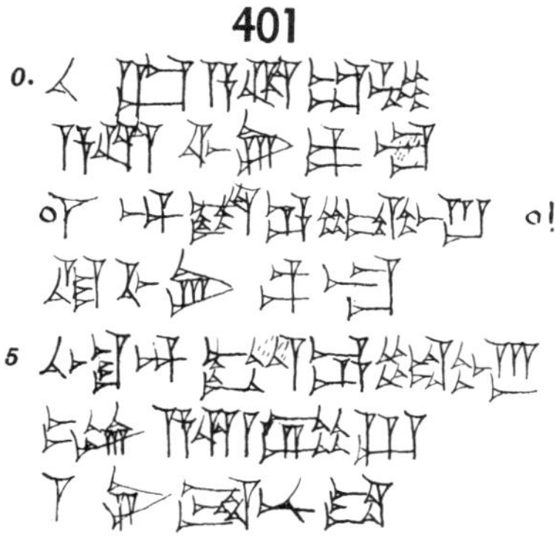

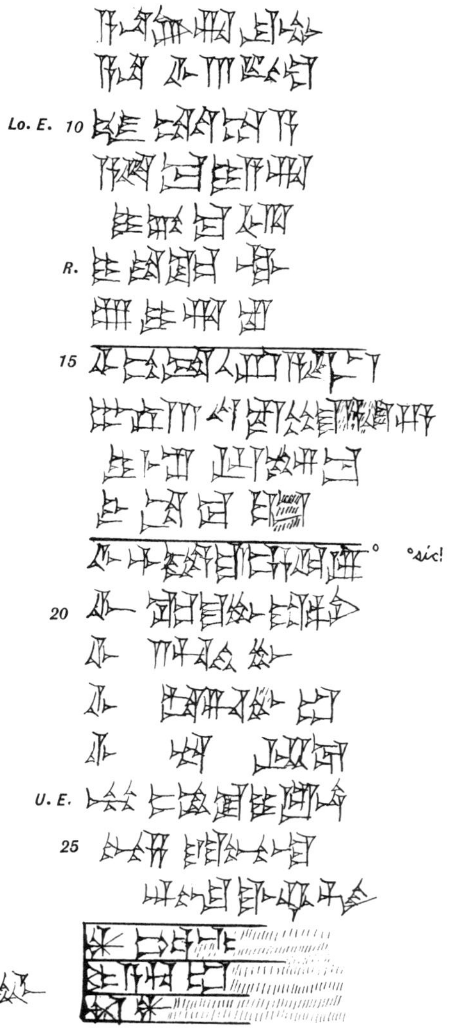

402

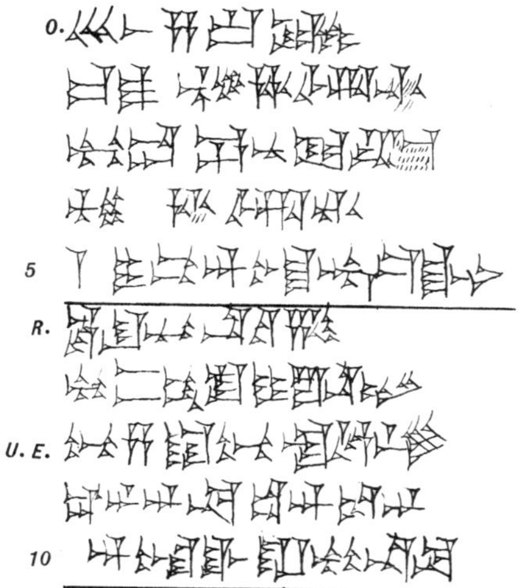

403

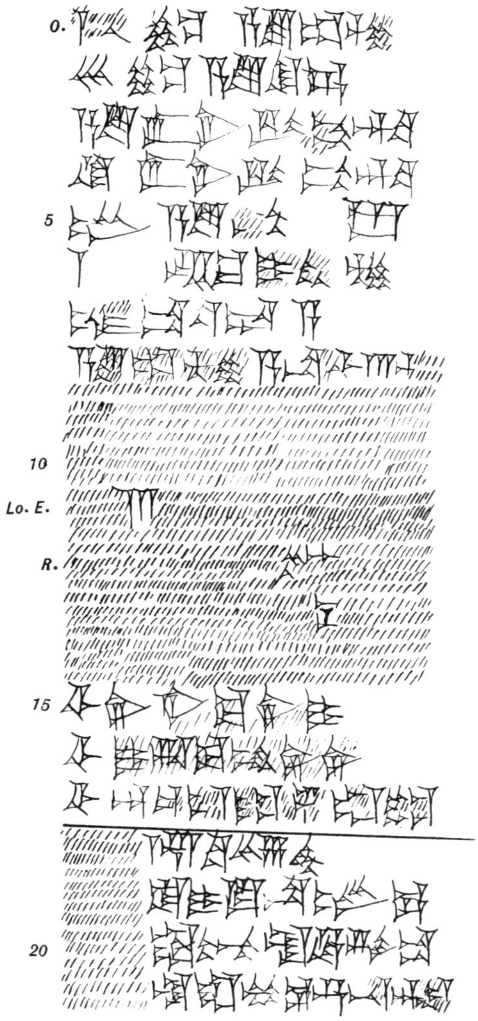

404

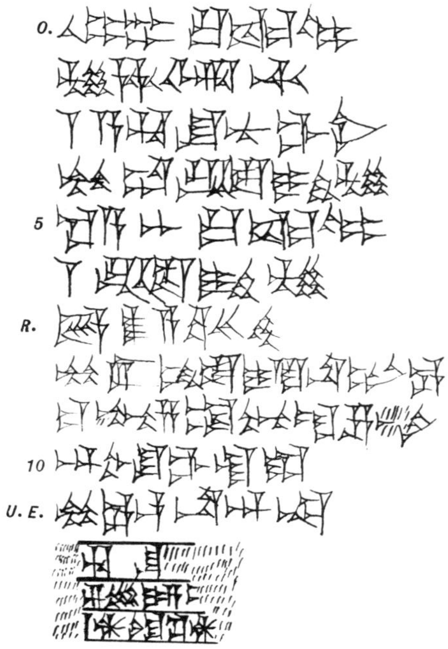

405

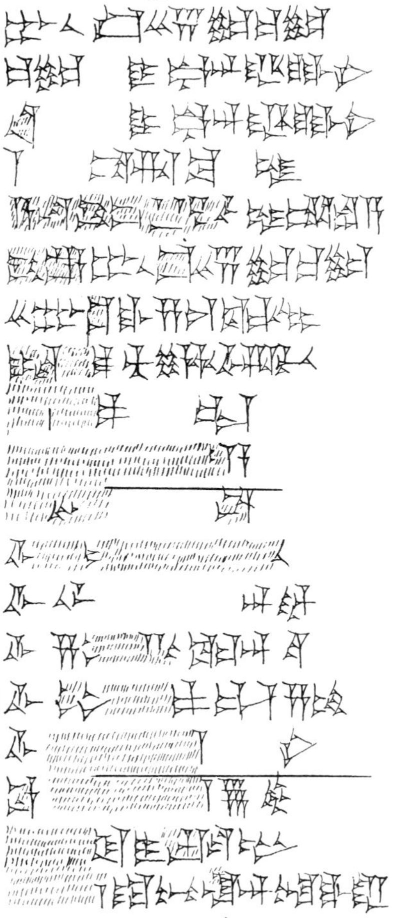

Indistinct seal impressions.

406

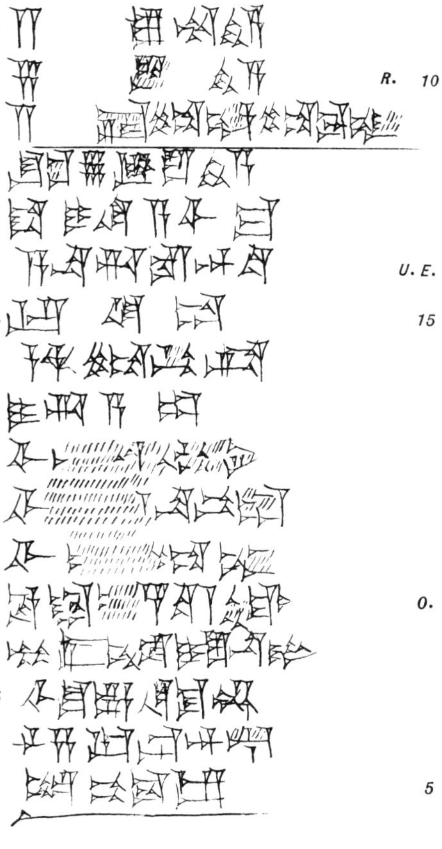

407

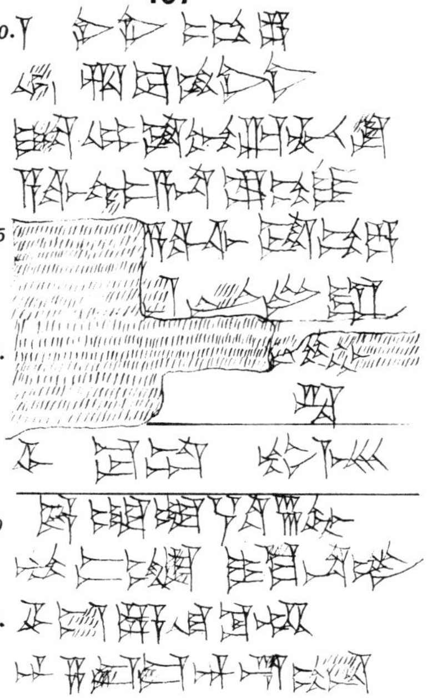

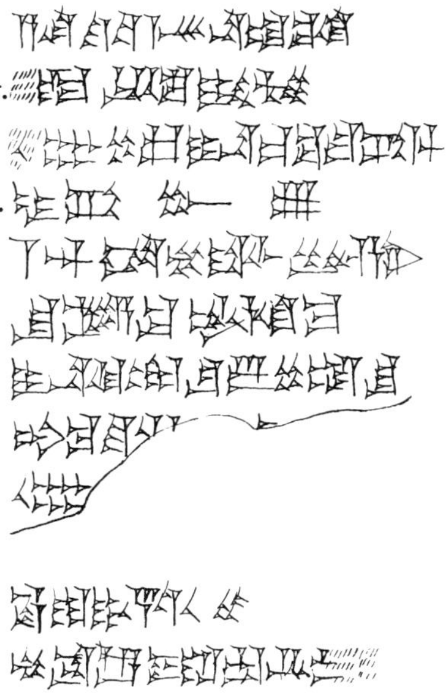

408

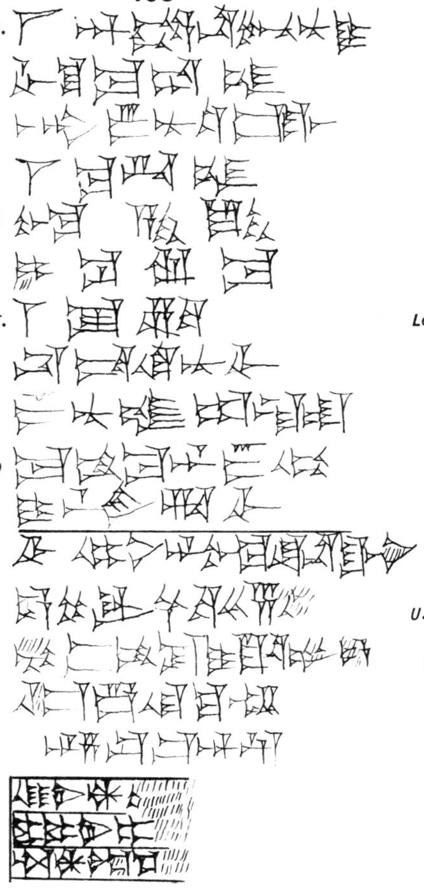

409

410

411

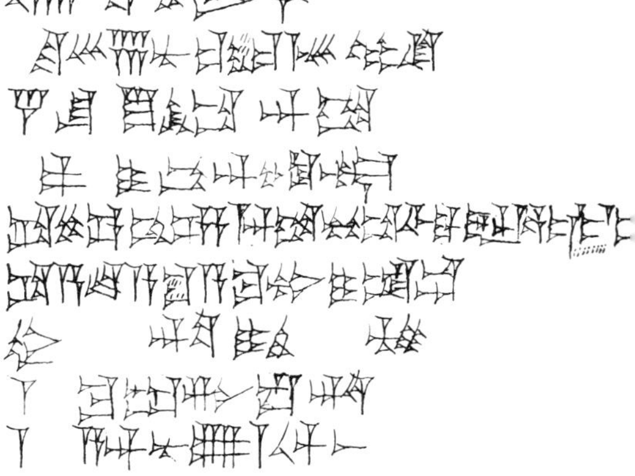

411 CONTINUED

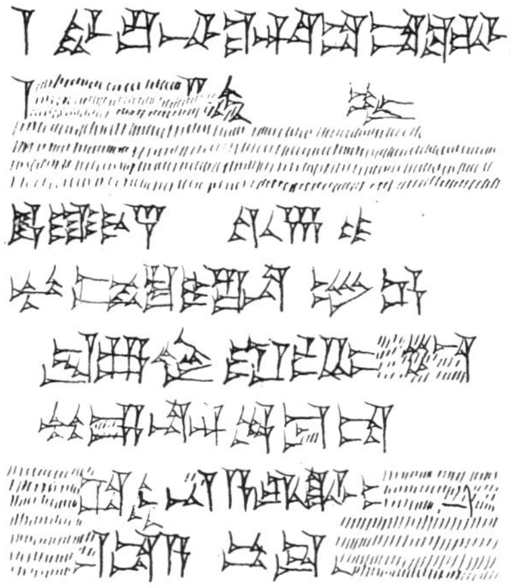

Indistinct seal impressions.

412

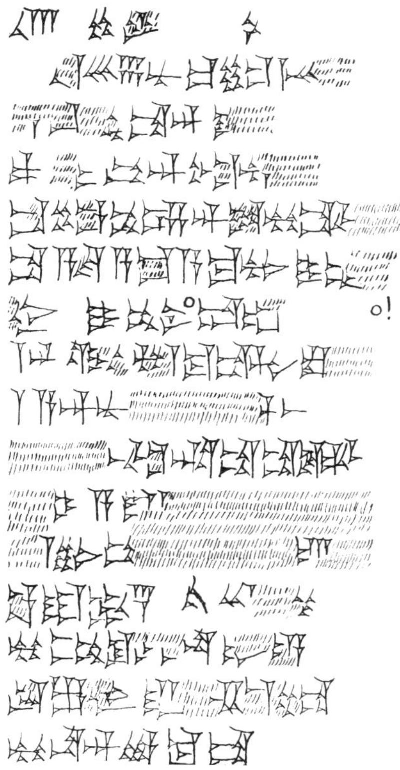

Indistinct seal impressions.

413

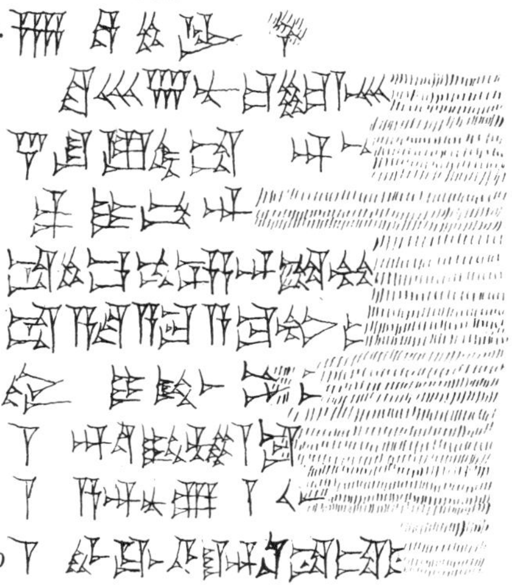

Indistinct seal impressions.

414

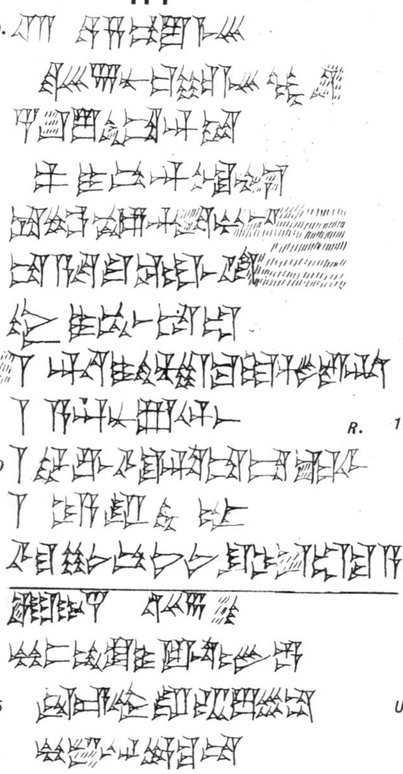

Indistinct seal impressions.

415

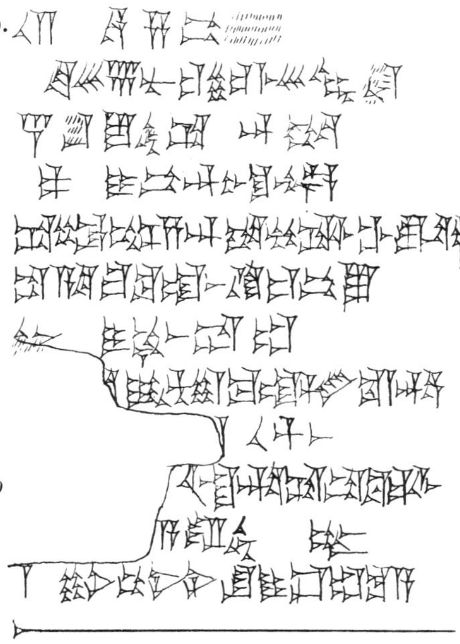

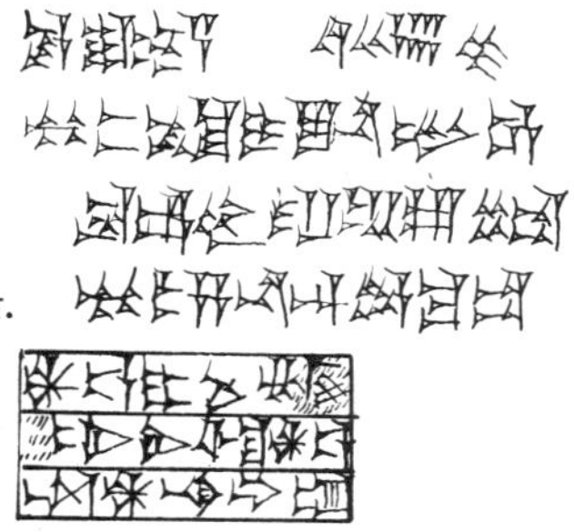

416

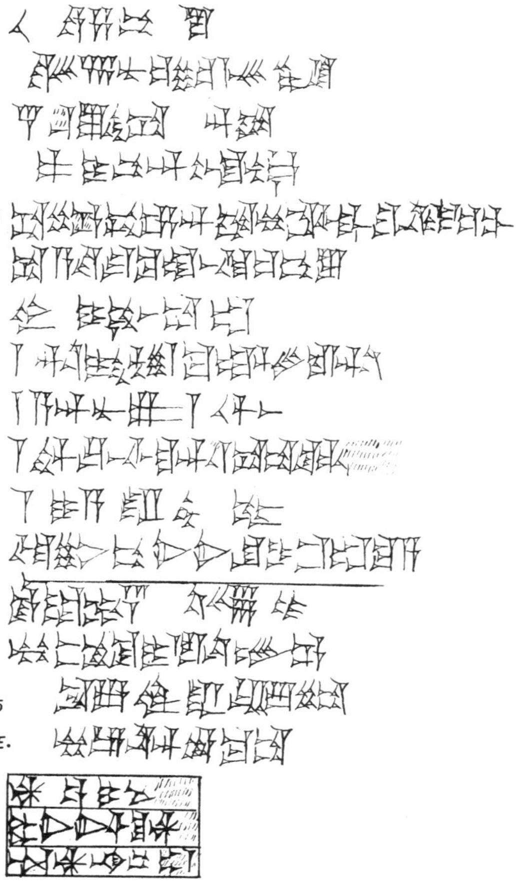

417

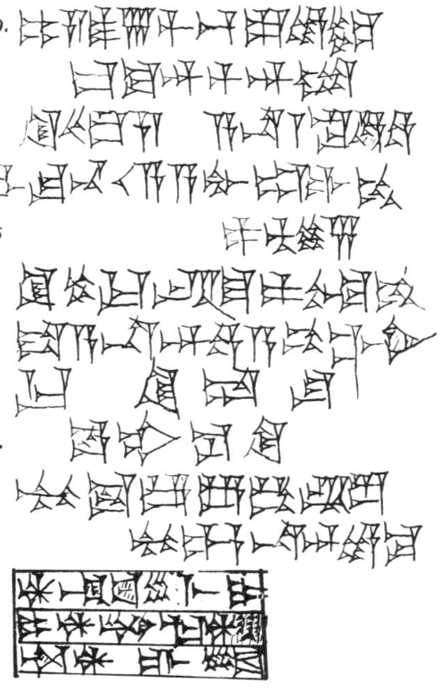

418

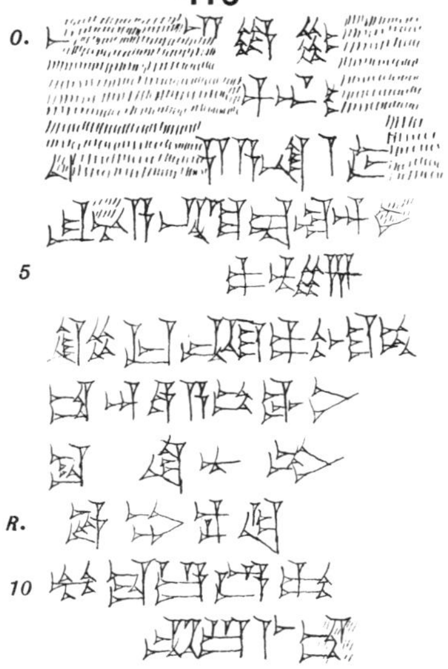

Indistinct seal impressions.

419 TABLET

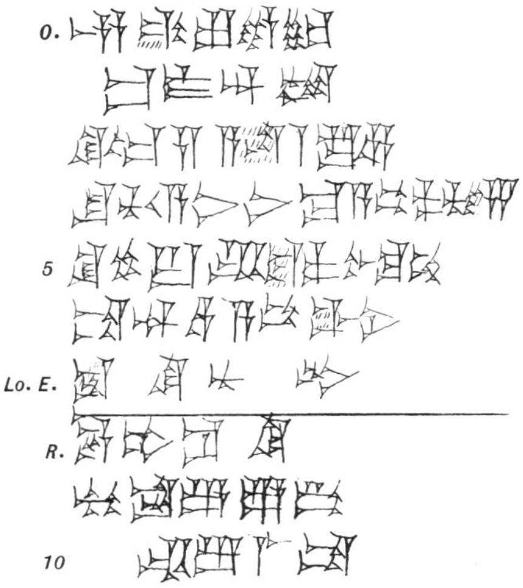

CASE

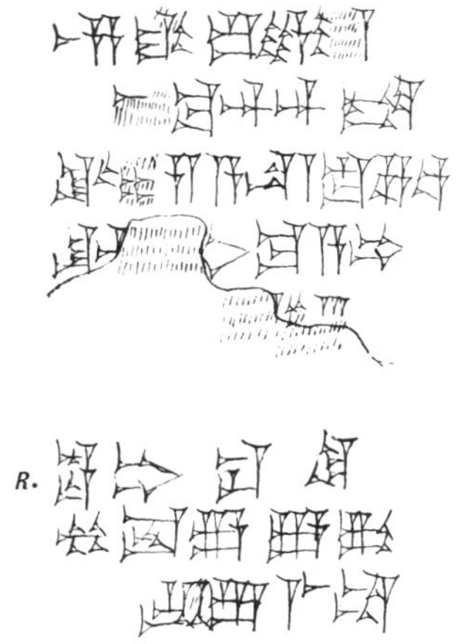

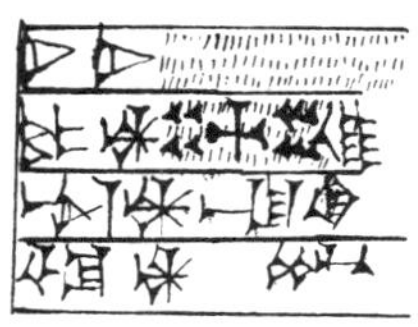

420

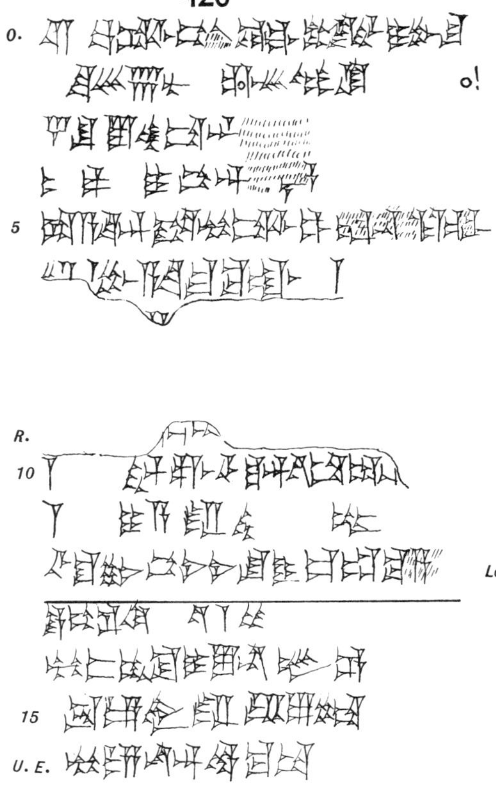

Indistinct seal impressions.

421

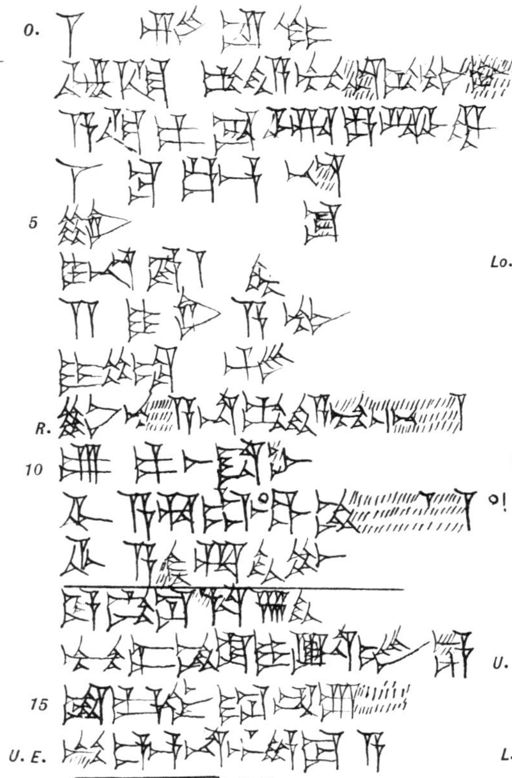

422

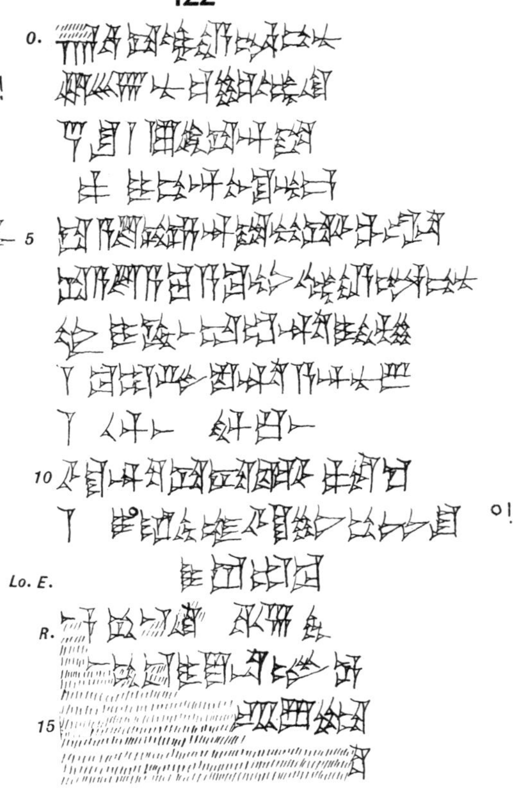

Indistinct seal impressions.

423

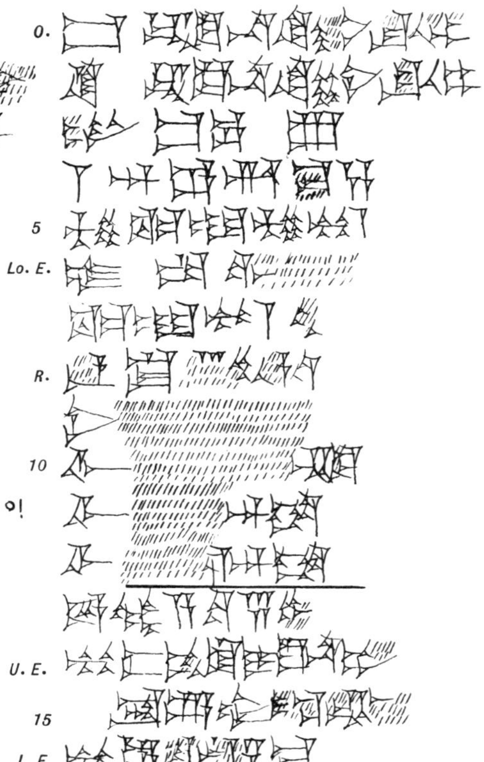

424

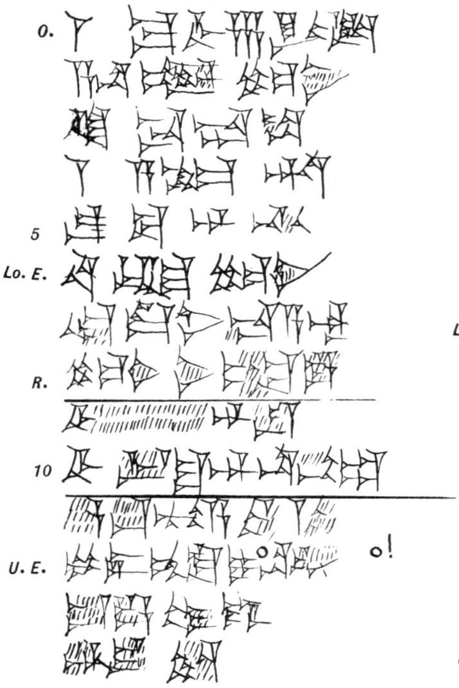

Indistinct seal impressions.

425

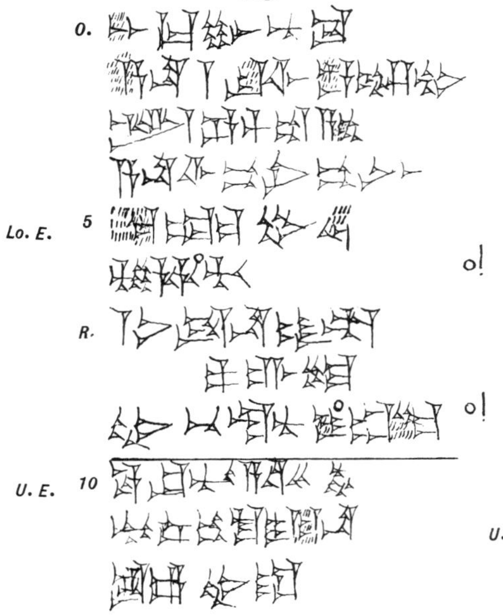

426

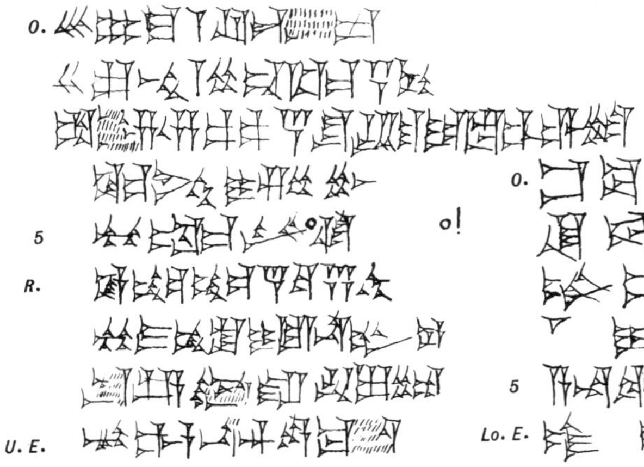

427

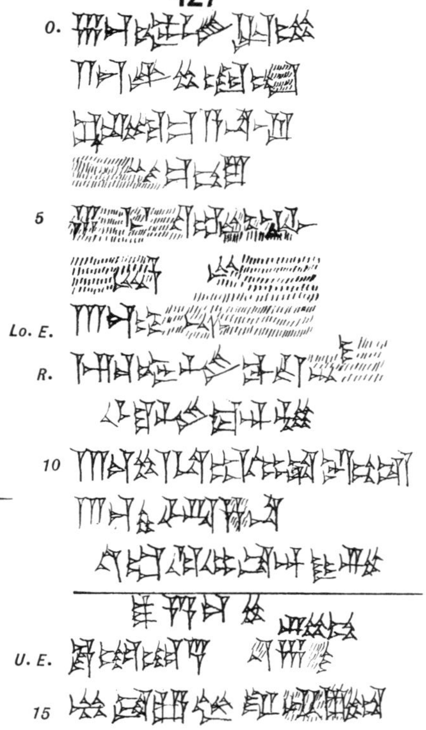

428

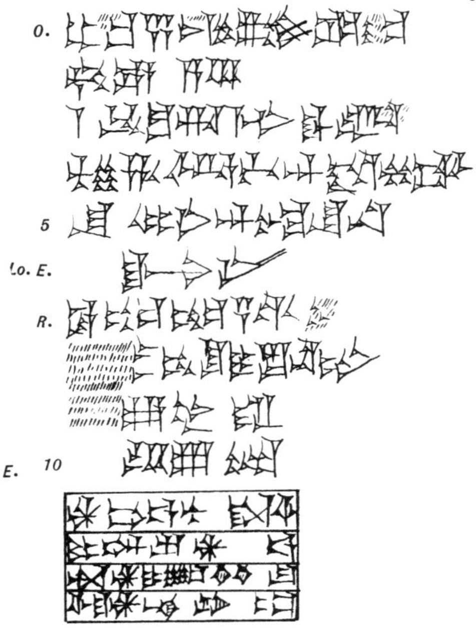

429

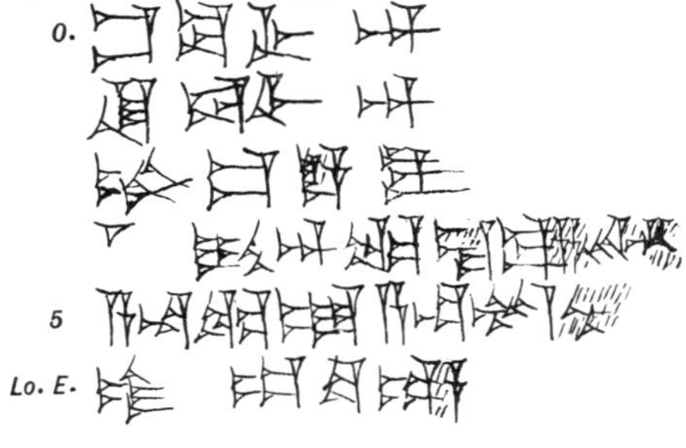

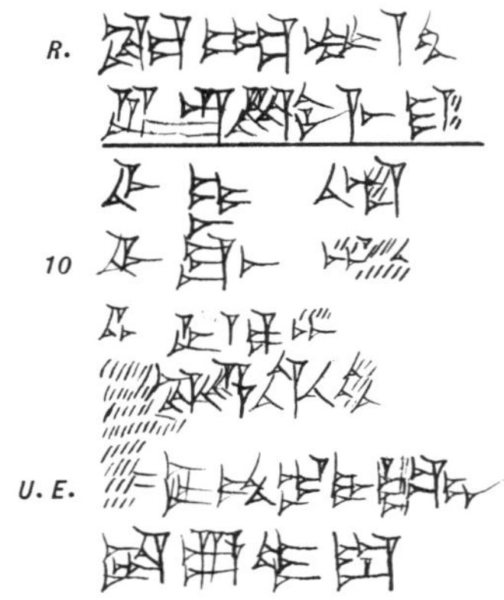

430

431

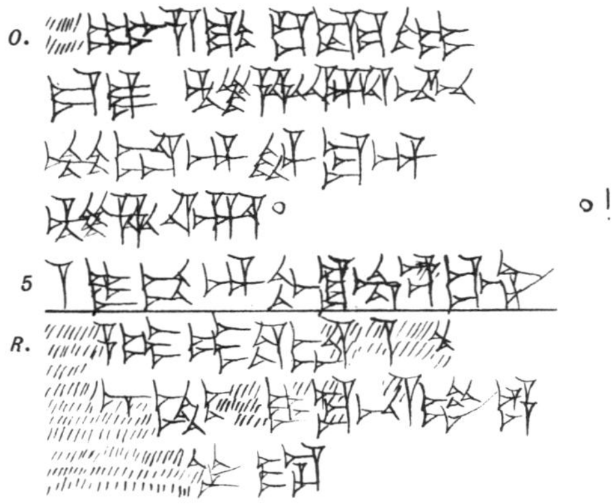

432

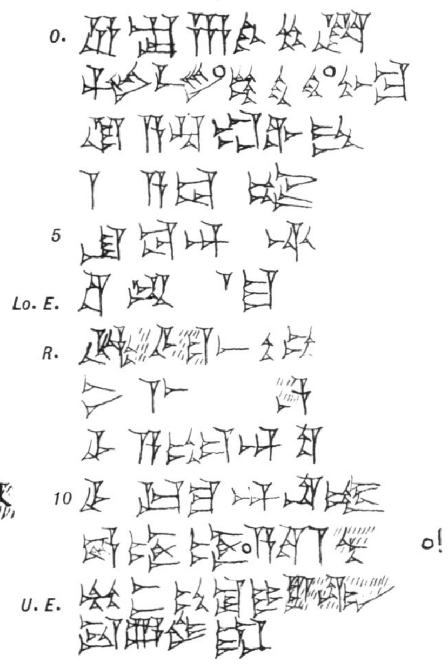

433

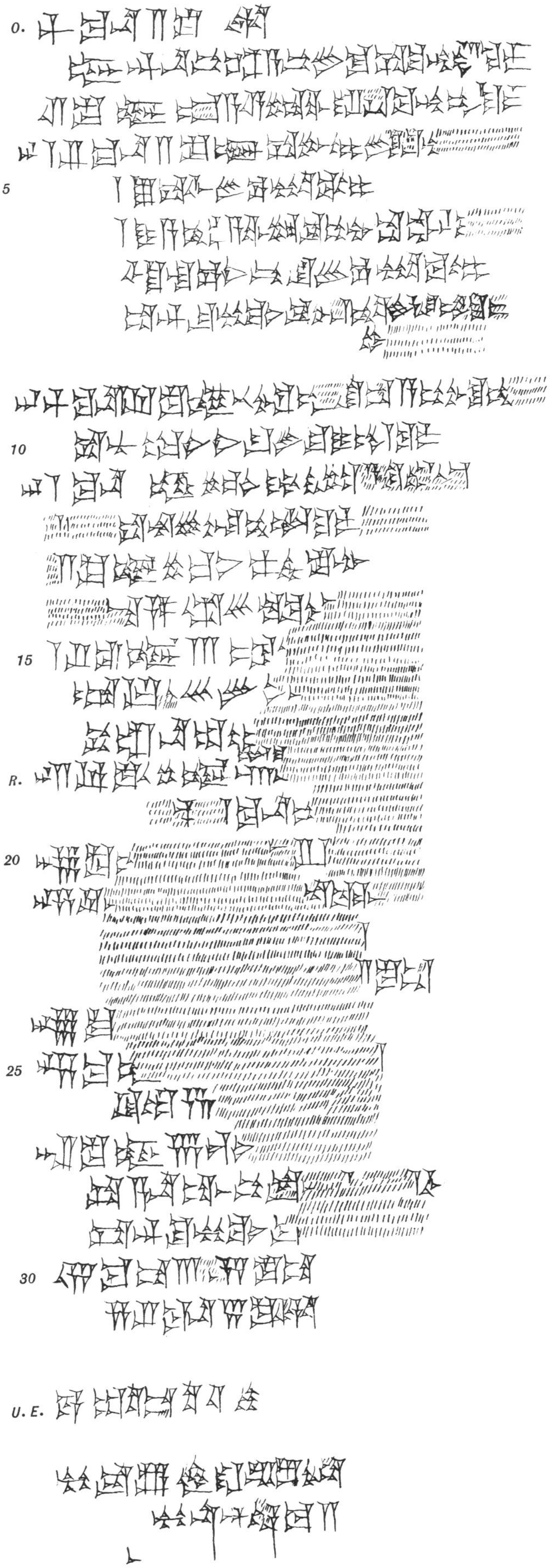

434

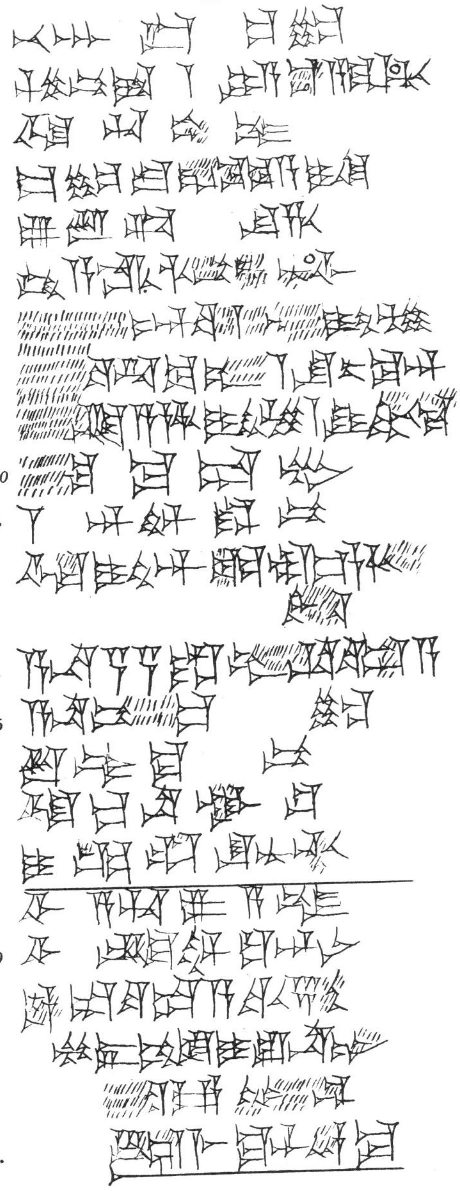

435

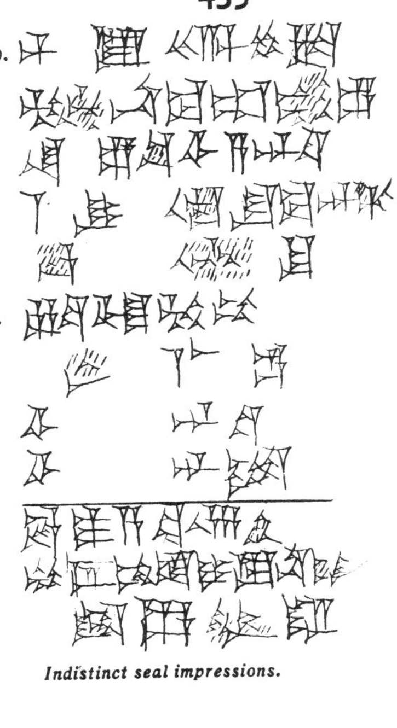

Indistinct seal impressions.

436

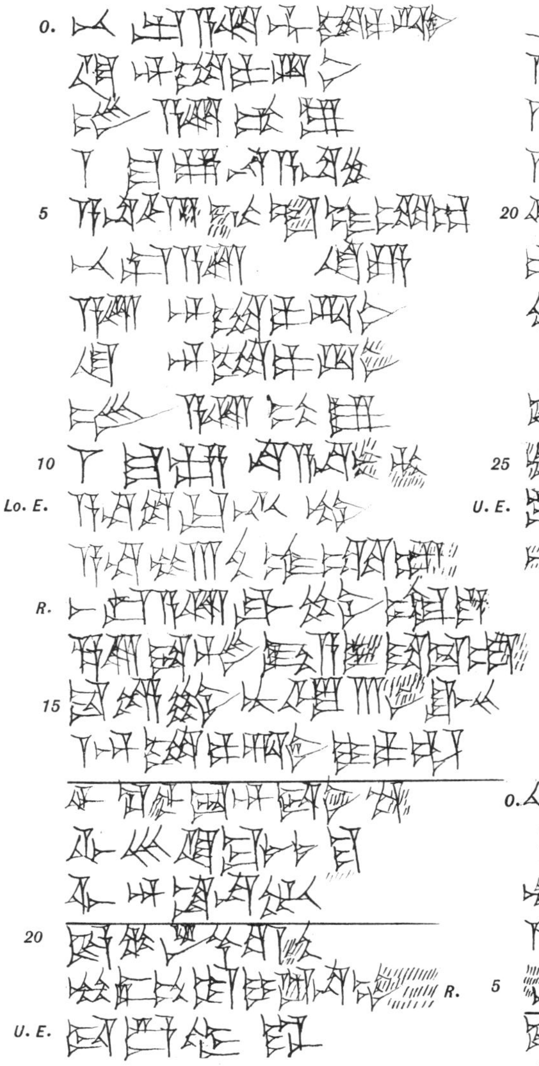

Indistinct seal impressions.

437

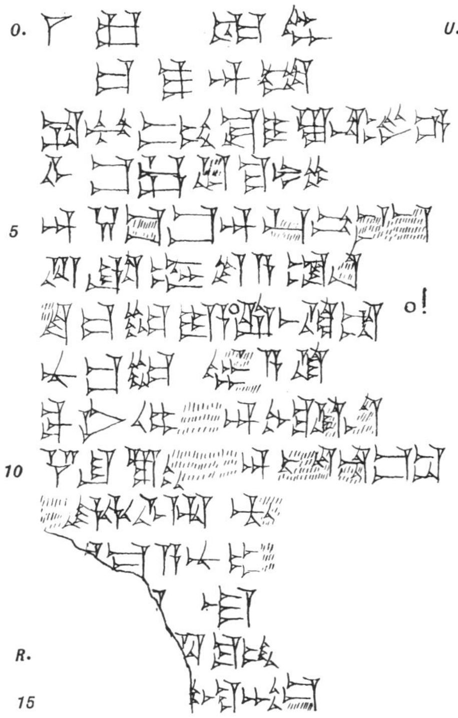

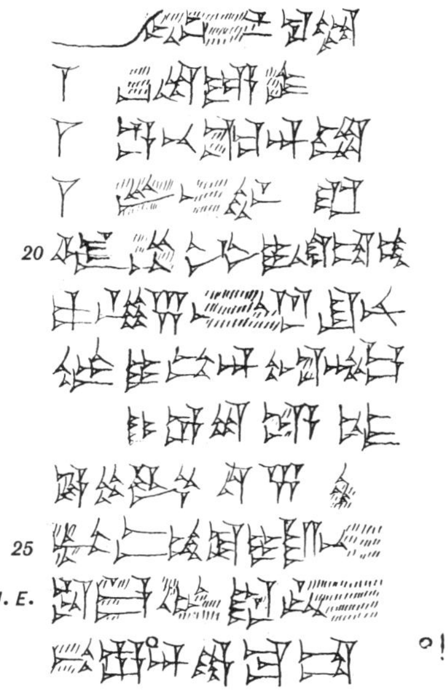

438

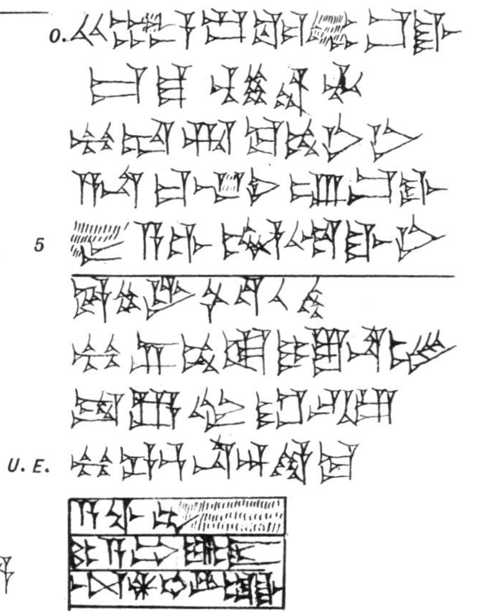

439

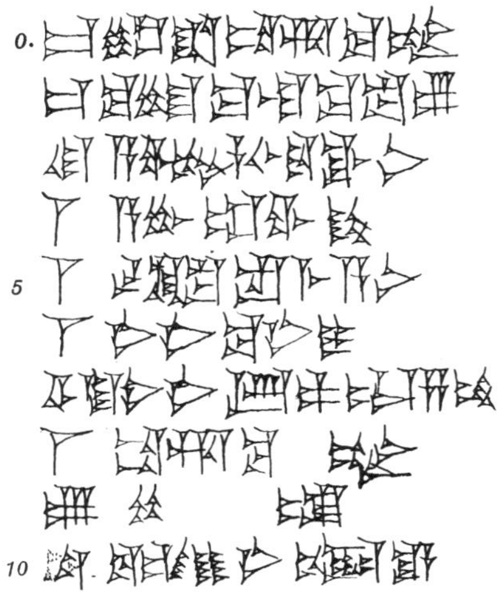

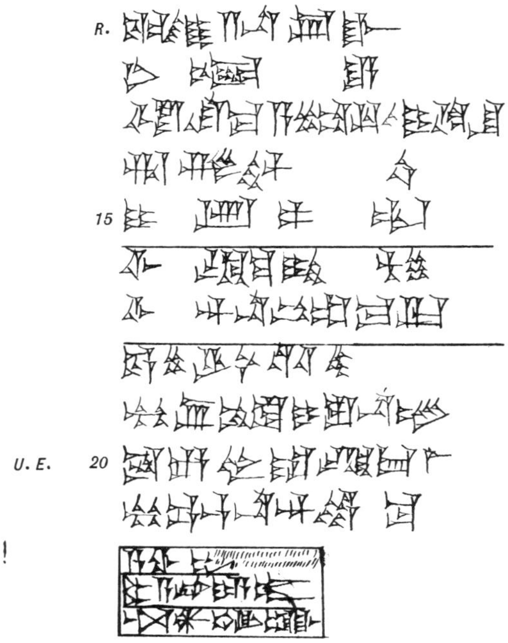

440

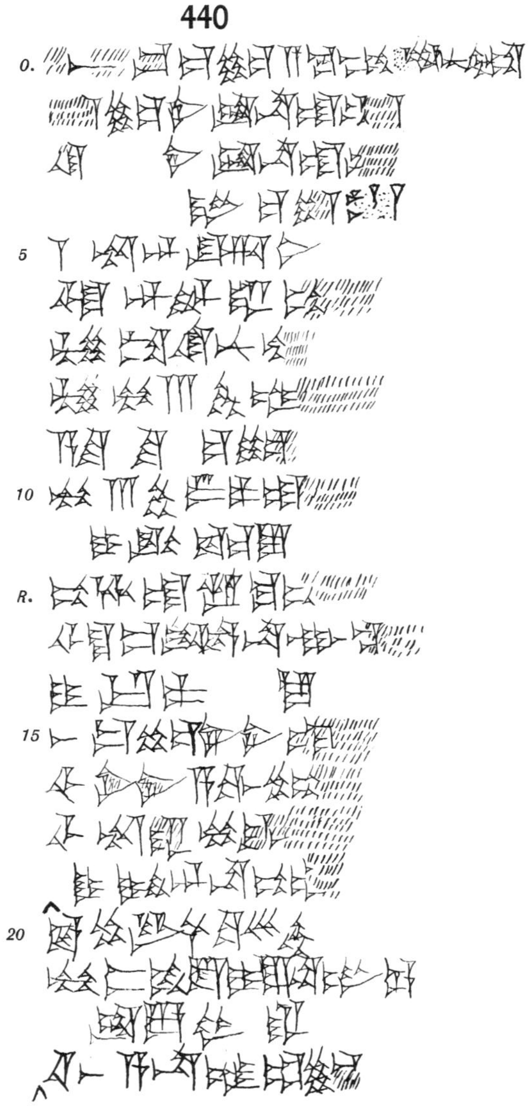

Indistinct seal impressions.

441

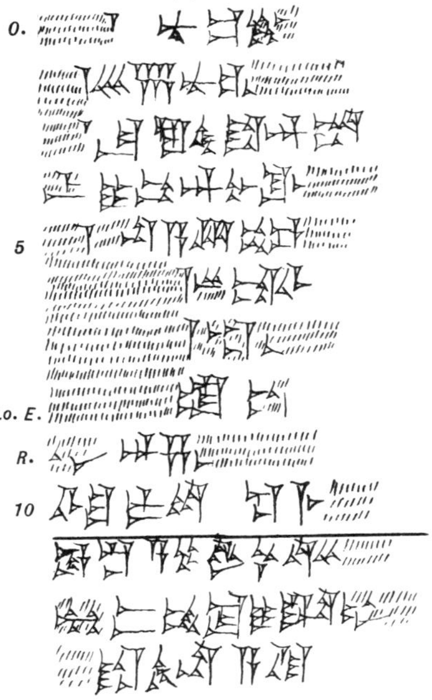

442

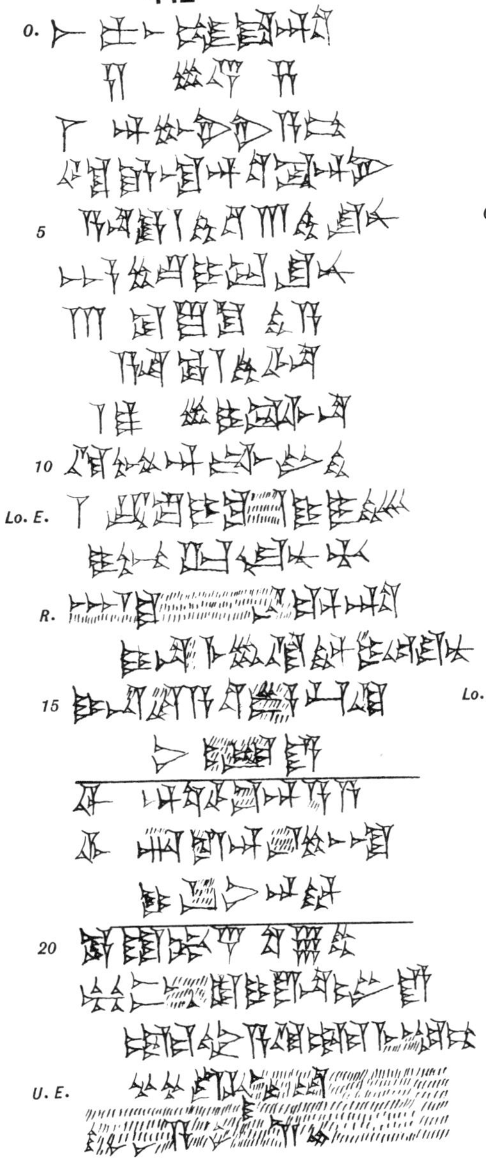

443

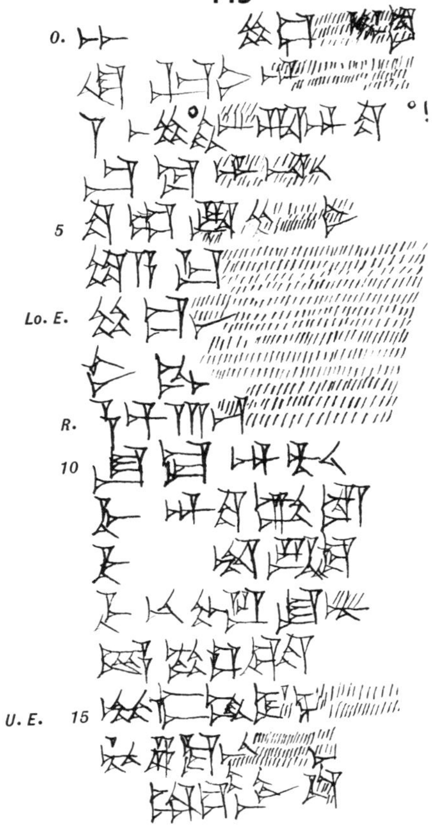

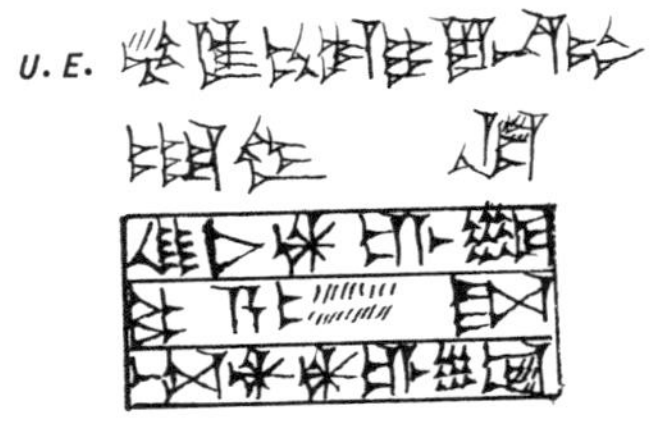

444

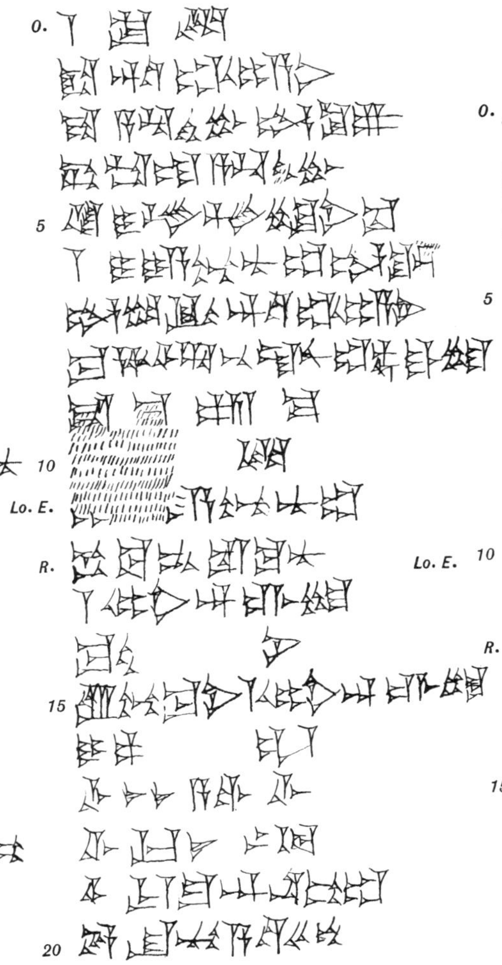

445

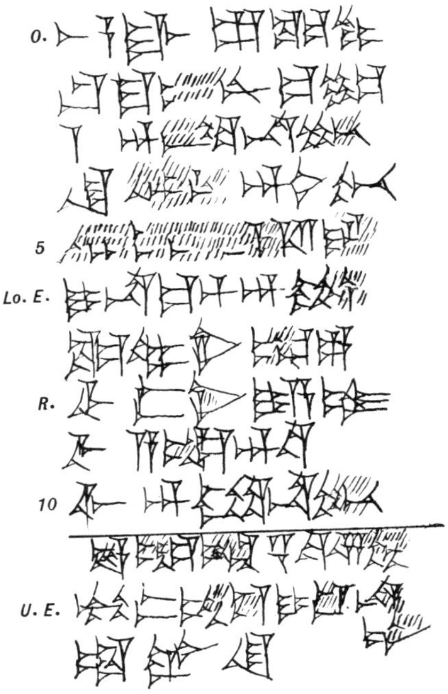

446

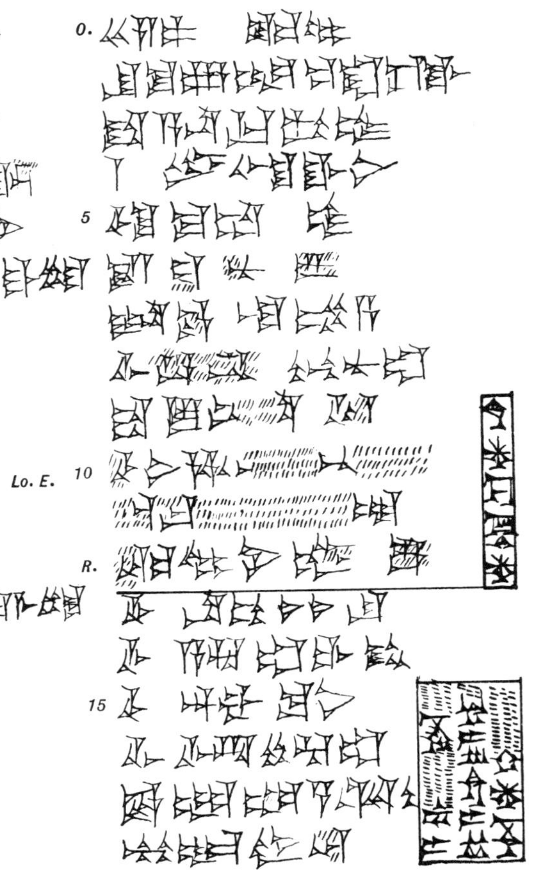

447

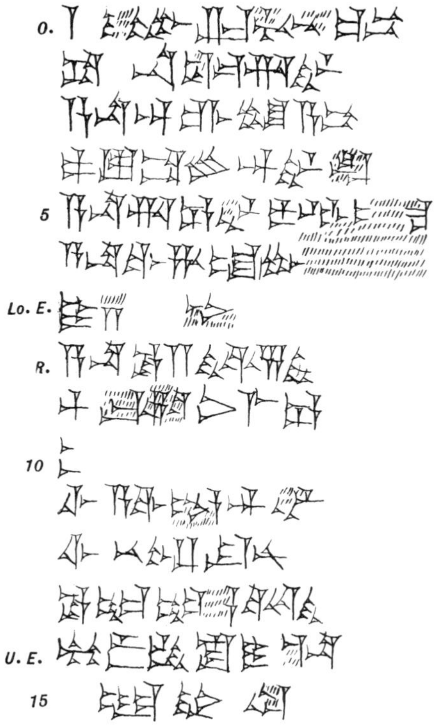

448

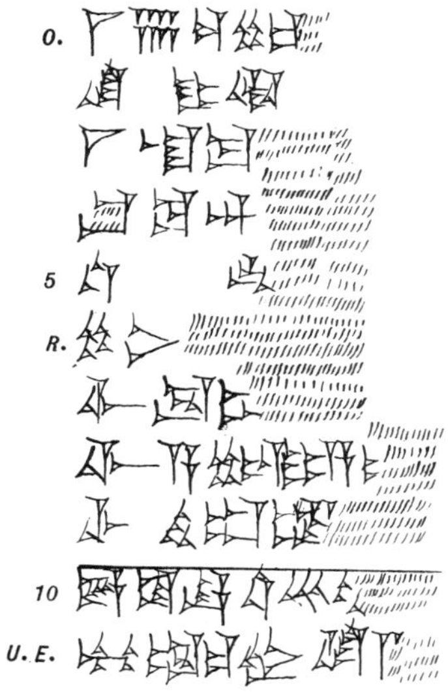

449

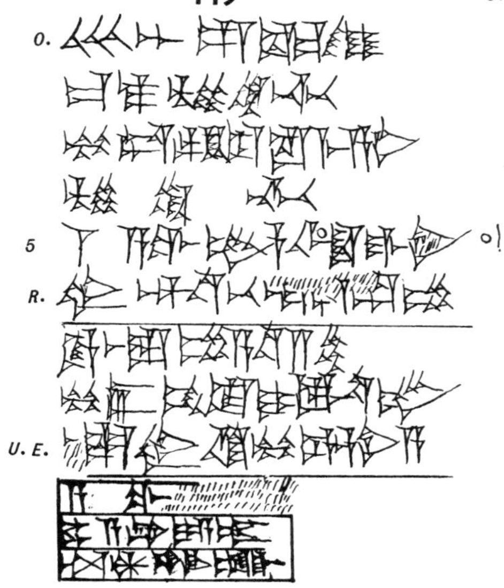

450

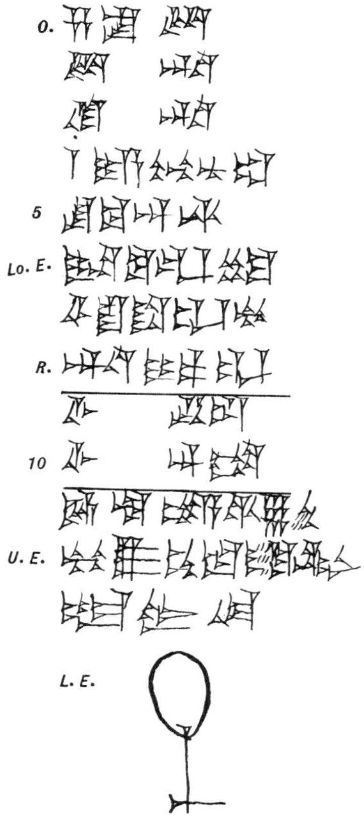

451

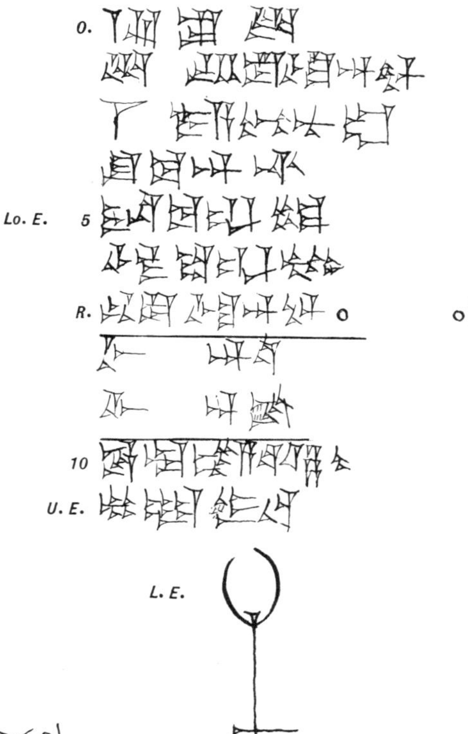

452

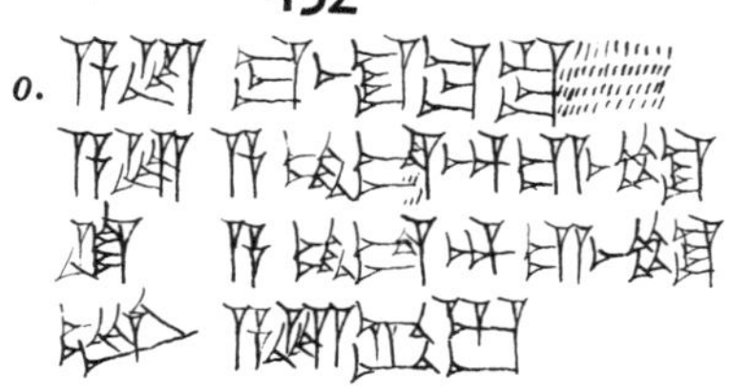

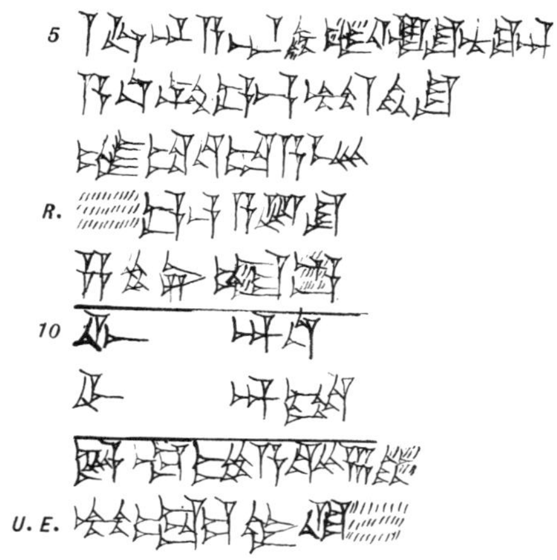

453

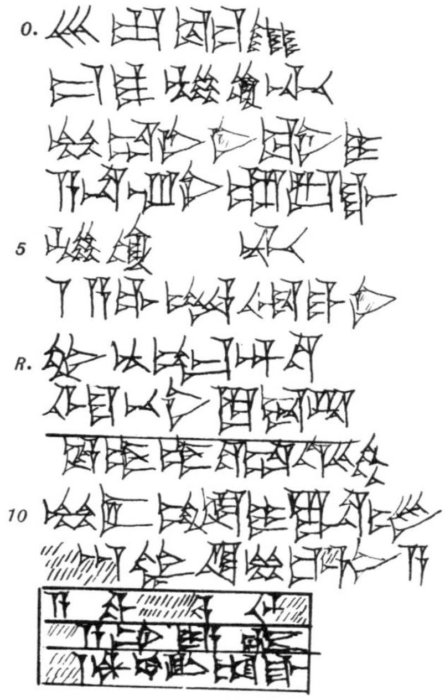

454

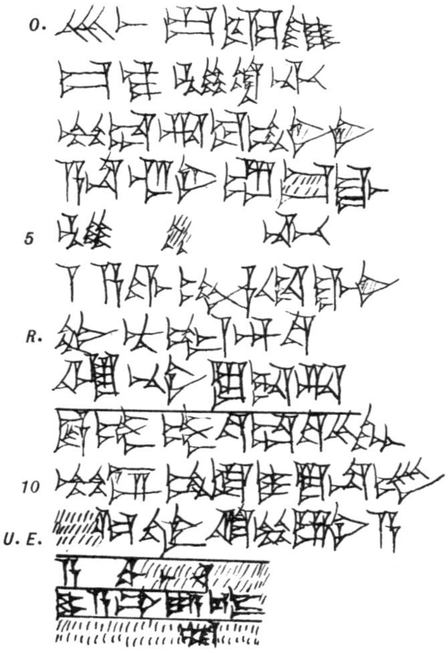

455

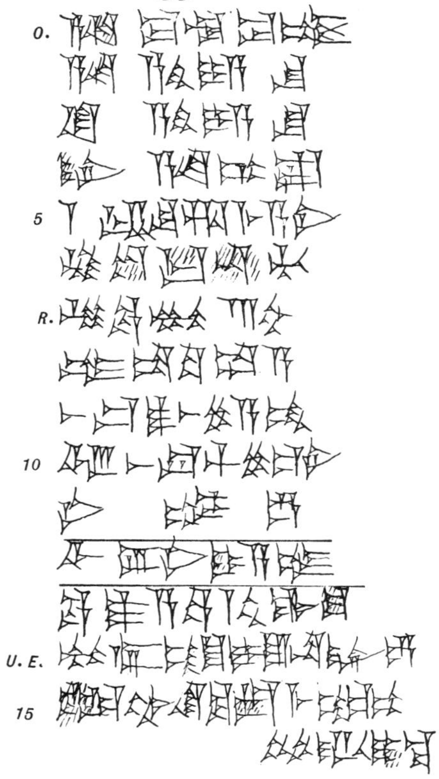

Indistinct seal impressions.

456

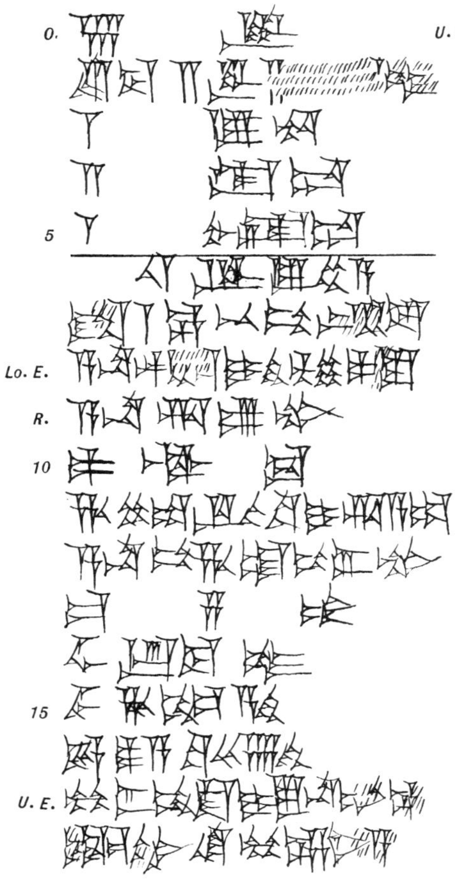

Indistinct seal impressions.

457

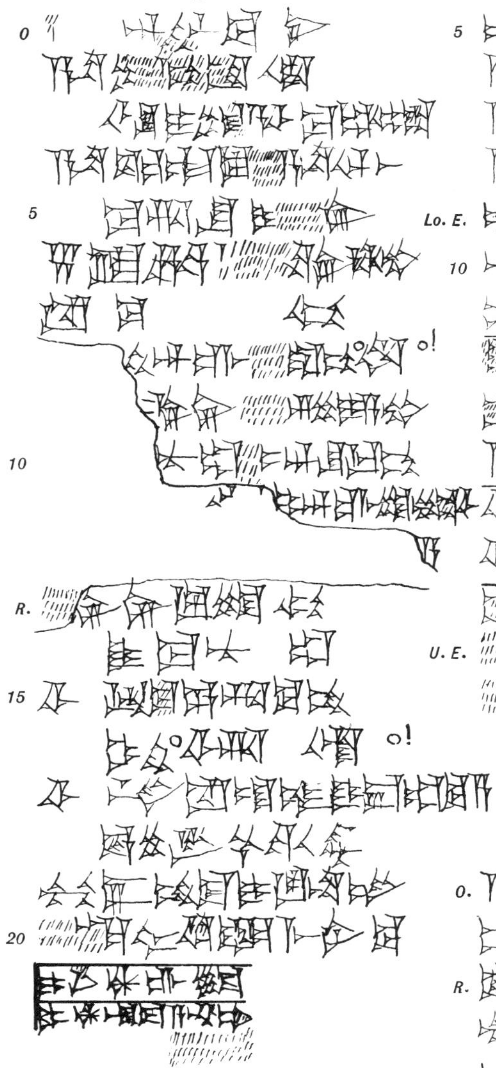

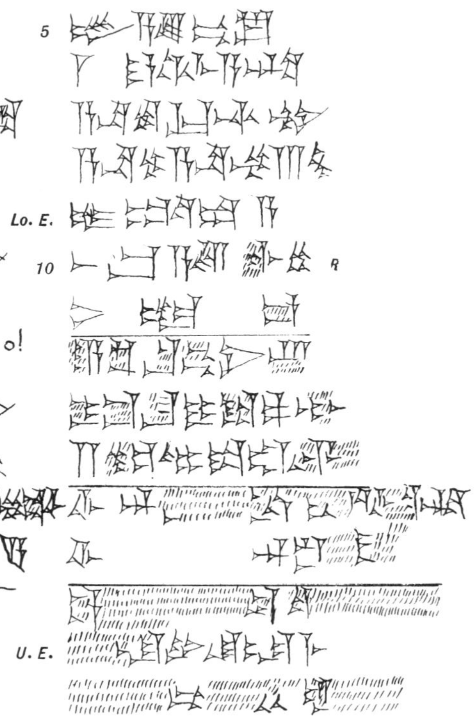

Indistinct seal impressions.

458

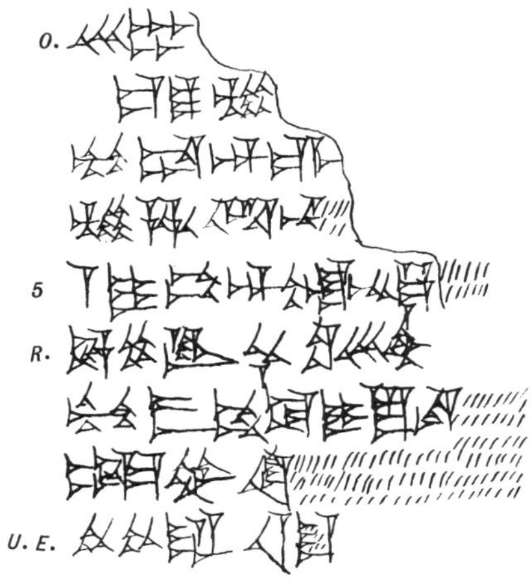

459

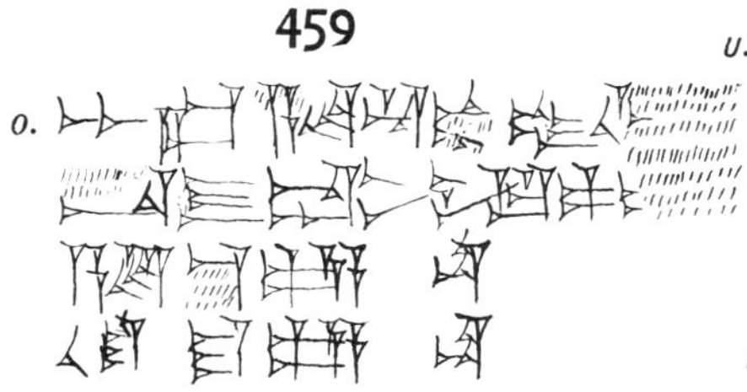

460

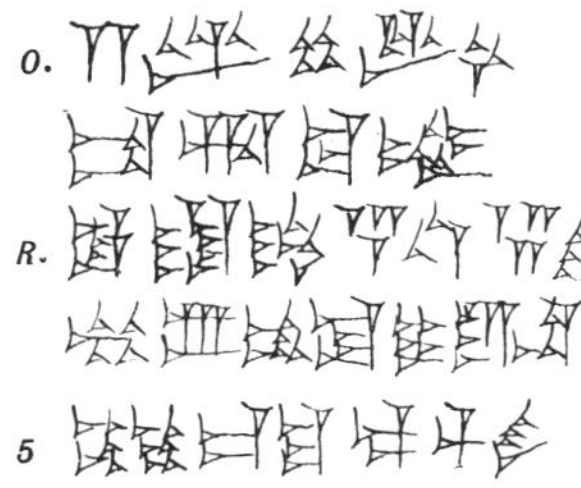

Indistinct seal impressions.

461

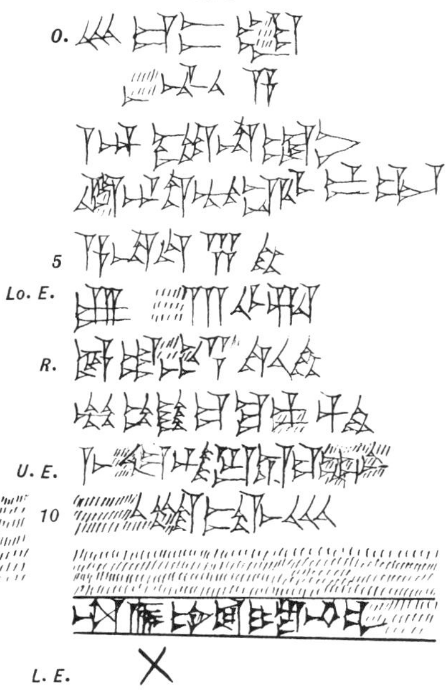

462

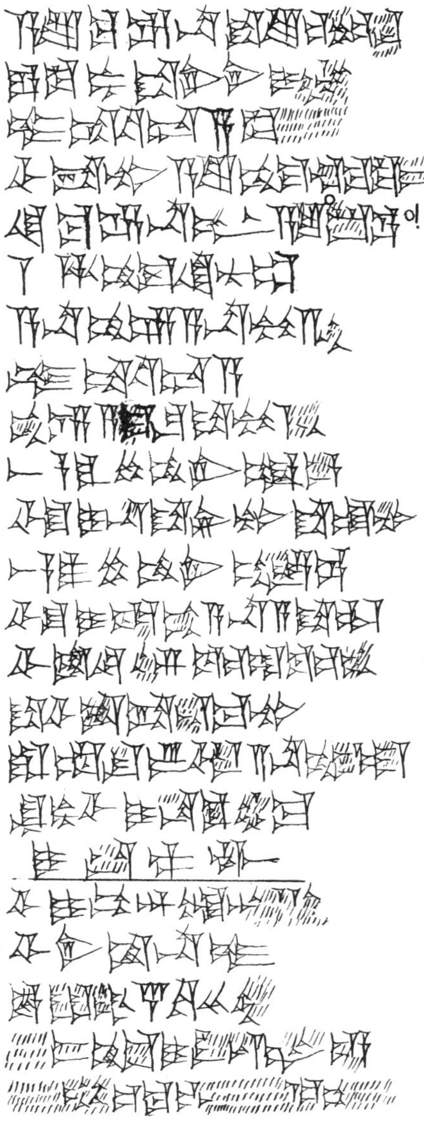

463

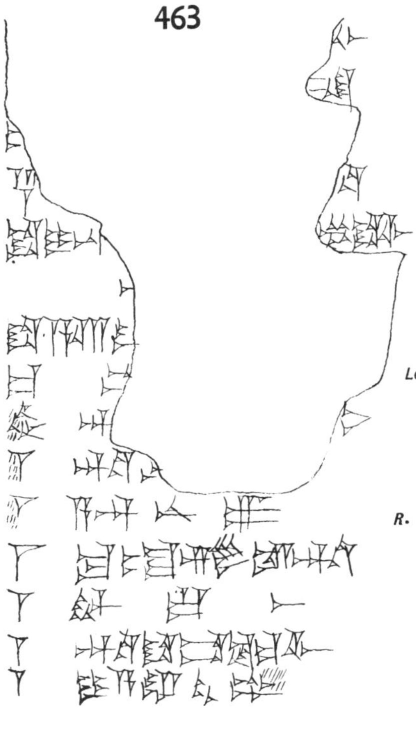

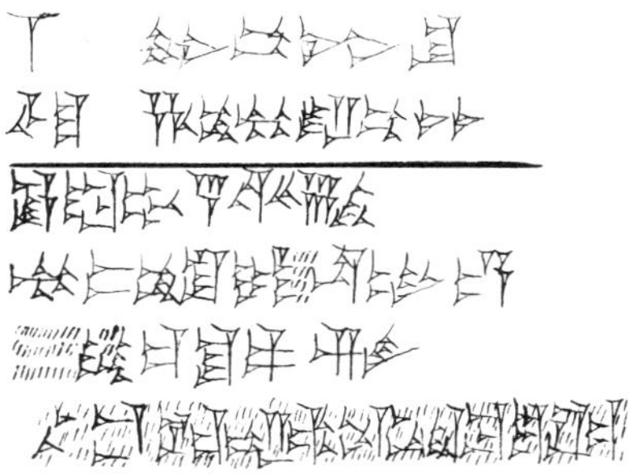

Indistinct seal impressions.

464

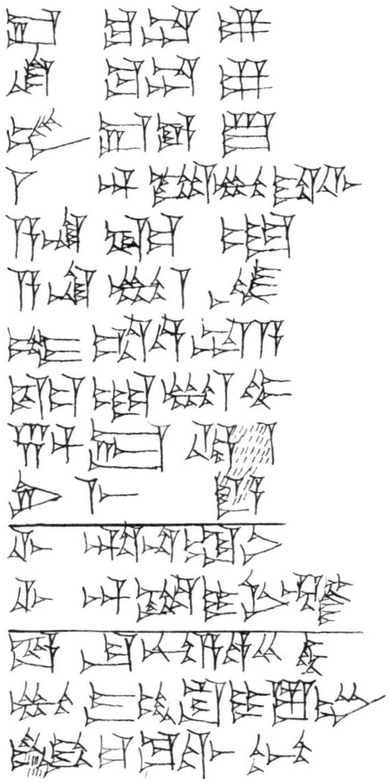

465

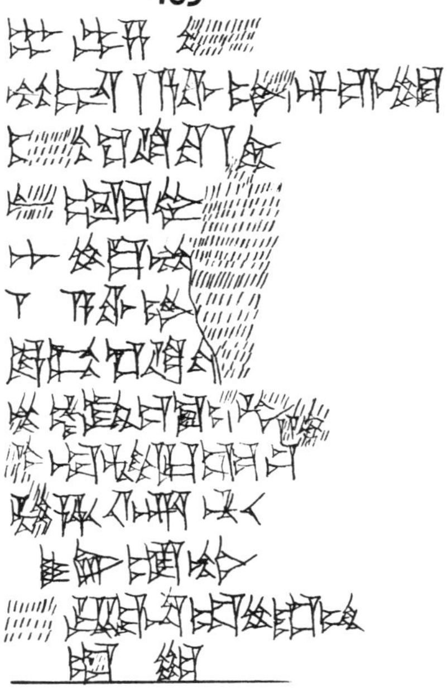

Indistinct seal impressions.

466

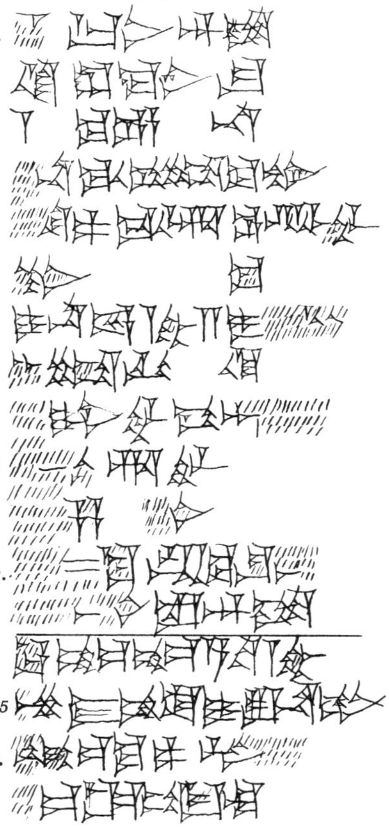

467

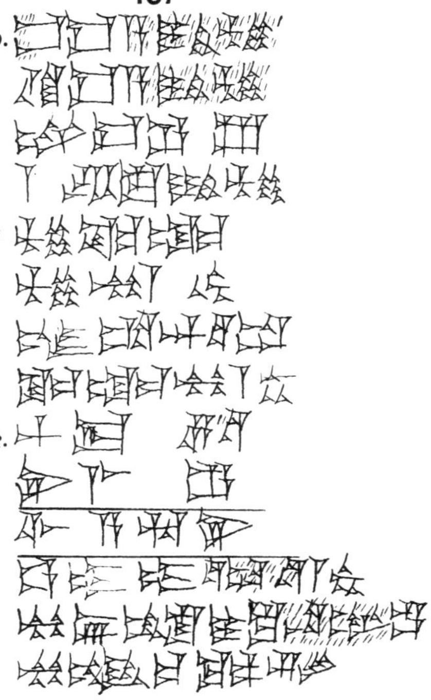

468

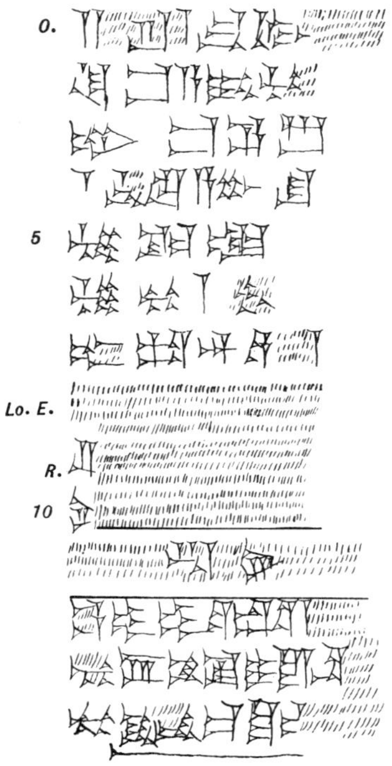

469

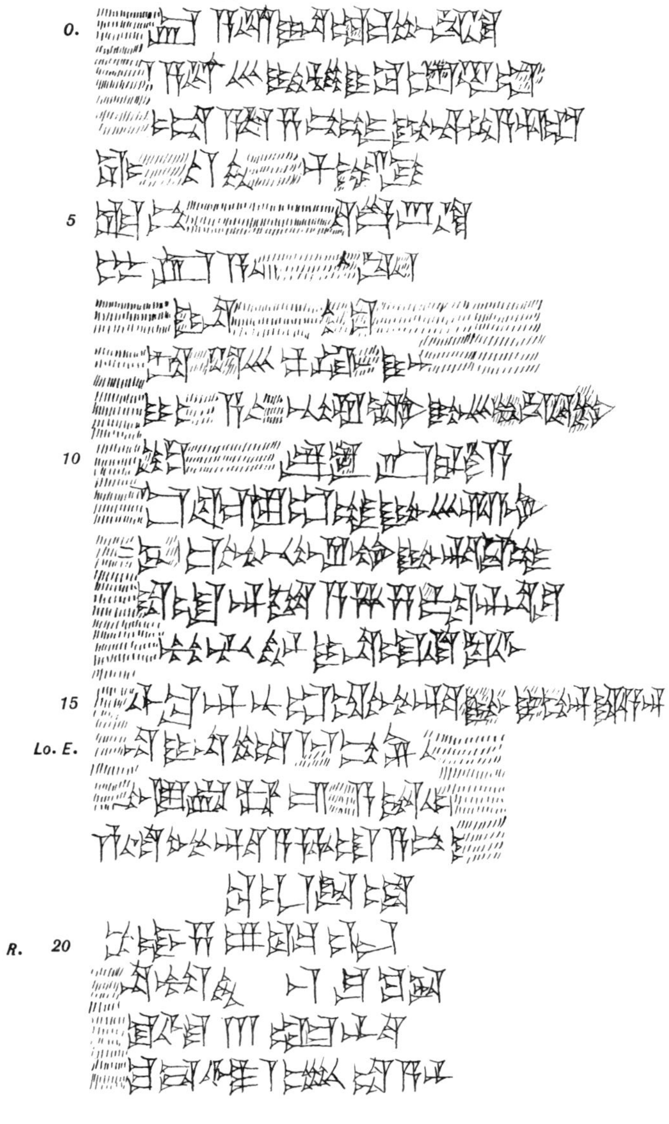

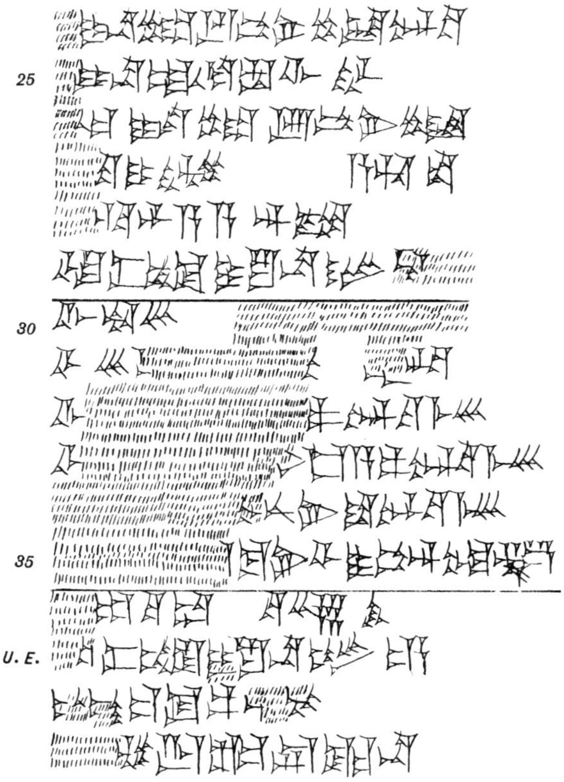

470

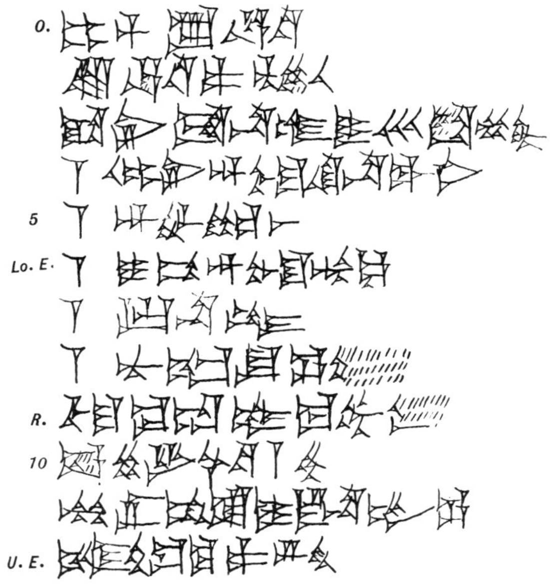

471

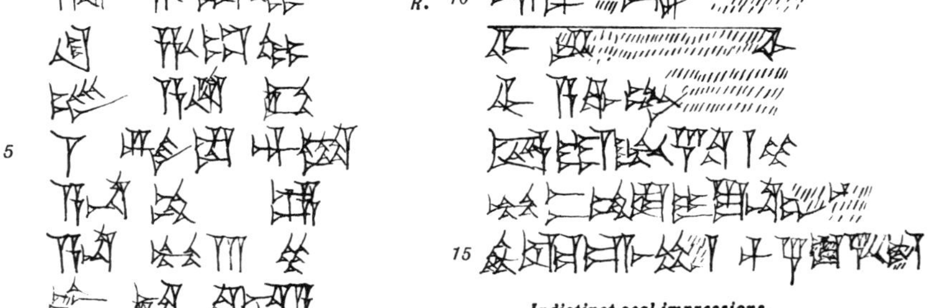

Indistinct seal impressions.

472

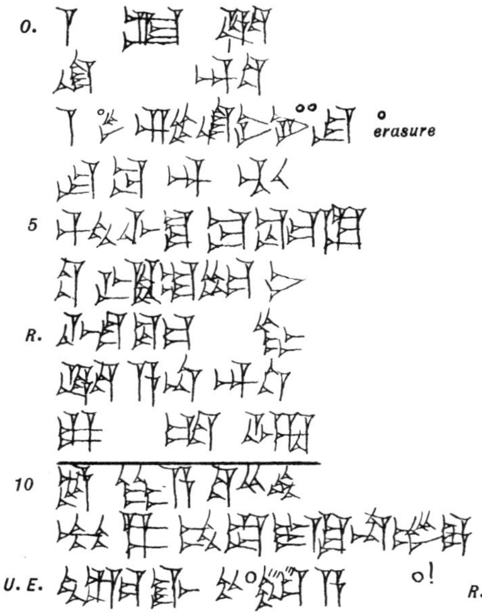

473

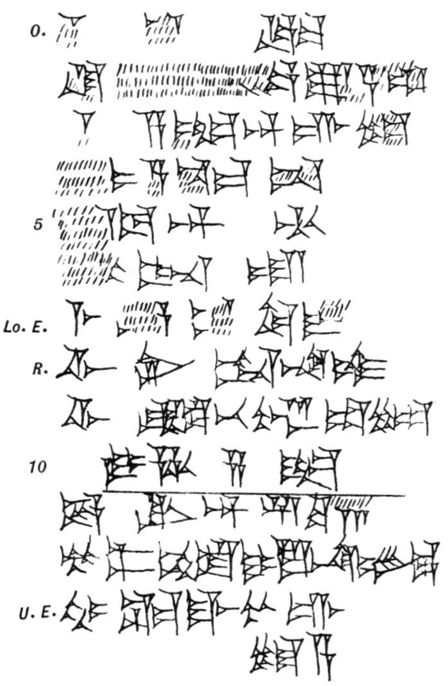

474

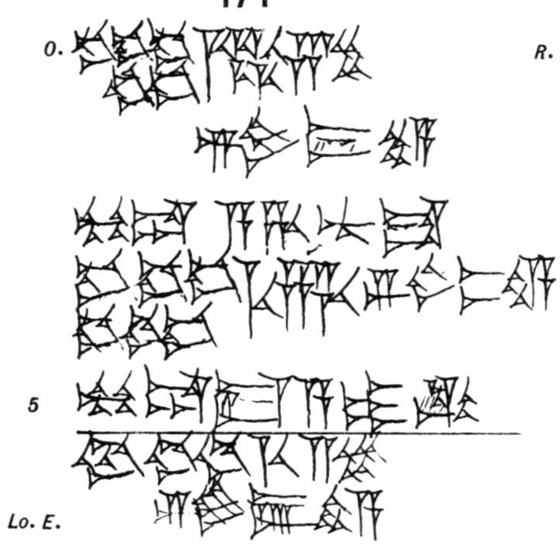

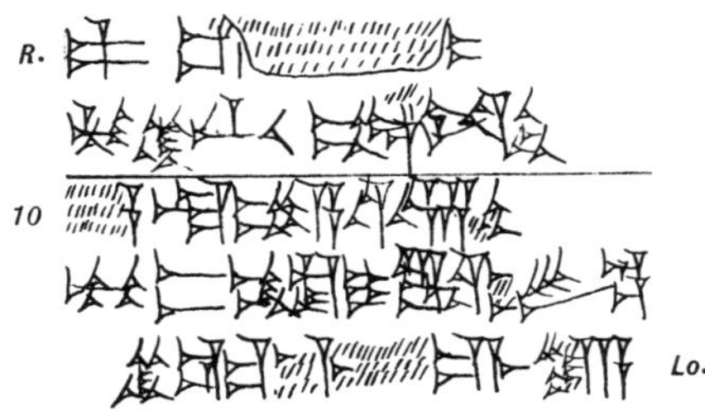

Indistinct seal impressions.

475

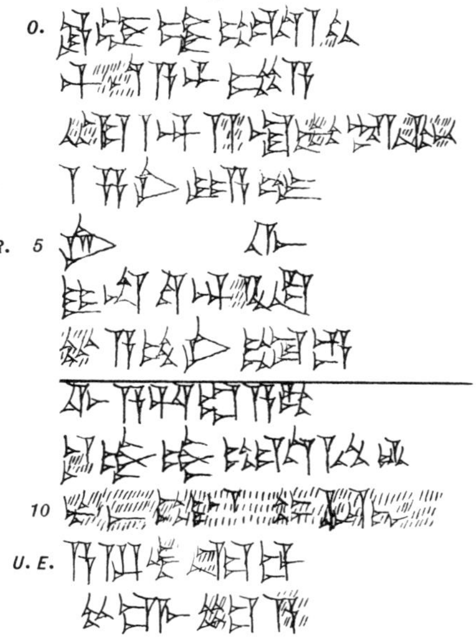

Indistinct seal impressions.

476

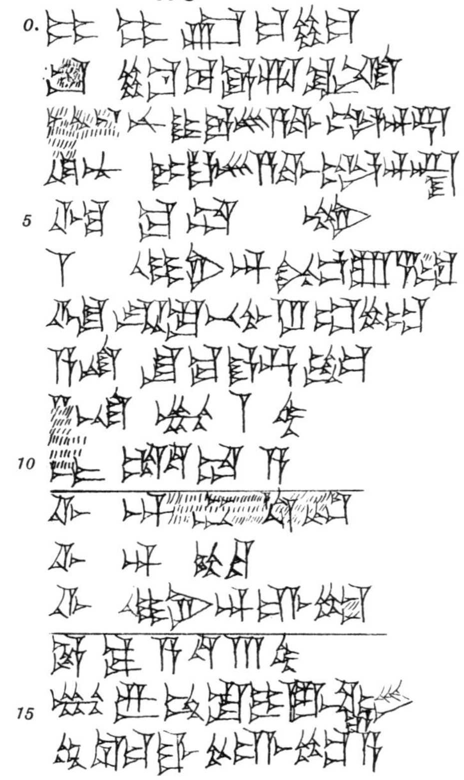

Indistinct seal impressions.

477

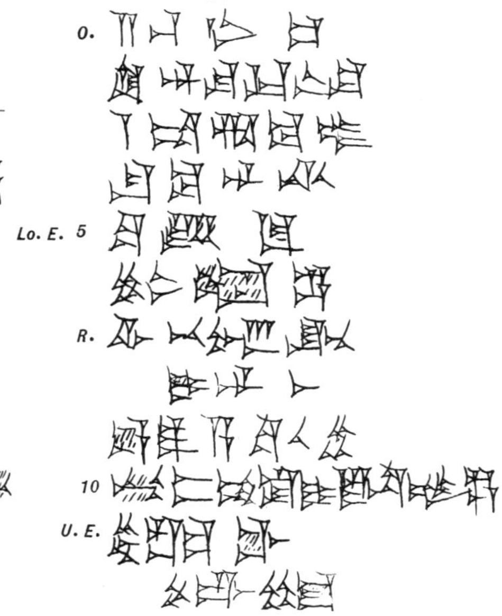

Indistinct seal impressions.

478

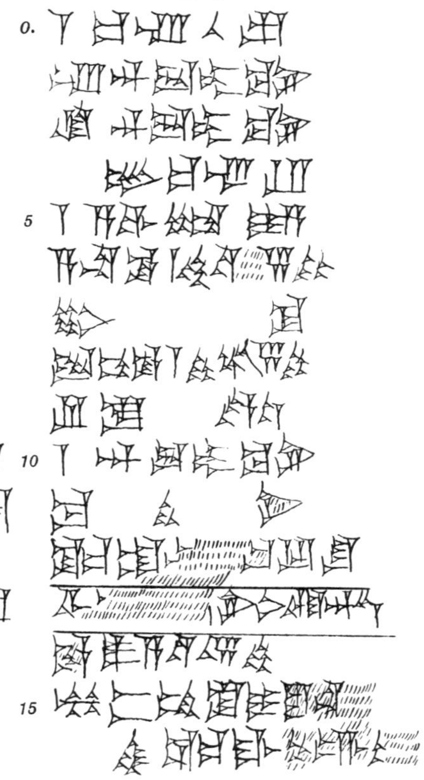

479

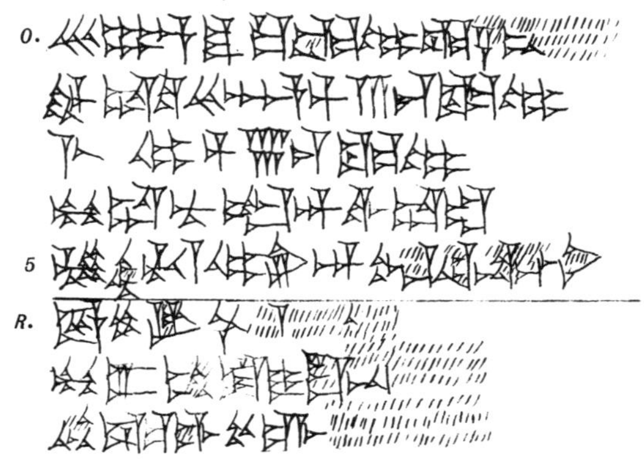

Indistinct seal impressions.

480

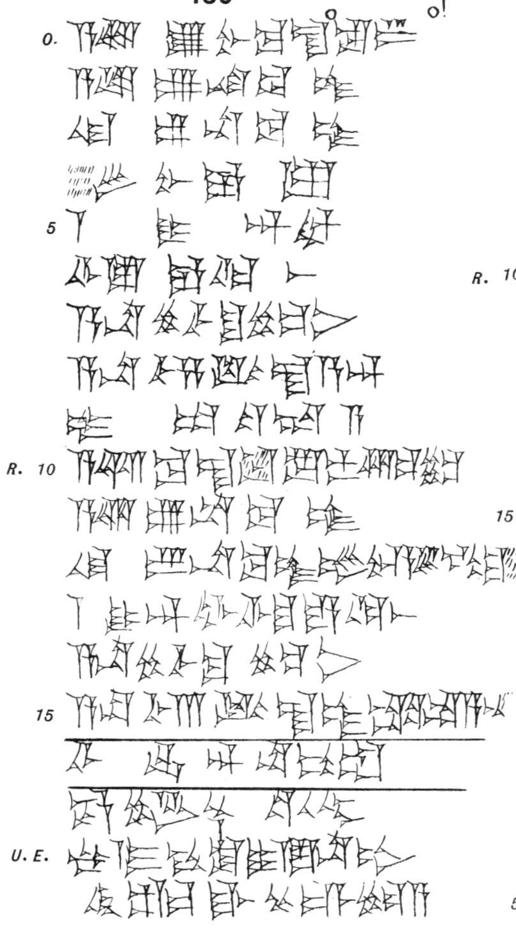

Indistinct seal impressions.

481

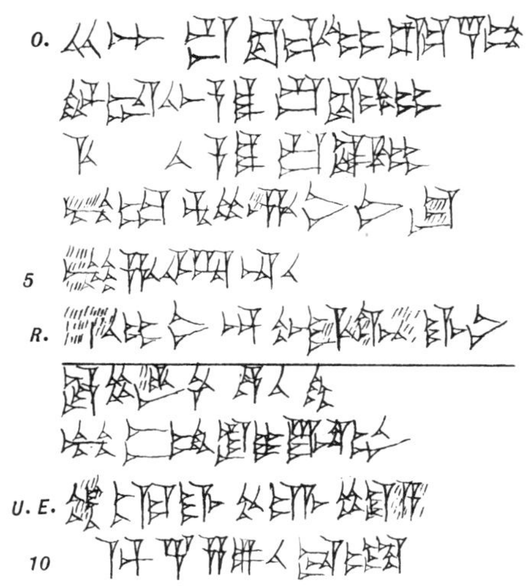

Indistinct seal impressions.

482

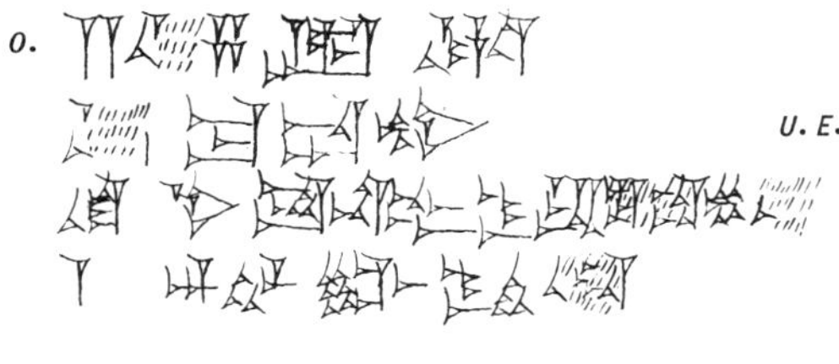

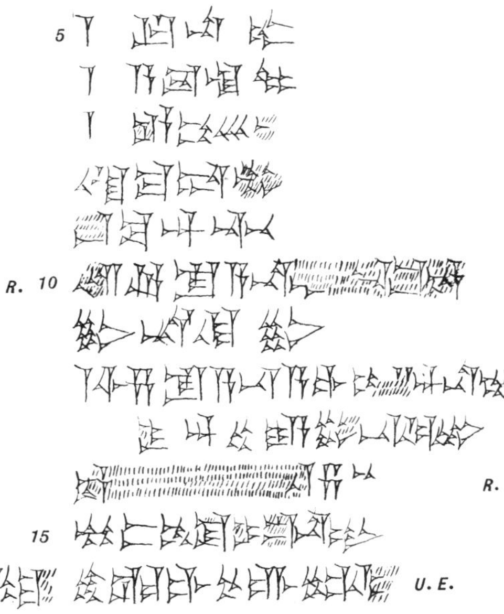

Indistinct seal impressic

483

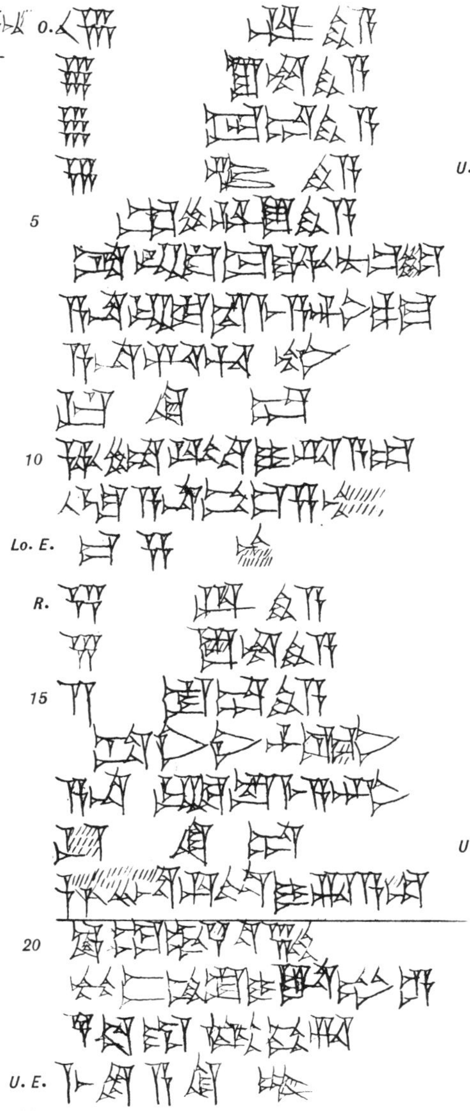

Indistinct seal impressions.

484

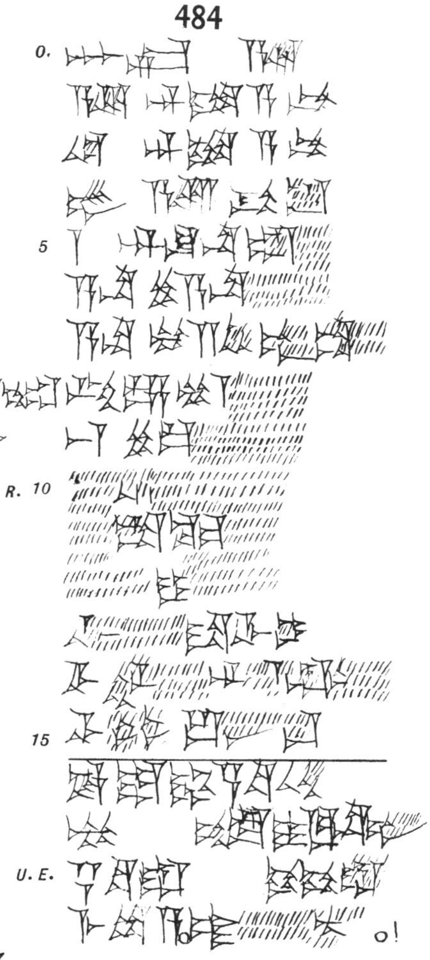

Indistinct seal impressions.

485

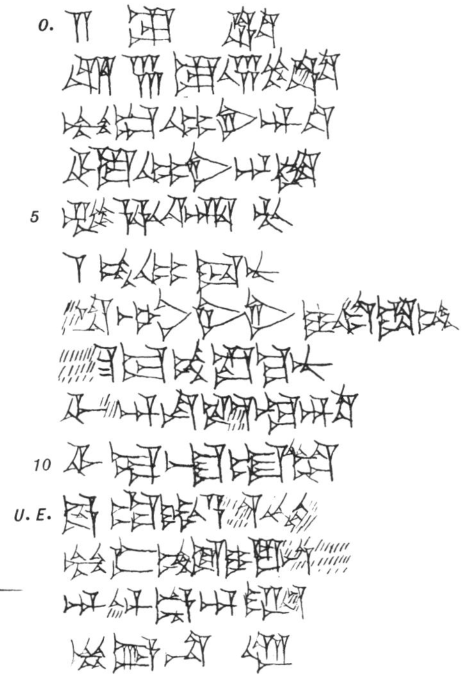

Indistinct seal impressions.

486

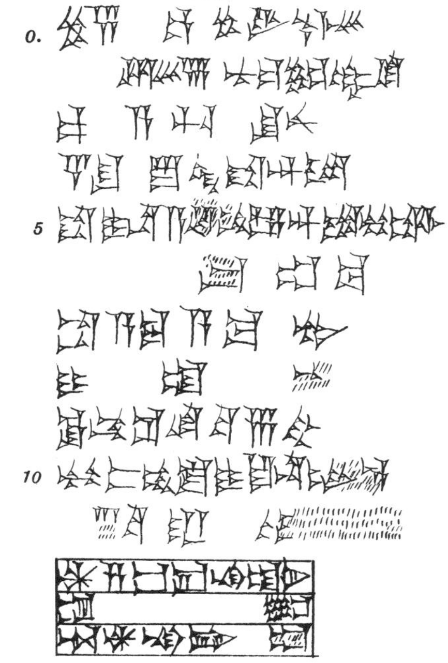

487

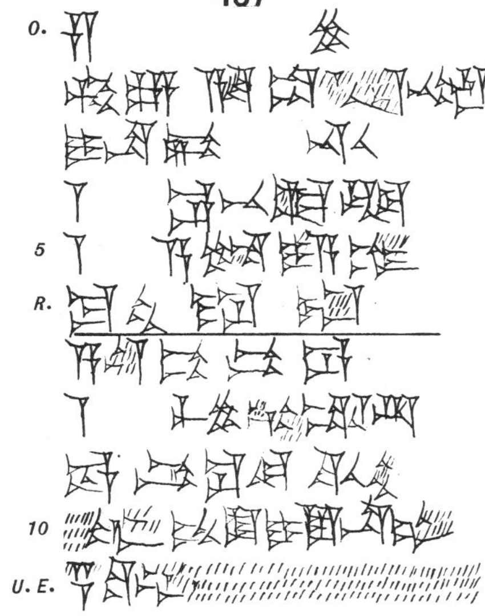

488

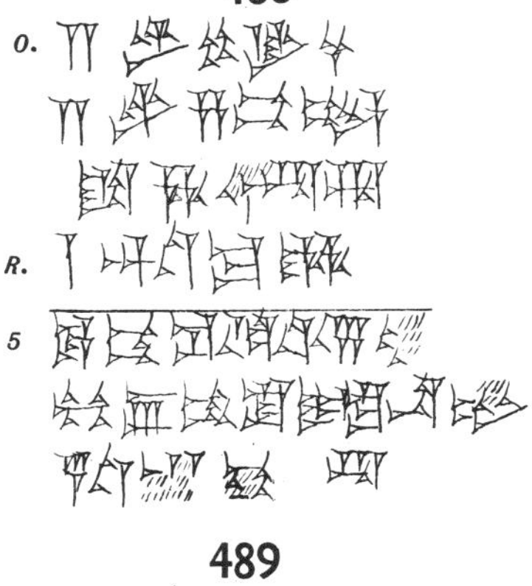

489

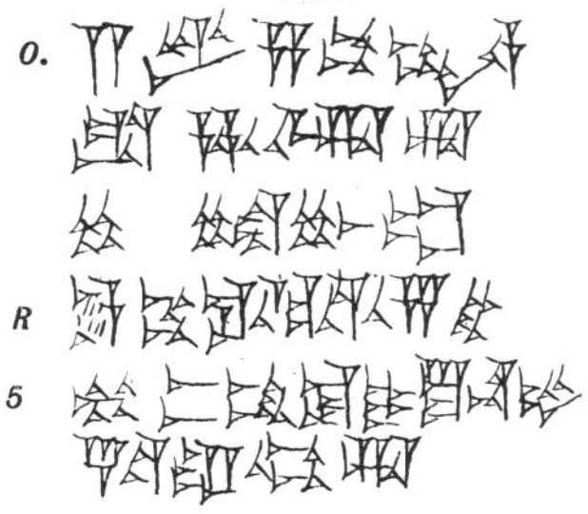

490

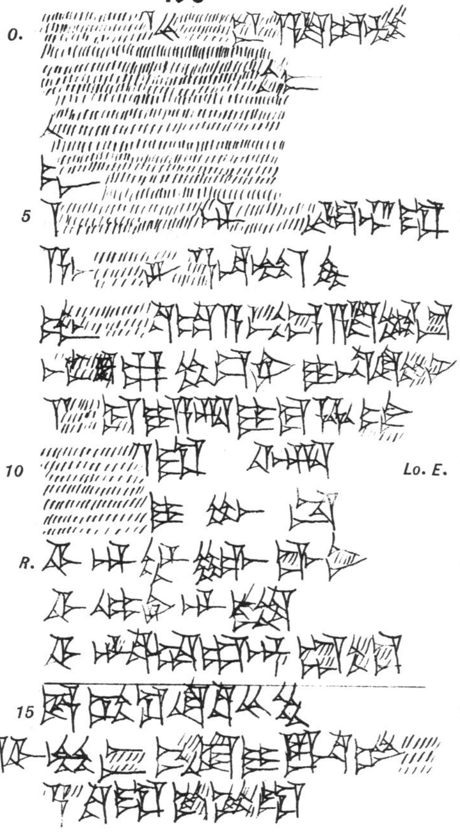

491

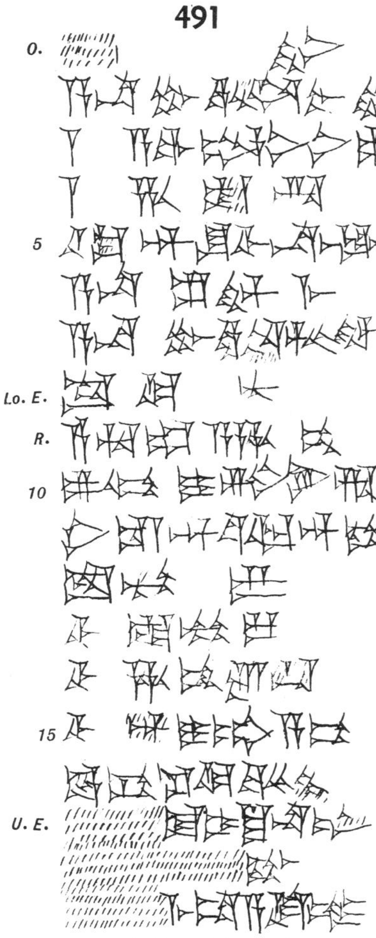

Indistinct seal impressions.

492

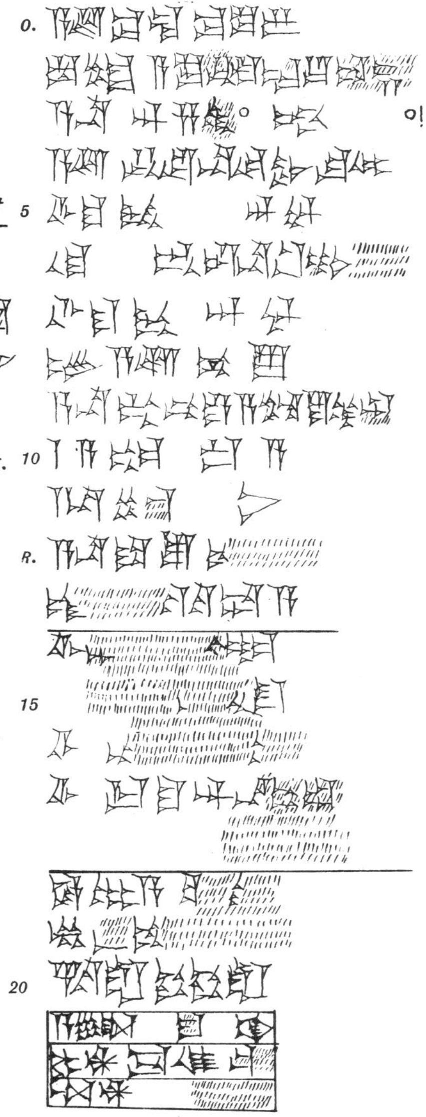

493

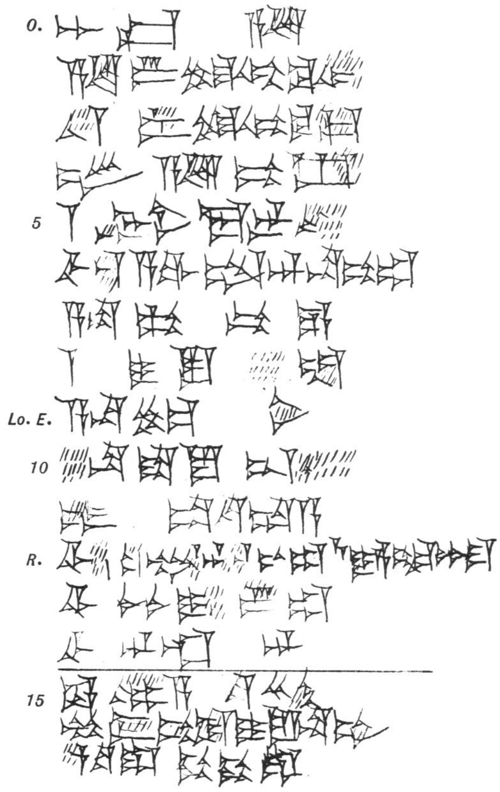

494

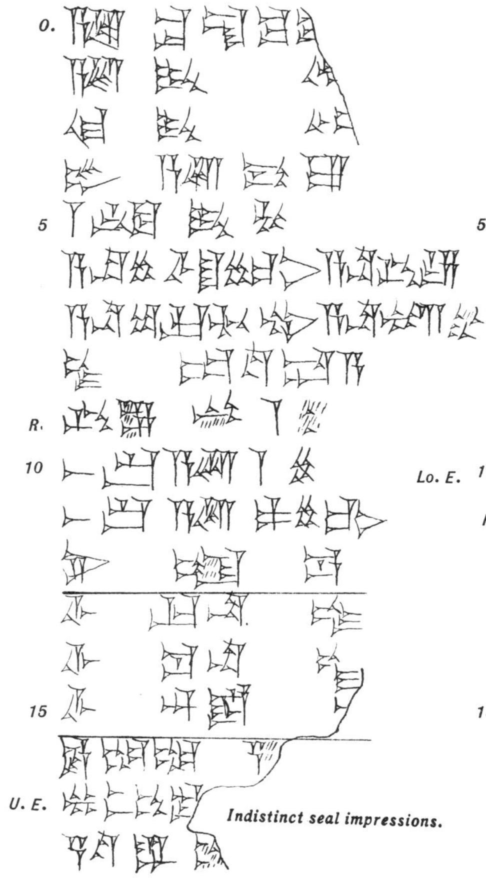

Indistinct seal impressions.

495

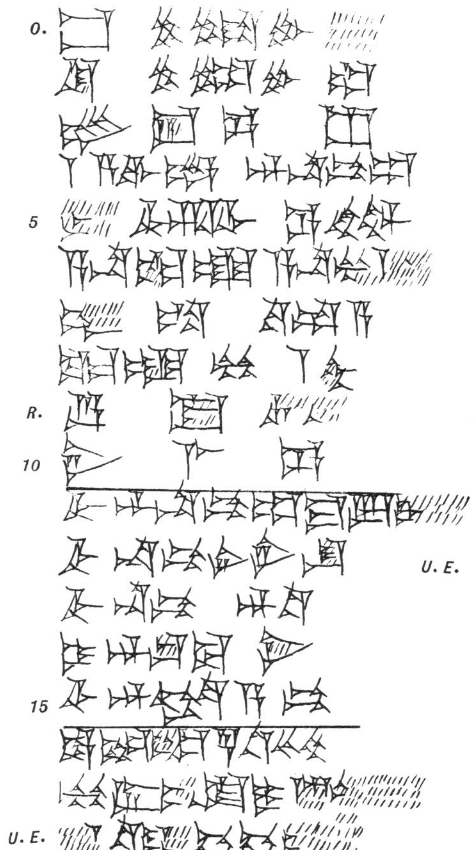

Indistinct seal impressions.

496

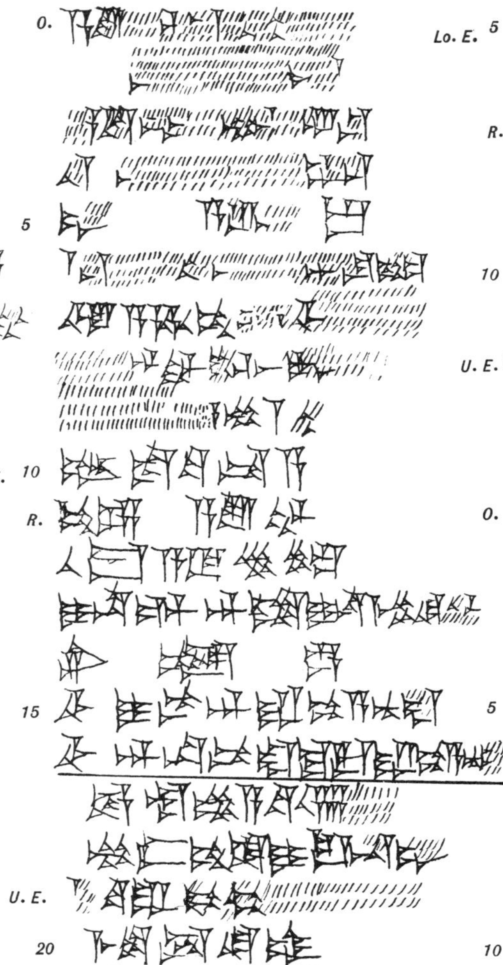

Indistinct seal impressions.

497

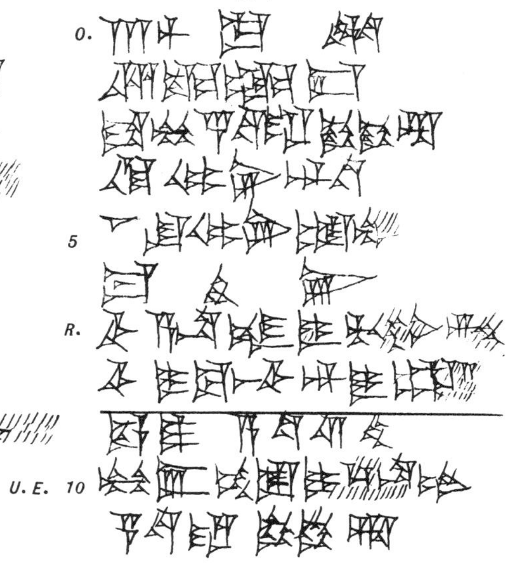

498

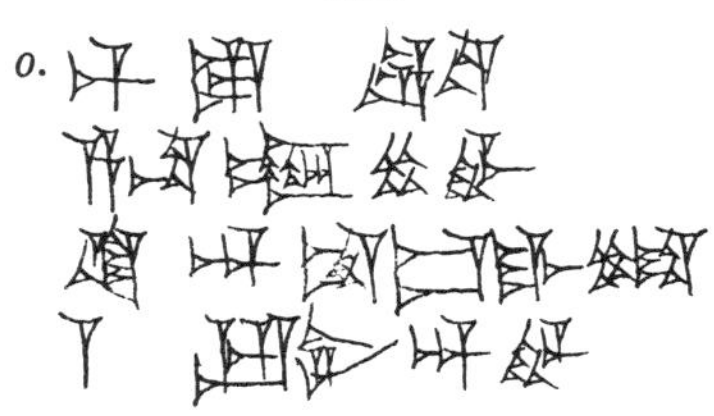

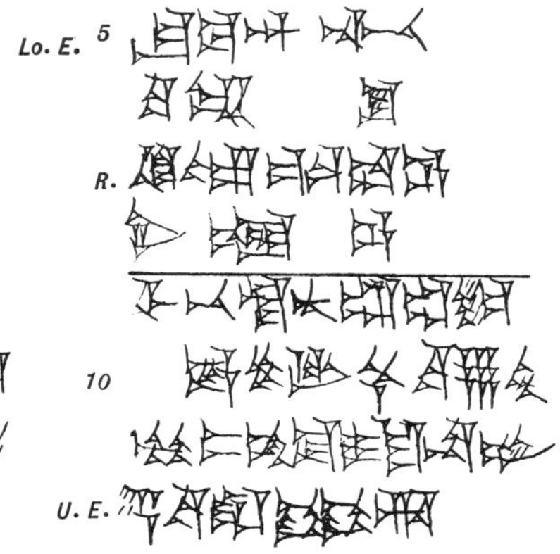

Indistinct seal impressions.

499

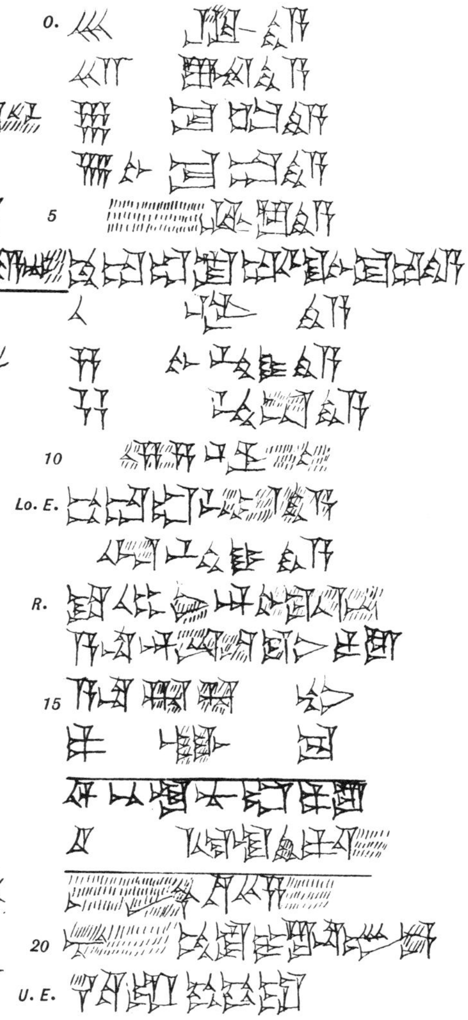

500

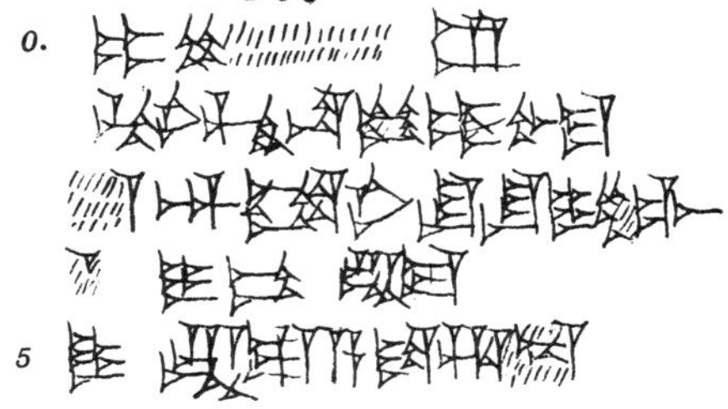

500 CONTINUED

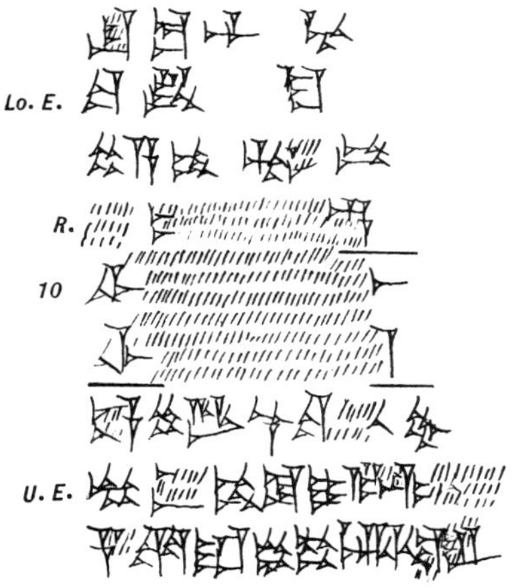

501

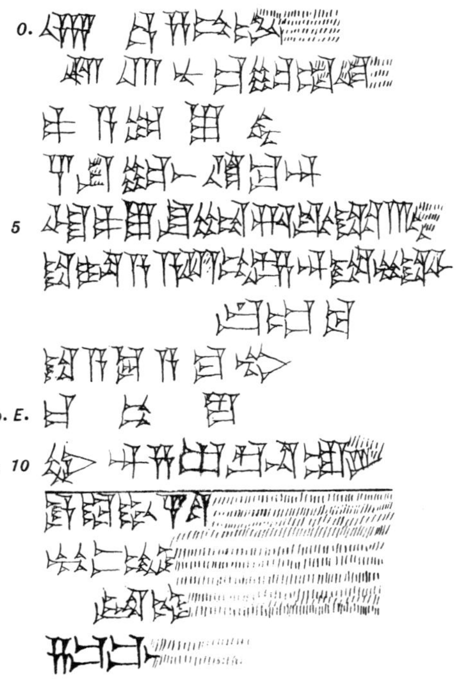

502

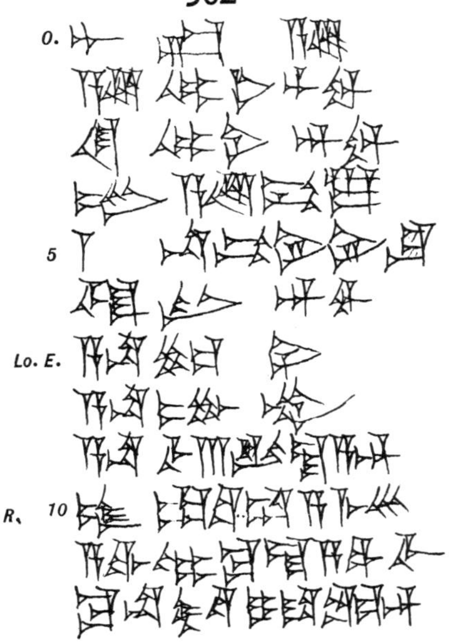

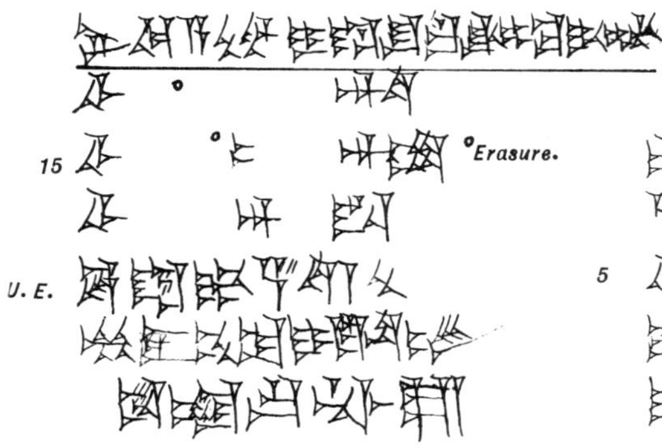

503

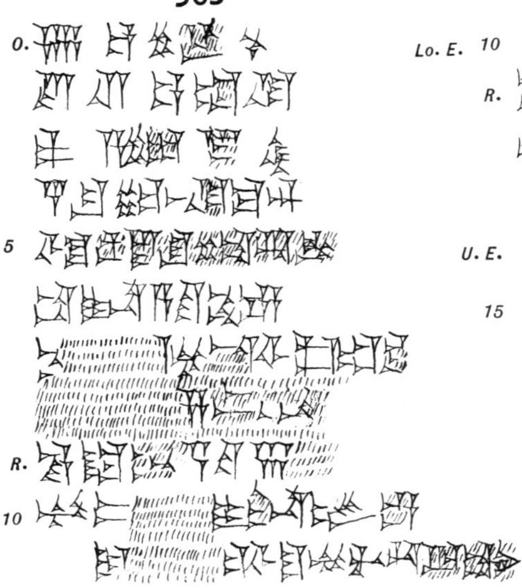

Indistinct seal impressions.

504

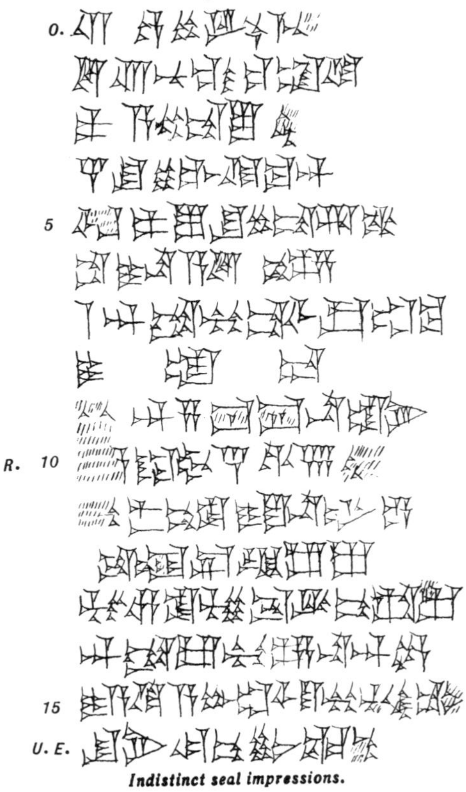

Indistinct seal impressions.

505

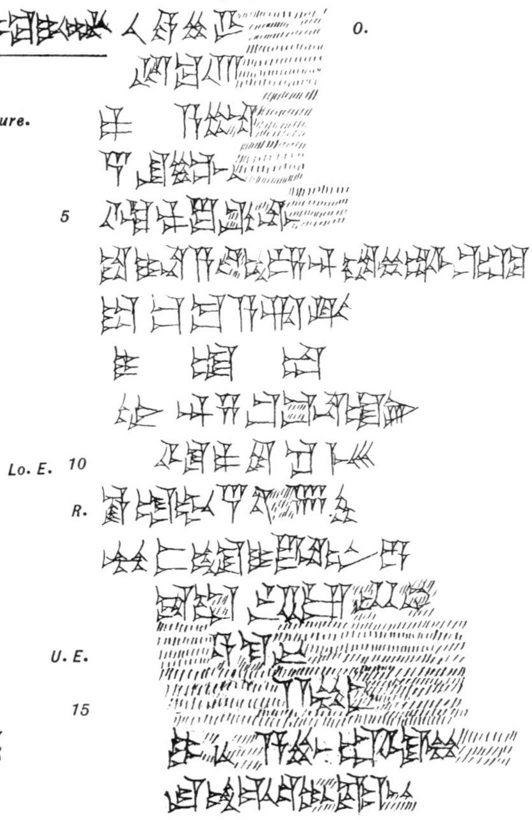

Indistinct seal impressions.

506

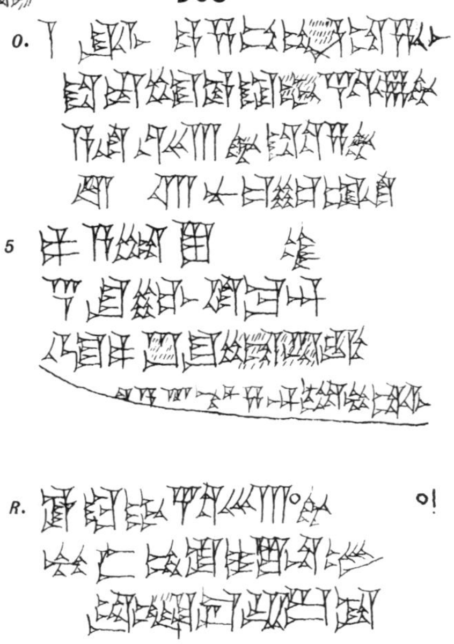

Indistinct seal impressions.

507

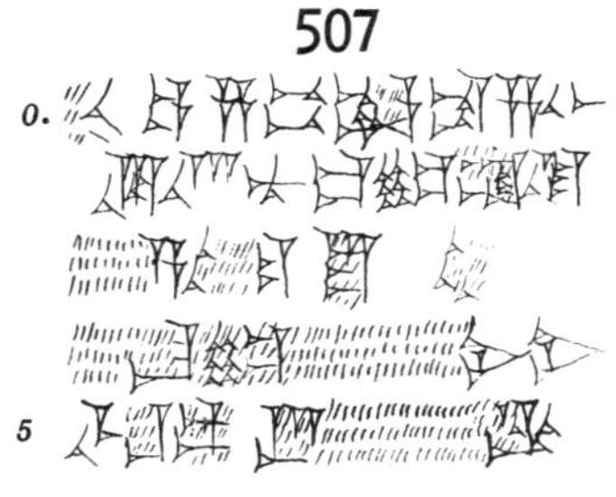

507 CONTINUED

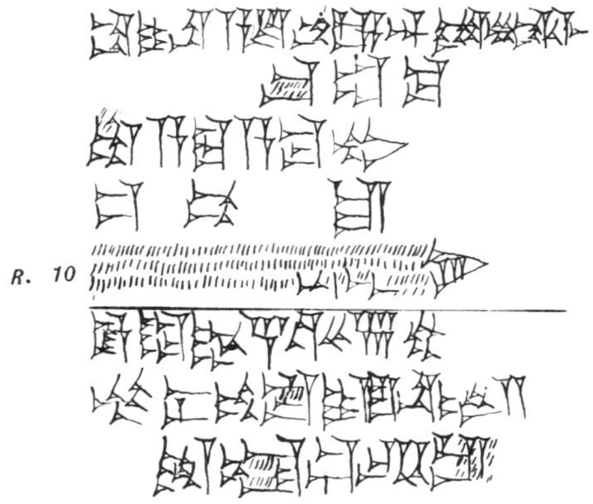

Indistinct seal impressions.

508

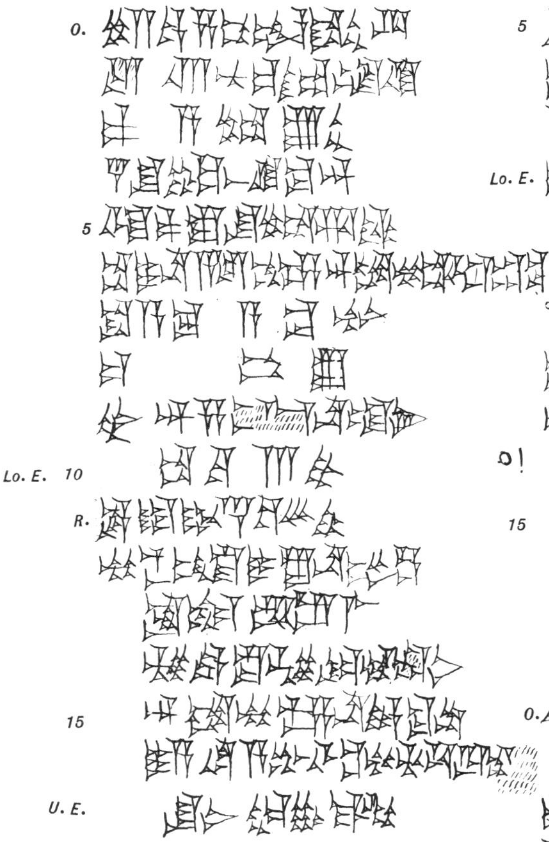

Indistinct seal impressions.

509

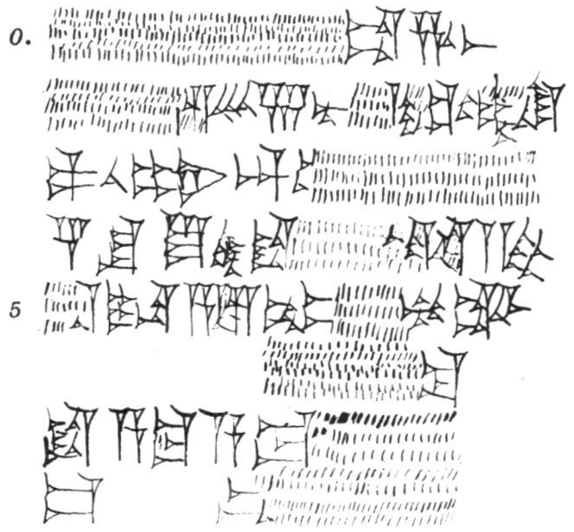

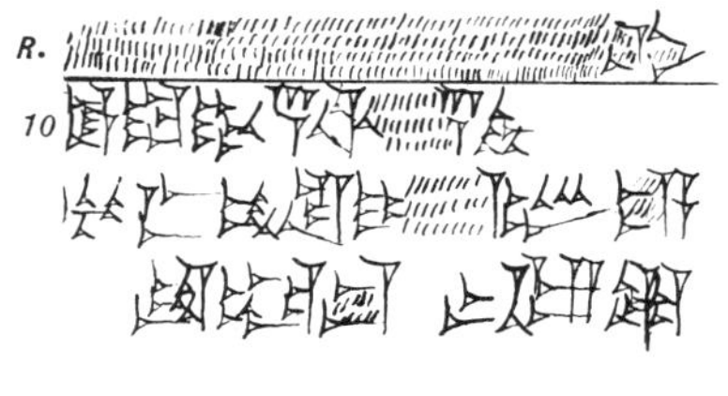

Indistinct seal impressions.

510

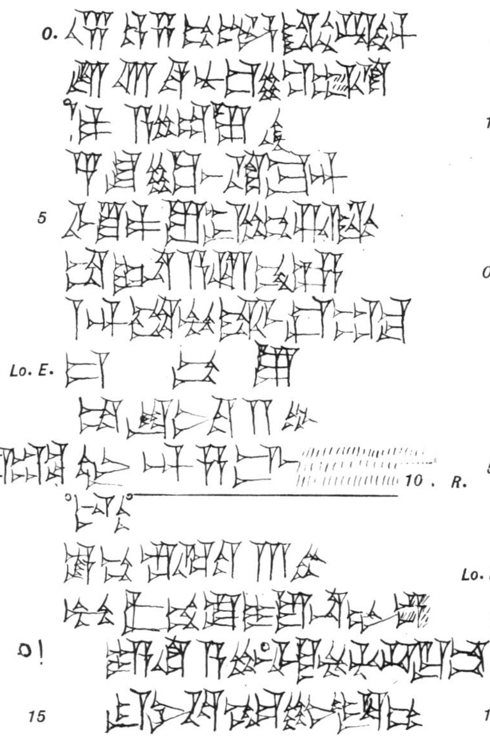

Indistinct seal impressions.

511

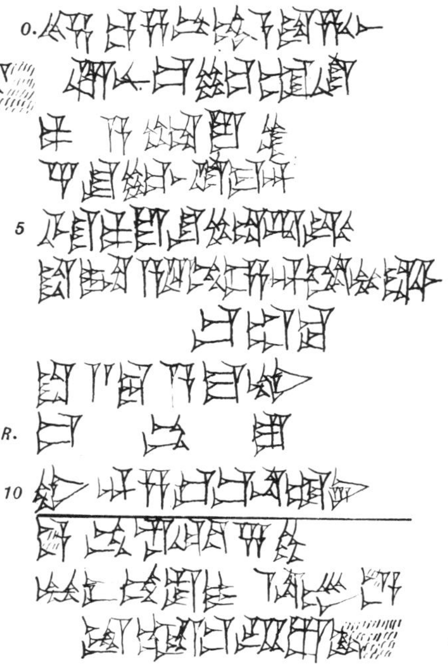

Indistinct seal impressions.

512

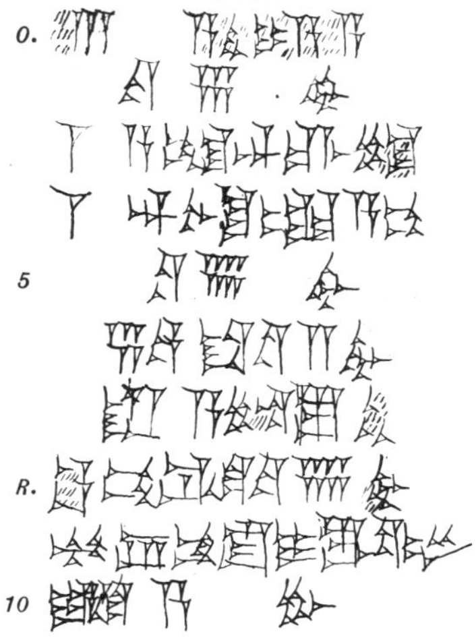

513

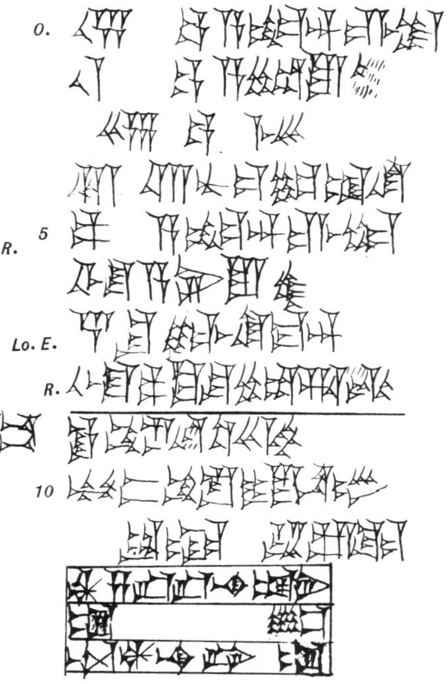

514

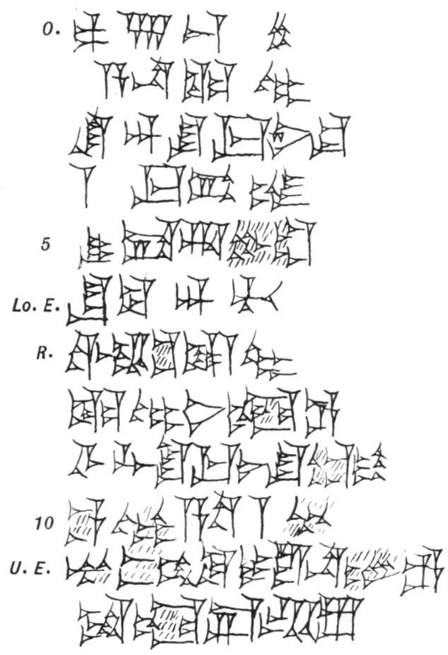

515

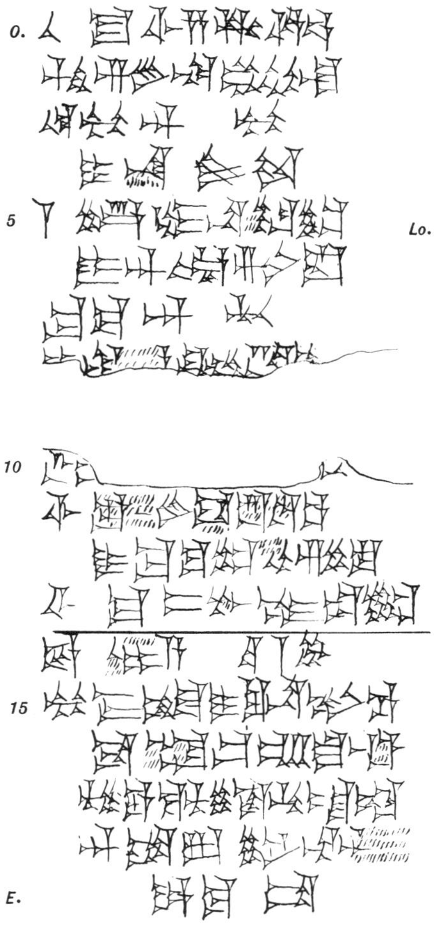

516

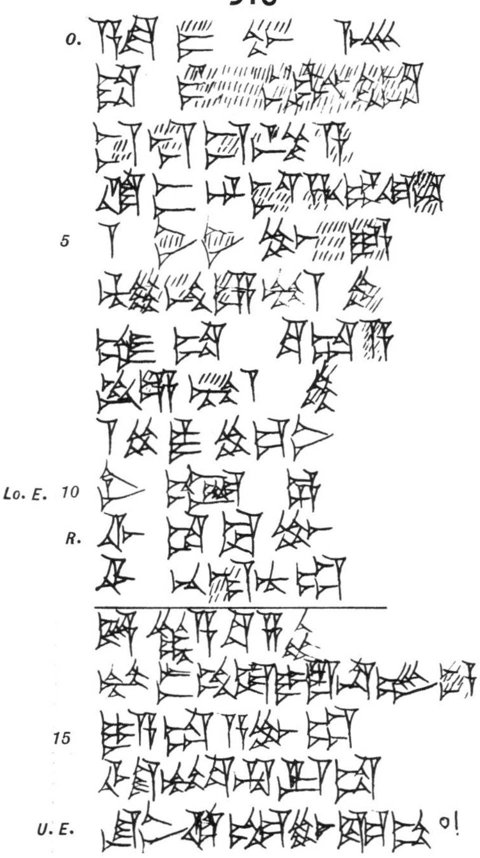

Indistinct seal impressions.

517

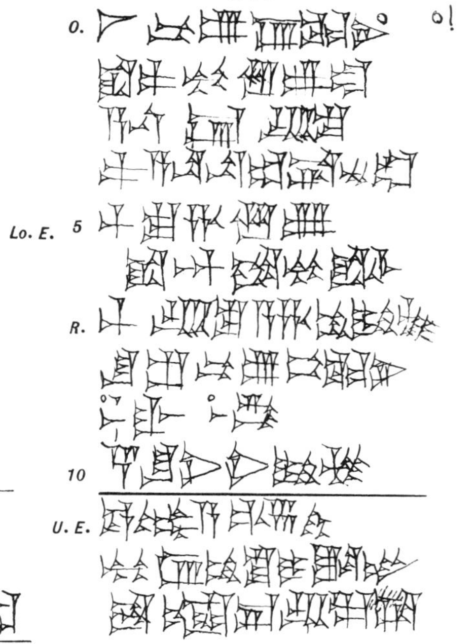

518

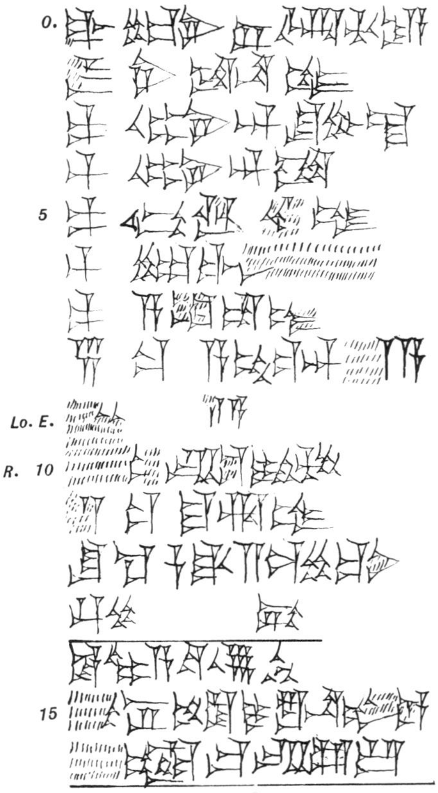

519

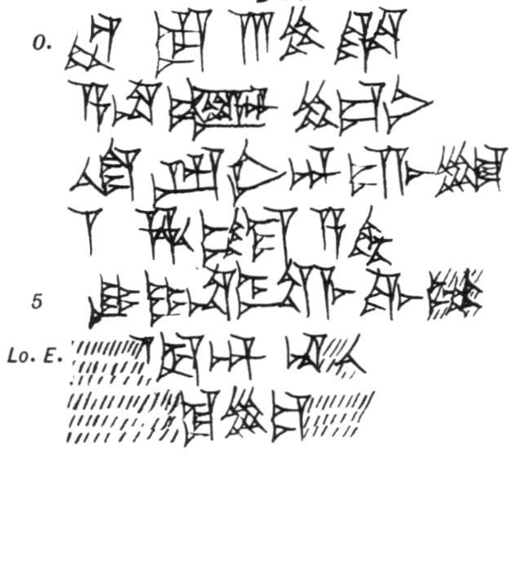

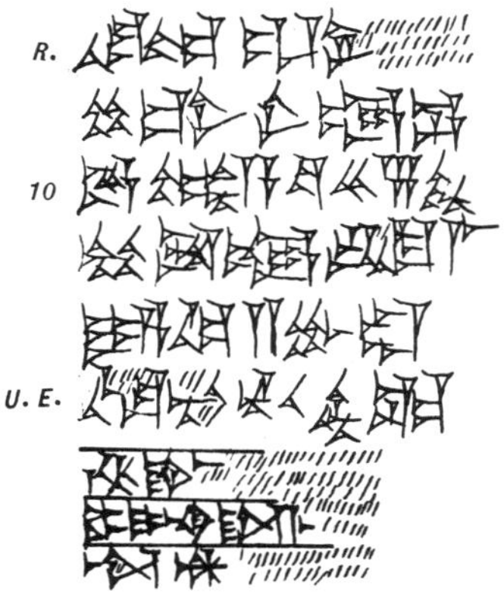

520

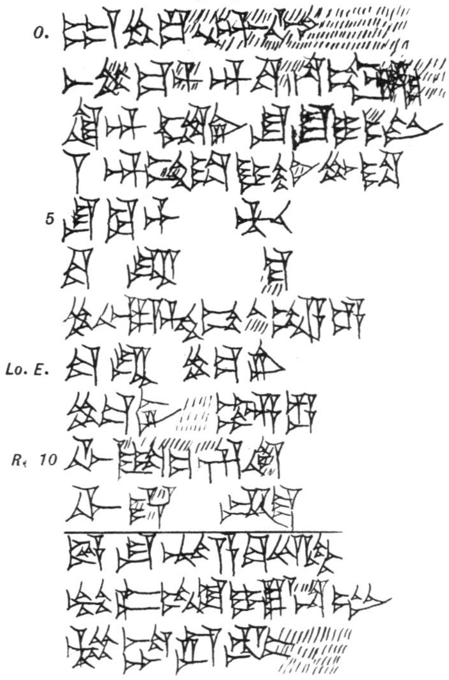

521

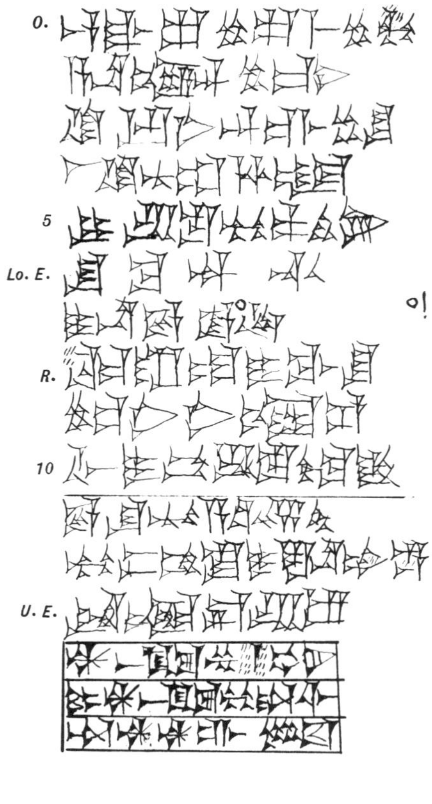

522

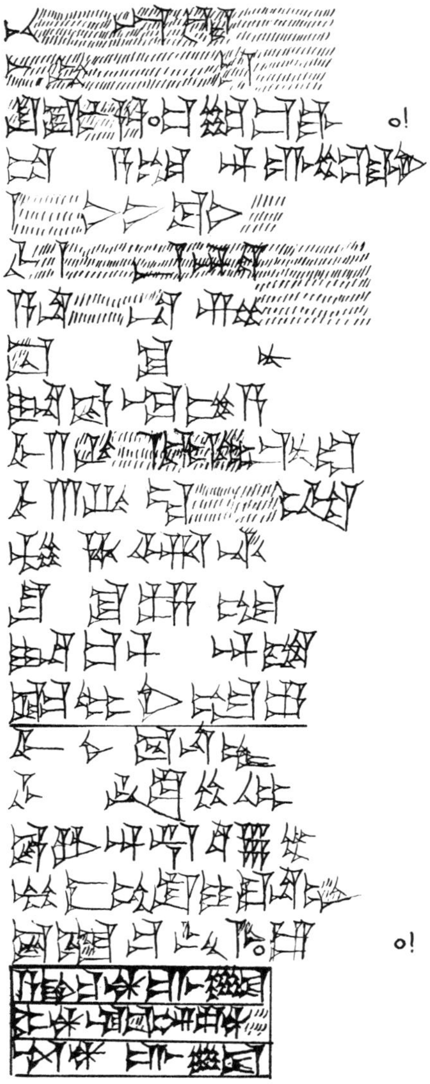

523

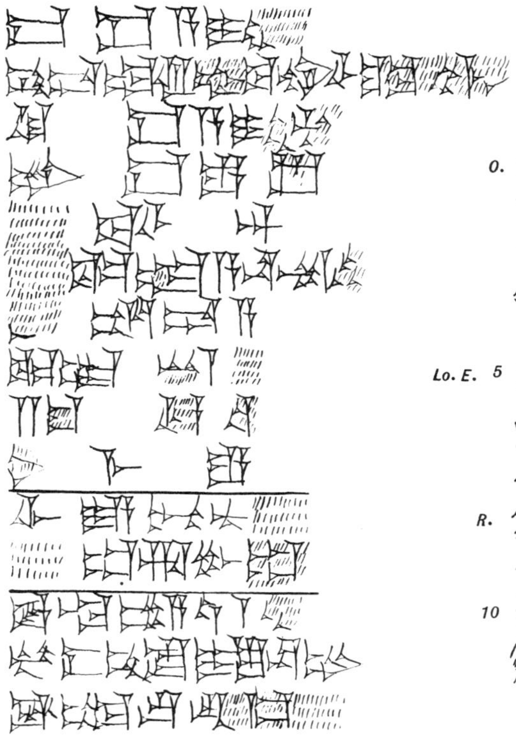

524

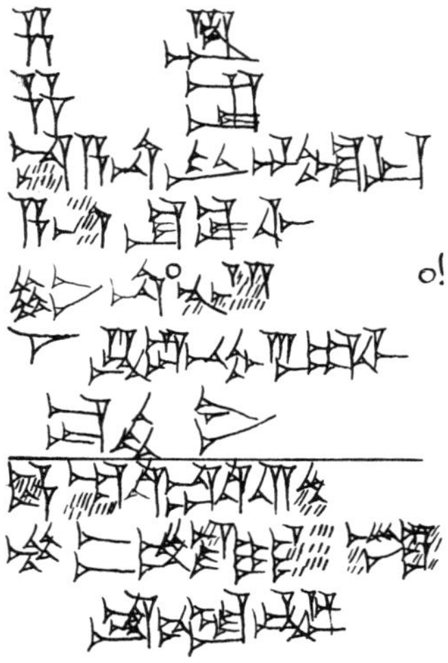

Indistinct seal impressions.

525

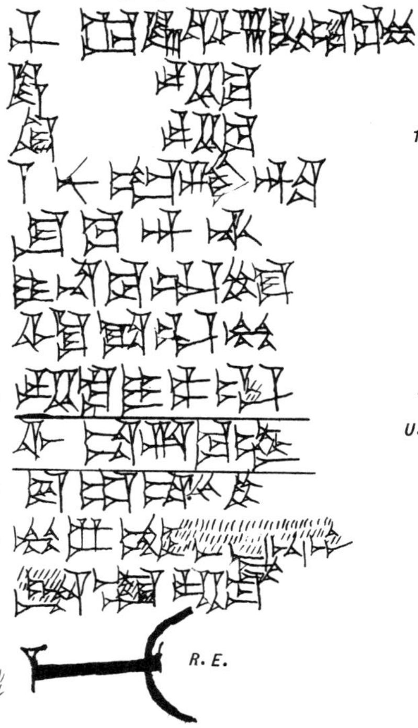

526

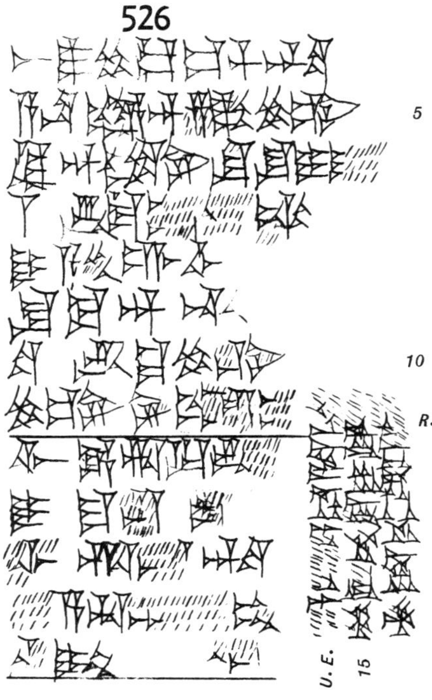

527

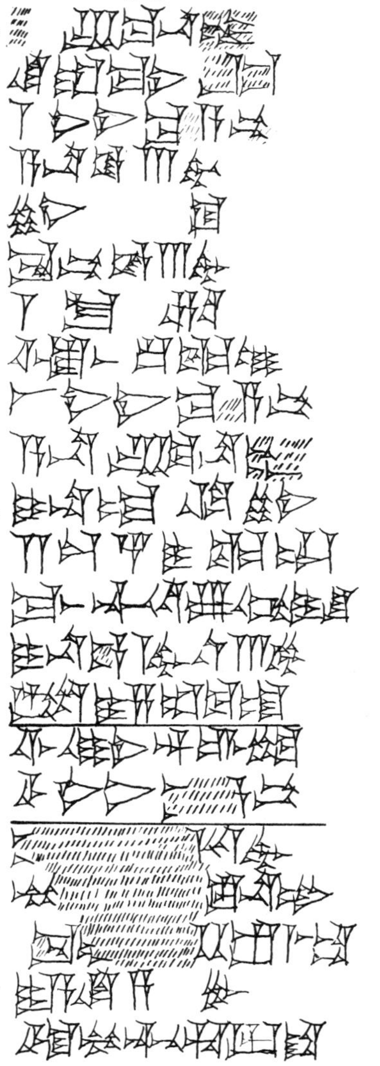

Indistinct seal impressions.

528

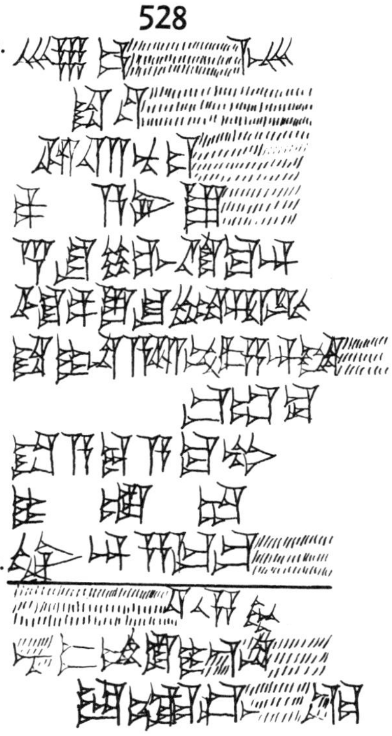

Indistinct seal impressions.

529

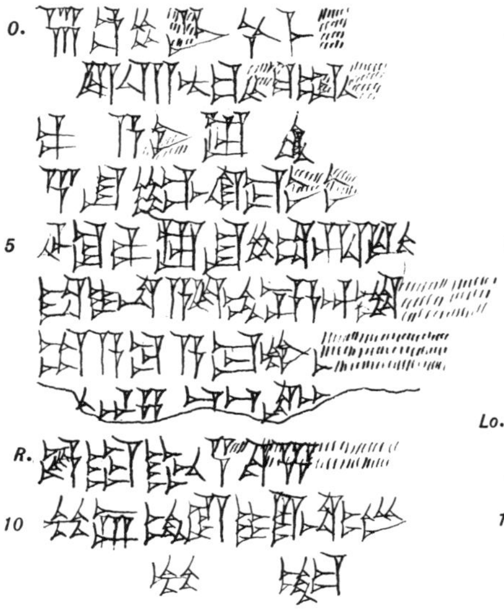

Indistinct seal impressions.

530

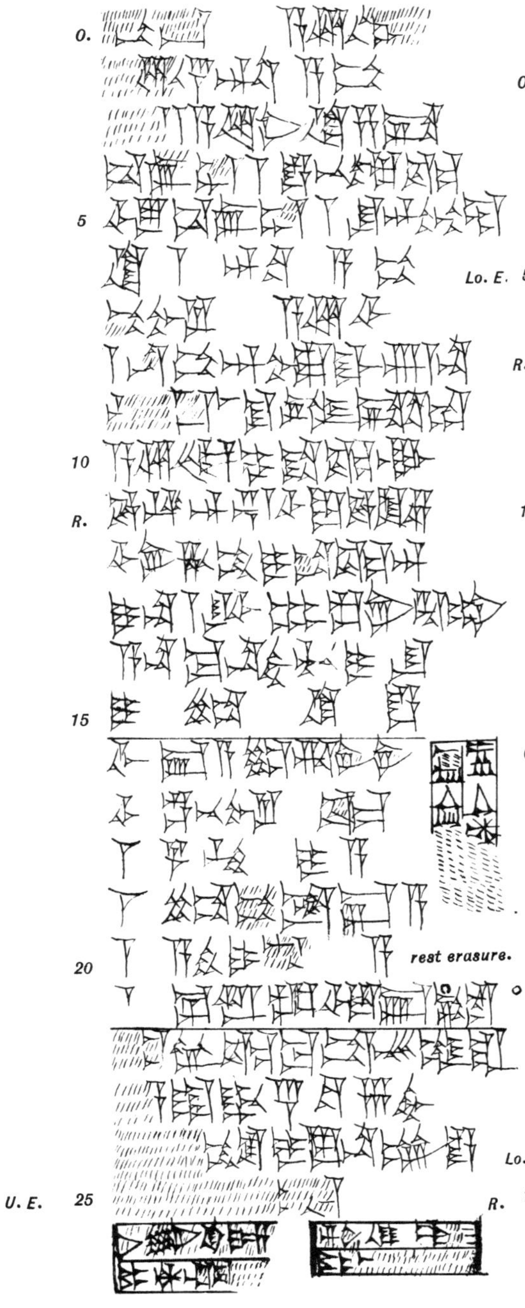

rest erasure.

531

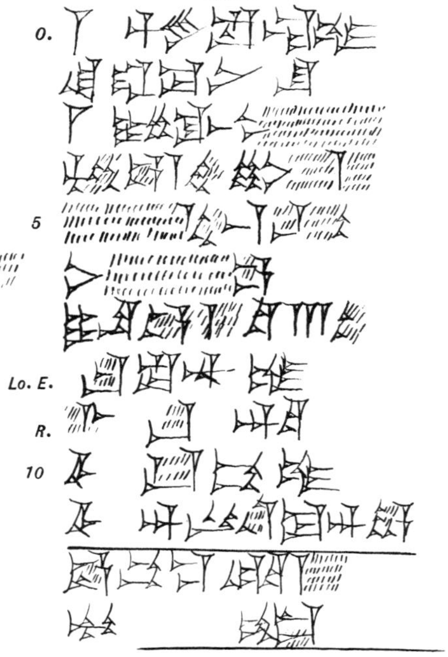

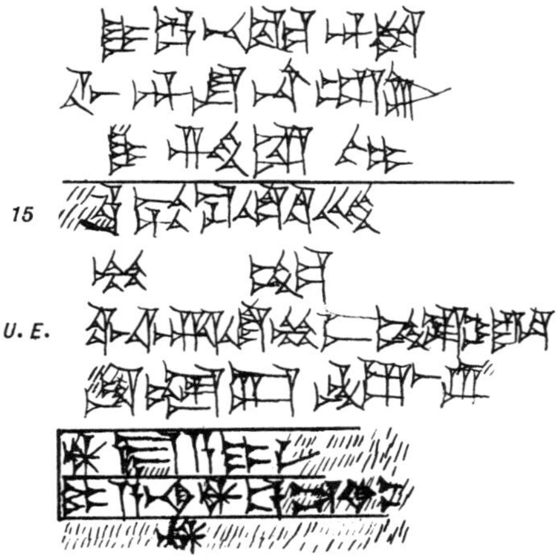

532

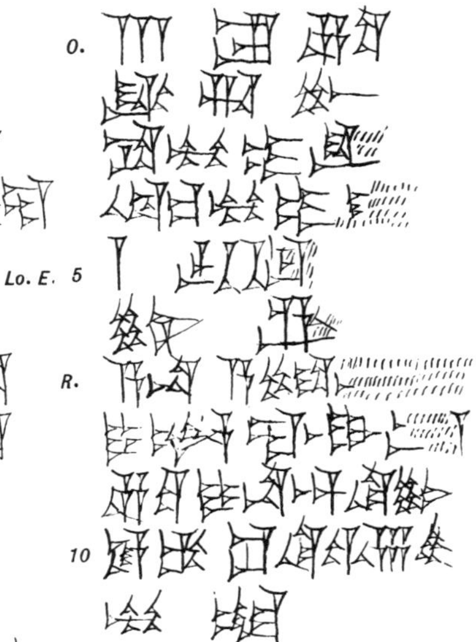

Indistinct seal impressions.

533

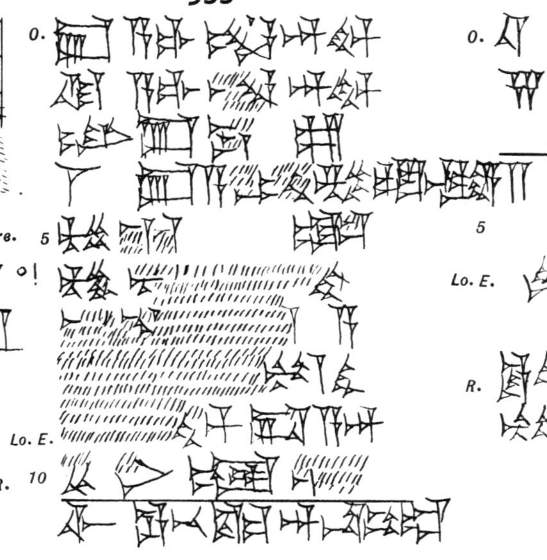

534

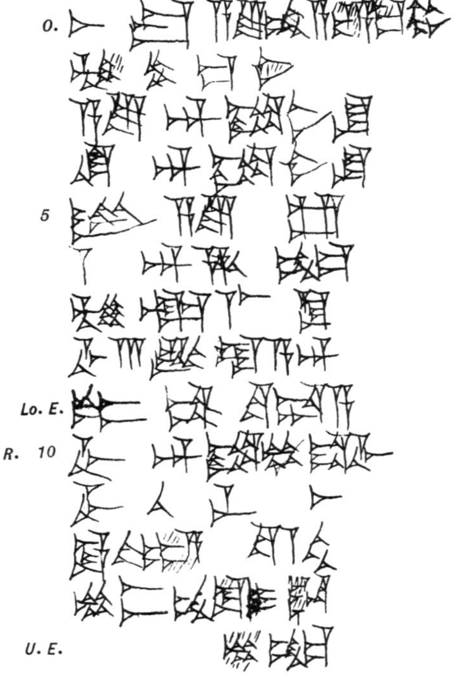

Indistinct seal impressions.

535

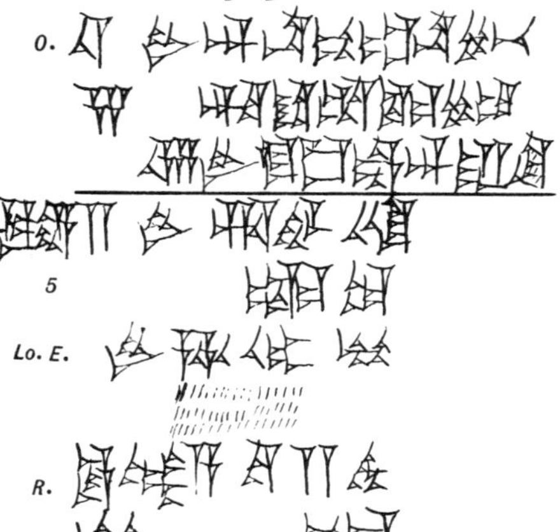

536 CASE

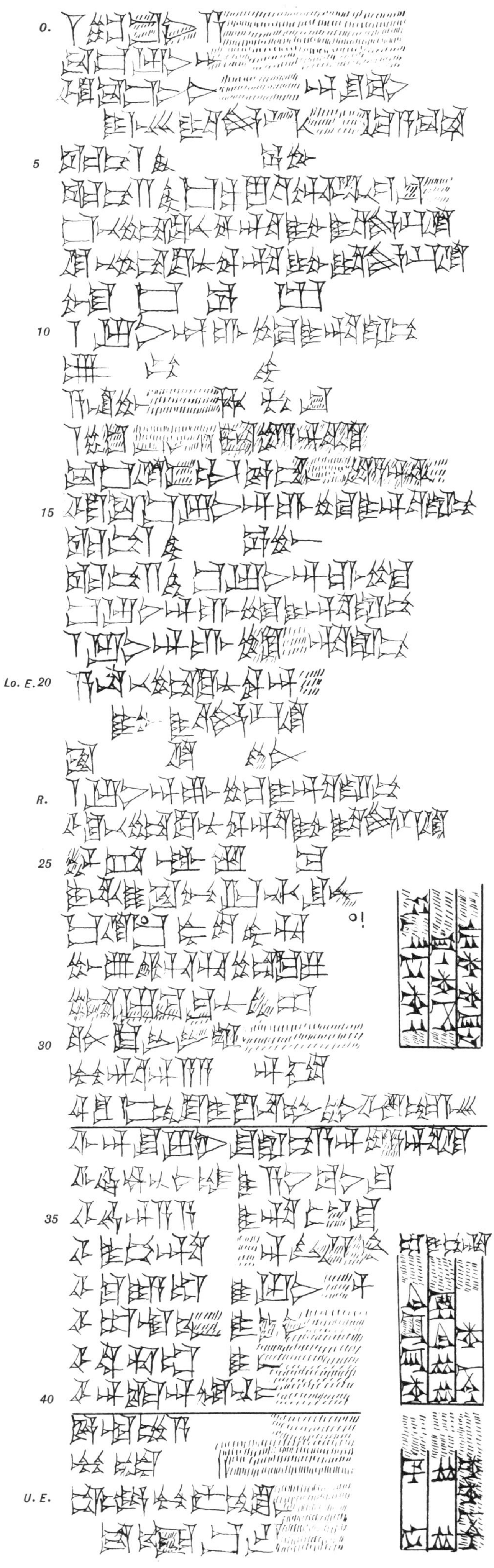

TABLET 537

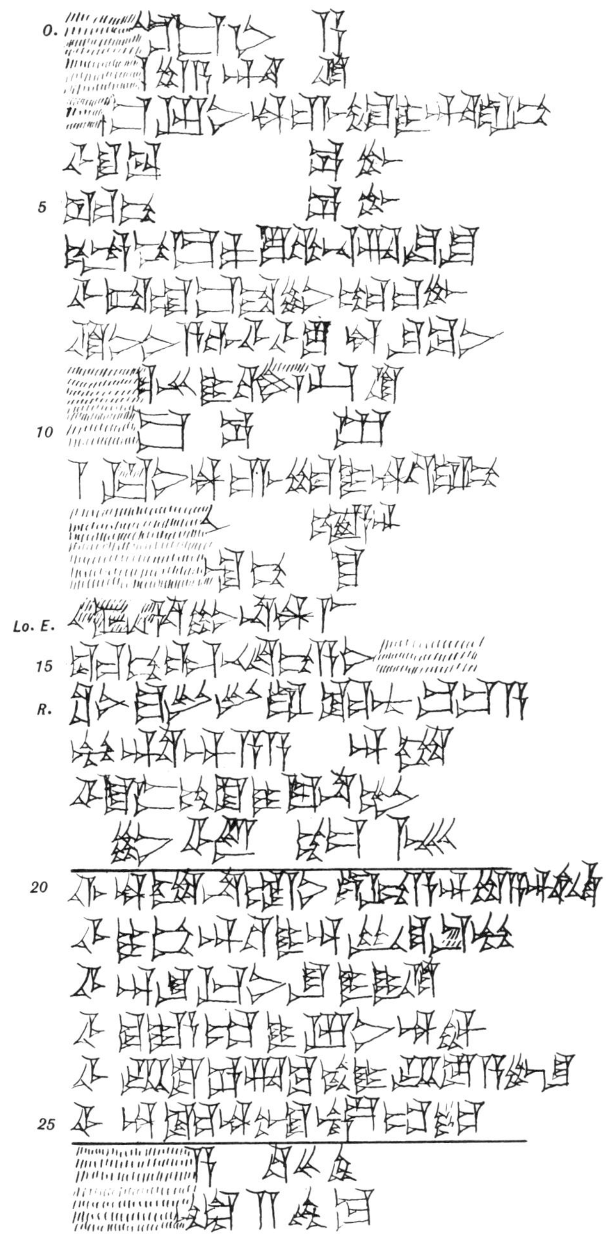

CASE

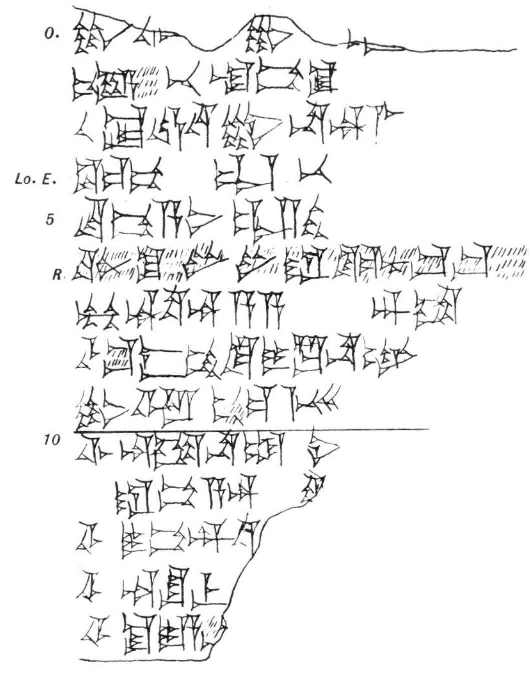

538

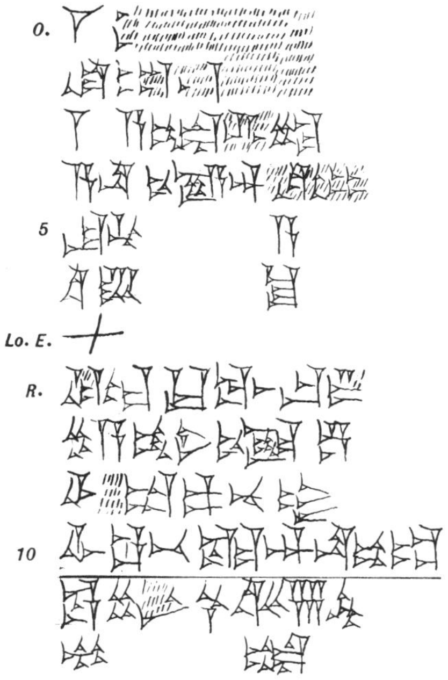

Indistinct seal impressions.

539

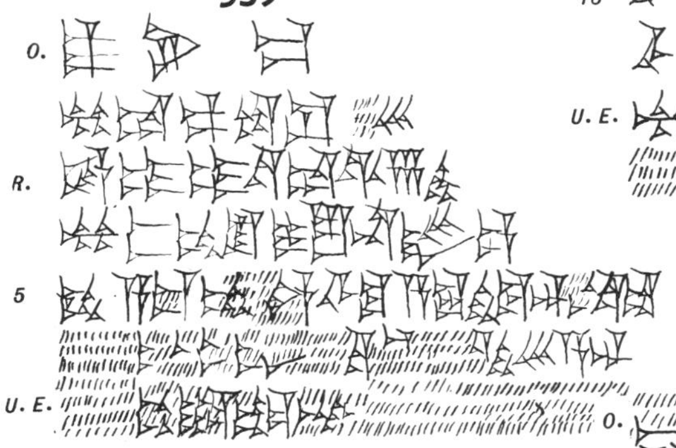

Indistinct seal impressions.

540

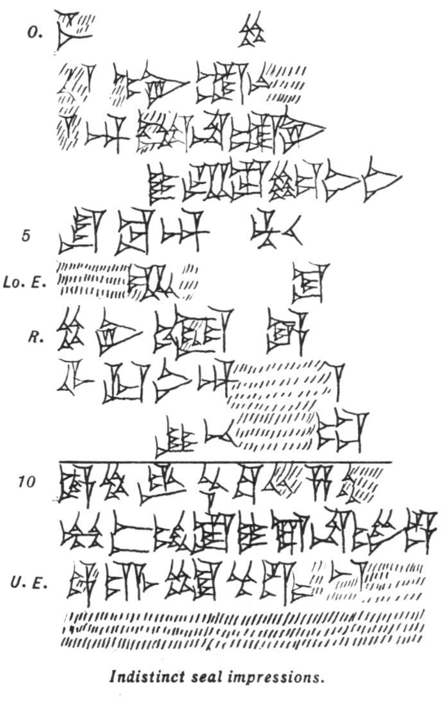

Indistinct seal impressions.

541

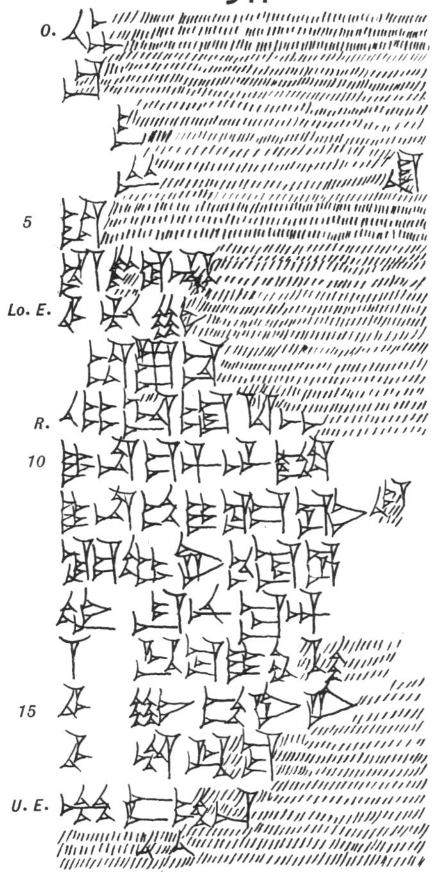

Indistinct seal impressions.

542

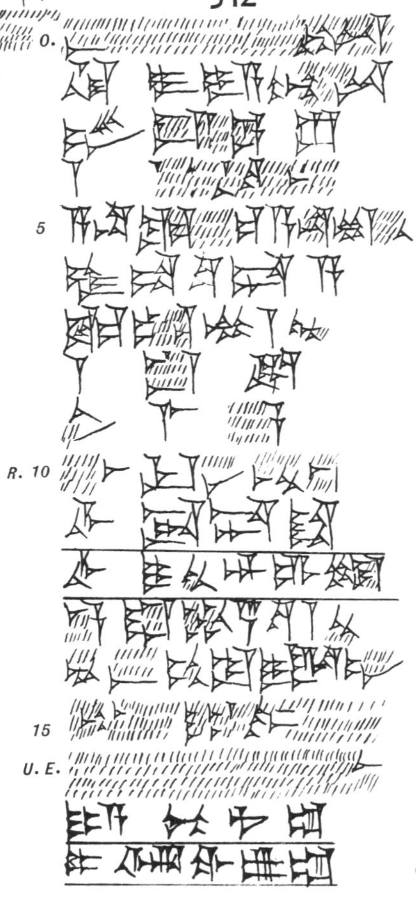

543

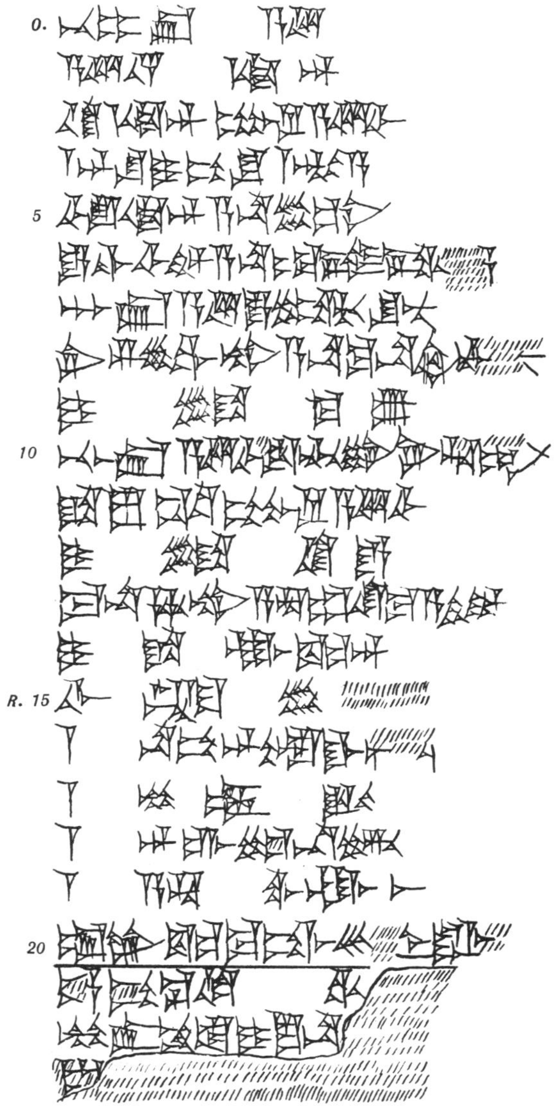

544

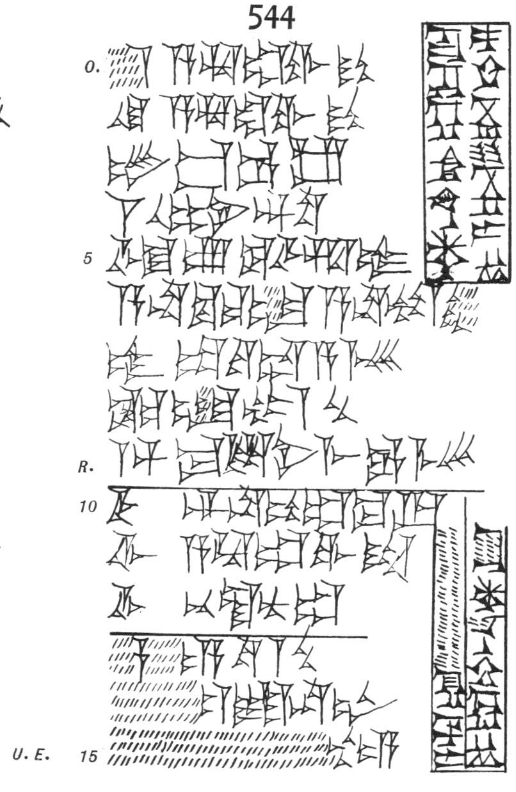

PLATE XCIV

545

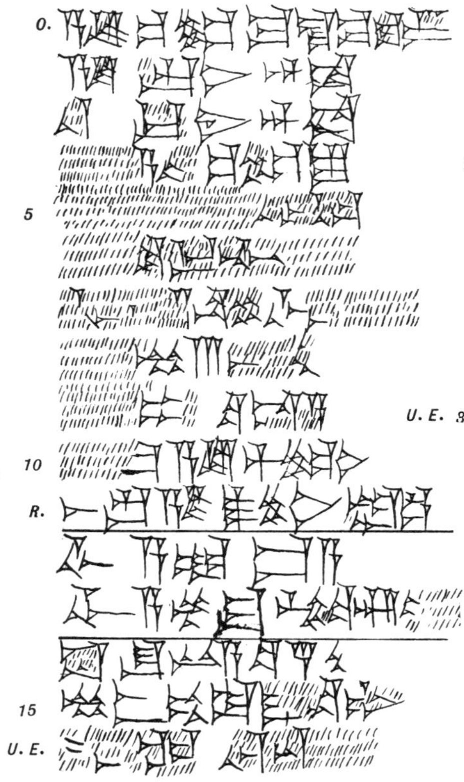

Indistinct seal impressions.

546

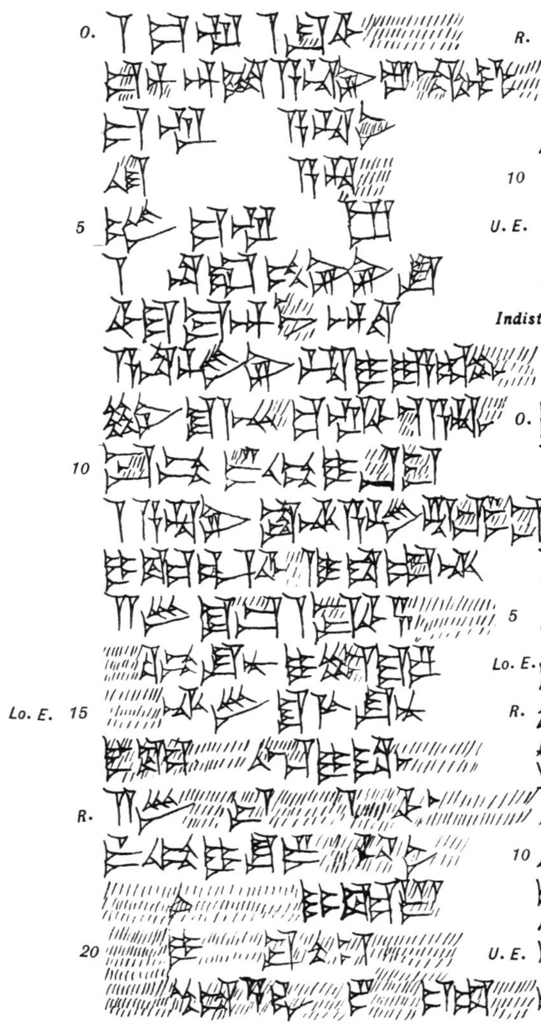

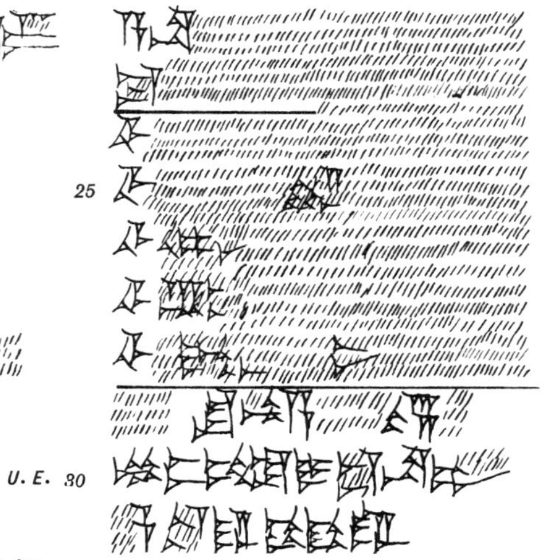

Indistinct seal impressions.

547

Indistinct seal impressions.

548

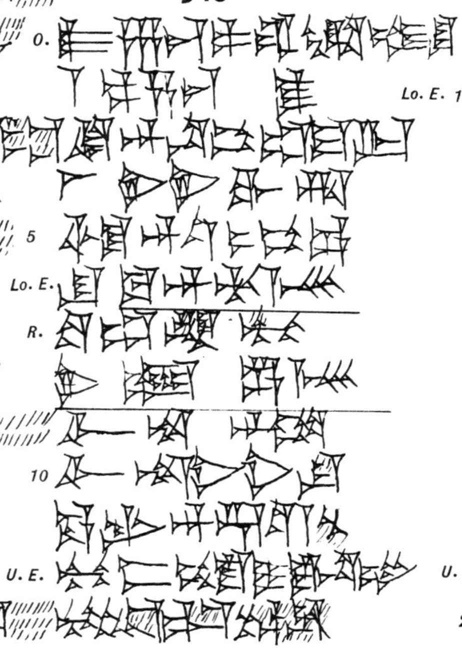

Indistinct seal impressions.

549

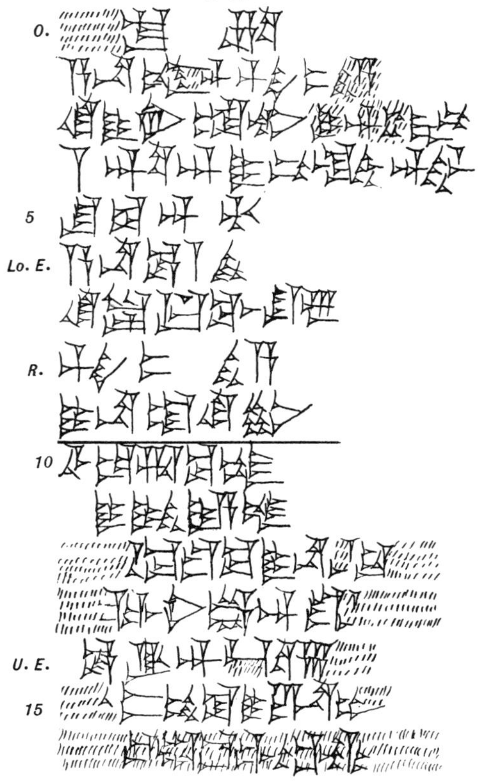

550

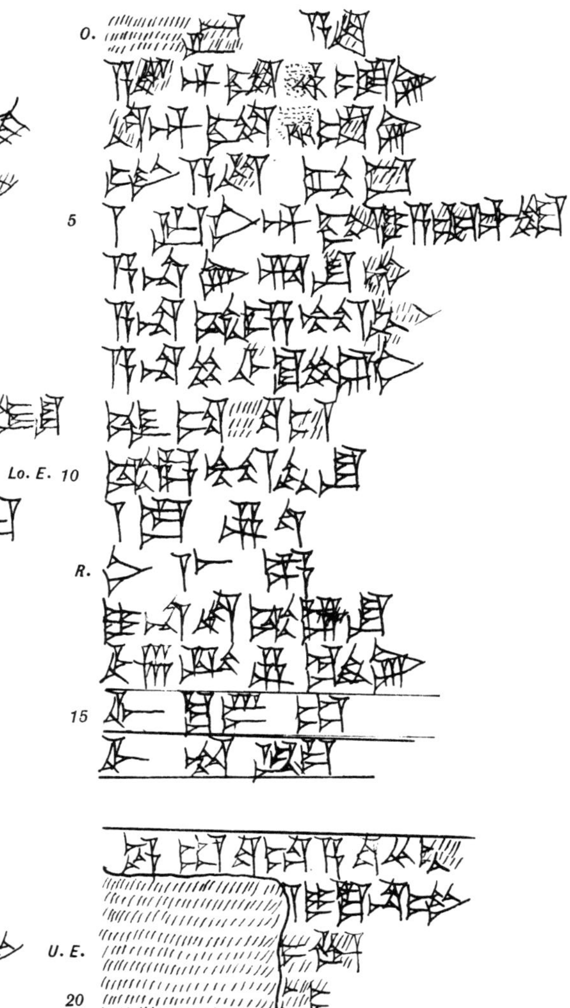

551

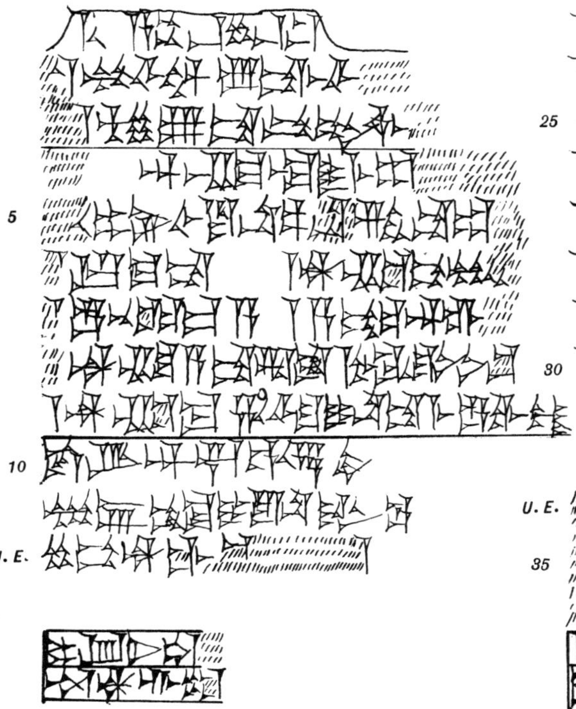

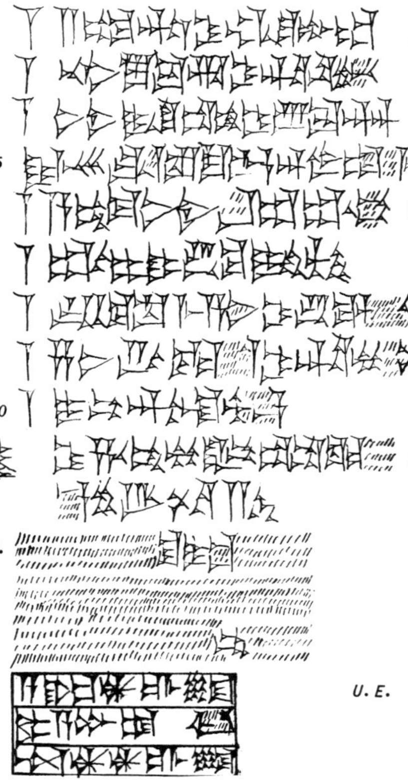

Indistinct seal impressions.

554

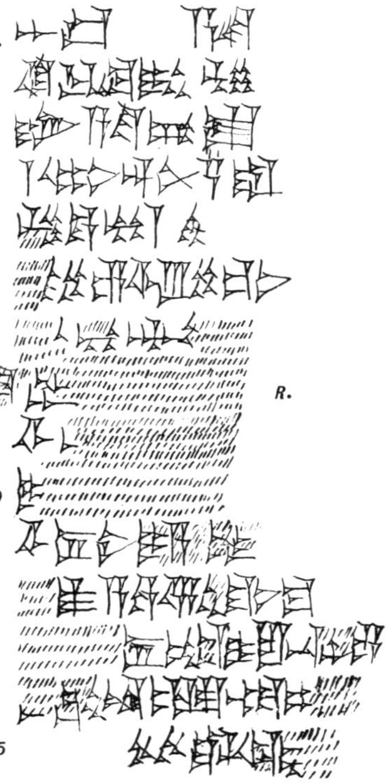

Indistinct seal impressions.

552

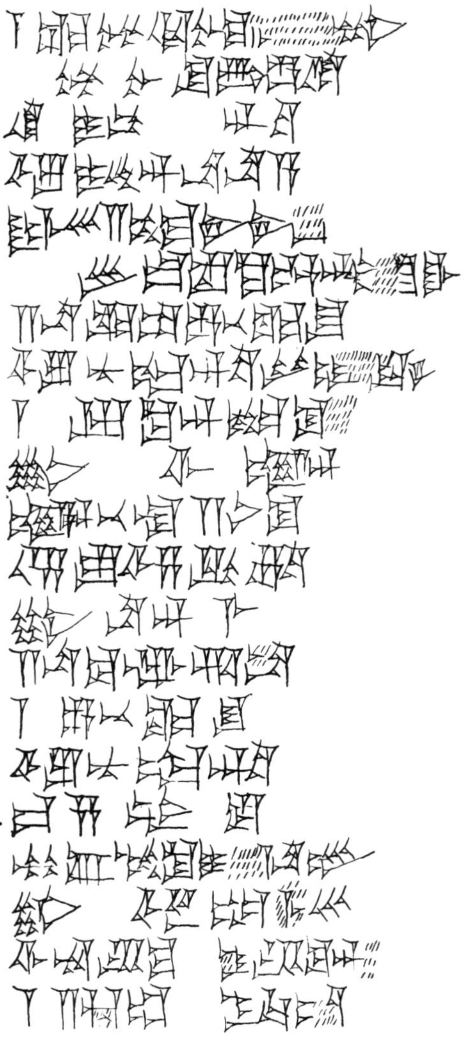

553

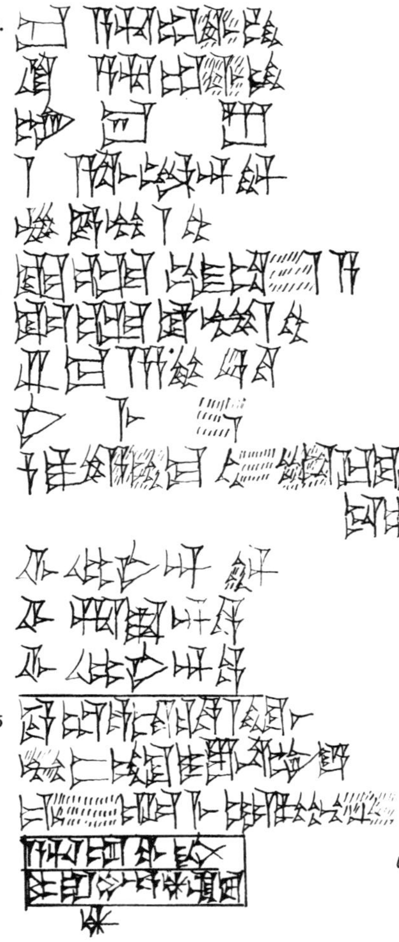

555

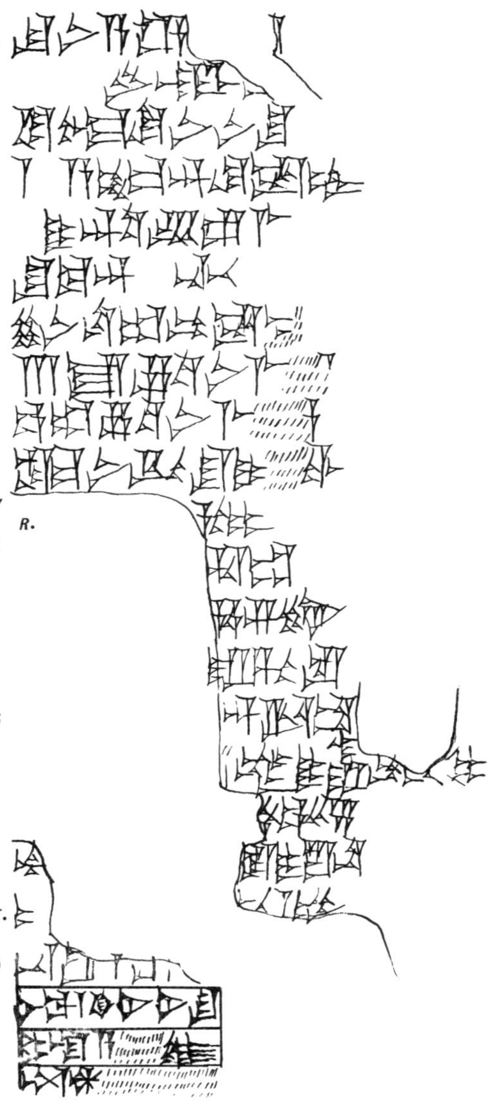

556

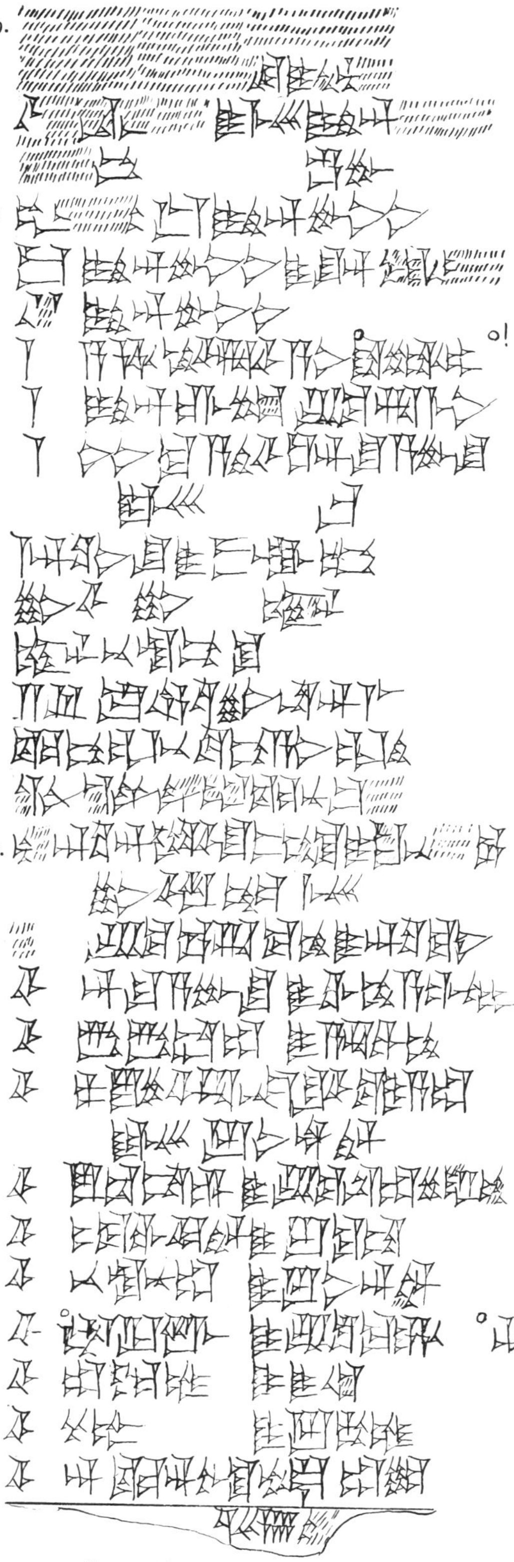

Case adds :

Indistinct seal impressions.

557

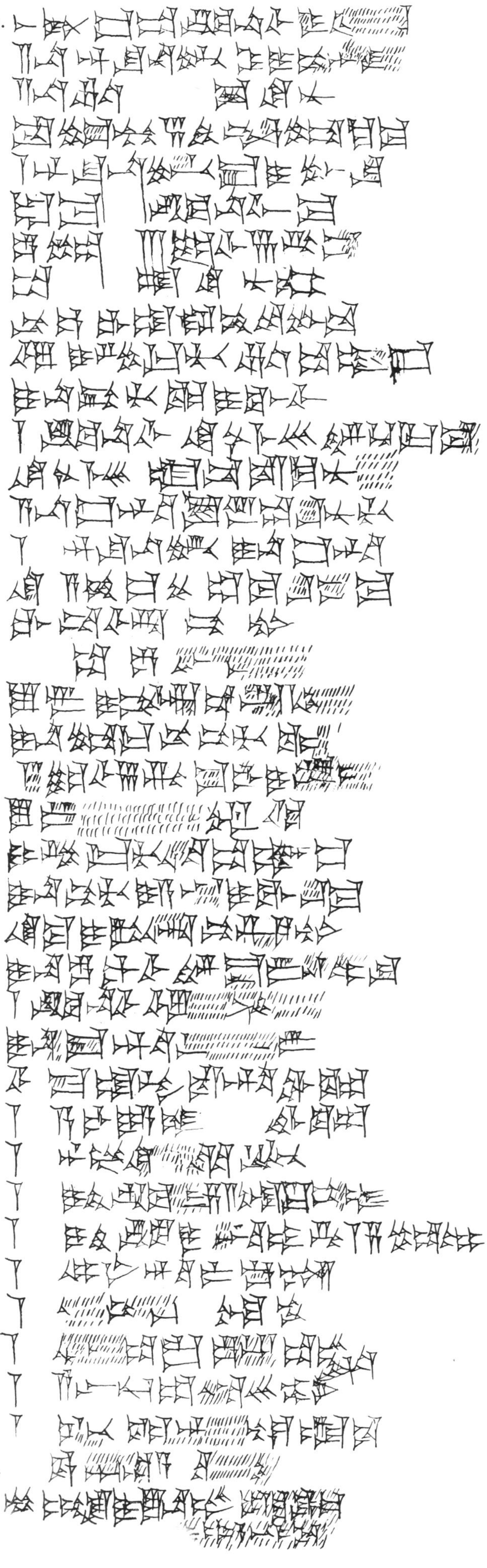

558

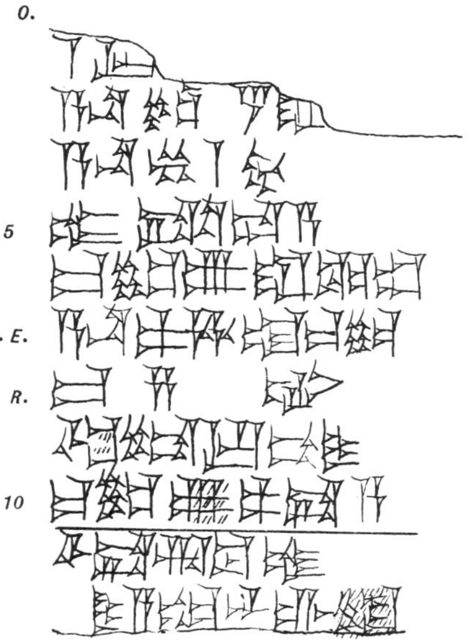

Indistinct seal impressions.

559

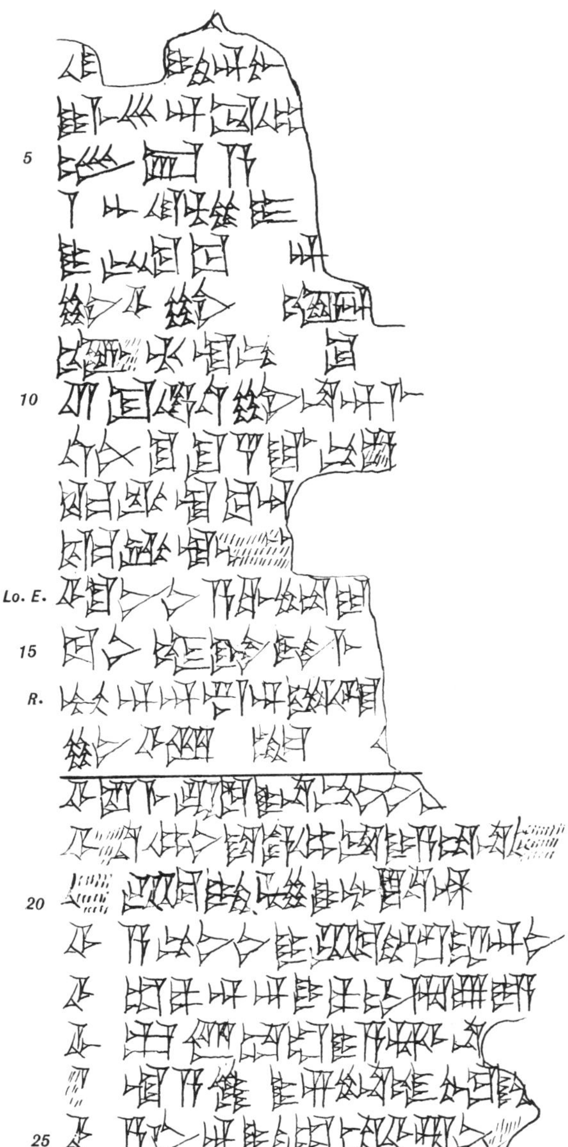

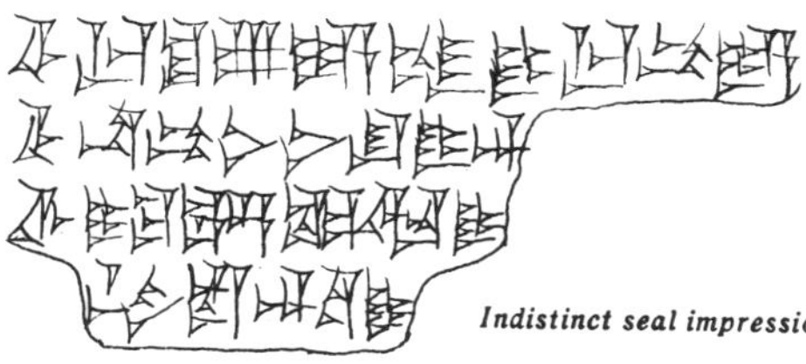

Indistinct seal impressions.

560

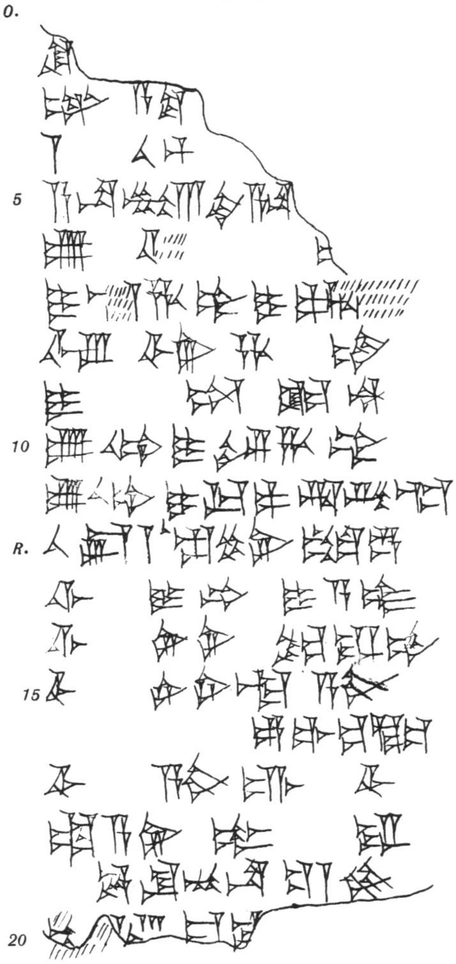

561

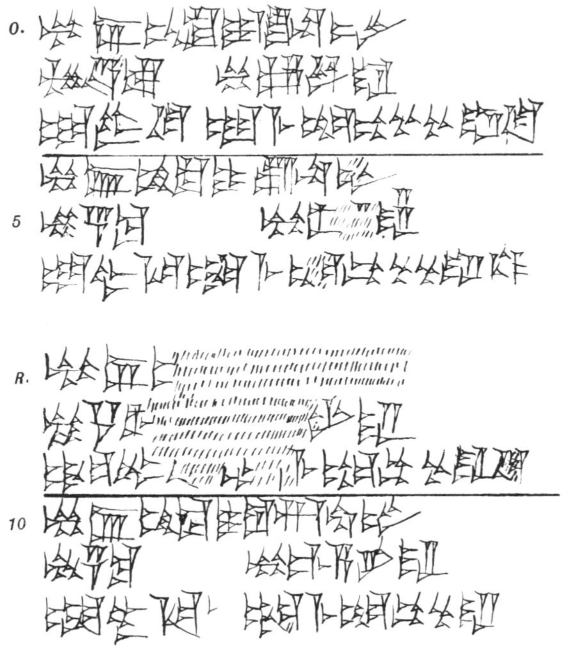

10 CASE

23 TABLET

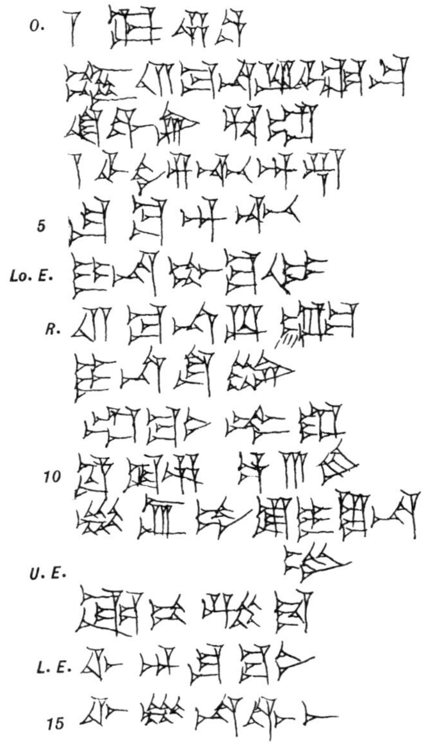

17 TABLET

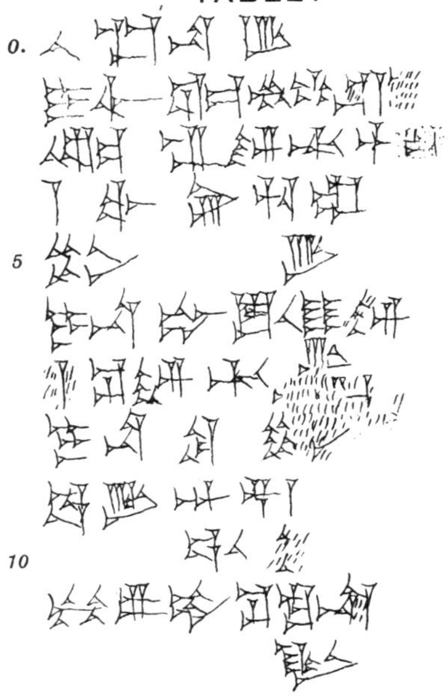

44 TABLET

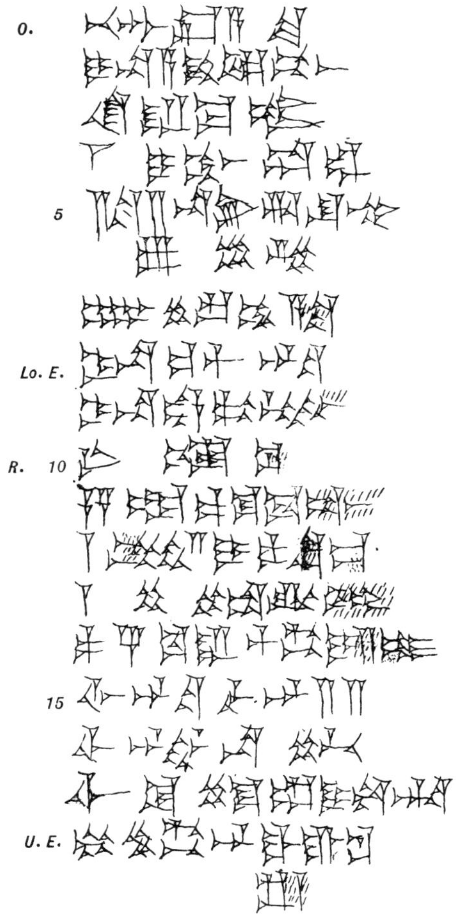

57 TABLET

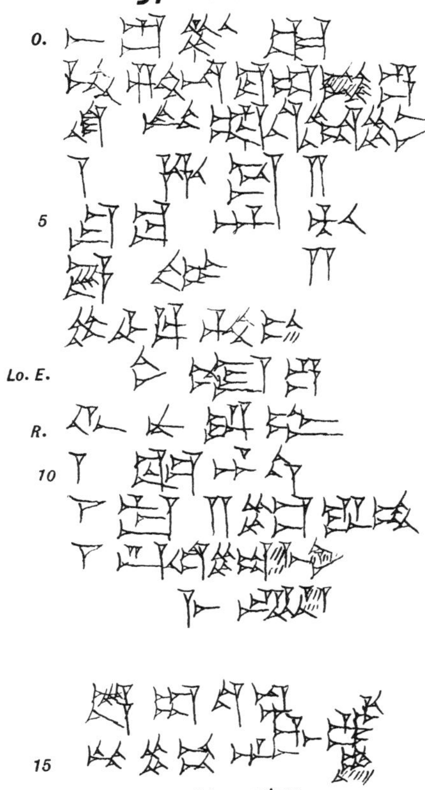

Indistinct seal impressions.

91 TABLET

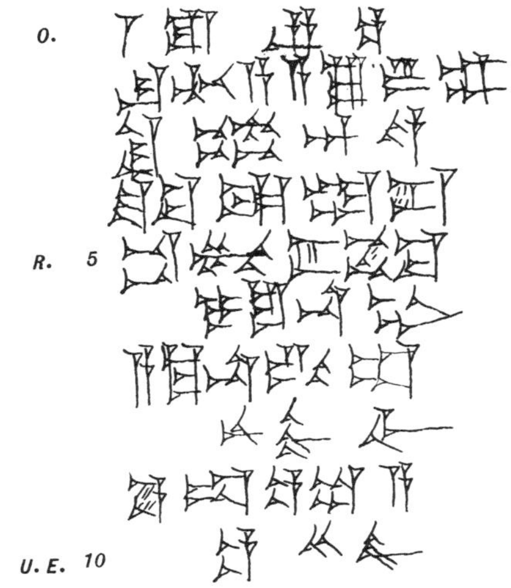

177 CASE

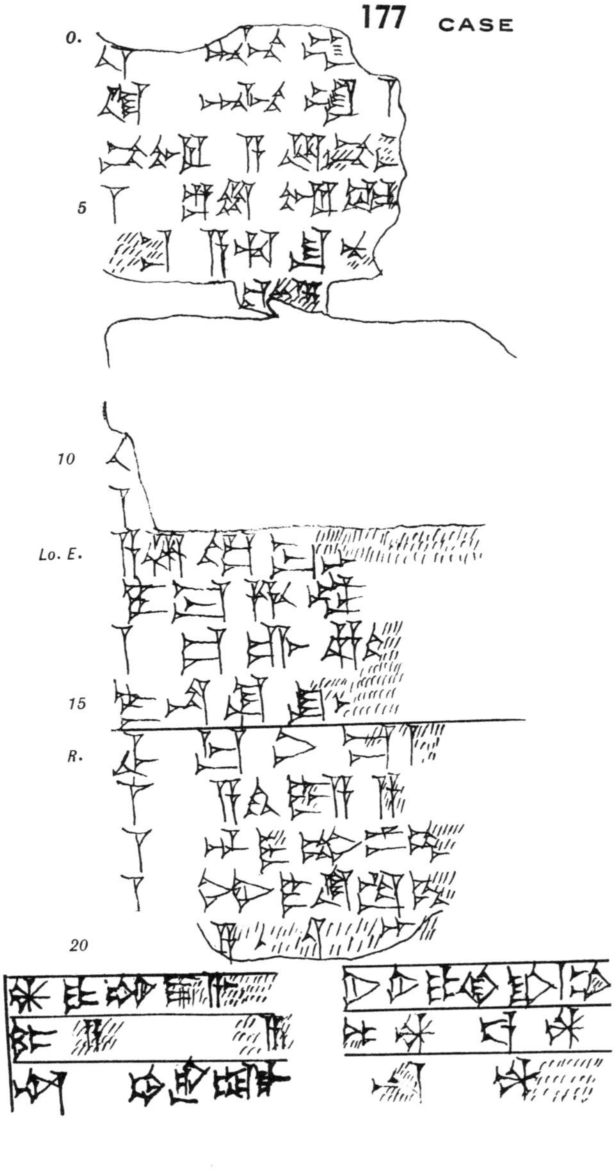

225 TABLET

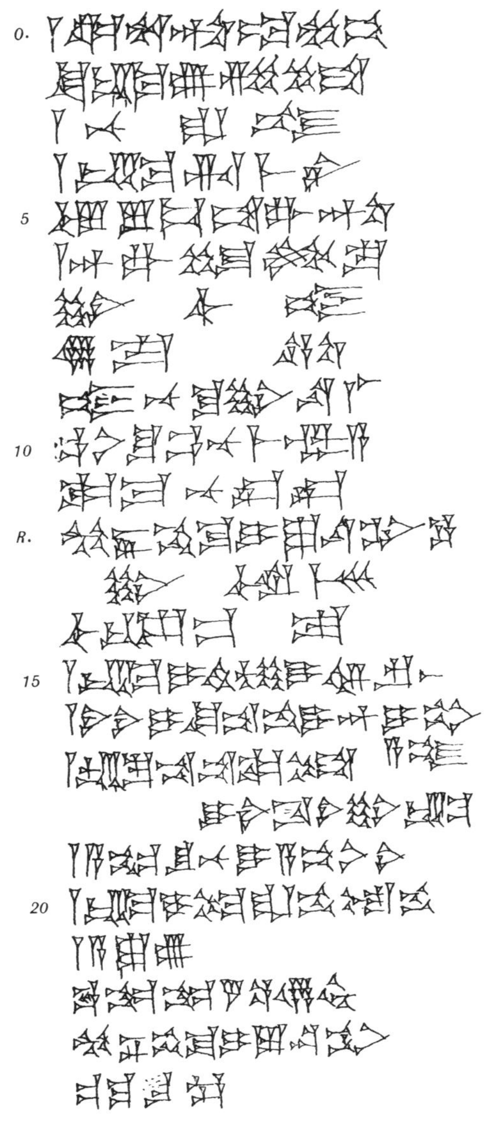

Indistinct seal impressions.

PLATE C

14

16

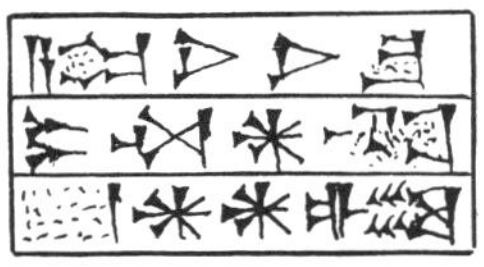

63

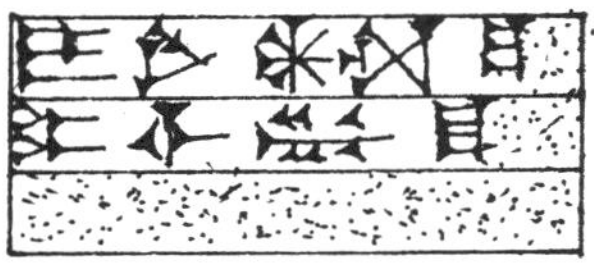

167

176

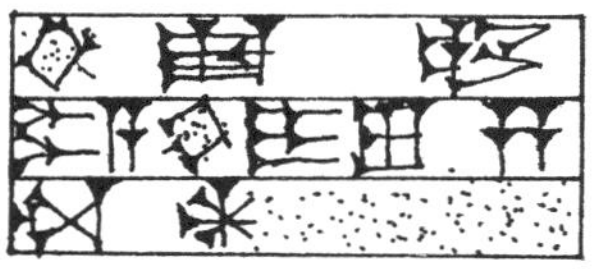

192

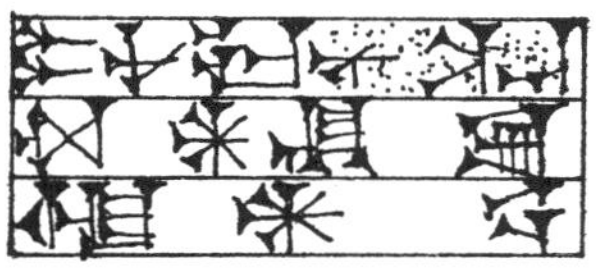

211

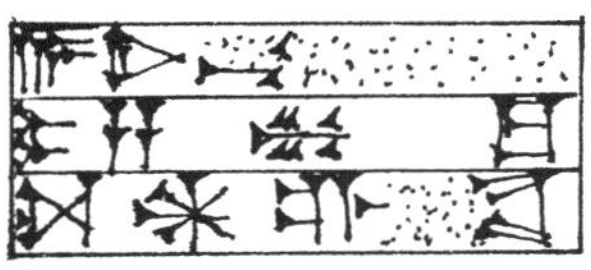

216

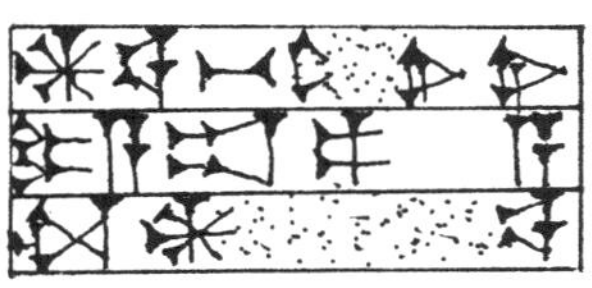

217

219

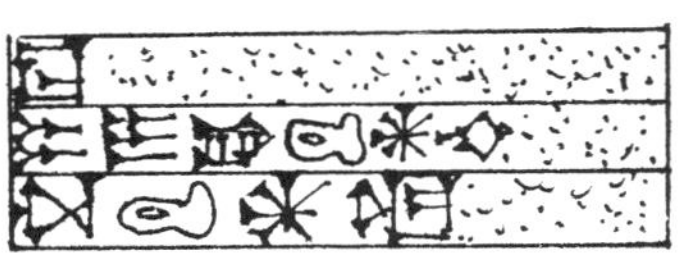

220

222

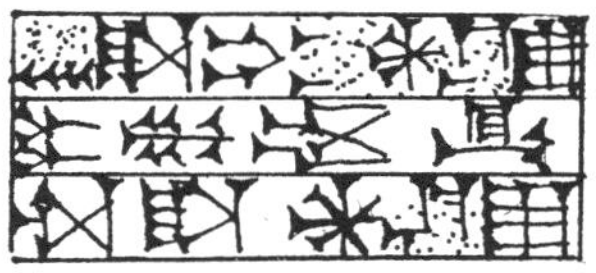

236

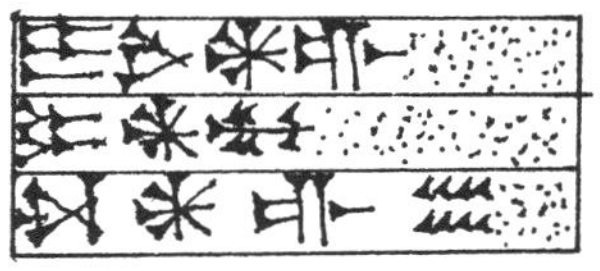

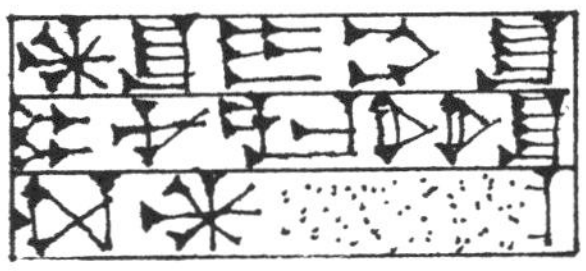

243

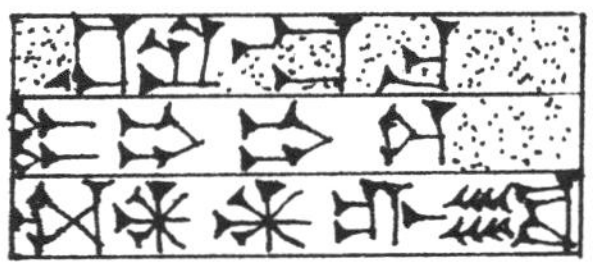

257

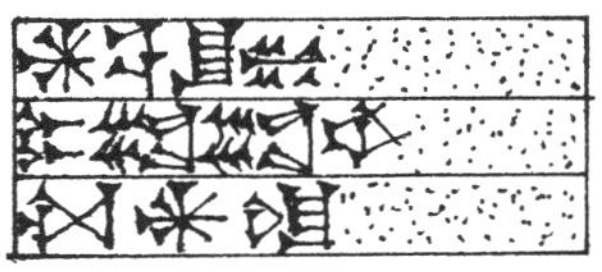

286

328

352

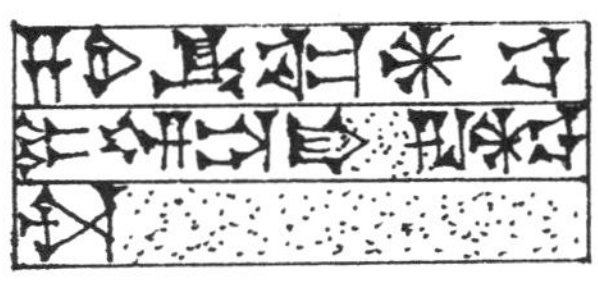

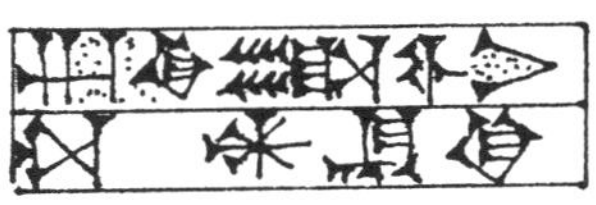

354

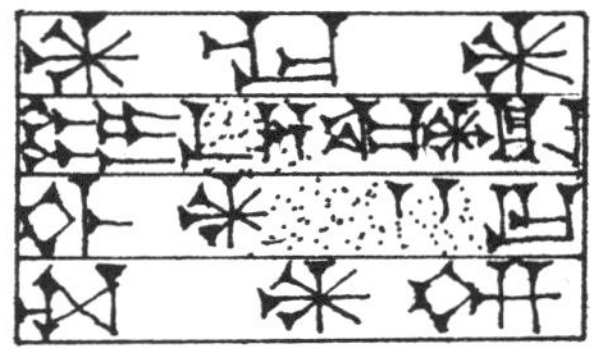

382

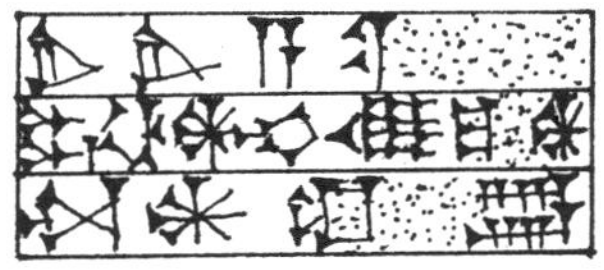

436

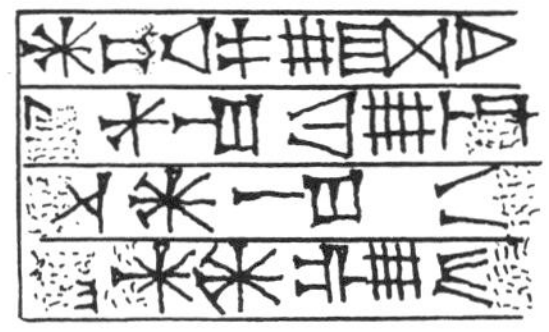

462

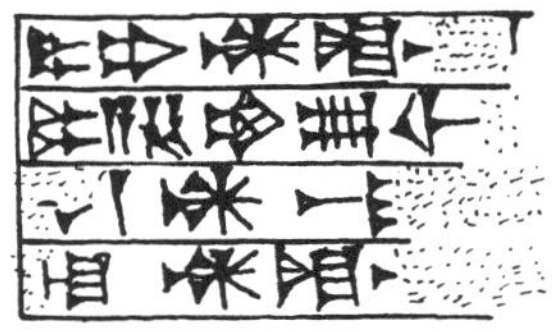

490

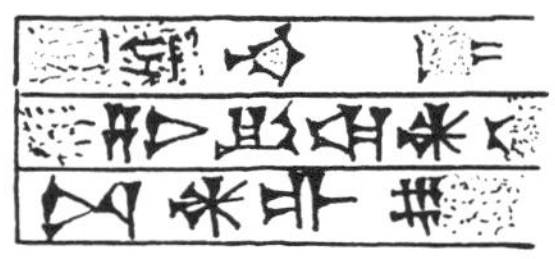

530

560

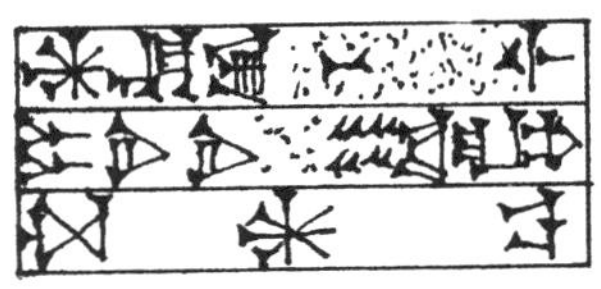